CCIE Routing and Switching Exam Certification Guide
Third Edition

Wendell Odom, CCIE No. 1624

Rus Healy, CCIE No. 15025

Contributing author: Naren Mehta, CCIE No. 9797

Cisco Press

800 East 96th Street
Indianapolis, Indiana 46240 USA

CCIE Routing and Switching Exam Certification Guide, Third Edition

Wendell Odom, CCIE No. 1624

Rus Healy, CCIE No. 15025

Contributing author: Naren Mehta, CCIE No. 9797

Copyright© 2008 Cisco Systems, Inc.

Published by:
Cisco Press
800 East 96th Street
Indianapolis, IN 46240 USA

Printed in the United States of America

First Printing   November   2007

Library of Congress Cataloging-in-Publication Data

Odom, Wendell.

CCIE routing and switching exam certification guide / Wendell Odom, Rus Healy ; contributing author, a Naren Mehta. -- 3rd ed.

p. cm.

ISBN 978-1-58720-196-7 (hardcover w/cd) 1. Electronic data processing personnel--Certification--Study guides. 2. Telecommunication--Switching systems--Examinations--Study guides. 3. Computer networks--Examinations--Study guides. 4. Internetworking (Telecommunication)--Examinations--Study guides. I. Healy, Rus. II. Mehta, Naren. III. Title.

QA76.3.B78475 2007

004.6'6--dc22

2007038136

ISBN-13: 978-1-58720-196-7

ISBN-10: 1-58720-196-8

Warning and Disclaimer

This book is designed to provide information about the Cisco CCIE Routing and Switching Written Exam, No. 350-001. Every effort has been made to make this book as complete and as accurate as possible, but no warranty or fitness is implied.

The information is provided on an "as is" basis. The authors, Cisco Press, and Cisco Systems, Inc. shall have neither liability nor responsibility to any person or entity with respect to any loss or damages arising from the information contained in this book or from the use of the discs or programs that may accompany it.

The opinions expressed in this book belong to the author and are not necessarily those of Cisco Systems, Inc.

Trademark Acknowledgments

All terms mentioned in this book that are known to be trademarks or service marks have been appropriately capitalized. Cisco Press or Cisco Systems, Inc., cannot attest to the accuracy of this information. Use of a term in this book should not be regarded as affecting the validity of any trademark or service mark.

Corporate and Government Sales

The publisher offers excellent discounts on this book when ordered in quantity for bulk purchases or special sales, which may include electronic versions and/or custom covers and content particular to your business, training goals, marketing focus, and branding interests. For more information, please contact: **U.S. Corporate and Government Sales**   1-800-382-3419   corpsales@pearsontechgroup.com

For sales outside the United States please contact: **International Sales**   international@pearsoned.com

Feedback Information

At Cisco Press, our goal is to create in-depth technical books of the highest quality and value. Each book is crafted with care and precision, undergoing rigorous development that involves the unique expertise of members from the professional technical community.

Readers' feedback is a natural continuation of this process. If you have any comments regarding how we could improve the quality of this book, or otherwise alter it to better suit your needs, you can contact us through e-mail at feedback@ciscopress.com. Please make sure to include the book title and ISBN in your message.

We greatly appreciate your assistance.

Publisher	Paul Boger
Associate Publisher	Dave Dusthimer
Cisco Representative	Anthony Wolfenden
Cisco Press Program Manager	Jeff Brady
Executive Editor	Brett Bartow
Managing Editor	Patrick Kanouse
Development Editor	Andrew Cupp
Senior Project Editor	San Dee Phillips
Copy Editor	Bill McManus
Technical Editors	Maurilio Gorito
	Rodney Guenther
	Paul Negron
Editorial Assistant	Vanessa Evans
Book and Cover Designer	Louisa Adair
Composition	Mark Shirar
Indexer	Tim Wright

Americas Headquarters	Asia Pacific Headquarters	Europe Headquarters
Cisco Systems, Inc.	Cisco Systems, Inc.	Cisco Systems International BV
170 West Tasman Drive	168 Robinson Road	Haarlerbergpark
San Jose, CA 95134-1706	#28-01 Capital Tower	Haarlerbergweg 13-19
USA	Singapore 068912	1101 CH Amsterdam
www.cisco.com	www.cisco.com	The Netherlands
Tel: 408 526-4000	Tel: +65 6317 7777	www-europe.cisco.com
800 553-NETS (6387)	Fax: +65 6317 7799	Tel: +31 0 800 020 0791
Fax: 408 527-0883		Fax: +31 0 20 357 1100

Cisco has more than 200 offices worldwide. Addresses, phone numbers, and fax numbers are listed on the Cisco Website at **www.cisco.com/go/offices.**

About the Authors

Wendell Odom, CCIE No. 1624, has been in the networking industry since 1981. He currently teaches QoS, MPLS, and CCNA courses for Skyline Advanced Technology Services (http://www.skyline-ats.com). Wendell also has worked as a network engineer, consultant, and systems engineer, and as an instructor and course developer. He is the author of all prior editions of *CCNA Exam Certification Guide* as well as *Cisco QOS Exam Certification Guide*, Second Edition, *Computer Networking First-Step*, *CCIE Routing and Switching Official Exam Certification Guide*, Second Edition, and *CCNA Video Mentor*, all from Cisco Press.

Rus Healy, CCIE No. 15025, wrote Chapter 20, "IP Version 6," and made updates, large and small, to most other chapters in updating the book for the Cisco CCIE Routing and Switching version 3.0 blueprint. He has worked on several Cisco Press projects, including the second edition of this book, as a technical reviewer. Rus is a principal SE with Annese & Associates, the largest Cisco Upstate New York Silver partner. He was instrumental in guiding Annese to Cisco Silver partnership and their three Cisco Advanced Specializations (Wireless LAN, Security, and Unified Communications).

In addition to the CCIE Routing and Switching certification, Rus holds Cisco CCDP and CCVP certifications, several Cisco Qualified Specialist certifications in Unified Communications, and the Cisco Technology Solution Specialist (TSS) designation in Unified Communications.

Along with his wife, Nancy, and children, Gwen and Trevor, Rus lives in the Finger Lakes region of New York. He and his family enjoy camping, boating, skiing, bicycling, and many other family activities. Rus is also an avid amateur radio contest operator, particularly using Morse Code. He was a member of the U.S. team in the 2002 World Radio Team Championship in Helsinki, Finland. Rus is also active in the Ontario County, New York chapter of Habitat for Humanity and in St Mary's Church in Honeoye, New York.

About the Contributing Author

Naren Mehta, CCIE No. 9797 (Routing and Switching, Security), author of Chapters 16 and 17, is a senior partner and director of training for an internationally known training and consulting company that specializes in providing customized, one-to-one training for CCIE lab students and consulting for Cisco networks. Naren has been in the training and consulting field for the past 17 years and has been teaching Cisco certification courses ranging from CCNA to CCIE (written and lab) for the past 9 years. His experience includes the analysis, design, installation, training, and support for various Cisco networks for the financial, manufacturing, utility, and healthcare industries. His specialty is explaining complex concepts in such a way that it becomes easier for anybody to understand them. Naren has been a source of inspiration, motivation, and encouragement for many of his students who wanted to pursue their CCIE lab certification and helped them pass their CCIE Routing and Switching and Security lab certification exams. He has an MBA in marketing and finance, a master's in industrial engineering, and a bachelor's in mechanical engineering.

About the Technical Reviewers

Maurilio Gorito, CCIE No. 3807 (Routing and Switching, WAN Switching, and Security), has more than 20 years of experience in networking, including Cisco networks and IBM/SNA environments, which includes the planning, designing, implementation, and troubleshooting of large IP networks running RIP, IGRP, EIGRP, BGP, OSPF, QoS, and SNA worldwide, including in Brazil and the United States. Maurilio has worked for Cisco since 2000 with the CCIE Team. As program manager he is responsible for managing the CCIE Routing and Switching track certification exams, and he has more than seven years of experience proctoring CCIE lab exams. He holds degrees in mathematics and pedagogy.

Rodney Guenther currently works at Skyline ATS as an instructor and consultant. He began his networking career at IBM in 1979 and pursued other opportunities as an independent consultant in 1992. He became the 48th certified Cisco instructor in 1995. During these 12 years he has been certified to teach close to 20 Cisco courses, from the Routing and Switching track, such as ICND, CCNA, and BCMSN; to all of the Cisco IBM SNA courses, such as CIP, SNAM, and DLSW; as well as several VoIP courses, such as CIPT, IPCC, BTS, SS7 Interconnect, and IPTD.

Paul Negron, CCIE No. 14856, CCSI No. 22752, has been involved with networking technologies for 15 years. He has been a senior instructor for Skyline ATS for the past 7 years. He has been involved with the designing of core network services for a number of service providers. He currently instructs all the CCIP-level courses, including Advanced BGP, MPLS, and the QoS course. Paul has 6 years of experience with satellite communications as well as 8 years of experience with Cisco platforms.

Dedications

For Edna Stellarea York: For the laughter, for the big family get togethers, and for loving all us grandkids so much. And of course, for the biscuits.

—Wendell

For my dad, Jim Healy, who has provided me with technical inspiration since my earliest years and who has always encouraged me to push myself toward lofty, worthy goals.

—Rus

Acknowledgments

Maurilio, Rodney, and Paul each did a nice job tech editing the book and finding the technical errors that can creep into a manuscript. Additionally, Maurilio helped tremendously with one of the most difficult challenges with this book: choosing what to cover and in what depth and what to not cover. Rodney gave us added perspective on the big picture and on keeping the audience in mind every step of the journey. Paulie helped (again) on the MPLS chapter and kept us on the straight and narrow. Many thanks to all three of you!

Drew Cupp did a great job for us on yet another book. Thanks Drew! In particular, Drew did a great job with the unique challenges for this book in which some chapters and sections were not changed at all, but some were changed a lot, with lots of renumbering chapters—which, oddly enough, introduces many opportunities to make mistakes that aren't easily found. Drew kept an eagle's eye view of the whole project, throughout the months, long after we would forget the details. Thanks for keeping us on track, in context, and fishing from the right side of the boat.

The wonderful and mostly hidden production folks did their usual great job. When every time you see how they reworded something, and think "Wow, why didn't I write that?" it makes me appreciate the kind of team we have at Cisco Press. Thanks for moving the book along to completion and helping make us look better along the way.

From Wendell Odom: The timing for revisions to the CCIE Routing and Switching written blueprint, and the development of this book, unfortunately coincided with the same timeline as the revisions of two CCNA-related books for which I'm the sole author. The timing presented a bit of a problem in getting this book done. I'm honored to say, though, that the problem was turned into an opportunity to bring Rus into the authoring team, a decision that I'm thrilled with. Rus took his responsibilities seriously, worked very hard, and watched every nook and cranny of content (a huge piece of the work on this book). He did a nice job writing and, almost as importantly, a nice job choosing where to add small topics and identifying what needed to be removed. Rus, thanks for the time, effort, attention, and care for this big book—and for the quality content as well.

On the personal side, thanks to the Mikes at Skyline for your incredible flexibility in having time to do all this writing. Thanks to Kris and Hannah for putting up with the sometimes inconvenient answers to the "when's your next deadline, dear/dad?" questions. And as usual, thanks to my Lord and Savior, Jesus Christ.

From Rus Healy: As this is my first authoring project for Cisco Press, I want to thank Wendell Odom first and foremost for his confidence in me and for inviting me to work with him on this book. I'm honored and delighted to have the opportunity, and I hope I've risen to the considerable challenge of doing "Wendell quality" work. I certainly have enjoyed the interaction and the sense of teamwork!

Over the last few years, Cisco Press has given me the opportunity to work on a number of books as a technical reviewer. I've really enjoyed working on these projects, and the opportunity means a lot to me—my thanks to the Cisco Press editors who have looked to me for those projects.

Most importantly, my sincere and heartfelt thanks to my wife, Nancy, and our kids, Gwen and Trevor, who gave up a fair amount of my time over several months while I worked on this book. Thanks for making it possible, gang!

This Book Is Safari Enabled

The Safari® Enabled icon on the cover of your favorite technology book means the book is available through Safari Bookshelf. When you buy this book, you get free access to the online edition for 45 days.

Safari Bookshelf is an electronic reference library that lets you easily search thousands of technical books, find code samples, download chapters, and access technical information whenever and wherever you need it.

To gain 45-day Safari Enabled access to this book:

- Go to http://www.ciscopress.com/safarienabled

- Complete the brief registration form

- Enter the coupon code Z3HX-GMKI-Z2ZV-QWIJ-QGMZ

If you have difficulty registering on Safari Bookshelf or accessing the online edition, please e-mail customer-service@safaribooksonline.com.

Contents at a Glance

Contents

Icons Used in This Book

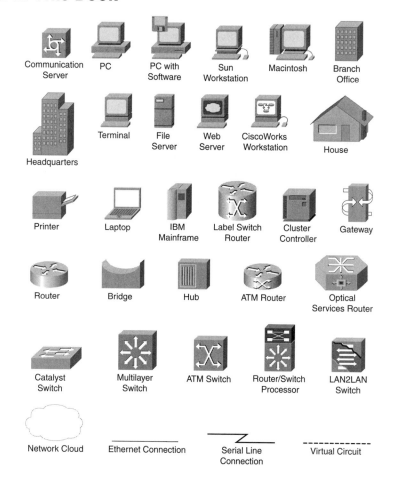

Command Syntax Conventions

The conventions used to present command syntax in this book are the same conventions used in the IOS Command Reference. The Command Reference describes these conventions as follows:

- **Boldface** indicates commands and keywords that are entered literally as shown. In actual configuration examples and output (not general command syntax), boldface indicates commands that are manually input by the user (such as a **show** command).

- *Italics* indicate arguments for which you supply actual values.

- Vertical bars | separate alternative, mutually exclusive elements.

- Square brackets [ ] indicate optional elements.

- Braces { } indicate a required choice.

- Braces within brackets [{ }] indicate a required choice within an optional element.

Foreword

CCIE Routing and Switching Exam Certification Guide, Third Edition, is an excellent self-study resource for the CCIE Routing and Switching written exam. Passing this exam is the first step to attaining the valued CCIE Routing and Switching certification and qualifies candidates for the CCIE Routing and Switching lab exam.

Gaining certification in Cisco technology is key to the continuing educational development of today's networking professional. Through certification programs, Cisco validates the skills and expertise required to effectively manage the modern enterprise network.

Cisco Press Exam Certification Guides and preparation materials offer exceptional—and flexible—access to the knowledge and information required to stay current in your field of expertise or to gain new skills. Whether used as a supplement to more traditional training or as a primary source of learning, these materials offer users the information and knowledge validation required to gain new understanding and proficiencies.

Developed in conjunction with the Cisco certifications and training team, Cisco Press books are the only self-study books authorized by Cisco and offer students a series of exam practice tools and resource materials to help ensure that learners fully grasp the concepts and information presented.

Additional authorized Cisco instructor-led courses, e-learning, labs, and simulations are available exclusively from Cisco Learning Solutions Partners worldwide. To learn more, visit http://www.cisco.com/go/training.

I hope that you find these materials to be an enriching and useful part of your exam preparation.

Erik Ullanderson
Manager, Global Certifications
Learning@Cisco
October 2007

Introduction

The Cisco Certified Internetwork Expert (CCIE) certification may be the most challenging and prestigious of all networking certifications. It has received numerous awards and certainly has built a reputation as one of the most difficult certifications to earn in all of the technology world. Having a CCIE certification opens doors professionally typically results in higher pay and looks great on a resume.

Cisco currently offers several CCIE certifications. This book covers the version 3.0 exam blueprint topics of the written exam for the CCIE Routing and Switching certification. The following list details the currently available CCIE certifications at the time of this book's publication; check http://www.cisco.com/go/ccie for the latest information. The certifications are listed in the order in which they were made available to the public.

- CCIE Routing and Switching
- CCIE Security
- CCIE Service Provider
- CCIE Voice
- CCIE Storage Networking

Each of the CCIE certifications requires the candidate to pass both a written exam and a one-day, hands-on lab exam. The written exam is intended to test your knowledge of theory, protocols, and configuration concepts that follow good design practices. The lab exam proves that you can configure and troubleshoot actual gear.

Why Should I Take the CCIE Routing and Switching Written Exam?

The first and most obvious reason to take the CCIE Routing and Switching written exam is that it is the first step toward obtaining the CCIE Routing and Switching certification. Also, you cannot schedule a CCIE lab exam until you pass the corresponding written exam. In short, if you want all the professional benefits of a CCIE Routing and Switching certification, you start by passing the written exam.

The benefits of getting a CCIE certification are varied, among which are the following:

- Better pay
- Career advancement opportunities
- Applies to certain minimum requirements for Cisco Silver and Gold Channel Partners, as well as those seeking Master Specialization, making you more valuable to Channel Partners

- Better movement through the problem-resolution process when calling the Cisco TAC

- Prestige

- Credibility for consultants and customer engineers, including the use of the Cisco CCIE logo

The other big reason to take the CCIE Routing and Switching written exam is that it recertifies an individual's associate-, professional-, and expert-level Cisco certifications. In other words, passing any CCIE written exam recertifies that person's CCNA, CCNP, CCIP, CCSP, CCDP, and so on. (Recertification requirements do change, so please verify the requirements at http://www.cisco.com/go/certifications.)

CCIE Routing and Switching Written Exam 350-001

The CCIE Routing and Switching written exam, as of the time of publication, consists of a two-hour exam administered at a proctored exam facility affiliated with Pearson VUE (http://www.vue.com/cisco). The exam typically includes approximately 100 multiple-choice questions. No simulation questions are currently part of the written exam.

As with most exams, everyone wants to know what is on the exam. Cisco provides general guidance as to topics on the exam in the CCIE Routing and Switching written exam blueprint, the most recent copy of which can be accessed from http://www.cisco.com/go/ccie.

Cisco changes both the CCIE written and lab blueprints over time, but Cisco seldom, if ever, changes the exam numbers. (Cisco changes the exam numbers of the associate- and professional-level certifications when it makes major changes to what is covered on those exams.) Knowing that the content will change over time, this book includes Appendix C, "CCIE Routing and Switching Exam Updates: Version 1.0." This appendix will include coverage of any newly added topics to the CCIE Routing and Switching written exam. When Cisco changes the blueprint, the authors will add content to cover the new topics at http://www.ciscopress.com/title/9781587201967 and make that content available to all readers who have bought the earlier edition of the book. For future printings, Cisco Press will put that new content into Appendix C.

The CCIE Routing and Switching written exam blueprint, as of the time of publication, is listed in Table I-1. Table I-1 also lists the chapter(s) that cover each topic.

Table 8-1 *CCIE Routing and Switching Written Exam Blueprint*

Blueprint Topic	Chapter(s)
I. General Networking Theory	
A. General Routing Concepts	4, 6, 7, 10
1. Link State and Distance Vector Protocols	7
2. Split Horizon	7

Table 8-1 *CCIE Routing and Switching Written Exam Blueprint (Continued)*

Blueprint Topic	Chapter(s)
3. Summarization	4, 10
4. Classful and a Classless Routing Protocol	6
5. Routing Decision Criteria	10
B. Routing Information Base (RIB) and Routing Protocols Interaction	10, 11
1. Administrative Distance	10
2. Routing Table	10
3. RIB and Forwarding Information Base Interaction	10, 11
C. Redistribution	10
1. Redistribution Between Routing	10
2. Troubleshooting Routing Loop	10
II. Bridging and LAN Switching	
A. Spanning Tree Protocol (STP)	1, 3, 18
1. 802.1d	3
2. 802.1w	3
3. 802.1s	3
4. Loopguard	3
5. Rootguard	3
6. Bridge Protocol Data Unit (BPDU) Guard	3
7. Storm Control	18
8. Rapid Spanning Tree Protocol (RSTP)	3
9. Unicast flooding	1
10. STP port roles, Failure propagation, and Loopguard Operation	3
B. LAN Switching	1, 2, 3
1. Trunks	2, 3
2. VLAN Trunking Protocol (VTP) Administrative Functions	2
C. Ethernet	1
1. Speed	1
2. Duplex	1
3. Ethernet	1

continues

Table 8-1 *CCIE Routing and Switching Written Exam Blueprint (Continued)*

Blueprint Topic	Chapter(s)
4. Fast Ethernet	1
5. Gigabit Ethernet	1
III. IP	
A. Addressing	4, 5
1. Subnetting	4
2. Hot Standby Routing Protocol (HSRP)	5
3. Gateway Load Balancing Protocol (GLBP)	5
4. Virtual Router Redundancy Protocol (VRRP)	5
5. Network Address Translation (NAT)	4
B. Services	5
1. Network Time Protocol (NTP)	5
2. Dynamic Host Control Protocol (DHCP)	5
3. Web Cache Communication Protocol (WCCP)	5
C. Network Management	
1. Logging and Syslog	5
IV. IP Routing	
A. OSPF	9
1. Standard OSPF Area	9
2. Stub Area	9
3. Totally Stub Area	9
4. Not-So-Stubby-Area (NSSA)	9
5. Totally NSSA	9
6. Link State Advertisement (LSA) Types	9
7. Adjacency on a Point-to-Point and on a Multi-Access (Broadcast)	9
8. OSPF Graceful Restart	9
9. Troubleshooting Failing Adjacency Formation to Fail	9
10. Troubleshooting of External Route Installation in the RIB	9
B. BGP	11
1. Protocol on Which BGP Peers Communicate	11
2. Next Hop	11

Table 8-1 *CCIE Routing and Switching Written Exam Blueprint (Continued)*

Blueprint Topic	Chapter(s)
3. Peering	11
4. Troubleshooting of BGP Route That Will Not Install in the Routing Table	11
C. EIGRP	8
1. Best Path	8
2. Loop Free Paths	8
3. EIGRP Operations When Alternate Loop Free Paths Are Available and When It Is Not Available	8
4. EIGRP Queries	8
5. Manual Summarization	8
6. Auto-Summarization	8
7. EIGRP Stubs	8
8. Troubleshooting of EIGRP Neighbor Adjacencies	8
D. Policy Routing	6, 12
1. Concept of policy routing	6, 12
V. QoS	
A. Modular QoS Command-Line (MQC) Applied To:	12, 13, 14
1. Network-Based Application Recognition (NBAR)	12
2. Class-Based Weighted Fair Queueing (CBWFQ) / Modified Deficit Round Robin (MDRR)	13, 14
3. Policing	14
4. Shaping	14
5. Marking	12, 14
6. Random Early Detection (RED)	13
VI. WAN	
A. Frame Relay	6, 15, 18
1. Local Management Interface (LMI)	6, 15
2. Traffic Shaping	15
3. Hub and Spoke routers	15
4. Dynamic Multipoint VPN (DMVPN)	18
5. DE	15

continues

Table 8-1 *CCIE Routing and Switching Written Exam Blueprint (Continued)*

Blueprint Topic	Chapter(s)
VII. IP Multicast	
A. Internet Group Management Protocol (IGMP) v2	16, 17
B. Group Addresses	16, 17
C. Shared Trees	17
D. Source Trees	17
E. Protocol Independent Multicast (PIM) Mechanic	17
F. PIM Sparse Mode	17
G. Auto-RP	17
H. Anycast RP	17
VIII. Security	
A. Extended IP Access Lists	18
B. Unicast Reverse Path Forwarding (uRPF)	18
C. IP Source Guard	18
D. Context Based Access Control (CBAC)	18
IX. MPLS (New)	
A. Label Switching Router (LSR)	19
B. Label Switched Path (LSP)	19
C. Route Descriptor	19
D. Label Format	19
E. Label imposition/disposition	19
F. Label Distribution	19
X. IPv6 (New)	
A. IPv6 Addressing and Types	20
B. IPv6 Neighbor Discovery	20
C. Basic IPv6 functionality Protocols	20
D. IPv6 Multicast and Related Multicast Protocols	20
E. Tunneling Techniques	20
F. OSPFv3	20
G. EIGRPv6	20

The blueprint tells you what major topics to study and by implication, what not to study. However, the blueprint does not provide many details about the scope and depth covered for each topic. As you prepare for the written exam, it is a good idea to study more details than you think you need to pass the exam, because the lab exam is considerably more rigorous than the written exam.

Knowing what topics Cisco does not list in the blueprint is also useful, particularly topics that Cisco has removed from earlier blueprints. For example, in 2005, Cisco announced the removal of ISDN/DDR, IS-IS, ATM, and SONET from the written exam blueprint, but it added wireless. In 2007, Cisco announced a new CCIE Routing and Switching written blueprint, referenced as "version 3.0" (the older blueprints did not have a version). This version 3.0 blueprint also added and removed topics; for example, it removed wireless coverage, but added MPLS and expanded IPv6. Always check http://www.cisco.com/go/ccie for the latest information regarding any other new or deleted blueprint topics. For any major changes, the authors will post a new version of Appendix C, which will add coverage of the new topics. Go to http://www.ciscopress.com/title/1587201968 for this book's web page, and look for a new Appendix C if the blueprint changes.

About the *CCIE Routing and Switching Official Exam Certification Guide*, Third Edition

This section provides a brief insight into the contents of the book, the major goals, and some of the book features that you will encounter when using this book.

Book Organization

This book contains nine major parts, which correspond to, and are in the same order as, the last nine major headings in the 10-heading CCIE Routing and Switching written blueprint. The topics under the first heading of the blueprint, "General Networking Theory," are covered in this book, but they are spread throughout the various parts of the book.

Each part of the book has one or more chapters. Some have a single chapter, such as Part VII, "Security." However, Part III, "IP Routing," has six chapters and a high page count.

Beyond the chapters in the nine major parts of the book, you will find several useful appendixes gathered in Part X. In particular, Appendix C, "CCIE Routing and Switching Exam Updates: Version 1.0," as mentioned earlier, will be updated with subsequent versions online at http://www.ciscopress.com/title/9781587201967 when appropriate to provide you with the most up-to-date material. Also included in Part X is a decimal to binary conversion chart for reference in Appendix B. There are also several useful appendixes that can only be accessed from the CD in the back of the book.

Following is a description of each part's coverage:

- **Part I, "LAN Switching" (Chapters 1–3)**

  This part focuses on LAN Layer 2 features, specifically Ethernet (Chapter 1), VLANs and trunking (Chapter 2), and Spanning Tree Protocol (Chapter 3).

- **Part II, "IP" (Chapters 4–5)**

  This part is titled "IP" to match the blueprint, but it might be better titled "TCP/IP" because it covers details across the spectrum of the TCP/IP protocol stack. It includes IP addressing (Chapter 4) and IP services such as DHCP and ARP (Chapter 5).

- **Part III, "IP Routing" (Chapters 6–11)**

  This part covers some of the more important topics on the exam and is easily the largest part of the book. It covers Layer 3 forwarding concepts (Chapter 6), followed by three routing protocol chapters, one each about RIP, EIGRP, and OSPF (Chapters 7 through 9, respectively). Following that, Chapter 10 covers route redistribution between IGPs. At the end, Chapter 11 hits the details of BGP.

- **Part IV, "QoS" (Chapters 12–14)**

  This part covers the more popular QoS tools, including some MQC-based tools, as well as several older tools, particularly FRTS. The chapters include coverage of classification and marking (Chapter 12), queuing and congestion avoidance (Chapter 13), plus shaping, policing, and link efficiency (Chapter 14).

- **Part V, "Wide-Area Networks" (Chapter 15)**

  The WAN coverage has generally shrunk with the last several changes to the CCIE Routing and Switching written blueprints, so Frame Relay is all that remains in this section. However, the latest blueprint revision includes another WAN topic, MPLS, which is covered in Chapter 19. MPLS is covered in Part VIII of this book to keep the order of book parts in synch with the blueprint.

- **Part VI, "IP Multicast" (Chapters 16–17)**

  This is one of the two parts of the book that cover topics that are mostly ignored for the CCNP exam. As a result, the text assumes that the reader has no knowledge of multicast before beginning this part. Chapter 16 covers multicast on LANs, including IGMP and how hosts join multicast groups. Chapter 17 covers multicast WAN topics.

- **Part VII, "Security" (Chapter 18)**

  Given the CCIE tracks for both Security and Voice, Cisco has a small dilemma regarding whether to cover those topics on CCIE Routing and Switching, and if so, in how much detail. This part covers a variety of security topics appropriate for CCIE Routing and Switching, in a single chapter. This chapter focuses on switch and router security. (Note that Voice, whose protocols were formerly covered on CCIE Routing and Switching, is not covered in the current blueprint or in this book.)

- **Part VIII, "MPLS" (Chapter 19)**

  As mentioned in the WAN section, MPLS is an addition to the latest blueprint and thus debuts with its own chapter. As with many larger topics in this book, the blueprint does not cover all parts of MPLS but rather focuses on enterprise-related topics such as core MPLS concepts and MPLS VPNs.

- **Part IX, "IP Version 6" (Chapter 20)**

  IPv6 is comprehensively addressed in the version 3.0 exam blueprint, so we've added a fairly lengthy chapter to cover it.

- **Part X, "Appendixes"**

  — **Appendix A, "Answers to the 'Do I Know This Already?' Quizzes"**

    This appendix lists answers and explanations for the questions at the beginning of each chapter.

— **Appendix B,** "Decimal to Binary Conversion Table"

This appendix lists the decimal values 0 through 255, with their binary equivalents.

— **Appendix C, "CCIE Routing and Switching Exam Updates: Version 1.0"**

As of the first printing of the book, this appendix contains only a few words that reference the web page for this book at http://www.ciscopress.com/title/9781587201967. As the blueprint evolves over time, the authors will post new materials at the website. Any future printings of the book will include the latest newly added materials in printed form inside Appendix C.

NOTE   Appendixes D through H are in printable, PDF format on the CD.

— **(CD-only) Appendix D, "IP Addressing Practice"**

This appendix lists several practice problems for IP subnetting and finding summary routes. The explanations to the answers use the shortcuts described in the book.

— **(CD-only) Appendix E, "Key Tables for CCIE Study"**

This appendix lists the most important tables from the core chapters of the book. The tables have much of the content removed so you can use them as an exercise. You can print the PDF and then fill in the table from memory, checking your answers against the completed tables in Appendix F.

— **(CD-only) Appendix F, "Solutions for Key Tables for CCIE Study"**

This appendix lists the completed tables from the Appendix E exercises so you can check your answers.

— **(CD-only) Appendix G, "IEEE 802.11 Fundamentals"**

Because wireless was removed from the version 3.0 blueprint, we've removed the two wireless chapters from the third edition of this book. However, there's a chance that wireless will return to the CCIE Routing and Switching blueprint in the future, so we're including those chapters as appendixes on the CD.

— **(CD-only) Appendix H, "Wireless LAN Solutions"**

Like Appendix G, Appendix H covers wireless materials that may be useful for future CCIE Routing and Switching study, if the blueprint is revised to once again include wireless coverage.

NOTE   There is also a glossary near the end of the book. You can use it to look up key terms and to find the definitions for the exercise at the end of each chapter.

Book Features

The core chapters of this book have several features that help you make the best use of your time:

- **"Do I Know This Already?" Quizzes**—Each chapter begins with a quiz that helps you to determine the amount of time you need to spend studying that chapter. If you score yourself strictly, and you miss only one question, then you may want to skip the core of the chapter and move on to the "Foundation Summary" section at the end of the chapter, which lets you review facts and spend time on other topics. If you miss more than one, you may want to spend some time reading the chapter or at least reading sections that cover topics about which you know you are weaker.

- **Foundation Topics**—These are the core sections of each chapter. They explain the protocols, concepts, and configuration for the topics in that chapter.

- **Foundation Summary**—The "Foundation Summary" section of this book departs from the typical features of the "Foundation Summary" section of other Cisco Press Exam Certification Guides. This section does not repeat any details from the "Foundation Topics" section; instead, it simply summarizes and lists facts related to the chapter but for which a longer or more detailed explanation is not warranted.

- **Key Topics**—Throughout the "Foundation Topics" section, a Key Topic icon has been placed beside the most important areas for review. After reading a chapter, when doing your final preparation for the exam, take the time to flip through the chapters, looking for the Key Topic icons, and review those paragraphs, tables, figures, and lists.

- **Fill in Key Tables from Memory**—The more important tables from the chapters have been copied to PDF files available on the CD as Appendix E. The tables have most of the information removed. After printing these mostly empty tables, you can use them to improve your memory of the facts in the table by trying to fill them out. This tool should be useful for memorizing key facts. CD-only Appendix F contains the completed tables so you can check your work.

- **CD-based practice exam**—The companion CD contains multiple-choice questions and a testing engine. The CD includes 300 questions unique to the CD. As part of your final preparation, you should practice with these questions to help you get used to the exam-taking process, as well as help refine and prove your knowledge of the exam topics.

- **Key Terms and Glossary**—The more important terms mentioned in each chapter are listed at the end of each chapter under the heading "Definitions." The glossary, found at the end of the book, lists all the terms from the chapters. When studying each chapter, you should review the key terms, and for those terms about which you are unsure of the definition, you can review the short definitions from the glossary.

- **Further Reading**—Each chapter includes a suggested set of books and websites for additional study on the same topics covered in that chapter. Often, these references will be useful tools for preparation for the CCIE Routing and Switching lab exam.

Part I: LAN Switching

Blueprint topics covered in this chapter:

This chapter covers the following subtopics from the Cisco CCIE Routing and Switching written exam blueprint. Refer to the full blueprint in Table I-1 in the Introduction for more details on the topics covered in each chapter and their context within the blueprint.

- LAN Switching

- Ethernet

- Speed

- Duplex

- Unicast Flooding

- Fast Ethernet

- Gigabit Ethernet

CHAPTER 1

Ethernet Basics

It's no surprise that the concepts, protocols, and commands related to Ethernet are a key part of the CCIE Routing and Switching written exam. Almost all campus networks today are built using Ethernet technology. Also, Ethernet technology is moving into the WAN with the emergence of metro Ethernet. Even in an IT world, where technology changes rapidly, you can expect that ten years from now, Ethernet will still be an important part of the CCIE Routing and Switching written and lab exams.

For this chapter, if I had to venture a guess, probably 100 percent of you reading this book know a fair amount about Ethernet basics already. I must admit, I was tempted to leave it out. However, I would also venture a guess that at least some of you have forgotten a few facts about Ethernet. So you can read the whole chapter if your Ethernet recollections are a bit fuzzy—or you could just hit the highlights. For exam preparation, it is typically useful to use all the refresher tools: take the "Do I Know This Already?" quiz, complete the definitions of the terms listed at the end of the chapter, print and complete the tables in Appendix E, "Key Tables for CCIE Study," and certainly answer all the CD-ROM questions concerning Ethernet.

"Do I Know This Already?" Quiz

Table 1-1 outlines the major headings in this chapter and the corresponding "Do I Know This Already?" quiz questions.

Table 1-1 *"Do I Know This Already?" Foundation Topics Section-to-Question Mapping*

Foundation Topics Section	Questions Covered in This Section	Score
Ethernet Layer 1: Wiring, Speed, and Duplex	1–5	
Ethernet Layer 2: Framing and Addressing	6–7	
Switching and Bridging Logic	8	
Total Score		

In order to best use this pre-chapter assessment, remember to score yourself strictly. You can find the answers in Appendix A, "Answers to the 'Do I Know This Already?' Quizzes."

1. Which of the following denotes the correct usage of pins on the RJ-45 connectors at the opposite ends of an Ethernet cross-over cable?

   a. 1 to 1

   b. 1 to 2

   c. 1 to 3

   d. 6 to 1

   e. 6 to 2

   f. 6 to 3

2. Which of the following denotes the correct usage of pins on the RJ-45 connectors at the opposite ends of an Ethernet straight-through cable?

   a. 1 to 1

   b. 1 to 2

   c. 1 to 3

   d. 6 to 1

   e. 6 to 2

   f. 6 to 3

3. Which of the following commands must be configured on a Cisco IOS switch interface to disable Ethernet auto-negotiation?

   a. **no auto-negotiate**

   b. **no auto**

   c. Both **speed** and **duplex**

   d. **duplex**

   e. **speed**

4. Consider an Ethernet cross-over cable between two 10/100 ports on Cisco switches. One switch has been configured for 100-Mbps full duplex. Which of the following is true about the other switch?

   a. It will use a speed of 10 Mbps.

   b. It will use a speed of 100 Mbps.

   c. It will use a duplex setting of half duplex.

   d. It will use a duplex setting of full duplex.

5. Consider an Ethernet cross-over cable between two 10/100/1000 ports on Cisco switches. One switch has been configured for half duplex, and the other for full duplex. The ports successfully negotiate a speed of 1 Gbps. Which of the following could occur as a result of the duplex mismatch?

- **a.** No frames can be received by the half-duplex switch without it believing an FCS error has occurred.

- **b.** CDP would detect the mismatch and change the full-duplex switch to half duplex.

- **c.** CDP would detect the mismatch and issue a log message to that effect.

- **d.** The half-duplex switch will erroneously believe collisions have occurred.

6. Which of the following Ethernet header type fields is a 2-byte field?

- **a.** DSAP

- **b.** Type (in SNAP header)

- **c.** Type (in Ethernet V2 header)

- **d.** LLC Control

7. Which of the following standards defines a Fast Ethernet standard?

- **a.** IEEE 802.1Q

- **b.** IEEE 802.3U

- **c.** IEEE 802.1X

- **d.** IEEE 802.3Z

- **e.** IEEE 802.3AB

- **f.** IEEE 802.1AD

8. Suppose a brand-new Cisco IOS–based switch has just been taken out of the box and cabled to several devices. One of the devices sends a frame. For which of the following destinations would a switch flood the frames out all ports (except the port upon which the frame was received)?

- **a.** Broadcasts

- **b.** Unknown unicasts

- **c.** Known unicasts

- **d.** Multicasts

Foundation Topics

Ethernet Layer 1: Wiring, Speed, and Duplex

Before making an Ethernet LAN functional, end-user devices, routers, and switches must be cabled correctly. To run with fewer transmission errors at higher speeds, and to support longer cable distances, variations of copper and optical cabling can be used. The different Ethernet specifications, cable types, and cable lengths per the various specifications are important for the exam, and are listed in the "Foundation Summary" section.

RJ-45 Pinouts and Category 5 Wiring

You should know the details of cross-over and straight-through Category 5 (Cat 5) or Cat 5e cabling for most any networking job. The EIA/TIA defines the cabling specifications for Ethernet LANs (http://www.eia.org and http://www.tiaonline.org), including the pinouts for the RJ-45 connects, as shown in Figure 1-1.

Figure 1-1 *RJ-45 Pinouts with Four-Pair UTP Cabling*

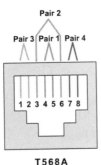
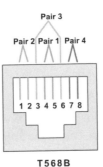

The most popular Ethernet standards (10BASE-T and 100BASE-TX) each use two twisted pairs (specifically pairs 2 and 3 shown in Figure 1-1), with one pair used for transmission in each direction. Depending on which pair a device uses to transmit and receive, either a straight-through or cross-over cable is required. Table 1-2 summarizes how the cabling and pinouts work.

Table 1-2 *Ethernet Cabling Types*

Type of Cable	Pinouts	Key Pins Connected
Straight-through	T568A (both ends) or T568B (both ends)	1 – 1; 2 – 2; 3 – 3; 6 – 6
Cross-over	T568A on one end, T568B on the other	1 – 3; 2 – 6; 3 – 1; 6 – 2

Many Ethernet standards use two twisted pairs, with one pair being used for transmission in each direction. For instance, a PC network interface card (NIC) transmits on pair 1,2 and receives on pair 3,6; switch ports do the opposite. So, a straight-through cable works well, connecting pair 1,2 on the PC (PC transmit pair) to the switch port's pair 1,2, on which the switch receives. When the two devices on the ends of the cable both transmit using the same pins, a cross-over cable is required. For instance, if two connected switches send using the pair at pins 3,6 and receive on pins 1,2, then the cable needs to connect the pair at 3,6 on one end to pins 1,2 at the other end, and vice versa.

> **NOTE** Cross-over cables can also be used between a pair of PCs, swapping the transmit pair on one end (1,2) with the receive pins at the other end (3,6).

Cisco also supports a switch feature that lets the switch figure out if the wrong cable is installed: *Auto-MDIX* (automatic medium-dependent interface crossover) detects the wrong cable and causes the switch to swap the pair it uses for transmitting and receiving, which solves the cabling problem. (As of publication, this feature is not supported on all Cisco switch models.)

Auto-negotiation, Speed, and Duplex

By default, each Cisco switch port uses *Ethernet auto-negotiation* to determine the speed and duplex setting (half or full). The switches can also set their duplex setting with the **duplex** interface subcommand, and their speed with—you guessed it—the **speed** interface subcommand.

Switches can dynamically detect the speed setting on a particular Ethernet segment by using a few different methods. Cisco switches (and many other devices) can sense the speed using the *Fast Link Pulses (FLP)* of the auto-negotiation process. However, if auto-negotiation is disabled on either end of the cable, the switch detects the speed anyway based on the incoming electrical signal. You can force a speed mismatch by statically configuring different speeds on either end of the cable, causing the link to no longer function.

Switches detect duplex settings through auto-negotiation only. If both ends have auto-negotiation enabled, the duplex is negotiated. However, if either device on the cable disables auto-negotiation, the devices without a configured duplex setting must assume a default. Cisco switches use a default duplex setting of half duplex (HDX) (for 10-Mbps and 100-Mbps interfaces) or full duplex (FDX) (for 1000-Mbps interfaces). To disable auto-negotiation on a Cisco switch port, you simply need to statically configure the speed and the duplex settings.

Ethernet devices can use FDX only when collisions cannot occur on the attached cable; a collision-free link can be guaranteed only when a shared hub is not in use. The next few topics review how Ethernet deals with collisions when they do occur, as well as what is different with Ethernet logic in cases where collisions cannot occur and FDX is allowed.

CSMA/CD

The original Ethernet specifications expected collisions to occur on the LAN. The media was shared, creating a literal electrical bus. Any electrical signal induced onto the wire could collide with a signal induced by another device. When two or more Ethernet frames overlap on the transmission medium at the same instant in time, a collision occurs; the collision results in bit errors and lost frames.

The original Ethernet specifications defined the *Carrier Sense Multiple Access with Collision Detection (CSMA/CD)* algorithm to deal with the inevitable collisions. CSMA/CD minimizes the number of collisions, but when they occur, CSMA/CD defines how the sending stations can recognize the collisions and retransmit the frame. The following list outlines the steps in the CSMA/CD process:

1. A device with a frame to send listens until the Ethernet is not busy (in other words, the device cannot sense a carrier signal on the Ethernet segment).

2. When the Ethernet is not busy, the sender begins sending the frame.

3. The sender listens to make sure that no collision occurred.

4. If there was a collision, all stations that sent a frame send a jamming signal to ensure that all stations recognize the collision.

5. After the jamming is complete, each sender of one of the original collided frames randomizes a timer and waits that long before resending. (Other stations that did not create the collision do not have to wait to send.)

6. After all timers expire, the original senders can begin again with Step 1.

Collision Domains and Switch Buffering

A *collision domain* is a set of devices that can send frames that collide with frames sent by another device in that same set of devices. Before the advent of LAN switches, Ethernets were either physically shared (10BASE2 and 10BASE5) or shared by virtue of shared hubs and their Layer 1 "repeat out all other ports" logic. Ethernet switches greatly reduce the number of possible collisions, both through frame buffering and through their more complete Layer 2 logic.

By definition of the term, Ethernet hubs:

■ Operate solely at Ethernet Layer 1

■ Repeat (regenerate) electrical signals to improve cabling distances

■ Forward signals received on a port out all other ports (no buffering)

As a result of a hub's logic, a hub creates a single *collision domain*. Switches, however, create a different collision domain per switch port, as shown in Figure 1-2.

Figure 1-2 *Collision Domains with Hubs and Switches*

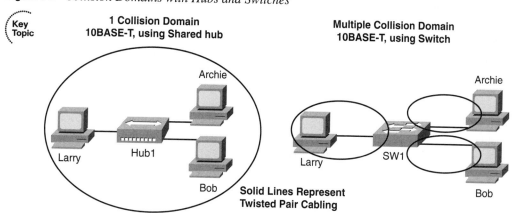

Switches have the same cabling and signal regeneration benefits as hubs, but switches do a lot more—including sometimes reducing or even eliminating collisions by buffering frames. When switches receive multiple frames on different switch ports, they store the frames in memory buffers to prevent collisions.

For instance, imagine that a switch receives three frames at the same time, entering three different ports, and they all must exit the same switch port. The switch simply stores two of the frames in memory, forwarding the frames sequentially. As a result, in Figure 1-2, the switch prevents any frame sent by Larry from colliding with a frame sent by Archie or Bob—which by definition puts each of the PCs attached to the switch in Figure 1-2 in different collision domains.

When a switch port connects via cable to a single other non-hub device—for instance, like the three PCs in Figure 1-2—no collisions can possibly occur. The only devices that could create a collision are the switch port and the one connected device—and they each have a separate twisted pair on which to transmit. Because collisions cannot occur, such segments can use full-duplex logic.

When a switch port connects to a hub, it needs to operate in HDX mode, because collisions might occur due to the logic used by the hub.

NOTE NICs operating in HDX mode use *loopback circuitry* when transmitting a frame. This circuitry loops the transmitted frame back to the receive side of the NIC, so that when the NIC receives a frame over the cable, the combined looped-back signal and received signal allows the NIC to notice that a collision has occurred.

Basic Switch Port Configuration

The three key configuration elements on a Cisco switch port are auto-negotiation, speed, and duplex. Cisco switches use auto-negotiation by default; it is then disabled if both the speed and duplex are manually configured. You can set the speed using the **speed** {**auto** | **10** | **100** | **1000**} interface subcommand, assuming the interface supports multiple speeds. You configure the duplex setting using the **duplex** {**auto** | **half** | **full**} interface subcommand.

Example 1-1 shows the manual configuration of the speed and duplex on the link between Switch1 and Switch4 from Figure 1-3, and the results of having mismatched duplex settings. (The book refers to specific switch commands used on IOS-based switches, referred to as "Catalyst IOS" by the Cisco CCIE blueprint.)

Figure 1-3 *Simple Switched Network with Trunk*

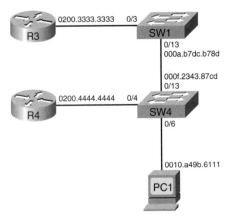

Example 1-1 *Manual Setting for Duplex and Speed, with Mismatched Duplex*

```
switch1# show interface fa 0/13
FastEthernet0/13 is up, line protocol is up
  Hardware is Fast Ethernet, address is 000a.b7dc.b78d (bia 000a.b7dc.b78d)
  MTU 1500 bytes, BW 100000 Kbit, DLY 100 usec,
     reliability 255/255, txload 1/255, rxload 1/255
  Encapsulation ARPA, loopback not set
  Keepalive set (10 sec)
  Full-duplex, 100Mb/s
! remaining lines omitted for brevity
! Below, Switch1's interface connecting to Switch4 is configured for 100 Mbps,
! HDX. Note that IOS rejects the first duplex command; you cannot set duplex until
! the speed is manually configured.
switch1# conf t
Enter configuration commands, one per line.  End with CNTL/Z.
switch1(config)# int fa 0/13
switch1(config-if)# duplex half
Duplex will not be set until speed is set to non-auto value
switch1(config-if)# speed 100
```

Example 1-1 *Manual Setting for Duplex and Speed, with Mismatched Duplex (Continued)*

```
05:08:41: %LINEPROTO-5-UPDOWN: Line protocol on Interface FastEthernet0/13, changed state
  to down
05:08:46: %LINEPROTO-5-UPDOWN: Line protocol on Interface FastEthernet0/13, changed state
  to up
switch1(config-if)# duplex half
!!!!!!!!!!!!!!!!!!!!!!!!!!!!!!!!!!!!!!!!!!!!!!!!!!!!!!!!!!!!!!!!!!!!!!!!!!!!!!!!!!!!!!!
! NOT SHOWN: Configuration for 100/half on Switch4's int fa 0/13.
!!!!!!!!!!!!!!!!!!!!!!!!!!!!!!!!!!!!!!!!!!!!!!!!!!!!!!!!!!!!!!!!!!!!!!!!!!!!!!!!!!!!!!!
! Now with both switches manually configured for speed and duplex, neither will be
! using Ethernet auto-negotiation. As a result, below the duplex setting on Switch1
! can be changed to FDX with Switch4 remaining configured to use HDX.
switch1# conf t
Enter configuration commands, one per line.  End with CNTL/Z.
switch1(config)# int fa 0/13
switch1(config-if)# duplex full
05:13:03: %LINEPROTO-5-UPDOWN: Line protocol on Interface FastEthernet0/13, changed state
  to down
05:13:08: %LINEPROTO-5-UPDOWN: Line protocol on Interface FastEthernet0/13, changed state
  to up
switch1(config-if)#^Z
switch1# sh int fa 0/13
FastEthernet0/13 is up, line protocol is up
! Lines omitted for brevity
  Full-duplex, 100Mb/s
! remaining lines omitted for brevity
! Below, Switch4 is shown to be HDX. Note
! the collisions counters at the end of the show interface command.
switch4# sh int fa 0/13
FastEthernet0/13 is up, line protocol is up (connected)
  Hardware is Fast Ethernet, address is 000f.2343.87cd (bia 000f.2343.87cd)
  MTU 1500 bytes, BW 100000 Kbit, DLY 1000 usec,
     reliability 255/255, txload 1/255, rxload 1/255
  Encapsulation ARPA, loopback not set
  Keepalive set (10 sec)
  Half-duplex, 100Mb/s
! Lines omitted for brevity
  5 minute output rate 583000 bits/sec, 117 packets/sec
     25654 packets input, 19935915 bytes, 0 no buffer
     Received 173 broadcasts (0 multicast)
     0 runts, 0 giants, 0 throttles
     0 input errors, 0 CRC, 0 frame, 0 overrun, 0 ignored
     0 watchdog, 173 multicast, 0 pause input
     0 input packets with dribble condition detected
     26151 packets output, 19608901 bytes, 0 underruns
     54 output errors, 5 collisions, 0 interface resets
     0 babbles, 54 late collision, 59 deferred
     0 lost carrier, 0 no carrier, 0 PAUSE output
     0 output buffer failures, 0 output buffers swapped out
```

continues

Example 1-1 *Manual Setting for Duplex and Speed, with Mismatched Duplex (Continued)*

```
02:40:49: %CDP-4-DUPLEX_MISMATCH: duplex mismatch discovered on FastEthernet0/13
(not full duplex), with Switch1 FastEthernet0/13 (full duplex).
! Above, CDP messages have been exchanged over the link between switches. CDP
! exchanges information about Duplex on the link, and can notice (but not fix)
! the mismatch.
```

The statistics on switch4 near the end of the example show collisions (detected in the time during which the first 64 bytes were being transmitted) and late collisions (after the first 64 bytes were transmitted). In an Ethernet that follows cabling length restrictions, collisions should be detected while the first 64 bytes are being transmitted. In this case, Switch1 is using FDX logic, meaning it sends frames anytime—including when Switch4 is sending frames. As a result, Switch4 receives frames anytime, and if sending at the time, it believes a collision has occurred. Switch4 has deferred 59 frames, meaning that it chose to wait before sending frames because it was currently receiving a frame. Also, the retransmission of the frames that Switch4 thought were destroyed due to a collision, but may not have been, causes duplicate frames to be received, occasionally causing application connections to fail and routers to lose neighbor relationships.

Ethernet Layer 2: Framing and Addressing

In this book, as in many Cisco courses and documents, the word *frame* refers to the bits and bytes that include the Layer 2 header and trailer, along with the data encapsulated by that header and trailer. The term *packet* is most often used to describe the Layer 3 header and data, without a Layer 2 header or trailer. Ethernet's Layer 2 specifications relate to the creation, forwarding, reception, and interpretation of Ethernet frames.

The original Ethernet specifications were owned by the combination of Digital Equipment Corp., Intel, and Xerox—hence the name "Ethernet (DIX)." Later, in the early 1980s, the IEEE standardized Ethernet, defining parts (Layer 1 and some of Layer 2) in the 802.3 *Media Access Control (MAC)* standard, and other parts of Layer 2 in the 802.2 *Logical Link Control (LLC)* standard. Later, the IEEE realized that the 1-byte DSAP field in the 802.2 LLC header was too small. As a result, the IEEE introduced a new frame format with a *Sub-Network Access Protocol (SNAP)* header after the 802.2 header, as shown in the third style of header in Figure 1-4. Finally, in 1997, the IEEE added the original DIX V2 framing to the 802.3 standard as well as shown in the top frame in Figure 1-40.

Table 1-3 lists the header fields, along with a brief explanation. The more important fields are explained in more detail after the table.

Figure 1-4 *Ethernet Framing Options*

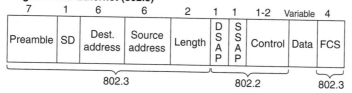

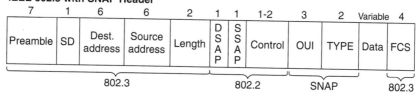

Table 1-3 *Ethernet Header Fields*

Field	Description
Preamble (DIX)	Provides synchronization and signal transitions to allow proper clocking of the transmitted signal. Consists of 62 alternating 1s and 0s, and ends with a pair of 1s.
Preamble and Start of Frame Delimiter (802.3)	Same purpose and binary value as DIX preamble; 802.3 simply renames the 8-byte DIX preamble as a 7-byte preamble and a 1-byte Start of Frame Delimiter (SFD).
Type (or Protocol Type) (DIX)	2-byte field that identifies the type of protocol or protocol header that follows the header. Allows the receiver of the frame to know how to process a received frame.
Length (802.3)	Describes the length, in bytes, of the data following the Length field, up to the Ethernet trailer. Allows an Ethernet receiver to predict the end of the received frame.
Destination Service Access Point (802.2)	DSAP; 1-byte protocol type field. The size limitations, along with other uses of the low-order bits, required the later addition of SNAP headers.
Source Service Access Point (802.2)	SSAP; 1-byte protocol type field that describes the upper-layer protocol that created the frame.

continues

Table 1-3 *Ethernet Header Fields (Continued)*

Field	Description
Control (802.2)	1- or 2-byte field that provides mechanisms for both connectionless and connection-oriented operation. Generally used only for connectionless operation by modern protocols, with a 1-byte value of 0x03.
Organizationally Unique Identifier (SNAP)	OUI; 3-byte field, generally unused today, providing a place for the sender of the frame to code the OUI representing the manufacturer of the Ethernet NIC.
Type (SNAP)	2-byte Type field, using same values as the DIX Type field, overcoming deficiencies with size and use of the DSAP field.

Types of Ethernet Addresses

Ethernet addresses, also frequently called MAC addresses, are 6 bytes in length, typically listed in hexadecimal form. There are three main types of Ethernet address, as listed in Table 1-4.

Table 1-4 *Three Types of Ethernet/MAC Address*

Type of Ethernet/MAC Address	Description and Notes
Unicast	Fancy term for an address that represents a single LAN interface. The I/G bit, the most significant bit in the most significant byte, is set to 0.
Broadcast	An address that means "all devices that reside on this LAN right now." Always a value of hex FFFFFFFFFFFF.
Multicast	A MAC address that implies some subset of all devices currently on the LAN. By definition, the I/G bit is set to 1.

Most engineers instinctively know how unicast and broadcast addresses are used in a typical network. When an Ethernet NIC needs to send a frame, it puts its own unicast address in the Source Address field of the header. If it wants to send the frame to a particular device on the LAN, the sender puts the other device's MAC address in the Ethernet header's Destination Address field. If the sender wants to send the frame to every device on the LAN, it sends the frame to the FFFF.FFFF.FFFF broadcast destination address. (A frame sent to the broadcast address is named a *broadcast* or *broadcast frame,* and frames sent to unicast MAC addresses are called *unicasts* or *unicast frames.*)

Multicast Ethernet frames are used to communicate with a possibly dynamic subset of the devices on a LAN. The most common use for Ethernet multicast addresses involves the use of IP multicast. For example, if only 3 of 100 users on a LAN want to watch the same video stream using an IP multicast–based video application, the application can send a single multicast frame. The three interested devices prepare by listening for frames sent to a particular multicast Ethernet address, processing frames destined for that address. Other devices may receive the frame, but they ignore its contents. Because the concept of Ethernet multicast is most often used today with IP multicast, most of the rest of the details of Ethernet multicast will be covered in Chapter 16, "Introduction to IP Multicasting."

Ethernet Address Formats

The IEEE intends for unicast addresses to be unique in the universe by administering the assignment of MAC addresses. The IEEE assigns each vendor a code to use as the first 3 bytes of its MAC addresses; that first half of the addresses is called the *Organizationally Unique Identifier (OUI)*. The IEEE expects each manufacturer to use its OUI for the first 3 bytes of the MAC assigned to any Ethernet product created by that vendor. The vendor then assigns a unique value in the low-order 3 bytes for each Ethernet card that it manufactures—thereby ensuring global uniqueness of MAC addresses. Figure 1-5 shows the basic Ethernet address format, along with some additional details.

Figure 1-5   *Ethernet Address Format*

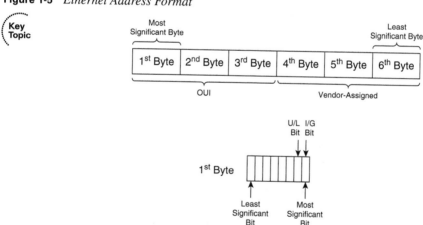

Note that Figure 1-5 shows the location of the most significant byte and most significant bit in each byte. IEEE documentation lists Ethernet addresses with the most significant byte on the left. However, inside each byte, the leftmost bit is the least significant bit, and the rightmost bit is the most significant bit. Many documents refer to the bit order as *canonical;* other documents refer to it as *little-endian*. Regardless of the term, the bit order inside each byte is important for understanding the meaning of the two most significant bits in an Ethernet address:

■   The Individual/Group (I/G) bit

■   The Universal/Local (U/L) bit

Table 1-5 summarizes the meaning of each bit.

Table 1-5 *I/G and U/L Bits*

Field	Meaning
I/G	Binary 0 means the address is a unicast; Binary 1 means the address is a multicast or broadcast.
U/L	Binary 0 means the address is vendor assigned; Binary 1 means the address has been administratively assigned, overriding the vendor-assigned address.

The I/G bit signifies whether the address represents an individual device or a group of devices, and the U/L bit identifies locally configured addresses. For instance, the Ethernet multicast addresses used by IP multicast implementations always start with 0x01005E. Hex 01 (the first byte of the address) converts to binary 00000001, with the most significant bit being 1, confirming the use of the I/G bit.

> **NOTE**   Often, when overriding the MAC address to use a local address, the device or device driver does not enforce the setting of the U/L bit to a value of 1.

Protocol Types and the 802.3 Length Field

Each of the three types of Ethernet header shown in Figure 1-4 has a field identifying the format of the Data field in the frame. Generically called a *Type* field, these fields allow the receiver of an Ethernet frame to know how to interpret the data in the received frame. For instance, a router might want to know whether the frame contains an IP packet, an IPX packet, and so on.

DIX and the revised IEEE framing use the Type field, also called the Protocol Type field. The originally-defined IEEE framing uses those same 2 bytes as a Length field. To distinguish the style of Ethernet header, the Ethernet Type field values begin at 1536, and the length of the Data field in an IEEE frame is limited to decimal 1500 or less. That way, an Ethernet NIC can easily determine whether the frame follows the DIX or original IEEE format.

The original IEEE frame used a 1-byte Protocol Type field (DSAP) for the 802.2 LLC standard type field. It also reserved the high-order 2 bits for other uses, similar to the I/G and U/L bits in MAC addresses. As a result, there were not enough possible combinations in the DSAP field for the needs of the market—so the IEEE had to define yet another type field, this one inside an additional IEEE SNAP header. Table 1-6 summarizes the meaning of the three main Type field options with Ethernet.

Table 1-6 *Ethernet Type Fields*

Type Field	Description
Protocol Type	DIX V2 Type field; 2 bytes; registered values now administered by the IEEE
DSAP	802.2 LLC; 1 byte, with 2 high-order bits reserved for other purposes; registered values now administered by the IEEE
SNAP	SNAP header; 2 bytes; uses same values as Ethernet Protocol Type; signified by an 802.2 DSAP of 0xAA

Switching and Bridging Logic

In this chapter so far, you have been reminded about the cabling details for Ethernet along with the formats and meanings of the fields inside Ethernet frames. A switch's ultimate goal is to deliver those frames to the appropriate destination(s) based on the destination MAC address in the frame header. Table 1-7 summarizes the logic used by switches when forwarding frames, which differs based on the type of destination Ethernet address and on whether the destination address has been added to its MAC address table.

Table 1-7 *LAN Switch Forwarding Behavior*

Type of Address	Switch Action
Known unicast	Forwards frame out the single interface associated with the destination address
Unknown unicast	Floods frame out all interfaces, except the interface on which the frame was received
Broadcast	Floods frame identically to unknown unicasts
Multicast	Floods frame identically to unknown unicasts, unless multicast optimizations are configured

For unicast forwarding to work most efficiently, switches need to know about all the unicast MAC addresses and out which interface the switch should forward frames sent to each MAC address. Switches learn MAC addresses, and the port to associate with them, by reading the source MAC address of received frames. You can see the learning process in Example 1-2, along with several other details of switch operation. Figure 1-6 lists the devices in the network associated with Example 1-2, along with their MAC addresses.

Figure 1-6 *Sample Network with MAC Addresses Shown*

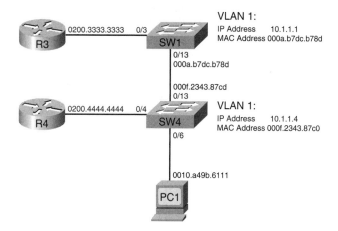

Example 1-2 *Command Output Showing MAC Address Table Learning*

```
Switch1# show mac-address-table dynamic
          Mac Address Table
-------------------------------------------

Vlan    Mac Address      Type       Ports
----    -----------      ----       -----
  1     000f.2343.87cd   DYNAMIC    Fa0/13
  1     0200.3333.3333   DYNAMIC    Fa0/3
  1     0200.4444.4444   DYNAMIC    Fa0/13
Total Mac Addresses for this criterion: 3
! Above, Switch1's MAC address table lists three dynamically learned addresses,
! including Switch4's FA 0/13 MAC.
! Below, Switch1 pings Switch4's management IP address.
Switch1# ping 10.1.1.4

Type escape sequence to abort.
Sending 5, 100-byte ICMP Echos to 10.1.1.4, timeout is 2 seconds:
!!!!!
Success rate is 100 percent (5/5), round-trip min/avg/max = 1/2/4 ms
! Below Switch1 now knows the MAC address associated with Switch4's management IP
! address. Each switch has a range of reserved MAC addresses, with the first MAC
! being used by the switch IP address, and the rest being assigned in sequence to
! the switch interfaces - note 0xcd (last byte of 2nd address in the table above)
! is for Switch4's FA 0/13 interface, and is 13 (decimal) larger than Switch4's
! base MAC address.
Switch1# show mac-address-table dynamic
          Mac Address Table
-------------------------------------------

Vlan    Mac Address      Type       Ports
----    -----------      ----       -----
  1     000f.2343.87c0   DYNAMIC    Fa0/13
  1     000f.2343.87cd   DYNAMIC    Fa0/13
  1     0200.3333.3333   DYNAMIC    Fa0/3
  1     0200.4444.4444   DYNAMIC    Fa0/13
Total Mac Addresses for this criterion: 4
! Not shown: PC1 ping 10.1.1.23 (R3) PC1's MAC in its MAC address table
-------------------------------------------

Vlan    Mac Address      Type       Ports
----    -----------      ----       -----
  1     000f.2343.87c0   DYNAMIC    Fa0/13
  1     000f.2343.87cd   DYNAMIC    Fa0/13
  1     0010.a49b.6111   DYNAMIC    Fa0/13
```

Example 1-2   *Command Output Showing MAC Address Table Learning (Continued)*

```
    1    0200.3333.3333    DYNAMIC    Fa0/3
    1    0200.4444.4444    DYNAMIC    Fa0/13
Total Mac Addresses for this criterion: 5
! Above, Switch1 learned the PC's MAC address, associated with FA 0/13,
! because the frames sent by the PC came into Switch1 over its FA 0/13.
! Below, Switch4's MAC address table shows PC1's MAC off its FA 0/6
switch4# show mac-address-table dynamic
          Mac Address Table
-------------------------------------------

Vlan    Mac Address       Type       Ports
----    -----------       --------   -----
    1    000a.b7dc.b780   DYNAMIC    Fa0/13
    1    000a.b7dc.b78d   DYNAMIC    Fa0/13
    1    0010.a49b.6111   DYNAMIC    Fa0/6
    1    0200.3333.3333   DYNAMIC    Fa0/13
    1    0200.4444.4444   DYNAMIC    Fa0/4
Total Mac Addresses for this criterion: 5
! Below, for example, the aging timeout (default 300 seconds) is shown, followed
! by a command just listing the mac address table entry for a single address.
switch4# show mac-address-table aging-time
Vlan    Aging Time
----    ----------
    1    300
switch4# show mac-address-table address 0200.3333.3333
          Mac Address Table
-------------------------------------------

Vlan    Mac Address       Type       Ports
----    -----------       --------   -----
    1    0200.3333.3333   DYNAMIC    Fa0/13
Total Mac Addresses for this criterion: 1
```

Foundation Summary

This section lists additional details and facts to round out the coverage of the topics in this chapter. Unlike most of the Cisco Press *Exam Certification Guides*, this "Foundation Summary" does not repeat information presented in the "Foundation Topics" section of the chapter. Please take the time to read and study the details in the "Foundation Topics" section of the chapter, as well as review items noted with a Key Topic icon.

Table 1-8 lists the different types of Ethernet and some distinguishing characteristics of each type.

Table 1-8 *Ethernet Standards*

Type of Ethernet	General Description
10BASE5	Commonly called "thick-net"; uses coaxial cabling
10BASE2	Commonly called "thin-net"; uses coaxial cabling
10BASE-T	First type of Ethernet to use twisted-pair cabling
DIX Ethernet Version 2	Layer 1 and Layer 2 specifications for original Ethernet, from Digital/Intel/Xerox; typically called DIX V2
IEEE 802.3	Called MAC due to the name of the IEEE committee (Media Access Control); original Layer 1 and 2 specifications, standardized using DIX V2 as a basis
IEEE 802.2	Called LLC due to the name of the IEEE committee (Logical Link Control); Layer 2 specification for header common to multiple IEEE LAN specifications
IEEE 802.3u	IEEE standard for Fast Ethernet (100 Mbps) over copper and optical cabling; typically called FastE
IEEE 802.3z	Gigabit Ethernet over optical cabling; typically called GigE
IEEE 802.3ab	Gigabit Ethernet over copper cabling

Switches forward frames when necessary, and do not forward when there is no need to do so, thus reducing overhead. To accomplish this, switches perform three actions:

■ Learn MAC addresses by examining the source MAC address of each received frame

■ Decide when to forward a frame or when to filter (not forward) a frame, based on the destination MAC address

■ Create a loop-free environment with other bridges by using the Spanning Tree Protocol

The internal processing algorithms used by switches vary among models and vendors; regardless, the internal processing can be categorized as one of the methods listed in Table 1-9.

Table 1-9 *Switch Internal Processing*

Switching Method	Description
Store-and-forward	The switch fully receives all bits in the frame (store) before forwarding the frame (forward). This allows the switch to check the FCS before forwarding the frame, thus ensuring that errored frames are not forwarded.
Cut-through	The switch performs the address table lookup as soon as the Destination Address field in the header is received. The first bits in the frame can be sent out the outbound port before the final bits in the incoming frame are received. This does not allow the switch to discard frames that fail the FCS check, but the forwarding action is faster, resulting in lower latency.
Fragment-free	This performs like cut-through switching, but the switch waits for 64 bytes to be received before forwarding the first bytes of the outgoing frame. According to Ethernet specifications, collisions should be detected during the first 64 bytes of the frame, so frames that are in error because of a collision will not be forwarded.

Table 1-10 lists some of the most popular Cisco IOS commands related to the topics in this chapter.

Table 1-10 *Catalyst IOS Commands for Catalyst Switch Configuration*

Command	Description
interface vlan 1	Global command; moves user to interface configuration mode for a VLAN interface
interface fastethernet *0/x*	Puts user in interface configuration mode for that interface
duplex {auto I full I half}	Used in interface configuration mode; sets duplex mode for the interface
speed {10 I 100 I 1000 I auto I nonegotiate}	Used in interface configuration mode; sets speed for the interface
show mac address-table [aging-time I count I dynamic I static] [address *hw-addr*] **[interface** *interface-id*] **[vlan** *vlan-id*]	Displays the MAC address table; the security option displays information about the restricted or static settings
show interface fastethernet 0/x	Displays interface status for a physical 10/100 interface
show interface vlan 1	Displays IP address configuration for VLAN

Table 1-11 outlines the types of UTP cabling.

Table 1-11 *UTP Cabling Reference*

UTP Category	Max Speed Rating	Description
1	—	Used for telephones, and not for data
2	4 Mbps	Originally intended to support Token Ring over UTP
3	10 Mbps	Can be used for telephones as well; popular option for Ethernet in years past, if Cat 3 cabling for phones was already in place
4	16 Mbps	Intended for the fast Token Ring speed option
5	1 Gbps	Very popular for cabling to the desktop
5e	1 Gbps	Added mainly for the support of copper cabling for Gigabit Ethernet
6	1 Gbps+	Intended as a replacement for Cat 5e, with capabilities to support multigigabit speeds

Table 1-12 lists the pertinent details of the Ethernet standards and the related cabling.

Table 1-12 *Ethernet Types and Cabling Standards*

Standard	Cabling	Maximum Single Cable Length
10BASE5	Thick coaxial	500 m
10BASE2	Thin coaxial	185 m
10BASE-T	UTP Cat 3, 4, 5, 5e, 6	100 m
100BASE-FX	Two strands, multimode	400 m
100BASE-T	UTP Cat 3, 4, 5, 5e, 6, 2 pair	100 m
100BASE-T4	UTP Cat 3, 4, 5, 5e, 6, 4 pair	100 m
100BASE-TX	UTP Cat 3, 4, 5, 5e, 6, or STP, 2 pair	100 m
1000BASE-LX	Long-wavelength laser, MM or SM fiber	10 km (SM) 3 km (MM)
1000BASE-SX	Short-wavelength laser, MM fiber	220 m with 62.5-micron fiber; 550 m with 50-micron fiber
1000BASE-ZX	Extended wavelength, SM fiber	100 km
1000BASE-CS	STP, 2 pair	25 m
1000BASE-T	UTP Cat 5, 5e, 6, 4 pair	100 m

Memory Builders

The CCIE Routing and Switching written exam, like all Cisco CCIE written exams, covers a fairly broad set of topics. This section provides some basic tools to help you exercise your memory about some of the broader topics covered in this chapter.

Fill in Key Tables from Memory

Appendix E, "Key Tables for CCIE Study," on the CD in the back of this book contains empty sets of some of the key summary tables in each chapter. Print Appendix E, refer to this chapter's tables in it, and fill in the tables from memory. Refer to Appendix F, "Solutions for Key Tables for CCIE Study," on the CD to check your answers.

Definitions

Next, take a few moments to write down the definitions for the following terms:

Auto-negotiation, half duplex, full duplex, cross-over cable, straight-through cable, unicast address, multicast address, broadcast address, loopback circuitry, I/G bit, U/L bit, CSMA/CD

Refer to the glossary to check your answers.

Further Reading

For a good reference for more information on the actual FLPs used by auto-negotiation, refer to the Fast Ethernet web page of the University of New Hampshire Research Computing Center's InterOperability Laboratory, at http://www.iol.unh.edu/services/testing/fe/training/.

Blueprint topics covered in this chapter:

This chapter covers the following subtopics from the Cisco CCIE Routing and Switching written exam blueprint. Refer to the full blueprint in Table I-1 in the Introduction for more details on the topics covered in each chapter and their context within the blueprint.

- Trunks

- VLAN Trunking Protocol (VTP) Administrative Functions

CHAPTER 2

Virtual LANs and VLAN Trunking

This chapter continues with the coverage of some of the most fundamental and important LAN topics with coverage of VLANs and VLAN trunking. As usual, for those of you current in your knowledge of the topics in this chapter, review the items next to the Key Point icons spread throughout the chapter, plus the "Foundation Summary," "Memory Builders," and "Q&A" sections at the end of the chapter.

"Do I Know This Already?" Quiz

Table 2-1 outlines the major headings in this chapter and the corresponding "Do I Know This Already?" quiz questions.

Table 2-1 *"Do I Know This Already?" Foundation Topics Section-to-Question Mapping*

Foundation Topics Section	Questions Covered in This Section	Score
Virtual LANs	1–2	
VLAN Trunking Protocol	3–5	
VLAN Trunking: ISL and 802.1Q	6–9	
Total Score		

In order to best use this pre-chapter assessment, remember to score yourself strictly. You can find the answers in Appendix A, "Answers to the 'Do I Know This Already?' Quizzes."

1. Assume that VLAN 28 does not yet exist on Switch1. Which of the following commands, issued from any part of global configuration mode (reached with the **configure terminal** exec command) would cause the VLAN to be created?

   a. **vlan 28**

   b. **vlan 28 name fred**

   c. **switchport vlan 28**

   d. **switchport access vlan 28**

   e. **switchport access 28**

2. Which of the following are the two primary motivations for using private VLANs?

   a. Better LAN security

   b. IP subnet conservation

   c. Better consistency in VLAN configuration details

   d. Reducing the impact of broadcasts on end-user devices

   e. Reducing the unnecessary flow of frames to switches that do not have any ports in the VLAN to which the frame belongs

3. Which of the following VLANs can be pruned by VTP on an 802.1Q trunk?

   a. 1–1023

   b. 1–1001

   c. 2–1001

   d. 1–1005

   e. 2–1005

4. An existing switched network has ten switches, with Switch1 and Switch2 being the only VTP servers in the network. The other switches are all VTP clients and have successfully learned about the VLANs from the VTP servers. The only configured VTP parameter on all switches is the VTP domain name (Larry). The VTP revision number is 201. What happens when a new, already-running VTP client switch, named Switch11, with domain name Larry and revision number 301, connects via a trunk to any of the other ten switches?

   a. No VLAN information changes; Switch11 ignores the VTP updates sent from the two existing VTP servers until the revision number reaches 302.

   b. The original ten switches replace their old VLAN configuration with the configuration in Switch11.

   c. Switch11 replaces its own VLAN configuration with the configuration sent to it by one of the original VTP servers.

   d. Switch11 merges its existing VLAN database with the database learned from the VTP servers, because Switch11 had a higher revision number.

5. An existing switched network has ten switches, with Switch1 and Switch2 being the only VTP servers in the network. The other switches are all VTP clients, and have successfully learned about the VLANs from the VTP server. The only configured VTP parameter is the VTP domain name (Larry). The VTP revision number is 201. What happens when an already-running VTP server switch, named Switch11, with domain name Larry and revision number 301, connects via a trunk to any of the other ten switches?

a. No VLAN information changes; all VTP updates between the original VTP domain and the new switch are ignored.

b. The original ten switches replace their old VLAN configuration with the configuration in Switch11.

c. Switch11 replaces its old VLAN configuration with the configuration sent to it by one of the original VTP servers.

d. Switch11 merges its existing VLAN database with the database learned from the VTP servers, because Switch11 had a higher revision number.

e. None of the other answers is correct.

6. Assume that two brand-new Cisco switches were removed from their cardboard boxes. PC1 was attached to one switch, PC2 was attached to the other, and the two switches were connected with a cross-over cable. The switch connection dynamically formed an 802.1Q trunk. When PC1 sends a frame to PC2, how many additional bytes of header are added to the frame before it passes over the trunk?

a. 0

b. 4

c. 8

d. 26

7. Assume that two brand-new Cisco Catalyst 3550 switches were connected with a cross-over cable. Before attaching the cable, one switch interface was configured with the **switchport trunk encapsulation dot1q**, **switchport mode trunk**, and **switchport nonegotiate** subcommands. Which of the following must be configured on the other switch before trunking will work between the switches?

a. **switchport trunk encapsulation dot1q**

b. **switchport mode trunk**

c. **switchport nonegotiate**

d. No configuration is required.

8. When configuring trunking on a Cisco router fa0/1 interface, under which configuration modes could the IP address associated with the native VLAN (VLAN 1 in this case) be configured?

   a. Interface fa 0/1 configuration mode

   b. Interface fa 0/1.1 configuration mode

   c. Interface fa 0/1.2 configuration mode

   d. None of the other answers is correct

9. Which of the following is false about 802.1Q?

   a. Encapsulates the entire frame inside an 802.1Q header and trailer

   b. Supports the use of a native VLAN

   c. Allows VTP to operate only on extended-range VLANs

   d. Is chosen over ISL by DTP

Foundation Topics

Virtual LANs

In an Ethernet LAN, a set of devices that receive a broadcast sent by any one of the devices in the same set is called a *broadcast domain*. On switches that have no concept of virtual LANs (VLAN), a switch simply forwards all broadcasts out all interfaces, except the interface on which it received the frame. As a result, all the interfaces on an individual switch are in the same broadcast domain. Also, if the switch connects to other switches and hubs, the interfaces on those switches and hubs are also in the same broadcast domain.

A *VLAN* is simply an administratively defined subset of switch ports that are in the same broadcast domain. Ports can be grouped into different VLANs on a single switch, and on multiple interconnected switches as well. By creating multiple VLANs, the switches create multiple broadcast domains. By doing so, a broadcast sent by a device in one VLAN is forwarded to the other devices in that same VLAN; however, the broadcast is not forwarded to devices in the other VLANs.

With VLANs and IP, best practices dictate a one-to-one relationship between VLANs and IP subnets. Simply put, the devices in a single VLAN are typically also in the same single IP subnet. Alternately, it is possible to put multiple subnets in one VLAN, and use secondary IP addresses on routers to route between the VLANs and subnets. Also, although not typically done, you can design a network to use one subnet on multiple VLANs, and use routers with proxy ARP enabled to forward traffic between hosts in those VLANs. (Private VLANs might be considered to consist of one subnet over multiple VLANs as well, as covered later in this chapter.) Ultimately, the CCIE written exams tend to focus more on the best use of technologies, so this book will assume that one subnet sits on one VLAN, unless otherwise stated.

Layer 2 switches forward frames between devices in the same VLAN, but they do not forward frames between two devices in different VLANs. To forward data between two VLANs, a multilayer switch (MLS) or router is needed. Chapter 6, "IP Forwarding (Routing)," covers the details of MLS.

VLAN Configuration

Configuring VLANs in a network of Cisco switches requires just a few simple steps:

Step 1   Create the VLAN itself.

Step 2   Associate the correct ports with that VLAN.

The challenge relates to how some background tasks differ depending on how the Cisco *VLAN Trunking Protocol (VTP)* is configured, and whether normal-range or extended-range VLANs are being used.

Using VLAN Database Mode to Create VLANs

To begin, consider Example 2-1, which shows some of the basic mechanics of VLAN creation in *VLAN database configuration mode*. VLAN database configuration mode allows the creation of VLANs, basic administrative settings for each VLAN, and verification of VTP configuration information. Only normal-range (VLANs 1–1005) VLANs can be configured in this mode, and the VLAN configuration is stored in a Flash file called vlan.dat.

Example 2-1 demonstrates VLAN database configuration mode, showing the configuration on Switch3 from Figure 2-1. The example shows VLANs 21 and 22 being created.

Figure 2-1 *Simple Access and Distribution*

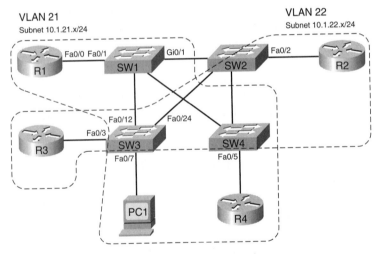

Example 2-1 *VLAN Creation in VLAN Database Mode–Switch3*

```
! Below, note that FA 0/12 and FA0/24 missing from the list, because they have
! dynamically become trunks, supporting multiple VLANs.
Switch3# show vlan brief
VLAN Name                             Status    Ports
---- -------------------------------- --------- -------------------------------
1    default                          active    Fa0/1, Fa0/2, Fa0/3, Fa0/4
                                                Fa0/5, Fa0/6, Fa0/7, Fa0/8
                                                Fa0/9, Fa0/10, Fa0/11, Fa0/13
                                                Fa0/14, Fa0/15, Fa0/16, Fa0/17
                                                Fa0/18, Fa0/19, Fa0/20, Fa0/21
                                                Fa0/22, Fa0/23
```

Example 2-1   *VLAN Creation in VLAN Database Mode–Switch3 (Continued)*

```
! Below, "unsup" means that this 2950 switch does not support FDDI and TR
1002 fddi-default              act/unsup
1003 token-ring-default        act/unsup
1004 fddinet-default           act/unsup
1005 trnet-default             act/unsup
! Below, vlan database moves user to VLAN database configuration mode.
! The vlan 21 command defines the VLAN, as seen in the next command output
! (show current), VLAN 21 is not in the "current" VLAN list.
Switch3# vlan database
Switch3(vlan)# vlan 21
VLAN 21 added:
    Name: VLAN0021
! The show current command lists the VLANs available to the IOS when the switch
! is in VTP Server mode. The command lists the VLANs in numeric order, with
! VLAN 21 missing.
Switch3(vlan)# show current
  VLAN ISL Id: 1
    Name: default
    Media Type: Ethernet
    VLAN 802.10 Id: 100001
    State: Operational
    MTU: 1500
    Backup CRF Mode: Disabled
    Remote SPAN VLAN: No

  VLAN ISL Id: 1002
    Name: fddi-default
    Media Type: FDDI
    VLAN 802.10 Id: 101002
    State: Operational
    MTU: 1500
    Backup CRF Mode: Disabled
    Remote SPAN VLAN: No
! Lines omitted for brevity
! Next, note that show proposed lists VLAN 21. The vlan 21 command
! creates the definition, but it must be "applied" before it is "current".
Switch3(vlan)# show proposed
  VLAN ISL Id: 1
    Name: default
    Media Type: Ethernet
    VLAN 802.10 Id: 100001
    State: Operational
    MTU: 1500
    Backup CRF Mode: Disabled
    Remote SPAN VLAN: No
```

continues

Example 2-1 *VLAN Creation in VLAN Database Mode–Switch3 (Continued)*

```
 VLAN ISL Id: 21
    Name: VLAN0021
    Media Type: Ethernet
    VLAN 802.10 Id: 100021
    State: Operational
    MTU: 1500
    Backup CRF Mode: Disabled
    Remote SPAN VLAN: No
! Lines omitted for brevity
! Next, you could apply to complete the addition of VLAN 21,
! abort to not make the changes and exit VLAN database mode, or
! reset to not make the changes but stay in VLAN database mode.
Switch3(vlan)# ?
VLAN database editing buffer manipulation commands:
   abort  Exit mode without applying the changes
   apply  Apply current changes and bump revision number
   exit   Apply changes, bump revision number, and exit mode
   no     Negate a command or set its defaults
   reset  Abandon current changes and reread current database
   show   Show database information
   vlan   Add, delete, or modify values associated with a single VLAN
   vtp    Perform VTP administrative functions.
! The apply command was used, making the addition of VLAN 21 complete.
Switch3(vlan)# apply
APPLY completed.
! A show current now would list VLAN 21.
Switch3(vlan)# vlan 22 name ccie-vlan-22
VLAN 22 added:
    Name: ccie-vlan-22
! Above and below, some variations on commands are shown, along with the
! creation of VLAN 22, with name ccie-vlan-22.
! Below, the vlan 22 option is used on show current and show proposed
! detailing the fact that the apply has not been done yet.
Switch3(vlan)# show current 22
VLAN 22 does not exist in current database
Switch3(vlan)# show proposed 22
   VLAN ISL Id: 22
! Lines omitted for brevity
! Finally, the user exits VLAN database mode using CTRL-Z, which does
! not inherently apply the change. CTRL-Z actually executes an abort.
Switch3(vlan)# ^Z
```

Key Topic

Using Configuration Mode to Put Interfaces into VLANs

To make a VLAN operational, the VLAN must be created, and then switch ports must be assigned to the VLAN. Example 2-2 shows how to associate the interfaces with the correct VLANs, once again on Switch3.

> **NOTE**   At the end of Example 2-1, VLAN 22 had not been successfully created. The
> assumption for Example 2-2 is that VLAN 22 has been successfully created.

Example 2-2 *Assigning Interfaces to VLANs–Switch3*

```
! First, the switchport access command assigns the VLAN numbers to the
! respective interfaces.

Switch3# config t
Enter configuration commands, one per line.  End with CNTL/Z.
Switch3(config)# int fa 0/3
Switch3(config-if)# switchport access vlan 22
Switch3(config-if)# int fa 0/7
Switch3(config-if)# switchport access vlan 21
Switch3(config-if)# ^Z
! Below, show vlan brief lists these same two interfaces as now being in
! VLANs 21 and 22, respectively.
Switch3# show vlan brief

VLAN Name                             Status    Ports
---- -------------------------------- --------- -------------------------------
1    default                          active    Fa0/1, Fa0/2, Fa0/4, Fa0/5
                                                Fa0/6, Fa0/8, Fa0/9, Fa0/10
                                                Fa0/11, Fa0/13, Fa0/14, Fa0/15
                                                Fa0/16, Fa0/17, Fa0/18, Fa0/19
                                                Fa0/20, Fa0/21, Fa0/22, Fa0/23
21   VLAN0021                         active    Fa0/7
22   ccie-vlan-22                     active    Fa0/3
! Lines omitted for brevity
! While the VLAN configuration is not shown in the running-config at this point,
! the switchport access command that assigns the VLAN for the interface is in the
! configuration, as seen with the show run int fa 0/3 command.
Switch3# show run int fa 0/3
interface FastEthernet0/3
switchport access vlan 22
```

Using Configuration Mode to Create VLANs

At this point, the two new VLANs (21 and 22) have been created on Switch3, and the two
interfaces are now in the correct VLANs. However, Cisco IOS switches support a different way to
create VLANs, using configuration mode, as shown in Example 2-3.

Example 2-3 *Creating VLANs in Configuration Mode–Switch3*

```
! First, VLAN 31 did not exist when the switchport access vlan 31 command was
! issued. As a result, the switch both created the VLAN and put interface fa0/8
! into that VLAN. Then, the vlan 32 global command was used to create a
```

continues

Example 2-3 *Creating VLANs in Configuration Mode–Switch3 (Continued)*

```
! VLAN from configuration mode, and the name subcommand was used to assign a
! non-default name.
Switch3# conf t
Enter configuration commands, one per line.  End with CNTL/Z.
Switch3(config)# int fa 0/8
Switch3(config-if)# switchport access vlan 31
% Access VLAN does not exist. Creating vlan 31
Switch3(config-if)# exit
Switch3(config)# vlan 32
Switch3(config-vlan)# name ccie-vlan-32
Switch3(config-vlan)# ^Z
Switch3# show vlan brief

VLAN Name                             Status    Ports
---- -------------------------------- --------- -------------------------------
1    default                          active    Fa0/1, Fa0/2, Fa0/4, Fa0/5
                                                Fa0/6, Fa0/9, Fa0/10, Fa0/11
                                                Fa0/13, Fa0/14, Fa0/15, Fa0/16
                                                Fa0/17, Fa0/18, Fa0/19, Fa0/20
                                                Fa0/21, Fa0/22, Fa0/23
21   VLAN0021                         active    Fa0/7
22   ccie-vlan-22                     active    Fa0/3
31   VLAN0031                         active    Fa0/8
32   ccie-vlan-32                     active
! Portions omitted for brevity
```

Example 2-3 shows how the **switchport access vlan** subcommand creates the VLAN, as needed, and assigns the interface to that VLAN. Note that in Example 2-3, the **show vlan brief** output lists fa0/8 as being in VLAN 31. Because no ports have been assigned to VLAN 32 as of yet, the final line in Example 2-3 simply does not list any interfaces.

The VLAN creation process is simple but laborious in a large network. If many VLANs exist, and they exist on multiple switches, instead of manually configuring the VLANs on each switch, you can use VTP to distribute the VLAN configuration of a VLAN to the rest of the switches. VTP will be discussed after a brief discussion of private VLANs.

Private VLANs

Engineers may design VLANs with many goals in mind. In many cases today, devices end up in the same VLAN just based on the physical locations of the wiring drops. Security is another motivating factor in VLAN design: devices in different VLANs do not overhear each other's broadcasts. Additionally, the separation of hosts into different VLANs and subnets requires an intervening router or multilayer switch between the subnets, and these types of devices typically provide more robust security features.

Regardless of the design motivations behind grouping devices into VLANs, good design practices typically call for the use of a single IP subnet per VLAN. In some cases, however, the need to increase security by separating devices into many small VLANs conflicts with the design goal of conserving the use of the available IP subnets. The Cisco private VLAN feature addresses this issue. Private VLANs allow a switch to separate ports as if they were on different VLANs, while consuming only a single subnet.

A common place to implement private VLANs is in the multitenant offerings of a service provider (SP). The SP can install a single router and a single switch. Then, the SP attaches devices from multiple customers to the switch. Private VLANs then allow the SP to use only a single subnet for the whole building, separating different customers' switch ports so that they cannot communicate directly, while supporting all customers with a single router and switch.

Conceptually, a private VLAN includes the following general characterizations of how ports communicate:

- Ports that need to communicate with all devices

- Ports that need to communicate with each other, and with shared devices, typically routers

- Ports that need to communicate only with shared devices

To support each category of allowed communications, a single private VLAN features a *primary VLAN* and one or more *secondary VLANs*. The ports in the primary VLAN are *promiscuous* in that they can send and receive frames with any other port, including ports assigned to secondary VLANs. Commonly accessed devices, such as routers and servers, are placed into the primary VLAN. Other ports, such as customer ports in the SP multitenant model, attach to one of the secondary VLANs.

Secondary VLANs are either *community VLANs* or *isolated VLANs*. The engineer picks the type based on whether the device is part of a set of ports that should be allowed to send frames back and forth (community VLAN ports), or whether the device port should not be allowed to talk to any other ports besides those on the primary VLAN (isolated VLAN). Table 2-2 summarizes the behavior of private VLAN communications between ports.

Table 2-2 *Private VLAN Communications Between Ports*

Description of Who Can Talk to Whom	Primary VLAN Ports	Community VLAN Ports[1]	Isolated VLAN Ports[1]
Talk to ports in primary VLAN (promiscuous ports)	Yes	Yes	Yes
Talk to ports in the same secondary VLAN (host ports)	N/A[2]	Yes	No
Talks to ports in another secondary VLAN	N/A[2]	No	No

[1]Community and isolated VLANs are secondary VLANs.

[2]Promiscuous ports, by definition in the primary VLAN, can talk to all other ports.

VLAN Trunking Protocol

VTP advertises VLAN configuration information to neighboring switches so that the VLAN configuration can be made on one switch, with all the other switches in the network learning the VLAN information dynamically. VTP advertises the VLAN ID, VLAN name, and VLAN type for each VLAN. However, VTP does not advertise any information about which ports (interfaces) should be in each VLAN, so the configuration to associate a switch interface with a particular VLAN (using the **switchport access vlan** command) must still be configured on each individual switch. Also, the existence of the VLAN IDs used for private VLANs is advertised, but the rest of the detailed private VLAN configuration is not advertised by VTP.

Each Cisco switch uses one of three VTP modes, as outlined in Table 2-3.

Table 2-3 *VTP Modes and Features**

Function	Server Mode	Client Mode	Transparent Mode
Originates VTP advertisements	Yes	Yes	No
Processes received advertisements to update its VLAN configuration	Yes	Yes	No
Forwards received VTP advertisements	Yes	Yes	Yes
Saves VLAN configuration in NVRAM or vlan.dat	Yes	Yes	Yes
Can create, modify, or delete VLANs using configuration commands	Yes	No	Yes

*CatOS switches support a fourth VTP mode (off), meaning that the switch does not create, listen to, or forward VTP updates.

VTP Process and Revision Numbers

The VTP update process begins when a switch administrator, from a VTP server switch, adds, deletes, or updates the configuration for a VLAN. When the new configuration occurs, the VTP server increments the old VTP *revision number* by 1, and advertises the entire VLAN configuration database along with the new revision number.

The VTP revision number concept allows switches to know when VLAN database changes have occurred. Upon receiving a VTP update, if the revision number in a received VTP update is larger than a switch's current revision number, it believes that there is a new version of the VLAN database. Figure 2-2 shows an example in which the old VTP revision number was 3, the server adds a new VLAN, incrementing the revision number to 4, and then propagates the VTP database to the other switches.

Figure 2-2   *VTP Revision Number Basic Operation*

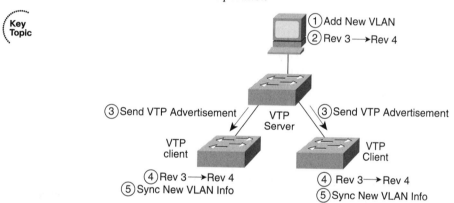

Cisco switches default to use VTP server mode, but they do not start sending VTP updates until the switch has been configured with a VTP domain name. At that point, the server begins to send its VTP updates, with a different database and revision number each time its VLAN configuration changes. However, the VTP clients in Figure 2-2 actually do not have to have the VTP domain name configured. If not configured, the client will assume it should use the VTP domain name in the first received VTP update. However, the client does need one small bit of configuration, namely, the VTP mode, as configured with the **vtp mode** global configuration command.

VTP clients and servers alike will accept VTP updates from other VTP server switches. When using VTP, for better availability, a switched network using VTP needs at least two VTP server switches. Under normal operations, a VLAN change could be made on one server switch, and the other VTP server (plus all the clients) would learn about the changes to the VLAN database. Once learned, both VTP servers and clients store the VLAN configuration in their respective vlan.dat files in flash memory; they do not store the VLAN configuration in NVRAM.

With multiple VTP servers installed in a LAN, it is possible to accidentally overwrite the VTP configuration in the network. If trunks fail and then changes are made on more than one VTP server, the VTP configuration databases could differ, with different configuration revision numbers. When the formerly-separated parts of the LAN reconnect using trunks, the VTP database with a higher revision number is propagated throughout the VTP domain, replacing some switches' VTP databases. Note also that because VTP clients can actually originate VTP updates, under the right circumstances, a VTP client can update the VTP database on another VTP client or server. See http://www.ciscopress.com/ 1587201968 and look for downloads, to download a document that describes how a client could update the VLAN database on another VTP client or server. In summary, for a newly-connected VTP server or client to change another switch's VTP database, the following must be true:

- The new link connecting the new switch is trunking.

- The new switch has the same VTP domain name as the other switches.

- The new switch's revision number is larger than that of the existing switches.

- The new switch must have the same password, if configured on the existing switches.

The revision number and VTP domain name can be easily seen with a Sniffer trace; to prevent DoS attacks with VTP, set VTP passwords, which are encoded as message digests (MD5) in the VTP updates. Also, some installations simply use VTP transparent mode on all switches, which prevents switches from ever listening to other switch VTP updates and erroneously deleting their VLAN configuration databases.

VTP Configuration

VTP sends updates out all active trunk interfaces (ISL or 802.1Q). However, with all default settings from Cisco, switches are in server mode, with no VTP domain name configured, and they do not send any VTP updates. Before any switches can learn VLAN information from another switch, at least one switch must have a bare-minimum VTP server configuration—specifically, a domain name.

Example 2-4 shows Switch3 configuring a VTP domain name to become a VTP server and advertise the VLANs it has configured. The example also lists several key VTP **show** commands. (Note that the example begins with VLANs 21 and 22 configured on Switch3, and all default settings for VTP on all four switches.)

Example 2-4 *VTP Configuration and* **show** *Command Example*

```
! First, Switch3 is configured with a VTP domain ID of CCIE-domain.
Switch3# conf t
Enter configuration commands, one per line.  End with CNTL/Z.
Switch3(config)# vtp domain CCIE-domain
Changing VTP domain name from NULL to CCIE-domain
Switch3(config)# ^Z
! Next, on Switch1, the VTP status shows the same revision as Switch3, and it
! learned the VTP domain name CCIE-domain. Note that Switch1 has no VTP-related
```

Example 2-4 *VTP Configuration and* **show** *Command Example (Continued)*

```
! configuration, so it is a VTP server; it learned the VTP domain name from.
! Switch3.
Switch1# sh vtp status
VTP Version                    : 2
Configuration Revision         : 2
Maximum VLANs supported locally : 1005
Number of existing VLANs       : 7
VTP Operating Mode             : Server
VTP Domain Name                : CCIE-domain
VTP Pruning Mode               : Disabled
VTP V2 Mode                    : Disabled
VTP Traps Generation           : Disabled
MD5 digest                     : 0x0E 0x07 0x9D 0x9A 0x27 0x10 0x6C 0x0B
Configuration last modified by 10.1.1.3 at 3-1-93 00:02:55
Local updater ID is 10.1.1.1 on interface Vl1 (lowest numbered VLAN interface found)
! The show vlan brief command lists the VLANs learned from Switch3.
Switch1# show vlan brief
VLAN Name                         Status    Ports
---- -------------------------------- --------- -------------------------------
1    default                          active    Fa0/1, Fa0/2, Fa0/3, Fa0/4
                                                Fa0/5, Fa0/6, Fa0/7, Fa0/10
                                                Fa0/11, Fa0/13, Fa0/14, Fa0/15
                                                Fa0/16, Fa0/17, Fa0/18, Fa0/19
                                                Fa0/20, Fa0/21, Fa0/22, Fa0/23
                                                Gi0/2

21   VLAN0021                         active
22   ccie-vlan-22                     active
1002 fddi-default                     active
1003 token-ring-default               active
1004 fddinet-default                  active
1005 trnet-default                    active
```

Example 2-4 shows examples of a few VTP configuration options. Table 2-4 provides a complete list, along with explanations.

Table 2-4 *VTP Configuration Options*

Key Topic

Option	Meaning
domain	Sends domain name in VTP updates. Received VTP update is ignored if it does not match a switch's domain name. One VTP domain name per switch is allowed.
password	Used to generate an MD5 hash that is included in VTP updates. Received VTP updates are ignored if the passwords on the sending and receiving switch do not match.
mode	Sets server, client, or transparent mode on the switch.

continues

Table 2-4 *VTP Configuration Options (Continued)*

Option	Meaning
version	Sets version 1 or 2. Servers and clients must match version to exchange VLAN configuration data. Transparent mode switches at version 2 forward version 1 or version 2 VTP updates.
pruning	Enables VTP pruning, which prevents flooding on a per-VLAN basis to switches that do not have any ports configured as members of that VLAN.
interface	Specifies from which interface a switch picks the source MAC address for VTP updates.

Normal-Range and Extended-Range VLANs

Some VLAN numbers are considered to be *normal*, whereas some others are considered to be *extended*. Normal-range VLANs are VLANs 1–1005, and can be advertised via VTP versions 1 and 2. These VLANs can be configured in VLAN database mode, with the details being stored in the vlan.dat file in Flash.

Extended-range VLANs range from 1006–4094, inclusive. However, these additional VLANs cannot be configured in VLAN database mode, nor stored in the vlan.dat file, nor advertised via VTP. In fact, to configure them, the switch must be in VTP transparent mode. (Also, you should take care to avoid using VLANs 1006–1024 for compatibility with CatOS-based switches.)

Both ISL and 802.1Q support extended-range VLANs today. Originally, ISL began life only supporting normal-range VLANs, using only 10 of the 15 bits reserved in the ISL header to identify the VLAN ID. The later-defined 802.1Q used a 12-bit VLAN ID field, thereby allowing support of the extended range. Following that, Cisco changed ISL to use 12 of its reserved 15 bits in the VLAN ID field, thereby supporting the extended range.

Table 2-5 summarizes VLAN numbers and provides some additional notes.

Table 2-5 *Valid VLAN Numbers, Normal and Extended*

VLAN Number	Normal or Extended?	Can Be Advertised and Pruned by VTP Versions 1 and 2?	Comments
0	Reserved	—	Not available for use
1	Normal	No	On Cisco switches, the default VLAN for all access ports; cannot be deleted or changed
2–1001	Normal	Yes	

Table 2-5   *Valid VLAN Numbers, Normal and Extended (Continued)*

VLAN Number	Normal or Extended?	Can Be Advertised and Pruned by VTP Versions 1 and 2?	Comments
1002–1005	Normal	No	Defined specifically for use with FDDI and TR translational bridging
1006–4094	Extended	No	

Storing VLAN Configuration

Catalyst IOS stores VLAN and VTP configuration in one of two places—either in a Flash file called vlan.dat or in the running configuration. (Remember that the term "Catalyst IOS" refers to a switch that uses IOS, not the Catalyst OS, which is often called CatOS.) IOS chooses the storage location in part based on the VTP mode, and in part based on whether the VLANs are normal-range VLANs or extended-range VLANs. Table 2-6 describes what happens based on what configuration mode is used to configure the VLANs, the VTP mode, and the VLAN range. (Note that VTP clients also store the VLAN configuration in vlan.dat, and they do not understand extended range VLANs.)

Table 2-6   *VLAN Configuration and Storage*

Key Topic

Function	When in VTP Server Mode	When in VTP Transparent Mode
Normal-range VLANs can be configured from	Both VLAN database and configuration modes	Both VLAN database and configuration modes
Extended-range VLANs can be configured from	Nowhere—cannot be configured	Configuration mode only
VTP and normal-range VLAN configuration commands are stored in	vlan.dat in Flash	Both vlan.dat in Flash and running configuration[1]
Extended-range VLAN configuration commands stored in	Nowhere—extended range not allowed in VTP server mode	Running configuration only

[1]When a switch reloads, if the VTP mode or domain name in the vlan.dat file and the startup-config file differ, the switch uses only the vlan.dat file's contents for VLAN configuration.

NOTE   The configuration characteristics referenced in Table 2-6 do not include the interface configuration command **switchport access vlan**; it includes the commands that create a VLAN (**vlan** command) and VTP configuration commands.

Of particular interest for those of you stronger with CatOS configuration skills is that when you erase the startup-config file, and reload the Cisco IOS switch, you do not actually erase the normal-range VLAN and VTP configuration information. To erase the VLAN and VTP configuration, you must use the **delete flash:vlan.dat** exec command. Also note that if multiple switches are in VTP server mode, if you delete vlan.dat on one switch and then reload it, as soon as the switch comes back up and brings up a trunk, it learns the old VLAN database via a VTP update from the other VTP server.

VLAN Trunking: ISL and 802.1Q

VLAN trunking allows switches, routers, and even PCs with the appropriate NICs to send traffic for multiple VLANs across a single link. In order to know to which VLAN a frame belongs, the sending switch, router, or PC adds a header to the original Ethernet frame, with that header having a field in which to place the VLAN ID of the associated VLAN. This section describes the protocol details for the two trunking protocols, followed by the details of how to configure trunking.

ISL and 802.1Q Concepts

If two devices are to perform trunking, they must agree to use either ISL or 802.1Q, because there are several differences between the two, as summarized in Table 2-7.

Table 2-7 *Comparing ISL and 802.1Q*

Feature	ISL	802.1Q
VLANs supported	Normal and extended range[1]	Normal and extended range
Protocol defined by	Cisco	IEEE
Encapsulates original frame or inserts tag	Encapsulates	Inserts tag
Supports native VLAN	No	Yes

[1]ISL originally supported only normal-range VLANs, but was later improved to support extended-range VLANs as well.

ISL and 802.1Q differ in how they add a header to the Ethernet frame before sending it over a trunk. ISL adds a new 26-byte header, plus a new trailer (to allow for the new FCS value), encapsulating the original frame. This encapsulating header uses the source address (listed as SA in Figure 2-3) of the device doing the trunking, instead of the source MAC of the original frame. ISL uses a multicast destination address (listed as DA in Figure 2-3) of either 0100.0C00.0000 or 0300.0C00.0000.

802.1Q inserts a 4-byte header, called a tag, into the original frame (right after the Source Address field). The original frame's addresses are left intact. Normally, an Ethernet controller would expect to find either an Ethernet Type field or 802.3 Length field right after the Source Address field. With an 802.1Q tag, the first 2 bytes after the Address fields holds a registered Ethernet type value of 0x8100, which implies that the frame includes an 802.1Q header. Because 802.1Q does not actually encapsulate the original frame, it is often called *frame tagging*. Figure 2-3 shows the contents of the headers used by both ISL and 802.1Q.

Figure 2-3 *ISL and 802.1Q Frame Marking Methods*

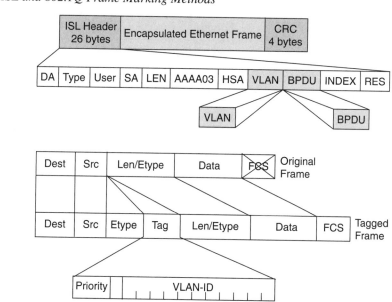

Finally, the last row from Table 2-7 refers to the *native VLAN*. 802.1Q does not tag frames sent inside the native VLAN. The native VLAN feature allows a switch to attempt to use 802.1Q trunking on an interface, but if the other device does not support trunking, the traffic for that one native VLAN can still be sent over the link. By default, the native VLAN is VLAN 1.

ISL and 802.1Q Configuration

Cisco switches use the *Dynamic Trunk Protocol (DTP)* to dynamically learn whether the device on the other end of the cable wants to perform trunking and, if so, which trunking protocol to use. DTP learns whether to trunk based on the DTP mode defined for an interface. Cisco switches default to use the DTP *desirable* mode, which means that the switch initiates sending DTP messages, hoping that the device on the other end of the segment replies with another DTP message. If a reply is received, DTP can detect whether both switches can trunk and, if so, which type of trunking to use. If both switches support both types of trunking, they choose to use ISL. (An upcoming section, "Trunk Configuration Compatibility," covers the different DTP modes and how they work.)

With the DTP mode set to desirable, switches can simply be connected, and they should dynamically form a trunk. You can, however, configure trunking details and verify the results with **show** commands. Table 2-8 lists some of the key Catalyst IOS commands related to trunking.

Table 2-8 *VLAN Trunking–Related Commands*

Key Topic

Command	Function
switchport | no switchport	Toggle defining whether to treat the interface as a switch interface (**switchport**) or as a router interface (**no switchport**)
switchport mode	Sets DTP negotiation parameters
switchport trunk	Sets trunking parameters if the interface is trunking
switchport access	Sets nontrunking-related parameters if the interface is not trunking
show interface trunk	Summary of trunk-related information
show interface *type number* **trunk**	Lists trunking details for a particular interface
show interface *type number* **switchport**	Lists nontrunking details for a particular interface

Figure 2-4 lists several details regarding Switch1's trunking configuration and status, as shown in Example 2-5. R1 is not configured to trunk, so Switch1 will fail to negotiate trunking. Switch2 is a Catalyst 3550, which supports both ISL and 802.1Q, so they will negotiate trunking and use ISL. Switch3 and Switch4 are Catalyst 2950s, which support only 802.1Q; as a result, Switch1 negotiates trunking, but picks 802.1Q as the trunking protocol.

Figure 2-4 *Trunking Configuration Reference for Example 2-5*

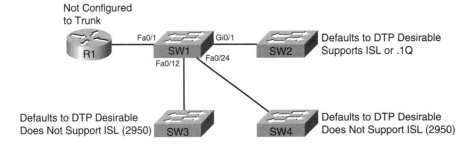

Example 2-5 *Trunking Configuration and **show** Command Example–Switch1*

```
! The administrative mode of dynamic desirable (trunking) and negotiate (trunking
! encapsulation) means that Switch1 attempted to negotiate to trunk, but the
! operational mode of static access means that trunking negotiation failed.
! The reference to "operational trunking encapsulation" of native means that
! no tagging occurs.
```

Example 2-5 *Trunking Configuration and* **show** *Command Example–Switch1 (Continued)*

```
Switch1# show int fa 0/1 switchport
Name: Fa0/1
Switchport: Enabled
Administrative Mode: dynamic desirable
Operational Mode: static access
Administrative Trunking Encapsulation: negotiate
Operational Trunking Encapsulation: native
Negotiation of Trunking: On
Access Mode VLAN: 1 (default)
Trunking Native Mode VLAN: 1 (default)
Administrative private-vlan host-association: none
Administrative private-vlan mapping: none
Operational private-vlan: none
Trunking VLANs Enabled: ALL
Pruning VLANs Enabled: 2-1001

Protected: false
Unknown unicast blocked: disabled
Unknown multicast blocked: disabled

Voice VLAN: none (Inactive)
Appliance trust: none
! Next, the show int gig 0/1 trunk command shows the configured mode
! (desirable), and the current status (N-ISL), meaning negotiated ISL. Note
! that the trunk supports the extended VLAN range as well.
Switch1# show int gig 0/1 trunk
Port        Mode        Encapsulation  Status        Native vlan
Gi0/1       desirable   n-isl          trunking      1

Port      Vlans allowed on trunk
Gi0/1     1-4094

Port      Vlans allowed and active in management domain
Gi0/1     1,21-22

Port      Vlans in spanning tree forwarding state and not pruned
Gi0/1     1,21-22
! Next, Switch1 lists all three trunks - the segments connecting to the other
! three switches - along with the type of encapsulation.
Switch1# show int trunk
Port      Mode        Encapsulation  Status        Native vlan
Fa0/12    desirable   n-802.1q       trunking      1
Fa0/24    desirable   n-802.1q       trunking      1
Gi0/1     desirable   n-isl          trunking      1

Port      Vlans allowed on trunk
Fa0/12    1-4094
```

continues

Example 2-5 *Trunking Configuration and* **show** *Command Example–Switch1 (Continued)*

```
Fa0/24    1-4094
Gi0/1     1-4094


Port      Vlans allowed and active in management domain
Fa0/12    1,21-22
Fa0/24    1,21-22
Gi0/1     1,21-22


Port      Vlans in spanning tree forwarding state and not pruned
Fa0/12    1,21-22
Fa0/24    1,21-22
Gi0/1     1,21-22
```

Allowed, Active, and Pruned VLANs

Although a trunk can support VLANs 1–4094, several mechanisms reduce the actual number of VLANs whose traffic flows over the trunk. First, VLANs can be administratively forbidden from existing over the trunk using the **switchport trunk allowed** interface subcommand. Also, any allowed VLANs must be configured on the switch before they are considered active on the trunk. Finally, VTP can prune VLANs from the trunk, with the switch simply ceasing to forward frames from that VLAN over the trunk.

The **show interface trunk** command lists the VLANs that fall into each category, as shown in the last command in Example 2-5. The categories are summarized as follows:

- **Allowed VLANs**—Each trunk allows all VLANs by default. However, VLANs can be removed or added to the list of allowed VLANs by using the **switchport trunk allowed** command.

- **Allowed and active**—To be active, a VLAN must be in the allowed list for the trunk (based on trunk configuration), and the VLAN must exist in the VLAN configuration on the switch. With PVST+, an STP instance is actively running on this trunk for the VLANs in this list.

- **Active and not pruned**—This list is a subset of the "allowed and active" list, with any VTP-pruned VLANs removed.

Trunk Configuration Compatibility

In most production networks, switch trunks are configured using the same standard throughout the network. For instance, rather than allow DTP to negotiate trunking,, many engineers configure trunk interfaces to always trunk (**switchport mode trunk**) and disable DTP on ports that should not trunk. IOS includes several commands that impact whether a particular segment becomes a trunk. Because many enterprises use a typical standard, it is easy to forget the nuances of how the related commands work. This section covers those small details.

Two IOS configuration commands impact if and when two switches form a trunk. The **switchport mode** and **switchport nonegotiate** interface subcommands define whether DTP even attempts to negotiate a trunk, and what rules it uses when the attempt is made. Additionally, the settings on the switch ports on either side of the segment dictate whether a trunk forms or not.

Table 2-9 summarizes the trunk configuration options. The first column suggests the configuration on one switch, with the last column listing the configuration options on the other switch that would result in a working trunk between the two switches.

Table 2-9 *Trunking Configuration Options That Lead to a Working Trunk*

Configuration Command on One Side[1]	Short Name	Meaning	To Trunk, Other Side Must Be
switchport mode trunk	Trunk	Always trunks on this end; sends DTP to help other side choose to trunk	On, desirable, auto
switchport mode trunk; **switchport nonegotiate**	Nonegotiate	Always trunks on this end; does not send DTP messages (good when other switch is a non-Cisco switch)	On
switchport mode dynamic desirable	Desirable	Sends DTP messages, and trunks if negotiation succeeds	On, desirable, auto
switchport mode dynamic auto	Auto	Replies to DTP messages, and trunks if negotiation succeeds	On, desirable
switchport mode access	Access	Never trunks; sends DTP to help other side reach same conclusion	(Never trunks)
switchport mode access; **switchport nonegotiate**	Access (with nonegotiate)	Never trunks; does not send DTP messages	(Never trunks)

[1]When the **switchport nonegotiate** command is not listed in the first column, the default (DTP negotiation is active) is assumed.

> **NOTE**   If an interface trunks, then the type of trunking (ISL or 802.1Q) is controlled by the setting on the **switchport trunk encapsulation** command. This command includes an option for dynamically negotiating the type (using DTP) or configuring one of the two types. See Example 2-5 for a sample of the syntax.

Configuring Trunking on Routers

VLAN trunking can be used on routers and hosts as well as on switches. However, routers do not support DTP, so you must manually configure them to support trunking. Additionally, you must manually configure a switch on the other end of the segment to trunk, because the router does not participate in DTP.

The majority of router trunking configurations use subinterfaces, with each subinterface being associated with one VLAN. The subinterface number does not have to match the VLAN ID; rather, the **encapsulation** command sits under each subinterface, with the associated VLAN ID being part of the **encapsulation** command. Also, because good design calls for one IP subnet per VLAN, if the router wants to forward IP packets between the VLANs, the router needs to have an IP address associated with each trunking subinterface.

You can configure 802.1Q native VLANs under a subinterface or under the physical interface on a router. If configured under a subinterface, you use the **encapsulation dot1q** *vlan-id* **native** subcommand, with the inclusion of the **native** keyword meaning that frames exiting this subinterface should not be tagged. As with other router trunking configurations, the associated IP address would be configured on that same subinterface. Alternately, if not configured on a subinterface, the router assumes that the native VLAN is associated with the physical interface. In this case, the **encapsulation** command is not needed under the physical interface; the associated IP address, however, would need to be configured under the physical interface.

Example 2-6 shows an example configuration for Router1 in Figure 2-1, both for ISL and 802.1Q. In this case, Router1 needs to forward packets between the subnets on VLANs 21 and 22. The first part of the example shows ISL configuration, with no native VLANs, and therefore only a subinterface being used for each VLAN. The second part of the example shows an alternative 802.1Q configuration, using the option of placing the native VLAN (VLAN 21) configuration on the physical interface.

Example 2-6   *Trunking Configuration on Router1*

Key
Topic

```
! Note the subinterface on the fa 0/0 interface, with the encapsulation
! command noting the type of trunking, as well as the VLAN number. The
! subinterface does not have to be the VLAN ID. Also note the IP addresses for
! each interface, allowing Router1 to route between VLANs.
interface fastethernet 0/0.1
 ip address 10.1.21.1 255.255.255.0
 encapsulation isl 21
!
interface fastethernet 0/0.2
 ip address 10.1.22.1 255.255.255.0
 encapsulation isl 22
! Next, an alternative 802.1Q configuration is shown. Note that this 802.1Q configuration
! places the IP address
! for VLAN 21 on the physical interface; the router simply associates the
! physical interface with the native VLAN. Alternatively, a subinterface could be
! used, with the encapsulation dot1q 21 native command specifying that the router
! should treat this VLAN as the native VLAN.
interface fastethernet 0/0
  ip address 10.1.21.1 255.255.255.0
!
interface fastethernet 0/0.2
  ip address 10.1.22.1 255.255.255.0
  encapsulation dot1q 22
```

Note also that the router does not have an explicitly defined allowed VLAN list. However, the allowed VLAN list is implied based on the configured VLANs. For instance, in this example, Router1 allows VLAN 1 (because it cannot be deleted), VLAN 21, and VLAN 22. A **show interface trunk** command on Switch1 would show only 1, 21, and 22 as the allowed VLANs on FA0/1.

802.1Q-in-Q Tunneling

Traditionally, VLANs have not extended beyond the WAN boundary. VLANs in one campus extend to a WAN edge router, but VLAN protocols are not used on the WAN.

Today, several emerging alternatives exist for the passage of VLAN traffic across a WAN, including 802.1Q-in-Q, Ethernet over MPLS (EoMPLS), and VLAN MPLS (VMPLS). While these topics are more applicable to the CCIE Service Provider certification, you should at least know the concept of 802.1 Q-in-Q tunneling.

Also known as Q-in-Q or Layer 2 protocol tunneling, 802.1Q-in-Q allows an SP to preserve 802.1Q VLAN tags across a WAN service. By doing so, VLANs actually span multiple geographically dispersed sites. Figure 2-5 shows the basic idea.

Figure 2-5 *Q-in-Q: Basic Operation*

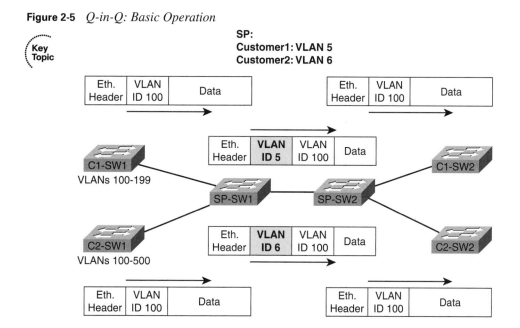

The ingress SP switch takes the 802.1Q frame, and then tags each frame entering the interface with an additional 802.1Q header. In this case, all of Customer1's frames are tagged as VLAN 5 as they pass over the WAN; Customer2's frames are tagged with VLAN 6. After removing the tag at egress, the customer switch sees the original 802.1Q frame, and can interpret the VLAN ID correctly. The receiving SP switch (SP-SW2 in this case) can keep the various customers' traffic separate based on the additional VLAN tags.

Using Q-in-Q, an SP can offer VLAN services, even when the customers use overlapping VLAN IDs. Customers get more flexibility for network design options, particularly with metro Ethernet services. Plus, CDP and VTP traffic passes transparently over the Q-in-Q service.

Foundation Summary

This section lists additional details and facts to round out the coverage of the topics in this chapter. Unlike most of the Cisco Press *Exam Certification Guides*, this "Foundation Summary" does not repeat information presented in the "Foundation Topics" section of the chapter. Please take the time to read and study the details in the "Foundation Topics" section of the chapter, as well as review items noted with a Key Topic icon.

Table 2-10 lists some of the most popular IOS commands related to the topics in this chapter. (The command syntax was copied from the *Catalyst 3550 Multilayer Switch Command Reference, 12.1(20)EA2*. Note that some switch platforms may have differences in the command syntax.)

Table 2-10   *Catalyst IOS Commands Related to Chapter 2*

Command	Description
show mac address-table [**aging-time** l **count** l **dynamic** l **static**] [**address** *hw-addr*] [**interface** *interface-id*] [**vlan** *vlan-id*]	Displays the MAC address table; the security option displays information about the restricted or static settings
show interfaces [*interface-id* l **vlan** *vlan-id*] **switchport** l **trunk**]	Displays detailed information about an interface operating as an access port or a trunk
show vlan [**brief** l **id** *vlan-id* l **name** *vlan-name* l *summary*]	EXEC command that lists information about VLAN
show vlan [*vlan*]	Displays VLAN information
show vtp status	Lists VTP configuration and status information
switchport mode {**access** l **dot1q-tunnel** l **dynamic** {**auto** l **desirable**} l **trunk**}	Configuration command setting nontrunking (**access**), trunking, and dynamic trunking (**auto** and **desirable**) parameters
switchport nonegotiate	Interface subcommand that disables DTP messages; interface must be configured as trunk or access port
switchport trunk {**allowed vlan** *vlan-list*} l {**encapsulation** {**dot1q** l **isl** l **negotiate**}} l {**native vlan** *vlan-id*} l {**pruning vlan** *vlan-list*}	Interface subcommand used to set parameters used when the port is trunking
switchport access vlan *vlan-id*	Interface subcommand that statically configures the interface as a member of that one VLAN

Table 2-11 lists the commands related to VLAN creation—both the VLAN database mode configuration commands (reached with the **vlan database** privileged mode command) and the normal configuration mode commands.

> **NOTE** Some command parameters may not be listed in Table 2-11.

Table 2-11 *Catalyst 3550 VLAN Database and Configuration Mode Command List*

VLAN Database	Configuration
vtp {**domain** *domain-name* | **password** *password* | **pruning** | **v2-mode** | {**server** | **client** | **transparent**} }	**vtp** {**domain** *domain-name* | **file** *filename* | **interface** *name* | **mode** {**client** | **server** | **transparent**} | **password** *password* | **pruning** | **version** *number*}
vlan *vlan-id* [**backupcrf** {**enable** | **disable**}] [**mtu** *mtu-size*] [**name** *vlan-name*] [**parent** *parent-vlan-id*] [**state** {**suspend** | **active**}]	**vlan** *vlan-id*[1]
show {**current** | **proposed** | **difference**}	No equivalent
apply | **abort** | **reset**	No equivalent

[1]Creates the VLAN and places the user in VLAN configuration mode, where commands matching the VLAN database mode options of the **vlan** command are used to set the same parameters.

Memory Builders

The CCIE Routing and Switching written exam, like all Cisco CCIE written exams, covers a fairly broad set of topics. This section provides some basic tools to help you exercise your memory about some of the broader topics covered in this chapter.

Fill in Key Tables from Memory

Appendix E, "Key Tables for CCIE Study," on the CD in the back of this book contains empty sets of some of the key summary tables in each chapter. Print Appendix E, refer to this chapter's tables in it, and fill in the tables from memory. Refer to Appendix F, "Solutions for Key Tables for CCIE Study," on the CD to check your answers.

Definitions

Next, take a few moments to write down the definitions for the following terms:

VLAN, broadcast domain, DTP, VTP pruning, 802.1Q, ISL, native VLAN, encapsulation, private VLAN, promiscuous port, community VLAN, isolated VLAN, 802.1Q-in-Q, Layer 2 protocol tunneling

Refer to the Glossary to check your answers.

Further Reading

The topics in this chapter tend to be covered in slightly more detail in CCNP Switching exam preparation books. For more details on these topics, refer to *Authorized Self-Study Guide: Building Cisco Multilayer Switched Networks (BCMSN)*, Fourth Edition, and *CCNP BCMSN Official Exam Certification Guide*, Fourth Edition.

Cisco LAN Switching, by Kennedy Clark and Kevin Hamilton, is an excellent reference for LAN-related topics in general, and certainly very useful for CCIE written and lab exam preparation.

Blueprint topics covered in this chapter:

This chapter covers the following subtopics from the Cisco CCIE Routing and Switching written exam blueprint. Refer to the full blueprint in Table I-1 in the Introduction for more details on the topics covered in each chapter and their context within the blueprint.

- 802.1d

- 802.1s

- 802.1w

- Loop Guard

- Root Guard

- Bridge Protocol Data Unit (BRDU) Guard

- STP Port Roles, Failure Propagation, and Loopguard Operation

- Rapid Spanning Tree Protocol (RSTP)

- Trunks

CHAPTER 3

Spanning Tree Protocol

Spanning Tree Protocol (STP) is probably one of the most widely known protocols covered on the CCIE Routing and Switching written exam. STP has been around a long time, is used in most every campus network today, and is covered extensively on the CCNP BCMSN exam. This chapter covers a broad range of topics related to STP.

"Do I Know This Already?" Quiz

Table 3-1 outlines the major headings in this chapter and the corresponding "Do I Know This Already?" quiz questions.

Table 3-1 *"Do I Know This Already?" Foundation Topics Section-to-Question Mapping*

Foundation Topics Section	Questions Covered in This Section	Score
802.1d Spanning Tree Protocol	1–6	
Optimizing Spanning Tree	7–9	
Protecting STP	10	
Total Score		

In order to best use this pre-chapter assessment, remember to score yourself strictly. You can find the answers in Appendix A, "Answers to the 'Do I Know This Already?' Quizzes."

1. Assume that a non-root 802.1d switch has ceased to receive Hello BPDUs. Which STP setting determines how long a non-root switch waits before trying to choose a new Root Port?

   a. Hello timer setting on the Root

   b. Maxage timer setting on the Root

   c. Forward Delay timer setting on the Root

   d. Hello timer setting on the non-root switch

   e. Maxage timer setting on the non-root switch

   f. Forward Delay timer setting on the non-root switch

2. Assume that a non-root 802.1d switch receives a Hello BPDU with the TCN flag set. Which STP setting determines how long the non-root switch waits before timing out CAM entries?

   a. Hello timer setting on the Root

   b. Maxage timer setting on the Root

   c. Forward Delay timer setting on the Root

   d. Hello timer setting on the non-root switch

   e. Maxage timer setting on the non-root switch

   f. Forward Delay timer setting on the non-root switch

3. Assume that non-root Switch1 (SW1) is blocking on a 802.1Q trunk connected to Switch2 (SW2). Both switches are in the same MST region. SW1 ceases to receive Hellos from SW2. What timers have an impact on how long Switch1 takes to both become the Designated Port on that link and reach forwarding state?

   a. Hello timer setting on the Root

   b. Maxage timer setting on the Root

   c. Forward Delay timer on the Root

   d. Hello timer setting on SW1

   e. Maxage timer setting on SW1

   f. Forward Delay timer on SW1

4. Which of the following statements are true regarding support of multiple spanning trees over an 802.1Q trunk?

   a. Only one common spanning tree can be supported.

   b. Cisco PVST+ supports multiple spanning trees if the switches are Cisco switches.

   c. 802.1Q supports multiple spanning trees when using IEEE 802.1s MST.

   d. Two PVST+ domains can pass over a region of non-Cisco switches using 802.1Q trunks by encapsulating non-native VLAN Hellos inside the native VLAN Hellos.

5. When a switch notices a failure, and the failure requires STP convergence, it notifies the Root by sending a TCN BPDU. Which of the following best describes why the notification is needed?

   a. To speed STP convergence by having the Root converge quickly.

   b. To allow the Root to keep accurate count of the number of topology changes.

   c. To trigger the process that causes all switches to use a short timer to help flush the CAM.

   d. There is no need for TCN today; it is a holdover from DEC's STP specification.

6. Two switches have four parallel Ethernet segments, none of which forms into an EtherChannel. Assuming 802.1d is in use, what is the maximum number of the eight ports (four on each switch) that stabilize into a forwarding state?

    a. 1

    b. 3

    c. 4

    d. 5

    e. 7

7. Two switches have four Ethernet segments connecting them, with the intention of using an EtherChannel. Port fa 0/1 on one switch is connected to port fa0/1 on the other switch; port fa0/2 is connected to the other switch's port fa0/2; and so on. An EtherChannel can still form using these four segments, even though some configuration settings do not match on the corresponding ports on each switch. Which settings do not have to match?

    a. DTP negotiation settings (auto/desirable/on)

    b. Allowed VLAN list

    c. STP per-VLAN port cost on the ports on a single switch

    d. If 802.1Q, native VLAN

8. IEEE 802.1w does not use the exact same port states as does 802.1d. Which of the following are valid 802.1w port states?

    a. Blocking

    b. Listening

    c. Learning

    d. Forwarding

    e. Disabled

    f. Discarding

9. What STP tools or protocols supply a "Maxage optimization," allowing a switch to bypass the wait for Maxage to expire when its Root Port stops receiving Hellos?

    a. Loop Guard

    b. UDLD

    c. UplinkFast

    d. BackboneFast

    e. IEEE 802.1w

10. A trunk between switches lost its physical transmit path in one direction only. Which of the following features protect against the STP problems caused by such an event?

   a. Loop Guard

   b. UDLD

   c. UplinkFast

   d. PortFast

Foundation Topics

802.1d Spanning Tree Protocol

Although many CCIE candidates already know STP well, the details are easily forgotten. For instance, you can install a campus LAN, possibly turn on a few STP optimizations and security features out of habit, and have a working LAN using STP—without ever really contemplating how STP does what it does. And in a network that makes good use of Layer 3 switching, each STP instance might span only three to four switches, making the STP issues much more manageable—but more forgettable in terms of helping you remember things you need to know for the exam. This chapter reviews the details of IEEE 802.1d STP, and then goes on to related topics—802.1w RSTP, multiple spanning trees, STP optimizations, and STP security features.

STP uses messaging between switches to stabilize the network into a logical, loop-free topology. To do so, STP causes some interfaces (popularly called *ports* when discussing STP) to simply not forward or receive traffic—in other words, the ports are in a *blocking* state. The remaining ports, in an STP *forwarding* state, together provide a loop-free path to every Ethernet segment in the network.

Choosing Which Ports Forward: Choosing Root Ports and Designated Ports

To determine which ports forward and block, STP follows a three-step process, as listed in Table 3-2. Following the table, each of the three steps is explained in more detail.

Table 3-2   *Three Major 802.1d STP Process Steps*

Major Step	Description
Elect the root switch	The switch with the lowest bridge ID wins; the standard bridge ID is 2-byte priority followed by a MAC address unique to that switch.
Determine each switch's Root Port	The one port on each switch with the least cost path back to the root.
Determine the Designated Port for each segment	When multiple switches connect to the same segment, this is the switch that forwards the least cost Hello onto a segment.

Electing a Root Switch

Only one switch can be the *root* of the spanning tree; to select the root, the switches hold an *election*. Each switch begins its STP logic by creating and sending an STP Hello bridge protocol data unit (BPDU) message, claiming to be the root switch. If a switch hears a *superior Hello*—a Hello with a lower bridge ID—it stops claiming to be root by ceasing to originate and send Hellos. Instead, the switch starts forwarding the superior Hellos received from the superior candidate. Eventually, all switches except the switch with the best bridge ID cease to originate Hellos; that one switch wins the election and becomes the root switch.

The original IEEE 802.1d bridge ID held two fields:

■ The 2-byte Priority field, which was designed to be configured on the various switches to affect the results of the STP election process.

■ A 6-byte MAC Address field, which was included as a tiebreaker, because each switch's bridge ID includes a MAC address value that should be unique to each switch. As a result, some switch must win the root election.

The format of the original 802.1d bridge ID has been redefined. Figure 3-1 shows the original and new format of the bridge IDs.

Figure 3-1 *IEEE 802.1d STP Bridge ID Formats*

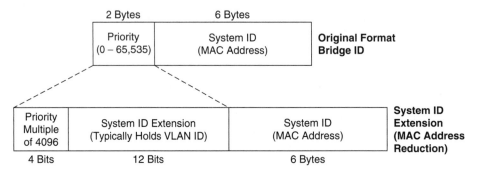

The format was changed mainly due to the advent of multiple spanning trees as supported by Per VLAN Spanning Tree Plus (PVST+) and IEEE 802.1s Multiple Spanning Trees (MST). With the old-style bridge ID format, a switch's bridge ID for each STP instance (possibly one per VLAN) was identical if the switch used a single MAC address when building the bridge ID. Having multiple STP instances with the same bridge ID was confusing, so vendors such as Cisco Systems used a different Ethernet BIA for each VLAN when creating the old-style bridge IDs. This provided a different bridge ID per VLAN, but it consumed a large number of reserved BIAs in each switch.

The System ID Extension allows a network to use multiple instances of STP, even one per VLAN, but without the need to consume a separate BIA on each switch for each STP instance. The System ID Extension field allows the VLAN ID to be placed into what was formerly the last 12 bits of the

Priority field. A switch can use a single MAC address to build bridge IDs, and with the VLAN number in the System ID Extension field still have a unique bridge ID in each VLAN. The use of the System ID Extension field is also called *MAC address reduction*, because of the need for many fewer reserved MAC addresses on each switch.

Determining the Root Port

Once the root is elected, the rest of the switches now need to determine their *Root Port (RP)*. The process proceeds as described in the following list:

1. The root creates and sends a Hello every Hello timer (2 seconds default).

2. Each switch that receives a Hello forwards the Hello after updating the following fields in the Hello: the cost, the forwarding switch's bridge ID, forwarder's port priority, and forwarder's port number.

3. Switches do not forward Hellos out ports that stabilize into a blocking state.

4. Of all the ports in which a switch receives Hellos, the port with the least calculated cost to the root is the RP.

A switch must examine the cost value in each Hello, plus the switch's STP port costs, in order to determine its least cost path to reach the root. To do so, the switch adds the cost listed in the Hello message to the switch's port cost of the port on which the Hello was received. For example, Figure 3-2 shows the loop network design and details several STP cost circulations.

Figure 3-2 *Calculating STP Costs to Determine RPs*

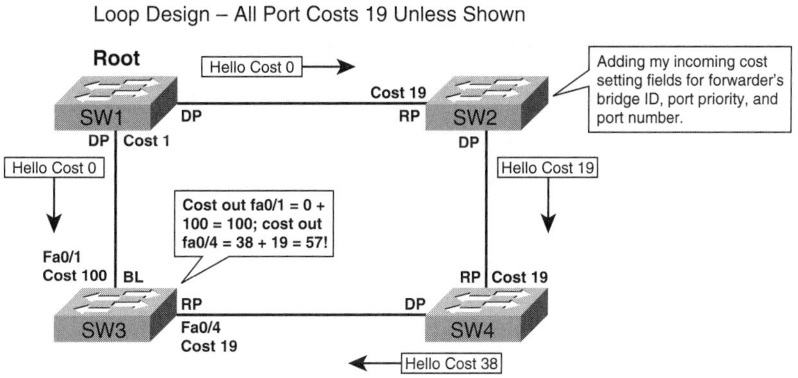

In Figure 3-2, SW1 happened to become root, and is originating Hellos of cost 0. SW3 receives two Hellos, one with cost 0 and one with cost 38. However, SW3 must then calculate its cost to reach the root, which is the advertised cost (0 and 38, respectively) plus SW3's port costs (100 and 19, respectively). As a result, although SW3 has a direct link to SW1, the calculated cost is lower out interface fa0/4 (cost 57) than it is out interface fa0/1 (cost 100), so SW3 chooses its fa0/4 interface as its RP.

> **NOTE** Many people think of STP costs as being associated with a segment; however, the cost is actually associated with interfaces. Good design practices dictate using the same STP cost on each end of a point-to-point Ethernet segment, but the values can be different.

While the costs shown in Figure 3-2 might seem a bit contrived, the same result would happen with default port costs if the link from SW1 to SW3 were Fast Ethernet (default cost 19), and the other links were Gigabit Ethernet (default cost 4). Table 3-3 lists the default port costs according to IEEE 802.1d. Note that the IEEE updated 802.1d in the late 1990s, changing the suggested default port costs.

Table 3-3 *Default Port Costs According to IEEE 802.1d*

Speed of Ethernet	Original IEEE Cost	Revised IEEE Cost
10 Mbps	100	100
100 Mbps	10	19
1 Gbps	1	4
10 Gbps	1	2

When a switch receives multiple Hellos with equal calculated cost, it uses the following tiebreakers:

1. Pick the lowest value of the forwarding switch's bridge ID.

2. Use the lowest port priority of the neighboring switch. The neighboring switch added its own port priority to the Hello before forwarding it.

3. Use the lowest internal port number (of the forwarding switch) as listed inside the received Hellos.

Note that if the first tiebreaker in this list fails to produce an RP, this switch must have multiple links to the same neighboring switch. The last two tiebreakers simply help decide which of the multiple parallel links to use.

Determining the Designated Port

A converged STP topology results in only one switch forwarding onto each LAN segment. The switch that forwards onto a LAN segment is called the *designated switch* for that segment, and the port that it uses to forward frames onto that segment is called the *Designated Port (DP)*. By definition, only the DP on that segment should forward frames onto the segment.

To win the right to be the DP, a switch must send the Hello with the *lowest advertised cost* onto the segment. For instance, consider the segment between SW3 and SW4 in Figure 3-2 before the DP has been determined on that segment. SW3 would get Hellos directly from SW1, compute its cost to the root over that path, and then forward the Hello out its fa 0/4 interface to SW4, with cost 100. Similarly, SW4 will forward a Hello with cost 38, as shown in Figure 3-2. SW4's fa 0/3 port becomes the DP due to its lower advertised cost.

Only the DP forwards Hellos onto a LAN segment as well. In the same example, SW4 keeps sending the cost-38 Hellos out the port, but SW3 stops sending its inferior Hellos.

When the cost is a tie, STP uses the same tiebreakers to choose the DP as when choosing an RP: lowest forwarder's bridge ID, lowest forwarder's port priority, and lowest forwarder's port number.

Converging to a New STP Topology

STP logic monitors the normal ongoing Hello process when the network topology is stable; when the Hello process changes, STP then needs to react and converge to a new STP topology. When STP has a stable topology, the following occurs:

1. The root switch generates a Hello regularly based on the Hello timer.

2. Each non-root switch regularly (based on the Hello timer) receives a copy of the root's Hello on its RP.

3. Each switch updates and forwards the Hello out its Designated Ports.

4. For each blocking port, the switch regularly receives a copy of the Hello from the DP on that segment. (The switches do not forward Hellos out blocking interfaces.)

When some deviation from these events occurs, STP knows that the topology has changed and that convergence needs to take place. For instance, one simple case might be that the root switch loses power; the rest of the switches will not hear any Hello messages, and after the Maxage timer expires (default 10 times Hello, or 20 seconds), the switches elect a new root based on the logic described earlier in this chapter.

For a more subtle example, consider Figure 3-3, which shows the same loop network as in Figure 3-2. In this case, however, the link from SW1 to SW2 has just failed.

Figure 3-3 *Reacting to Loss of Link Between SW1 and SW2*

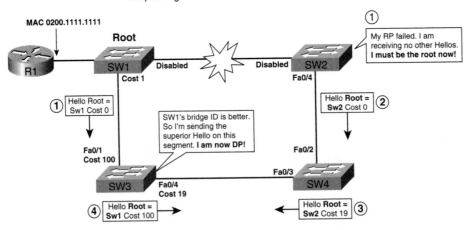

The following list describes some of the key steps from Figure 3-3:

1. SW2 ceases to receive Hellos on its RP.

2. Because SW2 is not receiving Hellos over any other path, it begins a new root election by claiming to be root and flooding Hellos out every port.

3. SW4 notices that the latest Hello implies a new root switch, but SW4 ends up with the same RP (for now). SW4 forwards the Hello out toward SW3 after updating the appropriate fields in the Hello.

4. SW3 receives the Hello from SW4, but it is inferior to the one SW3 receives from SW1. So, SW3 becomes the DP on the segment between itself and SW4, and starts forwarding the superior Hello on that port.

Remember, SW1 had won the earlier election; as of Steps 3 and 4, the Hellos from SW1 and SW2 are competing, and the one claiming SW1 as root will again win. The rest of the process results with SW3's fa0/4 as DP, SW4's fa 0/3 as RP, SW4's fa 0/2 as DP, and SW3's fa 0/4 as RP.

Topology Change Notification and Updating the CAM

When STP reconvergence occurs, some Content Addressable Memory (CAM) entries might be invalid (CAM is the Cisco term for what's more generically called the MAC address table, switching table, or bridging table on a switch). For instance, before the link failure shown in Figure 3-3, SW3's CAM might have had an entry for 0200.1111.1111 (Router1's MAC address) pointing out fa0/4 to SW4. (Remember, at the beginning of the scenario described in Figure 3-3,

SW3 was blocking on its fa0/1 interface back to SW1.) When the link between SW1 and SW2 failed, SW3 would need to change its CAM entry for 0200.1111.111 to point out port fa0/1.

To update the CAMs, two things need to occur:

- All switches need to be notified to time out their CAM entries.

- Each switch needs to use a short timer, equivalent to the Forward Delay timer (default 15 seconds), to time out the CAM entries.

Because some switches might not directly notice a change in the STP topology, any switch that detects a change in the STP topology has a responsibility to notify the rest of the switches. To do so, a switch simply notifies the root switch in the form of a *Topology Change Notification (TCN)* BPDU. The TCN goes up the tree to the root. After that, the root notifies all the rest of the switches. The process runs as follows:

1. A switch experiencing the STP port state change sends a TCN BPDU out its Root Port; it repeats this message every Hello time until it is acknowledged.

2. The next switch receiving that TCN BPDU sends back an acknowledgement via its next forwarded Hello BPDU by marking the *Topology Change Acknowledgement (TCA)* bit in the Hello.

3. The switch that was the DP on the segment in the first two steps repeats the first two steps, sending a TCN BPDU out its Root Port, and awaiting acknowledgement from the DP on that segment.

By each successive switch repeating Steps 1 and 2, eventually the root receives a TCN BPDU. Once received, the root sets the TCA flag on the next several Hellos, which are forwarded to all switches in the network, notifying them that a change has occurred. A switch receiving a Hello BPDU with the TCA flag set uses the short (Forward Delay time) timer to time out entries in the CAM.

Transitioning from Blocking to Forwarding

When STP reconverges to a new, stable topology, some ports that were blocking might have been designated as DP or RP, so these ports need to be in a forwarding state. However, the transition from blocking to forwarding state cannot be made immediately without the risk of causing loops.

To transition to forwarding state but also prevent temporary loops, a switch first puts a formerly blocking port into *listening* state, and then into *learning* state, with each state lasting for the length of time defined by the forward delay timer (by default, 15 seconds). Table 3-4 summarizes the key points about all of the 802.1d STP port states.

Table 3-4 *IEEE 802.1d Spanning Tree Interface States*

State	Forwards Data Frames?	Learn Source MACs of Received Frames?	Transitory or Stable State?
Blocking	No	No	Stable
Listening	No	No	Transitory
Learning	No	Yes	Transitory
Forwarding	Yes	Yes	Stable
Disabled	No	No	Stable

In summary, when STP logic senses a change in the topology, it converges, possibly picking different ports as RP, DP, or neither. Any switch changing its RPs or DPs sends a TCN BPDU to the root at this point. For the ports newly designated as RP or DP, 802.1d STP first uses the listening and learning states before reaching the forwarding state. (The transition from forwarding to blocking can be made immediately.)

Per-VLAN Spanning Tree and STP over Trunks

If only one instance of STP was used for a switched network with redundant links but with multiple VLANs, several ports would be in a blocking state, unused under stable conditions. The redundant links would essentially be used for backup purposes.

The Cisco Per VLAN Spanning Tree Plus (PVST+) feature creates an STP instance for each VLAN. By tuning STP configuration per VLAN, each STP instance can use a different root switch and have different interfaces block. As a result, the traffic load can be balanced across the available links. For instance, in the common building design with distribution and access links in Figure 3-4, focus on the left side of the figure. In this case, the access layer switches block on different ports on VLANs 1 and 2, with different root switches.

Figure 3-4 *Operation of PVST+ for Better Load Balancing*

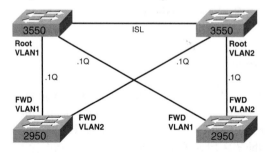

With different root switches and with default port costs, the access layer switches end up sending VLAN1 traffic over one uplink and VLAN2 traffic over another uplink.

Using 802.1Q with STP requires some extra thought as to how it works. 802.1Q does not support PVST+ natively; however, Cisco switches do support PVST+ over 802.1Q trunks. So, with all Cisco switches, and PVST+ (which is enabled by default), PVST+ works fine.

When using 802.1Q with non-Cisco switches, the switches must follow the IEEE standard completely, so the trunks support only a *Common Spanning Tree (CST)*. With standard 802.1Q, only one instance of STP runs only over the native VLAN, and that one STP topology is used for all VLANs. Although using only one STP instance reduces the STP messaging overhead, it does not allow load balancing by using multiple STP instances, as was shown with PVST+ in Figure 3-4.

When building networks using a mix of Cisco and non-Cisco switches, along with 802.1Q trunking, you can still take advantage of multiple STP instances in the Cisco portion of the network. Figure 3-5 shows two general options in which two CST regions of non-Cisco switches connect to two regions of Cisco PVST+ supporting switches.

Figure 3-5   *Combining Standard IEEE 802.1Q and CST with PVST+*

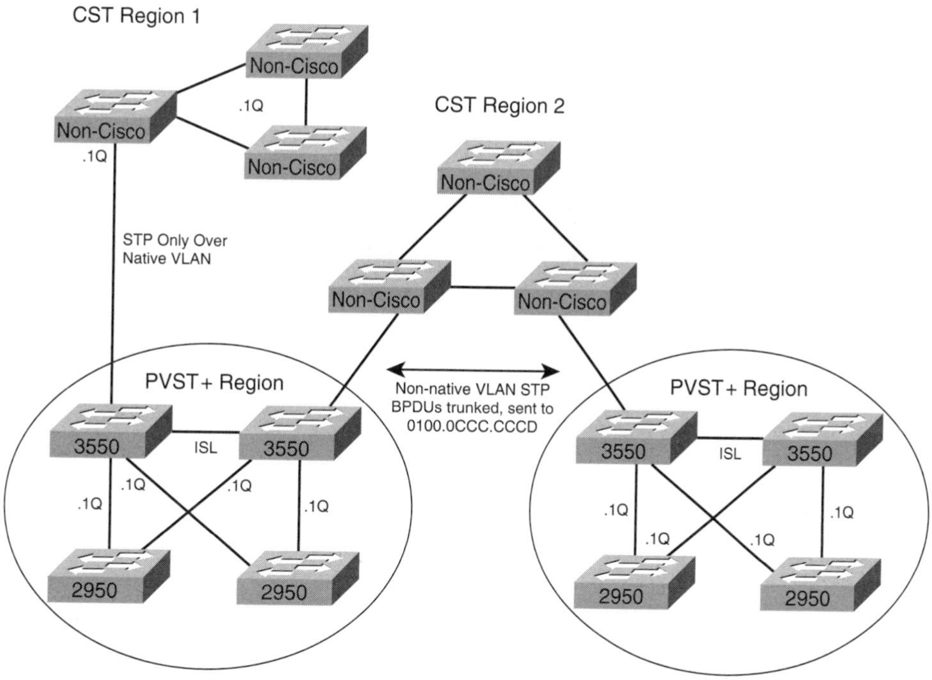

The left side of Figure 3-5 shows an example in which the CST region is not used for transit between multiple PVST+ regions. In this case, none of the PVST+ per-VLAN STP information needs to pass over the CST region. The PVST+ region maps the single CST instance to each of the PVST+ STP instances.

The rest of Figure 3-5 shows two PVST+ regions, separated by a single CST region (CST Region 2). In this case, the PVST+ per-VLAN STP information needs to pass through the CST region. To do so, PVST+ treats the CST region as a single link and tunnels the PVST+ BPDUs across the CST region. The tunnel is created by sending the BPDUs using a multicast destination MAC of 0100.0CCC.CCCD, with the BPDUs being VLAN tagged with the correct VLAN ID. As a result, the non-Cisco switches forward the BPDUs as a multicast, and do not interpret the frames as BPDUs. When a forwarded BPDU reaches the first Cisco PVST+ switch in the other PVST+ region, the switch, listening for multicasts to 0100.0CCC.CCCD, reads and interprets the BPDU.

> **NOTE** 802.1Q, along with 802.1s Multiple-instance Spanning Tree (MST), allows 802.1Q trunks for support multiple STP instances. MST is covered later in this chapter.

STP Configuration and Analysis

Example 3-1, based on Figure 3-6, shows some of the basic STP configuration and **show** commands. Take care to note that many of the upcoming commands allow the parameters to be set for all VLANs by omitting the VLAN parameter, or set per VLAN by including a VLAN parameter. Example 3-1 begins with SW1 coincidentally becoming the root switch. After that, SW2 is configured to become root, and SW3 changes its Root Port as a result of a configured port cost in VLAN 1.

Figure 3-6 *Network Used with Example 3-1*

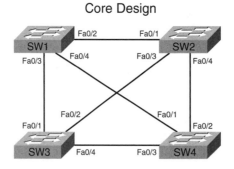

Example 3-1 *STP Basic Configuration and* **show** *Commands*

```
! First, note the Root ID column lists the root's bridge ID as two parts,
! first the priority, followed by the MAC address of the root. The root cost of
! 0 implies that SW1 (where the command is executed) is the root.
SW1#sh spanning-tree root

                                     Root    Hello Max Fwd
Vlan                   Root ID       Cost    Time  Age Dly  Root Port
---------------        -----------   ------  ----- --- ---  -----------
VLAN0001               32769 000a.b7dc.b780      0    2   20  15
VLAN0011               32779 000a.b7dc.b780      0    2   20  15
VLAN0012               32780 000a.b7dc.b780      0    2   20  15
VLAN0021               32789 000a.b7dc.b780      0    2   20  15
VLAN0022               32790 000a.b7dc.b780      0    2   20  15
```

Example 3-1 *STP Basic Configuration and* **show** *Commands (Continued)*

```
! The next command confirms that SW1 believes that it is the root of VLAN 1.
SW1#sh spanning-tree vlan 1 root detail
  Root ID    Priority    32769
             Address     000a.b7dc.b780
             This bridge is the root
             Hello Time   2 sec  Max Age 20 sec  Forward Delay 15 sec
! Next, SW2 is configured with a lower (better) priority than SW1,
! so it becomes the root. Note that because SW2 is defaulting to use
! the system ID extension, the actual priority must be configured as a
! multiple of 4096.
SW2#conf t
Enter configuration commands, one per line.  End with CNTL/Z.
SW2(config)#spanning-tree vlan 1 priority ?
  <0-61440>  bridge priority in increments of 4096

SW2(config)#spanning-tree vlan 1 priority 28672
SW2(config)#^Z
SW2#sh spanning-tree vlan 1 root detail
VLAN0001
  Root ID    Priority    28673
             Address     0011.92b0.f500
             This bridge is the root
             Hello Time   2 sec  Max Age 20 sec  Forward Delay 15 sec
! The System ID Extension field of the bridge ID is implied next. The output
! does not separate the 4-bit Priority field from the System ID field. The output
! actually shows the first 2 bytes of the bridge ID, in decimal. For VLAN1,
! the priority is 28,763, which is the configured 28,672 plus the VLAN ID,
! because the VLAN ID value is used in the System ID field in order to implement
! the MAC address reduction feature. The other VLANs have a base priority
! of 32768, plus the VLAN ID - for example, VLAN11 has priority 32779,
! (priority 32,768 plus VLAN 11), VLAN12 has 32780, and so on.
SW2#sh spanning-tree root priority
VLAN0001          28673
VLAN0011          32779
VLAN0012          32780
VLAN0021          32789
VLAN0022          32790
! Below, SW3 shows a Root Port of Fa 0/2, with cost 19. SW3 gets Hellos
! directly from the root (SW2) with cost 0, and adds its default cost (19).
! This next command also details the breakdown of the priority and system ID.
SW3#sh spanning-tree vlan 1
VLAN0001
  Spanning tree enabled protocol ieee
  Root ID    Priority    28673
             Address     0011.92b0.f500
             Cost        19
```

continues

Example 3-1 *STP Basic Configuration and* **show** *Commands (Continued)*

```
               Port          2 (FastEthernet0/2)
               Hello Time    2 sec  Max Age 20 sec  Forward Delay 15 sec


  Bridge ID  Priority     32769  (priority 32768 sys-id-ext 1)
             Address       000e.837b.3100
             Hello Time    2 sec  Max Age 20 sec  Forward Delay 15 sec
             Aging Time 300

Interface        Role Sts Cost      Prio.Nbr Type
---------------- ---- --- --------- -------- --------------------------------
Fa0/1            Altn BLK 19        128.1    P2p
Fa0/2            Root FWD 19        128.2    P2p
Fa0/4            Desg FWD 19        128.4    P2p
Fa0/13           Desg FWD 100       128.13   Shr
! Above, the port state of BLK and FWD for each port is shown, as well as the
! Root port and the Designated Ports.
! Below, Switch3's VLAN 1 port cost is changed on its Root Port (fa0/2),
! causing SW3 to reconverge, and pick a new RP.
SW3#conf t
Enter configuration commands, one per line.  End with CNTL/Z.
SW3(config)#int fa 0/2
SW3(config-if)#spanning-tree vlan 1 cost 100
SW3(config-if)#^Z
! The next command was done immediately after changing the port cost on
! SW3. Note the state listed as "LIS," meaning listen. STP has already
! chosen fa 0/1 as the new RP, but it must now transition through listening
! and learning states.
SW3#sh spanning-tree vlan 1
VLAN0001
  Spanning tree enabled protocol ieee
  Root ID    Priority    28673
             Address      0011.92b0.f500
             Cost         38
             Port          1 (FastEthernet0/1)
             Hello Time    2 sec  Max Age 20 sec  Forward Delay 15 sec


  Bridge ID  Priority     32769  (priority 32768 sys-id-ext 1)
             Address       000e.837b.3100
             Hello Time    2 sec  Max Age 20 sec  Forward Delay 15 sec
             Aging Time 15
Interface        Role Sts Cost      Prio.Nbr Type
---------------- ---- --- --------- -------- --------------------------------
Fa0/1            Root LIS 19        128.1    P2p
Fa0/2            Altn BLK 100       128.2    P2p
Fa0/4            Desg FWD 19        128.4    P2p
Fa0/13           Desg FWD 100       128.13   Shr
```

The preceding example shows one way to configure the priority to a lower value to become the root. Optionally, the **spanning-tree vlan** *vlan-id* **root** {**primary** | **secondary**} [**diameter** *diameter*] command could be used. This command causes the switch to set the priority lower. The optional **diameter** parameter causes this command to lower the Hello, Forward Delay, and Maxage timers. (This command does not get placed into the configuration, but rather it acts as a macro, being expanded into the commands to set priority and the timers.)

> **NOTE** When using the **primary** option, the **spanning-tree vlan** command sets the priority to 24,576 if the current root has a priority larger than 24,576. If the current root's priority is 24,576 or less, this command sets this switch's priority to 4096 less than the current root. With the **secondary** keyword, this switch's priority is set to 28,672. Also note that this logic applies to when the configuration command is executed; it does not dynamically change the priority if another switch later advertises a better priority.

Optimizing Spanning Tree

Left to default settings, IEEE 802.1d STP works, but convergence might take up to a minute or more for the entire network. For instance, when the root fails, a switch must wait on the 20-second Maxage timer to expire. Then, newly forwarding ports spend 15 seconds each in listening and learning states, which makes convergence take 50 seconds for that one switch.

Over the years, Cisco added features to its STP code, and later the IEEE made improvements as well. This section covers the key optimizations to STP.

PortFast, UplinkFast, and BackboneFast

The Cisco-proprietary PortFast, UplinkFast, and BackboneFast features each solve specific STP problems. Table 3-5 summarizes when each is most useful, and the short version of how they improve convergence time.

Table 3-5 *PortFast, UplinkFast, and BackboneFast*

Key Topic

Feature	Requirements for Use	How Convergence Is Optimized
PortFast	Used on access ports that are not connected to other switches or hubs	Immediately puts the port into forwarding state once the port is physically working
UplinkFast	Used on access layer switches that have multiple uplinks to distribution/core switches	Immediately replaces a lost RP with an alternate RP, immediately forwards on the RP, and triggers updates of all switches' CAMs
BackboneFast	Used to detect indirect link failures, typically in the network core	Avoids waiting for Maxage to expire when its RP ceases to receive Hellos; does so by querying the switch attached to its RP

PortFast

PortFast optimizes convergence by simply ignoring listening and learning states on ports. In effect, convergence happens instantly on ports with PortFast enabled. Of course, if another switch is connected to a port on which PortFast is enabled, loops may occur. So, PortFast is intended for access links attached to single end-user devices. To be safe, you should also enable the BPDU Guard and Root Guard features when using PortFast, as covered later in this chapter.

UplinkFast

UplinkFast optimizes convergence when an uplink fails on an access layer switch. For good STP design, access layer switches should not become root or become transit switches. (A transit switch is a switch that forwards frames between other switches.) Figure 3-7 shows the actions taken when UplinkFast is enabled on a switch, and then when the Root Port fails.

Figure 3-7 *UplinkFast Operations*

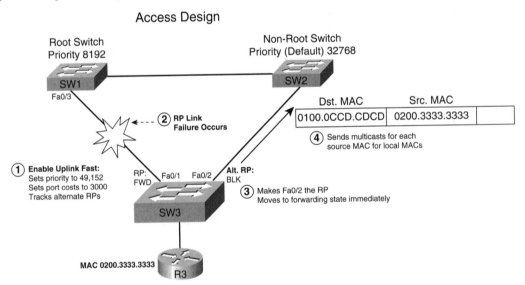

Upon enabling UplinkFast globally in a switch, the switch takes three actions:

- Increases the root priority to 49,152

- Sets the post costs to 3000

- Tracks alternate RPs, which are ports in which root Hellos are being received

As a result of these steps, SW3 can become root if necessary, but it is unlikely to do so given the large root priority value. Also, the very large costs on each link make the switch unlikely to be used as a transit switch. When the RP port does fail, SW3 can fail over to an alternate uplink as the new RP and forward immediately.

The final step in Uplink Fast logic causes the switches to time-out the correct entries in their CAMs, but it does not use the TCN process. Instead, the access switch finds all the MAC addresses of local devices and sends one multicast frame with each local MAC address as the source MAC—causing all the other switches to update their CAMs. The access switch also clears out the rest of the entries in its own CAM.

BackboneFast

BackboneFast optimizes convergence for any generalized topological case, improving convergence when an *indirect failure* occurs. When some direct failures occur (for instance, a switch's RP interface fails), the switch does not have to wait for Maxage to expire. However, when another switch's direct link fails, resulting in lost Hellos for other switches, the downstream switches indirectly learn of the failure because they cease to receive Hellos. Any time a switch learns of an STP failure indirectly, the switch must wait for Maxage to expire before trying to change the STP topology.

BackboneFast simply causes switches that indirectly learn of a potential STP failure to ask their upstream neighbors if they know about the failure. To do so, when the first Hello goes missing, a BackboneFast switch sends a *Root Link Query (RLQ)* BPDU out the port in which the missing Hello should have arrived. The RLQ asks the neighboring switch if that neighboring switch is still receiving Hellos from the root. If that neighboring switch had a direct link failure, it can tell the original switch (via another RLQ) that this path to the root is lost. Once known, the switch experiencing the indirect link failure can go ahead and converge without waiting for Maxage to expire.

> **NOTE**   All switches must have BackboneFast configured for it to work correctly.

PortFast, UplinkFast, and BackboneFast Configuration

Configuration of these three STP optimizing tools is relatively easy, as summarized in Table 3-6.

Table 3-6   *PortFast, UplinkFast, and BackboneFast Configuration*

Feature	Configuration Command
PortFast	**spanning-tree portfast** (interface subcommand)
	spanning-tree portfast default (global)
UplinkFast	**spanning-tree uplinkfast** [**max-update-rate** *rate*] (global)
BackboneFast	**spanning-tree backbonefast** (global)

PortChannels

When a network design includes multiple parallel segments between the same pair of switches, one switch ends up in a forwarding state on all the links, but the other switch blocks all but one of the ports of those parallel segments. As a result, only one of the links can be used at any point in time. Using *Fast EtherChannel (FEC)* (using FastE segments) and *Gigabit EtherChannel (GEC)* (using GigE segments) allows the combined links to be treated as one link from an STP perspective, so that all the parallel physical segments are used. (When configuring a Cisco switch, a group of segments comprising an FEC or GEC is called a *PortChannel*.) Most campus designs today use a minimum of two segments per trunk, in a PortChannel, for better availability. That way, as long as at least one of the links in the EtherChannel is up, the STP path cannot fail, and no STP convergence is required.

Load Balancing Across PortChannels

When a switch decides to forward a frame out a PortChannel, the switch must also decide which physical link to use to send each frame. To use the multiple links, Cisco switches load balance the traffic over the links in an EtherChannel based on the switch's global load-balancing configuration.

Load-balancing methods differ depending on the model of switch and software revision. Generally, load balancing is based on the contents of the Layer 2, 3, and/or 4 headers. If load balancing is based on only one header field in the frame, a bitmap of the low-order bits is used; if more than one header field is used, an XOR of the low-order bits is used.

For the best balancing effect, the header fields on which balancing is based need to vary among the mix of frames sent over the PortChannel. For instance, for a Layer 2 PortChannel connected to an access layer switch, most of the traffic going from the access layer switch to the distribution layer switch is probably going from clients to the default router. So most of the frames have different source MAC addresses, but the same destination MAC address. For packets coming back from a distribution switch toward the access layer switch, many of the frames might have a source address of that same router, with differing destination MAC addresses. So, you could balance based on source MAC at the access layer switch, and based on destination MAC at the distribution layer switch—or balance based on both fields on both switches. The goal is simply to use a balancing method for which the fields in the frames vary.

The **port-channel load-balance** *type* command sets the type of load balancing. The *type* options include using source and destination MAC, IP addresses, and TCP and UDP ports—either a single field or both the source and destination.

PortChannel Discovery and Configuration

You can explicitly configure interfaces to be in a PortChannel by using the **channel-group** *number* **mode on** interface subcommand. You would simply put the same command under each of the physical interfaces inside the PortChannel, using the same PortChannel number.

You can also use dynamic protocols to allow neighboring switches to figure out which ports should be part of the same PortChannel. Those protocols are the Cisco-proprietary *Port Aggregation Protocol (PAgP)* and the IEEE 802.1AD *Link Aggregation Control Protocol (LACP)*. To dynamically form a PortChannel using PAgP, you still use the **channel-group** command, with a mode of **auto** or **desirable**. To use LACP to dynamically create a PortChannel, use a mode of **active** or **passive**. Table 3-7 lists and describes the modes and their meanings.

Table 3-7 *PAgP and LACP Configuration Settings and Recommendations*

PAgP Setting	LACP 802.1AD Setting	Action
on	on	Disables PAgP or LACP, and forces the port into the PortChannel
off	off	Disables PAgP or LACP, and prevents the port from being part of a PortChannel
auto	passive	Uses PAgP or LACP, but waits on other side to send first PAgP or LACP message
desirable	active	Uses PAgP or LACP, and initiates the negotiation

NOTE Using **auto** (PAgP) or **passive** (LACP) on both switches prevents a PortChannel from forming dynamically. Cisco recommends the use of desirable mode (PAgP) or active mode (LACP) on ports that you intend to be part of a PortChannel.

When PAgP or LACP negotiate to form a PortChannel, the messages include the exchange of some key configuration information. As you might imagine, they exchange a system ID to determine which ports connect to the same two switches. The two switches then exchange other information about the candidate links for a PortChannel; several items must be identical on the links for them to be dynamically added to the PortChannel, as follows:

- Same speed and duplex settings.

- If not trunking, same access VLAN.

- If trunking, same trunk type, allowed VLANs, and native VLAN.

- On a single switch, each port in a PortChannel must have the same STP cost per VLAN on all links in the PortChannel.

- No ports can have SPAN configured.

When PAgP or LACP completes the process, a new PortChannel interface exists, and is used as if it were a single port for STP purposes, with balancing taking place based on the global load-balancing method configured on each switch.

Rapid Spanning Tree Protocol

IEEE 802.1w *Rapid Spanning Tree Protocol (RSTP)* enhances the 802.1d standard with one goal in mind: improving STP convergence. To do so, RSTP defines new variations on BPDUs between switches, new port states, and new port roles, all with the capability to operate backwardly compatible with 802.1d switches. The key components of speeding convergence with 802.1w are as follows:

- Waiting for only three missed Hellos on an RP before reacting (versus ten missed Hellos via the Maxage timer with 802.1d)

- New processes that allow transition from the disabled state (replaces the blocking state in 802.1d) to learning state, bypassing the concept of an 802.1d listening state

- Standardization of features like Cisco PortFast, UplinkFast, and BackboneFast

- An additional feature to allow a backup DP when a switch has multiple ports connected to the same shared LAN segment

To support these new processes, RSTP uses the same familiar Hello BPDUs, using some previously undefined bits to create the new features. For instance, RSTP defines a Hello message option for the same purpose as the Cisco proprietary RLQ used by the Cisco BackboneFast feature.

RSTP takes advantage of a switched network topology by categorizing ports, using a different link type to describe each. RSTP takes advantage of the fact that STP logic can be simplified in some cases, based on what is attached to each port, thereby allowing faster convergence. Table 3-8 lists the three RSTP link types.

Table 3-8 *RSTP Link Types*

Link Type	Description
Point-to-point	Connects a switch to one other switch; Cisco switches treat FDX links in which Hellos are received as point-to-point links.
Shared	Connects a switch to a hub; the important factor is that switches are reachable off that port.
Edge	Connects a switch to a single end-user device.

In most modern LAN designs with no shared hubs, all links would be either the point-to-point (a link between two switches) or edge link type. RSTP knows that link-type edge means the port is cabled to one device, and the device is not a switch. So, RSTP treats edge links with the same logic as Cisco PortFast—in fact, the same **spanning-tree portfast** command defines a port as link-type edge to RSTP. In other words, RSTP puts edge links into forwarding state immediately.

RSTP takes advantage of point-to-point links (which by definition connect a switch to another switch) by asking the other switch about its status. For instance, if one switch fails to receive its periodic Hello on a point-to-point link, it will query the neighbor. The neighbor will reply, stating whether it also lost its path to the root. It is the same logic as BackboneFast, but using IEEE standard messages to achieve the same goal.

RSTP also redefines the port states used with 802.1d, in part because the listening state is no longer needed. Table 3-9 compares the port states defined by each protocol.

Table 3-9 *RSTP and STP Port States*

Administrative State	STP State (802.1d)	RSTP State (802.1w)
Disabled	Disabled	Discarding
Enabled	Blocking	Discarding
Enabled	Listening	Discarding
Enabled	Learning	Learning
Enabled	Forwarding	Forwarding

In RSTP, a discarding state means that the port does not forward frames, receive frames, or learn source MAC addresses, regardless of whether the port was shut down, failed, or simply does not have a reason to forward. Once RSTP decides to transition from discarding to forwarding state (for example, a newly selected RP), it goes immediately to the learning state. From that point on, the process continues just as it does with 802.1d. RSTP no longer needs the listening state because of its active querying to neighbors, which guarantees no loops during convergence.

RSTP uses the term *port role* to refer to whether a port acts as an RP or a DP. RSTP uses the RP and DP port roles just as 802.1d does; however, RSTP adds several other roles, as listed in Table 3-10.

Table 3-10 *RSTP and STP Port Roles*

RSTP Role	Definition
Root Port	Same as 802.1d Root Port.
Designated Port	Same as 802.1d Designated Port.
Alternate Port	Same as the Alternate Port concept in UplinkFast; an alternate Root Port.
Backup Port	A port that is attached to the same link-type shared link as another port on the same switch, but the other port is the DP for that segment. The Backup Port is ready to take over if the DP fails.

The Alternate Port concept is like the UplinkFast concept—it offers protection against the loss of a switch's RP by keeping track of the Alternate Ports with a path to the root. The concept and general operation is identical to UplinkFast, although RSTP might converge more quickly via its active messaging between switches.

The Backup Port role has no equivalent with Cisco-proprietary features; it simply provides protection against losing the DP attached to a shared link when the switch has another physical port attached to the same shared LAN.

You can enable RSTP in a Cisco switch by using the **spanning-tree mode rapid-pvst** global command. Alternatively, you can simply enable 802.1s MST, which by definition uses 802.1w RSTP.

Rapid Per VLAN Spanning Tree Plus (RPVST+)

RPVST+ is a combination of PVST+ and RSTP. This combination provides the subsecond convergence of RSTP with the advantages of PVST+ described in the previous section. Thus, RPVST+ and PVST+ share the same characteristics such as convergence time, Hello behavior, the election process, port states, and so forth. RPVST+ is compatible with MSTP and PVST+.

Configuring RPVST+ is straightforward. In global configuration mode, issue the **spanning-tree mode rapid-pvst** command. Then, optionally, on an interface (VLAN, physical, or PortChannel), configure the **spanning-tree link-type point-to-point** command. This configures the port for fast changeover to the forwarding state.

See the "Further Reading" section for a source of more information on RPVST+.

Multiple Spanning Trees: IEEE 802.1s

IEEE 802.1s *Multiple Spanning Trees (MST)*, sometimes referred to as *Multiple Instance STP (MISTP)* or *Multiple STP (MSTP)*, defines a way to use multiple instances of STP in a network that uses 802.1Q trunking. The following are some of the main benefits of 802.1s:

- Like PVST+, it allows the tuning of STP parameters so that while some ports block for one VLAN, the same port can forward in another VLAN.

- Always uses 802.1w RSTP, for faster convergence.

- Does not require an STP instance for each VLAN; rather, the best designs use one STP instance per redundant path.

If the network consists of all MST-capable switches, MST is relatively simple to understand. A group of switches that together uses MST is called an *MST region*; to create an MST region, the switches need to be configured as follows:

1. Globally enable MST, and enter MST configuration mode by using the **spanning-tree mode mst** command.

2. From MST configuration mode, create an MST region name (up to 32 characters) by using the **name** subcommand.

3. From MST configuration mode, create an MST revision number by using the **revision** command.

4. From MST configuration mode, map VLANs to an MST STP instance by using the **instance** command.

The key to MST configuration is to configure the same parameters on all the switches in the region. For instance, if you match VLANs 1–4 to MST instance 1 on one switch, and VLANs 5–8 to MST instance 1 on another switch, the two switches will not consider themselves to be in the same MST region, even though their region names and revision numbers are identical.

For example, in Figure 3-8, an MST region has been defined, along with connections to non-MST switches. Focusing on the left side of the figure, inside the MST region, you really need only two instances of STP—one each for roughly half of the VLANs. With two instances, the access layer switches will forward on their links to SW1 for one set of VLANs using one MST instance, and forward on their links to SW2 for the other set of VLANs using the second MST instance.

Figure 3-8 *MST Operations*

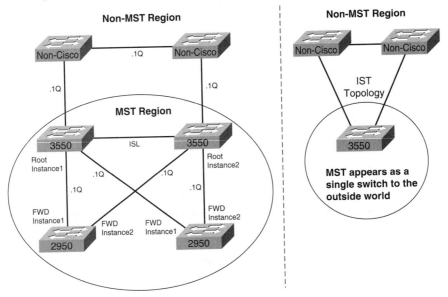

One of the key benefits of MST versus PVST+ is that it requires only one MST instance for a group of VLANs. If this MST region had hundreds of VLANs, and used PVST+, hundreds of sets of STP messages would be used. With MST, only one set of STP messages is needed for each MST instance.

When connecting an MST region to a non-MST region or to a different MST region, MST makes the entire MST region appear to be a single switch, as shown on the right side of Figure 3-8. An MST region can guarantee loop-free behavior inside the MST region. To prevent loops over the CST links connecting the MST region to a non-MST region, MST participates in an STP instance with the switches outside the MST region. This additional STP instance is called the *Internal Spanning Tree (IST)*. When participating in STP with the external switches, the MST region is made to appear as if it is a single switch; the right side of Figure 3-8 depicts the STP view of the left side of the figure, as seen by the external switches.

Protecting STP

The final section in this chapter covers four switch configuration tools that protect STP from different types of problems or attacks, depending on whether a port is a trunk or an access port.

Root Guard and BPDU Guard: Protecting Access Ports

Network designers probably do not intend for end users to connect a switch to an access port that is intended for attaching end-user devices. However, it happens—for instance, someone just may need a few more ports in the meeting room down the hall, so they figure they could just plug a small, cheap switch into the wall socket.

The STP topology can be changed based on one of these unexpected and undesired switches being added to the network. For instance, this newly added and unexpected switch might have the lowest bridge ID and become the root. To prevent such problems, BPDU Guard and Root Guard can be enabled on these access ports to monitor for incoming BPDUs—BPDUs that should not enter those ports, because they are intended for single end-user devices. Both features can be used together. Their base operations are as follows:

- **BPDU Guard**—Enabled per port; error disables the port upon receipt of any BPDU.

- **Root Guard**—Enabled per port; ignores any received superior BPDUs to prevent a switch connected to this port from becoming root. Upon receipt of superior BPDUs, this switch puts the port in a loop-inconsistent state, ceasing forwarding and receiving frames until the superior BPDUs cease.

With BPDU Guard, the port does not recover from the *err-disabled* state unless additional configuration is added. You can tell the switch to change from err-disabled state back to an up state after a certain amount of time. With Root Guard, the port recovers when the undesired superior BPDUs are no longer received.

UDLD and Loop Guard: Protecting Trunks

Both UniDirectional Link Detection (UDLD) and Loop Guard protect a switch trunk port from causing loops. Both features prevent switch ports from errantly moving from a blocking to a forwarding state when a unidirectional link exists in the network.

Unidirectional links are simply links for which one of the two transmission paths on the link has failed, but not both. This can happen as a result of miscabling, cutting one fiber cable, unplugging one fiber, GBIC problems, or other reasons. Although UDLD was developed for fiber links because of the unidirectional nature of fiber optic cabling—and therefore the much greater likelihood of a unidirectional link failure in a fiber cable—this feature also supports copper links. Because STP monitors incoming BPDUs to know when to reconverge the network, adjacent switches on a unidirectional link could both become forwarding, causing a loop, as shown in Figure 3-9.

Figure 3-9 *STP Problems with Unidirectional Links*

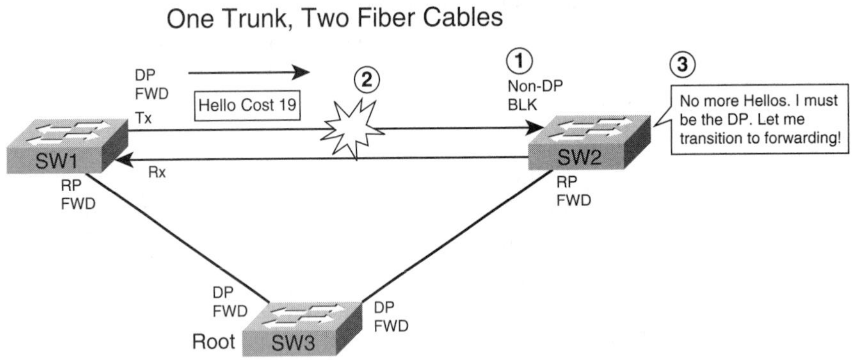

One Trunk, Two Fiber Cables

DP
FWD
Tx   Hello Cost 19

②
①
Non-DP
BLK

③
No more Hellos. I must
be the DP. Let me
transition to forwarding!

SW1
RP
FWD   Rx

SW2
RP
FWD

DP
FWD
Root   SW3   DP
FWD

Figure 3-9 shows the fiber link between SW1 and SW2 with both cables. SW2 starts in a blocking state, but as a result of the failure on SW1's transmit path, SW2 ceases to hear Hellos from SW1. SW2 then transitions to forwarding state, and now all trunks on all switches are forwarding. Even with the failure of SW1's transmit cable, frames will now loop counter-clockwise in the network.

UDLD uses two modes to attack the unidirectional link problem. As described next, both modes, along with Loop Guard, solve the STP problem shown in Figure 3-9:

■ **UDLD**—Uses Layer 2 messaging to decide when a switch can no longer receive frames from a neighbor. The switch whose transmit interface did not fail is placed into an err-disabled state.

■ **UDLD aggressive mode**—Attempts to reconnect with the other switch (eight times) after realizing no messages have been received. If the other switch does not reply to the repeated additional messages, both sides become err-disabled.

■ **Loop Guard**—When normal BPDUs are no longer received, the port does not go through normal STP convergence, but rather falls into an STP *loop-inconsistent* state.

In all cases, the formerly blocking port that would now cause a loop is prevented from migrating to a forwarding state. With both types of UDLD, the switch can be configured to automatically transition out of err-disabled state. With Loop Guard, the switch automatically puts the port back into its former STP state when the original Hellos are received again.

Foundation Summary

This section lists additional details and facts to round out the coverage of the topics in this chapter. Unlike most of the Cisco Press *Exam Certification Guides*, this "Foundation Summary" does not repeat information presented in the "Foundation Topics" section of the chapter. Please take the time to read and study the details in the "Foundation Topics" section of the chapter, as well as review items noted with a Key Topic icon.

Table 3-11 lists the protocols mentioned in this chapter and their respective standards documents.

Table 3-11 *Protocols and Standards for Chapter 3*

Name	Standards Body
RSTP	IEEE 802.1w
MST	IEEE 802.1s
STP	IEEE 802.1d
LACP	IEEE 802.1AD
Dot1Q trunking	IEEE 802.1Q
PVST+	Cisco
RPVST+	Cisco
PagP	Cisco

Table 3-12 lists the three key timers that impact STP convergence.

3-12 *IEEE 802.1d STP Timers*

Timer	Default	Purpose
Hello	2 sec	Interval at which the root sends Hellos
Forward Delay	15 sec	Time that switch leaves a port in listening state and learning state; also used as the short CAM timeout timer
Maxage	20 sec	Time without hearing a Hello before believing that the root has failed

Table 3-13 lists some of the key IOS commands related to the topics in this chapter. (The command syntax for switch commands was taken from the *Catalyst 3550 Multilayer Switch Command Reference, 12.1(20)EA2.*) Also refer to Table 3-5 for several other commands.

Table 3-13 *Command Reference for Chapter 3*

Command	Description
spanning-tree mode {**mst** | **pvst** | **rapid-pvst**}	Global config command that sets the STP mode
[**no**] **spanning-tree vlan x**	Enables or disables STP inside a particular VLAN when using PVST+
spanning-tree vlan *vlan-id* {**forward-time** *seconds* | **hello-time** *seconds* | **max-age** *seconds* | **priority** *priority* | {**root** {**primary** | **secondary**} [**diameter** *net-diameter* [**hello-time** *seconds*]]}}	Global config command to set a variety of STP parameters
spanning-tree vlan *x* **cost** *y*	Interface subcommand used to set interface costs, per VLAN
spanning-tree vlan *x* **port-priority** *y*	Interface subcommand used to set port priority, per VLAN
channel-group *channel-group-number* **mode** {**auto** [**non-silent**] | **desirable** [**non-silent**] | **on** | **active** | **passive**}	Interface subcommand that places the interface into a port channel, and sets the negotiation parameters
channel-protocol {**lacp** | **pagp**}	Interface subcommand to define which protocol to use for EtherChannel negotiation
interface port-channel *port-channel-number*	Global command that allows configuration of parameters for the EtherChannel
spanning-tree portfast	Interface subcommand that enables PortFast on the interface
spanning-tree uplinkfast	Global command that enables UplinkFast
spanning-tree backbonefast	Global command that enables BackboneFast
spanning-tree mst *instance-id* **priority** *priority*	Global command used to set the priority of an MST instance
spanning-tree mst configuration	Global command that puts user in MST configuration mode
show spanning-tree root | **brief** | **summary**	EXEC command to show various details about STP operation
show spanning-tree uplinkfast | **backbonefast**	EXEC command to show various details about UplinkFast and BackboneFast

Memory Builders

The CCIE Routing and Switching written exam, like all Cisco CCIE written exams, covers a fairly broad set of topics. This section provides some basic tools to help you exercise your memory about some of the broader topics covered in this chapter.

Fill in Key Tables from Memory

Appendix E, "Key Tables for CCIE Study," on the CD in the back of this book contains empty sets of some of the key summary tables in each chapter. Print Appendix E, refer to this chapter's tables in it, and fill in the tables from memory. Refer to Appendix F, "Solutions for Key Tables for CCIE Study," on the CD to check your answers.

Definitions

Next, take a few moments to write down the definitions for the following terms:

CST, STP, MST, RSTP, Hello timer, Maxage timer, Forward Delay timer, blocking state, forwarding state, listening state, learning state, disabled state, alternate state, discarding state, backup state, Root Port, Designated Port, superior BPDU, PVST+, RPVST+, UplinkFast, BackboneFast, PortFast, Root Guard, BPDU Guard, UDLD, Loop Guard, LACP, PAgP

Refer to the CD-based glossary to check your answers.

Further Reading

The topics in this chapter tend to be covered in slightly more detail in CCNP Switching exam preparation books. For more details on these topics, refer to *CCNP BCMSN Official Exam Certification Guide*, Fourth Edition, and *Authorized Self-Study Guide: Building Cisco Multilayer Switched Networks (BCMSN)*, Fourth Edition.

Cisco LAN Switching, by Kennedy Clark and Kevin Hamilton, covers STP logic and operations in detail.

MSTP, PVST+, and Rapid PVST+ (RPVST+) configuration are covered in the "Configuring STP" document at http://www.cisco.com/univercd/cc/td/doc/product/lan/cat3560/12225see/scg/swstp.htm.

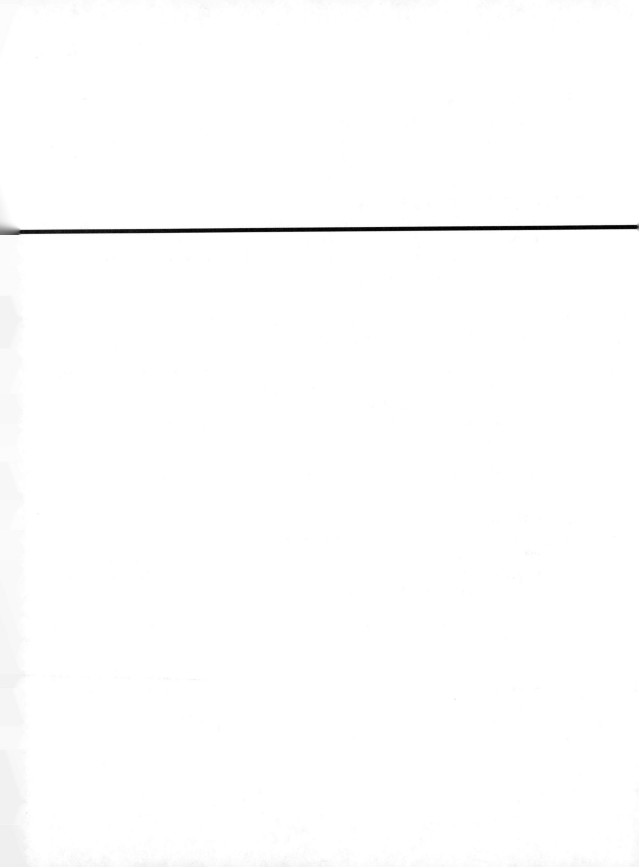

Part II: IP

Blueprint topics covered in this chapter:

This chapter covers the following subtopics from the Cisco CCIE Routing and Switching written exam blueprint. Refer to the full blueprint in Table I-1 in the Introduction for more details on the topics covered in each chapter and their context within the blueprint.

- Addressing

- Subnetting

- Summarization

- Network Address Translation (NAT)

CHAPTER 4

IP Addressing

Complete mastery of IP addressing and subnetting is required for any candidate to have a reasonable chance at passing both the CCIE written and lab exam. In fact, even the CCNA exam has fairly rigorous coverage of IP addressing and the related protocols. For the CCIE exam, understanding these topics is required to answer much deeper questions—for instance, a question might ask for the interpretation of the output of a **show ip bgp** command and a configuration snippet to decide what routes would be summarized into a new prefix. To answer such questions, the basic concepts and math behind subnetting need to be very familiar.

"Do I Know This Already?" Quiz

Table 4-1 outlines the major headings in this chapter and the corresponding "Do I Know This Already?" quiz questions.

Table 4-1 *"Do I Know This Already?" Foundation Topics Section-to-Question Mapping*

Foundation Topics Section	Questions Covered in This Section	Score
IP Addressing and Subnetting	1–4	
CIDR, Private Addresses, and NAT	5–8	
Total Score		

In order to best use this pre-chapter assessment, remember to score yourself strictly. You can find the answers in Appendix A, "Answers to the 'Do I Know This Already?' Quizzes."

1. In what subnet does address 192.168.23.197/27 reside?

    a. 192.168.23.0

    b. 192.168.23.128

    c. 192.168.23.160

    d. 192.168.23.192

    e. 192.168.23.196

2. Router1 has four LAN interfaces, with IP addresses 10.1.1.1/24, 10.1.2.1/24, 10.1.3.1/24, and 10.1.4.1/24. What is the smallest summary route that could be advertised out a WAN link connecting Router1 to the rest of the network, if subnets not listed here were allowed to be included in the summary?

    a. 10.1.2.0/22

    b. 10.1.0.0/22

    c. 10.1.0.0/21

    d. 10.1.0.0/16

3. Router1 has four LAN interfaces, with IP addresses 10.22.14.1/23, 10.22.18.1/23, 10.22.12.1/23, and 10.22.16.1/23. Which one of the answers lists the smallest summary route(s) that could be advertised by R1 without also including subnets not listed in this question?

    a. 10.22.12.0/21

    b. 10.22.8.0/21

    c. 10.22.8.0/21 and 10.22.16.0/21

    d. 10.22.12.0/22 and 10.22.16.0/22

4. Which two of the following VLSM subnets, when taken as a pair, overlap?

    a. 10.22.21.128/26

    b. 10.22.22.128/26

    c. 10.22.22.0/27

    d. 10.22.20.0/23

    e. 10.22.16.0/22

5. Which of the following protocols or tools includes a feature like route summarization, plus administrative rules for global address assignment, with a goal of reducing the size of Internet routing tables?

    a. Classless interdomain routing

    b. Route summarization

    c. Supernetting

    d. Private IP addressing

6. Which of the following terms refers to a NAT feature that allows for significantly fewer IP addresses in the enterprise network as compared with the required public registered IP addresses?

    a. Static NAT

    b. Dynamic NAT

    c. Dynamic NAT with overloading

    d. PAT

    e. VAT

7. Consider an enterprise network using private class A network 10.0.0.0, and using NAT to translate to IP addresses in registered class C network 205.1.1.0. Host 10.1.1.1 has an open www session to Internet web server 198.133.219.25. Which of the following terms refers to the destination address of a packet, sent by the web server back to the client, when the packet has not yet made it back to the enterprise's NAT router?

    a. Inside Local

    b. Inside Global

    c. Outside Local

    d. Outside Global

8. Router1 has its fa0/0 interface, address 10.1.2.3/24, connected to an enterprise network. Router1's S0/1 interface connects to an ISP, with the interface using a publicly-registered IP address of 171.1.1.1/30,. Which of the following commands could be part of a valid NAT overload configuration, with 171.1.1.1 used as the public IP address?

    a. **ip nat inside source list 1 int s0/1 overload**

    b. **ip nat inside source list 1 pool fred overload**

    c. **ip nat inside source list 1 171.1.1.1 overload**

    d. None of the answers is correct.

Foundation Topics

IP Addressing and Subnetting

You need a postal address to receive letters; similarly, computers must use an IP address to be able to send and receive data using the TCP/IP protocols. Just as the postal service dictates the format and meaning of a postal address to aid the efficient delivery of mail, the TCP/IP protocol suite imposes some rules about IP address assignment so that routers can efficiently forward packets between IP hosts. This chapter begins with coverage of the format and meaning of IP addresses, with required consideration for how they are grouped to aid the routing process.

IP Addressing and Subnetting Review

First, here's a quick review of some of the core facts about IPv4 addresses that should be fairly familiar to you:

- 32-bit binary number.

- Written in "dotted decimal" notation (for example, 1.2.3.4), with each decimal octet representing 8 bits.

- Addresses are assigned to network interfaces, so computers or routers with multiple interfaces have multiple IP addresses.

- A computer with an IP address assigned to an interface is an *IP host*.

- A group of IP hosts that are not separated from each other by an IP router are in the same grouping.

- These groupings are called *networks*, *subnets*, or *prefixes*, depending on the context.

- IP hosts separated from another set of IP hosts by a router must be in separate groupings (network/subnet/prefix).

IP addresses may be analyzed using *classful* or *classless* logic, depending on the situation. Classful logic simply means that the main class A, B, and C rules from RFC 791 are considered. The next several pages present a classful view of IP addresses, as reviewed in Table 4-2.

With classful addressing, class A, B, and C networks can be identified as such by their first several bits (shown in the last column of Table 4-1) or by the range of decimal values for their first octets. Also, each class A, B, or C address has two parts (when not subnetted): a *network part* and a *host part*. The size of each is implied by the class, and can be stated explicitly using the default mask for that class of network. For instance, mask 255.0.0.0, the default mask for class A networks, has 8 binary 1s and 24 binary 0s, representing the size of the network and host parts, respectively.

Table 4-2   *Classful Network Review*

Class of Address	Size of Network and Host Parts of the Addresses	Range of First Octet Values	Default Mask for Each Class of Network	Identifying Bits at Beginning of Address
A	8/24	1–126	255.0.0.0	0
B	16/16	128–191	255.255.0.0	10
C	24/8	192–223	255.255.255.0	110
D	—	224–239	—	1110
E	—	240–255	—	1111

Subnetting a Classful Network Number

With classful addressing, and no subnetting, an entire class A, B, or C network is needed on each individual instance of a data link. For example, Figure 4-1 shows a sample internetwork, with dashed-line circles representing the set of hosts that must be in the same IP network—in this case requiring three networks. Figure 4-1 shows two options for how IP addresses may be assigned and grouped together for this internetwork topology.

Figure 4-1   *Sample Internetwork with Two Alternatives for Address Assignment—Without and With Subnetting*

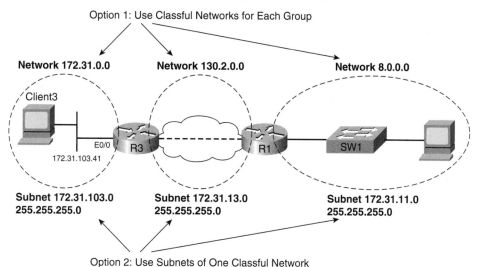

Option 1 uses three classful networks; however, it wastes a lot of IP addresses. For example, all hosts in class A network 8.0.0.0 must reside on the LAN on the right side of the figure.

Of course, the much more reasonable alternative is to reserve one classful IP network number, and use *subnetting* to subdivide that network into at least three subdivisions, called *subnets*. Option 2 (bottom of Figure 4-1) shows how to subdivide a class A, B, or C network into subnets.

To create subnets, the IP addresses must have three fields instead of just two—the network, *subnet*, and host. When using classful logic to interpret IP addresses, the size of the network part is still defined by classful rules—either 8, 16, or 24 bits based on class. To create the subnet field, the host field is shortened, as shown in Figure 4-2.

Figure 4-2 *Formats of IP Addresses when Subnetting*

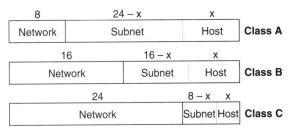

> **NOTE** The term *internetwork* refers to a collection of computers and networking hardware; because TCP/IP discussions frequently use the term *network* to refer to a classful class A, B, or C IP network, this book uses the term internetwork to refer to an entire network topology, as shown in Figure 4-1.

To determine the size of each field in a subnetted IP address, you can follow the three easy steps shown in Table 4-3. Note that Figure 4-1 also showed alternative addressing for using subnets, with the last column in Table 4-3 showing the size of each field for that particular example, which used class B network 172.31.0.0, mask 255.255.255.0.

Table 4-3 *Finding the Size of the Network, Subnet, and Host Fields in an IP Address*

Name of Part of the Address	Process to Find Its Size	Size per Figure 4-1 Example
Network	8, 16, or 24 bits based on class rules	16
Subnet	32 minus network and host bits	8
Host	Equal to the number of binary 0s in the mask	8

Comments on Classless Addressing

The terms *classless* and *classful* can be applied to three popular topics that are all related to IP. This chapter explains classful and classless IP addressing, which are relatively simple concepts. Two other chapters explain the other uses of the terms classless and classful: Chapter 6, "IP Forwarding (Routing)," describes classless/classful routing, and Chapter 7, "RIP Version 2," covers classless/classful routing protocols.

Classless IP addressing, simply put, means that class A, B, and C rules are ignored. Each address is viewed as a two-part address, formally called the *prefix* and the *host* parts of the address. The prefix simply states how many of the beginning bits of an IP address identify or define the group. It is the same idea as using the combined network and subnet parts of an address to identify a subnet. All the hosts with identical prefixes are in effect in the same group, which can be called a *subnet* or a *prefix*.

Just as a classful subnet must be listed with the subnet mask to know exactly which addresses are in the subnet, a prefix must be listed with its *prefix length*. The prefix itself is a dotted-decimal number. It is typically followed by a / symbol, after which the prefix length is listed. The prefix length is a decimal number that denotes the length (in bits) of the prefix. For example, 172.31.13.0/24 means a prefix of 172.31.13.0 and a prefix length of 24 bits. Also, the prefix can be implied by a subnet mask, with the number of 1s in the binary version of the mask implying the prefix length.

Classless and classful addressing are mainly just two ways to think about IP address formats. For the exam, make sure to understand both perspectives and the terminology used by each.

Subnetting Math

Knowing how to interpret the meaning of addresses and masks, routes and masks in the routing table, addresses and masks in ACLs, and configure route-filtering are all very important topics for the CCIE Routing and Switching written and lab exams. This section covers the binary math briefly, with coverage of some tricks to do the math quickly without binary math. Several subsequent chapters cover the configuration details of features that require this math.

Dissecting the Component Parts of an IP Address

First, deducing the size of the three parts (classful view) or two parts (classless view) of an IP address is important, because it allows you to analyze information about that subnet and other subnets. Every internetwork requires some number of subnets, and some number of hosts per subnet. Analyzing the format of an existing address, based on the mask or prefix length, allows you to determine whether enough hosts per subnet exist, or whether enough subnets exist to support the number of hosts. The following list summarizes some of the common math facts about subnetting related to the format of IP addresses:

- If a subnet has been defined with y host bits, there are $2^y - 2$ valid usable IP addresses in the subnet, because two numeric values are reserved.

- One reserved IP address in each subnet is the subnet number itself. This number, by definition, has binary 0s for all host bits. This number represents the subnet, and is typically seen in routing tables.

- The other reserved IP address in the subnet is the subnet broadcast address, which by definition has binary 1s for all host bits. This number can be used as a destination IP address to send a packet to all hosts in the subnet.

- When you are thinking classfully, if the mask implies x subnet bits, then 2^x possible subnets exist for that classful network, assuming the same mask is used throughout the network.

- Although there are no truly reserved values for the subnet numbers, two (lowest and highest values) may be discouraged from use in some cases:

  — **Zero subnet**—The subnet field is all binary 0s; in decimal, each zero subnet is the exact same dotted-decimal number as the classful network number, potentially causing confusion.

  — **Broadcast subnet**—The subnet field is all binary 1s; in decimal, this subnet's broadcast address is the same as the network-wide broadcast address, potentially causing confusion.

In Cisco routers, by default, zero subnets and broadcast subnets work fine. You can disable the use of the zero subnet with the **no ip subnet-zero** global command. The only time that using the zero subnet typically causes problems is when classful routing protocols are used.

Finding Subnet Numbers and Valid Range of IP Addresses—Binary

When examining an IP address and mask, the process of finding the subnet number, the broadcast address, and the range of valid IP addresses is as fundamental to networking as is addition and subtraction for advanced math. Possibly more so for the CCIE Routing and Switching lab exam, mastery of the math behind subnetting, which is the same basic math behind route summarization and filtering, will improve your speed completing complex configurations on the exam.

The range of valid IP addresses in a subnet begins with the number that is one larger than the subnet number, and ends with the address that is one smaller than the broadcast address for the subnet. So, to determine the range of valid addresses, just calculate the subnet number and broadcast address, which can be done as follows:

- **To derive the subnet number**—Perform a bit-wise Boolean AND between the IP address and mask

- **To derive the broadcast address**—Change all host bits in the subnet number from 0s to 1s

A bitwise Boolean AND means that you place two long binary numbers on top of each other, and then AND the two bits that line up vertically. (A Boolean AND results in a binary 1 only if both bits are 1; otherwise, the result is 0.) Table 4-4 shows an easy example based on subnet 172.31.103.0/24 from Figure 4-1.

Table 4-4 *Binary Math to Calculate the Subnet Number and Broadcast Address*

Address	172.31.103.41	1010 1100 0001 1111 0110 0111 **0010 1001**
Mask	255.255.255.0	1111 1111 1111 1111 1111 1111 **0000 0000**
Subnet Number (Result of AND)	172.31.103.0	1010 1100 0001 1111 0110 0111 **0000 0000**
Broadcast	172.31.103.255	1010 1100 0001 1111 0110 0111 **1111 1111**

Probably most everyone reading this already knew that the decimal subnet number and broadcast addresses shown in Table 4-4 were correct, even without looking at the binary math. The important part is to recall the binary process, and practice until you can confidently and consistently find the answer without using any binary math at all. The only parts of the math that typically trip people up are the binary to decimal and decimal to binary conversions. When working in binary, keep in mind that you will not have a calculator for the written exam, and that when converting to decimal, you always convert 8 bits at a time—even if an octet contains some prefix bits and some host bits. (Appendix B, "Decimal to Binary Conversion Table," contains a conversion table for your reference.)

Decimal Shortcuts to Find the Subnet Number and Valid Range of IP Addresses

Many of the IP addressing and routing related problems on the exam come back to the ability to solve a couple of classic basic problems. One of those problems runs as follows:

> Given an IP address and mask (or prefix length), determine the subnet number/prefix, broad-cast address, and range of valid IP addresses.

If you personally can already solve such problems with only a few seconds' thought, even with tricky masks, then you can skip this section of the chapter. If you cannot solve such questions easily and quickly, this section can help you learn some math shortcuts that allow you to find the answers without needing to use any Boolean math.

> **NOTE**   The next several pages of this chapter describe some algorithms you can use to find many important details related to IP addressing, without needing to convert to and from binary. In my experience, some people simply work better performing the math in binary until the answers simply start popping into their heads. Others find that the decimal shortcuts are more effective.
>
> If you use the decimal shortcuts, it is best to practice them until you no longer really use the exact steps listed in this book; rather, the processes should become second nature. To that end, CD-only Appendix D, "IP Addressing Practice," lists several practice problems for each of the algorithms presented in this chapter.

To solve the "find the subnet/broadcast/range of addresses" type of problem, at least three of the four octets should have pretty simple math. For example, with a nice, easy mask like 255.255.255.0, the logic used to find the subnet number and broadcast address is intuitive to most people. The more challenging cases occur when the mask or prefix does not divide the host field at a byte boundary. For instance, the same IP address 172.31.103.41, with mask 255.255.252.0 (prefix /22), is actually in subnet 172.31.100.0. Working with the third octet in this example is the hard part, because the mask value for that octet is not 0 or 255; for the upcoming process, this octet is called the *interesting octet*. The following process finds the subnet number, using decimal math, even with a challenging mask:

Step 1   Find the mask octets of value 255; copy down the same octets from the IP address.

Step 2   Find the mask octets of value 0; write down 0s for the same octets.

Step 3   If one octet has not yet been filled in, that octet is the interesting octet. Find the subnet mask's value in the interesting octet, and subtract it from 256. Call this number the "magic number."

Step 4   Find the integer multiple of the magic number that is closest to, but not larger than, the interesting octet's value.

An example certainly helps, as shown in Table 4-5, with 172.31.103.41, mask 255.255.252.0. The table separates the address into its four component octets. In this example, the first, second, and fourth octets of the subnet number are easily found from Steps 1 and 2 in the process. Because the interesting octet is the third octet, the magic number is 256 – 252, or 4. The integer multiple of 4, closest to 103 but not exceeding 103, is 100—making 100 the subnet number's value in the third octet. (Note that you can use this same process even with an easy mask, and Steps 1 and 2 will give you the complete subnet number.)

Table 4-5 *Quick Math to Find the Subnet Number—172.31.103.41, 255.255.252.0*

	Octet				Comments
	1	**2**	**3**	**4**	
Address	172	31	103	41	
Mask	255	255	252	0	Equivalent to /22.
Subnet number results after Steps 1 and 2	172	31		0	Magic number will be 256 − 252 = 4.
Subnet number after completing the interesting octet	172	31	**100**	0	100 is the multiple of 4 closest to, but not exceeding, 103.

A similar process can be used to determine the subnet broadcast address. This process assumes that the mask is tricky. The detailed steps are as follows:

Step 1   Start with the subnet number.

Step 2   Decide which octet is interesting, based on which octet of the mask does not have a 0 or 255.

Step 3   For octets to the left of the interesting octet, copy down the subnet number's values into the place where you are writing down the broadcast address.

Step 4   For any octets to the right of the interesting octet, write down 255 for the broadcast address.

Step 5   Calculate the magic number: find the subnet mask's value in the interesting octet and subtract it from 256.

Step 6   Take the subnet number's interesting octet value, add the magic number to it, and subtract 1. Fill in the broadcast address's interesting octet with this number.

Table 4-6 shows the 172.31.103.41/22 example again, using this process to find the subnet broadcast address.

Table 4-6 *Quick Math to Find the Broadcast Address—172.31.103.41, 255.255.252.0*

	Octet				Comments
	1	**2**	**3**	**4**	
Subnet number (per Step 1)	172	31	100	0	
Mask (for reference)	255	255	252	0	Equivalent to /22
Results after Steps 1 to 4	172	31		255	Magic number will be 256 − 252 = 4
Subnet number after completing the empty octet	172	31	**103**	255	Subnet's third octet (100), plus magic number (4), minus 1 is 103

> **NOTE**   If you have read the last few pages to improve your speed at dissecting a subnet without requiring binary math, it is probably a good time to pull out the CD in the back of the book. CD-only Appendix D, "IP Addressing Practice," contains several practice problems for finding the subnet and broadcast address, as well as for many other math related to IP addressing.

Determining All Subnets of a Network—Binary

Another common question, typically simply a portion of a more challenging question on the CCIE written exam, relates to finding all subnets of a network. The base underlying question might be as follows:

> Given a particular class A, B, or C network, and a mask/prefix length used on all subnets of that network, what are the actual subnet numbers?

The answers can be found using binary or using a simple decimal algorithm. This section first shows how to answer the question using binary, using the following steps. Note that the steps include details that are not really necessary for the math part of the problem; these steps are mainly helpful for practicing the process.

Step 1   Write down the binary version of the classful network number; that value is actually the zero subnet as well.

Step 2   Draw two vertical lines through the number, one separating the network and subnet parts of the number, the other separating the subnet and host part.

Step 3   Calculate the number of subnets, including the zero and broadcast subnet, based on 2^y, where y is the number of subnet bits.

Step 4   Write down $y-1$ copies of the binary network number below the first one, but leave the subnet field blank.

Step 5   Using the subnet field as a binary counter, write down values, top to bottom, in which the next value is 1 greater than the previous.

Step 6   Convert the binary numbers, 8 bits at a time, back to decimal.

This process takes advantage of a couple of facts about the binary form of IP subnet numbers:

■   All subnets of a classful network have the same value in the network portion of the subnet number.

■   All subnets of any classful network have binary 0s in the host portion of the subnet number.

Step 4 in the process simply makes you write down the network and host parts of each subnet number, because those values are easily predicted. To find the different subnet numbers, you then just need to discover all possible different combinations of binary digits in the subnet field, because that is the only part of the subnet numbers that differs from subnet to subnet.

For example, consider the same class B network 172.31.0.0, with static length subnet masking (SLSM) assumed, and a mask of 255.255.224.0. Note that this example uses 3 subnet bits, so there will be 2^3 subnets. Table 4-7 lists the example.

Table 4-7 *Binary Method to Find All Subnets—Steps 1 Through 4*

Subnet	Octet				
	1	2		3	4
Network number/zero subnet	10101100	000 11111	000	00000	00000000
2nd subnet	10101100	000 11111		00000	00000000
3rd subnet	10101100	000 11111		00000	00000000
4th subnet	10101100	000 11111		00000	00000000
5th subnet	10101100	000 11111		00000	00000000
6th subnet	10101100	000 11111		00000	00000000
7th subnet	10101100	000 11111		00000	00000000
8th subnet (2^y = 8); broadcast subnet	10101100	000 11111		00000	00000000

At this point, you have the zero subnet recorded at the top, and you are ready to use the subnet field (the missing bits in the table) as a counter to find all possible values. Table 4-8 completes the process.

Table 4-8 *Binary Method to Find All Subnets—Step 5*

Subnet	Octet				
	1	2		3	4
Network number/zero subnet	10101100	00011111	000	00000	00000000
2nd subnet	10101100	00011111	001	00000	00000000
3rd subnet	10101100	00011111	010	00000	00000000
4th subnet	10101100	00011111	011	00000	00000000
5th subnet	10101100	00011111	100	00000	00000000
6th subnet	10101100	00011111	101	00000	00000000
7th subnet	10101100	00011111	110	00000	00000000
8th subnet (2^y = 8); broadcast subnet	10101100	00011111	111	00000	00000000

The final step to determine all subnets is simply to convert the values back to decimal. Take care to always convert 8 bits at a time. In this case, you end up with the following subnets: 172.31.0.0, 172.31.32.0, 172.31.64.0, 172.31.96.0, 172.31.128.0, 172.31.160.0, 172.31.192.0, and 172.31.224.0.

Determining All Subnets of a Network—Decimal

You may have noticed the trend in the third octet values in the subnets listed in the previous paragraph. When assuming SLSM, the subnet numbers in decimal do have a regular increment value, which turns out to be the value of the magic number. For example, instead of the binary math in the previous section, you could have thought the following:

- The interesting octet is the third octet.

- The magic number is 256 − 224 = 32.

- 172.31.0.0 is the zero subnet, because it is the same number as the network number.

- The other subnet numbers are increments of the magic number inside the interesting octet.

If that logic already clicks in your head, you can skip to the next section in this chapter. If not, the rest of this section outlines an decimal algorithm that takes a little longer pass at the same general logic. First, the question and the algorithm assume that the same subnet mask is used on all subnets of this one classful network—a feature sometimes called *static length subnet masking (SLSM)*. In contrast, *variable length subnet masking (VLSM)* means that different masks are used in the same classful network. The algorithm assumes a subnet field of 8 bits or less just to keep the steps uncluttered; for longer subnet fields, the algorithm can be easily extrapolated.

Key Topic

Step 1   Write down the classful network number in decimal.

Step 2   For the first (lowest numeric) subnet number, copy the entire network number. That is the first subnet number, and is also the zero subnet.

Step 3   Decide which octet contains the entire subnet field; call this octet the interesting octet. (Remember, this algorithm assumes 8 subnet bits or less, so the entire subnet field will be in a single interesting octet.)

Step 4   Calculate the magic number by subtracting the mask's interesting octet value from 256.

Step 5   Copy down the previous subnet number's noninteresting octets onto the next line as the next subnet number; only one octet is missing at this point.

Step 6   Add the magic number to the previous subnet's interesting octet, and write that down as the next subnet number's interesting octet, completing the next subnet number.

Step 7   Repeat Steps 5 and 6 until the new interesting octet is 256. That subnet is not valid. The previously calculated subnet is the last valid subnet, and also the broadcast subnet.

For example, consider the same class B network 172.31.0.0, with SLSM assumed, and a mask of 255.255.224.0. Table 4-9 lists the example.

Table 4-9   *Subnet List Chart—172.31.0.0/255.255.224.0*

	Octet				Comments
	1	**2**	**3**	**4**	
Network number	172	31	0	0	Step 1 from the process.
Mask	255	255	224	0	Magic number is 256 − 224 = 32.
Subnet zero	172	31	0	0	Step 2 from the process.
First subnet	172	31	32	0	Steps 5 and 6; previous interesting octet 0, plus magic number (32).
Next subnet	172	31	64	0	32 plus magic number is 64.
Next subnet	172	31	96	0	64 plus magic number is 96.
Next subnet	172	31	128	0	96 plus magic number is 128.
Next subnet	172	31	160	0	128 plus magic number is 160.
Next subnet	172	31	192	0	160 plus magic number is 192.
Last subnet (broadcast)	172	31	224	0	The broadcast subnet in this case.
Invalid; easy-to-recognize stopping point	172	31	256	0	256 is out of range; when writing this one down, note that it is invalid, and that the previous one is the last valid subnet.

You can use this process repeatedly as needed until the answers start jumping out at you without the table and step-wise algorithm. For more practice, refer to CD-only Appendix D.

VLSM Subnet Allocation

So far in this chapter, most of the discussion has been about examining existing addresses and subnets. Before deploying new networks, or new parts of a network, you must give some thought to the ranges of IP addresses to be allocated. Also, when assigning subnets for different locations, you should assign the subnets with thought for how routes could then be summarized. This section covers some of the key concepts related to subnet allocation and summarization. (This section focuses on the concepts behind summarization; the configuration of route summarization is routing protocol–specific and thus is covered in the individual chapters covering routing protocols.)

Many organizations purposefully use SLSM to simplify operations. Additionally, many internetworks also use private IP network 10.0.0.0, with an SLSM prefix length of /24, and use NAT for connecting to the Internet. By using SLSM, particularly with a nice, easy prefix like /24, operations and troubleshooting can be a lot easier.

In some cases, VLSM is required or preferred when allocating addresses. VLSM is typically chosen when the address space is constrained to some degree. The VLSM subnet assignment strategy covered here complies with the strategy you may remember from the Cisco BSCI course or from reading the Cisco Press CCNP Routing certification books.

Similar to when assigning subnets with SLSM, you should use an easily summarized block of addresses for a new part of the network. Because VLSM network addresses are likely constrained to some degree, you should choose the specific subnets wisely. The general rules for choosing wisely are as follows:

Step 1   Determine the shortest prefix length (in other words, the largest block) required.

Step 2   Divide the available address block into equal-sized prefixes based on the shortest prefix from Step 1.

Step 3   Allocate the largest required subnets/prefixes from the beginning of the IP address block, leaving some equal-sized unallocated address blocks at the end of the original large address block.

Step 4   Choose an unallocated block that you will further subdivide by repeating the first three steps, using the shortest required prefix length (largest address block) for the remaining subnets.

Step 5   When allocating very small address blocks for use on links between routers, consider using subnets at the end of the address range. This leaves the largest consecutive blocks available in case future requirements change.

For instance, imagine that a network engineer plans a new site installation. He allocates the 172.31.28.0/23 address block for the new site, expecting to use the block as a single summarized route. When planning, the engineer then subdivides 172.31.28.0/23 per the subnet requirements for the new installation, as shown in Figure 4-3. The figure shows three iterations through the VLSM subnet assignment process, because the requirements call for three different subnet sizes. Each iteration divides a remaining block into equal sizes, based on the prefix requirements of the subnets allocated at that step. Note that the small /30 prefixes were allocated from the end of the address range, leaving the largest possible consecutive address range for future growth.

Figure 4-3 *Example of VLSM Subnet Allocation Process*

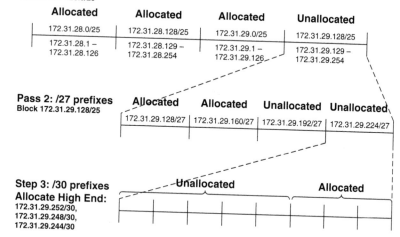

Route Summarization Concepts

The ability to recognize and define how to most efficiently summarize existing address ranges is an important skill on both the written and lab exams. For the written exam, the question may not be as straightforward as, "What is the most efficient summarization of the following subnets?" Rather, the math required for such a question might simply be part of a larger question. Certainly, such math is required for the lab exam. This section looks at the math behind finding the best summarization; other chapters cover specific configuration commands.

Good IP address assignment practices should always consider the capabilities for route summarization. For instance, if a division of a company needs 15 subnets, an engineer needs to allocate those 15 subnets from the unused portions of the address block available to that internetwork. However, assigning subnets 10.1.101.0/24 through 10.1.115.0/24 would be a poor choice, because those do not easily summarize. Rather, allocate a range of addresses that can be easily summarized into a single route. For instance, subnets 10.1.96.0/24 through 10.1.110.0/24 can be summarized as a single 10.1.96.0/20 route, making those routes a better choice.

There are two main ways to think of the word "best" when you are looking for the "best summarization":

- **Inclusive summary routes**—A single summarized route that is as small a range of addresses as possible, while including all routes/subnets shown, and *possibly including subnets that do not currently exist.*

- **Exclusive summary routes**—As few as possible summarized routes that include all to-be-summarized address ranges, but *excluding all other routes/subnets*.

NOTE The terms *inclusive summary*, *exclusive summary*, and *candidate summary* are simply terms I invented for this book and will continue to use later in the chapter.

For instance, with the VLSM example in Figure 4-3, the network engineer purposefully planned so that an inclusive summary of 172.31.28.0/23 could be used. Even though not all subnets are yet allocated from that address range, the engineer is likely saving the rest of that address range for future subnets at that site, so summarizing using an inclusive summary is reasonable. In other cases, typically when trying to summarize routes in an internetwork for which summarization was not planned, the summarization must exclude routes that are not explicitly listed, because those address ranges may actually be used in another part of the internetwork.

Finding Inclusive Summary Routes—Binary

Finding the best inclusive summary lends itself to a formal binary process, as well as to a formal decimal process. The binary process runs as follows:

Step 1   Write down the binary version of each component subnet, one on top of the other.

Step 2   Inspect the binary values to find how many consecutive bits have the exact same value in all component subnets. That number of bits is the prefix length.

Step 3   Write a new 32-bit number at the bottom of the list by copying y bits from the prior number, y being the prefix length. Write binary 0s for the remaining bits. This is the inclusive summary.

Step 4   Convert the new number to decimal, 8 bits at a time.

Table 4-10 shows an example of this process, using four routes, 172.31.20.0, .21.0, .22.0, and .23.0, all with prefix /24. The second example adds 172.31.24.0 to that same list.

Table 4-10   *Example of Finding the Best Inclusive Summary—Binary*

	Octet 1	Octet 2	Octet 3		Octet 4
172.31.20.0/24	10101100	00011111	000101	00	00000000
172.31.21.0/24	10101100	00011111	000101	01	00000000
172.31.22.0/24	10101100	00011111	000101	10	00000000
172.31.23.0/24	10101100	00011111	000101	11	00000000
Prefix length: 22					
Inclusive summary	10101100	00011111	000101	00	00000000

The trickiest part is Step 2, in which you have to simply look at the binary values and find the point at which the bits are no longer equal. You can shorten the process by, in this case, noticing that all component subnets begin with 172.31, meaning that the first 16 bits will certainly have the same values.

Finding Inclusive Summary Routes—Decimal

To find the same inclusive summary using only decimal math, use the following process. The process works just fine with variable prefix lengths and nonconsecutive subnets.

Step 1   Count the number of subnets; then, find the smallest value of y, such that $2^y =>$ that number of subnets.

Step 2   For the next step, use a prefix length based on the longest prefix length of the component subnets, minus y.

Step 3   Pretend that the lowest numeric subnet number in the list of component subnets is an IP address. Using the new, smaller prefix from Step 2, calculate the subnet number in which this pretend address resides.

Step 4   Repeat Step 3 for the largest numeric component subnet number and the same prefix. If it is the same subnet derived as in Step 3, the resulting subnet is the best summarized route, using the new prefix.

Step 5   If Steps 3 and 4 do not yield the same resulting subnet, repeat Steps 3 and 4 with another new prefix length of 1 less than the last prefix length.

Table 4-11 shows two examples of the process. The first example has four routes, 172.31.20.0, .21.0, .22.0, and .23.0, all with prefix /24. The second example adds 172.31.24.0 to that same list.

Table 4-11   *Example of Finding the Best Summarizations*

Step	Range of .20.0, .21.0, .22.0, and .23.0, /24	Same Range, Plus 172.31.24.0
Step 1	$2^2 = 4$, $y = 2$	$2^3 = 8$, $y = 3$
Step 2	$24 - 2 = 22$	$24 - 3 = 21$
Step 3	Smallest subnet 172.31.20.0, with /22, yields **172.31.20.0/22**	Smallest subnet 172.31.20.0, with /21, yields **172.31.16.0/21**
Step 4	Largest subnet 172.31.23.0, with /22, yields **172.31.20.0/22**	Largest subnet 172.31.24.0, with /21, yields **172.31.24.0/21**
Step 5	—	$21 - 1 = 20$; new prefix
Step 3, 2nd time	—	172.31.16.0/20
Step 4, 2nd time	—	172.31.16.0/20; the same as prior step, so that is the answer

With the first example, Steps 3 and 4 yielded the same answer, which means that the best inclusive summary had been found. With the second example, a second pass through the process was required. CD-only Appendix D contains several practice problems to help you develop speed and make this process second nature.

Finding Exclusive Summary Routes—Binary

A similar process, listed next, can be used to find the exclusive summary. Keep in mind that the best exclusive summary can be comprised of multiple summary routes. Once again, to keep it simple, the process assumes SLSM.

Step 1   Find the best *inclusive* summary route; call it a *candidate exclusive* summary route.

Step 2   Determine if the candidate summary includes any address ranges it should not. To do so, compare the summary's implied address range with the implied address ranges of the component subnets.

Step 3   If the candidate summary only includes addresses in the ranges implied by the component subnets, the candidate summary is part of the best exclusive summarization of the original component subnets.

Step 4   If instead the candidate summary includes some addresses that match the candidate summary routes and some addresses that do not, split the current candidate summary in half, into two new candidate summary routes, each with a prefix 1 *longer* than before.

Step 5   If the candidate summary only includes addresses outside the ranges implied by the component subnets, the candidate summary is not part of the best exclusive summarization, and it should not be split further.

Step 6   Repeat Steps 2 through 4 for each of the two possible candidate summary routes created at Step 4.

For example, take the same five subnets used with the inclusive example—172.31.20.0/24, .21.0, .22.0, .23.0, and .24.0. The best inclusive summary is 172.31.16.0/20, which implies an address range of 172.31.16.0 to 172.31.31.255—clearly, it includes more addresses than the original five subnets. So, repeat the process of splitting the summary in half, and repeating, until summaries are found that do not include any unnecessary address ranges. Figure 4-4 shows the idea behind the logic.

The process starts with one candidate summary. If it includes some addresses that need to be summarized and some addresses it should not summarize, split it in half, and try again with each half. Eventually, the best exclusive summary routes are found, or the splitting keeps happening until you get back to the original routes. In fact, in this case, after a few more splits (not shown), the process ends up splitting to 172.31.24.0/24, which is one of the original routes—meaning that 172.31.24.0/24 cannot be summarized any further in this example.

Figure 4-4 *Example of Process to Find Exclusive Summary Routes*

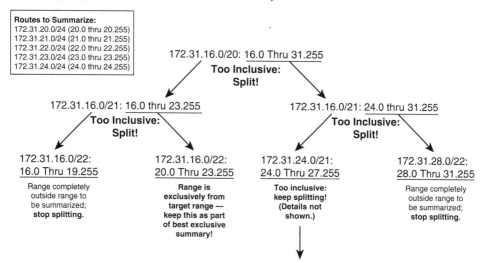

CIDR, Private Addresses, and NAT

The sky was falling in the early 1990s in that the commercialization of the Internet was rapidly depleting the IP Version 4 address space. Also, Internet routers' routing tables were doubling annually (at least). Without some changes, the incredible growth of the Internet in the 1990s would have been stifled.

To solve the problems associated with this rapid growth, several short-term solutions were created, as well as an ultimate long-term solution. The short-term solutions included classless interdomain routing (CIDR), which helps reduce the size of routing tables by aggregating routes, and Network Address Translation (NAT), which reduces the number of required public IP addresses used by each organization or company. This section covers the details of CIDR and NAT, plus a few related features. The long-term solution to this problem, IPv6, is covered in Chapter 20, "IP Version 6."

Classless Interdomain Routing

CIDR is a convention defined in RFCs 1517 through 1520 that calls for aggregating routes for multiple classful network numbers into a single routing table entry. The primary goal of CIDR is to improve the scalability of Internet routers' routing tables. Imagine the implications of an Internet router being burdened by carrying a route to every class A, B, and C network on the planet!

CIDR uses both technical tools and administrative strategies to reduce the size of the Internet routing tables. Technically, CIDR uses route summarization, but with Internet scale in mind.

For instance, CIDR might be used to allow a large ISP to control a range of IP addresses from 198.0.0.0 to 198.255.255.255, with the improvements to routing shown in Figure 4-5.

Figure 4-5 *Typical Use of CIDR*

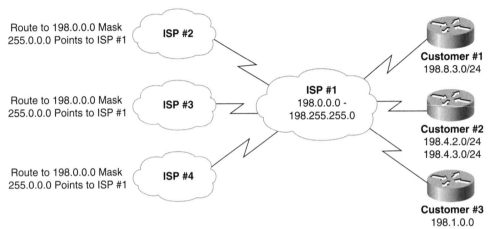

ISPs 2, 3, and 4 need only one route (198.0.0.0/8) in their routing tables to be able to forward packets to all destinations that begin with 198. Note that this summary actually summarizes multiple class C networks—a typical feature of CIDR. ISP 1's routers contain more detailed routing entries for addresses beginning with 198, based on where they allocate IP addresses for their customers. ISP 1 would reduce its routing tables similarly with large ranges used by the other ISPs.

CIDR attacks the problem of large routing tables via administrative means as well. As shown in Figure 4-5, ISPs are assigned contiguous blocks of addresses to use when assigning addresses for their customers. Likewise, regional authorities are assigned large address blocks, so when individual companies ask for registered public IP addresses, they ask their regional registry to assign them an address block. As a result, addresses assigned by the regional agency will at least be aggregatable into one large geographic region of the world. For instance, the Latin American and Caribbean Internet Addresses Registry (LACNIC, http://www.lacnic.net) administers the IP address space of the Latin American and Caribbean region (LAC) on behalf of the Internet community.

In some cases, the term CIDR is used a little more generally than the original intent of the RFCs. Some texts use the term CIDR synonymously with the term route summarization. Others use the term CIDR to refer to the process of summarizing multiple classful networks together. In other cases, when an ISP assigns subsets of a classful network to a customer who does not need an entire class C network, the ISP is essentially performing subnetting; once again, this idea sometimes gets categorized as CIDR. But CIDR itself refers to the administrative assignment of large address blocks, and the related summarized routes, for the purpose of reducing the size of the Internet routing tables.

> **NOTE** Because CIDR defines how to combine routes for multiple classful networks into a single route, some people think of this process as being the opposite of subnetting. As a result, many people refer to CIDR's summarization results as *supernetting*.

Private Addressing

One of the issues with Internet growth was the assignment of all possible network numbers to a small number of companies or organizations. Private IP addressing helps to mitigate this problem by allowing computers that will never be directly connected to the Internet to not use public, Internet-routable addresses. For IP hosts that will purposefully have no direct Internet connectivity, you can use several reserved network numbers, as defined in RFC 1918 and listed in Table 4-12.

Table 4-12 *RFC 1918 Private Address Space*

Range of IP Addresses	Class of Networks	Number of Networks
10.0.0.0 to 10.255.255.255	A	1
172.16.0.0 to 172.31.255.255	B	16
192.168.0.0 to 192.168.255.255	C	256

In other words, any organization can use these network numbers. However, no organization is allowed to advertise these networks using a routing protocol on the Internet. Furthermore, all Internet routers should be configured to reject these routes.

Network Address Translation

NAT, defined in RFC 1631, allows a host that does not have a valid registered IP address to communicate with other hosts on the Internet. NAT has gained such wide-spread acceptance that the majority of enterprise IP networks today use private IP addresses for most hosts on the network and use a small block of public IP addresses, with NAT translating between the two.

NAT translates, or changes, one or both IP addresses inside a packet as it passes through a router. (Many firewalls also perform NAT; for the CCIE Routing and Switching exam, you do not need to know NAT implementation details on firewalls.) In most cases, NAT changes the (typically private range) addresses used inside an enterprise network into address from the public IP address space. For instance, Figure 4-6 shows static NAT in operation; the enterprise has registered class C network 200.1.1.0/24, and uses private class A network 10.0.0.0/8 for the hosts inside its network.

Figure 4-6 *Basic NAT Concept*

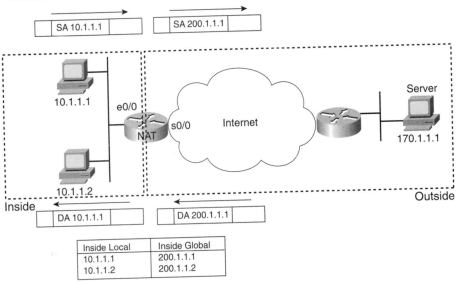

Beginning with the packets sent from a PC on the left to the server on the right, the private IP source address 10.1.1.1 is translated to a public IP address of 200.1.1.1. The client sends a packet with source address 10.1.1.1, but the NAT router changes the source to 200.1.1.1—a registered public IP address. Once the server receives a packet with source IP address 200.1.1.1, the server thinks it is talking to host 200.1.1.1, so it replies with a packet sent to destination 200.1.1.1. The NAT router then translates the destination address (200.1.1.1) back to 10.1.1.1.

Figure 4-6 provides a good backdrop for the introduction of a couple of key terms, *Inside Local* and *Inside Global*. Both terms take the perspective of the owner of the enterprise network. In Figure 4-6, address 10.1.1.1 is the Inside Local address, and 200.1.1.1 is the Inside Global address. Both addresses represent the client PC on the left, which is *inside the enterprise network*. Address 10.1.1.1 is from the enterprise's IP address space, which is only *locally* routable inside the enterprise—hence the term Inside Local. Address 200.1.1.1 represents the local host, but the address is from the globally routable public IP address space—hence the name Inside Global. Table 4-13 lists and describes the four main NAT address terms.

Table 4-13 *NAT Terminology*

Name	Location of Host Represented by Address	IP Address Space in Which Address Exists
Inside Local address	Inside the enterprise network	Part of the enterprise IP address space; typically a private IP address
Inside Global address	Inside the enterprise network	Part of the public IP address space

Key Topic

Table 4-13 *NAT Terminology (Continued)*

Name	Location of Host Represented by Address	IP Address Space in Which Address Exists
Outside Local address	In the public Internet; or, outside the enterprise network	Part of the enterprise IP address space; typically a private IP address
Outside Global address	In the public Internet; or, outside the enterprise network	Part of the public IP address space

Static NAT

Static NAT works just like the example in Figure 4-6, but with the IP addresses statically mapped to each other via configuration commands. With static NAT:

- A particular Inside Local address always maps to the same Inside Global (public) IP address.

- If used, each Outside Local address always maps to the same Outside Global (public) IP address.

- Static NAT does not conserve public IP addresses.

Although static NAT does not help with IP address conservation, static NAT does allow an engineer to make an inside server host available to clients on the Internet, because the inside server will always use the same public IP address.

Example 4-1 shows a basic static NAT configuration based on Figure 4-6. Conceptually, the NAT router has to identify which interfaces are inside (attach to the enterprise's IP address space) or outside (attach to the public IP address space). Also, the mapping between each Inside Local and Inside Global IP address must be made. (Although not needed for this example, outside addresses can also be statically mapped.)

Example 4-1 *Static NAT Configuration*

```
!!!!!!!!!!!!!!!!!!!!!!!!!!!!!!!!!!!!!!!!!!!!!!!!!!!!!!!!!!!!!!!!!!!!!!!!!!!!!!!!!!!!
! E0/0 attaches to the internal Private IP space, so it is configured as an inside
! interface.
interface Ethernet0/0
 ip address 10.1.1.3 255.255.255.0
 ip nat inside
! S0/0 is attached to the public Internet, so it is defined as an outside
! interface.
interface Serial0/0
 ip address 200.1.1.251 255.255.255.0
 ip nat outside
```

continues

Example 4-1 *Static NAT Configuration (Continued)*

```
! Next, two inside addresses are mapped, with the first address stating the
! Inside Local address, and the next stating the Inside Global address.
ip nat inside source static 10.1.1.2 200.1.1.2
ip nat inside source static 10.1.1.1 200.1.1.1
! Below, the NAT table lists the permanent static entries from the configuration.
NAT# show ip nat translations
Pro Inside global      Inside local     Outside local     Outside global
--- 200.1.1.1          10.1.1.1         ---               --
--- 200.1.1.2          10.1.1.2         ---               ---
```

The router is performing NAT only for inside addresses. As a result, the router processes packets entering E0/0—packets that could be sent by inside hosts—by examining the source IP address. Any packets with a source IP address listed in the Inside Local column of the **show ip nat translations** command output (10.1.1.1 or 10.1.1.2) will be translated to source address 200.1.1.1 or 200.1.1.2, respectively, per the NAT table. Likewise, the router examines the destination IP address of packets entering S0/0, because those packets would be destined for inside hosts. Any such packets with a destination of 200.1.1.1 or .2 will be translated to 10.1.1.1 or .2, respectively.

In cases with static outside addresses being configured, the router also looks at the destination IP address of packets sent from the inside to the outside interfaces, and the source IP address of packets sent from outside interfaces to inside interfaces.

Dynamic NAT Without PAT

Dynamic NAT (without PAT), like static NAT, creates a one-to-one mapping between an Inside Local and Inside Global address. However, unlike static NAT, it does so by defining a set or pool of Inside Local and Inside Global addresses, and dynamically mapping pairs of addresses as needed. For example, Figure 4-7 shows a pool of five Inside Global IP addresses—200.1.1.1 through 200.1.1.5. NAT has also been configured to translate any Inside Local addresses whose address starts with 10.1.1.

The numbers 1, 2, and 3 in Figure 4-7 refer to the following sequence of events:

1. Host 10.1.1.2 starts by sending its first packet to the server at 170.1.1.1.

2. As the packet enters the NAT router, the router applies some matching logic to decide if the packet should have NAT applied. Because the logic has been configured to mean "translate Inside Local addresses that start with 10.1.1," the router dynamically adds an entry in the NAT table for 10.1.1.2 as an Inside Local address.

3. The NAT router needs to allocate a corresponding IP address from the pool of valid Inside Global addresses. It picks the first one available (200.1.1.1 in this case) and adds it to the NAT table to complete the entry.

Figure 4-7 *Dynamic NAT*

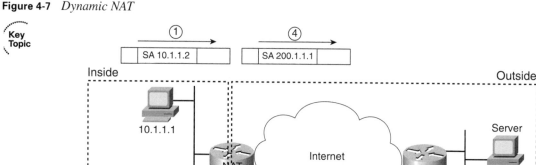

With the completion of step 3, the NAT router can actually translate the source IP address, and forward the packet. Note that as long as the dynamic NAT entry exists in the NAT table, only host 10.1.1.2 can use Inside Global IP address 200.1.1.1.

Overloading NAT with Port Address Translation

As mentioned earlier, NAT is one of the key features that helped to reduce the speed at which the IPv4 address space was being depleted. *NAT overloading*, also known as *Port Address Translation* (*PAT*), is the NAT feature that actually provides the significant savings of IP addresses. The key to understanding how PAT works is to consider the following: From a server's perspective, there is no significant difference between 100 different TCP connections, each from a different host, and 100 different TCP connections all from the same host.

PAT works by making large numbers of TCP or UDP flows from many Inside Local hosts appear to be the same number of large flows from one (or a few) host's Inside Global addresses. With PAT, instead of just translating the IP address, NAT also translates the port numbers as necessary. And because the port number fields are 16 bits in length, each Inside Global IP address can support over 65,000 concurrent TCP and UDP flows. For instance, in a network with 1000 hosts, a single public IP address used as the only Inside Global address could handle an average of six concurrent flows from each host to and from hosts on the Internet.

Dynamic NAT and PAT Configuration

Like static NAT, dynamic NAT configuration begins with identifying the inside and outside interfaces. Additionally, the set of Inside Local addresses is configured with the **ip nat inside** global command. If you are using a pool of public Inside Global addresses, the set of addresses is defined by the **ip nat pool** command. Example 4-2 shows a dynamic NAT configuration based on the internetwork shown in Figure 4-7. The example defines 256 Inside Local addresses and two Inside Global addresses.

Example 4-2 *Dynamic NAT Configuration*

Key
Topic

```
! First, the ip nat pool fred command lists a range of IP addresses. The ip nat
! inside source list 1 pool fred command points to ACL 1 as the list of Inside
! Local addresses, with a cross-reference to the pool name.
interface Ethernet0/0
 ip address 10.1.1.3 255.255.255.0
 ip nat inside
!
interface Serial0/0
 ip address 200.1.1.251 255.255.255.0
 ip nat outside
!
ip nat pool fred 200.1.1.1 200.1.1.2 netmask 255.255.255.252
ip nat inside source list 1 pool fred
!
access-list 1 permit 10.1.1.0 0.0.0.255
! Next, the NAT table begins as an empty table, because no dynamic entries had
! been created at that point.
NAT# show ip nat translations

! The NAT statistics show that no hits or misses have occurred. Hits occur when
! NAT looks for a mapping, and finds one. Misses occur when NAT looks for a NAT
! table entry, does not find one, and then needs to dynamically add one.
NAT# show ip nat statistics
Total active translations: 0 (0 static, 0 dynamic; 0 extended)
Outside interfaces:
  Serial0/0
Inside interfaces:
  Ethernet0/0
Hits: 0  Misses: 0
Expired translations: 0
Dynamic mappings:
-- Inside Source
access-list 1 pool fred refcount 0
 pool fred: netmask 255.255.255.252
    start 200.1.1.1 end 200.1.1.2
    type generic, total addresses 2, allocated 0 (0%), misses 0
! At this point, a Telnet session from 10.1.1.1 to 170.1.1.1 started.
```

Example 4-2 *Dynamic NAT Configuration (Continued)*

```
! Below, the 1 "miss" means that the first packet from 10.1.1.2 did not have a
! matching entry in the table, but that packet triggered NAT to add an entry to the
! NAT table. Host 10.1.1.2 has then sent 69 more packets, noted as "hits" because
! there was an entry in the table.
NAT# show ip nat statistics
Total active translations: 1 (0 static, 1 dynamic; 0 extended)
Outside interfaces:
  Serial0/0
Inside interfaces:
  Ethernet0/0
Hits: 69  Misses: 1
Expired translations: 0
Dynamic mappings:
-- Inside Source
access-list 1 pool fred refcount 1
 pool fred: netmask 255.255.255.252
    start 200.1.1.1 end 200.1.1.2
    type generic, total addresses 2, allocated 1 (50%), misses 0
! The dynamic NAT entry is now displayed in the table.
NAT# show ip nat translations
Pro Inside global      Inside local      Outside local      Outside global
--- 200.1.1.1          10.1.1.2          ---                ---
! Below, the configuration uses PAT via the overload parameter. Could have used the
! ip nat inside source list 1 int s0/0 overload command instead, using a single
! IP Inside Global IP address.
NAT(config)# no ip nat inside source list 1 pool fred
NAT(config)# ip nat inside source list 1 pool fred overload
! To test, the dynamic NAT entries were cleared after changing the NAT
! configuration. Before the next command was issued, host 10.1.1.1 had created two
! Telnet connections, and host 10.1.1.2 created 1 more TCP connection.
NAT# clear ip nat translations *
! Before the next command was issued, host 10.1.1.1 had created two
! Telnet connections, and host 10.1.1.2 created 1 more TCP connection. Note that
! all three dynamically mapped flows use common Inside Global 200.1.1.1.
NAT# show ip nat translations
Pro Inside global      Inside local      Outside local      Outside global
tcp 200.1.1.1:3212     10.1.1.1:3212     170.1.1.1:23       170.1.1.1:23
tcp 200.1.1.1:3213     10.1.1.1:3213     170.1.1.1:23       170.1.1.1:23
tcp 200.1.1.1:38913    10.1.1.2:38913    170.1.1.1:23       170.1.1.1:23
```

Foundation Summary

This section lists additional details and facts to round out the coverage of the topics in this chapter. Unlike most of the Cisco Press *Exam Certification Guides*, this "Foundation Summary" does not repeat information presented in the "Foundation Topics" section of the chapter. Please take the time to read and study the details in the "Foundation Topics" section of the chapter, as well as review items noted with a Key Topic icon.

Table 4-14 lists and briefly explains several variations on NAT.

Table 4-14 *Variations on NAT*

Name	Function
Static NAT	Statically correlates the same public IP address for use by the same local host every time. Does not conserve IP addresses.
Dynamic NAT	Pools the available public IP addresses, shared among a group of local hosts, but with only one local host at a time using a public IP address. Does not conserve IP addresses.
Dynamic NAT with overload (PAT)	Like dynamic NAT, but multiple local hosts share a single public IP address by multiplexing using TCP and UDP port numbers. Conserves IP addresses.
NAT for overlapping address	Can be done with any of the first three types. Translates both source and destination addresses, instead of just the source (for packets going from enterprise to the Internet).

Table 4-15 lists the protocols mentioned in this chapter and their respective standards documents.

Table 4-15 *Protocols and Standards for Chapter 4*

Name	Standardized In
IP	RFC 791
Subnetting	RFC 950
NAT	RFC 1631
Private addressing	RFC 1918
CIDR	RFCs 1517–1520

Table 4-16 lists and describes some of the most commonly used IOS commands related to the topics in this chapter.

Table 4-16   *Command Reference for Chapter 4*

Command	Description
ip address *ip-address mask* [**secondary**]	Interface subcommand to assign an IPv4 address
ip nat {**inside** I **outside**}	Interface subcommand; identifies inside or outside part of network
ip nat inside source {**list** {*access-list-number* I *access-list-name*} I **route-map** *name*} {**interface** *type number* I **pool** *pool-name*} [**overload**]	Global command that defines the set of inside addresses for which NAT will be performed, and corresponding outside addresses
ip nat inside destination list {*access-list-number* I *name*} **pool** *name*	Global command used with destination NAT
ip nat outside source {**list** {*access-list-number* I *access-list-name*} I **route-map** *name*} **pool** *pool-name* [**add-route**]	Global command used with both destination and dynamic NAT
ip nat pool *name start-ip end-ip* {**netmask** *netmask* I **prefix-length** *prefix-length*}[**type rotary**]	Global command to create a pool of addresses for dynamic NAT
show ip nat statistics	Lists counters for packets and for NAT table entries, as well as basic configuration information
show ip nat translations [**verbose**]	Displays the NAT table
clear ip nat translation {***** I [**inside** *global-ip local-ip*] [**outside** *local-ip global-ip*]}	Clears all or some of the dynamic entries in the NAT table, depending on which parameters are used
debug ip nat	Issues log messages describing each packet whose IP address is translated with NAT
show ip interface [*type number*] [**brief**]	Lists information about IPv4 on interfaces

Figure 4-8 shows the IP header format.

Figure 4-8 *IP Header*

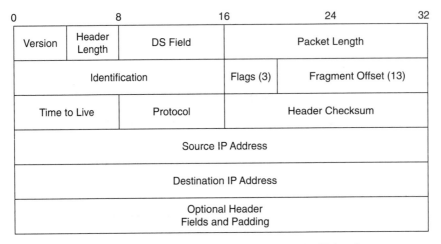

Table 4-17 lists the terms and meanings of the fields inside the IP header.

Table 4-17 *IP Header Fields*

Field	Meaning
Version	Version of the IP protocol. Most networks use IPv4 today, with IPv6 becoming more popular. The header format reflects IPv4.
Header Length	Defines the length of the IP header, including optional fields. Because the length of the IP header must always be a multiple of 4, the IP header length (IHL) is multiplied by 4 to give the actual number of bytes.
DS Field	Differentiated Services Field. This byte was originally called the Type of Service (ToS) byte, but was redefined by RFC 2474 as the DS Field. It is used for marking packets for the purpose of applying different quality of service (QoS) levels to different packets.
Packet Length	Identifies the entire length of the IP packet, including the data.
Identification	Used by the IP packet fragmentation process. If a single packet is fragmented into multiple packets, all fragments of the original packet contain the same identifier, so that the original packet can be reassembled.
Flags	3 bits used by the IP packet fragmentation process.
Fragment Offset	A number set in a fragment of a larger packet that identifies the fragment's location in the larger original packet.
Time to Live (TTL)	A value used to prevent routing loops. Routers decrement this field by 1 each time the packet is forwarded; once it decrements to 0, the packet is discarded.
Protocol	A field that identifies the contents of the data portion of the IP packet. For example, protocol 6 implies a TCP header is the first thing in the IP packet data field.

Table 4-17 *IP Header Fields (Continued)*

Field	Meaning
Header Checksum	A value used to store a frame check sequence (FCS) value, whose purpose is to determine if any bit errors occurred in the IP header (not the data) during transmission.
Source IP Address	The 32-bit IP address of the sender of the packet.
Destination IP Address	The 32-bit IP address of the intended recipient of the packet.
Optional Header Fields and Padding	IP supports additional header fields for future expansion via optional headers. Also, if these optional headers do not use a multiple of 4 bytes, padding bytes are added, comprised of all binary 0s, so that the header is a multiple of 4 bytes in length.

Table 4-18 lists some of the more common IP protocol field values.

Table 4-18 *IP Protocol Field Values*

Protocol Name	Protocol Number
ICMP	1
TCP	6
UDP	17
EIGRP	88
OSPF	89
PIM	103

Memory Builders

The CCIE Routing and Switching written exam, like all Cisco CCIE written exams, covers a fairly broad set of topics. This section provides some basic tools to help you exercise your memory about some of the broader topics covered in this chapter.

Fill in Key Tables from Memory

Appendix E, "Key Tables for CCIE Study," on the CD in the back of this book contains empty sets of some of the key summary tables in each chapter. Print Appendix E, refer to this chapter's tables in it, and fill in the tables from memory. Refer to Appendix F, "Solutions for Key Tables for CCIE Study," on the CD to check your answers.

Definitions

Next, take a few moments to write down the definitions for the following terms:

subnet, prefix, classless IP addressing, classful IP addressing, CIDR, NAT, IPv4, subnet broadcast address, subnet number, subnet zero, broadcast subnet, subnet mask, private addresses, SLSM, VLSM, Inside Local address, Inside Global address, Outside Local address, Outside Global address, PAT, overloading, quartet

Refer to the glossary to check your answers.

Further Reading

All topics in this chapter are covered to varying depth for the CCNP Routing exam. For more details on these topics, refer to *CCNP BSCI Official Exam Certification Guide*, Fourth Edition, and *Authorized Self-Study Guide: Building Scalable Cisco Internetworks (BSCI)*, Third Edition.

Blueprint topics covered in this chapter:

This chapter covers the following subtopics from the Cisco CCIE Routing and Switching written exam blueprint. Refer to the full blueprint in Table I-1 in the Introduction for more details on the topics covered in each chapter and their context within the blueprint.

- Hot Standby Router Protocol (HSRP)

- Gateway Load Balancing Protocol (GLBP)

- Virtual Router Redundancy Protocol (VRRP)

- Dynamic Host Configuration Protocol (DHCP)

- Network Time Protocol (NTP)

- Web Cache Communication Protocol (WCCP)

- Network Management

- Logging and Syslog

IP Services

IP relies on several protocols to perform a variety of tasks related to the process of routing packets. This chapter provides a reference for the most popular of these protocols. In addition, this chapter covers a number of management-related protocols and other blueprint topics related to IP services.

"Do I Know This Already?" Quiz

Table 5-1 outlines the major headings in this chapter and the corresponding "Do I Know This Already?" quiz questions.

Table 5-1 *"Do I Know This Already?" Foundation Topics Section-to-Question Mapping*

Foundation Topics Section	Questions Covered in This Section	Score
ARP, Proxy ARP, Reverse ARP, BOOTP, and DHCP	1–3	
HSRP, VRRP, and GLBP	4–6	
Network Time Protocol	7	
SNMP	8–9	
Web Cache Communication Protocol	10–11	
Total Score		

In order to best use this pre-chapter assessment, remember to score yourself strictly. You can find the answers in Appendix A, "Answers to the 'Do I Know This Already?' Quizzes."

1. Two hosts, named PC1 and PC2, sit on subnet 172.16.1.0/24, along with router R1. A web server sits on subnet 172.16.2.0/24, which is connected to another interface of R1. At some point, both PC1 and PC2 send an ARP request before they successfully send packets to the web server. With PC1, R1 makes a normal ARP reply, but for PC2, R1 uses a proxy ARP reply. Which two of the following answers could be true given the stated behavior in this network?

   a. PC2 set the proxy flag in the ARP request.

   b. PC2 encapsulated the ARP request inside an IP packet.

    c. PC2's ARP broadcast implied that PC2 was looking for the web server's MAC address.

    d. PC2 has a subnet mask of 255.255.0.0.

    e. R1's proxy ARP reply contains the web server's MAC address.

2. Host PC3 is using DHCP to discover its IP address. Only one router attaches to PC3's subnet, using its fa0/0 interface, with an **ip helper-address 10.5.5.5** command on that same interface. That same router interface has an **ip address 10.4.5.6 255.255.252.0** command configured as well. Which of the following are true about PC3's DHCP request?

    a. The destination IP address of the DHCP request packet is set to 10.5.5.5 by the router.

    b. The DHCP request packet's source IP address is unchanged by the router.

    c. The DHCP request is encapsulated inside a new IP packet, with source IP address 10.4.5.6 and destination 10.5.5.5.

    d. The DHCP request's source IP address is changed to 10.4.5.255.

    e. The DHCP request's source IP address is changed to 10.4.7.255.

3. Which of the following statements are true about BOOTP, but not true about RARP?

    a. The client can be assigned a different IP address on different occasions, because the server can allocate a pool of IP addresses for allocation to a set of clients.

    b. The server can be on a different subnet from the client.

    c. The client's MAC address must be configured on the server, with a one-to-one mapping to the IP address to be assigned to the client with that MAC address.

    d. The client can discover its IP address, subnet mask, and default gateway IP address.

4. R1 is HSRP active for virtual IP address 172.16.1.1, with HSRP priority set to 115. R1 is tracking three separate interfaces. An engineer configures the same HSRP group on R2, also connected to the same subnet, only using the **standby 1 ip 172.16.1.1** command, and no other HSRP-related commands. Which of the following would cause R2 to take over as HSRP active?

    a. R1 experiences failures on tracked interfaces, totaling 16 or more lost points.

    b. R1 experiences failures on tracked interfaces, totaling 15 or more lost points.

    c. R2 could configure a priority of 116 or greater.

    d. R1's fa0/0 interface fails.

    e. R2 would take over immediately.

5. Which Cisco IOS feature does HSRP, GLBP, and VRRP use to determine when an interface fails for active switching purposes?

    a. Each protocol has a built-in method of tracking interfaces.

    b. When a physical interface goes down, the redundancy protocol uses this automatically as a basis for switching.

    c. Each protocol uses its own hello mechanism for determining which interfaces are up or down.

    d. The Cisco IOS object tracking feature.

6. Which is the correct term for using more than one HSRP group to provide load balancing for HSRP?

    a. LBHSRP

    b. LSHSRP

    c. RHSRP

    d. MHSRP

    e. None of these. HSRP does not support load balancing.

7. Which of the following NTP modes in a Cisco router requires a predefinition of the IP address of an NTP server?

    a. Server mode

    b. Static client mode

    c. Broadcast client mode

    d. Symmetric active mode

8. Which of the following are true about SNMP security?

    a. SNMP Version 1 calls for the use of community strings that are passed as clear text.

    b. SNMP Version 2c calls for the use of community strings that are passed as MD5 message digests generated with private keys.

    c. SNMP Version 3 allows for authentication using MD5 message digests generated with private keys.

    d. SNMP Version 3 authentication also requires concurrent use of encryption, typically done with DES.

9. Which of the following statements are true regarding features of SNMP based on the SNMP version?

    a. SNMP Version 2 added the GetNext protocol message to SNMP.

    b. SNMP Version 3 added the Inform protocol message to SNMP.

    c. SNMP Version 2 added the Inform protocol message to SNMP.

    d. SNMP Version 3 expanded the SNMP Response protocol message so that it must be used by managers in response to Traps sent by agents.

    e. SNMP Version 3 enhanced SNMP Version 2 security features but not other features.

10. WCCP uses what protocol and port for communication between content engines and WCCP routers?

   a. UDP 2048

   b. TCP 2048

   c. UDP 4082

   d. TCP 4082

11. In a WCCP cluster, which content engine becomes the lead engine after the cluster stabilizes?

   a. The content engine with the lowest IP address.

   b. The content engine with the highest IP address.

   c. There is no such thing as a lead content engine; the correct term is designated content engine.

   d. All content engines have equal precedence for redundancy and the fastest possible load sharing.

Foundation Topics

ARP, Proxy ARP, Reverse ARP, BOOTP, and DHCP

The heading for this section may seem like a laundry list of a lot of different protocols. However, these five protocols do have one central theme, namely that they help a host learn information so that it can successfully send and receive IP packets. Specifically, ARP and proxy ARP define methods for a host to learn another host's MAC address, whereas the core functions of RARP, BOOTP, and DHCP define how a host can discover its own IP address, plus additional related information.

ARP and Proxy ARP

You would imagine that anyone getting this far in their CCIE study would already have a solid understanding of the Address Resolution Protocol (ARP, RFC 826). However, proxy ARP (RFC 1027) is often ignored, in part because of its lack of use today. To see how they both work, Figure 5-1 shows an example of each, with Fred and Barney both trying to reach the web server at IP address 10.1.2.200.

Figure 5-1 *Comparing ARP and Proxy ARP*

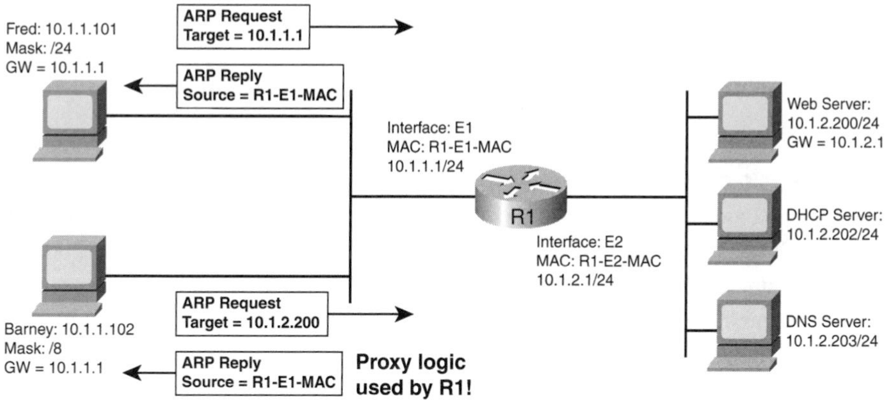

Fred follows a normal ARP process, broadcasting an ARP request, with R1's E1 IP address as the target. The ARP message has a *Target* field of all 0s for the MAC address that needs to be learned, and a target IP address of the IP address whose MAC address it is searching, namely 10.1.1.1 in this case. The ARP reply lists the MAC address associated with the IP address, in this case, the MAC address of R1's E1 interface.

> **NOTE** The ARP message itself does not include an IP header, although it does have destination and source IP addresses in the same relative position as an IP header. The ARP request lists an IP destination of 255.255.255.255. The ARP Ethernet protocol type is 0x0806, whereas IP packets have an Ethernet protocol type of 0x0800.

Proxy ARP uses the exact same ARP message as ARP, but the ARP request is actually requesting a MAC address that is not on the local subnet. Because the ARP request is broadcast on the local subnet, it will not be heard by the target host—so if a router can route packets to that target host, the router issues a proxy ARP reply on behalf of that target.

For instance, Barney places the web server's IP address (10.1.2.200) in the Target field, because Barney thinks that he is on the same subnet as the web server due to Barney's mask of 255.0.0.0. The ARP request is a LAN broadcast, so R1, being a well-behaved router, does not forward the ARP broadcast. However, knowing that the ARP request will never get to the subnet where 10.1.2.200 resides, R1 saves the day by replying to the ARP on behalf of the web server. R1 takes the web server's place in the ARP process, hence the name *proxy* ARP. Also, note that R1's ARP reply contains R1's E1 MAC address, so that Barney will forward frames to R1 when Barney wants to send a packet to the web server.

Before the advent of DHCP, many networks relied on proxy ARP, configuring hosts to use the default masks in their respective networks. Regardless of whether the proxy version is used, the end result is that the host learns a router's MAC address to forward packets to another subnet.

RARP, BOOTP, and DHCP

The ARP and proxy ARP processes both occur after a host knows its IP address and subnet mask. RARP, BOOTP, and DHCP represent the evolution of protocols defined to help a host dynamically learn its IP address. All three protocols require the client host to send a broadcast to begin discovery, and all three rely on a server to hear the request and supply an IP address to the client. Figure 5-2 shows the basic processes with RARP and BOOTP.

Figure 5-2 *RARP and BOOTP—Basic Processes*

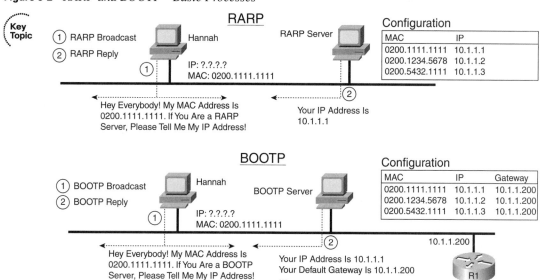

A RARP request is a host's attempt to find its own IP address. So RARP uses the same old ARP message, but the ARP request lists a MAC address target of its own MAC address and a target IP address of 0.0.0.0. A preconfigured RARP server, which must be on the same subnet as the client, receives the request and performs a table lookup in its configuration. If that target MAC address listed in the ARP request is configured on the RARP server, the RARP server sends an ARP reply, after entering the configured IP address in the Source IP address field.

BOOTP was defined in part to improve IP address assignment features of RARP. BOOTP uses a completely different set of messages, defined by RFC 951, with the commands encapsulated inside an IP and UDP header. With the correct router configuration, a router can forward the BOOTP packets to other subnets—allowing the deployment of a centrally located BOOTP server. Also, BOOTP supports the assignment of many other tidbits of information, including the subnet mask, default gateway, DNS addresses, and its namesake, the IP address of a boot (or image) server. However, BOOTP does not solve the configuration burden of RARP, still requiring that the server be preconfigured with the MAC addresses and IP addresses of each client.

DHCP

DHCP represents the next step in the evolution of dynamic IP address assignment. Building on the format of BOOTP protocols, DHCP focuses on dynamically assigning a variety of information and provides flexible messaging to allow for future changes, without requiring predefinition of MAC addresses for each client. DHCP also includes temporary leasing of IP addresses, enabling address reclamation, pooling of IP addresses, and, recently, dynamic registration of client DNS fully qualified domain names (FQDNs). (See http://www.ietf.org for more information on FQDN registration.)

DHCP servers typically reside in a centralized location, with remote routers forwarding the LAN-broadcast DHCP requests to the DHCP server by changing the request's destination address to match the DHCP server. This feature is called DHCP relay agent. For instance, in Figure 5-1, if Fred and Barney were to use DHCP, with the DHCP server at 10.1.2.202, R1 would change Fred's DHCP request from a source and destination of 255.255.255.255 to a source of 10.1.1.255 (directed broadcast of Fred's subnet) and destination of 10.1.2.202. The DHCP request would then be routed to the DHCP server, and the DHCP response would be forwarded to destination 10.1.1.255. The router would then broadcast the DHCP response back onto that subnet, as the destination address is Fred's subnet's broadcast address. The only configuration requirement on the router is an **ip helper-address 10.1.2.202** interface subcommand on its E1 interface.

Alternatively, R1 could be configured as a DHCP server—a feature that is not often configured on routers in production networks but is certainly fair game for the CCIE written and lab exams. Configuring DHCP on a router consists of several required steps:

Step 1   Configure a DHCP pool.

Step 2   Configure the router to exclude its own IP address from the DHCP pool.

Step 3   Disable DHCP conflict logging or configure a DHCP database agent.

The DHCP pool includes key items such as the subnet (using the **network** command within DHCP pool configuration), default gateway (*default-router*), and the length of time for which the DHCP lease is valid (*lease*). Other items, including the DNS domain name and any DHCP options, are also defined within the DHCP pool.

Although not strictly necessary in DHCP configuration, it is certainly a best practice to configure the router to make its own IP address in the DHCP pool subnet unavailable for allocation via DHCP. The same is true for any other static IP addresses within the DHCP pool range, such as those of servers and other routers. Exclude host IP addresses from the DHCP process using the **ip dhcp excluded-address** command.

> **NOTE**   The **ip dhcp excluded-address** command is one of the relatively few Cisco IOS **ip** commands that is a global configuration command rather than an interface command.

The Cisco IOS DHCP server also provides a mechanism for logging DHCP address conflicts to a central server called a DHCP database agent. IOS requires that you either disable conflict logging by using the **no ip dhcp conflict-logging** command or configure a DHCP database agent on a server by using the **ip dhcp database** command. Example 5-1 shows R1's configuration for a DHCP relay agent, as well as an alternative for R1 to provide DNS services for subnet 10.1.1.0/24.

Example 5-1 *DHCP Configuration Options—R1, Figure 5-1*

```
! UDP broadcasts coming in E0 will be forwarded as unicasts to 10.1.2.202.
! The source IP will be changed to 10.1.1.255, so that the reply packets will be
! broadcast back out E0.
interface Ethernet1
 ip address 10.1.1.1 255.255.255.0
 ip helper-address 10.1.2.202
! Below, an alternative configuration, with R1 as the DHCP server. R1 assigns IP
! addresses other than the excluded first 20 IP addresses in the subnet, and informs the
! clients of their IP addresses, mask, DNS, and default router. Leases are for 0 days,
! 0 hours, and 20 minutes.
ip dhcp excluded-address 10.1.1.0 10.1.1.20
!
ip dhcp pool subnet1
   network 10.1.0.0 255.255.255.0
   dns-server 10.1.2.203
   default-router 10.1.1.1
   lease 0 0 20
```

Table 5-2 summarizes some of the key comparison points with RARP, BOOTP, and DHCP.

Table 5-2 *Comparing RARP, BOOTP, and DHCP*

Feature	RARP	BOOTP	DHCP
Relies on server to allocate IP addresses	Yes	Yes	Yes
Encapsulates messages inside IP and UDP, so they can be forwarded to a remote server	No	Yes	Yes
Client can discover its own mask, gateway, DNS, and download server	No	Yes	Yes
Dynamic address assignment from a pool of IP addresses, without requiring knowledge of client MACs	No	No	Yes
Allows temporary lease of IP address	No	No	Yes
Includes extensions for registering client's FQDN with a DNS	No	No	Yes

HSRP, VRRP, and GLBP

IP hosts can use several methods of deciding which default router or default gateway to use—DHCP, BOOTP, ICMP Router Discovery Protocol (IRDP), manual configuration, or even by running a routing protocol (although having hosts run a routing protocol is not common today). The most typical methods—using DHCP or manual configuration—result in the host knowing a single IP address of its default gateway. Hot Standby Router Protocol (HSRP), Virtual Router Redundancy Protocol (VRRP), and Gateway Load Balancing Protocol (GLBP) represent a chronological list of some of the best tools for overcoming the issues related to a host knowing a single IP address as its path to get outside the subnet.

HSRP allows multiple routers to share a virtual IP and MAC address so that the end-user hosts do not realize when a failure occurs. Some of the key HSRP features are as follows:

- Virtual IP address and virtual MAC active on the Master router

- Standby routers listen for Hellos from the Active router, defaulting to a 3-second hello interval and 10-second dead interval

- Highest priority (IOS default 100, range 1–255) determines the Active router, with preemption disabled by default

- Supports tracking, whereby a router's priority is decreased when a tracked object (interface or route) fails

- Up to 255 HSRP groups per interface, enabling an administrative form of load balancing

- Virtual MAC of 0000.0C07.AC*xx*, where *xx* is the hex HSRP group

- Virtual IP address must be in the same subnet as the routers' interfaces on the same LAN

- Virtual IP address must be different from any of routers' individual interface IP addresses

- Supports clear-text and MD5 authentication (through a key chain)

Example 5-2 shows a typical HSRP configuration, with two groups configured. Routers R1 and R2 are attached to the same subnet, 10.1.1.0/24, both with WAN links (S0/0.1) connecting them to the rest of an enterprise network. Cisco IOS provides the tracking mechanism shown in Example 5-2 to permit many processes, including HSRP, VRRP, and GLBP, to track interface states. A tracking object can track based on the line protocol (shown here) or the IP routing table. The example contains the details and explanation of the configuration.

Example 5-2 *HSRP Configuration*

```
! First, on Router R1, a tracking object must be configured so that
! HSRP can track the interface state.
track 13 interface Serial0/0.1 line-protocol
! Next, on Router R1, two HSRP groups are configured. R1 has a higher priority
! in group 21, with R2 having a higher priority in group 22. R1 is set to preempt
! in group 21, as well as to track interface s0/0.1 for both groups.
interface FastEthernet0/0
 ip address 10.1.1.2 255.255.255.0
 standby 21 ip 10.1.1.21
```

Example 5-2 *HSRP Configuration (Continued)*

```
 standby 21 priority 105
 standby 21 preempt
 standby 21 track 13
 standby 22 ip 10.1.1.22
 standby 22 track 13
! Next, R2 is configured with a higher priority for HSRP group 22, and with
! HSRP tracking enabled in both groups. The tracking "decrement" used by R2,
! when S0/0.1 fails, is set to 9 (instead of the default of 10).
! A tracking object must be configured first, as on R1.
track 23 interface Serial0/0.1 line-protocol
interface FastEthernet0/0
 ip address 10.1.1.1 255.255.255.0
 standby 21 ip 10.1.1.21
 standby 21 track 23
 standby 22 ip 10.1.1.22
 standby 22 priority 105
 standby 22 track 23 decrement 9
!!!!!!!!!!!!!!!!!!!!!!!!!!!!!!!!!!!!!!!!!!!!!!!!!!!!!!!!!!!!!!!!!!!!!!!!!!!!!!!!!!!!!
! On R1 below, for group 21, the output shows that R1 is active, with R2
! (10.1.1.2) as standby.
! R1 is tracking s0/0.1, with a default "decrement" of 10, meaning that the
! configured priority of 105 will be decremented by 10 if s0/0.1 fails.
Router1#sh standby fa0/0
FastEthernet0/0 - Group 21
  State is Active
    2 state changes, last state change 00:00:45
  Virtual IP address is 10.1.1.21
  Active virtual MAC address is 0000.0c07.ac15
    Local virtual MAC address is 0000.0c07.ac15 (v1 default)
  Hello time 3 sec, hold time 10 sec
    Next hello sent in 2.900 secs
  Preemption enabled
  Active router is local
  Standby router is 10.1.1.2, priority 100 (expires in 7.897 sec)
  Priority 105 (configured 105)
    Track object 13 state Up decrement 10
  IP redundancy name is "hsrp-Fa0/0-21" (default)
! output omitted
! NOT SHOWN—R1 shuts down S0.0.1, lowering its priority in group 21 by 10.
! The debug below shows the reduced priority value. However, R2 does not become
! active, because R2's configuration did not include a standby 21 preempt command.
Router1# debug standby
*Mar  1 00:24:04.122: HSRP: Fa0/0 Grp 21 Hello  out 10.1.1.1 Active  pri 95 vIP 10.1.1.21
```

Because HSRP uses only one Active router at a time, any other HSRP routers are idle. To provide load sharing in an HSRP configuration, the concept of Multiple HSRP, or MHSRP, was developed. In MHSRP, two or more HSRP groups are configured on each HSRP LAN interface, where the configured priority determines which router will be active for each HSRP group.

MHSRP requires that each DHCP client and statically configured host is issued a default gateway corresponding to one of the HSRP groups and requires that they're distributed appropriately. Thus, in an MHSRP configuration with two routers and two groups, all other things being equal, half of the hosts should have one HSRP group address as its default gateway, and the other half of the hosts should use the other HSRP group address. If you now revisit Example 5-2, you will see that it is an MHSRP configuration.

HSRP is Cisco proprietary, has been out a long time, and is widely popular. VRRP (RFC 3768) provides a standardized protocol to perform almost the exact same function. The Cisco VRRP implementation has the same goals in mind as HSRP but with these differences:

- VRRP uses a multicast virtual MAC address (0000.5E00.01*xx*, where *xx* is the hex VRRP group number).

- VRRP uses the IOS object tracking feature, rather than its own internal tracking mechanism, to track interface states for failover purposes.

- VRRP defaults to use pre-emption, but HSRP defaults to not use pre-emption. Both can be configured to either use pre-emption or not.

- The VRRP term *Master* means the same thing as the HSRP term *Active*.

- In VRRP, the VRRP group IP address is the interface IP address of one of the VRRP routers.

GLBP is a newer Cisco-proprietary tool that adds load-balancing features in addition to gateway-redundancy features. Hosts still point to a default gateway IP address, but GLBP causes different hosts to send their traffic to one of up to four routers in a GLBP group. To do so, the GLBP Active Virtual Gateway (AVG) assigns each router in the group a unique virtual MAC address, following the format 0007.B400.*xxyy*, where *xx* is the GLBP group number, and *yy* is a different number for each router (01, 02, 03, or 04). When a client ARPs for the (virtual) IP address of its default gateway, the GLBP AVG replies with one of the four possible virtual MACs. By replying to ARP requests with different virtual MACs, the hosts in that subnet will in effect balance the traffic across the routers, rather than send all traffic to the one active router.

Cisco IOS devices with GLBP support permit configuring up to 1024 GLBP groups per physical interface and up to four hosts per GLBP group.

Network Time Protocol

NTP Version 3 (RFC 1305) allows IP hosts to synchronize their time-of-day clocks with a common source clock. For instance, routers and switches can synchronize their clocks to make event correlation from an SNMP management station more meaningful, by ensuring that any events and traps have accurate time stamps.

By design, most routers and switches use NTP *client mode*, adjusting their clocks based on the time as known by an NTP server. NTP defines the messages that flow between client and server, and the algorithms a client uses to adjust its clock. Routers and switches can also be configured as NTP servers, as well as using NTP *symmetric active mode*—a mode in which the router or switch mutually synchronizes with another NTP host.

NTP servers may reference other NTP servers to obtain a more accurate clock source as defined by the *stratum level* of the ultimate source clock. For instance, atomic clocks and Global Positioning System (GPS) satellite transmissions provide a source of stratum 1 (lowest/best possible stratum level). For an enterprise network, the routers and switches can refer to a low-stratum NTP source on the Internet, or purpose-built rack-mounted NTP servers, with built-in GPS capabilities, can be deployed.

Example 5-3 shows a sample NTP configuration on four routers, all sharing the same 10.1.1.0/24 Ethernet subnet. Router R1 will be configured as an NTP server. R2 acts as an *NTP static client* by virtue of the static configuration referencing R1's IP address. R3 acts as an *NTP broadcast client* by listening for R1's NTP broadcasts on the Ethernet. Finally, R4 acts in NTP symmetric active mode, configured with the **ntp peer** command.

Example 5-3 *NTP Configuration*

```
!!!!!!!!!!!!!!!!!!!!!!!!!!!!!!!!!!!!!!!!!!!!!!!!!!!!!!!!!!!!!!!!!!!!!!!!!!!!!!!!!!!!!!
! First, R1's configuration, the ntp broadcast command under interface fa0/0
! causes NTP to broadcast NTP updates on that interface. The first three of the
! four global NTP commands configure authentication; these commands are identical
! on all the routers.
R1# show running-config
interface FastEthernet0/0
 ntp broadcast
!
ntp authentication-key 1 md5 1514190900 7
ntp authenticate
ntp trusted-key 1
ntp master 7
! Below, the "127.127.7.1" notation implies that this router is the NTP clock
! source. The clock is synchronized, with stratum level 7, as configured on the
! ntp master 7 command above.
R1# show ntp associations
```

Example 5-3 *NTP Configuration (Continued)*

```
        address         ref clock    st  when  poll reach  delay  offset   disp
*~127.127.7.1         127.127.7.1     6   22    64  377    0.0    0.00    0.0
 * master (synced), # master (unsynced), + selected, - candidate, ~ configured
R1# show ntp status
Clock is synchronized, stratum 7, reference is 127.127.7.1
nominal freq is 249.5901 Hz, actual freq is 249.5901 Hz, precision is 2**16
reference time is C54483CC.E26EE853 (13:49:00.884 UTC Tue Nov 16 2004)
clock offset is 0.0000 msec, root delay is 0.00 msec
root dispersion is 0.02 msec, peer dispersion is 0.02 msec
! R2 is configured below as an NTP static client. Note that the ntp clock-period
! command is automatically generated as part of the synchronization process, and
! should not be added to the configuration manually.
R2# show run | begin ntp
ntp authentication-key 1 md5 1514190900 7
ntp authenticate
ntp trusted-key 1
ntp clock-period 17208144
ntp server 10.1.1.1
end
! Next, R3 has been configured as an NTP broadcast client. The ntp broadcast client
! command on R3 tells it to listen for the broadcasts from R1. This configuration
! relies on the ntp broadcast subcommand on R1's Fa0/0 interface, as shown at the
! beginning of this example.
R3# show run
interface Ethernet0/0
 ntp broadcast client
! R4's configuration is listed, with the ntp peer
! command implying the use of symmetric active mode.
R4# show run | beg ntp
ntp authentication-key 1 md5 0002010300 7
ntp authenticate
ntp trusted-key 1
ntp clock-period 17208233
ntp peer 10.1.1.1
```

SNMP

This section of the chapter summarizes some of the core Simple Network Management Protocol (SNMP) concepts and details, particularly with regard to features of different SNMP versions. SNMP or, more formally, the *Internet Standard Management Framework*, uses a structure in which the device being managed (the SNMP agent) has information that the management software (the SNMP manager) wants to display to someone operating the network. Each SNMP agent keeps a database, called a *Management Information Base (MIB)*, that holds a large variety of data about the operation of the device on which the agent resides. The manager collects the data by using SNMP.

SNMP has been defined with four major functional areas to support the core function of allowing managers to manage agents:

- **Data Definition**—The syntax conventions for how to define the data to an agent or manager. These specifications are called the *Structure of Management Information (SMI)*.

- **MIBs**—Over 100 Internet standards define different MIBs, each for a different technology area, with countless vendor-proprietary MIBs as well. The MIB definitions conform to the appropriate SMI version.

- **Protocols**—The messages used by agents and managers to exchange management data.

- **Security and Administration**—Definitions for how to secure the exchange of data between agents and managers.

Interestingly, by separating SNMP into these major functional areas, each part has been improved and expanded independently over the years. However, it is important to know a few of the main features added for each official SNMP version, as well as for a pseudo-version called SNMPv2c, as summarized in Table 5-3.

Table 5-3 *SNMP Version Summaries*

SNMP Version	Description
1	Uses SMIv1, simple authentication with communities, but used MIB-I originally.
2	Uses SMIv2, removed requirement for communities, added GetBulk and Inform messages, but began with MIB-II originally.
2c	Pseudo-release (RFC 1905) that allowed SNMPv1-style communities with SNMPv2; otherwise, equivalent to SNMPv2.
3	Mostly identical to SNMPv2, but adds significantly better security, although it supports communities for backward compatibility. Uses MIB-II.

Table 5-3 hits the highlights of the comparison points between the various SNMP versions. As you might expect, each release builds on the previous one. For example, SNMPv1 defined *community strings* for use as simple clear-text passwords. SNMPv2 removed the requirement for community strings—however, backward compatibility for SNMP communities was defined via an optional RFC (1901). Even SNMPv3, with much better security, supports communities to allow backward compatibility.

> **NOTE**   The use of SNMPv1 communities with SNMPv2, based on RFC 1901, has popularly been called *SNMP Version 2c*, with *c* referring to "communities," although it is arguably not a legitimate full version of SNMP.

The next few sections provide a bit more depth about the SNMP protocol, with additional details about some of the version differences.

SNMP Protocol Messages

The SNMPv1 and SNMPv2 protocol messages (RFC 3416) define how a manager and agent, or even two managers, can communicate information. For instance, a manager can use three different messages to get MIB variable data from agents, with an SNMP *Response* message returned by the agent to the manager supplying the MIB data. SNMP uses UDP exclusively for transport, using the SNMP Response message to both acknowledge receipt of other protocol messages and supply SNMP information.

Table 5-4 summarizes the key information about each of the SNMP protocol messages, including the SNMP version in which the message first appeared.

Table 5-4   *SNMP Protocol Messages (RFCs 1157 and 1905)*

Message	Initial Version	Response Message	Typically Sent By	Main Purpose
Get	1	Response	Manager	A request for a single variable's value.
GetNext	1	Response	Manager	A request for the next single MIB leaf variable in the MIB tree.
GetBulk	2	Response	Manager	A request for multiple consecutive MIB variables with one request. Useful for getting complex structures, for example, an IP routing table.
Response	1	None	Agent	Used to respond with the information in Get and Set requests.
Set	1	Response	Manager	Sent by a manager to an agent to tell the agent to set a variable to a particular value. The agent replies with a Response message.
Trap	1	None	Agent	Allows agents to send unsolicited information to an SNMP manager. The manager does not reply with any SNMP message.
Inform	2	Response	Manager	A message used between SNMP managers to allow MIB data to be exchanged.

The three variations of the SNMP Get message, and the SNMP Response message, are typically used when someone is actively using an SNMP manager. When a user of the SNMP manager asks for information, the manager sends one of the three types of Get commands to the agent. The agent replies with an SNMP Response message. The different variations of the Get command are useful, particularly when the manager wants to view large portions of the MIB. An agent's entire MIB—whose structure can vary from agent to agent—can be discovered with successive GetNext requests, or with GetBulk requests, using a process called a *MIB walk*.

The SNMP Set command allows the manager to change something on the agent. For example, the user of the management software can specify that a router interface should be shut down; the management station can then issue a Set command for a MIB variable on the agent. The agent sets the variable, which tells Cisco IOS Software to shut down the interface.

SNMP Traps are unsolicited messages sent by the agent to the management station. For example, when an interface fails, a router's SNMP agent could send a Trap to the SNMP manager. The management software could then highlight the failure information on a screen, e-mail first-level support personnel, page support, and so on. Also of note, there is no specific message in response to the receipt of a Trap; technically, of the messages in Table 5-4, only the Trap and Response messages do not expect to receive any kind of acknowledging message.

Finally, the Inform message allows two SNMP managers to exchange MIB information about agents that they both manage.

SNMP MIBs

SNMP Versions 1 and 2 included a standard generic MIB, with initial MIB-I (version 1, RFC 1156) and MIB-II (version 2, RFC 1213). MIB-II was actually created in between the release of SNMPv1 and v2, with SNMPv1 supporting MIB-II as well. After the creation of the MIB-II specification, the IETF SNMP working group changed the strategy for MIB definition. Instead of the SNMP working group creating standard MIBs, other working groups, in many different technology areas, were tasked with creating MIB definitions for their respective technologies. As a result, hundreds of standardized MIBs are defined. Additionally, vendors create their own vendor-proprietary MIBs.

The Remote Monitoring MIB (RMON, RFC 2819) is a particularly important standardized MIB outside MIB-II. An SNMP agent that supports the RMON MIB can be programmed, through SNMP Set commands, to capture packets, calculate statistics, monitor thresholds for specific MIB variables, report back to the management station when thresholds are reached, and perform other tasks. With RMON, a network can be populated with a number of monitoring probes, with SNMP messaging used to gather the information as needed.

SNMP Security

SNMPv3 added solid security to the existing SNMPv2 and SNMPv2c specifications. SNMPv3 adds two main branches of security to SNMPv2: authentication and encryption. SNMPv3 specifies the use of MD5 and SHA to create a message digest for each SNMPv3 protocol message. Doing so enables authentication of endpoints and prevents data modification and masquerade types of attacks. Additionally, SNMPv3 managers and agents can use Digital Encryption Standard (DES) to encrypt the messages, providing better privacy. (SNMPv3 suggests future support of Advanced Encryption Standard [AES] as well, but that is not a part of the original SNMPv3 specifications.) The encryption feature remains separate due to the U.S. government export restrictions on DES technology.

Syslog

Event logging is nothing new to most CCIE candidates. Routers and switches, among other devices, maintain event logs that reveal a great deal about the operating conditions of that device, along with valuable time-stamp information to help troubleshoot problems or chains of events that take place.

By default, Cisco routers and switches do not log events to nonvolatile memory. They can be configured to do so using the **logging buffered** command, with an additional argument to specify the size of the log buffer. Configuring a router, for example, for SNMP management provides a means of passing critical events from the event log, as they occur, to a network management station in the form of traps. SNMP is, however, fairly involved to configure. Furthermore, if it's not secured properly, SNMP also opens attack vectors to the device. However, disabling SNMP and watching event logs manually is at best tedious, and this approach simply does not scale.

 Syslog, described in RFC 3164, is a lightweight event-notification protocol that provides a middle ground between manually monitoring event logs and a full-blown SNMP implementation. It provides real-time event notification by sending messages that enter the event log to a Syslog server that you specify. Syslog uses UDP port 514 by default.

Cisco IOS devices configured for Syslog, by default, send all events that enter the event log to the Syslog server. You can also configure Syslog to send only specific classes of events to the server.

Syslog is a clear-text protocol that provides event notifications without requiring difficult, time-intensive configuration or opening attack vectors. In fact, it's quite simple to configure basic Syslog operation:

Step 1   Install a Syslog server on a workstation with a fixed IP address.

Step 2   Configure the logging process to send events to the Syslog server's IP address using the **logging host** command.

Step 3   Configure any options, such as which severity levels (0–7) you want to send to the Syslog server using the **logging trap** command.

Web Cache Communication Protocol

To ease pressure on congested WAN links in networks with many hosts, Cisco developed WCCP to coordinate the work of edge routers and content engines (also known as cache engines). Content engines collect frequently accessed data, usually HTTP traffic, locally, so that when hosts access the same pages the content can be delivered from the cache engine rather than crossing the WAN. WCCP differs from web proxy operation in that the hosts accessing the content have no knowledge that the content engine is involved in a given transaction.

WCCP works by allowing edge routers to communicate with content engines to make each aware of the other's presence and to permit the router to redirect traffic to the content engine as appropriate. Figure 5-3 shows how WCCP functions between a router and a content engine when a user requests a web object using HTTP.

Figure 5-3   *WCCP Operations Between a Router and a Content Engine*

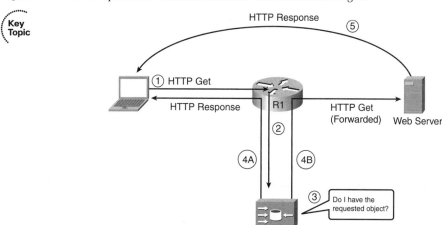

The figure shows the following steps, with the main decision point on the content engine coming at Step 4:

Step 1   The client sends an HTTP Get request with a destination address of the web server, as normal.

Step 2   The router's WCCP function notices the HTTP Get request and redirects the packet to the content engine.

Step 3   The content engine looks at its disk storage cache to discover if the requested object is cached.

Step 4A   If the object is cached, the content engine sends an HTTP response, which includes the object, back to the client.

Step 4B   If the object is not cached, the content engine sends the original HTTP Get request on to the original server.

Step 5   If Step 4B was taken, the server replies to the client, with no knowledge that the packet was ever redirected to a content engine.

Using WCCP, which uses UDP port 2048, a router and a content engine, or a pool of content engines (known as a cluster), become aware of each other. In a cluster of content engines, the content engines also communicate with each other using WCCP. Up to 32 content engines can communicate with a single router using WCCPv1. If more than one content engine is present, the one with the lowest IP address is elected as the lead engine.

WCCP also provides a means for content engines within a cluster to become aware of each other. content engines request information on the cluster members from the WCCP router, which replies with a list. This permits the lead content engine to determine how traffic should be distributed to the cluster.

In WCCPv1, only one router can redirect traffic to a content engine or a cluster of content engines. In WCCPv2, multiple routers and multiple content engines can be configured as a WCCP service group. This expansion permits much better scalability in content caching. Furthermore, WCCPv1 supports only HTTP traffic (TCP port 80, specifically). WCCPv2 supports several other traffic types and has other benefits compared to WCCPv1:

- Supports TCP and UDP traffic other than TCP port 80, including FTP caching, FTP proxy handling, web caching for ports other than 80, Real Audio, video, and telephony.

- Permits segmenting caching services provided by a caching cluster to a particular protocol or protocols, and uses a priority system for deciding which cluster to use for a particular cached protocol.

- Supports multicast to simplify configuration.

- Supports multiple routers (up to 32 per cluster) for redundancy and load distribution. (All content engines in a cluster must be configured to communicate with all routers in that cluster.)

- Provides for MD5 security in WCCP communication using the global configuration command **ip wccp password** *password.*

- Provides load distribution.

- Supports transparent error handling.

When you enable WCCP globally on a router, the default version used is WCCPv2. Because the WCCP version is configured globally for a router, the version number affects all interfaces. However, multiple services can run on a router at the same time. Routers and content engines can also simultaneously participate in more than one service group. These WCCP settings are configured on a per-interface basis.

Configuring WCCP on a router is not difficult because a lot of the configuration in a caching scenario takes place on the content engines; the routers need only minimal configuration. Example 5-4 shows a WCCPv2 configuration using MD5 authentication and multicast for WCCP communication.

Example 5-4   *WCCP Configuration Example*

```
! First we enable WCCP globally on the router,
! specifying a service (web caching), a multicast address for
! the WCCP communication, and an MD5 password:
ip wccp web-cache group-address 239.128.1.100 password cisco
! Next we configure an interface to redirect WCCP web-cache
! traffic outbound to a content engine:
int fa0/0
 ip wccp web-cache redirect out
! Finally, inbound traffic on interface fa0/1 is excluded from redirection:
int fa0/1
 ip wccp redirect exclude in
```

Finally, WCCP can make use of access lists to filter traffic only for certain clients (or to exclude WCCP use for certain clients) using the **ip wccp web-cache redirect-list** *access-list* global command. WCCP can also use ACLs to determine which types of redirected traffic the router should accept from content engines, using the global command **ip wccp web-cache group-list** *access-list*.

Foundation Summary

This section lists additional details and facts to round out the coverage of the topics in this chapter. Unlike most of the Cisco Press Exam Certification Guides, this "Foundation Summary" does not repeat information presented in the "Foundation Topics" section of the chapter. Please take the time to read and study the details in the "Foundation Topics" section of the chapter, as well as review items noted with a Key Topic icon.

Table 5-5 lists the protocols mentioned in this chapter and their respective standards documents.

Table 5-5 *Protocols and Standards for Chapter 5*

Name	Standardized In
ARP	RFC 826
Proxy ARP	RFC 1027
RARP	RFC 903
BOOTP	RFC 951
DHCP	RFC 2131
DHCP FQDN option	Internet-Draft
HSRP	Cisco proprietary
VRRP	RFC 3768
GLBP	Cisco proprietary
CDP	Cisco proprietary
NTP	RFC 1305
Syslog	RFC 3164
SNMP Version 1	RFCs 1155, 1156, 1157, 1212, 1213, 1215
SNMP Version 2	RFCs 1902–1907, 3416
SNMP Version 2c	RFC 1901
SNMP Version 3	RFCs 2578–2580, 3410–3415
Good Starting Point:	RFC 3410

Table 5-6 lists some of the most popular Cisco IOS commands related to the topics in this chapter.

Table 5-6   Command Reference for Chapter 5

Command	Description
ip dhcp pool *name*	Creates DHCP pool
default-router *address* [*address2...address8*]	DHCP pool subcommand to list the gateways
dns-server *address* [*address2...address8*]	DHCP pool subcommand to list DNS servers
lease {*days* [*hours*][*minutes*]	**infinite**}	DHCP pool subcommand to define the lease length
network *network-number* [*mask*	*prefix-length*]	DHCP pool subcommand to define IP addresses that can be assigned
ip dhcp excluded-address [*low-address high-address*]	DHCP pool subcommand to disallow these addresses from being assigned
host *address* [*mask*	*prefix-length*]	DHCP pool subcommand, used with *hardware-address* or *client-identifier*, to predefine a single host's IP address
hardware-address *hardware-address type*	DHCP pool subcommand to define MAC address; works with **host** command
show ip dhcp binding [*ip-address*]	Lists addresses allocated by DHCP
show ip dhcp server statistics	Lists stats for DHCP server operations
standby [*group-number*] **ip** [*ip-address* [**secondary**]]	Interface subcommand to enable an HSRP group and define the virtual IP address
track *object-number* **interface** *type-number* {**line-protocol**	**ip routing**}	Configures a tracking object that can be used by HSRP, VRRP, or GLBP to track the status of an interface
standby [*group-number*] **preempt** [**delay** {**minimum** *delay*	**reload** *delay*	**sync** *delay*}]	Interface subcommand to enable pre-emption and set delay timers
show track [*object-number* [**brief**]	**interface** [**brief**]	**ip route** [**brief**]	**resolution**	**timers**]	Displays status of tracked objects
standby [*group-number*] **priority** *priority*	Interface subcommand to set the HSRP group priority for this router
standby [*group-number*] **timers** [**msec**] *hellotime* [**msec**] *holdtime*	Interface subcommand to set HSRP group timers
standby [*group-number*] **track** *object-number*	Interface subcommand to enable HSRP to track defined objects, usually for the purpose of switching active routers on an event related to that object
show standby [*type number* [*group*]] [**brief**	**all**]	Lists HSRP statistics
ntp peer *ip-address* [**version** *number*] [**key** *keyid*] [**source** *interface*] [**prefer**]	Global command to enable symmetric active mode NTP

Table 5-6 Command Reference for Chapter 5 *(Continued)*

Command	Description
ntp server *ip-address* [**version** *number*] [**key** *keyid*] [**source** *interface*] [**prefer**]	Global command to enable static client mode NTP
ntp broadcast [**version** *number*]	Interface subcommand on an NTP server to cause NTP broadcasts on the interface
ntp broadcast client	Interface subcommand on an NTP client to cause it to listen for NTP broadcasts
ntp master [*stratum*]	Global command to enable NTP server
show ntp associations	Lists associations with other NTP servers and clients
show ntp status	Displays synchronization status, stratum level, and other basic information
logging trap *level*	Sets the severity level for Syslog messages; arguments are 0–7, where 0=emergencies, 1=alerts, 2=critical, 3=errors, 4=warnings, 5=notifications, 6=informational, 7=debugging (default)
logging host {{*ip-address* | *hostname*} | {**ipv6** *ipv6-address* | *hostname*}} [**transport** {**udp** [**port** *port-number*] | **tcp** [**port** *port-number*]}] [**alarm** [*severity*]]	Configures the IP or IPv6 address or hostname to which to send Syslog messages and permits setting the transport protocol and port number
ip wccp {**web-cache** | *service-number*} [**service-list** *service-access-list*] [**mode** {**open** | **closed**}] [**group-address** *multicast-address*] [**redirect-list** *access-list*] [**group-list** *access-list*] [**password** [**0-7**] *password*]	Enables WCCP and configures filtering and service parameters
ip wccp {**web-cache** | *service-number*} **redirect** {**in** | **out**}	Interface configuration command to enable WCCP and configure it for outbound or inbound service
show ip wccp	Displays WCCP configuration settings and statistics

Memory Builders

The CCIE Routing and Switching written exam, like all Cisco CCIE written exams, covers a fairly broad set of topics. This section provides some basic tools to help you exercise your memory about some of the broader topics covered in this chapter.

Fill in Key Tables from Memory

Appendix E, "Key Tables for CCIE Study," on the CD in the back of this book contains empty sets of some of the key summary tables in each chapter. Print Appendix E, refer to this chapter's tables in it, and fill in the tables from memory. Refer to Appendix F, "Solutions for Key Tables for CCIE Study," on the CD to check your answers.

Definitions

Next, take a few moments to write down the definitions for the following terms:

> HSRP, VRRP, GLBP, ARP, RARP, proxy ARP, BOOTP, DHCP, NTP symmetric active mode, NTP server mode, NTP client mode, NTP, virtual IP address, VRRP Master router, SNMP agent, SNMP manager, Get, GetNext, GetBulk, MIB-I, MIB-II, Response, Trap, Set, Inform, SMI, MIB, MIB walk, lead content engine

Refer to the glossary to check your answers.

Further Reading

More information about several of the topics in this chapter can be easily found in a large number of books and online documentation. The RFCs listed in Table 5-5 of the "Foundation Summary" section also provide a great deal of background information for this chapter. Here are a few references for more information about some of the less popular topics covered in this chapter:

- **Proxy ARP**—http://www.cisco.com/en/US/tech/tk648/tk361/
  technologies_tech_note09186a0080094adb.shtml.

- **GLBP**—http://www.cisco.com/en/US/partner/products/sw/iosswrel/ps1839/
  products_white_paper09186a00801541c8.shtml.

- **VRRP**—http://www.cisco.com/univercd/cc/td/doc/product/software/ios120/120newft/
  120limit/120st/120st18/st_vrrpx.htm.

- **SNMP**—Any further reading of SNMP-related RFCs should begin with RFC 3410, which provides a great overview of the releases and points to the more important of the vast number of SNMP-related RFCs.

Part III: IP Routing

Blueprint topics covered in this chapter:

This chapter covers the following subtopics from the Cisco CCIE Routing and Switching written exam blueprint. Refer to the full blueprint in Table I-1 in the Introduction for more details on the topics covered in each chapter and their context within the blueprint.

- Classful and Classless Routing Protocols

- Frame Relay

- Local Management Interface (LMI)

- Concepts of Policy Routing

IP Forwarding (Routing)

Chapter 6 begins the largest part of the book. This part of the book, containing Chapters 7 through 11, focuses on the topics that are the most important and popular for both the CCIE Routing and Switching written and practical (lab) exams.

Chapter 6 begins with coverage of the details of the forwarding plane—the actual forwarding of IP packets. This process of forwarding IP packets is often called *IP routing*, or simply *routing*. Also, many people also refer to IP routing as the *data plane*, meaning the plane (topic) related to the end-user data.

Chapters 7 through 11 cover the details of the IP *control plane*. In contrast to the term data plane, the control plane relates to the communication of control information—in short, routing protocols like OSPF and BGP. These chapters cover the routing protocols on the exam, one chapter per routing protocol, plus an additional chapter on redistribution and route summarization.

"Do I Know This Already?" Quiz

Table 6-1 outlines the major headings in this chapter and the corresponding "Do I Know This Already?" quiz questions.

Table 6-1 *"Do I Know This Already?" Foundation Topics Section-to-Question Mapping*

Foundation Topics Section	Questions Covered in This Section	Score
IP Forwarding	1–6	
Multilayer Switching	7–8	
Policy Routing	9–10	
Total Score		

In order to best use this pre-chapter assessment, remember to score yourself strictly. You can find the answers in Appendix A, "Answers to the 'Do I Know This Already?' Quizzes."

1. What command is used to enable CEF globally for IP packets?

   a. **enable cef**

   b. **ip enable cef**

   c. **ip cef**

   d. **cef enable**

   e. **cef enable ip**

   f. **cef ip**

2. Which of the follow triggers an update to a CEF FIB?

   a. Receipt of a Frame Relay InARP message with previously unknown information

   b. Receipt of a LAN ARP reply message with previously unknown information

   c. Addition of a new route to the IP routing table by EIGRP

   d. Addition of a new route to the IP routing table by adding an **ip route** command

   e. The removal of a route from the IP routing table by EIGRP

3. Router1 has a Frame Relay access link attached to its s0/0 interface. Router1 has a PVC connecting it to Router3. What action triggers Router3 to send an InARP message over the PVC to Router1?

   a. Receipt of a CDP multicast on the PVC connected to Router1

   b. Receipt of an InARP request from Router1

   c. Receipt of a packet that needs to be routed to Router1

   d. Receipt of a Frame Relay message stating the PVC to Router1 is up

4. Three routers are attached to the same Frame Relay network, have a full mesh of PVCs, and use IP addresses 10.1.1.1/24 (R1), 10.1.1.2/24 (R2), and 10.1.1.3 (R3). R1 has its IP address configured on its physical interface; R2 and R3 have their IP addresses configured on multipoint subinterfaces. Assuming all the Frame Relay PVCs are up and working, and the router interfaces have been administratively enabled, which of the following is true?

   a. R1 can ping 10.1.1.2.

   b. R2 cannot ping 10.1.1.3.

   c. R3 can ping 10.1.1.2.

   d. In this case, R1 must rely on mapping via InARP to be able to ping 10.1.1.3.

5. Three routers are attached to the same Frame Relay network, with a partial mesh of PVCs: R1-R2 and R1-R3. The routers use IP addresses 10.1.1.1/24 (R1), 10.1.1.2/24 (R2), and 10.1.1.3/24 (R3). R1 has its IP address configured on its physical interface; R2 has its IP address configured on a multipoint subinterface; and R3 has its IP address configured on a point-to-point subinterface. Assuming all the Frame Relay PVCs are up and working, and the router interfaces have been administratively enabled, which of the following is true? Assume no **frame-relay map** commands have been configured.

    a. R1 can ping 10.1.1.2.

    b. R2 can ping 10.1.1.3.

    c. R3 can ping 10.1.1.1.

    d. R3's **ping 10.1.1.2** command results in R3 not sending the ICMP Echo packet.

    e. R2's **ping 10.1.1.3** command results in R2 not sending the ICMP Echo packet.

6. Router1 has an OSPF-learned route to 10.1.1.0/24 as its only route to a subnet on class A network 10.0.0.0. It also has a default route. When Router1 receives a packet destined for 10.1.2.3, it discards the packet. Which of the following commands would make Router1 use the default route for those packets in the future?

    a. **ip classless** subcommand of **router ospf**

    b. **no ip classful** subcommand of **router ospf**

    c. **ip classless** global command

    d. **no ip classless** global command

    e. **no ip classful** global command

7. Which of the following commands is used on a Cisco IOS Layer 3 switch to use the interface as a *routed interface* instead of a *switched interface*?

    a. **ip routing** global command

    b. **ip routing** interface subcommand

    c. **ip address** interface subcommand

    d. **switchport access layer-3** interface subcommand

    e. **no switchport** interface subcommand

8. On a Cisco 3550 switch with Enterprise Edition software, the first line of the output of a **show interface vlan 55** command lists the state as "Vlan 55 is down, line protocol is down down." Which of the following might be causing that state to occur?

   a. VLAN interface has not been **no shut** yet.

   b. The **ip routing** global command is missing from the configuration.

   c. On at least one interface in the VLAN, a cable that was previously plugged in has been unplugged.

   d. VTP mode is set to transparent.

   e. The VLAN has not yet been created on this switch.

9. Imagine a route map used for policy routing, in which the route map has a **set interface default serial0/0** command. Serial0/0 is a point-to-point link to another router. A packet arrives at this router, and the packet matches the policy routing **route-map** clause whose only **set** command is the one just mentioned. Which of the following general characterizations is true?

   a. The packet will be routed out interface s0/0; if s0/0 is down, it will be routed using the default route from the routing table.

   b. The packet will be routed using the default route in the routing table; if there is no default, the packet will be routed out s0/0.

   c. The packet will be routed using the best match of the destination address with the routing table; if no match is made, the packet will be routed out s0/0.

   d. The packet will be routed out interface s0/0; if s0/0 is down, the packet will be discarded.

10. Router1 has an fa0/0 interface and two point-to-point WAN links back to the core of the network (s0/0 and s0/1, respectively). Router1 accepts routing information only over s0/0, which Router1 uses as its primary link. When s0/0 fails, Router1 uses policy routing to forward the traffic out the relatively slower s0/1 link. Which of the following **set** commands in Router1's policy routing route map could have been used to achieve this function?

    a. **set ip default next-hop**

    b. **set ip next-hop**

    c. **set ip default interface**

    d. **set ip interface**

Foundation Topics

IP Forwarding

IP forwarding, or *IP routing*, is simply the process of receiving an IP packet, making a decision of where to send the packet next, and then forwarding the packet. The forwarding process needs to be relatively simple, or at least streamlined, for a router to forward large volumes of packets. Ignoring the details of several Cisco optimizations to the forwarding process for a moment, the internal forwarding logic in a router works basically as shown in Figure 6-1.

Figure 6-1 *Forwarding Process at Router3, Destination Server1*

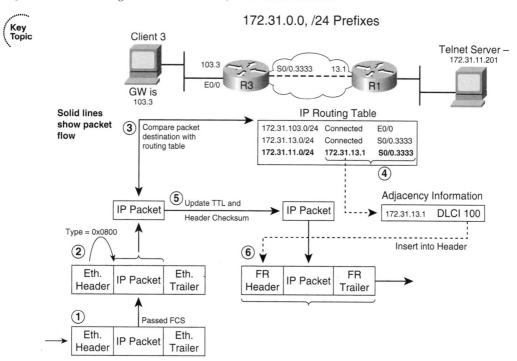

The following list summarizes the key steps shown in Figure 6-1.

1. A router receives the frame and checks the received frame check sequence (FCS); if errors occurred, the frame is discarded. The router makes no attempt to recover the lost packet.

2. If no errors occurred, the router checks the Ethernet Type field for the packet type, and extracts the packet. The Data Link header and trailer can now be discarded.

3. Assuming an IP packet, the router checks its IP routing table for the most specific prefix match of the packet's destination IP address.

4. The matched routing table entry includes the outgoing interface and next-hop router; this information points the router to the adjacency information needed to build a new Data Link frame.

5. Before creating a new frame, the router updates the IP header TTL field, requiring a recomputation of the IP header checksum.

6. The router encapsulates the IP packet in a new Data Link header (including the destination address) and trailer (including a new FCS) to create a new frame.

The preceding list is a generic view of the process; next, a few words on how Cisco routers can optimize the routing process by using Cisco Express Forwarding (CEF).

Process Switching, Fast Switching, and Cisco Express Forwarding

Steps 3 and 4 from the generic routing logic shown in the preceding section are the most computation-intensive tasks in the routing process. A router must find the best route to use for every packet, requiring some form of table lookup of routing information. Also, a new Data Link header and trailer must be created, and the information to put in the header (like the destination Data Link address) must be found in another table.

Cisco has created several different methods to optimize the forwarding processing inside routers, termed *switching paths*. This section examines the two most likely methods to exist in Cisco router networks today: fast switching and CEF.

With fast switching, the first packet to a specific destination IP address is *process switched*, meaning that it follows the same general algorithm as in Figure 6-1. With the first packet, the router adds an entry to the *fast-switching cache*, sometimes called the *route cache*. The cache has the destination IP address, the next-hop information, and the data link header information that needs to be added to the packet before forwarding (as in Step 6 in Figure 6-1). Future packets to the same destination address match the cache entry, so it takes the router less time to process and forward the packet.

Although it is much better than process switching, fast switching has a few drawbacks. The first packet must be process switched. The cache entries are timed out relatively quickly, because otherwise the cache could get overly large as it has an entry per each destination address, not per destination subnet/prefix. Also, load balancing can only occur per destination with fast switching.

CEF overcomes the main shortcoming of fast switching. CEF optimizes the route lookup process by using a construct called the *Forwarding Information Base (FIB)*. The FIB contains information about all the known routes in the routing table. Rather than use a table that is updated when new flows appear, as did the Cisco earlier fast-switching technology, CEF loads FIB entries as routes are added and removed from the routing table. CEF does not have to time out the entries in the FIB, does not require the first packet to a destination to be process switched, and allows much more effective load balancing over equal-cost routes.

When a new packet arrives, CEF routers first search the FIB. Cisco designed the CEF FIB structure as a special kind of tree, called an *mtrie*, that significantly reduces the time taken to match the packet destination address to the right CEF FIB entry.

The matched FIB entry points to an entry in the CEF *adjacency table*. The adjacency table lists the outgoing interface, along with all the information needed to build the Data Link header and trailer before sending the packet. When a router forwards a packet using CEF, it easily and quickly finds the corresponding CEF FIB entry, after which it has a pointer to the adjacency table entry— which tells the router how to forward the packet.

Table 6-2 summarizes a few key points about the three main options for router switching paths.

Table 6-2 *Matching Logic and Load-Balancing Options for Each Switching Path*

Switching Path	Tables that Hold the Forwarding Information	Load-Balancing Method
Process switching	Routing table	Per packet
Fast switching	Fast-switching cache (per flow route cache)	Per destination IP address
CEF	FIB and adjacency tables	Per a hash of the packet source and destination, or per packet

The **ip cef** global configuration command enables CEF for all interfaces on a Cisco router. The **no ip route-cache cef** interface subcommand can then be used to selectively disable CEF on an interface. On many of the higher-end Cisco platforms, CEF processing can be distributed to the linecards. Similarly, Cisco multilayer switches use CEF for Layer 3 forwarding, by loading CEF tables into the forwarding ASICs.

Building Adjacency Information: ARP and Inverse ARP

The CEF adjacency table entries list an outgoing interface and a Layer 2 and Layer 3 address reachable via that interface. The table also includes the entire data link header that should be used to reach that next-hop (adjacent) device.

The CEF adjacency table must be built based on the IP routing table, plus other sources. The IP routing table entries include the outgoing interfaces to use and the next-hop device's IP address. To complete the adjacency table entry for that next hop, the router needs to know the Data Link layer address to use to reach the next device. Once known, the router can build the CEF adjacency table entry for that next-hop router. For instance, for Router3 in Figure 6-1 to reach next-hop router 172.31.13.1 (Router1), out interface s0/0.3333, Router3 needed to know the right Data-Link connection identifier (DLCI) to use. So, to build the adjacency table entries, CEF uses the IP ARP cache, Frame Relay mapping information, and other sources of Layer 3-to-Layer 2 mapping information.

First, a quick review of IP ARP. The ARP protocol dynamically learns the MAC address of another IP host on the same LAN. The host that needs to learn the other host's MAC address sends an ARP request, sent to the LAN broadcast address, hoping to receive an ARP reply (a LAN unicast) from the other host. The reply, of course, supplies the needed MAC address information.

Frame Relay Inverse ARP

IP ARP is widely understood and relatively simple. As a result, it is hard to ask difficult questions about ARP on an exam. However, the topics of Frame Relay Inverse ARP (InARP), its use, defaults, and when static mapping must be used lend themselves to being the source of tricky exam questions. So, this section covers Frame Relay InARP to show some of the nuances of when and how it is used.

InARP discovers the DLCI to use to reach a particular adjacent IP address. However, as the term *Inverse* ARP implies, the process differs from ARP on LANs; with InARP, routers already know the Data Link address (DLCI), and need to learn the corresponding IP address. Figure 6-2 shows an example InARP flow.

Figure 6-2 *Frame Relay InARP*

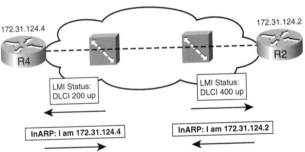

Unlike on LANs, a packet does not need to arrive at the router to trigger the InARP protocol; instead, an LMI status message triggers InARP. After receiving an LMI PVC Up message, each router announces its own IP address over the VC, using an InARP message, as defined in RFC 1293. Interestingly, if you disable LMI, then the InARP process no longer works, because nothing triggers a router to send an InARP message.

NOTE In production Frame Relay networks, the configuration details are chosen to purposefully avoid some of the pitfalls that are covered in the next several pages of this chapter. For example, when using mainly point-to-point subinterfaces, with a different subnet per VC, all the problems described in the rest of the Frame Relay coverage in this chapter can be avoided.

While InARP itself is relatively simple, implementation details differ based on the type of subinterface used in a router. For a closer look at implementation, Figure 6-3 shows an example Frame Relay topology with a partial mesh and a single subnet, in which each router uses a different interface type for its Frame Relay configuration. (You would not typically choose to configure

Frame Relay on physical, point-to-point and multipoint subinterfaces in the same design—indeed, it wreaks havoc with routing protocols if you do so. This example does so just to show in more detail in the examples how InARP really works.) Example 6-1 points out some of the basic **show** and **debug** commands related to Frame Relay InARP, and one of the oddities about InARP relating to point-to-point subinterfaces.

Figure 6-3   *Frame Relay Topology for Frame Relay InARP Examples*

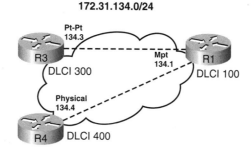

> **NOTE**   All figures with Frame Relay networks in this book use Global DLCI conventions unless otherwise stated. For instance, in Figure 6-3, DLCI 300 listed beside Router3 means that, due to Local DLCI assignment conventions by the service provider, all other routers (like Router4) use DLCI 300 to address their respective VCs back to Router3.

Example 6-1   *Frame Relay InARP* **show** *and* **debug** *Commands*

```
! First, Router1 configures Frame Relay on a multipoint subinterface.
Router1# sh run
! Lines omitted for brevity
interface Serial0/0
 encapsulation frame-relay
interface Serial0/0.11 multipoint
 ip address 172.31.134.1 255.255.255.0
 frame-relay interface-dlci 300
 frame-relay interface-dlci 400
! Lines omitted for brevity
! Next, the serial interface is shut and no shut, and the earlier InARP entries
! are cleared, so the example can show the InARP process.
Router1# conf t
Enter configuration commands, one per line.  End with CNTL/Z.
Router1(config)# int s 0/0
Router1(config-if)# do clear frame-relay inarp
Router1(config-if)# shut
Router1(config-if)# no shut
Router1(config-if)# ^Z
```

continues

Example 6-1 *Frame Relay InARP* **show** *and* **debug** *Commands (Continued)*

```
! Messages resulting from the debug frame-relay event command show the
! received InARP messages on Router1. Note the hex values 0xAC1F8603 and
! 0xAC1F8604, which in decimal are 172.31.134.3 and 172.31.134.4 (Router3
! and Router4, respectively).
Router1# debug frame-relay events
*Mar  1 00:09:45.334: Serial0/0.11: FR ARP input
*Mar  1 00:09:45.334: datagramstart = 0x392BA0E, datagramsize = 34
*Mar  1 00:09:45.334: FR encap = 0x48C10300
*Mar  1 00:09:45.334: 80 00 00 00 08 06 00 0F 08 00 02 04 00 09 00 00
*Mar  1 00:09:45.334: AC 1F 86 03 48 C1 AC 1F 86 01 01 02 00 00
*Mar  1 00:09:45.334:
*Mar  1 00:09:45.334: Serial0/0.11: FR ARP input
*Mar  1 00:09:45.334: datagramstart = 0x392B8CE, datagramsize = 34
*Mar  1 00:09:45.338: FR encap = 0x64010300
*Mar  1 00:09:45.338: 80 00 00 00 08 06 00 0F 08 00 02 04 00 09 00 00
*Mar  1 00:09:45.338: AC 1F 86 04 64 01 AC 1F 86 01 01 02 00 00
! Next, note the show frame-relay map command output does include a "dynamic"
! keyword, meaning that the entries were learned with InARP.
Router1# show frame-relay map
Serial0/0.11 (up): ip 172.31.134.3 dlci 300(0x12C,0x48C0), dynamic,
            broadcast,, status defined, active
Serial0/0.11 (up): ip 172.31.134.4 dlci 400(0x190,0x6400), dynamic,
            broadcast,, status defined, active
! On Router3, show frame-relay map only lists a single entry as well, but
! the format is different. Because Router3 uses a point-to-point subinterface,
! the entry was not learned with InARP, and the command output does not include
! the word "dynamic." Also note the absence of any Layer 3 addresses.
Router3# show frame-relay map
Serial0/0.3333 (up): point-to-point dlci, dlci 100(0x64,0x1840), broadcast
            status defined, active
```

NOTE Example 6-1 included the use of the **do** command inside configuration mode. The **do** command, followed by any **exec** command, can be used from inside configuration mode to issue an **exec** command, without having to leave configuration mode.

The example **show** commands from Router1 detail the fact that InARP was used; however, the last **show** command in Example 6-1 details how Router3 actually did not use the received InARP information. Cisco IOS Software knows that only one VC is associated with a point-to-point subinterface; any other IP hosts in the same subnet as a point-to-point subinterface can be reached only by that single DLCI. So, any received InARP information related to that DLCI is unnecessary.

For instance, whenever Router3 needs to forward a packet to Router1 (172.31.134.1), or any other host in subnet 172.31.134.0/24, Router3 already knows from its configuration to send the packet over the only possible DLCI on that point-to-point subinterface—namely, DLCI 100. So, although all three types of interfaces used for Frame Relay configuration support InARP by default, point-to-point subinterfaces ignore the received InARP information.

Static Configuration of Frame Relay Mapping Information

In Figure 6-3, Router3 already knows how to forward frames to Router4, but the reverse is not true. Router3 uses logic like this: "For packets needing to get to a next-hop router that is in subnet 172.31.124.0/24, send them out the one DLCI on that point-to-point subinterface—DLCI 100." The packet then goes over that VC to Router1, which in turn routes the packet to Router4.

In the admittedly poor design shown in Figure 6-3, however, Router4 cannot use the same kind of logic as Router3, as its Frame Relay details are configured on its physical interface. To reach Router3, Router4 needs to send frames over DLCI 100 back to Router1, and let Router1 forward the packet on to Router3. In this case, InARP does not help, because InARP messages only flow across a VC, and are not forwarded; note that there is no VC between Router4 and Router3.

The solution is to add a **frame-relay map** command to Router4's configuration, as shown in Example 6-2. The example begins before Router4 has added the **frame-relay map** command, and then shows the results after having added the command.

Example 6-2 *Using the* **frame-relay map** *Command—Router4*

```
! Router4 only lists a single entry in the show frame-relay map command
! output, because Router4 only has a single VC, which connects back to Router1.
! With only 1 VC, Router4 could only have learned of 1 other router via InARP.
Router4# sh run
! lines omitted for brevity
interface Serial0/0
 ip address 172.31.134.4 255.255.255.0
 encapsulation frame-relay
Router4# show frame-relay map
Serial0/0 (up): ip 172.31.134.1 dlci 100(0x64,0x1840), dynamic,
                broadcast,, status defined, active
! Next, proof that Router4 cannot send packets to Router3's Frame Relay IP address.
Router4# ping 172.31.134.3

Type escape sequence to abort.
Sending 5, 100-byte ICMP Echos to 172.31.134.3, timeout is 2 seconds:
.....
Success rate is 0 percent (0/5)
! Next, static mapping information is added to Router4 using the frame-relay map
! interface subcommand. Note that the command uses DLCI 100, so that any packets
! sent by Router4 to 172.31.134.3 (Router3) will go over the VC to Router1, which
! will then need to route the packet to Router3. The broadcast keyword tells
```

continues

Example 6-2 *Using the* **frame-relay map** *Command—Router4 (Continued)*

```
! Router4 to send copies of broadcasts over this VC.
Router4# conf t
Enter configuration commands, one per line.  End with CNTL/Z.
Router4(config)# int s0/0
Router4(config-if)# frame-relay map ip 172.31.134.3 100 broadcast
Router4(config-if)# ^Z
Router4# ping 172.31.134.3
Type escape sequence to abort.
Sending 5, 100-byte ICMP Echos to 172.31.134.3, timeout is 2 seconds:
!!!!!
Success rate is 100 percent (5/5), round-trip min/avg/max = 20/20/20 ms
```

> **NOTE**   Remember, Router3 did not need a **frame-relay map** command, due to the logic used for a point-to-point subinterface.

Keep in mind that you probably would not choose to build a network like the one shown in Figure 6-3 using different subinterface types on the remote routers, nor would you typically put all three non-fully-meshed routers into the same subnet unless you were seriously constrained in your IP address space.

In cases where you do use a topology like that shown in Figure 6-3, you can use the configuration described in the last few pages. Alternatively, if both Router3 and Router4 had used multipoint subinterfaces, they would both have needed **frame-relay map** commands, because these two routers could not have heard InARP messages from the other router. However, if both Router3 and Router4 had used point-to-point subinterfaces, neither would have required a **frame-relay map** command, due to the "use this VC to reach all addresses in this subnet" logic.

Disabling InARP

In most cases for production networks, using InARP makes sense. However, InARP can be disabled on multipoint and physical interfaces using the **no frame-relay inverse-arp** interface subcommand. InARP can be disabled for all VCs on the interface/subinterface, all VCs on the interface/subinterface for a particular Layer 3 protocol, and even for a particular Layer 3 protocol per DLCI.

Interestingly, the **no frame-relay inverse-arp** command not only tells the router to stop sending InARP messages, but also tells the router to ignore received InARP messages. For instance, the **no frame-relay inverse-arp ip 400** subinterface subcommand on Router1 in Example 6-2 not only prevents Router1 from sending InARP messages over DLCI 400 to Router4, but also causes Router1 to ignore the InARP received over DLCI 400.

Table 6-3 summarizes some of the key details about Frame Relay Inverse ARP settings in IOS.

Table 6-3   *Facts and Behavior Related to InARP*

Fact/Behavior	Point-to-Point	Multipoint or Physical
Does InARP require LMI?	Always	Always
Is InARP enabled by default?	Yes	Yes
Can InARP be disabled?	No	Yes
Ignores received InARP messages?	Always[1]	When InARP is disabled

[1]Point-to-point interfaces ignore InARP messages because of their "send all packets for addresses in this subnet using the only DLCI on the subinterface" logic.

Classless and Classful Routing

So far this chapter has reviewed the basic forwarding process for IP packets in a Cisco router. The logic requires matching the packet destination with the routing table, or with the CEF FIB if CEF is enabled, or with other tables for the other options Cisco uses for route table lookup. (Those options include fast switching in routers and NetFlow switching in multilayer switches, both of which populate an optimized forwarding table based on flows, but not on the contents of the routing table.)

Classless routing and *classful routing* relate to the logic used to match the routing table, specifically for when the default route is used. Regardless of the use of any optimized forwarding methods (for instance, CEF), the following statements are true about classless and classful routing:

- **Classless routing**—When a default route exists, and no specific match is made when comparing the destination of the packet and the routing table, the default route is used.

- **Classful routing**—When a default route exists, and the class A, B, or C network for the destination IP address does not exist at all in the routing table, the default route is used. If any part of that classful network exists in the routing table, but the packet does not match any of the existing subnets of that classful network, the router does not use the default route and thus discards the packet.

Typically, classful routing works well in enterprise networks only when all the enterprise routes are known by all routers, and the default is used only to reach the Internet-facing routers. Conversely, for enterprise routers that normally do not know all the routes—for instance, if a remote router has only a few connected routes to network 10.0.0.0 and a default route pointing back to a core site— classless routing is required. For instance, in an OSPF design using stubby areas, default routes are injected into the non-backbone areas, instead of advertising all routes to specific subnets. As a result, classless routing is required in routers in the stubby area, because otherwise non-backbone area routers would not be able to forward packets to all parts of the network.

Classless and classful routing logic is controlled by the **ip classless** global configuration command. The **ip classless** command enables classless routing, and the **no ip classless** command enables classful routing.

No single chapter in this book covers the details of the three uses of the terms classful and classless. Table 6-4 summarizes and compares the three uses of these terms.

Table 6-4 *Comparing the Use of the Terms Classless and Classful*

As the Terms Pertain to . . .	Meaning of "Classless"	Meaning of "Classful"
Addressing (Chapter 4)	Class A, B, and C rules are not used; addresses have two parts, the prefix and host.	Class A, B, and C rules are used; addresses have three parts, the network, subnet, and host.
Routing (Chapter 6)	If no specific routes are matched for a given packet, the router forwards based on the default route.	The router first attempts a match of the classful network. If found, but none of the routes in that classful network matches the destination of a given packet, the default route is not used.
Routing protocols (Chapters 7–10)	Routing protocol does not need to assume details about the mask, as it is included in the routing updates; supports VLSM and discontiguous networks. Classless routing protocols: RIPv2, EIGRP, OSPF, and IS-IS.	Routing protocol does need to assume details about the mask, as it is not included in the routing updates; does not support VLSM and discontiguous networks. Classful routing protocols: RIPv1 and IGRP.

Multilayer Switching

Multilayer Switching (MLS) refers to the process by which a LAN switch, which operates at least at Layer 2, also uses logic and protocols from layers other than Layer 2 to forward data. The term *Layer 3 switching* refers specifically to the use of the Layer 3 destination address, compared to the routing table (or equivalent), to make the forwarding decision. (The latest switch hardware and software from Cisco uses CEF switching to optimize the forwarding of packets at Layer 3.)

MLS Logic

Layer 3 switching configuration works similarly to router configuration—IP addresses are assigned to interfaces, and routing protocols are defined. The routing protocol configuration works just like a router; however, the interface configuration on MLS switches differs slightly from routers, using VLAN interfaces, routed interfaces, and PortChannel interfaces.

VLAN interfaces give a Layer 3 switch a Layer 3 interface attached to a VLAN. Cisco sometimes refers to these interfaces as *switched virtual interfaces (SVIs)*. To route between VLANs, a switch simply needs a virtual interface attached to each VLAN, and each VLAN interface needs an IP address in the respective subnets used on those VLANs.

> **NOTE** Although it is not a requirement, the devices in a VLAN are typically configured in the same single IP subnet. However, you can use secondary IP addresses on VLAN interfaces to configure multiple subnets in one VLAN, just like on other router interfaces.

When using VLAN interfaces, the switch must take one noticeable but simple additional step when routing a packet. Like typical routers, MLS makes a routing decision to forward a packet. As with routers, the routes in an MLS routing table entry list an outgoing interface (a VLAN interface in this case), as well as a next-hop layer 3 address. The adjacency information (for example, the IP ARP table or the CEF adjacency table) lists the VLAN number and the next-hop device's MAC address to which the packet should be forwarded—again, typical of normal router operation.

At this point, a true router would know everything it needs to know to forward the packet. An MLS switch, however, then also needs to use Layer 2 logic to decide out which physical interface to physically forward the packet. The switch will simply find the next-hop device's MAC address in the CAM and forward the frame to that address based on the CAM.

Using Routed Ports and PortChannels with MLS

In some point-to-point topologies, VLAN interfaces are not required. For instance, when an MLS switch connects to a router using a cable from a switch interface to a router's LAN interface, and the only two devices in that subnet are the router and that one physical interface on the MLS switch, the MLS switch can be configured to treat that one interface as a *routed port*. (Another typical topology for using router ports is when two MLS switches connect for the purpose of routing between the switches, again creating a case with only two devices in the VLAN/subnet.)

A routed port on an MLS switch has the following characteristics:

- The interface is not in any VLAN (not even VLAN 1).

- The switch does not keep any Layer 2 switching table information for the interface.

- Layer 3 settings, such as the IP address, are configured under the physical interface—just like a router.

- The adjacency table lists the outgoing physical interface or PortChannel, which means that Layer 2 switching logic is not required in these cases.

Ethernet PortChannels can be used as routed interfaces as well. To do so, as on physical routed interfaces, the **no switchport** command should be configured. (For PortChannels, the physical interfaces in the PortChannel must also be configured with the **no switchport** command.) Also, when using a PortChannel as a routed interface, PortChannel load balancing should be based on Layer 3 addresses because the Layer 2 addresses will mostly be the MAC addresses of the two MLS switches on either end of the PortChannel. PortChannels may also be used as Layer 2 interfaces when doing MLS. In that case, VLAN interfaces would be configured with IP address, and the PortChannel would simply act as any other Layer 2 interface.

Table 6-4 lists some of the specifics about each type of Layer 3 interface.

Table 6-5 *MLS Layer 3 Interfaces*

Interface	Forwarding to Adjacent Device	Configuration Requirements
VLAN interface	Uses Layer 2 logic and L2 MAC address table	Create VLAN interface; VLAN must also exist
Physical (routed) interface	Forwards out physical interface	Use **no switchport** command to create a routed interface
PortChannel (switched) interface	Not applicable; just used as another Layer 2 forwarding path	No special configuration; useful in conjunction with VLAN interfaces
PortChannel (routed) interface	Balances across links in PortChannel	Needs **no switchport** command in order to be used as a routed interface; optionally change load-balancing method

MLS Configuration

The upcoming MLS configuration example is designed to show all of the configuration options. The network design is shown in Figures 6-4 and 6-5. In Figure 6-4, the physical topology is shown, with routed ports, VLAN trunks, a routed PortChannel, and access links. Figure 6-5 shows the same network, with a Layer 3 view of the subnets used in the network.

Figure 6-4 *Physical Topology: Example Using MLS*

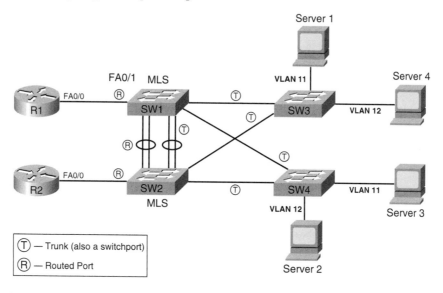

Figure 6-5 *Layer 3 Topology View: Example Using MLS*

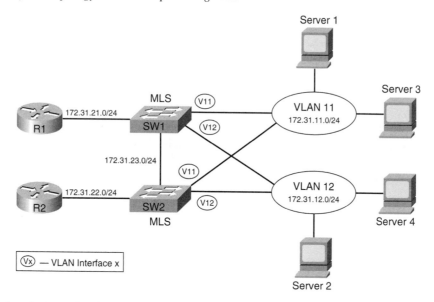

A few design points bear discussion before jumping into the configuration. First, SW1 and SW2 need Layer 2 connectivity to support traffic in VLANs 11 and 12. In other words, you need a Layer 2 trunk between SW1 and SW2, and for several reasons. Focusing on the Layer 2 portions of the network on the right side of Figure 6-4, SW1 and SW2, both distribution MLS switches, connect to SW3 and SW4, which are access layer switches. SW1 and SW2 are responsible for providing full connectivity in VLANs 11 and 12. To fully take advantage of the redundant links, SW1 and SW2 need a Layer 2 path between each other. Additionally, this design uses SW1 and SW2 as Layer 3 switches, so the hosts in VLANs 11 and 12 will use SW1 or SW2 as their default gateway. For better availability, the two switches should use HSRP, VRRP, or GLBP. Regardless of which protocol is used, both SW1 and SW2 need to be in VLANs 11 and 12, with connectivity in those VLANs, to be effective as default gateways.

In addition to a Layer 2 trunk between SW1 and SW2, to provide effective routing, it makes sense for SW1 and SW2 to have a routed path between each other as well. Certainly, SW1 needs to be able to route packets to router R1, and SW2 needs to be able to route packets to router R2. However, routing between SW1 and SW2 allows for easy convergence if R1 or R2 fails.

Figure 6-4 shows two alternatives for routed connectivity between SW1 and SW2, and one option for Layer 2 connectivity. For Layer 2 connectivity, a VLAN trunk needs to be used between the two switches. Figure 6-4 shows a pair of trunks between SW1 and SW2 (labeled with a circled T) as a Layer 2 PortChannel. The PortChannel would support the VLAN 11 and 12 traffic.

To support routed traffic, the figure shows two alternatives: simply route over the Layer 2 PortChannel using VLAN interfaces, or use a separate routed PortChannel. First, to use the Layer 2 PortChannel, SW1 and SW2 could simply configure VLAN interfaces in VLANs 11 and 12. The alternative configuration uses a second PortChannel that will be used as a routed PortChannel. However, the routed PortChannel does not function as a Layer 2 path between the switches, so the original Layer 2 PortChannel must still be used for Layer 2 connectivity. Upcoming Example 6-3 shows both configurations.

Finally, a quick comment about PortChannels is needed. This design uses PortChannels between the switches, but they are not required. Most links between switches today use at least two links in a PortChannel, for the typical reasons—better availability, better convergence, and less STP overhead. This design includes the PortChannel to point out a small difference between the routed interface configuration and the routed PortChannel configuration.

Example 6-3 shows the configuration for SW1, with some details on SW2.

Example 6-3 *MLS-Related Configuration on Switch1*

```
! Below, note that the switch is in VTP transparent mode, and VLANs 11 and 12 are
! configured, as required. Also note the ip routing global command, without which
! the switch will not perform Layer 3 switching of IP packets.
vlan 11
!
vlan 12
! The ip routing global command is required before the MLS will perform
! Layer 3 forwarding.
ip routing
```

Example 6-3   *MLS-Related Configuration on Switch1 (Continued)*

```
!
vtp domain CCIE-domain
vtp mode transparent
! Next the no switchport command makes PortChannel a routed port. On a routed
! port, an IP address can be added to the interface.
interface Port-channel1
 no switchport
 ip address 172.31.23.201 255.255.255.0
! Below, similar configuration on the interface connected to Router1.
interface FastEthernet0/1
 no switchport
 ip address 172.31.21.201 255.255.255.0
! Next, the configuration shows basic PortChannel commands, with the
! no switchport command being required due to the same command on PortChannel.
interface GigabitEthernet0/1
 no switchport
 no ip address
 channel-group 1 mode desirable
!
interface GigabitEthernet0/2
 no switchport
 no ip address
 channel-group 1 mode desirable
! Next, interface VLAN 11 gives Switch1 an IP presence in VLAN11. Devices in VLAN
! 11 can use 172.31.11.201 as their default gateway. However, using HSRP is
! better, so Switch1 has been configured to be HSRP primary in VLAN11, and Switch2
! to be primary in VLAN12, with tracking so that if Switch1 loses its connection
! to Router1, HSRP will fail over to Switch2.
interface Vlan11
 ip address 172.31.11.201 255.255.255.0
 no ip redirects
 standby 11 ip 172.31.11.254
 standby 11 priority 90
 standby 11 track FastEthernet0/1
! Below, VLAN12 has similar configuration settings, but with a higher (better)
! HSRP priority than Switch2's VLAN 12 interface.
interface Vlan12
 ip address 172.31.12.201 255.255.255.0
 no ip redirects
 standby 12 ip 172.31.12.254
 standby 12 priority 110
 standby 12 track FastEthernet0/1
```

> **NOTE**   For MLS switches to route using VLAN interfaces, two other actions are required: The corresponding VLANs must be created, and the **ip routing** global command must have been configured. (MLS switches will not perform Layer 3 routing without the **ip routing** command, which is not enabled by default.) If the VLAN interface is created before either of those actions, the VLAN interface sits in a "down and down" state. If the VLAN is created next, the VLAN interface is in an "up and down" state. Finally, after adding the **ip routing** command, the interface is in an "up and up" state.

As stated earlier, the routed PortChannel is not required in this topology. It was included to show an example of the configuration, and to provide a backdrop from which to discuss the differences. However, as configured, SW1 and SW2 are Layer 3 adjacent over the routed PortChannel as well as via their VLAN 11 and 12 interfaces. So, they could exchange IGP routing updates over three separate subnets. In such a design, the routed PortChannel was probably added so that it would be the normal Layer 3 path between SW1 and SW2; care should be taken to tune the IGP implementation so that this route is chosen instead of the routes over the VLAN interfaces.

Policy Routing

All the options for IP forwarding (routing) in this chapter had one thing in common: The destination IP address in the packet header was the only thing in the packet that was used to determine how the packet was forwarded. Policy routing allows a router to make routing decisions based on information besides the destination IP address.

Policy routing's logic begins with the **ip policy** command on an interface. This command tells IOS to process incoming packets with different logic before the normal forwarding logic takes place. (To be specific, policy routing intercepts the packet after Step 2, but before Step 3, in the routing process shown in Figure 6-1.) IOS compares the received packets using the **route map** referenced in the **ip policy** command. Figure 6-6 shows the basic logic.

Specifying the matching criteria for policy routing is relatively simple compared to defining the routing instructions using the **set** command. The route maps used by policy routing must match either based on referring to an ACL (numbered or named IP ACL, using the **match ip address** command) or based on packet length (using the **match length** command). To specify the routing instructions—in other words, where to forward the packet next—the **set** command is used. Table 6-5 lists the **set** commands, and provides some insight into their differences.

Figure 6-6 *Basic Policy Routing Logic*

Key
Topic

[Flowchart: Policy Routing Enabled? — No → (down). Yes → Match 1st Clause? — Yes → Permit or Deny?; No → Match 2nd Clause? — Yes → Permit or Deny?; No → Match Last Clause? — Yes → Permit or Deny?; No → (down). Permit or Deny? — Permit → Route Based on **set** Command; Deny → Destination Based Routing (Normal).]

Table 6-6 *Policy Routing Instructions (***set*** Commands)*

Key
Topic

Command	Comments
set ip next-hop *ip-address* [. . . *ip-address*]	Next-hop addresses must be in a connected subnet; forwards to the first address in the list for which the associated interface is up.
set ip default next-hop *ip-address* [. . . *ip-address*]	Same logic as previous command, except policy routing first attempts to route based on the routing table.
set interface *interface-type interface-number* [. . . *interface-type interface-number*]	Forwards packets using the first interface in the list that is up.
set default interface *interface-type interface-number* [. . . *interface-type interface-number*]	Same logic as previous command, except policy routing first attempts to route based on the routing table.
set ip precedence *number*	*name*	Sets IP precedence bits; can be decimal value or ASCII name.
set ip tos [*number*]	Sets entire ToS byte; numeric value is in decimal.

The first four **set** commands in Table 6-5 are the most important ones to consider. Essentially, you set either the next-hop IP address or the outgoing interface. Use the outgoing interface option only when it is unambiguous—for instance, do not refer to a LAN interface or multipoint Frame Relay subinterface. Most importantly, note the behavior of the **default** keyword in the **set** commands. Use of the **default** keyword essentially means that policy routing tries the default (destination based) routing first, and resorts to using the **set** command details only when the router finds no matching route in the routing table.

The remaining **set** commands set the bits inside the ToS byte of the packet; refer to Chapter 12, "Classification and Marking," for more information about the ToS byte and QoS settings. Note that you can have multiple **set** commands in the same **route-map** clause. For instance, you may want to define the next-hop IP address and mark the packet's ToS at the same time.

Figure 6-7 shows a variation on the same network used earlier in this chapter. Router3 and Router4 are now at the same site, connected to the same LAN, and each has PVCs connecting to Router1 and Router2.

Figure 6-7 *Policy Routing Example on Router3*

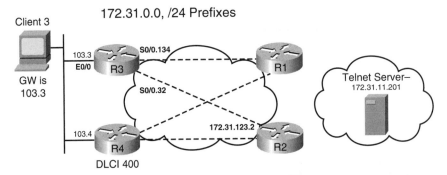

Example 6-4 shows three separate policy routing configurations on Router3. The first configuration forwards Telnet traffic over the PVC to Router2 (next hop 172.31.123.2). The next configuration does the same thing, but this time using the **set interface** command. The final option shows a nonworking case with Router3 specifying its LAN interface as an outgoing interface.

Example 6-4 *Policy Routing Example on Router3*

```
! Below, Router3 is configured with three route maps, one of which is enabled on
! interface e0/0 with the ip policy route-map to-R2-nexthop command. The two
! route maps that are not referenced in the ip policy command are used
! later in the configuration.
Router3# sh run
! Lines omitted for brevity
interface Ethernet0/0
 mac-address 0200.3333.3333
 ip address 172.31.104.3 255.255.255.0
```

Example 6-4   *Policy Routing Example on Router3 (Continued)*

Key
Topic

```
 ip policy route-map to-R2-nexthop
 !
interface Serial0/0.32 point-to-point
 ip address 172.31.123.3 255.255.255.0
 frame-relay interface-dlci 200
 !
interface Serial0/0.3333 point-to-point
 ip address 172.31.134.3 255.255.255.0
 frame-relay interface-dlci 100
 !
access-list 111 permit tcp any any eq telnet
! This route-map matches all telnet, and picks a route through R2.
route-map to-R2-nexthop permit 10
 match ip address 111
 set ip next-hop 172.31.123.2
! This route-map matches all telnet, and picks a route out E0/0.
route-map to-R4-outgoing permit 10
 match ip address 111
 set interface Ethernet0/0
! This route-map matches all telnet, and picks a route out S0/0.32.
route-map to-R2-outgoing permit 10
 match ip address 111
 set interface Serial0/0.32
! debugging is enabled to prove policy routing is working on Router3.
Router3# debug ip policy
Policy routing debugging is on
! Not shown, a Client3 tries to telnet to 172.31.11.201
! Below, a sample of the debug messages created for a single policy-routed packet.
06:21:57: IP: route map to-R2-nexthop, item 10, permit
06:21:57: IP: Ethernet0/0 to Serial0/0.32 172.31.123.2
!!!!!!!!!!!!!!!!!!!!!!!!!!!!!!!!!!!!!!!!!!!!!!!!!!!!!!!!!!!!!!!!!!!!!!!!!!!!!!!!!!!
! Next, Router3 uses a different route-map. This one sets the outgoing interface to
! S0/0.32.  The Outgoing interface option works, because it is a point-to-point
! subinterface
Router3# conf t
Enter configuration commands, one per line.  End with CNTL/Z.
Router3(config)# int e 0/0
Router3(config-if)# ip policy route-map to-R2-outgoing
Router3(config-if)# ^Z
! Not shown, the same user with default gateway of Router3 tries to telnet again.
! Below, the sample debug messages are identical as the previous set of messages.
!!!!!!!!!!!!!!!!!!!!!!!!!!!!!!!!!!!!!!!!!!!!!!!!!!!!!!!!!!!!!!!!!!!!!!!!!!!!!!!!!!!!
06:40:51: IP: route map to-R2-outgoing, item 10, permit
06:40:51: IP: Ethernet0/0 to Serial0/0.32 172.31.123.2
! Next, switching to a third route-map that sets the outgoing interface to E0/0.
Router3# conf t
Enter configuration commands, one per line.  End with CNTL/Z.
```

continues

Example 6-4 *Policy Routing Example on Router3 (Continued)*

```
Router3(config)# int e 0/0
Router3(config-if)# ip policy route-map to-R4-outgoing
Router3(config-if)# ^Z
! Not shown, the same user with default gateway of Router3 tries to telnet again.
! Router3 actually sends an ARP request out e0/0, looking for
! the IP address in the destination of the packet - 172.31.11.201, the address
! to which the user is telnetting.  Also below, Router3 shows that the ARP table
! entry for 172.31.11.201 is incomplete.
Router3# sh ip arp
Protocol  Address          Age (min)  Hardware Addr   Type   Interface
Internet  172.31.11.201           0   Incomplete      ARPA
Internet  172.31.104.3            -   0200.3333.3333  ARPA   Ethernet0/0
Internet  172.31.104.4            0   0200.4444.4444  ARPA   Ethernet0/0
```

The first two route maps in the example were relatively simple, with the last route map showing why specifying a multi-access outgoing interface is problematic. In the first two cases, the telnet works fine; to verify that it was working, the **debug ip policy** command was required.

The third route map (to-R4-outgoing) sets the output interface to Router3's E0/0 interface. Because Router3 does not have an associated next-hop IP address, Router3 sends an ARP request asking for 172.31.11.201's MAC address. As shown in the **show ip arp** command output, Router3 never completes its ARP entry. To work around the problem, assuming that the goal is to forward the packets to Router4 next, the configuration in Router3 should refer to the next-hop IP address instead of the outgoing interface E0/0.

NOTE Policy Routing for this particular topology fails due to a couple of tricky side effects of ARP. At first glance, you might think that the only thing required to make the to-R4-outgoing policy work is for R4 to enable proxy ARP. In fact, if R4 is then configured with an **ip proxy-arp** interface subcommand, R4 does indeed reply to R3's ARP for 172.31.11.201. R4 lists its own MAC address in the ARP reply. However, R3 rejects the ARP reply, because of a basic check performed on ARPs. R3's only IP route matching address 172.31.11.201 points over the WAN interface, and routers check ARP replies to make sure they list a sensible interface. From R3's perspective, the only sensible interface is one through which the destination might possibly be reached. So, R3's logic dictates that it should never hear an ARP reply regarding 172.31.11.201 coming in its fa0/0 interface, so R3 rejects the (proxy) ARP reply from R4. To see all of this working in a lab, re-create the topology, and use the **debug ip arp** and **debug policy** commands.

Foundation Summary

This section lists additional details and facts to round out the coverage of the topics in this chapter. Unlike most of the Cisco Press *Exam Certification Guides*, this "Foundation Summary" does not repeat information presented in the "Foundation Topics" section of the chapter. Please take the time to read and study the details in the "Foundation Topics" section of the chapter, as well as review items noted with a Key Topic icon.

Table 6-7 lists the protocols mentioned in or pertinent to this chapter and their respective standards documents.

Table 6-7 *Protocols and Standards for Chapter 7*

Name	Standardized In
Address Resolution Protocol (ARP)	RFC 826
Reverse Address Resolution Protocol (RARP)	RFC 903
Frame Relay Inverse ARP (InARP)	RFC 2390
Frame Relay Multiprotocol Encapsulation	RFC 2427
Differentiated Services Code Point (DSCP)	RFC 2474

Table 6-8 lists some of the key IOS commands related to the topics in this chapter. (The command syntax for switch commands was taken from the *Catalyst 3560 Multilayer Switch Command Reference, 12.2(25)SEE*.) Router-specific commands were taken from the IOS 12.3 mainline command reference.)

Table 6-8 *Command Reference for Chapter 6*

Command	Description
[no] **ip classless**	Enables classless (**ip classless**) or classful (**no ip classless**) forwarding
show ip arp	EXEC command that displays the contents of the IP ARP cache
show frame-relay map	Router **exec** command that lists the mapping information between Frame Relay DLCIs and Layer 3 addresses
frame-relay interface-dlci	Configuration command that associates a particular DLCI with a subinterface
[no] **switchport**	Switch interface subcommand that toggles an interface between a Layer 2 switched function (**switchport**) and a routed port (**no switchport**)

continues

Table 6-8   *Command Reference for Chapter 6 (Continued)*

Command	Description
clear frame-relay inarp	Router **exec** command that clears all InARP-learned entries from the Frame Relay mapping table
[no] ip route-cache cef	Interface subcommand that enables or disables CEF switching on an interface
[no] ip cef	Global configuration command to enable (or disable) CEF on all interfaces
debug frame-relay events	Displays messages about various events, including InARP messages
show frame-relay map	Displays information about Layer 3 to Layer 2 mapping with Frame Relay
frame-relay map *protocol protocol-address* {*dlci*} [**broadcast**] [**ietf** | **cisco**]	Interface subcommand that maps a Layer 3 address to a DLCI
[no] frame-relay inverse-arp [*protocol*] [*dlci*]	Interface subcommand that enables or disables InARP
[no] ip routing	Enables IP routing; defaults to **no ip routing** on a multilayer switch
ip policy route-map *map-tag*	Router interface subcommand that enables policy routing for the packets entering the interface

Refer to Table 6-6 for the list of **set** commands related to policy routing.

Memory Builders

The CCIE Routing and Switching written exam, like all Cisco CCIE written exams, covers a fairly broad set of topics. This section provides some basic tools to help you exercise your memory about some of the broader topics covered in this chapter.

Fill in Key Tables from Memory

Appendix E, "Key Tables for CCIE Study," on the CD in the back of this book contains empty sets of some of the key summary tables in each chapter. Print Appendix E, refer to this chapter's tables in it, and fill in the tables from memory. Refer to Appendix F, "Solutions for Key Tables for CCIE Study," on the CD to check your answers.

Definitions

Next, take a few moments to write down the definitions for the following terms:

policy routing, process switching, CEF, MLS, ARP, proxy ARP, routed interface, InARP, fast switching, TTL, classless routing, classful routing, FIB, adjacency table, control plane, switched interface, data plane, IP routing, IP forwarding

Refer to the Glossary to check your answers.

Further Reading

For a good reference on load balancing with CEF, refer to http://cisco.com/en/US/partner/tech/tk827/tk831/technologies_tech_note09186a0080094806.shtml. This website requires a CCO account.

Blueprint topics covered in this chapter:

This chapter covers the following subtopics from the Cisco CCIE Routing and Switching written exam blueprint. Refer to the full blueprint in Table I-1 in the Introduction for more details on the topics covered in each chapter and their context within the blueprint.

- Link State and Distance Vector Protocols

- Split Horizon

CHAPTER 7

RIP Version 2

Chapters 7 through 9 and 11 each focus on a single routing protocol. This chapter covers Routing Information Protocol (RIP) Version 2, including most of the features, concepts, and commands. Chapter 10, "IGP Route Redistribution, Route Summarization, and Default Routing," covers some RIP details, in particular, route redistribution between RIP and other routing protocols, and route summarization.

Although RIPv2 has been removed from the latest version of the CCIE Routing and Switching qualification exam blueprint (exam version 3 at the time of this publication), we have kept this chapter on RIPv2 in this edition because of its many parallels to the other IGPs covered in the CCIE blueprint. As a result, this information may help you to gain perspective on the other IGP topics and to understand the route redistribution examples in Chapter 10. Furthermore, it is one of two distance vector interior routing protocols, a topic on which exam questions are possible.

"Do I Know This Already?" Quiz

Table 7-1 outlines the major headings in this chapter and the corresponding "Do I Know This Already?" quiz questions.

Table 7-1 *"Do I Know This Already?" Foundation Topics Section-to-Question Mapping*

Foundation Topics Section	Questions Covered in This Section	Score
RIP Version 2 Basics	1–2	
RIP Convergence and Loop Prevention	3–5	
RIP Configuration	6–7	
Total Score		

In order to best use this pre-chapter assessment, remember to score yourself strictly. You can find the answers in Appendix A, "Answers to the 'Do I Know This Already?' Quizzes."

1. Which of the following items are true of RIP Version 2?

   a. Supports VLSM

   b. Sends Hellos to 224.0.0.9

   c. Allows for route tagging

   d. Defines infinity as 255 hops

   e. Authentication requires 3DES

2. In an internetwork that solely uses RIP, once the network is stable and converged, which of the following is true?

   a. Routers send RIP updates every 30 seconds.

   b. Routers send RIP updates every 90 seconds.

   c. Routers send Hellos every 10 seconds, and send updates only when routes change.

   d. A routing update sent out a router's s0/0 interface includes all RIP routes in the IP routing table.

   e. A RIP update's routes list the same metric as is shown in that router's IP routing table.

3. R1 previously had heard about only one route to 10.1.1.0/24, metric 3, via an update received on its s0/0 interface, so it put that route in its routing table. R1 gets an update from that same neighboring router, but the same route now has metric 16. R1 immediately sends a RIP update out s0/0 that advertises a metric 16 route for that same subnet. Which of the following are true for this scenario?

   a. Split horizon must have been disabled on R1's s0/0 interface.

   b. R1's update is a triggered update.

   c. R1's metric 16 route advertisement is an example of a poison reverse route.

   d. The incoming metric 16 route was the result of a counting-to-infinity problem.

4. R1 is in a network that uses RIPv2 exclusively, and RIP has learned dozens of subnets via several neighbors. Which of the following commands display the current value of at least one route's Invalid timer?

   a. **show ip route**

   b. **show ip rip database**

   c. **debug ip rip**

   d. **debug ip rip event**

5. R1 is in a network that uses RIPv2 exclusively, and RIP has learned dozens of subnets via several neighbors. From privileged EXEC mode, the network engineer types in the command **clear ip route**. What happens?

    a. R1 removes all routes from its IP routing table.

    b. R1 removes only RIP routes from its IP routing table.

    c. After the command, R1 will relearn its routes when the neighboring router's Update timers cause them to send their next updates.

    d. R1 immediately sends updates on all interfaces, poisoning all routes, so that all neighbors immediately send triggered updates—which allow R1 to immediately relearn its routes.

    e. R1 will relearn its routes immediately by sending RIP requests out all its interfaces.

    f. None of the other answers is correct.

6. R1 has been configured for RIPv2, including a **network 10.0.0.0** command. Which of the following statements are true about R1's RIP behavior?

    a. R1 will send advertisements out any of its interfaces in network 10.

    b. R1 will process received advertisements in any of its interfaces in network 10.

    c. R1 will send updates only after receiving a RIP Hello message from a neighboring router.

    d. R1 can disable the sending of routing updates on an interface using the **passive-interface** interface subcommand.

    e. R1 will advertise the subnets of any of its interfaces connected to subnets of network 10.

7. Which of the following represents a default setting for the Cisco IOS implementation of RIPv2?

    a. Split horizon is enabled on all types of interfaces.

    b. Split horizon is disabled on Frame Relay physical interfaces and multipoint subinterfaces.

    c. The default authentication mode, normally set with the **ip rip authentication mode** interface subcommand, is MD5 authentication.

    d. RIP will send triggered updates when a route changes.

Foundation Topics

RIP Version 2 Basics

CCIE candidates may already know many of the features and configuration options of RIP. Although RIPv2 is no longer on the CCIE Routing and Switching qualification exam blueprint, it is clearly helpful to understand its operations to strengthen your grasp on IGPs in general and the differences between distance vector and link-state protocols. This chapter summarizes RIPv2's protocol features and concepts. Table 7-2 provides a high-level overview of RIPv2's operation.

Table 7-2 *RIP Feature Summary*

Function	Description
Transport	UDP, port 520.
Metric	Hop count, with 15 as the maximum usable metric, and 16 considered to be infinite.
Hello interval	None; RIP relies on the regular full routing updates instead.
Update destination	Local subnet broadcast (255.255.255.255) for RIPv1; 224.0.0.9 multicast for RIPv2.
Update interval	30 seconds.
Full or partial updates	Full updates each interval. For on-demand circuits, allows RIP to send full updates once, and then remain silent until changes occur, per RFC 2091. Full updates each interval.
Triggered updates	Yes, when routes change.
Multiple routes to the same subnet	Allows installing 1 to 6 (default 4) equal-metric routes to the same subnet in a single routing table.
Authentication*	Allows both plain-text and MD5 authentication.
Subnet mask in updates*	RIPv2 transmits the subnet mask with each route, thereby supporting VLSM, making RIPv2 classless. This feature also allows RIPv2 to support discontiguous networks.
VLSM*	Supported as a result of the inclusion of subnet masks in the routing updates.

Table 7-2 *RIP Feature Summary (Continued)*

Function	Description
Route Tags*	Allows RIP to tag routes as they are redistributed into RIP.
Next Hop field*	Supports the assignment of a next-hop IP address for a route, allowing a router to advertise a next-hop router that is different from itself.

* RIPv2-only features

RIP exchanges routes by sending RIP updates on each interface based on an Update timer (update interval). A RIP router advertises its connected routes, as well as other RIP-learned routes that are in the router's IP routing table. Note that RIP does not keep a separate topology table. RIP routers do not form neighbor relationships, nor do they use a Hello protocol—each router simply sends updates, with destination address 224.0.0.9. (Note: RIPv1 uses broadcast address 255.255.255.255.)

RIPv2 uses the same hop-count metric as RIPv1, with 15 being the largest valid metric, and 16 considered to be infinity. Interestingly, a RIP router does not put its own metric in the route of a sent routing update; rather, it first adds 1 to each metric when building the update. For instance, if RouterA has a route with metric 2, it advertises that route with metric 3—in effect, telling the receiving router what its metric should be.

When Cisco RIP routers learn multiple routes to the same subnet, the lowest-metric route is chosen, of course. If multiple equal-hop routes exist, the router (by default) installs up to 4 such routes in its routing table, or between 1 and 6 of such routes, based on the **ip maximum-paths** *number* command under the **router rip** command.

RIP Convergence and Loop Prevention

The most interesting and complicated part of RIP relates to loop-prevention methods used during convergence after a route has failed. Some protocols, like OSPF, IS-IS, and EIGRP, include loop prevention as a side effect of their underlying route computations. However, RIP, like other distance vector protocols, uses several loop-prevention tools. Unfortunately, these loop-prevention tools also significantly increase convergence time—a fact that is certainly the biggest negative feature of RIP, even for RIPv2. Table 7-3 summarizes some of the key features and terms related to RIP convergence, with further explanations following the table.

Table 7-3 *RIP Features Related to Convergence and Loop Prevention*

Function	Description
Split horizon	Instead of advertising all routes out a particular interface, RIP omits the routes whose outgoing interface field matches the interface out which the update would be sent.
Triggered update	The immediate sending of a new update when routing information changes, instead of waiting for the Update timer to expire.

continues

Table 7-3 *RIP Features Related to Convergence and Loop Prevention (Continued)*

Function	Description
Route poisoning	The process of sending an infinite-metric (hop count 16) route in routing updates when that route fails.
Poison reverse	The act of advertising a poisoned route (metric 16) out an interface, but in reaction to receiving that same poisoned route in an update received on that same interface.
Update timer	The timer that specifies the time interval over which updates are sent. Each interface uses an independent timer, defaulting to 30 seconds.
Holddown timer	A per-route timer (default 180 seconds) that begins when a route's metric changes to a larger value. The router does not add an alternative route for this subnet to its routing table until the Holddown timer for that route expires.
Invalid timer	A per-route timer that increases until it receives a routing update that confirms the route is still valid, upon which the timer is reset to 0. If the updates cease, the Invalid timer will grow until it reaches the timer setting (default 180 seconds), after which the route is considered invalid.
Flush (Garbage) timer	A per-route timer that is reset and grows with the Invalid timer. When the Flush timer mark is reached (default 240 seconds), the router removes the route from the routing table and accepts new routes to the failed subnet.

The rest of this section shows examples of the convergence features, using RIP **show** and **debug** command output to show examples of their use. Figure 7-1 shows the sample internetwork that is used in these examples of the various loop-prevention tools.

Figure 7-1 *Sample Internetwork Used for Loop-Prevention Examples*

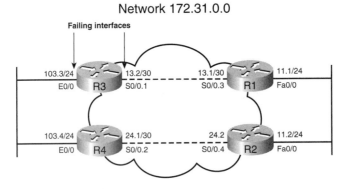

Network 172.31.0.0

Converged Steady-State Operation

Example 7-1 shows a few details of R1's operation while all interfaces in Figure 7-1 are up and working. The example lists the basic (and identical) RIP configuration on all four routers; configuration will be covered in more detail later in the chapter. As configured, all four routers are using only RIPv2, on all interfaces shown in Figure 7-1. Read the comments in Example 7-1 for explanations of the output.

Example 7-1   *Steady-State RIP Operation in Figure 7-1*

```
! All routers use the same three lines of RIP configuration.
router rip
 network 172.31.0.0
 version 2
! Below, the show ip protocol command lists many of RIP's operational settings,
! including RIP timers, version used, and neighbors from which RIP updates have
! been received (listed as "Routing Information Sources").
R1# show ip protocol
Routing Protocol is "rip"
  Sending updates every 30 seconds, next due in 24 seconds
  Invalid after 180 seconds, hold down 180, flushed after 240
  Outgoing update filter list for all interfaces is not set
  Incoming update filter list for all interfaces is not set
  Redistributing: rip
  Default version control: send version 2, receive version 2
    Interface             Send  Recv  Triggered RIP  Key-chain
    FastEthernet0/0       2     2
    Serial0/0.3           2     2
  Automatic network summarization is in effect
  Maximum path: 4
  Routing for Networks:
    172.31.0.0
  Routing Information Sources:
    Gateway         Distance      Last Update
    172.31.11.2          120      00:00:15
    172.31.13.2          120      00:00:08
  Distance: (default is 120)
! Below, the current Invalid timer is listed by each RIP route. Note that it took
! about 3 seconds between the above show ip protocols command and the upcoming
! show ip route command, so the last update from 172.31.13.2 (above)
! was 8 seconds; 3 seconds later, the Invalid timer for a route learned from
! 172.31.13.2 is now 11 seconds.
R1# show ip route
Codes: C - connected, S - static, R - RIP, M - mobile, B - BGP
       D - EIGRP, EX - EIGRP external, O - OSPF, IA - OSPF inter area
       N1 - OSPF NSSA external type 1, N2 - OSPF NSSA external type 2
       E1 - OSPF external type 1, E2 - OSPF external type 2
       i - IS-IS, su - IS-IS summary, L1 - IS-IS level-1, L2 - IS-IS level-2
       ia - IS-IS inter area, * - candidate default, U - per-user static route
       o - ODR, P - periodic downloaded static route
```

continues

Example 7-1 *Steady-State RIP Operation in Figure 7-1 (Continued)*

```
Gateway of last resort is not set

    172.31.0.0/16 is variably subnetted, 4 subnets, 2 masks
R      172.31.24.0/30 [120/1] via 172.31.11.2, 00:00:18, FastEthernet0/0
C      172.31.11.0/24 is directly connected, FastEthernet0/0
C      172.31.13.0/30 is directly connected, Serial0/0.3
R      172.31.103.0/24 [120/1] via 172.31.13.2, 00:00:11, Serial0/0.3
! Below, the show ip rip database command lists information for each route
! considered by RIP.
R1# show ip rip database
172.31.0.0/16     auto-summary
172.31.11.0/24    directly connected, FastEthernet0/0
172.31.13.0/30    directly connected, Serial0/0.3
172.31.24.0/30
    [1] via 172.31.11.2, 00:00:01, FastEthernet0/0
172.31.103.0/24
[1] via 172.31.13.2, 00:00:23, Serial0/0.3
```

> **NOTE**   The **show ip rip database** command lists all RIP learned routes, and all connected routes that RIP is advertising.

Triggered (Flash) Updates and Poisoned Routes

When RIP knows for sure that a route to a subnet has failed, RIPv2 can converge to an alternate route typically in less than a minute. Example 7-2 details the steps behind one such example, using Figure 7-1, with the steps outlined in the following list (the comments in Example 7-2 refer to these steps by number):

1. RIP **debug** messages show R1's RIP updates, including R1's use of split horizon.

2. R3's E0/0 interface is shut down, simulating a failure.

3. R3 immediately sends a triggered update (also called a flash update), because R3 knows for sure that the route has failed. R3's advertised route is a poisoned route to 172.31.103.0/24.

4. R1 immediately (due to triggered updates) advertises a poison reverse route for 172.31.103.0/24, back to R3, and sends a triggered update out its fa0/0 interface.

5. R1 removes its route to 172.31.103.0/24 from its routing table.

6. R1 waits for R2's next update, sent based on R2's Update timer on its fa0/0 interface. That update includes a route to 172.31.103.0/24. R1 adds that route to its routing table.

Example 7-2   *R1's Convergence for 172.31.103.0/24 upon R3's E0/0 Interface Failure*

```
! First, the debug ip rip command enables RIP debugging. This command will show
! messages that show every route in the sent and received updates.
R1# debug ip rip
RIP protocol debugging is on
! (Step 1) Below, the output exhibits split horizon—for example, 172.31.103.0/24
! is not advertised out s0/0.3, but it is advertised out fa0/0.
*Mar  3 22:44:08.176: RIP: sending v2 update to 224.0.0.9 via Serial0/0.3 (172.31.13.1)
*Mar  3 22:44:08.176: RIP: build update entries
*Mar  3 22:44:08.176:   172.31.11.0/24 via 0.0.0.0, metric 1, tag 0
*Mar  3 22:44:08.176:   172.31.24.0/30 via 0.0.0.0, metric 2, tag 0
*Mar  3 22:44:12.575: RIP: sending v2 update to 224.0.0.9 via FastEthernet0/0 (172.31.11.1)
*Mar  3 22:44:12.575: RIP: build update entries
*Mar  3 22:44:12.575:   172.31.13.0/30 via 0.0.0.0, metric 1, tag 0
*Mar  3 22:44:12.575:   172.31.103.0/24 via 0.0.0.0, metric 2, tag 0
! Next, R1 receives a RIP update from R3. The metric 1 route in the update below
! is R1's best route, and is placed into R1's routing table. Note that the metric
! in the received update is R1's actual metric to reach the route.
*Mar  3 22:44:21.265: RIP: received v2 update from 172.31.13.2 on Serial0/0.3
*Mar  3 22:44:21.269:       172.31.24.0/30 via 0.0.0.0 in 2 hops
*Mar  3 22:44:21.269:       172.31.103.0/24 via 0.0.0.0 in 1 hops
! (Step 2) R3's E0/0 interface is shut down at this point. (Not shown).
! (Step 3) Below, R1 receives a triggered update, with two poison routes from R3—
! the same two routes that R3 advertised in the previous routing update above.
! Note that the triggered update only includes changed routes, with full updates
! continuing on the same update interval.
*Mar  3 22:44:46.338: RIP: received v2 update from 172.31.13.2 on Serial0/0.3
*Mar  3 22:44:46.338:       172.31.24.0/30 via 0.0.0.0 in 16 hops  (inaccessible)
*Mar  3 22:44:46.338:       172.31.103.0/24 via 0.0.0.0 in 16 hops  (inaccessible)
! (Step 4) Above, R1 reacts to its receipt of poisoned routes, sending a triggered
! update out its fa0/0 interface. Note that the debug refers to the triggered
! update as a flash update.
*Mar  3 22:44:48.341: RIP: sending v2 flash update to 224.0.0.9 via FastEthernet 0/0
  (172.31.11.1)
*Mar  3 22:44:48.341: RIP: build flash update entries
*Mar  3 22:44:48.341:   172.31.103.0/24 via 0.0.0.0, metric 16, tag 0
! (Step 4) R1 also sends a triggered update out s0/0.3 to R3, which includes
! a poison reverse route to 172.31.103.0/24, back to R3. R1 does not send back a
! poison route to 172.31.24.0, because R1's route to 172.31.24.0 was
! pointing towards R2, not R3—so R1's route to 172.31.24.0/24 did not fail.
*Mar  3 22:44:48.341: RIP: sending v2 flash update to 224.0.0.9 via Serial0/0.3
(172.31.13.1)
! (Step 5) Below, note the absence of a route to 103.0/24 in R1's routing table.
R1# show ip route 172.31.103.0
% Subnet not in table
! (Step 6) Below, 23 seconds since the previous debug message, R2's next routing
! update arrives at R1, advertising 172.31.103.0/24. Following that, R1 now has
! a 2-hop route, through R2, to 172.31.103.0/24.
```

continues

Example 7-2 *R1's Convergence for 172.31.103.0/24 upon R3's E0/0 Interface Failure (Continued)*

```
*Mar  3 22:45:11.271: RIP: received v2 update from 172.31.11.2 on FastEthernet0/0
*Mar  3 22:45:11.271:      172.31.24.0/30 via 0.0.0.0 in 1 hops
*Mar  3 22:45:11.271:      172.31.103.0/24 via 0.0.0.0 in 2 hops
R1# show ip route 172.31.103.0
Routing entry for 172.31.103.0/24
  Known via "rip", distance 120, metric 2
  Redistributing via rip
  Last update from 172.31.11.2 on FastEthernet0/0, 00:00:01 ago
  Routing Descriptor Blocks:
  * 172.31.11.2, from 172.31.11.2, 00:00:01 ago, via FastEthernet0/0
Route metric is 2, traffic share count is 1
```

If you examine the **debug** message time stamps in Example 7-2, you will see that between 25 and 45 seconds passed from when R1 heard the poisoned routes until R1 heard R2's new routing update with a now-best route to 172.31.103.0/24. While not on par with EIGRP or OSPF, this convergence is reasonably fast for RIP.

> **NOTE** Do not confuse the term *triggered update* with the term *triggered extensions to RIP.* RFC 2091 defines how RIP can choose to send full updates only once, and then be silent, to support demand circuits. The feature is enabled per interface by the **ip rip triggered** interface subcommand.

RIP Convergence When Routing Updates Cease

When a router ceases to receive routing updates, RIP must wait for some timers to expire before it decides that routes previously learned from the now-silent router can be considered to be failed routes. To deal with such cases, RIP uses its Invalid, Flush, and Holddown timers to prevent loops. Coincidentally, RIP's convergence time increases to several minutes as a result.

Example 7-3 details just such a case, where R1 simply ceases to hear RIP updates from R3. (To create the failure, R3's s0/0.1 subinterface was shut down, simulating failure of a Frame Relay PVC.) The example uses the internetwork illustrated in Figure 7-1 again, and begins with all interfaces up, and all four routes known in each of the four routers. The example follows this sequence (the comments in Example 7-3 refer to these steps by number):

1. R3's s0/0.1 subinterface fails, but R1's Frame Relay subinterface stays up—so R1 must use its timers to detect route failures.

2. R1's Invalid and Flush timers for route 172.31.103.0/24 grow because it does not hear any further updates from R3.

3. After the Invalid timer expires (180 seconds) for R1's route to 172.31.103.0/24, R1 begins a Holddown timer for the route. Holddown starts at (default) 180 seconds, and counts down.

4. The Flush timer expires after a total 240 seconds, or 60 seconds past the Invalid timer. As a result, R1 flushes the route to 172.31.103.0/24 from its routing table, which also removes the Holddown timer for the route.

Example 7-3 *R1 Ceases to Hear R3's Updates: Invalid, Flush, and Holddown Timers Required*

```
! First, the debug ip rip event command is used, which displays messages when
! updates are sent and received, but does not display the contents of the updates.
R1# debug ip rip event
RIP event debugging is on
! (Step 1) Not Shown: R3's S0/0.1 subinterface is shut down.
! (Step 2) Below, the Invalid timer for 172.31.103.0/24 has reached 35, meaning
! that 35 seconds have passed since the last received update from which this route
! was learned. An Invalid timer over 30 seconds means that at least one RIP
! update was not received.
R1# show ip route
Codes: C - connected, S - static, R - RIP, M - mobile, B - BGP
       D - EIGRP, EX - EIGRP external, O - OSPF, IA - OSPF inter area
       N1 - OSPF NSSA external type 1, N2 - OSPF NSSA external type 2
       E1 - OSPF external type 1, E2 - OSPF external type 2
       i - IS-IS, su - IS-IS summary, L1 - IS-IS level-1, L2 - IS-IS level-2
       ia - IS-IS inter area, * - candidate default, U - per-user static route
       o - ODR, P - periodic downloaded static route

Gateway of last resort is not set

     172.31.0.0/16 is variably subnetted, 4 subnets, 2 masks
R       172.31.24.0/30 [120/1] via 172.31.11.2, 00:00:09, FastEthernet0/0
C       172.31.11.0/24 is directly connected, FastEthernet0/0
C       172.31.13.0/30 is directly connected, Serial0/0.3
R       172.31.103.0/24 [120/1] via 172.31.13.2, 00:00:35, Serial0/0.3
! Below, one example set of debug messages are shown. (Many more debug messages
! occurred while waiting for convergence, but those were omitted.) The messages
! about R1's received updates from R2 occur every 30 seconds or so. The contents
! include a 2-hop route to 172.31.103.0/24, which R1 ignores until the Flush timer
! expires.
*Mar  3 21:59:58.921: RIP: received v2 update from 172.31.11.2 on FastEthernet0/0
*Mar  3 21:59:58.921: RIP: Update contains 2 routes
! (Step 3) Below, the Invalid timer expires, roughly 3 minutes after the failure.
! Note that the route is listed as "possibly down," which occurs when the
! Invalid timer has expired but the Flush timer has not. Note that the show ip
! route command does not list the Flush timer settings, but the upcoming show
! ip route 172.31.103.0 command does.
R1# show ip route
Codes: C - connected, S - static, R - RIP, M - mobile, B - BGP
       D - EIGRP, EX - EIGRP external, O - OSPF, IA - OSPF inter area
       N1 - OSPF NSSA external type 1, N2 - OSPF NSSA external type 2
       E1 - OSPF external type 1, E2 - OSPF external type 2
```

continues

Example 7-3   *R1 Ceases to Hear R3's Updates: Invalid, Flush, and Holddown Timers Required (Continued)*

```
        i - IS-IS, su - IS-IS summary, L1 - IS-IS level-1, L2 - IS-IS level-2
        ia - IS-IS inter area, * - candidate default, U - per-user static route
        o - ODR, P - periodic downloaded static route

Gateway of last resort is not set

        172.31.0.0/16 is variably subnetted, 4 subnets, 2 masks
R       172.31.24.0/30 [120/1] via 172.31.11.2, 00:00:20, FastEthernet0/0
C       172.31.11.0/24 is directly connected, FastEthernet0/0
C       172.31.13.0/30 is directly connected, Serial0/0.3
R       172.31.103.0/24 is possibly down,
          routing via 172.31.13.2, Serial0/0.3
! (Step 3) Next, the command shows the metric as inaccessible, meaning an
! infinite metric, as well as the current Flush timer (3:23), which counts up.
! Also, the Holddown timer for this route has started (at 180 seconds), with 159
! seconds in its countdown. The Holddown timer prevents R1 from using the route
! heard from R2.

R1# show ip route 172.31.103.0
Routing entry for 172.31.103.0/24
  Known via "rip", distance 120, metric 4294967295 (inaccessible)
  Redistributing via rip
  Last update from 172.31.13.2 on Serial0/0.3, 00:03:23 ago
  Hold down timer expires in 159 secs
! (Step 4) Below, just after 4 minutes has passed, the Flush timer has expired,
! and the route to 172.31.103.0/24 has been flushed from the routing table.
R1# show ip route 172.31.103.0
% Subnet not in table
```

At the end of the example, the only remaining step for convergence is for R1 to receive R2's next regular full routing update, which includes a two-hop route to 172.31.103.0/24. R2 will send that update based on R2's regular update interval. R1 would place that route in its routing table, completing convergence.

Note that either the Flush timer or the Holddown timer must expire before new routing information would be used in this case. Here, the Flush timer for route 172.31.103.0/24 expired first, resulting in the route being removed from R1's routing table. When the route is flushed (removed), any associated timers are also removed, including the Holddown timer. Had the Holddown timer been smaller, and had it expired before the Flush timer, R1 would have been able to use the route advertised by R2 at that point in time.

Convergence Extras

Convergence in Example 7-3 took a little over 4 minutes, but it could be improved in some cases. The RIP timers can be tuned with the **timers basic** *update invalid hold-down flush* subcommand under **router rip**, although care should be taken when changing these timers. The timers should be consistent across routers, and smaller values increase the chance of routing loops being formed during convergence.

The **clear ip route** * command also speeds convergence by removing all routes from the routing table, along with any per-route timers. In Example 7-3, the **clear ip route 172.31.103.0** command would have worked as well, just deleting that one route. Because the **clear** command bypasses loop-prevention features by deleting the route and timers, it can be risky, but it certainly speeds convergence. Also, after the **clear** command, R1 would immediately issue RIP request packets, which cause the neighboring routers to send full routing updates to R1, instead of waiting on their next update time.

RIP Configuration

This chapter does not go into detail on configuring RIPv2. However, make sure to review the list of RIPv2 configuration commands, and command syntax, listed in Table 7-6 of the "Foundation Summary" section for this chapter.

Figure 7-2 shows the internetwork that will be used to illustrate RIP configuration concepts in Example 7-4. Note that most of the subnets are part of network 172.31.0.0, except where noted.

Figure 7-2 *Sample Internetwork Used for RIP Configuration Examples*

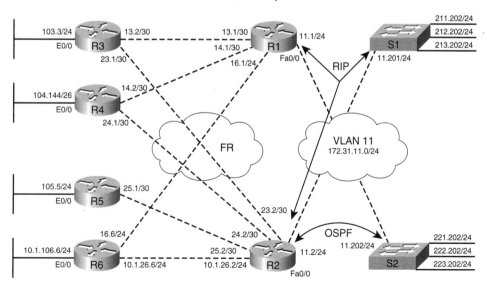

Network 172.31.0.0, Except where Shown

Enabling RIP and the Effects of Autosummarization

Example 7-4 covers basic RIP configuration, the meaning and implication of the RIP **network** command, and the effects of the default setting for autosummarization. To examine just those functions, Example 7-4 shows the related RIP configuration on R1, R2, and R6, along with some command output.

Example 7-4 *Basic RIP Configuration on R1, R2, R4, and S1*

```
! First, the three lines of configuration are the same on R1 and S1
! (Point 1): the version 2 command tells R1 to send and receive only RIPv2
! updates, and to ignore RIPv1 updates. The network command must have a classful
! network as the parameter.
router rip
  version 2
  network 172.31.0.0
! Next, the configuration for R2 and R6 is shown, which includes a network 10.0.0.0
! command, enabling RIP on their interfaces in network 10.0.0.0.
router rip
  version 2
  network 10.0.0.0
  network 172.31.0.0
! Below, R1 shows that only v2 updates are being sent and received, and that
! autosummarization is in effect.
R1# sh ip protocol
Routing Protocol is "rip"
  Sending updates every 30 seconds, next due in 26 seconds
  Invalid after 180 seconds, hold down 180, flushed after 240
  Outgoing update filter list for all interfaces is not set
  Incoming update filter list for all interfaces is not set
  Redistributing: rip
  Default version control: send version 2, receive version 2
    Interface           Send  Recv  Triggered RIP  Key-chain
    FastEthernet0/0      2     2                    carkeys
    Serial0/0.3          2     2
    Serial0/0.4          2     2                    anothersetofkeys
    Serial0/0.6          2     2
  Automatic network summarization is in effect
  Maximum path: 4
  Routing for Networks:
! lines omitted for brevity
! Below, the show ip route 10.0.0.0 command lists all of R1's known routes to
! network 10.0.0.0; the only route is for 10.0.0.0/8, because R2 and R6
! automatically summarize (by default) at the classful network boundary.
R1# show ip route 10.0.0.0
```

Example 7-4 *Basic RIP Configuration on R1, R2, R4, and S1 (Continued)*

```
Routing entry for 10.0.0.0/8
  Known via "rip", distance 120, metric 1
  Redistributing via rip
  Last update from 172.31.11.2 on FastEthernet0/0, 00:00:01 ago
  Routing Descriptor Blocks:
    172.31.16.6, from 172.31.16.6, 00:00:08 ago, via Serial0/0.6
      Route metric is 1, traffic share count is 1
  * 172.31.11.2, from 172.31.11.2, 00:00:01 ago, via FastEthernet0/0
Route metric is 1, traffic share count is 1
```

A couple of points from this example need a little more explanation. The RIP **network** command only allows for a classful network as a parameter, which in turn enables RIP on all of that router's interfaces that are part of that network. Enabling RIP on an interface makes the router begin sending RIP updates, listening for RIP updates (UDP port 520), and advertising that interface's connected subnet.

Because the RIP **network** command has no way to simply match one interface at a time, a RIP configuration may enable these three functions on an interface for which some or all of these functions are not required. The three RIP functions can be individually disabled on an interface with some effort. Table 7-4 lists these three functions, along with how to disable each feature.

Table 7-4 *RIP Per-Interface Actions, and How to Disable Them When Enabled*

Key
Topic

RIP Function	How to Disable
Sending RIP updates	Make the interface passive: configure **router rip**, followed by **passive-interface** *type number*
Listening for RIP updates	Filter all incoming routes using a distribute list
Advertising the connected subnet	Filter outbound advertisements on other interfaces using distribute lists, filtering an interface's connected subnet

Another way you can limit advertisements on multiaccess networks is to use the **neighbor** *ip-address* **RIP** subcommand. This command tells RIP to send unicast RIP updates to that neighbor. For instance, when using a multipoint Frame Relay subinterface, there may be four routers reachable using that subinterface. If you want to send RIP updates to only one of them, make the interface passive, and then use the **neighbor** command to cause RIP to send updates, but only to that one neighbor.

RIP uses *autosummarization* at classful network boundaries by default. In Example 7-4, R2 and R6 connect to parts of classful networks 10.0.0.0/8 and network 172.31.0.0/16. Advertisements sent out interfaces in network 172.31.0.0/16 advertise a summarized route of the complete class A network 10.0.0.0/8. In the example, R2 and R6 both advertise a summarized network 10.0.0.0 to R1. As a result, as seen with the **show ip route 10.0.0.0** command on R1, R1 knows two equal-cost routes to classful network 10.0.0.0. In this case, R1 would send some packets meant for subnet 10.1.106.0/24 through R2 first, a seemingly poor choice. To advertise the subnets of network 10.0.0.0, R2 and R6 could be configured with the **no auto-summary** command under **router rip**.

Note that RIPv2 allows for discontiguous networks, but autosummarization must be disabled for a design using discontiguous networks to work.

RIP Authentication

RIP authentication, much like EIGRP and OSPF authentication, requires the creation of keys and requires authentication to be enabled on an interface. The keys are used either as clear-text passwords or as the secret (private) key used in an MD5 calculation.

Multiple keys are allowed, and are grouped together using a construct called a *key chain*. A key chain is simply a set of related keys, each of which has a different number and may be restricted to a time period. By allowing multiple related keys in a key chain, with each key valid during specified time periods, the engineer can easily plan for migration to new keys in the future. (NTP is recommended when keys are restricted by time ranges.)

Cisco IOS enables the RIP (and OSPF and EIGRP) authentication process on a per-interface basis, referring to the key chain that holds the keys with the **ip authentication key-chain** *name* interface subcommand. The router looks in the key chain and selects the key(s) valid at that particular time. With RIP, the type of authentication (clear-text password or MD5 digest) is chosen per interface as well, using the **ip rip authentication mode {text | md5}** interface subcommand. If this command is omitted, the authentication type defaults to **text**, meaning that the key is used as a clear-text password

RIP Next-Hop Feature and Split Horizon

This section covers the split horizon and next-hop features of RIPv2. These two features do not typically need to be considered at the same time, but in some cases they do.

First, Cisco IOS controls the split horizon setting per interface, using the [**no**] **ip split-horizon** interface subcommand. Split horizon is on by default, except for cases in which Frame Relay is configured with the IP address on the physical interface.

The RIPv2 next-hop feature allows a RIP router to advertise a different next-hop router than the advertising router.

Although this is not a common requirement, this little-known feature permits a RIP router to point to a different next hop than it would normally provide to another RIP router, permitting a form of traffic engineering.

RIP Offset Lists

RIP *offset lists* allow RIP to add to a route's metric, either before sending an update, or for routes received in an update. The offset list refers to an ACL (standard, extended, or named) to match the routes; the router then adds the specified *offset*, or extra metric, to any matching routes. Any routes not matched by the offset list are unchanged. The offset list also specifies which routing updates to examine by referring to a direction (in or out) and, optionally, an interface. If the interface is omitted from the command, all updates for the defined direction are examined.

Route Filtering with Distribute Lists and Prefix Lists

Outbound and inbound RIP updates can be filtered at any interface, or for the entire RIP process. To filter the routes, the **distribute-list** command is used under **router rip**, referencing an IP ACL or an IP prefix list. Any subnets matched with a **permit** clause in the ACL make it through; any that match with a **deny** action are filtered. The distribution list filtering can be performed for either direction of flow (in or out) and, optionally, for a particular interface. If the interface option is omitted, all updates coming into or out of the RIP process are filtered. (Routes can also be filtered at redistribution points, a topic covered in Chapter 10.)

The generic command, when creating a RIP distribution list that uses an ACL, is

```
distribute-list {access-list-number | name} {in | out} [interface-type interface-number]
```

A RIP distribute list might refer to a prefix list instead of an ACL to match routes. Prefix lists are designed to match a range of subnets, as well as a range of subnet masks associated with the subnets. The distribute list must still define the direction of the updates to be examined (in or out), and optionally an interface.

Chapter 10 includes a more complete discussion of the syntax and formatting of prefix lists; this chapter focuses on how to call and use a prefix list for RIP. To reference a prefix list, use the following **router rip** subcommand:

```
distribute-list {prefix list-name} {in | out } [interface-type interface-number]
```

Foundation Summary

This section lists additional details and facts to round out the coverage of the topics in this chapter. Unlike most of the Cisco Press *Exam Certification Guides*, this "Foundation Summary" does not repeat information presented in the "Foundation Topics" section of the chapter. Please take the time to read and study the details in the "Foundation Topics" section of the chapter, as well as review items noted with a Key Topic icon.

Table 7-5 lists the protocols mentioned in this chapter and their respective standards documents.

Table 7-5 *Protocols and Standards for Chapter 7*

Protocol or Feature	Standard
RIP (Version 1)	RFC 1058
RIP (Version 2)	RFC 2453
RIP Update Authentication	RFC 2082
RIP Triggered Extensions for On-Demand Circuits	RFC 2091

Table 7-6 lists some of the most significant Cisco IOS commands related to the topics in this chapter.

Table 7-6 *Command Reference for Chapter 7*

Command	Command Mode and Description
router rip	Global config; puts user in RIP configuration mode
network *ip-address*	RIP config mode; defines classful network, with all interfaces in that network sending and able to receive RIP advertisements
distribute-list [*access-list-number* | *name* | **prefix** *name*] | {**in** | **out**} [*interface-type* | *interface-number*]	RIP config mode; defines ACL or prefix list to filter RIP updates
ip split-horizon	Interface subcommand; enables or disables split horizon
passive-interface [**default**] {*interface-type interface-number*}	RIP config mode; causes RIP to stop sending updates on the specified interface
timers basic *update invalid holddown flush*	RIP config mode; sets the values for RIP timers
version {**1** | **2**}	RIP config mode; sets the RIP version to version 1 or version 2

Table 7-6 *Command Reference for Chapter 7 (Continued)*

Command	Command Mode and Description
offset-list {*access-list-number* | *access-list-name*} {**in** | **out**} *offset* [*interface-type interface-number*]	RIP config mode; defines rules for RIP to add to the metrics of particular routes
neighbor *ip-address*	RIP config mode; identifies a neighbor to which unicast RIP updates will be sent
show ip route rip	User mode; displays all routes in the IP routing table learned by RIP
show ip rip database	User mode; lists all routes learned by RIP, even if a route is not in the routing table because of a route with lower administrative distance
debug ip rip	Enable mode; displays details of RIP processing
show ip protocols	User mode; lists RIP timer settings, current protocol status, autosummarization actions, and update sources
clear ip route {*network* [*mask*] | ***}**	Enable mode; clears the routing table entry, and with RIP, sends RIP requests, quickly rebuilding the routing table
show ip interface [*type number*] [**brief**]	User mode; lists many interface settings, including split horizon
key chain *name-of-chain*	Global config; defines name of key chain for routing protocol authentication
key *key-id*	Key config mode; identifies a key by number
key *string*	Key config mode; defines the text of the key
send-lifetime [*start-time* {**infinite** | *end-time* | **duration** *seconds*}]	Key config mode; defines when the key is valid to be used for sent updates
accept-lifetime [*start-time* {**infinite** | *end-time* | **duration** *seconds*}]	Key config mode; defines when the key is valid for received updates
ip rip authentication key-chain *name-of-chain*	Interface mode; enables RIP authentication on the interface
ip rip authentication mode {**text** | **md5**}	Interface mode; defines RIP authentication as clear text (default) or MD5

Memory Builders

The CCIE Routing and Switching written exam, like all Cisco CCIE written exams, covers a fairly broad set of topics. This section provides some basic tools to help you exercise your memory about some of the broader topics covered in this chapter.

Fill in Key Tables from Memory

Appendix E, "Key Tables for CCIE Study," on the CD in the back of this book contains empty sets of some of the key summary tables in each chapter. Print Appendix E, refer to this chapter's tables in it, and fill in the tables from memory. Refer to Appendix F, "Solutions for Key Tables for CCIE Study," on the CD to check your answers.

Definitions

Next, take a few moments to write down the definitions for the following terms:

Holddown timer, Invalid timer, Flush timer, Garbage timer, authentication, Update timer, triggered updates, flash updates, split horizon, route poisoning, poison reverse, counting to infinity, hello interval, full update, partial update, Route Tag field, Next Hop field, Triggered Extensions to RIP for On-Demand Circuits, MD5, offset list, prefix list, distribution list, distance vector, metric

Refer to the glossary to check your answers.

Further Reading

This chapter focuses on TCP/IP protocols; much more information can be found in the RFCs mentioned throughout the chapter.

The RIP RFCs listed in Table 7-5 provide good references for RIP concepts.

Jeff Doyle's *Routing TCP/IP*, Volume I, Second Edition, (Cisco Press), has several excellent configuration examples and provides a complete explanation of RIPv2 concepts.

Blueprint topics covered in this chapter:

This chapter covers the following subtopics from the Cisco CCIE Routing and Switching written exam blueprint. Refer to the full blueprint in Table I-1 in the Introduction for more details on the topics covered in each chapter and their context within the blueprint.

- Best Path

- Loop Free Paths

- EIGRP Operations when Alternate Loop-free Paths Are Available and when No Alternate Loop-free Paths Are Available

- EIGRP Queries

- Manual Summarization

- Autosummarization

- EIGRP Stubs

- Troubleshooting EIGRP Neighbor Adjacencies

CHAPTER 8

EIGRP

This chapter covers most of the features, concepts, and commands related to EIGRP. Chapter 10, "IGP Route Redistribution, Route Summarization, and Default Routing," covers a few other details of EIGRP—in particular, route redistribution, route filtering when redistributing, and route summarization.

"Do I Know This Already?" Quiz

Table 8-1 outlines the major headings in this chapter and the corresponding "Do I Know This Already?" quiz questions.

Table 8-1 *"Do I Know This Already?" Foundation Topics Section-to-Question Mapping*

Foundation Topics Section	Questions Covered in This Section	Score
EIGRP Basics and Steady-State Operation	1–4	
EIGRP Convergence	5–7	
EIGRP Configuration	8–9	
Total Score		

In order to best use this pre-chapter assessment, remember to score yourself strictly. You can find the answers in Appendix A, "Answers to the 'Do I Know This Already?' Quizzes."

1. Which of the following items are true of EIGRP?

    a. Authentication can be done using MD5 or clear text.

    b. Uses UDP port 88.

    c. Sends full or partial updates as needed.

    d. Multicasts updates to 224.0.0.10.

2. Four routers (R1, R2, R3, and R4) are attached to the same VLAN. R1 has been configured for an EIGRP Hello timer of 3. R2 has been configured with a **metric weights 0 0 0 1 0 0** command. R3 has been configured with a hold time of 11 seconds. Their IP addresses are

10.1.1.1, 10.1.1.2, 10.1.1.3, and 10.1.1.4, with /24 prefixes, except R4, which has a /23 prefix configured. All other related parameters are set to their default. Select the routers that are able to collectively form neighbor relationships.

   a. R1

   b. R2

   c. R3

   d. R4

   e. None of them can form a neighbor relationship.

3. In the following command output, what do the numbers in the column labeled "H" represent?

```
R1# show ip eigrp neighbors
IP-EIGRP neighbors for process 1
H   Address                 Interface      Hold Uptime    SRTT   RTO   Q    Seq
                                           (sec)          (ms)         Cnt  Num
2   172.31.11.2             Fa0/0          4 00:03:10     1      4500  0    233
1   172.31.11.202           Fa0/0          11 00:04:43    1      4500  0    81
0   172.31.11.201           Fa0/0          14 00:05:11    1927   5000  0    84
```

   a. The current Hold Time countdown

   b. The number of seconds before a Hello is expected

   c. The order in which the neighbors came up

   d. None of the other answers is correct

4. Which of the following is not true regarding the EIGRP Update message?

   a. Updates require an acknowledgement with an Ack message.

   b. Updates can be sent to multicast address 224.0.0.10.

   c. Updates are sent as unicasts when they are retransmitted.

   d. Updates always include all routes known by a router, with partial routing information distributed as part of the EIGRP Reply message.

5. The output of a **show ip eigrp topology** command lists information about subnet 10.1.1.0/24, with two successors, and three routes listed on lines beginning with "via." How many feasible successor routes exist for 10.1.1.0/24?

   a. 0

   b. 1

   c. 2

   d. 3

   e. Cannot determine from the information given

6. The following command output shows R11's topology information for subnet 10.1.1.0/24. Then R11 and R12 (IP address 10.1.11.2) are connected to the same LAN segment. Then R11's EIGRP Hold Time expires for neighbor R12. Which of the following is true about R11's first reaction to the loss of its neighbor R12?

```
R11# show ip eigrp topology
! lines omitted for brevity
P 10.1.1.0/24, 1 successors, FD is 1456
        via 10.1.11.2 (1456/1024), FastEthernet0/0
        via 10.1.14.2 (1756/1424), Serial0/0.4
```

  a. R11 sends Updates to all neighbors poisoning its route to 10.1.1.0/24.

  b. R11 replaces the old route through 10.1.11.2 with the feasible successor route through 10.1.14.2.

  c. R11 sends Query messages to all other neighbors to ensure that the alternate route through 10.1.14.2 is loop free, before using the route.

  d. R11 first Queries only neighbors on interface fa0/0 for alternative routes before Querying the rest of its neighbors.

7. EIGRP router R11 has just changed its route to subnet 10.1.2.0/24 to the active state, and has sent a Query to five neighbors. Which of the following is true about the next step taken by R11?

  a. R11 adds a new route to 10.1.2.0/24 to the routing table as soon as it receives an EIGRP Reply that describes a new route to 10.1.2.0/24.

  b. R11 can add a new route to 10.1.2.0/24 after receiving Reply messages from all 5 neighbors.

  c. R11 can add a new route for 10.1.2.0/24 to the routing table, even without five Reply messages, once the Hold timer expires.

  d. R11 can add a new route for 10.1.2.0/24 to the routing table, even without five Reply messages, once the Dead timer expires.

8. EIGRP router R11 has five interfaces, with IP address 10.1.1.11/24 (interface fa0/0), 10.1.2.11/24, 10.1.3.11/24, 10.1.4.11/24, and 10.1.5.11/24. Its EIGRP configuration is shown below. Which of the following answers is true regarding this router?

```
router eigrp 1
 network 10.1.0.0 0.0.3.255
 passive-interface fa0/0
```

  a. R11 will send EIGRP Updates out fa0/0, but not process received EIGRP Updates.

  b. R11 will advertise connected subnets 10.1.3.0/24 and 10.1.4.0/24.

  c. R11 will advertise subnets 10.1.1.0/24 and 10.1.2.0/24, as well as attempt to send Hellos and Updates on the related interfaces.

  d. The **network** command does not match any interfaces, so EIGRP will essentially do nothing.

9. EIGRP router Br1 is a branch router with two Frame Relay subinterfaces (s0/0.1 and s0/0.2) connecting it to distribution routers. It also has one LAN interface, fa0/0. No other routers connect to the Br1 LAN. Which of the following scenarios prevent router Br1 from sending EIGRP Hellos out its fa0/0 interface?

   a. The inclusion of the **passive-interface fa0/0** command on Br1

   b. The inclusion of the **eigrp stub** command on Br1

   c. The inclusion of the **eigrp stub receive-only** command on Br1

   d. The lack of a **network** command that matches the IP address of Br1's fa0/0 interface

Foundation Topics

EIGRP Basics and Steady-State Operation

Many CCIE candidates have learned many of the details of EIGRP operation and configuration. EIGRP is widely deployed and is thoroughly covered on the CCNP BSCI exam. With that in mind, this chapter strives to review the key terms and concepts briefly, and get right to specific examples that detail EIGRP operation on a Cisco router. To that end, the chapter begins with Table 8-2, which lists some of the key features related to EIGRP.

Table 8-2 *EIGRP Feature Summary*

Feature	Description
Transport	IP, protocol type 88 (does not use UDP or TCP).
Metric	Based on constrained bandwidth and cumulative delay by default, and optionally load, reliability, and MTU.
Hello interval	Interval at which a router sends EIGRP Hello messages on an interface.
Hold timer	Timer used to determine when a neighboring router has failed, based on a router not receiving any EIGRP messages, including Hellos, in this timer period.
Update destination address	Normally sent to 224.0.0.10, with retransmissions being sent to each neighbor's unicast IP address.
Full or partial updates	Full updates are used when new neighbors are discovered; otherwise, partial updates are used.
Authentication	Supports MD5 authentication only.
VLSM/classless	EIGRP includes the mask with each route, also allowing it to support discontiguous networks and VLSM.
Route Tags	Allows EIGRP to tag routes as they are redistributed into EIGRP.
Next-hop field	Supports the advertisement of routes with a different next-hop router than the advertising router.
Manual route summarization	Allows route summarization at any point in the EIGRP network.
Multiprotocol	Supports the advertisement of IPX and AppleTalk routes.

Hellos, Neighbors, and Adjacencies

After a router has been configured for EIGRP, and its interfaces come up, it attempts to find neighbors by sending EIGRP *Hellos* (destination 224.0.0.10). Once a pair of routers have heard each other say Hello, they become adjacent—assuming several key conditions are met. Once neighbors pass the checks in the following list, they are considered to be adjacent. At that point, they can exchange routes and are listed in the output of the **show ip eigrp neighbor** command. Neighbors should always form when these conditions are met, regardless of link type.

- Must pass the authentication process

- Must use the same configured AS number

- Must believe that the source IP address of a received Hello is in that router's primary connected subnet on that interface

- K values must match

The wording of the third item in the list bears a little further scrutiny. The *primary subnet* of an interface is the subnet as implied by the **ip address** command that does not have the **secondary** keyword. An EIGRP router looks at the source IP address of a Hello; if the source IP address is a part of that router's primary subnet of the incoming interface, the Hello passes the IP address check.

This logic leaves open some interesting possibilities. For example, if the routers are misconfigured with different subnet masks, the check may still pass. If one router has configured 10.1.2.1/24, and the other has configured 10.1.2.2/23, they could become adjacent, assuming all the other checks pass. While EIGRP supports secondary IP addresses and subnets, EIGRP sources its messages from the address in the primary subnet, and the IP addresses of neighbors must be in the subnet of the primary subnets.

The last item in the list mentions K values; *K values* are constants that define the multipliers used by EIGRP when calculating metrics. The settings can be changed with a **router eigrp** subcommand **metric weights** *tos k1 k2 k3 k4 k5*. The command defaults to a setting of **0 1 0 1 0 0**, meaning that only bandwidth and delay are used to calculate the metric. (The examples in this chapter usually use the settings **0 0 0 1 0 0**, which removes bandwidth from the calculation and makes the metrics in the examples a little more obvious.)

Besides simply checking to see if the right parameters agree, the Hello messages also serve as an EIGRP keepalive. Adjacent routers continue to multicast Hellos based on each interface's EIGRP *hello interval*. If a router fails to hear from a neighbor for a number of seconds, defined by the EIGRP *Hold Time* for that neighbor, all routes through the neighbor are considered to have failed.

Example 8-1 shows how a router displays some of the basic information regarding EIGRP operations based on Figure 8-1. The example begins with four routers (R1, R2, S1, and S2) that have only their common LAN interfaces up, just to show the Hello process. By the end of the example, the R2-to-R5 PVC will come up, but the EIGRP adjacency will fail due to a K-value mismatch.

Figure 8-1 *Sample Internetwork Used for EIGRP Examples*

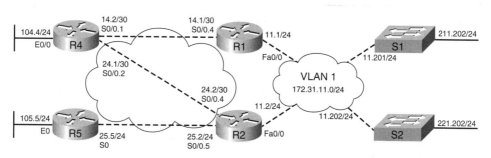

Example 8-1 *Forming EIGRP Adjacencies*

```
! First, a debug is initiated on R1.
R1# debug eigrp packet hello
EIGRP Packets debugging is on
    (HELLO)
Jan 11 13:27:19.714: EIGRP: Received HELLO on FastEthernet0/0 nbr 172.31.11.201
Jan 11 13:27:19.714:   AS 1, Flags 0x0, Seq 0/0 idbQ 0/0 iidbQ un/rely 0/0 peerQ
  un/rely 0/0
!!!!!!!!!!!!!!!!!!!!!!!!!!!!!!!!!!!!!!!!!!!!!!!!!!!!!!!!!!!!!!!!!!!!!!!!!!!!!!!!!!!
! S2's LAN interface brought up, not shown
! Below, a pair of log messages appear, announcing the new neighbor; this message
! appears due to the default router eigrp subcommand eigrp log-neighbor-changes.
Jan 11 13:27:19.995: EIGRP: New peer 172.31.11.202
Jan 11 13:27:19.995: %DUAL-5-NBRCHANGE: IP-EIGRP(0) 1: Neighbor 172.31.11.202
  (FastEthernet0/0) is up: new adjacency
!!!!!!!!!!!!!!!!!!!!!!!!!!!!!!!!!!!!!!!!!!!!!!!!!!!!!!!!!!!!!!!!!!!!!!!!!!!!!!!!!!!
! Next, only neighbors who become adjacent—those that pass all the required
! checks for the parameters—are listed. The Hold timer is shown; it starts at
! its maximum, and decrements towards 0, being reset upon the receipt of any EIGRP
! packet from that neighbor. The "H" column on the left states the order in
! which the neighbors became adjacent.
R1# show ip eigrp neighbors
IP-EIGRP neighbors for process 1
H   Address                 Interface       Hold Uptime   SRTT   RTO  Q   Seq
                                            (sec)         (ms)        Cnt Num
2   172.31.11.2             Fa0/0              4 00:03:10    1   4500  0   233
1   172.31.11.202           Fa0/0             11 00:04:43    1   4500  0   81
0   172.31.11.201           Fa0/0             14 00:05:11 1927   5000  0   84
! Below, the PVC between R2 and R5 came up, but R5's K values do not match R2's.
! Both messages below are log messages, with no debugs enabled on either router.
! Next message on R5 !!!!!!!!!!
03:55:51: %DUAL-5-NBRCHANGE: IP-EIGRP(0) 1: Neighbor 172.31.25.2 (Serial0) is down: K-value
  mismatch
! Next message on R2 !!!!!!!!!!
Jan 11 13:21:45.643: %DUAL-5-NBRCHANGE: IP-EIGRP(0) 1: Neighbor 172.31.25.5 (Serial0/0.5)
  is down: Interface Goodbye received
```

Note that when the PVC between R2 and R5 comes up, the message on R5 is pretty obvious, but the message at R2 says nothing about K values. Some later releases of Cisco IOS mistake invalid EIGRP K-value settings as a newer EIGRP message called a *Goodbye* message. Goodbye messages allow routers to tell each other that they are shutting down in a graceful fashion; be aware that this message may simply be the result of a K-value mismatch.

Interestingly, the Hello and Hold time parameters do not need to match for EIGRP neighbor relationships to form. In fact, a router does not use its own timers when monitoring a neighbor relationship—instead, it uses each neighbor's stated timers, as exchanged in the Hello messages. For example, in Example 8-1, R2 has been configured with Hello and Hold timer settings at 2 and 6 seconds, respectively, with R1 defaulting to 5 and 15 seconds. As R1 monitors its neighbor connection to R2, R1 resets the Hold timer to 6 seconds upon receipt of an EIGRP message. With a hello interval of 2 seconds, R1's listing for hold time for R2 shows it fluctuating between 6 and 4, assuming no Hellos are lost. Note the **show ip eigrp neighbors** command on R1 near the end of the example—under normal operation, this value fluctuates between 6 and 4 seconds. The other neighbors default to Hello and Hold time of 5 and 15, so R1's Hold time in the command output fluctuates between 15 and 10 for these neighbors, assuming no Hellos are lost.

EIGRP Updates

Once routers are adjacent, they can exchange routes using EIGRP *Update* messages. The process follows this general sequence:

1. Initially, full updates are sent, including all routes except those omitted due to split horizon.

2. Once all routes have been exchanged, the updates cease.

3. Future partial updates occur when one or more routes change.

4. If neighbors fail and recover, or new neighbor adjacencies are formed, full updates are sent.

EIGRP uses the *Reliable Transport Protocol (RTP)* to send the multicast EIGRP updates. EIGRP sends updates, waiting on a unicast EIGRP ACK message from each recipient. Figure 8-2 shows the general idea over a LAN.

Figure 8-2 *EIGRP Use of RTP on a LAN*

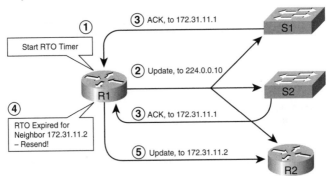

RTP allows the Updates to be sent as multicasts. If any neighbors fail to acknowledge receipt of the multicasted update, RTP resends Updates as unicasts just to those neighbors. The steps run as follows, using Figure 8-2 as an example:

1. The EIGRP sender (R1 in Figure 8-2) starts a *Retransmission Timeout (RTO)* timer for each neighbor when sending a reliable message like an Update. (Cisco IOS actually calculates a *Smoothed Round-Trip Time*, or SRTT, to each neighbor, and derives RTO from the SRTT; both values are shown in the **show ip eigrp neighbor** output. These values vary over time.)

2. R1 sends the multicast EIGRP Update.

3. R1 notes from which neighbors it receives an EIGRP ACK for the Update.

4. RTO expired before router R2 sent its EIGRP ACK.

5. R1 resends the Update, this time as a unicast, and only to the neighbor(s) that did not reply within the RTO time (R2 in this case).

This process allows efficient multicasting of updates under normal circumstances, and efficient retransmission when ACKs do not arrive in time.

EIGRP and RTP use a simple acknowledgement process with a window size of one message. Each Update packet has a sequence number, with the returned ACK message confirming receipt of the message by listing that same sequence number. Example 8-2 shows the location of the sequence number information in both **show** and **debug** commands. (In the example, R1 does a **no shut** on a loopback interface [IP address 172.31.151.1/24], with R1 sending an update advertising the newly-available route.)

Example 8-2 *Sequence Numbers in EIGRP Updates and ACKs*

```
! First, note the show ip eigrp neighbor output on router R2. The last column
! lists the sequence number last used by that neighbor to send a "reliable"
! packet. So, R2 expects R1's next reliable EIGRP message to have sequence number
! 225. Also, the RTO calculations are listed for each neighbor. Note
! that the SRTT value is 0 until some reliable packets are exchanged, as SRTT
! is calculated based on actual round-trip time measurements.
R2# sh ip eigrp neighbor
IP-EIGRP neighbors for process 1
H   Address              Interface     Hold Uptime    SRTT   RTO  Q   Seq
                                       (sec)          (ms)        Cnt Num
2   172.31.11.1          Fa0/0          5 01:14:03     1     200  0   224
1   172.31.11.202        Fa0/0         13 01:15:36     1     200  0   92
0   172.31.11.201        Fa0/0         13 01:16:04    257   1542  0   96
!!!!!!!!!!!!!!!!!!!!!!!!!!!!!!!!!!!!!!!!!!!!!!!!!!!!!!!!!!!!!!!!!!!!!!!!!!!!!!!!!!
! R1 - R1 - R1 - R1
! Next, the debug command on R1 enables debug for Update and Ack packets.
```

continues

Example 8-2 *Sequence Numbers in EIGRP Updates and ACKs (Continued)*

```
R1# debug eigrp packet update ack
EIGRP Packets debugging is on
    (UPDATE, ACK)
! Not Shown: R1's loop0 is "no shutdown," interface address 172.31.151.1/24.
! Below, the debug messages show R1's update, and each of the other three routers'
! Acks. Note R1's update has "sequence" 225, and the Acks list that same sequence
! number after the slash.
Jan 11 14:43:35.844: EIGRP: Enqueueing UPDATE on FastEthernet0/0 iidbQ un/rely 0/1 serno
  207-207
Jan 11 14:43:35.848: EIGRP: Sending UPDATE on FastEthernet0/0
Jan 11 14:43:35.848:   AS 1, Flags 0x0, Seq 225/0 idbQ 0/0 iidbQ un/rely 0/0 serno 207-207
Jan 11 14:43:35.848: EIGRP: Received ACK on FastEthernet0/0 nbr 172.31.11.202
Jan 11 14:43:35.852:   AS 1, Flags 0x0, Seq 0/225 idbQ 0/0 iidbQ un/rely 0/0 peerQ un/rely
  0/1
Jan 11 14:43:35.852: EIGRP: Received ACK on FastEthernet0/0 nbr 172.31.11.2
Jan 11 14:43:35.852:   AS 1, Flags 0x0, Seq 0/225 idbQ 0/0 iidbQ un/rely 0/0 peerQ un/rely
  0/1
```

The EIGRP Topology Table

EIGRP uses three tables: the neighbor table, the topology table, and the IP routing table. The neighbor table keeps state information regarding neighbors, and is displayed using the **show ip eigrp neighbors** command. EIGRP Update messages fill the routers' EIGRP topology tables. Based on the contents of the topology table, each router chooses its best routes and installs these routes in its respective IP routing table.

An EIGRP router calculates the metric for each route based on the components of the metric. When a neighboring router advertises a route, the Update includes the metric component values for each route. The router then considers the received metric values, as well its own interfaces settings, to calculate its own metric for each route. The default metric components are cumulative delay, in tens of microseconds, and the constraining bandwidth for the entire route, in bits per second. By setting the correct K values in the **metric weights** command, EIGRP can also consider link load, reliability, and MTU. Cisco recommends not using those values, in large part due to the fluctuation created by the rapidly changing calculated metrics and repeated routing reconvergence.

Figure 8-3 depicts the general logic relating to the metric components in a routing update, showing the units on the **bandwidth** and **delay** commands versus the contents of the updates.

> **NOTE** A router considers its interface delay settings, as defined with the **delay** interface subcommand, when calculating EIGRP metrics. The **delay** command's units are tens of microseconds, so a **delay 1** command sets the interface delay as 10 microseconds.

Figure 8-3   *EIGRP Update and Computing the Metric*

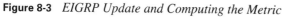

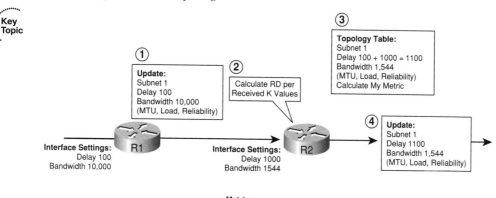

Because the received update includes the neighbor's metric components, a router can calculate the advertising neighbor's metric for a route—called the *reported distance (RD)*. A router can, of course, also calculate its own metric for a particular route, after adding its own interface delay and considering whether it should adjust the value for the constraining bandwidth. For example, consider the four steps outlined in Figure 8-3:

1. R1 advertises a route, with bandwidth = 10,000 and delay = 100.

2. R2 calculates the RD for this route per the received K values.

3. R2 updates its topology table, adding delay 1000 because the interface on which R2 received the update has a delay setting of 1000. It also uses a new bandwidth setting, because the received Update's bandwidth (10,000) was greater than R2's incoming interface's bandwidth (1544).

4. R2's update to another neighbor includes the new (cumulative) delay and the new (constraining) bandwidth.

Assuming default K-value settings, the EIGRP formula for the metric calculation is

$$\text{Metric} = 256 \,(10^7/\text{bandwidth}) + 256 \,(\text{delay})$$

The **show ip eigrp topology** command lists the RD and the locally computed metric for the entries in the EIGRP topology table. Example 8-3 shows a few details of where the RD and local metric can be seen in **show** command output. The example is based on Figure 8-1, with all routers and interfaces now working properly. Also, to keep things simple, the **delay** command has been used to set all links to **delay 1** (LANs), **delay 2** (WANs), or **delay 3** (loopbacks). Also, the **metric weights 0 0 0 1 0 0** command was used on each router, taking bandwidth out of the calculation, making the calculated metrics a little more meaningful in the command output.

Example 8-3 *EIGRP Topology Table*

```
! First, the numbers in parentheses show this router's (R1's) calculated metric,
! then a "/", then the RD. For example, S1 advertised the route to 211.0/24, with
! R1 calculating S1's metric (the RD) as 768. Delay 3 was set on S1's loopback
! (where 211.0/24 resides), so its metric was 3*256=768. R1's metric adds delay 1,
! for a metric of 4*256=1024.
R1# show ip eigrp topology
IP-EIGRP Topology Table for AS(1)/ID(172.31.16.1)

Codes: P - Passive, A - Active, U - Update, Q - Query, R - Reply,
       r - reply Status, s - sia Status
P 172.31.151.0/24, 1 successors, FD is 768
        via Connected, Loopback1
P 172.31.211.0/24, 1 successors, FD is 1024
        via 172.31.11.201 (1024/768), FastEthernet0/0
P 172.31.24.0/30, 1 successors, FD is 768
        via 172.31.11.2 (768/512), FastEthernet0/0
        via 172.31.14.2 (1024/512), Serial0/0.4
! Lines omitted for brevity
! Below, the metric in the IP routing table entries match the first number in
! the parentheses, as well as the number listed as "FD is…" in the output above.
R1# show ip route
! omitted legend for brevity
     172.31.0.0/16 is variably subnetted, 9 subnets, 2 masks
D       172.31.211.0/24 [90/1024] via 172.31.11.201, 00:29:42, FastEthernet0/0
D       172.31.24.0/30 [90/768] via 172.31.11.2, 00:29:44, FastEthernet0/0
! Lines omitted for brevity
```

Key
Topic

The **show ip eigrp topology** command lists a few additional very important concepts and terms related to how EIGRP chooses between multiple possible routes to the same prefix. First, the term *feasible distance (FD)* refers to this router's best calculated metric among all possible routes to reach a particular prefix. The FD is listed as "FD is *x*" in the command output. The route that has this best FD is called the *successor route*, and is installed in the routing table. The successor route's metric is by definition called the feasible distance, so that metric is what shows up in the routes shown with the **show ip route** command. These additional terms all relate to how EIGRP processes convergence events, which is explained next.

EIGRP Convergence

Once all the EIGRP routers have learned all the routes in the network, and placed the best routes (the successor routes) in their IP routing tables, their EIGRP processes simply continue to send Hellos, expect to receive Hellos, and look for any changes to the network. When those changes do occur, EIGRP must converge to use the best available routes. This section covers the three major components of EIGRP convergence: input events, local computation (which includes looking for feasible successors), and using active querying to find alternative routes.

Table 8-3 lists several of the key EIGRP terms related to convergence. Following the table, the text jumps right into what EIGRP does when a topology or metric change occurs.

Table 8-3 *EIGRP Features Related to Convergence*

EIGRP Convergence Function	Description
Reported distance (RD)	The metric (distance) of a route as reported by a neighboring router
Feasible distance (FD)	The metric value for the lowest-metric path to reach a particular subnet
Feasibility condition	When multiple routes to reach one subnet exist, the case in which one route's RD is lower than the FD
Successor route	The route to each destination prefix for which the metric is the lowest metric
Feasible successor (FS)	A route that is not a successor route but meets the feasibility condition; can be used when the successor route fails, without causing loops
Input event	Any occurrence that could change a router's EIGRP topology table
Local computation	An EIGRP router's reaction to an input event, leading to the use of a feasible successor or going active on a route

Input Events and Local Computation

An EIGRP router needs to react when an *input event* occurs. The obvious input events are when a router learns of new prefixes via newly received routing updates, when an interface fails, or when a neighbor fails. Because EIGRP sends updates only as a result of changed or new topology information, a router must consider the update and decide if any of its routes have changed.

When an input event implies that a route has failed, the router performs *local computation*, a fancy term for a process that can be boiled down to relatively simple logic. In short, the result of local computation is that the router either is able to choose a replacement route locally, without having to ask any neighbors, or is required to ask neighbors for help. Simply put, for a failed route, local computation does the following:

■ If FS routes exist, install the lowest-metric FS route into the routing table, and send Updates to neighbors to notify them of the new route.

■ If no FS route exists, actively query neighbors for a new route.

To be an FS route, a route must meet the *feasibility condition*, defined as follows:

The RD must be lower than this router's current FD for the route.

The local computation is best understood by looking at an example. Figure 8-4 shows the same network as in Figure 8-1, but with delay values shown. Example 8-4 begins with R4 using a successor route to 172.31.211.0/24, through R1. R4 also has an FS route to 172.31.211.0/24 through R2. The example shows what happens when the PVC from R1 to R4 fails, and R4's neighbor relationship with R1 fails, causing R4 to perform local computation and start using its FS route through R2.

Figure 8-4 *Network Used for EIGRP Convergence Examples*

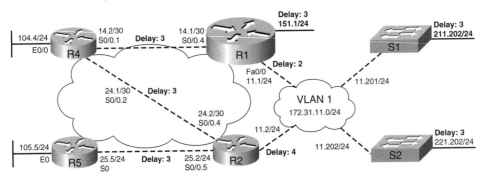

> **NOTE** The routers have disabled the use of bandwidth in the EIGRP metric calculation, so all metrics in Example 8-4 are multiples of 256.

Example 8-4 *Local Computation: R1-R4 Link Fails; R4 Finds an FS to 172.31.211.0/24 Through R2*

```
! First, the current successor route on R4 points out S0/0.1, to R1, metric 2048.
R4# show ip route
! lines omitted for brevity
      172.31.0.0/16 is variably subnetted, 9 subnets, 2 masks
D        172.31.211.0/24 [90/2048] via 172.31.14.1, 00:01:46, Serial0/0.1
! Below, the FD is listed as 2048 as well. The topology entry for the successor
! has the same 2048 metric listed as the first number in parentheses; the second
! number is the RD on R1 (1280). The second topology entry for this route lists
! metric 2560, RD 1792; with RD in the second route being less than the FD, this
! second route meets the feasibility condition, making it an FS route.
R4# show ip eigrp topology
IP-EIGRP Topology Table for AS(1)/ID(172.31.104.4)

Codes: P - Passive, A - Active, U - Update, Q - Query, R - Reply,
r - reply Status, s - sia Status
! lines omitted for brevity
P 172.31.211.0/24, 1 successors, FD is 2048
        via 172.31.14.1 (2048/1280), Serial0/0.1
        via 172.31.24.2 (2560/1792), Serial0/0.2
! Next, R4 loses Neighbor R1, with EIGRP Finite State Machine (FSM) debug on.
R4# debug eigrp fsm
```

Example 8-4   *Local Computation: R1-R4 Link Fails; R4 Finds an FS to 172.31.211.0/24 Through R2 (Continued)*

```
EIGRP FSM Events/Actions debugging is on
Jan 12 07:17:42.391: %DUAL-5-NBRCHANGE: IP-EIGRP(0) 1: Neighbor 172.31.14.1 (Serial0/0.1)
  is down: holding time expired
! Below, debug messages have been edited to only show messages relating to
! the route to 172.31.211.0/24. R4 looks for an FS, finds it, replaces the old
! successor with the FS, and sends updates telling neighbors about the new route.
Jan 12 07:17:42.399: DUAL: Destination 172.31.211.0/24
Jan 12 07:17:42.399: DUAL: Find FS for dest 172.31.211.0/24. FD is 2048, RD is 2048
Jan 12 07:17:42.399: DUAL: 172.31.14.1 metric 4294967295/4294967295
Jan 12 07:17:42.399: DUAL: 172.31.24.2 metric 2560/1792 found Dmin is 2560
Jan 12 07:17:42.399: DUAL: Removing dest 172.31.211.0/24, nexthop 172.31.14.1
Jan 12 07:17:42.403: DUAL: RT installed 172.31.211.0/24 via 172.31.24.2
Jan 12 07:17:42.403: DUAL: Send update about 172.31.211.0/24.  Reason: metric chg
Jan 12 07:17:42.403: DUAL: Send update about 172.31.211.0/24.  Reason: new if
! Finally, note that the FD is unchanged; the FD is never raised until the route
! has been actively queried. The new route info has been put in the routing table.
R4# show ip eigrp topology
! lines omitted for brevity
P 172.31.211.0/24, 1 successors, FD is 2048
        via 172.31.24.2 (2560/1792), Serial0/0.2
R4# show ip route
! Lines omitted for brevity
D       172.31.211.0/24 [90/2560] via 172.31.24.2, 00:00:25, Serial0/0.2
```

Key
Topic

Going Active on a Route

The second branch in the local computation logic causes the EIGRP router to ask its neighbors about their current best route to a subnet, hoping to find an available, loop-free alternative route to that subnet. When no FS route is found, the EIGRP router goes active for the route. *Going active* is jargon for the process of changing a route's status to active. Once the router is active, EIGRP multicasts *Query* messages to its neighbors, asking the neighbors if they have a valid route to the subnet. The neighbors should unicast EIGRP *Reply* packets back to the original router, stating whether or not they have a current loop-free route with which to reach that prefix.

Once a router receives Reply messages from all the neighbors to which it sent Queries, the router updates its topology table with all the new information learned in the Reply messages, recomputes metrics for any known routes, and chooses a new successor. Of course, if no routes to that subnet are found, this router simply does not add a route to the routing table.

> **NOTE**   The EIGRP term "active" refers to a route for which a router is currently using the Query process to find a loop-free alternative route. Conversely, a route is in passive state when it is not in an active state.

The neighboring routers view any received Query messages as an input event. Each neighbor router's behavior when receiving a Query can be summarized as follows:

1. If the router does not have an entry in its topology table for that subnet, it sends an EIGRP Reply packet stating that it has no route.

2. If the router's successor for that subnet is unchanged, or an FS is found, the neighbor sends back an EIGRP Reply message with the details of the route.

3. If the conditions in step 1 or 2 do not exist, the router itself goes active, and withholds its EIGRP response to the original Query, until all of its neighbors respond.

Note that the logic in the third step can result in a route for which the Active Querying process never completes. Routes that stay in active state too long are considered to be *stuck-in-active* routes. The related concepts are covered in the next section.

Example 8-5 shows an example of the Query process. The example is again based on Figure 8-4, with R4 again losing its neighbor relationship with R1. In this case, R4's local computation will not find an FS for its failed route to 172.31.151.0/24, so it must go active.

Example 8-5 *R1-R4 Link Fails; R4 Actively Queries for 172.31.151.0/24*

```
! First, the show ip eigrp topology command only lists the successor route, and no
! FS routes. This command does not list non-FS routes.
R4# show ip eigrp topo
! Lines omitted for brevity

P 172.31.151.0/24, 1 successors, FD is 1536
        via 172.31.14.1 (1536/768), Serial0/0.1
! Below, the show ip eigrp topology all-links command includes non-FS routes,
! in this case including the non-FS route to 151.0/24 through R2. Note that this
! alternate non-FS route's RD is 1792, which is more than the FD of 1536.
R4# show ip eigrp topology all-links
! Lines omitted for brevity

P 172.31.151.0/24, 1 successors, FD is 1536, serno 175
        via 172.31.14.1 (1536/768), Serial0/0.1
        via 172.31.24.2 (2560/1792), Serial0/0.2
! Next, the FSM debug is again enabled, and R4 loses neighbor R1.
R4# debug eigrp fsm
Jan 12 07:16:04.099: %DUAL-5-NBRCHANGE: IP-EIGRP(0) 1: Neighbor 172.31.14.1 (Serial0/0.1)
  is down: holding time expired
!!!!!!!!!!!!!!!!!!!!!!!!!!!!!!!!!!!!!!!!!!!!!!!!!!!!!!!!!!!!!!!!!!!!!!!!!!!!!!!!!!!!
! Below, R4 looks for an FS for route 172.31.151.0/24, and does not find one—
! so it enters active state. R4 sends a query to its one remaining neighbor (R2),
! and keeps track of the number of outstanding Queries (1). Upon receiving the
! Reply from R2, it can update its topology table, and repeat local computation,
! and use the now-best route through R2.
Jan 12 07:17:42.391: %DUAL-5-NBRCHANGE: IP-EIGRP(0) 1: Neighbor 172.31.14.1 (Serial0/0.1)
  is down: holding time expired
```

Key Topic

Key Topic

Example 8-5 *R1-R4 Link Fails; R4 Actively Queries for 172.31.151.0/24 (Continued)*

```
Jan 12 07:17:42.391: DUAL: linkdown: start - 172.31.14.1 via Serial0/0.1
Jan 12 07:17:42.391: DUAL: Destination 172.31.151.0/24
Jan 12 07:17:42.391: DUAL: Find FS for dest 172.31.151.0/24. FD is 1536, RD is 1536
Jan 12 07:17:42.395: DUAL:  172.31.14.1 metric 4294967295/4294967295
Jan 12 07:17:42.395: DUAL:  172.31.24.2 metric 2560/1792 not found Dmin is 2560
Jan 12 07:17:42.395: DUAL: Dest 172.31.151.0/24 entering active state.
Jan 12 07:17:42.395: DUAL: Set reply-status table. Count is 1.
Jan 12 07:17:42.395: DUAL: Not doing split horizon
Jan 12 07:17:42.459: DUAL: rcvreply: 172.31.151.0/24 via 172.31.24.2 metric 2560/1792
Jan 12 07:17:42.459: DUAL: reply count is 1
Jan 12 07:17:42.459: DUAL: Clearing handle 0, count now 0
Jan 12 07:17:42.463: DUAL: Freeing reply status table
Jan 12 07:17:42.463: DUAL: Find FS for dest 172.31.151.0/24. FD is 4294967295, RD is
  4294967295 found
Jan 12 07:17:42.463: DUAL: Removing dest 172.31.151.0/24, nexthop 172.31.14.1
Jan 12 07:17:42.463: DUAL: RT installed 172.31.151.0/24 via 172.31.24.2
Jan 12 07:17:42.467: DUAL: Send update about 172.31.151.0/24.  Reason: metric chg
Jan 12 07:17:42.467: DUAL: Send update about 172.31.151.0/24.  Reason: new if
! Next, note that because R4 actively queried for the route, the FD could change.
R4# show ip eigrp topo
IP-EIGRP Topology Table for AS(1)/ID(172.31.104.4)

Codes: P - Passive, A - Active, U - Update, Q - Query, R - Reply,
       r - reply Status, s - sia Status

P 172.31.151.0/24, 1 successors, FD is 2560
via 172.31.24.2 (2560/1792), Serial0/0.2
```

Of particular note in this example, look for the **debug** message starting with "Dual: rcvreply:" (highlighted). This message means that the router received an EIGRP Reply message, in this case from R2. The message includes R2's valid routing information for 172.31.151.0/24. Also note that the FD was recomputed, whereas it was not in Example 8-4 when an FS route was found.

> **NOTE** Query messages use reliable transmission via RTP and are multicasts; Reply messages are reliable and are unicasts. Both are acknowledged using Ack messages.

> **NOTE** The EIGRP term *Diffusing Update Algorithm (DUAL)* refers to the totality of the logic used by EIGRP to calculate new routes. The term is based on the logic used as Query messages go outward from a router, with the outward movement stopped when routers Reply.

Stuck-in-Active

Any router in active state for a route must wait for a Reply to each of its Query messages. It is possible for a router to wait several minutes for all the replies, because neighboring routers might also need to go active, and then their neighbors might need to go active, and so on—each withholding its Reply message until it in turn receives all of its Reply messages. In normal operation, the process should complete; to handle exception cases, EIGRP includes a timer called the *Active timer*, which limits the amount of time in which a route can stay active. If the Active timer expires before a router receives all of its Reply messages, the router places the route in a *stuck-in-active state*. The router also brings down any neighbors from which no corresponding Reply was received, thinking that any neighbors that did not send a Reply are having problems.

In some conditions—large, redundant networks, flapping interfaces, or networks with lots of packet loss, to name a few—neighbors might be working fine, but their Reply messages may not complete within the Active timer. To avoid the downside of having the route become stuck-in-active, and losing all routes through a possibly still-working neighbor, you can disable the Active timer by using the **timers active-time disabled** subcommand under **router eigrp**.

Limiting Query Scope

Although disabling the Active timer can prevent stuck-in-active routes, a better solution to the prolonged wait for Reply messages is to limit the scope of Query messages. By reducing the number of neighbors that receive the messages, and by limiting the number of hops away the queries flow, you can greatly reduce the time required to receive all Reply messages.

Two methods can be used to limit query scope. The first is route summarization. When a Query reaches a router that has a summarized route, but not the specific route in the query, the router immediately replies that it does not have that route. For instance, a router with the route 172.31.0.0/16 in its topology table, upon receiving a query for 172.31.151.0/24, immediately sends a Reply, stating it does not have a route to 172.31.151.0/24. With well-designed route summarization, EIGRP queries can be limited to a few hops. (Chapter 11, "IGP Redistribution, Route Summarization, and Default Routing," covers route summarization details.)

The use of EIGRP *stub routers* also limits the query scope. Stub routers, by definition, should not be used as transit routers for traffic. In Figure 8-4, R5 would be a classic candidate to be a stub router. Also, if R4 should not be used to forward traffic from R1 over to R2, or vice versa, R4 could be a stub as well. In either case, non-stub routers do not send Query messages to the stub routers, knowing that the stub routers should not be transit routers. (Stub router configuration is covered in the next section.)

EIGRP Configuration

This section explains the majority of the options for EIGRP configuration. The "Foundation Summary" section includes the full syntax of the commands, along with some comments, in Table 8-6.

EIGRP Configuration Example

Example 8-6 lists the configuration for R1, R2, R4, and R5 from Figure 8-4. The routers were configured based on the following design goals:

- Enable EIGRP on all interfaces.

■ Configure K values to ignore bandwidth.

■ Configure R5 as an EIGRP stub router.

■ Ensure that R2's LAN interface uses a Hello and Hold time of 2 and 6, respectively.

■ Configure R4 to allow 75 percent of interface bandwidth for EIGRP updates.

■ Advertise R4's LAN subnet, but do not attempt to send or receive EIGRP updates on the LAN.

Example 8-6 *Basic EIGRP Configuration on R1, R2, R4, and R5*

```
! Below, R1 EIGRP-related configuration
! The default metric weights are "0 1 0 1 0 0".
router eigrp 1
 network 172.31.0.0
 metric weights 0 0 0 1 0 0
! R2 EIGRP-related configuration
! Note the commands used to change the Hello and Hold Time values per interface.
! R2's Hellos advertise the timer values, and other routers on the LAN use these
! values on their neighbor relationship with R2. Also below, note the use of the
! inverse mask to match a subset of interfaces on a single network command.
interface FastEthernet0/0
 ip hello-interval eigrp 1 2
 ip hold-time eigrp 1 6
!
router eigrp 1
 network 10.0.0.0
 network 172.31.11.2 0.0.0.0
 network 172.31.24.0 0.0.1.255
 metric weights 0 0 0 1 0 0
! R4 EIGRP-related configuration
! Below, the percentage of the interface bandwidth used for EIGRP is changed. The
! value can go over 100% to allow for cases in which the bandwidth has
! been artificially lowered to impact the EIGRP metric. Also note that R4 makes
! its e0/0 interface passive, meaning no routes learned or advertised on E0/0.
interface Serial0/0.1 point-to-point
 bandwidth 64
 ip bandwidth-percent eigrp 1 150
!
router eigrp 1
 passive-interface Ethernet0/0
 network 172.31.0.0
 metric weights 0 0 0 1 0 0
! R5 EIGRP-related configuration
! Below, note R5's configuration as a stub area.
```

continues

Example 8-6 *Basic EIGRP Configuration on R1, R2, R4, and R5 (Continued)*

```
router eigrp 1
 network 172.31.0.0
 metric weights 0 0 0 1 0 0
 eigrp stub connected summary
```

EIGRP allows for better control of the three functions enabled on an interface by the EIGRP **network** command. (The three functions are advertising the connected subnet, sending routing updates, and receiving routing updates.) Like OSPF, the EIGRP **network** command supports configuration of an optional wildcard mask (as seen on R4 in Example 8-6), allowing each interface to be matched individually—and making it simple to enable EIGRP on a subset of interfaces. Also, a LAN subnet might have a single router attached to it, so there is no need to attempt to send or receive updates on those interfaces. By enabling EIGRP on the interface with a **network** command, and then configuring the **passive-interface** command, you can stop the router from sending Hellos. If a router does not send Hellos, it forms no neighbor adjacencies, and it then neither sends nor receives updates on that LAN.

Example 8-6 also shows R5 configured as an EIGRP stub router. R5 announces itself as a stub router via its EIGRP Hellos. As a result, R2 will not send Query messages to R5, limiting the scope of Query messages.

The **eigrp stub** command has several options, with the default options (**connected** and **summary**) shown on the last line of Example 8-6. (Note that the **eigrp stub** command was typed, and IOS added the **connected** and **summary** options in the configuration.) Table 8-4 lists the **eigrp stub** command options, and explains some of the logic behind using them.

Table 8-4 *Options on the* **eigrp stub** *Command*

Option	This Router Is Allowed To...
connected	Advertise connected routes, but only for interfaces matched with a **network** command.
summary	Advertise auto-summarized or statically configured summary routes.
static	Advertise static routes, assuming the **redistribute static** command is configured.
redistributed	Advertise redistributed routes, assuming redistribution is configured.
receive-only	Not advertise any routes. This option cannot be used with any other option.

Note that the stub option still requires the stub router to form neighbor relationships, even in receive-only mode. The stub router simply performs less work and reduces the query scope.

Example 8-6 also shows the EIGRP hello interval and hold time being set. These parameters can be set per interface using the interface subcommands **ip hello-interval eigrp** *asn seconds* and

ip hold-time eigrp *asn seconds*, respectively. The default EIGRP hello interval defaults to 5 seconds on most interfaces, with NBMA interfaces whose bandwidth is T1 or slower using a hello interval of 60 seconds. The hold time defaults to 15 and 180 seconds, respectively—three times the default hello interval. However, if you change the hello interval, the hold time default does not automatically change to three times the new hello interval; instead, it remains at 15 or 180 seconds.

EIGRP Load Balancing

EIGRP allows for up to six equal-metric routes to be installed into the IP routing table at the same time. However, because of the complex EIGRP metric calculation, metrics may often be close to each other, but not exactly equal. To allow for metrics that are somewhat close in value to be considered equal, and added to the IP routing table, you can use the **variance** *multiplier* command. The *multiplier* defines a value that is multiplied by the lowest metric (in other words, the FD, which is the metric of the successor route). If any other routes have a better metric than that product of variance * FD, those other routes are considered equal, and added to the routing table.

> **NOTE** EIGRP allows only FS routes to be considered for addition as a result of using the **variance** command. Otherwise, routing loops could occur.

Once the multiple routes for the same destination are in the routing table, EIGRP allows several options for balancing traffic across the routes. Table 8-5 summarizes the commands that impact how load balancing is done with EIGRP, plus the other commands related to installing multiple EIGRP routes into the same subnet. Note that these commands are all subcommands under **router eigrp**.

Table 8-5 *EIGRP Route Load-Balancing Commands*

Router EIGRP Subcommand	Meaning
variance	Any FS route whose metric is less than the variance value multiplied by the FD is added to the routing table (within the restrictions of the **maximum-paths** command).
maximum-paths {1..6}	The maximum number of routes to the same destination allowed in the routing table. Defaults to 4.
traffic-share balanced	The router balances across the routes, giving more packets to lower-metric routes.
traffic-share min	Although multiple routes are installed, sends traffic using only the lowest-metric route.
traffic-share balanced across-interfaces	If more routes exist than are allowed with the **maximum-paths** setting, the router chooses routes with different outgoing interfaces, for better balancing.
No **traffic-share** command configured	Balances evenly across routes, ignoring EIGRP metrics.

EIGRP Authentication

EIGRP authentication, much like OSPF authentication, requires the creation of keys and requires authentication to be enabled on a per-interface basis. The keys are used as the secret (private) key used in an MD5 calculation. (EIGRP does not support clear-text authentication.)

Multiple keys are allowed and are grouped together using a construct called a *key chain*. A key chain is simply a set of related keys, each of which has a different number and may be restricted to a time period. By allowing multiple related keys in a key chain, with each key valid during specified time periods, the engineer can easily plan for migration to new keys in the future. (NTP is recommended when keys are restricted by time ranges, because the local times on the routers must be synchronized for this feature to work correctly.)

Cisco IOS enables the EIGRP authentication process on a per-interface basis using the command **ip authentication mode eigrp** *asn* **md5**, and refers to the key chain that holds the keys with the **ip authentication key-chain eigrp** *asn key_name* interface subcommand. The router looks in the key chain and selects the key(s) valid at that particular time.

Example 8-7 shows the EIGRP authentication configuration for R1, R2, and R4, and includes a few additional comments. The network in Figure 8-1 is the basis for this example.

Example 8-7 *EIGRP Authentication (R1, R2, and R4)*

```
! First, R1 Config
! Chain "carkeys" will be used on R1's LAN. R1 will use key "fred" for
! about a month, and then start using "wilma."
key chain carkeys
 key 1
  key-string fred
  accept-lifetime 08:00:00 Jun 11 2007 08:00:00 Jul 11 2007
  send-lifetime 08:00:00 Jun 11 2007 08:00:00 Jul 11 2007
 key 2
  key-string wilma
  accept-lifetime 08:00:00 Jul 10 2007 08:00:00 Aug 11 2007
  send-lifetime 08:00:00 Jul 10 2007 08:00:00 Aug 11 2007
! Next, key chain "anothersetofkeys" defines the key to be
! used with R4.
key chain anothersetofkeys
 key 1
  key-string barney
! Next, R1's interface subcommands are shown.
! The key chain is referenced
! using the ip eigrp 1 authentication command.
interface FastEthernet0/0
 ip address 172.31.11.1 255.255.255.0
 ip authentication mode eigrp 1 md5
 ip authentication key-chain eigrp 1 carkeys
! Below, R1 enables EIGRP authentication on
```

Example 8-7 *EIGRP Authentication (R1, R2, and R4)*

```
! the subinterface connecting to R4.
interface Serial0/0.4 point-to-point
  ip address 172.31.14.1 255.255.255.252
  ip authentication mode eigrp 1 md5
  ip authentication key-chain eigrp 1 anothersetofkeys
! R2 Config - R2 Config - R2 Config
! Next, on R2, the key chain name (housekeys) differs with
! R1's key chain name (carkeys), but
! the key string "fred" is the same.
key chain housekeys
 key 1
  key-string fred
interface FastEthernet0/0
 ip address 172.31.11.2 255.255.255.0
 ip authentication mode eigrp 1 md5
 ip authentication key-chain eigrp 1 housekeys
! R4 Config - R4 Config - R4 Config
! Next, R4 enables EIGRP authentication on its subinterface connecting to R1.
key chain boatkeys
 key 1
  key-string barney
 !
interface Serial0/0.1 point-to-point
 ip address 172.31.14.2 255.255.255.252
 ip authentication mode eigrp 1 md5
 ip authentication key-chain eigrp 1 boatkeys
```

Although the comments in Example 8-7 explain the more important details, one other point needs to be made regarding the key lifetimes. The configuration shows that two of the keys' lifetimes overlap by a day. On that day, EIGRP would use the key with the lowest key number. By using such logic, you could start by configuring one key. Later, you could then add a second key on all the routers, with overlapping time periods, but still use the original key. Finally, you could either let the first key expire or delete the first key, allowing for easy key migration.

EIGRP Automatic Summarization

Key
Topic

EIGRP defaults to use automatic summarization, or autosummarization. Autosummarization can be disabled with the **no auto-summary** command under **router eigrp process**. Unless you particularly want a router to autosummarize using EIGRP, you should configure the **no auto-summary** command to disable this feature. (Note that EIGRP autosummarization works the same in concept as autosummarization with RIP, which discussed in the Chapter 7 section titled "Enabling RIP and the Effects of Autosummarization.")

EIGRP Split Horizon

EIGRP bounds its updates using split-horizon logic. Split horizon can be disabled on a per-interface basis by using the **no ip split-horizon eigrp** *asn* interface subcommand. Most interface types enable split horizon by default, with the notable exception of a physical serial interface configured for Frame Relay.

EIGRP Route Filtering

Outbound and inbound EIGRP updates can be filtered at any interface, or for the entire EIGRP process. To filter the routes, the **distribute-list** command is used under **router eigrp** *asn*, referencing an IP ACL.

The generic command, when creating an EIGRP distribution list that uses an ACL, is

```
distribute-list {access-list-number | name} {in | out} [interface-type interface-number]
```

Example 8-8 shows an inbound distribution list on router R2 (in the example in Figure 8-1), filtering routes in the 172.31.196.0/22 range. For this example, R2 now receives several /24 and /30 routes from S2, using EIGRP. The routes are in the range of 172.31.192.0/21, and the goal is to filter the upper half of that numeric range.

Example 8-8 *EIGRP Distribution List*

```
! The example begins with a list of the routes that should be filtered.
! Note that the longer-prefixes option below makes the command
! list all routes in the range.
! The highlighted lines are the ones that will be filtered.
R2# show ip route 172.31.192.0 255.255.248.0 longer-prefixes
! Lines omitted for brevity; in this case, the legend was deleted
172.31.0.0/16 is variably subnetted, 24 subnets, 3 masks
D       172.31.195.0/30 [120/1] via 172.31.11.202, 00:00:18, FastEthernet0/0
D       172.31.194.0/24 [120/1] via 172.31.11.202, 00:00:18, FastEthernet0/0
D       172.31.196.4/30 [120/1] via 172.31.11.202, 00:00:18, FastEthernet0/0
D       172.31.195.4/30 [120/1] via 172.31.11.202, 00:00:18, FastEthernet0/0
D       172.31.197.0/24 [120/1] via 172.31.11.202, 00:00:19, FastEthernet0/0
D       172.31.196.0/30 [120/1] via 172.31.11.202, 00:00:19, FastEthernet0/0
D       172.31.195.8/30 [120/1] via 172.31.11.202, 00:00:19, FastEthernet0/0
! R2's Configuration follows. access-list 2 denies all subnets in the
! 172.31.196.0/22 range, which is the set of subnets that needs to be filtered.
! The distribute-list 2 in FastEthernet0/0 command tells EIGRP to filter inbound
! EIGRP updates that come in fa0/0.
router eigrp 1
 network 10.0.0.0
 network 172.31.0.0
 distribute-list 2 in FastEthernet0/0
!
access-list 2 deny   172.31.196.0 0.0.3.255
access-list 2 permit any
```

Example 8-8 *EIGRP Distribution List (Continued)*

```
! Below, the results show three less subnets in the larger 172.31.192.0/21 range.
R2# show ip route 172.31.192.0 255.255.248.0 longer-prefixes
! Lines omitted for brevity; in this case, the legend was deleted
     172.31.0.0/16 is variably subnetted, 21 subnets, 3 masks
D        172.31.195.0/30 [90/1] via 172.31.11.202, 00:00:22, FastEthernet0/0
D        172.31.194.0/24 [90/1] via 172.31.11.202, 00:00:22, FastEthernet0/0
D        172.31.195.4/30 [90/1] via 172.31.11.202, 00:00:22, FastEthernet0/0
D        172.31.195.8/30 [90/1] via 172.31.11.202, 00:00:22, FastEthernet0/0
```

An EIGRP **distribute list** might refer to a **prefix list** instead of an ACL to match routes. Prefix lists are designed to match a range of subnets, as well as a range of subnet masks associated with the subnets. The **distribute list** must still define the direction of the updates to be examined (in or out), and optionally an interface.

Chapter 10 includes a more complete discussion of the syntax and formatting of prefix lists; this chapter focuses on how to call and use a prefix list for EIGRP route filtering. To reference a prefix list, use the following **router eigrp** *asn* subcommand:

distribute-list {**prefix** *list-name*} {**in** ¦ **out**} [*interface-type interface-number*]

Example 8-9 shows the execution of this syntax, with the prefix list denying all /30 routes from the range 172.31.192.0/21. The prefix list permits all other subnets.

Example 8-9 *EIGRP Prefix Lists*

```
! The example begins with a list of the routes that should be filtered.
! Note that the longer-prefixes option below makes the
! command list all routes in the range.
! The highlighted lines are the ones that will be filtered.
R2# show ip route 172.31.192.0 255.255.248.0 longer-prefixes
! Lines omitted for brevity; in this case, the legend was deleted
     172.31.0.0/16 is variably subnetted, 24 subnets, 3 masks
D        172.31.195.0/30 [90/1] via 172.31.11.202, 00:00:18, FastEthernet0/0
D        172.31.194.0/24 [90/1] via 172.31.11.202, 00:00:18, FastEthernet0/0
D        172.31.196.4/30 [90/1] via 172.31.11.202, 00:00:18, FastEthernet0/0
D        172.31.195.4/30 [90/1] via 172.31.11.202, 00:00:18, FastEthernet0/0
D        172.31.197.0/24 [90/1] via 172.31.11.202, 00:00:18, FastEthernet0/0
D        172.31.196.0/30 [90/1] via 172.31.11.202, 00:00:19, FastEthernet0/0
D        172.31.195.8/30 [90/1] via 172.31.11.202, 00:00:19, FastEthernet0/0
! R2's configuration follows. The "wo2" prefix list limits the mask range to
! only /30 with the "ge 30 le 30" parameters. It matches any subnets between
! 172.31.192.0 and 172.31.199.255.
! Note that the prefix-list commands are global commands.
router eigrp 1
 network 10.0.0.0
 network 172.31.0.0
 distribute-list prefix wo2 in FastEthernet0/0
```

continues

Example 8-9 *EIGRP Prefix Lists (Continued)*

```
!
ip prefix-list wo2 seq 5 deny 172.31.192.0/21 ge 30 le 30
ip prefix-list wo2 seq 10 permit 0.0.0.0/0 le 32
! Below, note the absence of /30 routes in the specified range, and the presence
! of the two /24 routes seen at the beginning of Example 8-8.
R2# show ip route 172.31.192.0 255.255.248.0 longer-prefixes
! Lines omitted for brevity; in this case, the legend was deleted
     172.31.0.0/16 is variably subnetted, 19 subnets, 3 masks
D       172.31.194.0/24 [90/1] via 172.31.11.202, 00:00:23, FastEthernet0/0
D       172.31.197.0/24 [90/1] via 172.31.11.202, 00:00:23, FastEthernet0/0
```

One key concept is worth noting before we move on: With EIGRP filtering, an incoming filter prevents topology information from entering the EIGRP topology table. That is, inbound filters do not affect the routing table directly, but because they keep routing information from the topology table, they have the same effect.

EIGRP Offset Lists

EIGRP *offset lists* allow EIGRP to add to a route's metric, either before sending an update, or for routes received in an update. The offset list refers to an ACL (standard, extended, or named) to match the routes; any matched routes have the specified *offset*, or extra metric, added to their metrics. Any routes not matched by the offset list are unchanged. The offset list also specifies which routing updates to examine by specifying a direction (in or out) and, optionally, an interface. If the interface is omitted from the command, all updates for the defined direction will be examined.

Offset lists are much more applicable to RIP (version 1 or 2) than EIGRP because RIP has such a limited metric range. With EIGRP, because of the metric's complexity, it is doubtful that you would manipulate EIGRP metrics this way. Because several other filtering methods and ways to influence EIGRP metrics are available, offset lists see limited use in EIGRP and are therefore not covered in more detail in this chapter.

Clearing the IP Routing Table

The **clear ip route** * command clears the IP routing table. However, because EIGRP keeps all possible routes in its topology table, a **clear ip route** * command does not cause EIGRP to send any messages or learn any new topology information; the router simply refills the IP routing table with the best routes from the existing topology table.

The **clear ip eigrp neighbor** command clears all neighbor relationships, which clears the entire topology table on the router. The neighbors then come back up, send new updates, and repopulate the topology and routing tables. The **clear** command also allows for clearing all neighbors that are reachable out an interface, or based on the neighbor's IP address. The generic syntax is

```
clear ip eigrp neighbors [ip-address | interface-type interface-number]
```

Foundation Summary

This section lists additional details and facts to round out the coverage of the topics in this chapter. Unlike most of the Cisco Press *Exam Certification Guides*, this "Foundation Summary" does not repeat information presented in the "Foundation Topics" section of the chapter. Please take the time to read and study the details in the "Foundation Topics" section of the chapter, as well as review items noted with a Key Topic icon.

Table 8-6 lists some of the most popular Cisco IOS commands related to the topics in this chapter. Also refer to Table 8-4 for a few additional commands related to load balancing.

Table 8-6 *Command Reference for Chapter 9*

Command	Command Mode and Description
router eigrp *as-number*	Global config; puts user in EIGRP configuration mode for that AS
network *ip-address* [*wildcard-mask*]	EIGRP config mode; defines matching parameters, compared to interface IP addresses, to pick interfaces on which to enable EIGRP
distribute-list [*access-list-number* | *name*] {**in** | **out**} [*interface-type* | *interface-number*]	EIGRP config mode; defines ACL or prefix list to use for filtering EIGRP updates
ip split-horizon eigrp *asn*	Interface subcommand; enables or disables split horizon
passive-interface [**default**] {*interface-type interface-number*}	EIGRP config mode; causes EIGRP to stop sending Hellos on the specified interface, and thereby to also stop receiving and/or sending updates
ip hello-interval eigrp *asn seconds*	Interface subcommand; sets the interval for periodic Hellos sent by this interface
ip hold-time eigrp *asn seconds*	Interface subcommand; sets the countdown timer to be used by a router's neighbor when monitoring for incoming EIGRP messages from this interface
auto-summary	EIGRP config mode; enables automatic summarization at classful network boundaries
metric weights *tos k1 k2 k3 k4 k5*	EIGRP config mode; defines the per-ToS K values to be used in EIGRP metric calculations
ip bandwidth-percent eigrp *asn percent*	Interface subcommand; defines the maximum percentage of interface bandwidth to be used for EIGRP messages

Table 8-6 *Command Reference for Chapter 9 (Continued)*

Command	Command Mode and Description
ip authentication mode eigrp *asn* **md5**	Enables MD5 authentication of EIGRP packets on an interface
ip authentication key-chain eigrp *asn key_chain_name*	Specifies the authentication key for EIGRP on an interface
distribute-list {*access-list-number* | *name*} {**in** | **out**} [*interface-type interface-number*]	Specifies an access list for filtering routing updates to/from the EIGRP topology table
distribute-list prefix *prefix_list_name* {**in** | **out**} [*interface-type interface-number*]	Specifies a prefix list for filtering routing updates to/from the EIGRP topology table
timers active-time [*time-limit* | **disabled**]	EIGRP config mode; sets the time limit for how long a route is in active state before becoming stuck-in-active
show ip route eigrp *asn*	User mode; displays all EIGRP routes in the IP routing table
show ip eigrp topology [*as-number* | [[*ip-address*] *mask*]] [**active** | **all-links** | **pending** | **summary** | **zero-successors**]	User mode; lists different parts of the EIGRP topology table, depending on the options used
show ip eigrp interfaces [*interface-type interface-number*] [*as-number*]	User mode; lists EIGRP protocol timers and statistics per interface
show ip eigrp traffic [*as-number*]	User mode; displays EIGRP traffic statistics
show ip protocols	User mode; lists EIGRP timer settings, current protocol status, automatic summarization actions, and update sources
show ip eigrp *asn* **neighbors**	User mode; lists EIGRP neighbors
clear ip eigrp neighbors [*ip-address* | *interface-type interface-number*]	Enable mode; disables current neighbor relationships, removing topology table entries associated with each neighbor
clear ip route {*network* [*mask*] | ***}	Enable mode; clears the routing table entries, which are then refilled based on the current topology table
show ip interface [*type number*]	User mode; lists many interface settings, including split horizon
eigrp log-neighbor-changes	EIGRP subcommand; displays log messages when neighbor status changes; enabled by default

Table 8-7 summarizes the types of EIGRP packets and their purposes.

Table 8-7   *EIGRP Message Summary*

Key
Topic

EIGRP Packet	Purpose
Hello	Identifies neighbors, exchanges parameters, and is sent periodically as a keepalive function
Update	Informs neighbors about routing information
Ack	Acknowledges Update, Query, and Response packets
Query	Asks neighboring routers to verify their route to a particular subnet
Reply	Sent by neighbors to reply to a Query
Goodbye	Used by a router to notify its neighbors when the router is gracefully shutting down

Memory Builders

The CCIE Routing and Switching written exam, like all Cisco CCIE written exams, covers a fairly broad set of topics. This section provides some basic tools to help you exercise your memory about some of the broader topics covered in this chapter.

Fill in Key Tables from Memory

Appendix E, "Key Tables for CCIE Study," on the CD in the back of this book contains empty sets of some of the key summary tables in each chapter. Print Appendix E, refer to this chapter's tables in it, and fill in the tables from memory. Refer to Appendix F, "Solutions for Key Tables for CCIE Study," on the CD to check your answers.

Definitions

Next, take a few moments to write down the definitions for the following terms:

hello interval, full update, partial update, Route Tag field, Next Hop field, MD5, DUAL, Hold timer, K value, neighbor, adjacency, RTP, SRTT, RTO, Update, Ack, query, Reply, Hello, Goodbye, RD, FD, feasibility condition, successor route, feasible successor, input event, local computation, active, passive, going active, stuck-in-active, query scope, EIGRP stub router, limiting query scope, variance

Refer to the glossary to check your answers.

Further Reading

Jeff Doyle's *Routing TCP/IP*, Volume I, Second Edition, (Cisco Press) has several excellent examples of configuration, as well as several examples of the DUAL algorithm and the Active Query process.

EIGRP Network Design Solutions, by Ivan Pepelnjak, contains wonderfully complete coverage of EIGRP. It also has great, detailed examples of the Query process.

Blueprint topics covered in this chapter:

This chapter covers the following subtopics from the Cisco CCIE Routing and Switching written exam blueprint. Refer to the full blueprint in Table I-1 in the Introduction for more details on the topics covered in each chapter and their context within the blueprint.

- Standard OSPF Area

- Stub OSPF Area

- Totally Stubby Area

- Not-So-Stubby Area (NSSA)

- Totally NSSA

- LSA Types

- Adjacency on Point-to-Point and Multiaccess Network Types

- OSPF Graceful Restart

- Troubleshooting Adjacency Failures

- Troubleshooting External Route Installation in the RIB

OSPF

This chapter covers OSPF, the only link-state routing protocol covered by the CCIE Routing and Switching exam blueprint. As with the other routing protocol chapters, this chapter includes most of the features, concepts, and commands related to OSPF. Chapter 10 "IGP Route Redistribution, Route Summarization, and Default Routing," covers a few other details of OSPF, in particular, route redistribution, route filtering in redistribution, and route summarization.

"Do I Know This Already?" Quiz

Table 9-1 outlines the major sections in this chapter and the corresponding "Do I Know This Already?" quiz questions.

Table 9-1   *"Do I Know This Already?" Foundation Topics Section-to-Question Mapping*

Foundation Topics Section	Questions Covered in This Section	Score
OSPF Database Exchange	1–5	
OSPF Design and LSAs	6–9	
OSPF Configuration	10–12	
Total Score		

In order to best use this pre-chapter assessment, remember to score yourself strictly. You can find the answers in Appendix A, "Answers to the 'Do I Know This Already?' Quizzes."

1. R1 has received an OSPF LSU from R2. Which of the following methods may be used by R1 to acknowledge receipt of the LSU from R2?

    a. TCP on R1 acknowledges using the TCP Acknowledgement field.

    b. R1 sends back an identical copy of the LSU.

    c. R1 sends back an LSAck to R2.

    d. R1 sends back a DD packet with LSA headers whose sequence numbers match the sequence numbers in the LSU.

2. Fredsco has an enterprise network with one core Frame Relay connected router, with a hub-and-spoke network of PVCs connecting to ten remote offices. The network uses OSPF exclusively. The core router (R-core) has all ten PVCs defined under multipoint subinterface s0/0.1. Each remote router also uses a multipoint subinterface. Fred, the engineer, configures an **ip ospf network non-broadcast** command under the subinterface on R-core and on the subinterfaces of the ten remote routers. Fred also assigns an IP address to each router from subnet 10.3.4.0/24, with R-core using the .100 address, and the remote offices using .1 through .10. Assuming all other related options are using defaults, which of the following would be true about this network?

    a. The OSPF hello interval would be 30 seconds.

    b. The OSPF dead interval would be 40 seconds.

    c. The remote routers could learn all routes to other remote routers' subnets, but only if R-core became the designated router.

    d. No designated router will be elected in subnet 10.3.4.0/24.

3. Which of the following interface subcommands, used on a multipoint Frame Relay subinterface, creates a requirement for a DR to be elected for the attached subnet?

    a. **ip ospf network point-to-multipoint**

    b. **ip ospf network point-to-multipoint non-broadcast**

    c. **ip ospf network non-broadcast**

    d. None of these answers is correct.

4. The following routers share the same LAN segment and have the stated OSPF settings: R1: RID 1.1.1.1, hello 10, priority 3; R2: RID 2.2.2.2, hello 9, priority 4; R3, RID 3.3.3.3, priority 3; and R4: RID 4.4.4.4, hello 10, priority 2. The LAN switch fails, recovers, and all routers attempt to elect an OSPF DR and form neighbor relationships at the same time. No other OSPF-related parameters were specifically set. Which of the following is true about negotiations and elections on this LAN?

    a. R1, R3, and R4 will expect Hellos from R2 every 9 seconds.

    b. R2 will become the DR but have no neighbors.

    c. R3 will become the BDR.

    d. R4's dead interval will be 40 seconds.

    e. All routers will use R2's hello interval of 9 once R2 becomes the designated router.

5. Which of the following must be true in order for two OSPF routers that share the same LAN data link to be able to become OSPF neighbors?

    a. Must be in the same area

    b. Must have the same LSRefresh setting

    c. Must have differing OSPF priorities

    d. Must have the same Hello timer, but can have different dead intervals

6. R1 is an OSPF ASBR that injects an E1 route for network 200.1.1.0/24 into the OSPF backbone area. R2 is an ABR connected to area 0 and to area 1. R2 also has an Ethernet interface in area 0, IP address 10.1.1.1/24, for which it is the designated router. R3 is a router internal to area 1. Enough links are up and working for the OSPF design to be working properly. Which of the following is true regarding this topology? (Assume no other routing protocols are running, and that area 1 is not a stub area.)

    a. R1 creates a type 7 LSA and floods it throughout area 0.

    b. R3 will not have a specific route to 200.1.1.0/24.

    c. R2 forwards the LSA that R1 created for 200.1.1.0/24 into area 1.

    d. R2 will create a type 2 LSA for subnet 10.1.1.0/24 and flood it throughout area 0.

7. R1 is an OSPF ASBR that injects an E1 route for network 200.1.1.0/24 into the OSPF backbone area. R2 is an ABR connected to area 0 and to area 1. R2 also has an Ethernet interface in area 0, IP address 10.1.1.1/24, for which it is the designated router. R3 is a router internal to area 1. Enough links are up and working for the OSPF design to be working properly. Which of the following are true regarding this topology? (Assume no other routing protocols are running, and that area 1 is a totally NSSA area.)

    a. R3 could inject internal routes into the OSPF domain.

    b. R3 will not have a specific route to 200.1.1.0/24.

    c. R2 forwards the LSA that R1 created for 200.1.1.0/24 into area 1.

    d. R2 will create a type 2 LSA for subnet 10.1.1.0/24 and flood it throughout area 0.

8. The routers in area 55 all have the **area 55 stub no-summary** command configured under the **router ospf** command. OSPF has converged, with all routers in area 55 holding an identical link-state database for area 55. All IP addresses inside the area come from the range 10.55.0.0/16; no other links outside area 55 use addresses in this range. R11 is the only ABR for the area. Which of the following is true about this design?

   a. The area is a stubby area.

   b. The area is a totally stubby area.

   c. The area is an NSSA.

   d. ABR R11 is not allowed to summarize the type 1 and 2 LSAs in area 55 into the 10.55.0.0/16 prefix due to the **no-summary** keyword.

   e. Routers internal to area 55 can have routes to specific subnets inside area 0.

   f. Routers internal to area 55 can have routes to E1, but not E2, OSPF routes.

9. R1 is an OSPF ASBR that injects an E1 route for network 200.1.1.0/24 into the OSPF backbone area. R2 is an ABR connected to area 0 and to area 1. R2 also has an Ethernet interface in area 0, IP address 10.1.1.1/24, for which it is the designated router. R3 is a router internal to area 1. Enough links are up and working for the OSPF design to be working properly. Which of the following are true regarding this topology? (Assume no other routing protocols are running, and that area 1 is not a stubby area.)

   a. R3's cost for the route to 200.1.1.0 will be the cost of the route as it was injected into the OSPF domain by R1, without considering any internal cost.

   b. R3's cost for the route to 200.1.1.0 will include the addition of R3's cost to reach R1, plus the external cost listed in the LSA.

   c. R3's cost for the route to 10.1.1.0/24 will be the same as its cost to reach ABR R2.

   d. R3's cost for the route to 10.1.1.0/24 will be the sum of its cost to reach ABR R2 plus the cost listed in the type 3 LSA created for 10.1.1.0/24 by ABR R2.

   e. It is impossible to characterize R3's cost to 10.1.1.0/24 because R3 uses a summary type 3 LSA, which hides some of the costs.

10. R1 and R2 each connect via Fast Ethernet interfaces to the same LAN, which should be in area 0. R1's IP address is 10.1.1.1/24, and R2's is 10.1.1.2/24. The only OSPF-related configuration is as follows:

```
hostname R1
router ospf 1
 network 0.0.0.0 255.255.255.255 area 0
 auto-cost reference-bandwidth 1000
 !
hostname R2
router ospf 2
 network 10.0.0.0 0.0.0.255 area 0
```

Which of the following statements are true about the configuration?

a. The **network** command on R2 does not match IP address 10.1.1.2, so R2 will not attempt to send Hellos or discover neighbors on the LAN.

b. The different process IDs in the **router ospf** command prevent the two routers from becoming neighbors on the LAN.

c. R2 will become the DR as a result of having a cost of 1 associated with its Fast Ethernet interface.

d. R1 and R2 could never become neighbors due to the difference in cost values.

e. R1's OSPF cost for its Fast Ethernet interface would be 10.

11. Which of the following are true about setting timers with OSPF?

a. The **ip ospf dead-interval minimal hello-multiplier 4** interface subcommand sets the hello interval to 4 ms.

b. The **ip ospf dead-interval minimal hello-multiplier 4** interface subcommand sets the dead interval to 4 seconds.

c. The **ip ospf dead-interval minimal hello-multiplier 4** interface subcommand sets the hello interval to 250 ms.

d. On all interfaces, the **ip ospf hello-interval 30** interface subcommand changes the hello interval from 10 to 30.

e. The **ip ospf hello-multiplier 5** interface subcommand sets the dead interval to five times the then-current hello interval.

f. Cisco IOS defaults the hello and dead intervals to 30/120 on interfaces using the OSPF nonbroadcast network type.

12. R1 has been configured for OSPF authentication on its fa0/0 interface as shown below. Which of the following is true about the configuration?

```
interface fa0/0
 ip ospf authentication-key hannah
 ip ospf authentication
 ip ospf message-digest-key 2 md5 jessie
router ospf 2
 area 0 authentication message-digest
```

a. R1 will attempt simple-text authentication on the LAN with key **hannah**.

b. R1 will attempt MD5 authentication on the LAN with key **jessie**.

c. R2 will attempt OSPF type 2 authentication on fa0/0.

d. R2 will attempt OSPF type 3 authentication on fa0/0.

Foundation Topics

Link-state routing protocols define the content and structure of data that describes network topology, and define the processes by which routers exchange that detailed topology information. The name "link state" refers to the fact that the topology information includes information about each data *link*, along with each link's current operational *state*. All the topological data together comprises the *link-state database (LSDB)*. Each link-state router applies the Dijkstra algorithm to the database to calculate the current-best routes to each subnet.

This chapter breaks down the OSPF coverage into three major sections. The first section details how the topology data is exchanged. The second section covers OSPF design and the contents of the LSDB, which comprises different types of *link-state advertisements (LSAs)*. (The second section covers both design and the LSDB because the design choices directly impact which types of LSAs are forwarded into the differing parts of an OSPF network.) The third section covers the majority of the OSPF configuration details of OSPF for this chapter, although a few configuration topics are interspersed in the first two sections.

> **NOTE** This chapter addresses the functions of OSPF Version 2. It ignores OSPF Version 3 (RFC 2740), which was introduced primarily to support IPv6 and is covered in detail in Chapter 20, "IP Version 6."

OSPF Database Exchange

OSPF defines five different messages that routers can use to exchange LSAs. The process by which LSAs are exchanged does not change whether a single area or multiple areas are used, so this section will use a single OSPF area (area 0).

OSPF Router IDs

Before an OSPF router can send any OSPF messages, it must choose a unique 32-bit dotted-decimal identifier called the OSPF *router identifier (RID)*. Cisco routers use the following sequence to choose their OSPF RID, only moving on to the next step in this list if the previous step did not supply the OSPF RID:

1. Use the router ID configured in the **router-id** *id* subcommand under **router ospf**.

2. Use the highest numeric IP address on any currently "up and up" loopback interface.

3. Use the highest numeric IP address on any currently "up and up" non-loopback interface.

The sequence and logic are very simple, but some details are hidden in the sequence:

- The interface from which the RID is taken does not have to be matched by an OSPF **network** command.

- OSPF does not have to advertise a route to reach the RID's subnet.

- The RID does not have to be reachable per the IP routing table.

- Steps 2 and 3 look at the then-current interface state to choose the RID when the OSPF process is started.

- Routers consider changing the OSPF RID when the OSPF process is restarted, or when the RID is changed via configuration.

- If a router's RID changes, the rest of the routers in the same area will have to perform a new SPF calculation.

- If the RID is configured with the **router-id** command, and the command remains unchanged, that router's RID will never change.

For these reasons, many people set their RIDs with the **router-id** command and use an obvious numbering scheme to make it easy to identify a router by its RID.

Becoming Neighbors, Exchanging Databases, and Becoming Adjacent

OSPF directly encapsulates the five different types of OSPF messages inside IP packets, using IP protocol 89, as listed in Table 9-2.

Table 9-2 *OSPF Messages*

Message	Description
Hello	Used to discover neighbors, bring a neighbor relationship to a 2-way state, and monitor a neighbor's responsiveness in case it fails
Database Description (DD or DBD)	Used to exchange brief versions of each LSA, typically on initial topology exchange, so that a router knows a list of that neighbor's LSAs
Link-State Request (LSR)	A packet that identifies one or more LSAs about which the sending router would like the neighbor to supply full details about the LSAs
Link-State Update (LSU)	A packet that contains fully detailed LSAs, typically sent in response to an LSR message
Link-State Acknowledgement (LSAck)	Sent to confirm receipt of an LSU message

These messages together allow routers to discover each other's presence (Hello), learn which LSAs are missing from their LSDBs (DD), request and reliably exchange the LSAs (LSR/LSU), and monitor their neighbors for any changes in the topology (Hello). Note that the LSAs themselves are not OSPF messages—an LSA is a data structure, held inside a router's LSDB, and exchanged inside LSU messages.

When a particular data link first comes up, OSPF routers first become neighbors using the Hello message. At that point, they exchange topology information using the other four OSPF messages. Figure 9-1 outlines the overall process between two routers.

Figure 9-1 *Overview of OSPF LSDB Exchange*

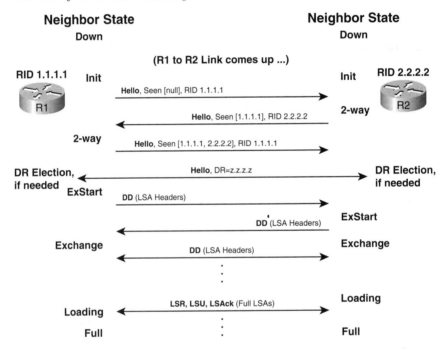

Figure 9-1 shows the overall message flow, along with the *neighbor state* on each router. An OSPF router keeps a state machine for each neighbor, listing the current neighbor state in the output of the **show ip ospf neighbor** command. These neighbor states change as the neighbors progress through their messaging; in this example, the neighbors settle into a *full state*, meaning *fully adjacent*, once the process is completed.

The "Foundation Summary" section at the end of this chapter includes a reference table (Table 9-13) listing the neighbor states and their meanings. The next few sections explain the details behind the process shown in Figure 9-1.

Becoming Neighbors: The Hello Process

Hello messages perform three major functions:

■ Discover other OSPF-speaking routers on common subnets

■ Check for agreement on some configuration parameters

■ Monitor health of the neighbors to react if the neighbor fails

To discover neighbors, Cisco OSPF routers listen for multicast Hello messages sent to 224.0.0.5—the *All OSPF Routers* multicast address—on any interfaces that have been enabled for OSPF. The Hellos are sourced from that router's primary IP address on the interface—in other words, Hellos are not sourced from secondary IP addresses. (OSPF routers will advertise secondary IP addresses, but they will not send Hellos from those IP addresses, and never form neighbor relationships using secondary addresses.) Furthermore, OSPF neighbors will become fully adjacent if one or both of the neighbors are using unnumbered interfaces for the connection between them.

After two routers discover each other by receiving Hellos from the other router, the routers perform the following parameter checks based on the receive Hellos:

■ Must pass the authentication process

■ Must be in the same primary subnet, including same subnet mask

■ Must be in the same OSPF area

■ Must be of the same area type (stub, NSSA, and so on)

■ Must not have duplicate RIDs

■ OSPF Hello and Dead timers must be equal

If any of these items do not match, the two routers simply do not form a neighbor relationship. Also of note is one important item that does not have to match: the OSPF process ID (PID), as configured in the **router ospf** *process-id* command. Also, the MTU must be equal for the DD packets to be successfully sent between neighbors, but this parameter check is technically not part of the Hello process.

The third important function for a Hello is to maintain a heartbeat function between neighbors. The neighbors send Hellos every *hello interval*; failure to receive a Hello within the longer *dead interval* causes a router to believe that its neighbor has failed. The hello interval defaults to 10 seconds on LAN interfaces and 30 seconds on T1 and slower WAN interfaces; the dead interval defaults to four times the hello interval.

Example 9-1 lists some basic OSPF command output related to the neighbor establishment with Hellos, and the hello and dead intervals.

Example 9-1 *Hello Mismatches and Basic Neighbor Parameters*

```
! Below, debug messages show that this router disagrees with the hello and dead
! intervals on router 10.1.111.4; The "C" and "R" mean "configured" and "received,"
! respectively, meaning that this router uses 30/120 for hello/dead, and the other
! router is trying to use 10/40.
R1# debug ip ospf hello
OSPF hello events debugging is on
Jan 12 06:41:20.940: OSPF: Mismatched hello parameters from 10.1.111.4
Jan 12 06:41:20.940: OSPF: Dead R 40 C 120, Hello R 10 C 30   Mask R 255.255.255.0 C
  255.255.255.0
! Below, R1's hello and dead intervals are listed for the same interface.
R1# show ip ospf int s 0/0.100
Serial0/0.100 is up, line protocol is up
  Internet Address 10.1.111.1/24, Area 0
  Process ID 1, Router ID 1.1.1.1, Network Type NON_BROADCAST, Cost: 64
  Transmit Delay is 1 sec, State DR, Priority 1
  Designated Router (ID) 1.1.1.1, Interface address 10.1.111.1
  No backup designated router on this network
  Timer intervals configured, Hello 30, Dead 120, Wait 120, Retransmit 5
! Lines omitted for brevity
! Below, R1 shows a neighbor on S0/0.100, in the full state, meaning the routers
! have completed LSDB exchange. Note the current Dead timer counts down, in this
! case from 2 minutes; the value of 1:58 means R1 last received a Hello from
! neighbor 10.1.111.6 two seconds ago.
R1# sh ip ospf neighbor 6.6.6.6
 Neighbor 6.6.6.6, interface address 10.1.111.6
    In the area 0 via interface Serial0/0.100
    Neighbor priority is 0, State is FULL, 8 state changes
    DR is 10.1.111.1 BDR is 0.0.0.0
    Poll interval 120
    Options is 0x42
    Dead timer due in 00:01:58
    Neighbor is up for 00:17:22
! Lines omitted for brevity
```

Flooding LSA Headers to Neighbors

When two routers hear Hellos, and the parameter check passes, they do not immediately send packets holding the LSAs. Instead, each router creates and sends *Database Description* (*DD*, or sometimes called *DBD*) packets, which contain the headers of each LSA. The headers include enough information to uniquely identify each LSA. Essentially, the routers exchange a list of all the LSAs they each know about; the next step in the process is letting a router request a new copy of any old or unknown LSAs.

The DD messages use an OSPF-defined simple error-recovery process. Each DD packet, which may contain several LSA headers, has an assigned sequence number. The receiver acknowledges a received DD packet by sending an identical DD packet back to the sender. The sender uses a window size of one packet, then waits for the acknowledgement before sending the next DD packet.

Database Descriptor Exchange: Master/Slave Relationship

As a neighbor relationship forms between two routers (specifically, at the ExStart stage of the neighborship), the neighbors determine which router is to be the master and which is to be the slave during the database exchange between them. The router with the higher RID becomes the master and initiates the database exchange. At that point, the master begins sending DD packets to the slave, and the slave acknowledges them as they are received. Only the master can increment sequence numbers in the DD exchange process.

Requesting, Getting, and Acknowledging LSAs

Once all LSA headers have been exchanged using DD packets, each neighboring router has a list of LSAs known by the neighbor. Using that knowledge, a router needs to request a full copy of each LSA that is missing from its LSDB.

To know whether a neighbor has a more recent copy of a particular LSA, a router looks at the sequence number of the LSA in its LSDB and compares it to the sequence number of that same LSA learned from the DD packet. Each LSA's sequence number is incremented every time the LSA changes. So, if a router received (via a DD packet) an LSA header with a later sequence number for a particular LSA (as compared with the LSA in the LSDB), that router knows that the neighbor has a more recent LSA. For example, R1 sent R2 an LSA header for the type 1 LSA that describes R1 itself, with sequence number 0x80000004. If R2's database already held that LSA, but with a sequence number of 0x80000003, then R2 would know that it needs to ask R1 to send the latest copy (sequence number 0x80000004) of that LSA.

> **NOTE** New LSAs begin with sequence number 0x80000001, increase, and then wrap back to 0x7FFFFFFF. If the LSA made it to sequence number 0x80000000, the LSA must be reflooded throughout the network.

Routers use *Link-State Request (LSR)* packets to request one or more LSAs from a neighbor. The neighboring router replies with *Link-State Update (LSU)* packets, which hold one or more full LSAs. As shown in Figure 9-1, both routers sit in a loading state while the LSR/LSA process continues. Once the process is complete, they settle into a *full* state, which means that the two routers should have fully exchanged their databases, resulting in identical copies of the LSDB entries for that area on both routers.

The LSR/LSA process uses a reliable protocol that has two options for acknowledging packets. First, an LSU can be acknowledged by the receiver of the LSU simply repeating the exact same LSU back to the sender. Alternatively, a router can send back an *LSAck* packet to acknowledge the packet, which contains a list of acknowledged LSA headers.

At the end of the process outlined in Figure 9-1, two neighbors have exchanged their LSDBs. As a result, their LSDBs should be identical. At this point, they can each independently run the Dijkstra Shortest Path First (SPF) algorithm to calculate the best routes from their own perspectives.

Designated Routers on LANs

OSPF optimizes the LSA flooding process on multiaccess data links by using the concept of a *designated router (DR)*. Without the concept of a DR, each pair of routers that share a data link would become fully adjacent neighbors. Each pair of routers would directly exchange their LSDBs with each other as shown in Figure 9-1. On a LAN with only six routers, without a DR, 15 different pairs of routers would exist, and 15 different instances of full database flooding would occur. OSPF uses a DR (and *backup DR*, or *BDR*) on a LAN or other multiaccess network. The flooding occurs through the DR, significantly reducing the unnecessary exchange of redundant LSAs.

> **NOTE** DRs have one other major function besides improving the efficiency of LSA flooding process. They also create a type 2 LSA that represents the subnet. LSA types are covered in the next major section, "OSPF Design and LSAs."

The next section goes through the basics of the DR/BDR process on LANs, which is followed by coverage of options of OSPF network types and how they impact OSPF flooding on Frame Relay links.

Designated Router Optimization on LANs

Figure 9-2 depicts the DR flooding optimization that occurs with sending DD packets over a LAN.

Figure 9-2 *DR Optimization on a LAN*

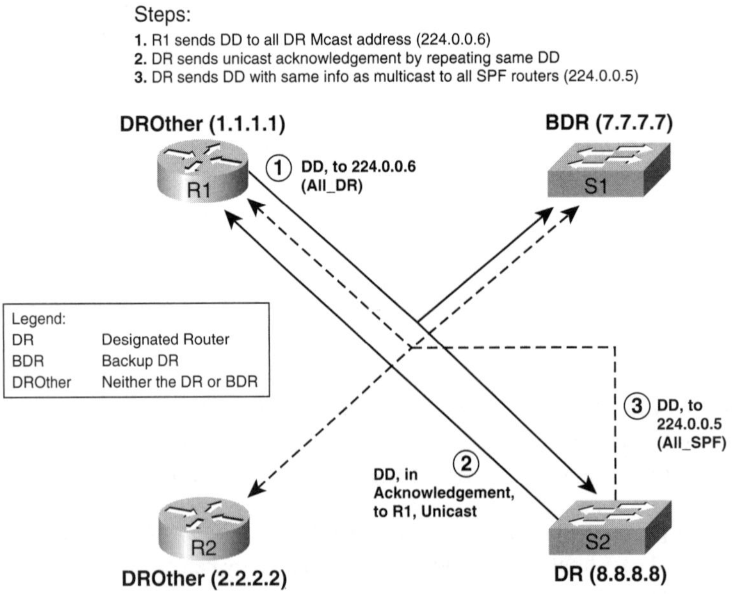

Steps:
1. R1 sends DD to all DR Mcast address (224.0.0.6)
2. DR sends unicast acknowledgement by repeating same DD
3. DR sends DD with same info as multicast to all SPF routers (224.0.0.5)

DROther (1.1.1.1)
BDR (7.7.7.7)
R1
S1

① DD, to 224.0.0.6 (All_DR)

Legend:
DR   Designated Router
BDR   Backup DR
DROther   Neither the DR or BDR

③ DD, to 224.0.0.5 (All_SPF)

② DD, in Acknowledgement, to R1, Unicast

R2
S2

DROther (2.2.2.2)
DR (8.8.8.8)

Routers that are not the DR (including the BDR) send DDs to the DR by sending them to multicast address 224.0.0.6, the All OSPF DR Routers multicast address. The DR then acknowledges the DDs with a unicast DD (Step 2 in Figure 9-2). The DR then floods a new DD packet to all OSPF routers (multicast address 224.0.0.5).

Figure 9-2 shows the three main steps, but the non-DR routers also need to acknowledge the DD packet sent in Step 3. Typically, the acknowledgment occurs by the other routers each replying with a unicast DD packet.

> **NOTE**   In topologies without a DR, the DD and LSU packets are typically sent to the 224.0.0.5 All OSPF Routers multicast IP address.

Example 9-2 shows the output of a **show ip ospf neighbor** command on R1 from Figure 9-2. Note that R1 is in a full state with S2, which is the DR, with OSPF RID 8.8.8.8. R1 is also in a full state with S1, the BDR, OSPF RID 7.7.7.7. However, R1 is in a 2WAY state with R2, RID 2.2.2.2.

Example 9-2   *The* **show ip ospf neighbor** *Command*

```
R1# sh ip ospf neighbor fa 0/0
Neighbor ID     Pri    State           Dead Time    Address      Interface
2.2.2.2          1     2WAY/DROTHER    00:00:35     10.1.1.2     FastEthernet0/0
7.7.7.7          1     FULL/BDR        00:00:38     10.1.1.3     FastEthernet0/0
8.8.8.8          1     FULL/DR         00:00:34     10.1.1.4     FastEthernet0/0
```

When a DR is used on a link, routers end up as DR, BDR, or neither; a router that is neither DR or BDR is called a *DROther* router. The DR and BDR form full adjacencies with all other neighbors on the link, so they reach a full state once the database exchange process is complete. However, two neighbors that are both DROthers do not become fully adjacent—they stop at the 2WAY state, as shown in Example 9-2. Stopping at the 2WAY state between two DROther routers is normal; it simply means that the Hello parameter-match check worked, but the neighbors do not need to proceed to the point of exchanging DD packets, because they do not need to when a DR is present.

To describe the fact that some neighbors do not directly exchange DD and LSU packets, OSPF makes a distinction between the terms *neighbors* and *adjacent*, as follows:

■ **Neighbors**—Two routers that share a common data link, that exchange Hello messages, and the Hellos must match for certain parameters.

■ **Adjacent (fully adjacent)**—Two neighbors that have completed the process of fully exchanging DD and LSU packets directly between each other.

Note that although DROther routers do not exchange DD and LSU packets directly with each other, like R1 and R2 in Figure 9-2, the DROther routers do end up with an identical copy of the LSDB entries by exchanging them with the DR.

DR Election on LANs

As noted in Figure 9-1, if a DR is elected, the election occurs after the routers have become neighbors, but before they send DD packets and reach the ExStart neighbor state. When an OSPF router reaches the 2-way state with the first neighbor on an interface, it has already received at least one Hello from that neighbor. If the Hello messages state a DR of 0.0.0.0—meaning none has been elected—the router waits before attempting to elect a DR. This typically occurs after a failure on the LAN. OSPF routers wait with the goal of giving all the routers on that subnet a chance to finish initializing after a failure so that all the routers can participate in the DR election—otherwise, the first router to become active would always become the DR. (The time period is called the OSPF *wait time*, which is set to the same value as the Dead timer.)

However, if the received Hellos already list the DR's RID, the router does not have to wait before beginning the election process. This typically occurs when one router lost its connection to the LAN, but other routers remained and continued to work. In this case, the newly-connected router does not attempt to elect a new DR, assuming the DR listed in the received Hello is indeed the current DR.

The election process allows for the possibility of many different scenarios for which routers may and may not become the DR or BDR. Generally speaking, the following rules govern the DR/BDR election process:

- Any router with its OSPF priority set to between 1–255 inclusive can try to become DR by putting its own RID into the DR field of its sent Hellos.

- Routers examine received Hellos, looking at other routers' priority settings, RIDs, and whether each neighbor claims to want to become the DR.

- If a received Hello implies a "better" potential DR, the router stops claiming to want to be DR and asserts that the better candidate should be the DR.

- The first criteria for "better" is the router with the highest priority.

- If the priorities tie, the router with the higher RID is better.

- The router not claiming to be the DR, but with the higher priority (or higher RID, in case priority is a tie) becomes the BDR.

- If a new router arrives after the election, or an existing router improves its priority, it cannot preempt the existing DR and take over as DR (or as BDR).

- When a DR is elected, and the DR fails, the BDR becomes DR, and a new election is held for a new BDR.

After the DR is elected, LSA flooding continues as illustrated previously in Figure 9-2.

Designated Routers on WANs and OSPF Network Types

Using a DR makes good sense on a LAN because it improves LSA flooding efficiency. Likewise, not using a DR on a point-to-point WAN link also makes sense, because with only two routers on the subnet, there is no inefficiency upon which to improve. However, on nonbroadcast multiaccess (NBMA) networks, arguments can be made regarding whether a DR is helpful. So, OSPF includes several options that include a choice of whether to use a DR on WAN interfaces.

Cisco router interfaces can be configured to use, or not use, a DR, plus a couple of other key behaviors, based on the *OSPF network type* for each interface. The OSPF network type determines that router's behavior regarding the following:

- Whether the router tries to elect a DR on that interface

- Whether the router must statically configure a neighbor (with the **neighbor** command), or find neighbors using the typical multicast Hello packets

- Whether more than two neighbors should be allowed on the same subnet

For instance, LAN interfaces default to use an OSPF network type of *broadcast*. OSPF broadcast networks elect a DR, use Hellos to dynamically find neighbors, and allow more than two routers to be in the same subnet on that LAN. For HDLC and PPP links, OSPF uses a network type of *point-to-point*, meaning that no DR is elected, only two IP addresses are in the subnet, and neighbors can be found through Hellos.

Table 9-3 summarizes the OSPF interface types and their meanings. Note that the interface type values can be set with the **ip ospf network** *type* interface subcommand; the first column in the table lists the exact keyword according to this command. Also, for cases in which a DR is not elected, all routers that become neighbors also attempt to become adjacent by the direct exchange of DD, LSR, and LSU packets.

Table 9-3 *OSPF Network Types*

Interface Type	Uses DR/BDR?	Default Hello Interval	Requires a neighbor Command?	More than Two Hosts Allowed in the Subnet?
Broadcast	Yes	10	No	Yes
Point-to-point[1]	No	10	No	No
Nonbroadcast[2] (NBMA)	Yes	30	Yes	Yes
Point-to-multipoint	No	30	No	Yes
Point-to-multipoint nonbroadcast	No	30	Yes	Yes
Loopback	No	—	—	No

[1] Default on Frame Relay point-to-point subinterfaces.

[2] Default on Frame Relay physical and multipoint subinterfaces.

Caveats Regarding OSPF Network Types over NBMA Networks

When configuring OSPF over Frame Relay, the OSPF network type concept can become a bit troublesome. In fact, many CCIE Routing and Switching lab preparation texts and lab books focus on the variety of combinations of OSPF network types used with Frame Relay for various interfaces/subinterfaces. The following list contains many of the key items you should check when looking at an OSPF configuration over Frame Relay, when the OSPF network types used on the various routers do not match:

■ Make sure the default Hello/Dead timers do not cause the Hello parameter check to fail. (See Table 9-3 for the defaults for each OSPF network type.)

■ If one router expects a DR to be elected, and the other does not, the neighbors may come up, and full LSAs be communicated. However, **show** command output may show odd information, and next-hop routers may not be reachable. So, make sure all routers in the same NBMA subnet use an OSPF network type that either does use a DR or does not.

■ If a DR is used, the DR and BDR must have a permanent virtual circuit (PVC) to every other router in the subnet. If not, not all routers will be able to learn routes, because the DR must forward the DD and LSU packets to each of the other routers. Routers that do not have a PVC to every other router should not be permitted to become a DR/BDR.

■ If one router requires a static **neighbor** command, typically the other router on the other end of the PVC does not require a **neighbor** command. For clarity, however, it is better to configure **neighbor** commands on both routers.

Two very simple options exist for making OSPF work over Frame Relay—both of which do not require a DR and do not require **neighbor** commands. If the design allows for the use of point-to-point subinterfaces, use those, take the default OSPF network type of point-to-point, and no additional work is required. If multipoint subinterfaces are needed, or if the configuration must not use subinterfaces, adding the **ip ospf network point-to-multipoint** command on all the routers works, without requiring additional effort to manually define neighbors or worry about which router becomes the DR.

Example of OSPF Network Types and NBMA

On NBMA networks with an OSPF network type that requires that a DR be elected, you must take care to make sure the correct DR is elected. The reason is that the DR and BDR must each have a PVC connecting it to all the DROther routers—otherwise, LSA flooding will not be possible. So, with partial meshes, the election should be influenced by configuring the routers' priority and RIDs such that the hub site of a hub-and-spoke partial mesh becomes the DR. Figure 9-3 shows an example network for which R1 should be the only router allowed to become DR or BDR.

Figure 9-3 *Network Used in the Frame Relay Priority and Network Type Example*

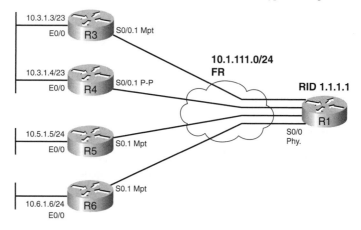

Example 9-3 depicts the following scenarios relating to DR election in Figure 9-3:

- The R1, R3, and R5 configuration is correct for operating with default OSPF network type nonbroadcast in a partial mesh.

- R6 has omitted the **ip ospf priority** interface subcommand, causing it to inadvisably become the DR.

- R4 will be used as an example of what not to do, in part to point out some interesting facts about OSPF **show** commands.

> **NOTE** Figure 9-3 and Example 9-3 do not depict a suggested design for Frame Relay and OSPF. With this topology, using point-to-point subinterfaces in all cases, using four small (/30) subnets, and defaulting to OSPF network type point-to-point would work well. Such a design, however, would not require any thought regarding the OSPF network type. So, this example is purposefully designed to provide a backdrop from which to show how the OSPF network types work.

Example 9-3 shows only the nondefault OSPF configuration settings; also, the routers have an obvious RID numbering scheme (1.1.1.1 for R1, 2.2.2.2 for R2, and so on).

Example 9-3 *Setting Priority on NBMA Networks*

```
! R1 configuration—the neighbor commands default to a priority value of 0,
! meaning R1's perception of that neighbor is priority 0.
router ospf 1
 log-adjacency-changes detail
 network 0.0.0.0 255.255.255.255 area 0
 neighbor 10.1.111.3
 neighbor 10.1.111.4
 neighbor 10.1.111.5
 neighbor 10.1.111.6
! R3 configuration—R3's interface priority is set to 0; R1 will use the higher
! of R3's announced priority 0 (based on R3's ip ospf priority interface
! subcommand) and the priority value on R1's neighbor command, which defaulted
! to 0. So, R3 will not ever become a DR/BDR.
interface Serial0/0.1 multipoint
 ip address 10.1.111.3 255.255.255.0
 ip ospf priority 0
 frame-relay interface-dlci 100
! R4 configuration—note from Figure 9-3 that R4 is using a point-to-point
! subinterface, with all defaults. This is not a typical use of a point-to-point
! subinterface, and is shown to make a few points later in the example.
router ospf 1
 network 0.0.0.0 255.255.255.255 area 0
! R5's configuration is equivalent to R3 in relation to the OSPF network type
! and its implications.
interface Serial0.1 multipoint
 ip address 10.1.111.5 255.255.255.0
 ip ospf priority 0
 frame-relay interface-dlci 100
!
router ospf 1
 network 0.0.0.0 255.255.255.255 area 0
! R6 configuration—R6 forgot to set the interface priority with the ip ospf
! priority 0 command, defaulting to priority 1.
router ospf 1
 network 0.0.0.0 255.255.255.255 area 0
```

Example 9-3 *Setting Priority on NBMA Networks (Continued)*

```
! Below, the results of R6's default interface priority of 1—R6, with RID
! 6.6.6.6, and an announced priority of 1, wins the DR election. Note that the
! command is issued on R1.
R1# show ip ospf neighbor
Neighbor ID     Pri   State          Dead Time   Address       Interface
6.6.6.6          1    FULL/DR        00:01:52    10.1.111.6    Serial0/0
3.3.3.3          0    FULL/DROTHER   00:01:46    10.1.111.3    Serial0/0
N/A              0    ATTEMPT/DROTHER   —         10.1.111.4    Serial0/0
5.5.5.5          0    FULL/DROTHER   00:01:47    10.1.111.5    Serial0/0
! Next, R1's neighbor command was automatically changed to "priority 1" based on
! the Hello, with priority 1, that R1 received from R6. To prevent this dynamic
! reconfiguration, you could add an ip ospf priority 0 command under R6's s0/0.1
! interface.
R1# show run | beg router ospf 1
router ospf 1
 network 0.0.0.0 255.255.255.255 area 0
 neighbor 10.1.111.6 priority 1
 neighbor 10.1.111.3
 neighbor 10.1.111.4
 neighbor 10.1.111.5
! lines omitted for brevity
! Below, R4 is OSPF network type "point to point," with Hello/dead of 10/40.
! R1's settings, based on Table 9-3, would be nonbroadcast, 30/120.
R4# show ip ospf int s 0/0.1
Serial0/0.1 is up, line protocol is up
  Internet Address 10.1.111.4/24, Area 0
  Process ID 1, Router ID 4.4.4.4, Network Type POINT_TO_POINT, Cost: 1562
  Transmit Delay is 1 sec, State POINT_TO_POINT,
  Timer intervals configured, Hello 10, Dead 40, Wait 40, Retransmit 5
! lines omitted for brevity
! Below, R4 changes its network type to yet a different value, one that expects
! neighbor commands, but does not expect a DR to be used.
R4# conf t
Enter configuration commands, one per line.  End with CNTL/Z.
R4(config)# int s 0/0.1
R4(config-subif)# ip ospf network point-to-multipoint non-broadcast
! Next, R1 and R4 become neighbors now that the Hello parameters match. Note that
! R1 believes that R4 is DROther.
R1# show ip ospf neighbor

Neighbor ID     Pri   State          Dead Time   Address       Interface
! lines omitted for brevity
4.4.4.4          1    FULL/DROTHER   00:01:56    10.1.111.4    Serial0/0
! Below, R4 agrees it is in a full state with R1, but does not list R1 as DR,
! because R4 is not using the concept of a DR at all due to R4's network type.
R4# sh ip ospf neigh
Neighbor ID     Pri   State          Dead Time   Address       Interface
1.1.1.1          0    FULL/  —       00:01:42    10.1.111.1    Serial0/0.1
```

The first and most important point from Example 9-3 is the actual behavior of the two ways to set the priority in the example. The *Cisco IOS Configuration Guide* at Cisco.com states that the OSPF **neighbor** command defines the priority of the neighbor. However, in practice, a router's **neighbor priority** setting is compared with the priority inside the Hello it receives from that neighbor— and the larger of the two values is used. In this example, R1's **neighbor 10.1.111.6** command (with default priority of 0) was overridden by R6's Hello, which was based on R6's default OSPF interface priority of 1. So, during DR election, R1 and R6 tied on OSPF priority, and R6 won due to its larger (6.6.6.6 versus 1.1.1.1) RID. R1 even automatically changed its **neighbor** command dynamically to **neighbor 10.1.111.6 priority 1** to reflect the correct priority for R6.

Also note that, although neighbors must be statically configured for some network types, the **neighbor** command needs to be configured on only one router. R3 and R5, with correct working configurations, did not actually need a **neighbor** command.

Finally, it might seem that all is now fine between R1 and R4 by the end of the example, but even though the neighbors are fully adjacent, R4 cannot route packets to R3, R5, or R6 over the Frame Relay network. For instance, R5 could have some routes that point to 10.1.111.4 (R4's Frame Relay IP address) as the next hop. However, because R5 is using a multipoint subinterface, R5 will not know what PVC to use to reach 10.1.111.4. (Chapter 6, "IP Forwarding (Routing)," covers how Frame Relay mapping occurs, and the logic used on multipoint and point-to-point subinterfaces.) In this case, the routers with multipoint subinterfaces would need to add **frame-relay map** commands; for example, R5 would need a **frame-relay map ip 10.1.111.4 100 broadcast** command, causing packets to next-hop 10.1.111.4 to go over DLCI 100 to R1, which would then route the packet on to R4. Keep in mind that R4's configuration is not a recommended configuration.

SPF Calculation

So far, this chapter has covered a lot of ground related to the exchange of LSAs. Regardless of the OSPF network type and whether DRs are used, once a router has new or different information in its LSDB, it uses the Dijkstra SPF algorithm to examine the LSAs in the LSDB and derive the math-equivalent of a figure of a network. This mathematical model has routers, links, costs for each link, and the current (up/down) status of each link. Figure 9-4 represents the SPF model of a sample network.

Figure 9-4 *Single-Area SPF Calculation: Conceptual View*

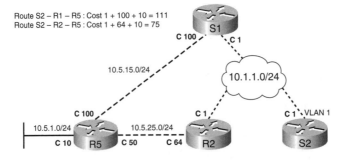

Humans can easily see the conclusion that the SPF algorithm will reach, even though the algorithm itself is fairly complicated. SPF on a router finds all possible routes to each subnet, adds the cost for each *outgoing* interface in that route, and then picks the path with the least cost. OSPF then places those least (shortest) cost routes into the routing table. For example, S2 calculates two possible routes to subnet 10.5.1.0/24, with the better route being out S2's VLAN 1 interface, with R2 as the next-hop router. Also note in Figure 9-4 that the cost values are per interface, and it is each outgoing interface's cost that SPF adds to come up with the total cost of the route.

Steady-State Operation

Even after a network has stabilized, all routers in the same area have the exact same LSAs, and each router has chosen its best routes using SPF, the following is still true of routers running OSPF:

- Each router sends Hellos, based on per-interface hello intervals.

- Each router expects to receive Hellos from neighbors within the dead interval on each interface; if not, the neighbor is considered to have failed.

- Each router originally advertising an LSA refloods each LSA (after incrementing its sequence number by 1) based on a per-LSA Link-State Refresh (LSRefresh) interval (default 30 minutes).

- Each router expects to have its LSA refreshed within each LSA's Maxage timer (default 60 minutes).

OSPF Design and LSAs

This section covers two major topics:

- OSPF design

- OSPF LSA types

Although these might seem to be separate concepts, most OSPF design choices directly impact the LSA types in a network and impose restrictions on which neighbors may exchange those LSAs. This section starts with an OSPF design and terminology review, and then moves on to LSA types. Toward the end of the section, OSPF area types are covered, including how each variation changes how LSAs flow through the different types of OSPF stubby areas.

OSPF Design Terms

OSPF design calls for grouping links into contiguous areas. Routers that connect to links in different areas are *Area Border Routers (ABRs)*. ABRs must connect to area 0, the *backbone area*, and one or more other areas as well. *Autonomous System Boundary Routers (ASBRs)* inject routes external to OSPF into the OSPF domain, having learned those routes from wide-ranging sources from the Border Gateway Protocol (BGP) on down to simple redistribution of static routes. Figure 9-5 shows the terms in the context of a simple OSPF design.

Figure 9-5 *OSPF Design Terminology*

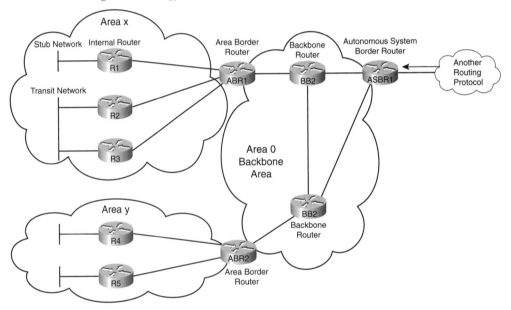

Networks can use a single OSPF area, but using OSPF areas helps speed convergence and reduce overhead in an OSPF network. Using areas provides the following benefits:

- Generally smaller per-area LSDBs, requiring less memory.

- Faster SPF computation due to the sparser LSDB.

- A link failure in one area only requires a partial SPF computation in other areas.

- Routes may only be summarized at ABRs (and ASBRs); having areas allows summarization, again shrinking the LSDB and improving SPF calculation performance.

When comparing the use of one area versus using many areas, the number of routers or subnets does not shrink, but the size of the LSDB on most routers should shrink. The LSDB shrinks because an ABR does not pass denser and more detailed type 1 and 2 LSAs from one area to another—instead, it passes type 3 summary LSAs. LSA types 1 and 2 can be thought of as the detailed topology information that causes most of the computing-intensive parts of the SPF algorithm; by representing these detailed type 1 and 2 LSAs in a different way in other areas, OSPF achieves its goal of reducing the effects of SPF.

OSPF Path Selection Process

OSPF has specific rules for selecting a path that crosses areas. Before studying the details of OSPF LSAs, it might help at this point to understand those rules:

- Take the shortest path to area 0.

- Take the shortest path across area 0 without traversing a nonzero area.

- Take the shortest path to the destination without traversing area 0.

Note that these conditions can result in both asymmetric routing and suboptimal routing across multiarea OSPF networks. For example, if the shortest path to a destination in area 0 is not also the least-cost path, OSPF behaves more like distance vector protocols than the link-state protocol that it is, which can cause headaches in both design and troubleshooting.

LSA Types and Network Types

Table 9-4 lists the LSA types and their descriptions for reference; following the table, each type is explained in more detail, in the context of a working network.

Table 9-4 *OSPF LSA Types*

LSA Type	Common Name	Description
1	Router	One per router, listing RID and all interface IP addresses. Represents stub networks as well.
2	Network	One per transit network. Created by the DR on the subnet, and represents the subnet and the router interfaces connected to the subnet.
3	Net Summary	Created by ABRs to represent one area's type 1 and 2 LSAs when being advertised into another area. Defines the links (subnets) in the origin area, and cost, but no topology data.
4	ASBR Summary	Like a type 3 LSA, except it advertises a host route used to reach an ASBR.
5	AS External	Created by ASBRs for external routes injected into OSPF.
6	Group Membership	Defined for MOSPF; not supported by Cisco IOS.
7	NSSA External	Created by ASBRs inside an NSSA area, instead of a type 5 LSA.
8	External Attributes	Not implemented in Cisco routers.
9–11	Opaque	Used as generic LSAs to allow for easy future extension of OSPF; for example, type 10 has been adapted for MPLS traffic engineering.

Before diving into the coverage of LSA types, two more definitions are needed:

- **Transit network**—A network over which two or more OSPF routers have become neighbors, so traffic can transit from one to the other.

- **Stub network**—A subnet on which a router has not formed any neighbor relationships.

Now on to the LSA types!

LSA Types 1 and 2

Each router creates and floods a type 1 LSA for itself. These LSAs describe the router, its interfaces (in that area), and a list of neighboring routers (in that area) on each interface. The LSA itself is identified by a *link-state ID (LSID)* equal to that router's RID.

Type 2 LSAs represent a transit subnet for which a DR has been elected. The LSID is the RID of the DR on that subnet. Note that type 2 LSAs are not created for subnets on which no DR has been elected.

Armed with an LSDB with all the type 1 and 2 LSAs inside an area, a router's SPF algorithm should be able to create a topological graph of the network, calculate the possible routes, and finally choose the best routes. For example, Figure 9-6 shows a sample internetwork that is used in several upcoming examples. Figure 9-7 shows a graphical view of the type 1 and type 2 LSAs created in area 3.

Figure 9-6 *Network Used in LSA Examples*

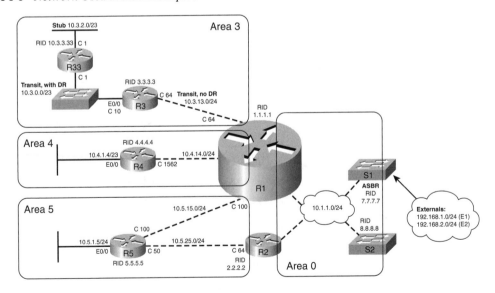

Figure 9-7 *Graph of Type 1 and 2 LSAs for Area 3*

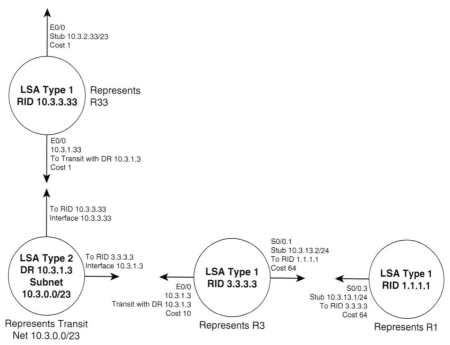

For subnets without a DR, the type 1 LSAs hold enough information for the SPF algorithm to create the math model of the topology. For example, R1 and R3 use point-to-point subinterfaces, and the OSPF point-to-point network type. SPF can match up the information shown in the type 1 LSAs for R1 and R3 in Figure 9-7 to know that the two routers are connected.

For transit networks with DRs, OSPF uses a type 2 LSA to model the subnet as a node in the SPF mathematical model. Because the SPF process treats the type 2 LSA as a node in the graph, this LSA is sometimes called a *pseudonode*. The type 2 LSA includes references to the RIDs of all routers that are currently neighbors of the DR on that subnet. That information, combined with the type 1 LSAs for each router connected to the subnet represented by the type 2 LSA, allows SPF to construct an accurate picture of the network.

Example 9-4 shows the LSAs in area 3 (Figures 9-6 and 9-7) via **show** commands.

Example 9-4 *LSA Types 1 and 2 in Area 3*

```
! R3's LSDB is shown, with type 1 LSAs listed as "Router Link States" and
! type 2 LSAs as "Net Link States." The command output shows a section for each LSA
! type, in sequential order.
R3# show ip ospf database
            OSPF Router with ID (3.3.3.3) (Process ID 1)
            Router Link States (Area 3)
```

continues

Example 9-4 *LSA Types 1 and 2 in Area 3 (Continued)*

```
Link ID          ADV Router       Age          Seq#          Checksum Link count
1.1.1.1          1.1.1.1          1203         0x80000025 0x0072C3 2
3.3.3.3          3.3.3.3          779          0x80000027 0x003FB0 3
10.3.3.33        10.3.3.33        899          0x80000020 0x002929 2


                 Net Link States (Area 3)
Link ID          ADV Router       Age          Seq#          Checksum
10.3.1.3         3.3.3.3          1290         0x8000001F 0x00249E
! Lines omitted for brevity
! Next, the specific LSA's link ID is included in the show command, listing detail
! for the one LSA type 2 inside area 3. Note that the "Link ID" is the DR's
! interface address on the subnet. The network keyword refers to the network LSAs (type 2 LSAs).
R3# show ip ospf database network 10.3.1.3
            OSPF Router with ID (3.3.3.3) (Process ID 1)
                Net Link States (Area 3)


Routing Bit Set on this LSA
LS age: 1304
Options: (No TOS-capability, DC)
LS Type: Network Links
Link State ID: 10.3.1.3 (address of Designated Router)
Advertising Router: 3.3.3.3
LS Seq Number: 8000001F
Checksum: 0x249E
Length: 32
Network Mask: /23
        Attached Router: 3.3.3.3
        Attached Router: 10.3.3.33
! Next, the type 1 LSA for R3 is listed. The link ID is the RID of R3. Note that
! the LSA includes reference to each stub and transit link connected to R3. The router
! keyword refers to the router LSAs (type 1 LSAs).
R3# show ip ospf database router 3.3.3.3
            OSPF Router with ID (3.3.3.3) (Process ID 1)
                Router Link States (Area 3)


  LS age: 804
  Options: (No TOS-capability, DC)
  LS Type: Router Links
  Link State ID: 3.3.3.3
  Advertising Router: 3.3.3.3
  LS Seq Number: 80000027
  Checksum: 0x3FB0
  Length: 60
  Number of Links: 3

    Link connected to: another Router (point-to-point)
    (Link ID) Neighboring Router ID: 1.1.1.1
    (Link Data) Router Interface address: 10.3.13.3
    Number of TOS metrics: 0
    TOS 0 Metrics: 64
```

Example 9-4 *LSA Types 1 and 2 in Area 3 (Continued)*

```
        Link connected to: a Stub Network
         (Link ID) Network/subnet number: 10.3.13.0
         (Link Data) Network Mask: 255.255.255.0
         Number of TOS metrics: 0
         TOS 0 Metrics: 64


! Note that R3's LSA refers to a transit network next, based on its DR RID -
! these lines allow OSPF to know that this router (R3) connects to the transit
! network whose type 2 LSA has LSID 10.3.1.3.

        Link connected to: a Transit Network
         (Link ID) Designated Router address: 10.3.1.3
         (Link Data) Router Interface address: 10.3.1.3
         Number of TOS metrics: 0
          TOS 0 Metrics: 10
! Below, the routes from R3 and R1 to 10.3.2.0/23 are shown. Note the cost values
! for each reflect the cumulative costs of the outgoing interfaces used to reach
! the subnet—for instance, R3's cost is the sum of its outgoing interface cost
! (10) plus R33's outgoing interface cost (1). R1's cost is based on three outgoing
! links: R1 (cost 64), R3 (cost 10), and R33 (cost 1), for a total of 75. Also
! note that the time listed in the route is the time since this LSA first arrived
! at the router, even if the LSA has been refreshed due to the LSRefresh interval.
R3# show ip route ospf 1 | include 10.3.2.0
O       10.3.2.0/23 [110/11] via 10.3.1.33, 17:08:33, Ethernet0/0
R1# show ip route ospf | include 10.3.2.0
O       10.3.2.0/23 [110/75] via 10.3.13.3, 17:10:15, Serial0/0.3
```

The **show ip ospf database** command lists the LSAs in that router's LSDB, with LSA type 1 LSAs (router LSAs) first, then type 2 (network link states), continuing sequentially through the LSA types. Also note that the LSDB for area 3 should be identical on R33, R3, and R1. However, on R1, the **show ip ospf database** command lists all of R1's LSDB entries, including LSAs from other areas, so using an internal router to look at the LSDB may be the best place to begin troubleshooting a problem. Also note the costs for the routes on R3 and R1 at the end of the example—the SPF algorithm simply added the outgoing costs along the routes, from each router's perspective.

NOTE To signify a network that is down, the appropriate type 1 or 2 LSA is changed to show a metric of 16,777,215 (2^{24} – 1), which is considered to be an infinite metric to OSPF.

LSA Type 3 and Inter-Area Costs

ABRs do not forward type 1 and 2 LSAs from one area to another. Instead, ABRs advertise type 3 LSAs into one area in order to represent subnets described in both the type 1 and 2 LSAs in another area. Each type 3 summary LSA describes a simple vector—the subnet, mask, and the ABR's cost to reach that subnet, as shown in Figure 9-8.

Figure 9-8 *Representation of Area 3 Subnets as Type 3 LSAs in Area 0*

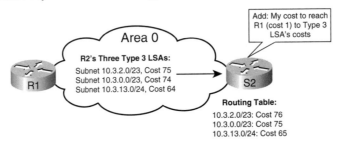

Example 9-5 focuses on the three subnets inside area 3, looking at the type 3 summary LSAs created for those subnets by ABR R1. Note that the example shows commands on S2; S2 has identical area 0 LSDB entries as compared with R1.

Example 9-5 *LSA Type 3 Created by R1 for Area 3's Subnets*

```
! S2, internal to area 0, does not have the type 1 and 2 LSAs seen by R3 back in
! Example 9-4. However, type 3 LSAs (listed as "Summary Net Links") show all
! three subnets inside area 3. R1 is listed as the advertising router because it
! created the type 3 LSAs.
S2# show ip ospf database
! Lines omitted for brevity
                 Summary Net Link States (Area 0)
Link ID          ADV Router      Age        Seq#        Checksum
10.3.0.0         1.1.1.1         257        0x80000001  0x00A63C
10.3.2.0         1.1.1.1         257        0x80000001  0x009A45
10.3.13.0        1.1.1.1         261        0x80000021  0x007747
! Lines omitted for brevity
! Below, note that the summary keyword is used to view type 3 LSAs. The metric
! reflects R1's cost to reach the subnet inside area 3.
S2# show ip ospf database summary 10.3.0.0
            OSPF Router with ID (8.8.8.8) (Process ID 1)
            Summary Net Link States (Area 0)

  Routing Bit Set on this LSA
  LS age: 341
  Options: (No TOS-capability, DC, Upward)
  LS Type: Summary Links(Network)
  Link State ID: 10.3.0.0 (summary Network Number)
  Advertising Router: 1.1.1.1
  LS Seq Number: 80000001
  Checksum: 0xA63C
  Length: 28
  Network Mask: /23
        TOS: 0   Metric: 74
! Next, S2's routes to all three subnets are listed. S2 calculates its cost
! based on its cost to reach R1, plus the cost listed in the type 3 LSA. For
```

Example 9-5 *LSA Type 3 Created by R1 for Area 3's Subnets (Continued)*

```
! example, the cost (above) in the type 3 LSA for 10.3.0.0/23 is 74; S2 adds
! that to S2's cost to reach ABR R1 (cost 1), for a metric of 75.
S2# show ip route ospf | include 10.3
O IA    10.3.13.0/24 [110/65] via 10.1.1.1, 00:16:04, Vlan1
O IA    10.3.0.0/23 [110/75] via 10.1.1.1, 00:05:08, Vlan1
O IA    10.3.2.0/23 [110/76] via 10.1.1.1, 00:05:12, Vlan1
! Next, S2's cost to reach RID 1.1.1.1 is listed as cost 1.
S2# show ip ospf border-routers
OSPF Process 1 internal Routing Table
Codes: i—Intra-area route, I—Inter-area route

i 1.1.1.1 [1] via 10.1.1.1, Vlan1, ABR, Area 0, SPF 18
i 2.2.2.2 [1] via 10.1.1.2, Vlan1, ABR, Area 0, SPF 18
i 7.7.7.7 [1] via 10.1.1.3, Vlan1, ASBR, Area 0, SPF 18
! Below, the show ip ospf statistics command lists the number of SPF calculations.
R1# show ip ospf stat
OSPF process ID 1
- - - - - - - - - - - - - - - - - - - - - - - - - - - - - - - - - - - -

  Area 0: SPF algorithm executed 6 times
  Area 3: SPF algorithm executed 15 times
  Area 4: SPF algorithm executed 6 times
  Area 5: SPF algorithm executed 5 times
! Lines omitted for brevity
```

Example 9-5 shows how S2 calculated its cost to the area 3 subnets. Routers calculate the cost for a route to a subnet defined in a type 3 LSA by adding the following items:

1. The calculated cost to reach the ABR that created and advertised the type 3 LSA.

2. The cost as listed in the type 3 LSA.

You can see the cost of the type 3 LSA with the **show ip ospf database summary** *link-id* command, and the cost to reach the advertising ABR with the **show ip ospf border-routers** command, as shown in Example 9-5.

The beauty of this two-step cost calculation process is that it allows a significant reduction in the number of SPF calculations. When a type 1 or 2 LSA changes in some way that affects the underlying routes—for instance, a link failure—each router in the area runs SPF, but routers inside other areas do not. For instance, if R3's E0/0 is shut down, all three routers in area 3 run SPF inside that area, and the counter for area 3 in the **show ip ospf statistics** command increments. However, routers not inside area 0 do not run SPF, even though they update their routing tables—a process called a *partial run*, *partial SPF*, or *partial calculation*.

For example, imagine that R3's LAN interface fails. R33 then updates its type 2 LSA, listing a metric of 16,777,215. R1 in turn updates its type 3 LSA for 10.3.0.0/23, flooding that throughout area 0. The next step shows the computational savings: S2, using the two-step calculation, simply adds its cost to R1 (still 1) to 16,777,215, finds the number out of range, and removes the route from the IP routing table. S2 did not have to actually run the SPF algorithm to discover a new SPF tree.

Of particular importance is that partial calculations happen without any route summarization. With OSPF, route summarization does help reduce the overall number of routes that require SPF calculations, but route summarization is not required for partial calculations to occur.

Removing Routes Advertised by Type 3 LSAs

When a router wants to remove a route advertised by a type 3 LSA from the LSDBs of its neighbors, it could simply remove that route from its LSDB and stop advertising it. The trouble with that approach is that the route might stick around for a while in other routers' LSDBs. Clearly, it is better to actively remove the failed route instead. As a result, the router that was advertising the failed route sets the route's age to the Maxage, as described in RFC 2328, and refloods it throughout the routing domain. This removes the route as quickly as possible from the domain, rather than waiting for it to age out slowly.

LSA Types 4 and 5, and External Route Types 1 and 2

OSPF allows for two types of external routes, aptly named types 1 and 2. The type determines whether only the external metric is considered by SPF when picking the best routes (external type 2, or E2), or whether both the external and internal metrics are added together to compute the metric (external type 1, or E1).

When an ASBR injects an E2 route, it creates a type 5 LSA for the subnet. The LSA lists the metric. The ASBR then floods the type 5 LSA throughout all areas. The other routers simply use the metric listed in the LSA; no need exists to add any cost on any links internal to the OSPF domain.

To support E1 routes, the ASBR creates and floods a type 5 LSA. When an ABR then floods the type 5 LSA into another area, the ABR creates a type 4 LSA, listing the ABR's metric to reach the ASBR that created the type 5 LSA. Other routers calculate their costs to reach E1 routes in a manner similar to how metrics for LSA type 3 routes are calculated—by calculating the cost to reach the ASBR, and then adding the cost listed in the type 5 LSA. Figure 9-9 outlines the mechanics of how the LSAs are propagated, and how the metrics are calculated.

Figure 9-9 *LSA Types 4 and 5 Propagation and the Effect on Type 1 External Routes*

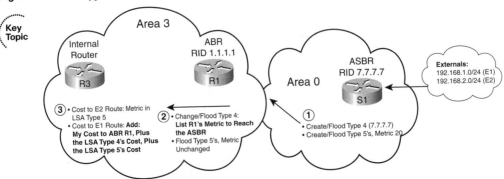

Note: Arrows Show Propagation of LSAs.

E1 routes by definition include the cost as assigned when the ASBR injected the route into OSPF, plus any cost inside the OSPF domain. To calculate the cost for the E1 route, a router inside a different area must use two steps to calculate the internal cost, and a third step to add the external cost. For example, when R3, internal to area 3, calculates the cost to reach 192.168.2.0/24 (an E1 route), R3 adds the following:

- R3's calculated area 3 cost to reach ABR R1 (RID 1.1.1.1).

- R1's cost to reach the ASBR that advertised the route (S2, RID 7.7.7.7). R1 announces this cost in the forwarded LSA type 4 that describes a host route to reach ASBR 7.7.7.7.

- The external metric for the route, as listed in the type 5 LSA created by the ASBR.

Example 9-6 shows the components of the metrics and LSAs for two external routes: 192.168.1.0/24 E1 with metric 20, and 192.168.2.0/24 E2, also with metric 20.

Example 9-6 *Calculating the Metric for External Types 1 and 2*

```
! R3 has learned the two LSA type 5s.
R3# show ip ospf database | begin Type-5
            Type-5 AS External Link States


Link ID         ADV Router      Age        Seq#       Checksum Tag
192.168.1.0     7.7.7.7         1916       0x8000002B 0x0080EF 0
192.168.2.0     7.7.7.7         1916       0x80000028 0x00FEF2 0
! Next, the detail for E2 192.168.2.0 is listed, with "metric type" referring
! to the external route type E2. (192.168.1.0, not shown, is type 1.)
R3# show ip ospf database external 192.168.2.0
            OSPF Router with ID (3.3.3.3) (Process ID 1)
        Type-5 AS External Link States


  Routing Bit Set on this LSA
  LS age: 1969
  Options: (No TOS-capability, DC)
  LS Type: AS External Link
  Link State ID: 192.168.2.0 (External Network Number)
  Advertising Router: 7.7.7.7
  LS Seq Number: 80000028
  Checksum: 0xFEF2
  Length: 36
  Network Mask: /24
    Metric Type: 2 (Larger than any link state path)
    TOS: 0
    Metric: 20
    Forward Address: 0.0.0.0
    External Route Tag: 0
! Next, R1's advertised cost of 1 between itself and the ASBR is listed. Note
! that S1's RID (7.7.7.7) is listed, with the ABR that forwarded the LSA into
```

continues

Example 9-6 *Calculating the Metric for External Types 1 and 2 (Continued)*

```
! area 3, R1 (RID 1.1.1.1) also listed.
R3# show ip ospf database asbr-summary
            OSPF Router with ID (3.3.3.3) (Process ID 1)
         Summary ASB Link States (Area 3)


  Routing Bit Set on this LSA
  LS age: 923
  Options: (No TOS-capability, DC, Upward)
  LS Type: Summary Links(AS Boundary Router)
  Link State ID: 7.7.7.7 (AS Boundary Router address)
  Advertising Router: 1.1.1.1
  LS Seq Number: 8000000A
  Checksum: 0x12FF
  Length: 28
  Network Mask: /0
    TOS: 0       Metric: 1
! Below, R3's calculated cost to R1 (64) and then to S2 (7.7.7.7) are listed. Note
! that the total of 65 is the cost 64 to reach the ABR, plus the cost 1 for the
! ABR to reach the ASBR.
R3# show ip ospf border-routers
OSPF Process 1 internal Routing Table
Codes: i—Intra-area route, I—Inter-area route

i 1.1.1.1 [64] via 10.3.13.1, Serial0/0.1, ABR, Area 3, SPF 30
I 7.7.7.7 [65] via 10.3.13.1, Serial0/0.1, ASBR, Area 3, SPF 30
! Below, each route is noted as E1 or E2, with the E1 route's metric including
! the external cost (20), plus cost to reach the ASBR (65).
R3# show ip route | include 192.168
O E1 192.168.1.0/24 [110/85] via 10.3.13.1, 00:50:34, Serial0/0.1
O E2 192.168.2.0/24 [110/20] via 10.3.13.1, 00:50:34, Serial0/0.1
```

OSPF Design in Light of LSA Types

OSPF's main design trade-offs consist of choosing links for particular areas, with the goal of speeding convergence, reducing memory and computing resources, and keeping routing tables small through route summarization. For instance, by using a larger number of areas, and the implied conversion of dense types 1 and 2 LSAs into sparser type 3 LSAs, the OSPF LSDBs can be made smaller. Also, link flaps in one area require SPF calculations only in that area, due to the partial calculation feature. Additionally, ABRs and ASBRs can be configured to summarize routes, reducing the number of type 3 LSAs introduced into other areas as well. (Route summarization is covered in Chapter 10, "IGP Route Summarization, Route Redistribution, and Default Routes.")

The OSPF design goals to reduce convergence time, reduce overhead processing, and improve network stability can be reached using the core OSPF protocols and features covered so far. Another key OSPF design tool, stubby areas, will be covered next.

NOTE   Before moving on, a comment is in order about the relative use of the word "summary" in OSPF. The typical uses within OSPF include the following:

- Type 3 LSAs are called *summary* LSAs in the OSPF RFCs.

- Type 5 and 7 external LSAs are sometimes called summary LSAs, because the LSAs cannot represent detailed topology information.

- The term *LSA summary* refers to the LSA headers that summarize LSAs and are sent inside DD packets.

- The term *summary* can also be used to refer to summary routes created with the **area range** and **summary-address** commands.

Stubby Areas

OSPF can further reduce overhead by treating each area with one of several variations of rules, based on a concept called a *stubby area*. Stubby areas take advantage of the fact that to reach subnets in other areas, routers in an area must forward the packets to some ABR. Without stubby areas, ABRs must advertise all the subnets into the area, so that the routers know about the subnets. With stubby areas, ABRs quit advertising type 5 (external) LSAs into the stubby area, but instead ABRs create and advertise default routes into the stubby area. As a result, internal routers use default routing to forward packets to the ABR anyway. However, the internal routers now have sparser LSDBs inside the area.

The classic case for a stubby area is an area with one ABR, but stubby areas can work well for areas with multiple ABRs as well. For example, the only way out of area 3 in Figure 9-6 is through the only ABR, R1. So, R1 could advertise a default route into area 3 instead of advertising any external type 5 LSAs.

Also in Figure 9-6, area 5 has two ABRs. If area 5 were a stubby area, both ABRs would inject default routes into the area. This configuration would work, but it may result in suboptimal routing.

OSPF defines several different types of stubby areas. By definition, all stubby areas stop type 5 (external) LSAs from being injected into them by the ABRs. However, depending on the variation, a stubby area may also prevent type 3 LSAs from being injected. The other variation includes whether a router inside the stubby area can redistribute routes into OSPF, thereby injecting an external route. Table 9-5 lists the variations on stubby areas, and their names.

Note in Table 9-5 that all four stub area types stop type 5 LSAs from entering the area. When the name includes "totally," type 3 LSAs are also not passed into the area, significantly reducing the size of the LSDB. If the name includes "NSSA," it means that external routes can be redistributed into OSPF by routers inside the stubby area; note that the LSAs for these external routes would be type 7.

Table 9-5 *OSPF Stubby Area Types*

Area Type	Stops Injection of Type 5 LSAs?	Stops Injection of Type 3 LSAs?	Allows Creation of Type 7 LSAs Inside the Area?
Stub	Yes	No	No
Totally stubby	Yes	Yes	No
Not-so-stubby area (NSSA)	Yes	No	Yes
Totally NSSA	Yes	Yes	Yes

Configuring a stub area is pretty simple—all routers in the area need the same stub settings, as configured in the **area stub** command. Table 9-6 lists the options.

Table 9-6 *Stub Area Configuration Options*

Stub Type	Router OSPF Subcommand
NSSA	**area** *area-id* **nssa**
Totally NSSA	**area** *area-id* **nssa no-summary**
Stub	**area** *area-id* **stub**
Totally stubby	**area** *area-id* **stub no-summary**

Example 9-7, based on Figure 9-6, shows the results of the following configuration:

- Area 3 is configured as a totally NSSA area.

- R3 will inject an external route to 192.168.21.0/24 as a type 7 LSA.

- Area 4 is configured as a totally stubby area.

- Area 5 is configured as simply stubby.

Example 9-7 *Stub Area Example*

```
! R3, in a totally NSSA area, knows intra-area routes (denoted with an "IA"
! near the front of the output line from show ip route), but the only
! inter-area route is the default route created and sent by R1, the ABR.
R3# show ip route ospf
     10.0.0.0/8 is variably subnetted, 3 subnets, 2 masks
O       10.3.2.0/23 [110/11] via 10.3.1.33, 00:00:00, Ethernet0/0
O*IA 0.0.0.0/0 [110/65] via 10.3.13.1, 00:00:00, Serial0/0.1
! Still on R3, the LSA type 3 summary, created by ABR R1, is shown first.
! Next, the External NSSA LSA type 7 LSA created by R3 is listed.
```

Example 9-7 *Stub Area Example (Continued)*

```
R3# show ip ospf database | begin Summary
        Summary Net Link States (Area 3)

Link ID          ADV Router       Age       Seq#        Checksum
0.0.0.0          1.1.1.1          704       0x80000004 0x00151A


        Type-7 AS External Link States (Area 3)

Link ID          ADV Router       Age       Seq#        Checksum Tag
192.168.21.0     3.3.3.3          17        0x80000003 0x00C12B 0

! R1, because it is attached to area 3, also has the R3-generated NSSA external
! LSA. Note the advertising router is R3, and it is an E2 external route.
R1# show ip ospf database nssa-external
            OSPF Router with ID (1.1.1.1) (Process ID 1)
        Type-7 AS External Link States (Area 3)


        Routing Bit Set on this LSA
        LS age: 188
        Options: (No TOS-capability, Type 7/5 translation, DC)
        LS Type: AS External Link
        Link State ID: 192.168.21.0 (External Network Number )
        Advertising Router: 3.3.3.3
        LS Seq Number: 80000003
        Checksum: 0xC12B
        Length: 36
        Network Mask: /24
          Metric Type: 2 (Larger than any link state path)
          TOS: 0
          Metric: 20
          Forward Address: 10.3.13.3
          External Route Tag: 0
! Below, the same command on R2, not in area 3, shows no type 7 LSAs. ABRs
! convert type 7 LSAs to type 5 LSAs before forwarding them into another area.
R2# show ip ospf database nssa-external

            OSPF Router with ID (2.2.2.2) (Process ID 2)
! Next, R2 does have a type 5 LSA for the subnet; R1 converts the type 7 to a type
! 5 before flooding it into other areas.
R2# show ip ospf database | begin Type-5
            Type-5 AS External Link States

Link ID          ADV Router       Age       Seq#        Checksum Tag
192.168.1.0      7.7.7.7          521       0x80000050 0x003615 0
192.168.2.0      7.7.7.7          521       0x8000004D 0x00B418 0
192.168.21.0     1.1.1.1          1778      0x80000019 0x006682 0
```

continues

Example 9-7 *Stub Area Example (Continued)*

```
! Below, R4 is in a totally stubby area, with only one inter-area route.
R4# show ip route ospf
O*IA 0.0.0.0/0 [110/1563] via 10.4.14.1, 00:11:59, Serial0/0.1


! R5, in a stubby area, has several inter-area routes, but none of the
! external routes (e.g. 192.168.1.0). R5's default points to R2.
R5# show ip route ospf
10.0.0.0/8 is variably subnetted, 7 subnets, 3 masks
O IA     10.3.13.0/24 [110/115] via 10.5.25.2, 13:45:49, Serial0.2
O IA     10.3.0.0/23 [110/125] via 10.5.25.2, 13:37:55, Serial0.2
O IA     10.1.1.0/24 [110/51] via 10.5.25.2, 13:45:49, Serial0.2
O IA     10.4.0.0/16 [110/1613] via 10.5.25.2, 13:45:49, Serial0.2
O*IA 0.0.0.0/0 [110/51] via 10.5.25.2, 13:45:49, Serial0.2

! Below, R5's costs on its two interfaces to R1 and R2 are highlighted. Note that
! the default route's metric (51) comes from the 50 below, plus an advertised
! cost of 1 in the summary (type 3) for default 0.0.0.0/0 generated by R2. R5
! simply chose to use the default route with the lower metric.
R5# sh ip ospf int brief
Interface   PID   Area        IP Address/Mask    Cost  State Nbrs F/C
Se0.1       1     5           10.5.15.5/24       64    P2P   1/1
Se0.2       1     5           10.5.25.5/24       50    P2P   1/1
Et0         1     5           10.5.1.5/24        10    DR    0/0


! Next, R2 changes the cost of its advertised summary from 1 to 15.
R2# conf t
Enter configuration commands, one per line.  End with CNTL/Z.
R2(config)# router ospf 2
R2(config-router)# area 5 default-cost 15
! Below, R5's metrics to both R1's and R2's default routes tie,
! so both are now in the routing table.
R5# show ip route ospf
! lines omitted for brevity
O*IA 0.0.0.0/0 [110/65] via 10.5.25.2, 00:00:44, Serial0.2
                 [110/65] via 10.5.15.1, 00:00:44, Serial0.1
```

The legend in the top of the output of a **show ip route** command lists several identifiers that pertain to OSPF. For example, the acronym "IA" refers to interarea OSPF routes, E1 refers to external type 1 routes, and E2 refers to external type 2 routes.

Graceful Restart

In steady-state operation, OSPF can react to changes in the routing domain and reconverge quickly. This is one of OSPF's strengths as an IGP. However, what happens when something goes really wrong is just as important as how things work under relatively stable conditions.

One of those "really wrong" things that sometimes happens is that a router requires a restart to its OSPF software process. To prevent various routing problems, including loops, that can take place when an OSPF router suddenly goes away while its OSPF software is restarting is the graceful restart process documented in RFC 3623. Cisco implemented its own version of graceful restart in Cisco IOS prior to RFC 3623; as a result, Cisco IOS supports both versions.

Graceful restart is also known as nonstop forwarding (NSF) in RFC 3623 because of the way it works. Graceful restart takes advantage of the fact that modern router architectures use separate routing and forwarding planes. It is possible to continue forwarding without loops while the routing process restarts, assuming the following conditions are true:

- The router whose OSPF process is restarting must notify its neighbors that the restart is going to take place by sending a "grace LSA."

- The LSA database remains stable during the restart.

- All of the neighbors support, and are configured for, graceful restart.

- The restart takes place within a specific "grace period."

- During restart, the neighboring fully adjacent routers must operate in "helper mode."

In Cisco IOS, CEF handles forwarding during graceful restart while OSPF rebuilds the RIB tables, provided that the preceding conditions are met. Both Cisco and IETF NSF support are enabled by default in Cisco IOS, beginning with version 12.4(6)T. Disabling it requires a routing process command for each NSF version, **nsf [cisco | ietf] helper disable**.

OSPF Path Choices That Do Not Use Cost

Under most circumstances, when an OSPF router runs the SPF algorithm and finds more than one possible route to reach a particular subnet, the router chooses the route with the least cost. However, OSPF does consider a few conditions other than cost when making this best-path decision. This short section explains the remaining factors that impact which route, or path, is considered best by the SPF algorithm.

Choosing the Best Type of Path

As mentioned earlier, some routes are considered to be intra-area routes, some are interarea routes, and two are types of external routes (E1 and E2). It is possible for a router to find multiple routes to reach a given subnet where the type of route (intra-area, interarea, E1, or E2) is different. In these cases, RFC 2328 specifies that the router should ignore the costs and instead chooses the best route based on the following order of preference:

1. Intra-area routes

2. Interarea routes

3. E1 routes

4. E2 routes

For example, if a router using OSPF finds one intra-area route for subnet 1 and one interarea route to reach that same subnet, the router ignores the costs and simply chooses the intra-area route. Similarly, if a router finds one interarea route, one E1 route, and one E2 route to reach the same subnet, that router chooses the interarea route, again regardless of the cost for each route.

Best-Path Side Effects of ABR Loop Prevention

The other item that affects OSPF best-path selection relates to some OSPF loop-avoidance features. Inside an area, OSPF uses Link State logic, but between areas OSPF acts much like a Distance Vector (DV) protocol in some regard. For example, the advertisement of a Type 3 LSA from one area to another hides the topology in the original area from the second area, just listing a destination subnet, metric (cost), and the ABR through which the subnet can be reached—all DV concepts.

OSPF does not use all the traditional DV loop avoidance features, but it does use some of the same underlying concepts, including Split Horizon. In OSPF's case, it applies Split Horizon for several types of LSAs so that an LSA is not advertised into one nonbackbone area and then advertised back into the backbone area. Figure 9-10 shows an example in which ABR1 and ABR2 both advertise Type 3 LSAs into area 1, but then they both choose to not forward a Type 3 LSA back into area 0.

Figure 9-10 *Split Horizon per Area with OSPF*

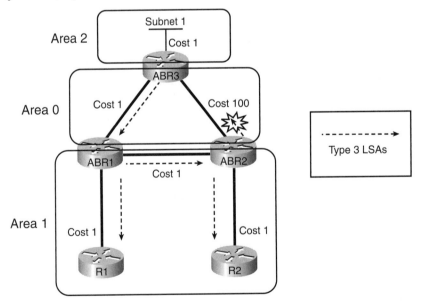

The figure shows the propagation of some of the LSAs for subnet 1 in this figure but not all. ABR3 generates a T3 LSA for subnet 1 and floods that LSA within area 0. ABR1 floods a T3 LSA for subnet 1 into area 1; however, when ABR2 gets that T3 LSA from ABR1, ABR2 does not flood a T3 LSA back into area 0. (To reduce clutter, the figure does not include arrowed lines for the opposite direction, in which ABR2 floods a T3 LSA into area 1, and then ABR1 chooses not to flood a T3 LSA back into area 0.)

More generically speaking, an ABR can learn about summary LSAs from other ABRs, inside the nonbackbone area, but the ABR will not then advertise another LSA back into area 0 for that subnet.

Although interesting, none of these facts impacts OSPF path selection. The second part of ABR loop prevention is the part that impacts path selection, as follows:

> ABRs ignore LSAs created by other ABRs, when learned through a nonbackbone area, when calculating least-cost paths. This prevents an ABR from choosing a path that goes into one nonbackbone area and then back into area 0 through some other ABR.

For example, without this rule, in the internetwork of Figure 9-11, router ABR2 would calculate a cost 3 path to subnet 1: from ABR2 to ABR1 inside area 1 and then from ABR1 to ABR3 in area 0. ABR2 would also calculate a cost 101 path to subnet 1, going from ABR2 through area 0 to ABR3. Clearly, the first of these two paths, with cost 3, is the least-cost path. However, ABRs use this additional loop-prevention rule, meaning that ABR2 ignores the T3 LSA advertised by ABR1 for subnet 1. This behavior prevents ABR2 from choosing the path through ABR2, so in actual practice, ABR2 would find only one possible path to subnet 1: the path directly from ABR2 to ABR3.

Figure 9-11 *Effect of ABR2 Ignoring Path to Subnet 1 Through Area 1*

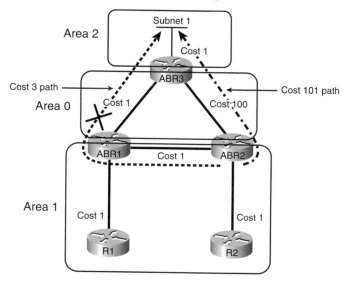

It is important to notice that the link between ABR1 and ABR2 is squarely inside nonbackbone area 1. If this link were in area 0, ABR2 would pick the best route to reach ABR3 as being ABR2—ABR1—ABR3, choosing the lower-cost route.

This loop-prevention rule has some even more interesting side effects for internal routers. Again in Figure 9-10, consider the routes calculated by internal router R2 to reach subnet 1. R2 learns a T3 LSA for subnet 1 from ABR1, with the cost listed as 2. To calculate the total cost for using ABR1 to reach subnet 1, R2 adds its cost to reach ABR1 (cost 2), totaling cost 4. Likewise, R2 learns a T3 LSA for subnet 1 from ABR2, with cost 101. R1 calculates its cost to reach ABR2 (cost 1) and adds that to 101 to arrive at cost 102 for this alternative route. As a result, R1 picks the route through ABR1 as the best route.

However, the story gets even more interesting with the topology in Figure 9-10. R2's next-hop router for the R2—ABR2—ABR1—ABR3 path is ABR2. So, R2 forwards packets destined to subnet 1 to ABR2 next. However, as noted just a few paragraphs ago, ABR2's route to reach subnet 1 points directly to ABR3. As a result, packets sent by R2, destined to subnet 1, actually take the path from R2 —ABR2—ABR3. As you can see, these decisions can result in arguably suboptimal routes, and even asymmetric routes, as would be the case in this particular example.

OSPF Configuration

This section covers the core OSPF configuration commands, along with the OSPF configuration topics not already covered previously in the chapter. (If you happened to skip the earlier parts of this chapter, planning to review OSPF configuration, make sure to go back and look at the earlier examples in the chapter. These examples cover OSPF stubby area configuration, OSPF network types, plus OSPF **neighbor** and **priority** commands.)

Example 9-8 shows configuration for the routers in Figure 9-6, with the following design goals in mind:

- Proving that OSPF PIDs do not have to match on separate routers

- Using the **network** command to match interfaces, thereby triggering neighbor discovery inside network 10.0.0.0

- Configuring S1's RID as 7.7.7.7

- Setting priorities on the backbone LAN to favor S1 and S2 to become the DR/BDR

- Configuring a minimal dead interval of 1 second, with hello multiplier of 4, yielding a 250-ms hello interval on the backbone LAN

Example 9-8 *OSPF Configuration Basics and OSPF Costs*

```
! R1 !!!!!!!!!!!!!!!!!!!!!!!!!!!!!!!!!!!!!!!!!!!!!!!!!!!!!!!!!!!!!!!!!!!!!!!!!!!!!!!!!
! R1 has been configured for a (minimal) 1-second dead interval, and 1/4-second
! (250 ms) hello interval based on 4 Hellos per 1-second dead interval.
interface FastEthernet0/0
 ip address 10.1.1.1 255.255.255.0
 ip ospf dead-interval minimal hello-multiplier 4
! R1 uses the same stub area configuration as in Example 9-7, with network
! commands matching based on the first two octets. Note that the network commands
! place each interface into the correct area.
router ospf 1
 area 3 nssa no-summary
 area 4 stub no-summary
 area 5 stub
 network 10.1.0.0 0.0.255.255 area 0
 network 10.3.0.0 0.0.255.255 area 3
 network 10.4.0.0 0.0.255.255 area 4
 network 10.5.0.0 0.0.255.255 area 5
! R2 !!!!!!!!!!!!!!!!!!!!!!!!!!!!!!!!!!!!!!!!!!!!!!!!!!!!!!!!!!!!!!!!!!!!!!!!!!!!!!!!
! The R2 configuration also uses the Fast Hello feature, otherwise it
! would not match hello and dead intervals with R1.
interface FastEthernet0/0
 ip address 10.1.1.2 255.255.255.0
 ip ospf dead-interval minimal hello-multiplier 4
! Below, R2 uses a different PID than R1, but the PID is only used locally.
! R1 and R2 will become neighbors. Also, all routers in a stubby area must be
! configured to be that type of stubby area; R2 does that for area 5 below.
router ospf 2
 area 5 stub
 network 10.1.0.0 0.0.255.255 area 0
 network 10.5.25.2 0.0.0.0 area 5
! R3 !!!!!!!!!!!!!!!!!!!!!!!!!!!!!!!!!!!!!!!!!!!!!!!!!!!!!!!!!!!!!!!!!!!!!!!!!!!!!!!!
!Note that R3's area 2 nssa no-summary command must match the settings
! on R1. Likewise, below, R4's stub settings must match R1's settings for area 4.
.
router ospf 1
 area 3 nssa no-summary
 network 10.0.0.0 0.255.255.255 area 3
! R4 !!!!!!!!!!!!!!!!!!!!!!!!!!!!!!!!!!!!!!!!!!!!!!!!!!!!!!!!!!!!!!!!!!!!!!!!!!!!!!!!
router ospf 1
 area 4 stub no-summary
 network 10.0.0.0 0.255.255.255 area 4
```

continues

Example 9-8 *OSPF Configuration Basics and OSPF Costs (Continued)*

```
! S1 !!!!!!!!!!!!!!!!!!!!!!!!!!!!!!!!!!!!!!!!!!!!!!!!!!!!!!!!!!!!!!!!!!!!!!!!!!!!!!!!
! S1 matches hello and dead intervals on the LAN. Also, it sets its OSPF
! priority to 255, the maximum value, hoping to become the DR.
interface Vlan1
 ip address 10.1.1.3 255.255.255.0
 ip ospf dead-interval minimal hello-multiplier 4
 ip ospf priority 255
! Below, S1 sets its RID manually, removing any reliance on an interface address.
router ospf 1
 router-id 7.7.7.7
 network 10.1.0.0 0.0.255.255 area 0
! S2 !!!!!!!!!!!!!!!!!!!!!!!!!!!!!!!!!!!!!!!!!!!!!!!!!!!!!!!!!!!!!!!!!!!!!!!!!!!!!!!!
! Below, S2 also matches timers, and sets its priority to 1 less than S1, hoping
! to be the BDR.
interface Vlan1
 ip address 10.1.1.4 255.255.255.0
 ip ospf dead-interval minimal hello-multiplier 4
 ip ospf priority 254
!
router ospf 1
 network 10.0.0.0 0.255.255.255 area 0
```

Key
Topic

Note that R3 and R4 do not need the **no-summary** option on the **area** command; this parameter is only needed at the ABR, in this case R1. The parameters are shown here to stress the variations of stubby areas.

OSPF Costs and Clearing the OSPF Process

Example 9-9 highlights a few details about clearing (restarting) the OSPF process, and looks at changes to OSPF costs. This example shows the following sequence:

1. R3's OSPF process is cleared, causing all neighbors to fail and restart.

2. R3's **log-adjacency-changes detail** configuration command (under **router ospf**) causes more detailed neighbor state change messages to appear.

3. R5 has tuned its cost settings with the **ip ospf cost 50** interface subcommand under S0.2 in order to prefer R2 over R1 for reaching the core.

4. R2 is configured to use a new reference bandwidth, changing its cost calculation per interface.

Example 9-9 *Changing RIDs, Clearing OSPF, and Cost Settings*

```
R3# clear ip ospf process
Reset ALL OSPF processes? [no]: y
! Above, all OSPF processes are cleared on R3. R3 has the log-adjacency-changes
! detail command configured, so that a message is generated at each state
! change, as shown below for neighbor R33 (RID 192.168.1.1). (Messages for
! other routers are omitted.)
```

Example 9-9 *Changing RIDs, Clearing OSPF, and Cost Settings (Continued)*

```
00:02:46: %OSPF-5-ADJCHG: Process 1, Nbr 192.168.1.1 on Ethernet0/0 from FULL to DOWN,
  Neighbor Down: Interface down or detached
00:02:53: %OSPF-5-ADJCHG: Process 1, Nbr 192.168.1.1 on Ethernet0/0 from DOWN to INIT,
  Received Hello
00:02:53: %OSPF-5-ADJCHG: Process 1, Nbr 192.168.1.1 on Ethernet0/0 from INIT to 2WAY,
  2-Way Received
00:02:53: %OSPF-5-ADJCHG: Process 1, Nbr 192.168.1.1 on Ethernet0/0 from 2WAY to EXSTART,
  AdjOK?
00:02:53: %OSPF-5-ADJCHG: Process 1, Nbr 192.168.1.1 on Ethernet0/0 from EXSTART
  to EXCHANGE, Negotiation Done
00:02:53: %OSPF-5-ADJCHG: Process 1, Nbr 192.168.1.1 on Ethernet0/0 from EXCHANGE
  to LOADING, Exchange Done
00:02:53: %OSPF-5-ADJCHG: Process 1, Nbr 192.168.1.1 on Ethernet0/0 from LOADING to FULL,
  Loading Done
! Next R5 has costs of 50 and 64, respectively, on interfaces s0.2 and s0.1.
R5# show ip ospf int brief
Interface    PID   Area        IP Address/Mask    Cost  State Nbrs F/C
Se0.2        1     5           10.5.25.5/24       50    P2P   1/1
Se0.1        1     5           10.5.15.5/24       64    P2P   1/1
Et0          1     5           10.5.1.5/24        10    DR    0/0
! Below, S0.1's cost was based on bandwidth of 64, using formula 10^8 / bandwidth,
! with bandwidth in bits/second.
R5# sh int s 0.1
Serial0.1 is up, line protocol is up
  Hardware is HD64570
  Internet address is 10.5.15.5/24
  MTU 1500 bytes, BW 1544 Kbit, DLY 20000 usec,
     reliability 255/255, txload 1/255, rxload 1/255
  Encapsulation FRAME-RELAY
  Last clearing of "show interface" counters never
! Next, R2's interface costs are shown, including the minimum cost 1 on fa0/0.
R2# sho ip ospf int brief
Interface    PID   Area        IP Address/Mask    Cost  State Nbrs F/C
Fa0/0        2     0           10.1.1.2/24        1     BDR   3/3
Se0/0.5      2     5           10.5.25.2/24       64    P2P   1/1
! Below, R2 changes its reference bandwidth from the default of 100 Mbps to
! 10,000 Mbps. That in turn changes R2's calculated cost values to be 100 times
! larger than before. Note that IOS allows this setting to differ on the routers,
! but recommends against it.
R2# conf t
Enter configuration commands, one per line.  End with CNTL/Z.
R2(config)# router ospf 2
R2(config-router)# auto-cost reference-bandwidth 10000
% OSPF: Reference bandwidth is changed.
        Please ensure reference bandwidth is consistent across all routers.
R2# show ip ospf int brief
Interface    PID   Area        IP Address/Mask    Cost  State Nbrs F/C
Fa0/0        2     0           10.1.1.2/24        100   BDR   3/3
Se0/0.5      2     5           10.5.25.2/24       6476  P2P   1/1
```

While Examples 9-8 and 9-9 show some details, the following list summarizes how IOS chooses OSPF interface costs:

1. Set the cost per neighbor using the **neighbor** *neighbor* **cost** *value* command. (This is valid only on OSPF network types that allow **neighbor** commands.)

2. Set the cost per interface using the **ip ospf cost** *value* interface subcommand.

3. Allow cost to default based on interface bandwidth and the OSPF Reference Bandwidth (Ref-BW) (default 10^8). The formula is Ref-BW / bandwidth (bps).

4. Default based on bandwidth, but change Ref-BW using the command **ospf auto-cost reference-bandwidth** value command within the OSPF process.

The only slightly tricky part of the cost calculation math is to keep the units straight, because the IOS interface bandwidth is kept in kbps, and the **auto-cost reference-bandwidth** command's units are Mbps. For instance, on R5 in Example 9-9, the cost is calculated as 100 Mbps divided by 1544 kbps, where 1544 kbps is equal to 1.544 Mbps. The result is rounded down to the nearest integer, 64 in this case. On R2's fa0/0, the bandwidth is 100,000 kbps, or 100 Mbps, making the calculation yield a cost of 1. After changing the reference bandwidth to 10,000, which means 10,000 Mbps, R2's calculated costs were 100 times larger.

> **NOTE**   When choosing the best routes to reach a subnet, OSPF also considers whether a route is an intra-area route, inter-area route, E1 route, or E2 route. OSPF prefers intra-area over all the rest, then interarea, then E1, and finally E2 routes. Under normal circumstances, routes to a single subnet should all be the same type; however, it is possible to have multiple route paths to reach a single subnet in the OSPF SPF tree, but with some of these routes being a different type. Example 10-7 in Chapter 10 demonstrates this.

Alternatives to the OSPF Network Command

As of Cisco IOS Software Release 12.3(11)T, OSPF configuration can completely omit the **network** command, instead relying on the **ip ospf** *process-id* **area** *area-id* interface subcommand. This new command enables OSPF on the interface and selects the area. For instance, on R3 in Example 9-8, the **network 10.3.0.0 0.0.255.255 area 3** command could have been deleted and replaced with the **ip ospf 1 area 3** command under S0/0.1 and e0/0.

The **network** and **ip ospf area** commands have some minor differences when secondary IP addresses are used. With the **network** command, OSPF advertises stub networks for any secondary IP subnets that are matched by the command. ("Secondary subnet" is jargon that refers to the subnet in which a secondary IP address resides.) The **ip ospf area** interface subcommand causes any and all secondary subnets on the interface to be advertised as stub networks—unless the optional **secondaries none** parameter is included at the end of the command.

OSPF Filtering

Intra-routing–protocol filtering presents some special challenges with link-state routing protocols like OSPF. Link-state protocols do not advertise routes—they advertise topology information. Also, SPF loop prevention relies on each router in the same area having an identical copy of the LSDB for that area. Filtering could conceivably make the LSDBs differ on different routers, causing routing irregularities.

IOS supports three variations of what could loosely be categorized as OSPF route filtering. These three major types of OSPF filtering are as follows:

■ **Filtering routes, not LSAs**—Using the **distribute-list in** command, a router can filter the *routes* its SPF process is attempting to add to its routing table, without affecting the LSDB.

■ **ABR type 3 LSA filtering**—A process of preventing an ABR from creating particular type 3 summary LSAs.

■ **Using the area range no-advertise option**—Another process to prevent an ABR from creating specific type 3 summary LSAs.

Each of these three topics is discussed in sequence in the next few sections.

Filtering Routes Using the distribute-list Command

For RIP and EIGRP, the **distribute-list** command can be used to filter incoming and outgoing routing updates. The process is straightforward, with the **distribute-list** command referring to ACLs or prefix lists. With OSPF, the **distribute-list** command filters what ends up in the IP routing table, and on only the router on which the **distribute-list** command is configured.

> **NOTE** The **distribute-list** command, when used for route distribution between OSPF and other routing protocols, does control what enters and leaves the LSDB. Chapter 10 covers more on route redistribution.

The following rules govern the use of distribute lists for OSPF, when not used for route redistribution with other routing protocols:

■ Distribute lists can be used only for inbound filtering, because filtering any outbound OSPF information would mean filtering LSAs, not routes.

■ The inbound logic does not filter inbound LSAs; it instead filters the routes that SPF chooses to add to that one router's routing table.

■ If the distribute list includes the incoming interface parameter, the incoming interface is checked as if it were the *outgoing interface* of the route.

That last bullet could use a little clarification. For example, if R2 learns routes via RIP or EIGRP updates that enter R2's s0/0 interface, those routes typically use R2's s0/0 interface as the outgoing interface of the routes. The OSPF LSAs may have been flooded into a router on several interfaces, so an OSPF router checks the outgoing interface of the route as if it had learned about the routes via updates coming in that interface.

Example 9-10 shows an example of two distribute lists on R5 from Figure 9-6. The example shows two options to achieve the same goal. In this case, R5 will filter the route to 10.4.8.0/24 via R5's S0.2 subinterface (to R2), instead using the route learned from R1. Later, it uses a **route map** to achieve the same result.

Example 9-10 *Filtering Routes with OSPF* **distribute-list** *Commands on R5*

```
! R5 has a route to 10.4.8.0/24 through R2 (10.5.25.2, s0.2)
R5# sh ip route ospf | incl 10.4.8.0
O IA    10.4.8.0/24 [110/1623] via 10.5.25.2, 00:00:28, Serial0.2
! Next, the distribute-list command refers to a prefix list that permits 10.4.8.0
! /24.
ip prefix-list prefix-9-4-8-0 seq 5 deny 10.4.8.0/24
ip prefix-list prefix-9-4-8-0 seq 10 permit 0.0.0.0/0 le 32
!
Router ospf 1
 distribute-list prefix prefix-9-4-8-0 in Serial0.2
! Below, note that R5's route through R2 is gone, and instead R5 uses its route
! through R1 (s0.1). But the LSDB is unchanged!
R5# sh ip route ospf | incl 10.4.8.0
O IA    10.4.8.0/24 [110/1636] via 10.5.15.1, 00:00:03, Serial0.1
! Not shown: the earlier distribute-list command is removed.
! Below, note that the distribute-list command with the route-map option does not
! have an option to refer to an interface, so the route map itself has been
! configured to refer to the advertising router's RID (2.2.2.2).
Router ospf 1
distribute-list route-map lose-9-4-8-0 in
! Next, ACL 48 matches the 10.4.8.0/24 prefix, with ACL 51 matching R2's RID.
access-list 48 permit 10.4.8.0
access-list 51 permit 2.2.2.2
! Below, the route map matches the prefix (based on ACL 48) and the advertising
! RID (ACL 51, matching R2's 2.2.2.2 RID). Clause 20 permits all other prefixes.
route-map lose-9-4-8-0 deny 10
match ip address 48
match ip route-source 51
route-map lose-9-4-8-0 permit 20
! Above, note the same results as the previous distribute list.
R5# sh ip route ospf | incl 10.4.8.0
O IA    10.4.8.0/24 [110/1636] via 10.5.15.1, 00:01:18, Serial0.1
```

Example 9-10 shows only two ways to filter the routes. The **distribute-list route-map** option, added in Cisco IOS Software Release 12.2(15)T, allows a much greater variety of matching parameters, and much more detailed logic with route maps. For instance, this example showed matching a prefix as well as the RID that advertised the LSA to R5, namely 2.2.2.2 (R2). Refer to Chapter 11 for a more complete review of route maps and the **match** command.

OSPF ABR LSA Type 3 Filtering

ABRs do not forward type 1 and 2 LSAs from one area into another, but instead create type 3 LSAs for each subnet defined in the type 1 and 2 LSAs. Type 3 LSAs do not contain detailed information about the topology of the originating area; instead, each type 3 LSA represents a subnet, and a cost from the ABR to that subnet. The earlier section "LSA Type 3 and Inter-Area Costs" covers the details and provides an example.

The *OSPF ABR type 3 LSA filtering* feature allows an ABR to filter type 3 LSAs at the point where the LSAs would normally be created. By filtering at the ABR, before the type 3 LSA is injected into another area, the requirement for identical LSDBs inside the area can be met, while still filtering LSAs.

To configure type 3 LSA filtering, you use the **area** *number* **filter-list prefix** *name* **in | out** command under **router ospf**. The referenced **prefix list** is used to match the subnets and masks to be filtered. The **area** *number* and the **in | out** option of the **area filter-list** command work together, as follows:

- When **in** is configured, IOS filters prefixes going into the configured area.

- When **out** is configured, IOS filters prefixes coming out of the configured area.

Example 9-11 should clarify the basic operation. ABR R1 will use two alternative **area filter-list** commands, both to filter subnet 10.3.2.0/23, the subnet that exists between R3 and R33 in Figure 9-6. Remember that R1 is connected to areas 0, 3, 4, and 5. The first **area filter-list** command shows filtering the LSA as it goes out of area 3; as a result, R2 will not inject the LSA into any of the other areas. The second case shows the same subnet being filtered going into area 0, meaning that the type 3 LSA for that subnet still gets into the area 4 and 5 LSDBs.

Example 9-11 *Type 3 LSA Filtering on R1 with the* **area filter-list** *Command*

```
! The command lists three lines of extracted output. One line is for the
! type 3 LSA in area 0, one is for area 4, and one is for area 5.
R1# show ip ospf data summary | include 10.3.2.0
        Link State ID: 10.3.2.0 (summary Network Number)
        Link State ID: 10.3.2.0 (summary Network Number)
        Link State ID: 10.3.2.0 (summary Network Number)
! Below, the two-line prefix list denies subnet 10.3.2.0/23, and then permits
! all others.
ip prefix-list filter-type3-9-3-2-0 seq 5 deny 10.3.2.0/23
ip prefix-list filter-type3-9-3-2-0 seq 10 permit 0.0.0.0/0 le 32
Next, the area filter-list command filters type 3 LSAs going out of area 3.
R1# conf t
Enter configuration commands, one per line.  End with CNTL/Z.
R1(config)# router ospf 1
```

Example 9-11   *Type 3 LSA Filtering on R1 with the* **area filter-list** *Command (Continued)*

```
R1(config-router)# area 3 filter-list prefix filter-type3-9-3-2-0 out
R1(config-router)# ^Z
! Below, R1 no longer has any type 3 LSAs, in areas 0, 4, and 5. For
! comparison, this command was issued a few commands ago, listing 1 line
! of output for each of the other 3 areas besides area 3.
R1# show ip ospf data | include 10.3.2.0
! Below, the previous area filter-list command is replaced by the next command
! below, which filters type 3 LSAs going into area 0, with the same prefix list.
area 0 filter-list prefix filter-type3-9-3-2-0 in
! Next, only 2 type 3 LSAs for 10.3.2.0 are shown—the ones in areas 4 and 5.
R1# show ip ospf data | include 10.3.2.0
  Link State ID: 10.3.2.0 (summary Network Number)
  Link State ID: 10.3.2.0 (summary Network Number)
! Below, the configuration for filtering type 3 LSAs with the area range command,
! which is explained following this example. The existing area filter-list
! commands from earlier in this chapter have been removed at this point.
R1(config-router)# area 3 range 10.3.2.0 255.255.254.0 not-advertise
R1# show ip ospf data summary ¦ include 10.3.2.0
R1#
```

Filtering Type 3 LSAs with the area range Command

The third method to filter OSPF routes is to filter type 3 LSAs at an ABR using the **area range** command. The **area range** command performs route summarization at ABRs, telling a router to cease advertising smaller subnets in a particular address range, instead creating a single type 3 LSA whose address and prefix encompass the smaller subnets.

When the **area range** command includes the **not-advertise** keyword, not only are the smaller component subnets not advertised as type 3 LSAs, the summary route is not advertised as a type 3 LSA either. As a result, this command has the same effect as the **area filter-list** command with the **out** keyword, filtering the LSA from going out to any other areas. An example **area range** command is shown at the end of Example 9-11.

Virtual Link Configuration

OSPF requires that each non-backbone area be connected to the backbone area (area 0). OSPF also requires that the routers in each area have a contiguous intra-area path to the other routers in the same area, because without that path, LSA flooding inside the area would fail. However, in some designs, meeting these requirements might be a challenge. You can use OSPF *virtual links* to overcome these problems.

For instance, in the top part of Figure 9-12, area 33 connects only to area 3, and not to area 0.

Figure 9-12 *The Need for Virtual Links*

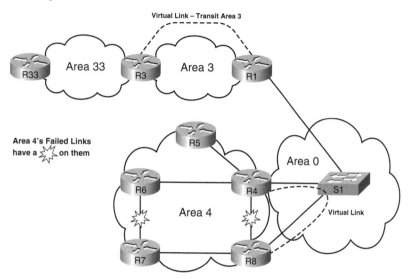

One straightforward solution to area 33's lack of connection to the backbone area would be to combine areas 3 and 33 into a single area, but OSPF virtual links could solve the problem as well. An OSPF virtual link allows a pair of routers to tunnel OSPF packets inside IP packets, across the IP network, to some other router that is not on the same data link. A virtual link between R3 and R1 gives area 33 a connection to area 0. Also note that R3 becomes an ABR, with a full copy of area 0's LSDB entries.

While the top part of Figure 9-10 simply shows a possibly poor OSPF area design, the lower part shows what could happen just because of a particular set of link failures. The figure shows several failed links that result in a *partitioned* area 4. As a result of the failures, R7 and R8 have no area 4 links connecting to the other three routers in area 4. A virtual link can be used to connect R4 and R8—the requirement being that both R4 and R8 connect to a common and working area— recombining the partitions through the virtual link. (A better solution than the virtual link in this particular topology might be to trunk on R4 and R8, create a small subnet through the LAN switch, and put it in area 4.)

Example 9-12 demonstrates a virtual link configuration between R33 and R1, as shown in Figure 9-12. Note that the virtual link cannot pass through a transit area that is a stubby area, so area 3 has been changed to no longer be a stubby area.

Example 9-12 *Virtual Link Between R3 and R1*

```
! R1 has not learned subnet 10.3.2.0 yet, because area 33 has no link to area 0.
R1# show ip route ospf | incl 10.3.2.0
R1#
! the area virtual link commands point to the other router's RID, and the
! transit area over which the virtual link exists—area 3 in this case. Note that
```

Example 9-12 *Virtual Link Between R3 and R1 (Continued)*

```
! timers can be set on the area virtual-link command, as well as authentication.
! It is important when authenticating virtual links to remember that
! the virtual links themselves are in area 0.
! R1 !!!!!!!!!!!!!!!!!!!!!!!!!!!!!!!!!!!!!!!!!!!!!!!!!!!!!!!!!!!!!!!!!!!!!!!!!!!!!!!!
router ospf 1
  area 3 virtual-link 3.3.3.3
! R3 !!!!!!!!!!!!!!!!!!!!!!!!!!!!!!!!!!!!!!!!!!!!!!!!!!!!!!!!!!!!!!!!!!!!!!!!!!!!!!!!
router ospf 1
  area 3 virtual-link 1.1.1.1
! Below, the status of the virtual link is listed.
R1# show ip ospf virtual-links
Virtual Link OSPF_VL0 to router 3.3.3.3 is up
  Run as demand circuit
  DoNotAge LSA allowed.
  Transit area 3, via interface Serial0/0.3, Cost of using 64
  Transmit Delay is 1 sec, State POINT_TO_POINT,
  Timer intervals configured, Hello 10, Dead 40, Wait 40, Retransmit 5
    Hello due in 00:00:02
    Adjacency State FULL (Hello suppressed)
    Index 3/6, retransmission queue length 0, number of retransmission 1
    First 0x0(0)/0x0(0) Next 0x0(0)/0x0(0)
    Last retransmission scan length is 1, maximum is 1
    Last retransmission scan time is 0 msec, maximum is 0 msec
! Because R1 and R3 are also sharing the same link, there is a neighbor
! relationship in area 3 that has been seen in the other examples, listed off
! interface s0/0.3. The new virtual link neighbor relationship is shown as well,
! with interface VL0 listed.
R1# show ip ospf nei
! Lines omitted for brevity
Neighbor ID     Pri   State        Dead Time   Address       Interface
3.3.3.3          0    FULL/ —         —         10.3.13.3     OSPF_VL0
3.3.3.3          0    FULL/ —      00:00:10     10.3.13.3     Serial0/0.3
! Below, subnet 10.3.2.0/23, now in area 33, is learned by R1 over the Vlink.
R1# show ip route ospf | incl 10.3.2.0
O IA    10.3.2.0/23 [110/75] via 10.3.13.3, 00:00:10, Serial0/0.3
```

Configuring OSPF Authentication

One of the keys to keeping OSPF authentication configuration straight is to remember that it differs significantly with RIPv2 and EIGRP, although some of the concepts are very similar. The basic rules for configuring OSPF authentication are as follows:

- Three types are available: type 0 (none), type 1 (clear text), and type 2 (MD5).

- Authentication is enabled per interface using the **ip ospf authentication** interface subcommand.

- The default authentication is type 0 (no authentication).

- The default can be redefined using the **area authentication** subcommand under **router ospf**.

- The keys are configured as interface subcommands.

- Multiple keys are allowed per interface; if configured, OSPF sends multiple copies of each message, one for each key.

Table 9-7 lists the three OSPF authentication types, along with the commands to enable each type, and the commands to define the authentication keys. Note that the three authentication types can be seen in the messages generated by the **debug ip ospf adjacency** command.

Table 9-7 *OSPF Authentication Types*

Type	Meaning	Enabling Interface Subcommand	Authentication Key Configuration Interface Subcommand
0	None	**ip ospf authentication null**	—
1	Clear text	**ip ospf authentication**	**ip ospf authentication-key** *key-value*
2	MD5	**ip ospf authentication message-digest**	**ip ospf message-digest-key** *key-number* **md5** *key-value*

Example 9-13 (again based on Figure 9-6) shows examples of type 1 and type 2 authentication configuration routers R1 and R2. (Note that S1 and S2 have been shut down for this example, but they would need the same configuration as shown on R1 and R2.) In this example, both R1 and R2 use their fa0/0 interfaces, so their authentication configuration will be identical. As such, the example shows only the configuration on R1.

Example 9-13 *OSPF Authentication Using Only Interface Subcommands*

```
! The two ip ospf commands are the same on R1 and R2. The first enables
! type 1 authentication, and the other defines the simple text key.
interface FastEthernet0/0
 ip ospf authentication
 ip ospf authentication-key key-t1
! Below, the neighbor relationship formed, proving that authentication works.
R1# show ip ospf neighbor fa 0/0
Neighbor ID     Pri   State          Dead Time   Address     Interface
2.2.2.2           1   FULL/BDR       00:00:37    10.1.1.2    FastEthernet0/0
! Next, each interface's OSPF authentication type can be seen in the last line
! or two in the output of the show ip ospf interface command.
R1# show ip ospf int fa 0/0
! Lines omitted for brevity
  Simple password authentication enabled

! Below, both R1 and R2 change to use type 2 authentication. Note that the key
! must be defined with the ip ospf message-digest-key interface subcommand. Key
```

Example 9-13 *OSPF Authentication Using Only Interface Subcommands*

```
! chains cannot be used.
interface FastEthernet0/0
 ip ospf authentication message-digest
 ip ospf message-digest-key 1 md5 key-t2
! Below, the command confirms type 2 (MD5) authentication, key number 1.
R1# show ip ospf int fa 0/0 | begin auth
! Lines omitted for brevity
Message digest authentication enabled
Youngest key id is 1
```

Example 9-13 shows two working examples of OSPF authentication, neither of which uses the **area** *number* **authentication** under **router ospf**. Some texts imply that the **area authentication** command is required—in fact, it was required prior to Cisco IOS Software Release 12.0. In later IOS releases, the **area authentication** command simply tells the router to change that router's default OSPF authentication type for all interfaces in that area. Table 9-8 summarizes the effects and syntax of the **area authentication** router subcommand.

Table 9-8 *Effect of the* **area authentication** *Command on OSPF Interface Authentication Settings*

area authentication Command	Interfaces in That Area Default to Use...
<no command>	Type 0
area *num* **authentication**	Type 1
area *num* **authentication message-digest**	Type 2

The keys themselves are kept in clear text in the configuration, unless you add the **service password-encryption** global command to the configuration.

The last piece of authentication configuration relates to OSPF virtual links. Because virtual links have no underlying interface on which to configure authentication, authentication is configured on the **area virtual-link** command itself. Table 9-9 shows the variations of the command options for configuring authentication on virtual links. Note that beyond the base **area** *number* **virtual-link** *rid* command, the parameters use similar keywords as compared with the equivalent interface subcommands.

Table 9-9 *Configuring OSPF Authentication on Virtual Links*

Type	Command Syntax for Virtual Links
0	**area** *num* **virtual-link** *router-id* **authentication null**
1	**area** *num* **virtual-link** *router-id* **authentication authentication-key** *key-value*
2	**area** *num* **virtual-link** *router-id* **authentication message-digest message-digest-key** *key-num* **md5** *key-value*

> **NOTE**   OSPF authentication is a good place for tricky CCIE lab questions—ones that can be solved in a few minutes if you know all the intricacies.

OSPF Stub Router Configuration

Defined in RFC 3137, and first supported in Cisco IOS Software Release 12.2(4)T, the OSPF *stub router* feature—not to be confused with stubby areas—allows a router to either temporarily or permanently be prevented from becoming a transit router. In this context, a transit router is simply one to which packets are forwarded, with the expectation that the transit router will forward the packet to yet another router. Conversely, non-transit routers only forward packets to and from locally attached subnets.

Figure 9-13 shows one typical case in which a stub router might be useful.

Figure 9-13   *OSPF Stub Router*

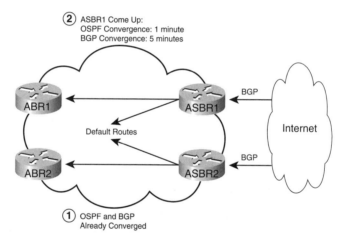

Both ASBR1 and ASBR2 advertise defaults into the network, expecting to have the capability to route to the Internet through BGP-learned routes. In this case, ASBR2 is already up, fully converged. However, if ASBR1 reloads, when it comes back up, OSPF is likely to converge faster than BGP. As a result, ASBR1 will advertise its default route, and OSPF routers may send packets to ASBR1, but ASBR1 will end up discarding the packets until BGP converges.

Using the stub router feature on the ASBRs solves the problem by making them advertise infinite metric routes (cost 16,777,215) for any transit routes—either for a configured time period or until BGP convergence is complete. To do so, under **router ospf**, the ASBRs would use either the **max-metric router-lsa on-startup** *announce-time* command or the **max-metric router-lsa on-startup wait-for-bgp** command. With the first version, the actual time period (in seconds) can be set. With the second, OSPF waits until BGP signals that convergence is complete or until 10 minutes pass, whichever comes first.

Foundation Summary

This section lists additional details and facts to round out the coverage of the topics in this chapter. Unlike most of the Cisco Press *Exam Certification Guides*, this "Foundation Summary" does not repeat information presented in the "Foundation Topics" section of the chapter. Please take the time to read and study the details in the "Foundation Topics" section of the chapter, as well as review items noted with a Key Topic icon.

Table 9-10 lists some of the key protocols regarding OSPF.

Table 9-10 *Protocols and Corresponding Standards for Chapter 9*

Name	Standard
OSPF Version 2	RFC 2328
The OSPF Opaque LSA Option	RFC 2370
The OSPF Not-So-Stubby Area (NSSA) Option	RFC 3101
OSPF Stub Router Advertisement	RFC 3137
Traffic Engineering (TE) Extensions to OSPF Version 2	RFC 3630
Graceful OSPF Restart	RFC 3623

Table 9-11 lists some of the most popular IOS commands related to the topics in this chapter. Also, refer to Tables 9-7 through 9-9 for references to OSPF authentication commands.

Table 9-11 *Command Reference for Chapter 9*

Command	Command Mode and Description
router ospf *process-id*	Global config; puts user in OSPF configuration mode for that PID.
network *ip-address* [wildcard-*mask*] **area** *area*	OSPF config mode; defines matching parameters, compared to interface IP addresses, to pick interfaces on which to enable OSPF.
ip ospf *process-id* **area** *area-id* [**secondaries none**]	Interface config mode; alternative to the **network** command for enabling OSPF on an interface.
neighbor *ip-address* [**priority** *number*] [**poll-interval** *seconds*] [**cost** *number*] [**database-filter all**]	OSPF config mode; used when neighbors must be defined, it identifies the neighbor's IP address, priority, cost, and poll interval.
auto-cost reference-bandwidth *ref-bw*	OSPF config mode; changes the numerator in the formula to calculate interface cost for all OSPF interfaces on that router.

Table 9-11 *Command Reference for Chapter 9*

Command	Command Mode and Description
router-id *ip-address*	OSPF config mode; statically sets the router ID.
ospf log-neighbor-changes [**detail**]	EIGRP subcommand; displays log messages when neighbor status changes. On by default.
passive-interface [**default**] {*interface-type interface-number*}	OSPF config mode; causes OSPF to stop sending Hellos on the specified interface. OSPF will still advertise the subnet as a stub network.
area *area-id* **stub** [**no-summary**]	OSPF config mode; sets the area type to stub or totally stubby.
area *area-id* **nssa** [**no-redistribution**] [**default-information-originate** [**metric**] [**metric-type**]] [**no-summary**]	OSPF config mode; sets the area type to NSSA or totally NSSA.
area *area-id* **default-cost** *cost*	OSPF config mode; sets the cost of default route created by ABRs and sent into stubby areas.
area *area-id* **nssa translate type7 suppress-fa**	OSPF config mode; sets an NSSA ABR to set the forwarding address to 0.0.0.0 for the type 5 LSAs it translates from type 7.
area *area-id* **range** *ip-address mask* [**advertise** I **not-advertise**] [**cost** *cost*]	OSPF config mode; summarizes routes into a larger prefix at ABRs. Optionally filters type 3 LSAs (**not-advertise** option).
area {*area-id*} **filter-list prefix** {*prefix-list-name* **in** I **out**}	OSPF config mode; filters type 3 LSA creation at ABR.
distribute-list [*ACL*] I [**route-map** *map-tag*] **in** [*int-type* I *int-number*]	OSPF config mode; defines ACL or prefix list to filter what OSPF puts into the routing table.
area *area-id* **virtual-link** *router-id* [**authentication** [**message-digest** I **null**]] [**hello-interval** *seconds*] [**retransmit-interval** *seconds*] [**transmit-delay** *seconds*] [**dead-interval** *seconds*] [[**authentication-key** *key*] I [**message-digest-key** *key-id* **md5** *key*]]	OSPF config mode; creates a virtual link, with typical interface configuration settings to overcome fact that the link is virtual.
ip ospf hello-interval *seconds*	Interface subcommand; sets the interval for periodic Hellos.
ip ospf dead-interval {*seconds* I **minimal hello-multiplier** *multiplier*}	Interface subcommand; defines the dead interval, or optionally the minimal dead interval of 1 second.
ip ospf name-lookup	Global command; causes the router to use DNS to correlate RIDs to host names for **show** command output.

Table 9-11   *Command Reference for Chapter 9*

Command	Command Mode and Description
ip ospf cost *interface-cost*	Interface subcommand; sets the cost.
ip ospf mtu-ignore	Interface subcommand; tells the router to ignore the check for equal MTUs that occurs when sending DD packets.
ip ospf network {**broadcast** | **non-broadcast** | {**point-to-multipoint** [**non-broadcast**] | **point-to-point**}}	Interface subcommand; sets the OSPF network type on an interface.
ip ospf priority *number-value*	Interface subcommand; sets the OSPF priority on an interface.
ip ospf retransmit-interval *seconds*	Interface subcommand; sets the time between LSA transmissions for adjacencies belonging to an interface.
ip ospf transmit-delay *seconds*	Interface subcommand; defines the estimated time expected for the transmission of an LSU.
max-metric router-lsa [**on-startup** {*announce-time* | **wait-for-bgp**}]	OSPF config mode; configures a stub router, delaying the point at which it can become a transit router.
show ip ospf border-routers	User mode; displays hidden LSAs for ABRs and ASBRs.
show ip ospf [*process-id* [*area-id*]] **database**	User mode; has many options not shown here. Displays the OSPF LSDB.
show ip ospf neighbor [*interface-type interface-number*] [*neighbor-id*] [**detail**]	User mode; lists information about OSPF neighbors.
show ip ospf [*process-id*] **summary-address**	User mode; lists information about route summaries in OSPF.
show ip ospf virtual-links	User mode; displays status and info about virtual links.
show ip route ospf	User mode; displays all OSPF routes in the IP routing table.
show ip ospf interface [*interface-type interface-number*] [**brief**]	User mode; lists OSPF protocol timers and statistics per interface.
show ip ospf statistics [**detail**]	User mode; displays OSPF SPF calculation statistics.
clear ip ospf [*pid*] {**process** | **redistribution** | **counters** [**neighbor** [*neighbor-interface*] [*neighbor-id*]]}	Enable mode; restarts the OSPF process, clears redistributed routes, or clears OSPF counters.
debug ip ospf hello	Enable mode; displays messages regarding Hellos, including Hello parameter mismatches.
debug ip ospf adj	Enable mode; displays messages regarding adjacency changes.
show ip ospf interface [*type number*] [**brief**]	User mode; lists many interface settings.

Table 9-12 summarizes many OSPF timers and their meaning.

Table 9-12 *OSPF Timer Summary*

Timer	Meaning
MaxAge	The maximum time an LSA can be in a router's LSDB, without receiving a newer copy of the LSA, before the LSA is removed. Default is 3600 seconds.
LSRefresh	The timer interval per LSA on which a router refloods an identical LSA, except for a 1-larger sequence number, to prevent the expiration of MaxAge. Default is 1800 seconds.
Hello	Per interface; time interval between Hellos. Default is 10 or 30 seconds, depending on interface type.
Dead	Per interface; time interval in which a Hello should be received from a neighbor. If not received, the neighbor is considered to have failed. Default is four times Hello.
Wait	Per interface; set to the same number as the dead interval. Defines the time a router will wait to get a Hello asserting a DR after reaching a 2WAY state with that neighbor.
Retransmission	Per interface; the time between sending an LSU, not receiving an acknowledgement, and then resending the LSU. Default is 5 seconds.
Inactivity	Countdown timer, per neighbor, used to detect when a neighbor has not been heard from for a complete dead interval. It starts equal to the dead interval, counts down, and is reset to be equal to the dead interval when each Hello is received.
Poll Interval	On NBMA networks, the period at which Hellos are sent to a neighbor when the neighbor is down. Default is 60 seconds.
Flood (Pacing)	Per interface; defines the interval between successive LSUs when flooding LSAs. Default is 33 ms.
Retransmission (Pacing)	Per interface; defines the interval between retransmitted packets as part of a single retransmission event. Default is 66 ms.
Lsa-group (Pacing)	Per OSPF process. LSA's LSRefresh intervals time out independently. This timer improves LSU reflooding efficiency by waiting, collecting several LSAs whose LSRefresh timers expire, and flooding all these LSAs together. Default is 240 seconds.

Table 9-13 lists OSPF neighbor states and their meaning.

Table 9-13 *OSPF Neighbor States*

State	Meaning
Down	No Hellos have been received from this neighbor for more than the dead interval.
Attempt	This router is sending Hellos to a manually configured neighbor.
Init	A Hello has been received from the neighbor, but it did not have the router's RID in it. This is a permanent state when Hello parameters do not match.
2WAY	A Hello has been received from the neighbor, and it has the router's RID in it. This is a stable state for pairs of DROther neighbors.
ExStart	Currently negotiating the DD sequence numbers and master/slave logic used for DD packets.
Exchange	Finished negotiating, and currently exchanging DD packets.
Loading	All DD packets exchanged, and currently pulling the complete LSDB entries with LSU packets.
Full	Neighbors are adjacent (fully adjacent), and should have identical LSDB entries for the area in which the link resides. Routing table calculations begin.

Table 9-14 lists several key OSPF numeric values.

Table 9-14 *OSPF Numeric Ranges*

Setting	Range of Values
Single interface cost	1 to 65,535 ($2^{16} - 1$)
Complete route cost	1 to 16,777,215 ($2^{24} - 1$)
Infinite route cost	16,777,215 ($2^{24} - 1$)
Reference bandwidth (units: Mbps)	1 to 4,294,967
OSPF PID	1 to 65,535 ($2^{16} - 1$)

Memory Builders

The *CCIE Routing and Switching* written exam, like all Cisco CCIE written exams, covers a fairly broad set of topics. This section provides some basic tools to help you exercise your memory about some of the broader topics covered in this chapter.

Fill in Key Tables from Memory

Appendix E, "Key Tables for CCIE Study," on the CD in the back of this book contains empty sets of some of the key summary tables in each chapter. Print Appendix E, refer to this chapter's tables in it, and fill in the tables from memory. Refer to Appendix F, "Solutions for Key Tables for CCIE Study," on the CD to check your answers.

Definitions

Next, take a few moments to write down the definitions for the following terms:

LSDB, Dijkstra, link-state routing protocol, LSA, LSU, DD, Hello, LSAck, RID, neighbor state, neighbor, adjacent, fully adjacent, 2-Way, 224.0.0.5, 224.0.0.6, area, stub area type, network type, external route, E1 route, E2 route, Hello timer, dead time/ interval, sequence number, DR, BDR, DROther, priority, LSA flooding, DR election, SPF calculation, partial SPF calculation, full SPF calculation, LSRefresh, hello time/ interval, Maxage, ABR, ASBR, internal router, backbone area, transit network, stub network, LSA type, stub area, NSSA, totally stubby area, totally NSSA area, virtual link, stub router, transit router, SPF algorithm, All OSPF DR Routers, All OSPF Routers, graceful restart

Refer to the glossary to check your answers.

Further Reading

Jeff Doyle's *Routing TCP/IP*, Volume I, Second Edition—every word a must for CCIE Routing and Switching.

Cisco OSPF Command and Configuration Handbook, by Dr. William Parkhurst, covers every OSPF-related command available in Cisco IOS at the time of that book's publication, with examples of each one.

Blueprint topics covered in this chapter:

This chapter covers the following subtopics from the Cisco CCIE Routing and Switching written exam blueprint. Refer to the full blueprint in Table I-1 in the Introduction for more details on the topics covered in each chapter and their context within the blueprint.

- General Routing Concepts

- Summarization

- Routing Decision Criteria

- Administrative Distance

- Routing Table

- Redistribution Between Routing Protocols

- Troubleshooting Routing Loops

IGP Route Redistribution, Route Summarization, and Default Routing

This chapter covers several topics related to the use of multiple IGP routing protocols. IGPs can use default routes to pull packets toward a small set of routers, with those routers having learned routes from some external source. IGPs can use route summarization with a single routing protocol, but it is often used at redistribution points between IGPs as well. Finally, route redistribution by definition involves moving routes from one routing source to another. This chapter takes a look at each topic.

For perspective, note that this chapter includes coverage of RIPv2 redistribution topics. Even though RIPv2 has been removed from the CCIE Routing and Switching qualifying exam blueprint, it is still possible that you might see exam questions on redistribution involving RIPv2. Therefore, this chapter includes coverage of that topic.

"Do I Know This Already?" Quiz

Table 10-1 outlines the major headings in this chapter and the corresponding "Do I Know This Already?" quiz questions.

Table 10-1 *"Do I Know This Already?" Foundation Topics Section-to-Question Mapping*

Foundation Topics Section	Questions Covered in This Section	Score
Route Maps, Prefix Lists, and Administrative Distance	1–2	
Route Redistribution	3–6	
Route Summarization	7	
Default Routes	8	
Total Score		

To best use this pre-chapter assessment, remember to score yourself strictly. You can find the answers in Appendix A, "Answers to the 'Do I Know This Already?' Quizzes."

1. A route map has several clauses. A route map's first clause has a **permit** action configured. The **match** command for this clause refers to an ACL that matches route 10.1.1.0/24 with a **permit** action, and matches route 10.1.2.0/24 with a **deny** action. If this route map is used for route redistribution, which of the following are true?

   a. The route map will attempt to redistribute 10.1.1.0/24.

   b. The question does not supply enough information to determine if 10.1.1.0/24 is redistributed.

   c. The route map will not attempt to redistribute 10.1.2.0/24.

   d. The question does not supply enough information to determine if 10.1.2.0/24 is redistributed.

2. Which of the following routes would be matched by this prefix list command: **ip prefix-list fred permit 10.128.0.0/9 ge 20**?

   a. 10.1.1.0 255.255.255.0

   b. 10.127.1.0 255.255.255.0

   c. 10.200.200.192 255.255.255.252

   d. 10.128.0.0 255.255.240.0

   e. None of these answers is correct.

3. A router is using the configuration shown below to redistribute routes. This router has several working interfaces with IP addresses in network 10.0.0.0, and has learned some network 10 routes with EIGRP and some with OSPF. Which of the following is true about the redistribution configuration?

```
router eigrp 1
 network 10.0.0.0
 redistribute ospf 2
!
router ospf 2
 network 10.0.0.0 0.255.255.255 area 3
 redistribute eigrp 1 subnets

R1# show ip route 15.0.0.0
Routing entry for 15.0.0.0/24, 5 known subnets
  Attached (2 connections)
  Redistributing via eigrp 1

O E1    10.6.11.0 [110/84] via 10.1.6.6, 00:21:52, Serial0/0/0.6
O E2    10.6.12.0 [110/20] via 10.1.6.6, 00:21:52, Serial0/0/0.6
C       10.1.6.0 is directly connected, Serial0/0/0.6
O IA    10.1.2.0 [110/65] via 10.1.1.5, 00:21:52, Serial0/0/0.5
C       10.1.1.0 is directly connected, Serial0/0/0.5
```

   a. EIGRP will not advertise any additional routes due to redistribution.

   b. OSPF will not advertise any additional routes due to redistribution.

   c. Routes redistributed into OSPF will be advertised as E1 routes.

   d. The **redistribute ospf 2** command would be rejected due to missing parameters.

4. Examine the following router configuration and excerpt from its IP routing table. Which routes could be redistributed into OSPF?

```
router eigrp 1
 network 12.0.0.0
router ospf 2
 redistribute eigrp 1 subnets
 network 13.0.0.0 0.255.255.255 area 3
An excerpt from the routing table is shown next:
C        12.1.6.0 is directly connected, Serial0/0/0.6
D        12.0.0.0/8 [90/2172416] via 13.1.1.1, 00:01:30, Serial0/0/0.5
C        13.1.1.0 is directly connected, Serial0/0/0.5
```

   a. 12.1.6.0

   b. 12.0.0.0

   c. 13.1.1.0

   d. None of these answers is correct

5. Two corporations merged. The network engineers decided to redistribute between one company's EIGRP network and the other company's OSPF network, using two mutually redistributing routers (R1 and R2) for redundancy. Assume that as many defaults as is possible are used for the redistribution configuration. Assume that one of the subnets in the OSPF domain is 10.1.1.0/24. Which of the following is true about a possible suboptimal route to 10.1.1.0/24 on R1—a route that sends packets through the EIGRP domain, and through R2 into the OSPF domain?

   a. The suboptimal routes will occur unless the configuration filters routes at R1.

   b. R1's administrative distance must be manipulated, such that OSPF routes have an administrative distance less than EIGRP's default of 90.

   c. EIGRP prevents the suboptimal routes by default.

   d. Using route tags is the only way to prevent the suboptimal routes.

6. Which of the following statements is true about the type of routes created when redistributing routes?

   a. Routes redistributed into OSPF default to be external type 2.

   b. Routes redistributed into EIGRP default to external, but can be set to internal with a route map.

   c. Routes redistributed into RIP are external by default.

   d. Routes redistributed into OSPF by a router in an NSSA area default to be external type 1.

7. Which of the following is not true about route summarization?

   a. The advertised summary is assigned the same metric as the lowest-metric component subnet.

   b. The router does not advertise the summary when its routing table does not have any of the component subnets.

   c. The router does not advertise the component subnets.

   d. Summarization, when used with redistribution, prevents all cases of suboptimal routes.

8. Which of the following is/are true regarding the **default-information originate** router subcommand?

   a. It is not supported by EIGRP.

   b. It causes OSPF to advertise a default route, but only if a static route to 0.0.0.0/0 is in that router's routing table.

   c. The **always** keyword on the **default-information originate** command, when used for OSPF, means OSPF will originate a default route even if no default route exists in its own IP routing table.

   d. None of the other answers are correct.

Foundation Topics

Route Maps, Prefix Lists, and Administrative Distance

Route maps, IP prefix lists, and administrative distance (AD) must be well understood to do well with route redistribution topics on the CCIE Routing and Switching written exam. This section focuses on the tools themselves, followed by coverage of route redistribution.

Configuring Route Maps with the route-map Command

Route maps provide programming logic similar to the If/Then/Else logic seen in other programming languages. A single route map has one or more **route-map** commands in it, and routers process **route-map** commands in sequential order based on sequence numbers. Each **route-map** command has underlying matching parameters, configured with the aptly named **match** command. (To match all packets, the **route-map** clause simply omits the **match** command.) Each **route-map** command also has one or more optional **set** commands that you can use to manipulate information—for instance, to set the metric for some redistributed routes. The general rules for route maps are as follows:

- Each **route-map** command must have an explicitly configured name, with all commands that use the same name being part of the same route map.

- Each **route-map** command has an action (**permit** or **deny**).

- Each **route-map** command in the same route map has a unique sequence number, allowing deletion and insertion of single **route-map** commands.

- When a route map is used for redistribution, the route map processes routes taken from the then-current routing table.

- The route map is processed sequentially based on the sequence numbers.

- Once a particular route is matched by the route map, it is not processed beyond that matching **route-map** command (specific to route redistribution).

- When a route is matched in a **route-map** statement, if the **route-map** command has a **permit** parameter, the route is redistributed (specific to route redistribution).

- When a route is matched in a **route-map** statement, if the **route-map** statement has a **deny** parameter, the route is not redistributed (specific to route redistribution).

Route maps can be confusing at times, especially when using the **deny** option on the **route-map** command. To help make sure the logic is clear before getting into redistribution, Figure 10-1 shows a logic diagram for an example route map. (This example is contrived to demonstrate some nuances of route map logic; a better, more efficient route map could be created to achieve the same results.) In the figure, R1 has eight loopback interfaces configured to be in class A networks 32 through 39. Figure 10-1 shows how the contrived **route-map picky** would process the routes.

Figure 10-1 *Route Map Logic Example*

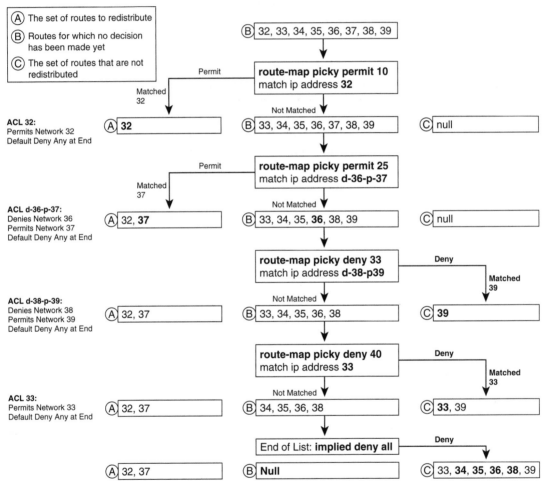

First, a few clarifications about the meaning of Figure 10-1 are in order. The top of the figure begins with the set of connected networks (32 through 39), labeled with a "B," which is the set of routes still being considered for redistribution. Moving down the figure, four separate **route-map** commands sit inside this single route map. Each **route-map** clause (the clause includes the underlying **match** and **set** commands) in turn moves routes from the list of possible routes ("B")

to either the list of routes to redistribute ("A") or the list to not redistribute ("C"). By the bottom of the figure, all routes will be noted as either to be redistributed or not to be redistributed.

The route map chooses to redistribute a route only if the **route-map** command has a **permit** option; the only time a **route-map** clause chooses to *not redistribute* a route is when the clause has a **deny** option. Ignoring the matching logic for a moment, the first two **route-map** commands (sequence numbers 10 and 25) use the **permit** option. As a result of those clauses, routes are either added to the list of routes to redistribute ("A") or left in the list of candidate routes ("B"). The third and fourth clauses (sequence numbers 33 and 40) use the **deny** option, so those clauses cause routes to be either added to the list of routes to not redistribute ("C"), or left in the list of candidate routes ("B"). In effect, once a **route-map** clause has matched a route, that route is flagged either as to be redistributed or as not to be redistributed, and the route is no longer processed by the route map.

One point that can sometimes be confused is that if a route is denied by an ACL used by a **match** command, it does not mean that the route is prevented from being redistributed. For instance, the **match ip address 32** command in clause 10 refers to ACL 32, which has one explicit *access control entry (ACE)* that matches network 32, with a **permit** action. Of course, ACL 32 has an implied deny all at the end, so ACL 32 permits network 32, and denies 33 through 39. However, denying networks 33 through 39 in the ACL does not mean that those routes are not redistributed—it simply means that those routes do not match **route-map** clause 10, so those routes are eligible for consideration by a later **route-map** clause.

The following list summarizes the key points about route map logic when used for redistribution:

- **route-map** commands with the **permit** option either cause a route to be redistributed or leave the route in the list of routes to be examined by the next **route-map** clause.

- **route-map** commands with the **deny** option either filter the route or leave the route in the list of routes to be examined by the next **route-map** clause.

- If a clause's **match** commands use an ACL, an ACL match with the **deny** action does not cause the route to be filtered. Instead, it just means that route does not match that particular **route-map** clause.

- The **route-map** command includes an implied deny all clause at the end; to configure a permit all, use the **route-map** command, with a **permit** action, but without a **match** command.

Route Map match Commands for Route Redistribution

Route maps use the **match** command to define the fields and values used for matching the routes being processed. If more than one **match** command is configured in a single **route-map** clause, a route is matched only if all the **match** commands' parameters match the route. The logic in each

match command itself is relatively straightforward. Table 10-2 lists the **match** command options when used for IGP route redistribution.

Table 10-2 *match Command Options for IGP Redistribution*

match Command	Description
match interface *interface-type interface-number* [*... interface-type interface-number*]	Looks at outgoing interface of routes
***match ip address** {[*access-list-number* I *access-list-name*] I *prefix-list prefix-list-name*}	Examines route prefix and prefix length
***match ip next-hop** {*access-list-number* I *access-list-name*}	Examines route's next-hop address
***match ip route-source** {*access-list-number* I *access-list-name*}	Matches advertising router's IP address
match metric *metric-value*	Matches route's metric
match route-type {**internal** I **external** [**type-1** I **type-2**] I **level-1** I **level-2**}	Matches route type
match tag *tag-value* [*...tag-value*]	Tag must have been set earlier

*Can reference multiple numbered and named ACLs on a single command.

Route Map set Commands for Route Redistribution

When used for redistribution, route maps have an implied action—either to allow the route to be redistributed or to filter the route so that it is not redistributed. As described earlier in this chapter, that choice is implied by the **permit** or **deny** option on the **route-map** command. Route maps can also change information about the redistributed routes by using the **set** command. Table 10-3 lists the **set** command options when used for IGP route redistribution.

Table 10-3 *set Command Options for IGP Redistribution*

set Command	Description
set level {**level-1** I **level-2** I **level-1-2** I **stub-area** I **backbone**}	Defines database(s) into which the route is redistributed
set metric *metric-value*	Sets the route's metric for OSPF, RIP, and IS-IS
set metric *bandwidth delay reliability loading mtu*	Sets the IGRP/EIGRP route's metric values
set metric-type {**internal** I **external** I **type-1** I **type-2**}	Sets type of route for IS-IS and OSPF
set tag *tag-value*	Sets the unitless tag value in the route

IP Prefix Lists

IP prefix lists provide mechanisms to match two components of an IP route:

- The route prefix (the subnet number)

- The prefix length (the subnet mask)

The **redistribute** command cannot directly reference a prefix list, but a route map can refer to a prefix list by using the **match** command.

A prefix list itself has similar characteristics to a route map. The list consists of one or more statements with the same text name. Each statement has a sequence number to allow deletion of individual commands, and insertion of commands into a particular sequence position. Each command has a **permit** or **deny** action—but because it is used only for matching packets, the **permit** or **deny** keyword just implies whether a route is matched (**permit**) or not (**deny**). The generic command syntax is as follows:

```
ip prefix-list list-name [seq seq-value] {deny network/length | permit network/
length}[ge ge-value] [le le-value]
```

The sometimes tricky and interesting part of working with prefix lists is that the meaning of the *network/length*, *ge-value*, and *le-value* parameters changes depending on the syntax. The *network/ length* parameters define the values to use to match the route prefix. For example, a *network/length* of 10.0.0.0/8 means "any route that begins with a 10 in the first octet." The **ge** and **le** options are used for comparison to the prefix length—in other words, to the number of binary 1s in the subnet mask. For instance, **ge 20 le 22** matches only routes whose masks are /20, /21, or /22. So, prefix list logic can be summarized into a two-step comparison process for each route:

1. The *route's prefix* must be within the range of addresses implied by the **prefix-list** command's *network/length* parameters.

2. The *route's prefix length* must match the *range of prefixes* implied by the **prefix-list** command.

The potentially tricky part of the logic relates to knowing the range of prefix lengths checked by this logic. The range is defined by the *ge-value* and *le-value* parameters, which stand for *greater-than-or-equal-to* and *less-than-or-equal-to*. Table 10-4 formalizes the logic, including the default values for *ge-value* and *le-value*. In the table, note that *conf-length* refers to the prefix length configured in the *network/prefix* (required) parameter, and *route-length* refers to the prefix length of a route being examined by the prefix list.

Table 10-4 *LE and GE Parameters on IP Prefix List, and the Implied Range of Prefix Lengths*

Prefix List Parameters	Range of Prefix Lengths
Neither	*conf-length = route-length*
Only **le**	*conf-length <= route-length <= le-value*
Only **ge**	*ge-value <= route-length <= 32*
Both **ge** and **le**	*ge-value <= route-length <= le-value*

Several examples can really help nail down prefix list logic. The following routes will be examined by a variety of prefix lists, with the routes numbered for easier reference:

1. 10.0.0.0/8

2. 10.128.0.0/9

3. 10.1.1.0/24

4. 10.1.2.0/24

5. 10.128.10.4/30

6. 10.128.10.8/30

Next, Table 10-5 shows the results of seven different one-line prefix lists applied to these six example routes. The table lists the matching parameters in the **prefix-list** commands, omitting the first part of the commands. The table explains which of the six routes would match the listed prefix list, and why.

Table 10-5 *Example Prefix Lists Applied to the List of Routes*

prefix-list Command Parameters	Routes Matched	Results
10.0.0.0/8	1	Without **ge** or **le** configured, both the prefix (10.0.0.0) and length (8) must be an exact match.
10.128.0.0/9	None	Without **ge** or **le** configured, the prefix (10.128.0.0) and length (9) must be an exact match, only the second route in the list is matched by this prefix list.
10.0.0.0/8 ge 9	2–6	The 10.0.0.0/8 means "all routes whose first octet is 10," effectively representing an address range. The prefix length must be between 9 and 32, inclusive.
10.0.0.0/8 ge 24 le 24	3, 4	The 10.0.0.0/8 means "all routes whose first octet is 10," and the prefix range is 24 to 24—meaning only routes with prefix length 24.

Table 10-5 *Example Prefix Lists Applied to the List of Routes (Continued)*

prefix-list Command Parameters	Routes Matched	Results
10.0.0.0/8 le 28	1–4	The prefix length needs to be between 8 and 28, inclusive.
0.0.0.0/0	None	0.0.0.0/0 means "match all prefixes, with prefix length of exactly 0." So, it would match all routes' prefixes, but none of their prefix lengths. Only a default route would match this prefix list.
0.0.0.0/0 le 32	All	The range implied by 0.0.0.0/0 is all IPv4 addresses. The **le 32** then implies any prefix length between 0 and 32, inclusive. This is the syntax for "match all" prefix list logic.

Administrative Distance

A single router can learn routes using multiple IP routing protocols, as well as via connected and static routes. When a router learns a particular route from multiple sources, the router cannot use the metrics to determine the best route, because the metrics are based on different units. So, the router uses each route's *administrative distance (AD)* to determine which is best, with the lower number being better. Table 10-6 lists the default AD values for the various routing sources.

Table 10-6 *Administrative Distances*

Key Topic

Route Type	Administrative Distance
Connected	0
Static	1
EIGRP summary route	5
EBGP	20
EIGRP (internal)	90
IGRP	100
OSPF	110
IS-IS	115
RIP	120
EIGRP (external)	170
iBGP	200
Unreachable	255

The defaults can be changed by using the **distance** command. The command differs amongst all three IGPs covered in this book. The generic versions of the **distance** router subcommand for RIP, EIGRP, and OSPF, respectively, are as follows:

```
distance distance
distance eigrp internal-distance external-distance
distance ospf {[intra-area dist1] [inter-area dist2] [external dist3]}
```

As you can see, EIGRP and OSPF can set a different AD depending on the type of route as well, whereas RIP cannot. You can also use the **distance** command to set a router's view of the AD per route, as is covered later in this chapter.

Route Redistribution

Although using a single routing protocol throughout an enterprise might be preferred, many enterprises use multiple routing protocols due to business mergers and acquisitions, organizational history, or in some cases for technical reasons. Route redistribution allows one or more routers to take routes learned via one routing protocol and advertise those routes via another routing protocol so that all parts of the internetwork can be reached.

To perform redistribution, one or more routers run both routing protocols, with each routing protocol placing routes into that router's routing table. Then, each routing protocol can take all or some of the other routing protocol's routes from the routing table and advertise those routes. This section begins by looking at the mechanics of how to perform simple redistribution on a single router, and ends with discussion of tools and issues that matter most when redistributing on multiple routers.

Mechanics of the redistribute Command

The **redistribute** router subcommand tells one routing protocol to take routes from another routing protocol. This command can simply redistribute all routes or, by using matching logic, redistribute only a subset of the routes. The **redistribute** command also supports actions for setting some parameters about the redistributed routes—for example, the metric.

The full syntax of the **redistribute** command is as follows:

```
redistribute protocol [process-id] [level-1 | level-1-2 | level-2] [as-number] [metric
metric-value] [metric-type type-value] [match {internal | external 1 | external 2}] [tag
tag-value] [route-map map-tag] [subnets]
```

The **redistribute** command identifies the routing source from which routes are taken, and the **router** command identifies the routing process into which the routes are advertised. For example, the command **redistribute eigrp 1** tells the router to *take routes from* EIGRP process 1; if that command were under **router rip**, the routes would be redistributed into RIP, enabling other RIP routers in the network to see some or all routes coming from EIGRP AS 1.

The **redistribute** command has a lot of other parameters as well, most of which will be described in upcoming examples. The first few examples use the network shown in Figure 10-2. In this network, each IGP uses a different class A network just to make the results of redistribution more obvious. Also note that the numbering convention is such that each of R1's connected WAN subnets has 1 as the third octet, and each LAN subnet off R3, R4, and R5 has 2 as the third octet.

Figure 10-2 *Sample Network for Default Route Examples*

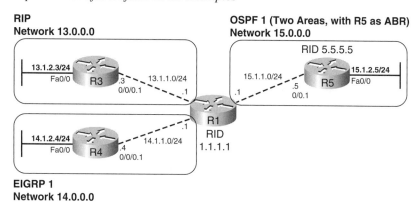

Redistribution Using Default Settings

The first example configuration meets the following design goals:

- R1 redistributes between each pair of IGPs—RIP, EIGRP, and OSPF.

- Default metrics are used whenever possible; when required, the metrics are configured on the **redistribute** command.

- Redistribution into OSPF uses the non-default **subnets** parameter, which causes subnets to be advertised into OSPF.

- All other settings use default values.

Example 10-1 shows R1's configuration for each routing protocol, along with **show** commands from all four routers to highlight the results of the redistribution.

Example 10-1 *Route Redistribution with Minimal Options*

```
! EIGRP redistributes from OSPF (process ID 1) and RIP. EIGRP must
! set the metric, as it has no default values. It also uses the
! no auto-summary command so that subnets will be redistributed into
! EIGRP.
```

continues

Example 10-1 *Route Redistribution with Minimal Options (Continued)*

```
router eigrp 1
 redistribute ospf 1 metric 1544 5 255 1 1500
 redistribute rip metric 1544 5 255 1 1500
 network 14.0.0.0
 no auto-summary
! OSPF redistributes from EIGRP (ASN 1) and RIP. OSPF defaults the
! metric to 20 for redistributed IGP routes. It must also use the
! subnets option in order to redistribute subnets.
router ospf 1
 router-id 1.1.1.1
 redistribute eigrp 1 subnets
 redistribute rip subnets
 network 15.0.0.0 0.255.255.255 area 0
! RIP redistributes from OSPF (process ID 1) and EIGRP (ASN 1). RIP
! must set the metric, as it has no default values. It also uses the
! no auto-summary command so that subnets will be redistributed into
! EIGRP.
router rip
 version 2
 redistribute eigrp 1 metric 2
 redistribute ospf 1 metric 3
 network 13.0.0.0
 no auto-summary
! R1 has a connected route (x.x.1.0) in networks 13, 14, and 15, as well as
! an IGP-learned route (x.x.2.0).
R1# show ip route
! lines omitted for brevity
      10.0.0.0/24 is subnetted, 1 subnets
C        10.1.1.0 is directly connected, FastEthernet0/0
      13.0.0.0/24 is subnetted, 2 subnets
C        13.1.1.0 is directly connected, Serial0/0/0.3
R        13.1.2.0 [120/1] via 13.1.1.3, 00:00:07, Serial0/0/0.3
      14.0.0.0/24 is subnetted, 2 subnets
D        14.1.2.0 [90/2172416] via 14.1.1.4, 00:58:20, Serial0/0/0.4
C        14.1.1.0 is directly connected, Serial0/0/0.4
      15.0.0.0/24 is subnetted, 2 subnets
O IA     15.1.2.0 [110/65] via 15.1.1.5, 00:04:25, Serial0/0/0.5
C        15.1.1.0 is directly connected, Serial0/0/0.5
! R3 learned two routes each from nets 14 and 15.
! Compare the metrics set on R1's RIP redistribute command to the metrics below.
R3# show ip route rip
      14.0.0.0/24 is subnetted, 2 subnets
R        14.1.2.0 [120/2] via 13.1.1.1, 00:00:19, Serial0/0/0.1
R        14.1.1.0 [120/2] via 13.1.1.1, 00:00:19, Serial0/0/0.1
      15.0.0.0/24 is subnetted, 2 subnets
R        15.1.2.0 [120/3] via 13.1.1.1, 00:00:19, Serial0/0/0.1
R        15.1.1.0 [120/3] via 13.1.1.1, 00:00:19, Serial0/0/0.1
```

Example 10-1 *Route Redistribution with Minimal Options (Continued)*

```
! R4 learned two routes each from nets 13 and 15.
! EIGRP injected the routes as external (EX), which are considered AD 170.
R4# show ip route eigrp
        13.0.0.0/24 is subnetted, 2 subnets
D EX    13.1.1.0 [170/2171136] via 14.1.1.1, 00:09:57, Serial0/0/0.1
D EX    13.1.2.0 [170/2171136] via 14.1.1.1, 00:09:57, Serial0/0/0.1
        15.0.0.0/24 is subnetted, 2 subnets
D EX    15.1.2.0 [170/2171136] via 14.1.1.1, 01:00:27, Serial0/0/0.1
D EX    15.1.1.0 [170/2171136] via 14.1.1.1, 01:00:27, Serial0/0/0.1
! R5 learned two routes each from nets 13 and 14.
! OSPF by default injected the routes as external type 2, cost 20.
R5# show ip route ospf
        13.0.0.0/24 is subnetted, 2 subnets
O E2    13.1.1.0 [110/20] via 15.1.1.1, 00:36:12, Serial0/0.1
O E2    13.1.2.0 [110/20] via 15.1.1.1, 00:36:12, Serial0/0.1
        14.0.0.0/24 is subnetted, 2 subnets
O E2    14.1.2.0 [110/20] via 15.1.1.1, 00:29:56, Serial0/0.1
O E2    14.1.1.0 [110/20] via 15.1.1.1, 00:36:12, Serial0/0.1
! As a backbone router, OSPF on R1 created type 5 LSAs for the four E2 subnets.
! If R1 had been inside an NSSA stub area, it would have created type 7 LSAs.
R5# show ip ospf data | begin Type-5
        Type-5 AS External Link States

Link ID         ADV Router      Age       Seq#        Checksum Tag
13.1.1.0        1.1.1.1         1444      0x80000002 0x000785 0
13.1.2.0        1.1.1.1         1444      0x80000002 0x00FB8F 0
14.1.1.0        1.1.1.1         1444      0x80000002 0x00F991 0
14.1.2.0        1.1.1.1         1444      0x80000002 0x00EE9B 0
```

Metrics must be set via configuration when redistributing into RIP and EIGRP, whereas OSPF uses default values. In the example, the two **redistribute** commands under **router rip** used hop counts of 2 and 3 just so the metrics could be easily seen in the **show ip route** command output on R3. The EIGRP metric in the **redistribute** command must include all five metric components, even if the last three are ignored by EIGRP's metric calculation (as they are by default). The command **redistribute rip metric 1544 5 255 1 1500** lists EIGRP metric components of bandwidth, delay, reliability, load, and MTU, in order. OSPF defaults to cost 20 when redistributing from an IGP, and 1 when redistributing from BGP.

The **redistribute** command redistributes only routes in that router's current IP routing table. When redistributing from a given routing protocol, the **redistribute** command takes routes listed in the IP routing table as being learned from that routing protocol. Interestingly, the **redistribute** command can also pick up connected routes. For example, R1 has an OSPF route to 15.1.2.0/24, and a connected route to 15.1.1.0/24. However, R3 (RIP) and R4 (EIGRP) redistribute both of these routes—the OSPF-learned route and one connected route—as a result of their respective

redistribute ospf commands. As it turns out, the **redistribute** command causes the router to use the following logic to choose which routes to redistribute from a particular IGP protocol:

1. Take all routes in my routing table that were learned by the routing protocol from which routes are being redistributed.

2. Take all connected subnets matched by that routing protocol's **network** commands.

Example 10-1 shows several instances of exactly how this two-part logic works. For instance, R3 (RIP) learns about connected subnet 14.1.1.0/24, because RIP redistributes from EIGRP, and R1's EIGRP **network 14.0.0.0** command matches that subnet.

The **redistribute** command includes a **subnets** option, but only OSPF needs to use it. By default, when redistributing into OSPF, OSPF redistributes only routes for classful networks, ignoring subnets. By including the **subnets** option, OSPF redistributes subnets as well. The other IGPs redistribute subnets automatically; however, if at a network boundary, the RIP or EIGRP **auto-summary** setting would still cause summarization to use the classful network. In Example 10-1, if either RIP or EIGRP had used **auto-summary**, each redistributed network would show just the classful networks. For example, if RIP had configured **auto-summary** in Example 10-1, R3 would have a route to networks 14.0.0.0/8 and 15.0.0.0/8, but no routes to subnets inside those class A networks.

Setting Metrics, Metric Types, and Tags

Cisco IOS provides three mechanisms for setting the metrics of redistributed routes, as follows:

1. Call a route map from the **redistribute** command, with the route map using the **set metric** command. This method allows different metrics for different routes.

2. Use the **metric** option on the **redistribute** command. This sets the same metric for all routes redistributed by that **redistribute** command.

3. Use the **default-metric** command under the **router** command. This command sets the metric for all redistributed routes whose metric was not set by either of the other two methods.

The list implies the order of precedence if more than one method defines a metric. For instance, if a route's metric is set by all three methods, the route map's metric is used. If the metric is set on the **redistribute** command and there is a **default-metric** command as well, the setting on the **redistribute** command takes precedence.

The **redistribute** command also allows a setting for the *metric-type* option, which really refers to the route type. For example, routes redistributed into OSPF must be OSPF external routes, but they can be either external type 1 (E1) or type 2 (E2) routes. Table 10-7 summarizes the defaults for metrics and metric types.

Table 10-7 *Default Metrics and Route Metric Types in IGP Route Redistribution*

IGP into Which Routes Are Redistributed	Default Metric	Default (and Possible) Metric Types
RIP	None	RIP has no concept of external routes
EIGRP	None	External
OSPF	20/1*	E2 (E1 or E2)
IS-IS	0	L1 (L1, L2, L1/L2, or external)

* OSPF uses cost 20 when redistributing from an IGP, and cost 1 when redistributing from BGP.

Redistributing a Subset of Routes Using a Route Map

Route maps can be referenced by any **redistribute** command. The route map may actually let all the routes through, setting different route attributes (for example, metrics) for different routes. Or it may match some routes with a **deny** clause, which prevents the route from being redistributed. (Refer to Figure 10-1 for a review of route map logic.)

Figure 10-3 and Example 10-2 show an example of mutual redistribution between EIGRP and OSPF, with some routes being either filtered or changed using route maps.

Figure 10-3 *OSPF and EIGRP Mutual Redistribution Using Route Maps*

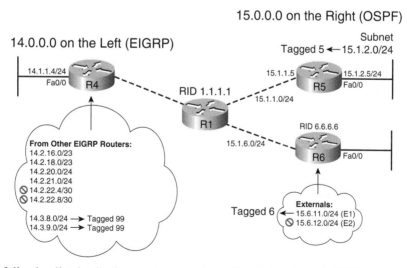

The following list details the requirements for redistribution from OSPF into EIGRP. These requirements use R1's perspective, because it is the router doing the redistribution.

■ Routes with next-hop address 15.1.1.5 (R5) should be redistributed, with route tag 5.

- E1 routes sourced by R6 (RID 6.6.6.6) should be redistributed, and assigned a route tag of 6.

- No other routes should be redistributed.

The requirements for redistributing routes from EIGRP into OSPF are as follows, again from R1's perspective:

- Routes beginning with 14.2, and with masks /23 and /24, should be redistributed, with metric set to 300.

- Other routes beginning with 14.2 should not be redistributed.

- Routes beginning with 14.3 should be redistributed, with route tag 99.

- No other routes should be redistributed.

Most of the explanation of the configuration is provided in the comments in Example 10-2, with a few additional comments following the example.

Example 10-2 *Route Redistribution Using Route Maps*

```
! No metrics are set on the redistribute commands; either the default metric
! is used, or the route maps set the metrics. The default-metric command
! sets the unused EIGRP metric parameters to "1" because something must be
! configured, but the values are unimportant.
router eigrp 1
 redistribute ospf 1 route-map ospf-into-eigrp
 network 14.0.0.0
 default-metric 1544 5 1 1 1
 no auto-summary
! While this configuration strives to use other options besides the options
! directly on the redistribute command, when used by OSPF, you must still
! include the subnets keyword for OSPF to learn subnets from other IGPs.
router ospf 1
 router-id 1.1.1.1
 redistribute eigrp 1 subnets route-map eigrp-into-ospf
 network 15.0.0.0 0.255.255.255 area 0
! ACL A-14-3-x-x matches all addresses that begin 14.3. ACL A-15-1-1-5 matches
! exactly IP address 15.1.1.5. ACL A-6-6-6-6 matches exactly address 6.6.6.6.
ip access-list standard A-14-3-x-x
 permit 14.3.0.0 0.0.255.255
ip access-list standard A-15-1-1-5
 permit 15.1.1.5
ip access-list standard A-6-6-6-6
 permit 6.6.6.6
! The prefix lists matches prefixes in the range 14.2.0.0 through 14.2.255.255,
! with prefix length 23 or 24.
ip prefix-list e-into-o seq 5 permit 14.2.0.0/16 ge 23 le 24
```

Example 10-2 *Route Redistribution Using Route Maps (Continued)*

```
! route-map ospf-into-eigrp was called by the redistribute command under router
! eigrp, meaning that it controls redistribution from OSPF into EIGRP.
! Clause 10 matches OSPF routes whose next hop is 15.1.1.5, which is R5's serial
! IP address. R1's only route that meets this criteria is 15.1.2.0/24. This route
! will be redistributed because the route-map clause 10 has a permit action.
! The route tag is also set to 5.
route-map ospf-into-eigrp permit 10
 match ip next-hop A-15-1-1-5
 set tag 5
! Clause 15 matches OSPF routes whose LSAs are sourced by router with RID 6.6.6.6,
! namely R6, and also have metric type E1. R6 sources two external routes, but
! only 15.6.11.0/24 is E1. The route is tagged 6.
route-map ospf-into-eigrp permit 15
 match ip route-source A-6-6-6-6
 match route-type external type-1
 set tag 6
! route-map eigrp-into-ospf was called by the redistribute command under router
! ospf, meaning that it controls redistribution from EIGRP into OSPF.
! Clause 10 matches using a prefix list, which in turn matches prefixes that begin
! with 14.2, and which have either a /23 or /24 prefix length. By implication, it
! does not match prefix length /30. The metric is set to 300 for these routes.
route-map eigrp-into-ospf permit 10
 match ip address prefix-list e-into-o
 set metric 300
! Clause 18 matches routes that begin 14.3. They are tagged with a 99.
route-map eigrp-into-ospf permit 18
 match ip address A-14-3-x-x
 set tag 99
! Next, the example shows the routes that could be redistributed, and then
! shows the results of the redistribution, pointing out which routes were
! redistributed. First, the example shows, on R1, all routes that R1 could
! try to redistribute into EIGRP.
R1# show ip route 15.0.0.0
Routing entry for 15.0.0.0/24, 5 known subnets
Attached (2 connections)
Redistributing via eigrp 1

O E1    15.6.11.0 [110/84] via 15.1.6.6, 00:21:52, Serial0/0/0.6
O E2    15.6.12.0 [110/20] via 15.1.6.6, 00:21:52, Serial0/0/0.6
C       15.1.6.0 is directly connected, Serial0/0/0.6
O IA    15.1.2.0 [110/65] via 15.1.1.5, 00:21:52, Serial0/0/0.5
C       15.1.1.0 is directly connected, Serial0/0/0.5
! R4 sees only two of the five routes from 15.0.0.0, because only two matched either of
! the route-map clauses. The other three routes matched the default deny clause.
R4# show ip route 15.0.0.0
Routing entry for 15.0.0.0/24, 2 known subnets
```

continues

Example 10-2 *Route Redistribution Using Route Maps (Continued)*

```
Redistributing via eigrp 1
D EX    15.6.11.0 [170/2171136] via 14.1.1.1, 00:22:21, Serial0/0/0.1
D EX    15.1.2.0 [170/2171136] via 14.1.1.1, 00:22:21, Serial0/0/0.1
! Still on R4, the show ip eigrp topology command displays the tag. This command
! filters the output so that just one line of output lists the tag values.
R4# sho ip eigrp topo 15.6.1.0 255.255.255.0 | incl tag
        Administrator tag is 5 (0x00000005)
R4# sho ip eigrp topo 15.6.11.0 255.255.255.0 | incl tag
        Administrator tag is 6 (0x00000006)
```

```
! Next, the example shows the possible routes that could be redistributed from
! EIGRP into OSPF.
! The next command (R1) lists all routes that could be redistributed into OSPF.
R1# show ip route 14.0.0.0
Routing entry for 14.0.0.0/8, 10 known subnets
  Attached (1 connections)
  Variably subnetted with 3 masks
  Redistributing via eigrp 1, ospf 1

D       14.3.9.0/24 [90/2297856] via 14.1.1.4, 00:34:48, Serial0/0/0.4
D       14.3.8.0/24 [90/2297856] via 14.1.1.4, 00:34:52, Serial0/0/0.4
D       14.1.2.0/24 [90/2172416] via 14.1.1.4, 00:39:27, Serial0/0/0.4
C       14.1.1.0/24 is directly connected, Serial0/0/0.4
D       14.2.22.8/30 [90/2297856] via 14.1.1.4, 00:35:49, Serial0/0/0.4
D       14.2.20.0/24 [90/2297856] via 14.1.1.4, 00:36:12, Serial0/0/0.4
D       14.2.21.0/24 [90/2297856] via 14.1.1.4, 00:36:08, Serial0/0/0.4
D       14.2.16.0/23 [90/2297856] via 14.1.1.4, 00:36:34, Serial0/0/0.4
D       14.2.22.4/30 [90/2297856] via 14.1.1.4, 00:35:53, Serial0/0/0.4
D       14.2.18.0/23 [90/2297856] via 14.1.1.4, 00:36:23, Serial0/0/0.4
```

```
! Next, on R5, note that the two /30 routes beginning with 14.2 were correctly
! prevented from getting into OSPF. It also filtered the redistribution of the
! two routes that begin with 14.1. As a result, R5 knows only 6 routes in
! network 14.0.0.0, whereas R1 had 10 subnets of that network it could have
! redistributed. Also below, note that the /23 and /24 routes inside 14.2 have
! metric 300.
R5# show ip route 14.0.0.0
Routing entry for 14.0.0.0/8, 6 known subnets
  Variably subnetted with 2 masks

O E2    14.3.9.0/24 [110/20] via 15.1.1.1, 00:22:41, Serial0/0.1
O E2    14.3.8.0/24 [110/20] via 15.1.1.1, 00:22:41, Serial0/0.1
O E2    14.2.20.0/24 [110/300] via 15.1.1.1, 00:22:41, Serial0/0.1
O E2    14.2.21.0/24 [110/300] via 15.1.1.1, 00:22:41, Serial0/0.1
O E2    14.2.16.0/23 [110/300] via 15.1.1.1, 00:22:41, Serial0/0.1
O E2    14.2.18.0/23 [110/300] via 15.1.1.1, 00:22:41, Serial0/0.1
! The show ip ospf database command confirms that the route tag was set
! correctly.
R5# show ip ospf data external 14.3.8.0 | incl Tag
External Route Tag: 99
```

> **NOTE**   Route maps have an implied **deny** clause at the end of the route map. This implied **deny** clause matches all packets. As a result, any routes not matched in the explicitly configured **route-map** clauses match the implied **deny** clause, and are filtered. Both route maps in the example used the implied **deny** clause to actually filter the routes.

Mutual Redistribution at Multiple Routers

When multiple routers redistribute between the same two routing protocol domains, several potential problems can occur. One type of problem occurs on the redistributing routers, because those routers will learn a route to most subnets via both routing protocols. That router uses the AD to determine the best route when comparing the best routes from each of the two routing protocols; this typically results in some routes using suboptimal paths. For example, Figure 10-4 shows a sample network, with R3 choosing its AD 110 OSPF route to 10.1.2.0/24 over the probably better AD 120 RIP route.

Figure 10-4   *OSPF and RIP Redistribution*

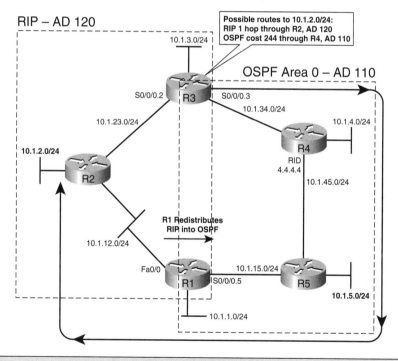

> **NOTE**   The OSPF configuration for this network matches only the interfaces implied by the OSPF box in Figure 10-4. RIP does not have a *wildcard-mask* option on the **network** command, so R1's and R3's **network** commands will match all of their interfaces, as all are in network 10.0.0.0.

In Figure 10-4, R3 learns of subnet 10.1.2.0/24 via RIP updates from R2. Also, R1 learns of the subnet with RIP and redistributes the route into OSPF, and then R3 learns of a route to 10.1.2.0/24 via OSPF. R3 chooses the route with the lower administrative distance; with all default settings, OSPF's AD of 110 is better that RIP's 120.

If both R1 and R3 mutually redistribute between RIP and OSPF, the suboptimal route problem would occur on either R1 or R3 for each RIP subnet, all depending on timing. Example 10-3 shows the redistribution configuration, along with R3 having the suboptimal route shown in Figure 10-4. However, after R1's fa0/0 interface flaps, R1 now has a suboptimal route to 10.1.2.0/24, but R3 has an optimal route.

Example 10-3 *Suboptimal Routing at Different Redistribution Points*

```
! R1's related configuration follows:
router ospf 1
 router-id 1.1.1.1
 redistribute rip subnets
 network 10.1.15.1 0.0.0.0 area 0
!
router rip
 redistribute ospf 1
 network 10.0.0.0
 default-metric 1
! R3's related configuration follows:
router ospf 1
 router-id 3.3.3.3
 redistribute rip subnets
 network 10.1.34.3 0.0.0.0 area 0
!
router rip
 redistribute ospf 1
 network 10.0.0.0
 default-metric 1
! R3 begins with an AD 120 OSPF route, and not a RIP route, to 10.1.2.0/24.
R3# sh ip route | incl 10.1.2.0
O E2    10.1.2.0 [110/20] via 10.1.34.4, 00:02:01, Serial0/0/0.4
! R1 has a RIP route to 10.1.2.0/24, and redistributes it into OSPF, causing R3
! to learn an OSPF route to 10.1.2.0/24.
R1# sh ip route | incl 10.1.2.0
R       10.1.2.0 [120/1] via 10.1.12.2, 00:00:08, FastEthernet0/0
! Next, R1 loses its RIP route to 10.1.2.0/24, causing R3 to lose its OSPF route.
R1# conf t
Enter configuration commands, one per line.  End with CNTL/Z.
R1(config)# int fa 0/0
R1(config-if)# shut
! R3 loses its OSPF route, but can then insert the RIP route into its table.
```

Example 10-3 *Suboptimal Routing at Different Redistribution Points (Continued)*

```
R3# sh ip route | incl 10.1.2.0
R        10.1.2.0 [120/1] via 10.1.23.2, 00:00:12, Serial0/0/0.2
! Not shown: R1 brings up its fa0/0 again
! However, R1 now has the suboptimal route to 10.1.2.0/24, through OSPF.
R1# sh ip route | incl 10.1.2.0
O E2     10.1.2.0 [110/20] via 10.1.15.5, 00:00:09, Serial0/0/0.5
```

The key concept behind this seemingly odd example is that a redistributing router processes only the current contents of its IP routing table. When this network first came up, R1 learned its RIP route to 10.1.2.0/24, and redistributed into OSPF, *before* R3 could do the same. So, R3 was faced with the choice of putting the AD 110 (OSPF) or AD 120 (RIP) route into its routing table, and R3 chose the lower AD OSPF route. Because R3 never had the RIP route to 10.1.2.0/24 in its routing table, R3 could not redistribute that RIP route into OSPF.

Later, when R1's fa0/0 failed (as shown in Example 10-3), R3 had time to remove the OSPF route and add the RIP route for 10.1.2.0/24 to its routing table—which then allowed R3 to redistribute that RIP route into OSPF, causing R1 to have the suboptimal route.

To solve this type of problem, the redistributing routers must have some awareness of which routes came from the other routing domain. In particular, the lower-AD routing protocol needs to decide which routes came from the higher-AD routing protocol, and either use a different AD for those routes or filter the routes. The next few sections show a few different methods of preventing this type of problem.

Preventing Suboptimal Routes by Setting the Administrative Distance

One simple and elegant solution to the problem of suboptimal routes on redistributing routers is to flag the redistributed routes with a higher AD. A route's AD is not advertised by the routing protocol; however, a single router can be configured such that it assigns different AD values to different routes, which then impacts that one router's choice of which routes end up in that router's routing table. For example, back in Figure 10-4 and Example 10-3, R3 could have assigned the OSPF-learned route to 10.1.2.0/24 an AD higher than 120, thereby preventing the original problem.

Figure 10-5 shows a more complete example, with a route from the RIP domain (10.1.2.0/24) and another from the OSPF domain (10.1.4.0/24). Redistributing router R3 will learn the two routes both from RIP and OSPF. By configuring R3's logic to treat OSPF internal routes with default AD 110, and OSPF external routes with AD 180 (or any other value larger than RIP's default of 120), R3 will choose the optimal path for both RIP and OSPF routes.

Figure 10-5 *The Effect of Differing ADs for Internal and External Routes*

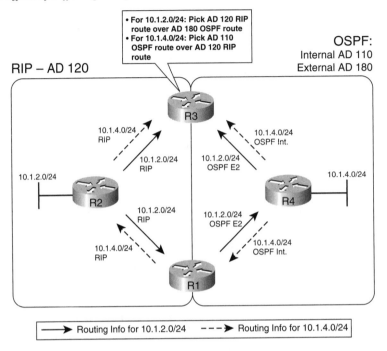

```
        ┌────────────────────────────────────┐
        │ • For 10.1.2.0/24: Pick AD 120 RIP │
        │   route over AD 180 OSPF route     │
        │ • For 10.1.4.0/24: Pick AD 110     │
        │   OSPF route over AD 120 RIP       │
        │   route                            │
        └────────────────────────────────────┘
```

Example 10-4 shows how to configure both R1 and R3 to use a different AD for external routes by using the **distance ospf external 180** command, under the **router ospf** process.

Example 10-4 *Preventing Suboptimal Routes with the* **distance** *Router Subcommand*

```
! Both R1's and R3's configurations look like they do in Example 10-3's, but with the
! addition of the distance command.
router ospf 1
 distance ospf external 180
! R3 has a more optimal RIP route to 10.1.2.0/24, as does R1.
R3# sh ip route | incl 10.1.2.0
R      10.1.2.0 [120/1] via 10.1.23.2, 00:00:19, Serial0/0/0.2
! R1 next…
R1# show ip route | incl 10.1.2.0_
R      10.1.2.0 [120/1] via 10.1.12.2, 00:00:11, FastEthernet0/0
! R1 loses its next-hop interface for the RIP route, so now its OSPF route, with
! AD 180, is its only and best route to 10.1.2.0/24.
R1# conf t
Enter configuration commands, one per line.  End with CNTL/Z.
R1(config)# int fa 0/0
R1(config-if)# shut
R1(config-if)# do sh ip route | incl 10.1.2.0
O E2    10.1.2.0 [180/20] via 10.1.15.5, 00:00:05, Serial0/0/0.5
```

EIGRP supports the exact same concept by default, using AD 170 for external routes and 90 for internal routes. In fact, if EIGRP were used instead of OSPF in this example, neither R1 nor R3 would have experienced any of the suboptimal routing. You can reset EIGRP's distance for internal and external routes by using the **distance eigrp** router subcommand. (At presstime, neither the IS-IS nor RIP **distance** commands support setting external route ADs and internal route ADs to different values.)

In some cases, the requirements may not allow for setting all external routes' ADs to another value. For instance, if R4 injected some legitimate external routes into OSPF, the configuration in Example 10-4 would result in either R1 or R3 having a suboptimal route to those external routes that pointed through the RIP domain. In those cases, the **distance** router subcommand can be used in a different way, influencing some or all of the routes that come from a particular router. The syntax is as follows:

```
distance {distance-value ip-address {wildcard-mask} [ip-standard-list] [ip-extended-
    list]
```

This command sets three key pieces of information: the AD to be set, the IP address of the router advertising the routes, and, optionally, an ACL with which to match routes. With RIP, EIGRP, and IS-IS, this command identifies a neighboring router's interface address using the *ip-address wildcard-mask* parameters. With OSPF, those same parameters identify the RID of the router owning (creating) the LSA for the route. The optional ACL then identifies the subset of routes for which the AD will be set. The logic boils down to something like this:

> Set this AD value for all routes, learned from a router that is defined by the IP address and wildcard mask, and for which the ACL permits the route.

Example 10-5 shows how the command could be used to solve the same suboptimal route problem on R1 and R3, while not causing suboptimal routing for other external routes. The design goals are summarized as follows:

- Set a router's local AD for its OSPF routes for subnets in the RIP domain to a value of 179, thereby making the RIP routes to those subnets better than the OSPF routes to those same subnets.

- Do not set the AD for any other routes.

Example 10-5 *Using the **distance** Command to Reset Particular Routes' ADs*

```
! R1 config. Note that the command refers to 3.3.3.3, which is R3's RID. Other
! commands not related to resetting the AD are omitted. Of particular importance,
! the distance command on R1 refers to R3's OSPF RID, because R3 created the OSPF
! LSAs that we are trying to match—the LSAs created when R3 injected the
! routes redistributed from RIP.
router ospf 1
 distance 179 3.3.3.3 0.0.0.0 only-rip-routes
```

continues

Example 10-5 *Using the* **distance** *Command to Reset Particular Routes' ADs (Continued)*

```
!
ip access-list standard only-rip-routes
 permit 10.1.12.0
 permit 10.1.3.0
 permit 10.1.2.0
 permit 10.1.23.0
! R3 config. Note that the command refers to 1.1.1.1, which is R1's RID. Other
! commands not related to resetting the AD are omitted. Also, the only-rip-routes
! ACL is identical to R1's only-rip-routes ACL.
router ospf 1
distance 179 1.1.1.1 0.0.0.0 only-rip-routes
```

Preventing Suboptimal Routes by Using Route Tags

Another method of preventing suboptimal routing on the redistributing routers is to simply filter the problematic routes. Using subnet 10.1.2.0/24 as an example again, R3 could use an incoming **distribute-list** command to filter the OSPF route to 10.1.2.0/24, allowing R3 to use its RIP route to 10.1.2.0/24. R1 would need to perform similar route filtering as well to prevent its suboptimal route.

Performing simple route filtering based on IP subnet number works, but the redistributing routers will need to be reconfigured every time subnets change in the higher-AD routing domain. The administrative effort can be improved by adding *route tagging* to the process. By tagging all routes taken from the higher-AD domain and advertised into the lower-AD domain, the **distribute-list** command can make a simple check for that tag. Figure 10-6 shows the use of this idea for subnet 10.1.2.0/24.

Route tags are simply unitless integer values in the data structure of a route. These tags, typically either 16 or 32 bits long depending on the routing protocol, allow a router to imply something about a route that was redistributed from another routing protocol. For instance, R1 can tag its OSPF-advertised route to 10.1.2.0/24 with a tag—say, 9999. OSPF does not define what a tag of 9999 means, but the OSPF protocol includes the tag field in the LSA so that it can be used for administrative purposes. Later, R3 can filter routes based on their tag, solving the suboptimal route problem.

Figure 10-6 and Example 10-6 depict an example of route tagging and route filtering, used to solve the same old problem with suboptimal routes. R1 and R3 tag all redistributed RIP routes with tag 9999 as they enter the OSPF domain, and then R1 and R3 filter incoming OSPF routes based on the tags. This design works well because R1 can tag all redistributed RIP routes, thereby removing the need to change the configuration every time a new subnet is added to the RIP domain. (Note that both R1 and R3 will tag routes injected from RIP into OSPF as 9999, and both will then filter OSPF-learned routes with tag 9999. Figure 10-6 just shows one direction to keep the figure less cluttered.)

Figure 10-6   *Filtering with Reliance on Route Tags*

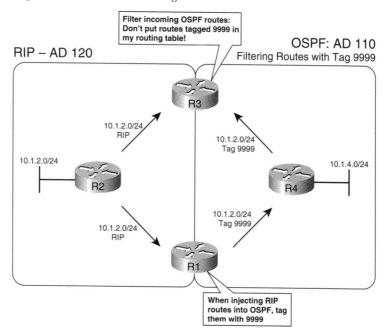

Example 10-6   *Using Route Tags and Distribute Lists to Prevent Suboptimal Routes at Redistributing Routers*

```
! R1 config. The redistribute command calls the route map that tags routes taken
! from RIP as 9999. distribute-list looks at routes learned in OSPF that were
! earlier tagged by R3.
router ospf 1
 redistribute rip subnets route-map tag-rip-9999
 network 10.1.15.1 0.0.0.0 area 0
 distribute-list route-map check-tag-9999 in
! Clause 10, a deny clause, matches all tagged 9999 routes—so those
! routes are filtered. Clause 20 permits all other routes, because with no match
! subcommand, the clause is considered to "match all."
route-map check-tag-9999 deny 10
 match tag 9999
!
route-map check-tag-9999 permit 20
! tag-rip-9999 matches all routes (it has no match command), and then
! tags them all with tag 9999. This route-map is used only for routes taken from
! RIP into OSPF.
route-map tag-rip-9999 permit 10
 set tag 9999

! R3 Config
! The R3 configuration does not have to use the same names for route maps, but
```

continues

Example 10-6 *Using Route Tags and Distribute Lists to Prevent Suboptimal Routes at Redistributing Routers (Continued)*

```
! the essential elements are identical, so the route maps are not repeated here.
router ospf 1
 redistribute rip subnets route-map tag-rip-9999
 network 10.1.34.3 0.0.0.0 area 0
 distribute-list route-map check-tag-9999 in
! R3 (shown) and R1 have RIP routes to 10.1.2.0, as well as other routes from the
! RIP domain. Also, note that the OSPF LSDB shows the tagged values on the routes.
R3# show ip route | incl 10.1.2.0
R        10.1.2.0 [120/1] via 10.1.23.2, 00:00:26, Serial0/0/0.2
R3# sh ip ospf data  begin Type-5
               Type-5 AS External Link States

Link ID         ADV Router      Age       Seq#       Checksum Tag
10.1.1.0        1.1.1.1         834       0x80000006 0x00CE86 9999
10.1.1.0        3.3.3.3         458       0x80000003 0x0098B7 9999
10.1.2.0        1.1.1.1         834       0x80000006 0x00C390 9999
10.1.2.0        3.3.3.3         458       0x80000003 0x008DC1 9999
! lines omitted for brevity
! Next, the unfortunate side effect of filtering the routes—R3 does not have an
! alternative route to RIP subnets, although OSPF internal routers (like R4
! in Figure 10-6) will.
R3# conf t
Enter configuration commands, one per line.  End with CNTL/Z.
R3(config)# int s0/0/0.2
R3(config-subif)# shut
R3(config-subif)# ^Z
R3# sh ip route | incl 10.1.2.0
R3#
```

The last few lines of the example show the largest negative of using route filtering to prevent the suboptimal routes. When R3 loses connectivity to R2, R3 does not use the alternate route through the OSPF domain. R3's filtering of those routes occurs regardless of whether R3's RIP routes are available or not. As a result, using a solution that manipulates the AD may ultimately be the better solution to this suboptimal-routing problem.

Using Metrics and Metric Types to Influence Redistributed Routes

A different set of issues can occur for a router that is internal to a single routing domain, like R4 and R5 in Figure 10-4. The issue is simple—with multiple redistributing routers, an internal router learns multiple routes to the same subnet, so it must pick the best route. As covered earlier in the chapter, the redistributing routers can set the metrics; by setting those metrics with meaningful values, the internal routers can be influenced to use a particular redistribution point.

Interestingly, internal routers may not use metric as their first consideration when choosing the best route. For instance, an OSPF internal router will first take an intra-area route over an inter-area route, regardless of their metrics. Table 10-8 lists the criteria an internal router will use when picking the best route, before considering the metrics of the different routes.

Table 10-8 *IGP Order of Precedence for Choosing Routes Before Considering the Metric*

IGP	Order of Precedence of Metric
RIP	No other considerations
EIGRP	Internal, then external
OSPF	Intra-area, inter-area, E1, then E2*
IS-IS	L1, L2, external

* For E2 routes whose metric ties, OSPF also checks the cost to the advertising ASBR.

To illustrate some of these details, Example 10-7 focuses on R4 and its routes to 10.1.2.0/24 and 10.1.5.0/24 from Figure 10-4. The example shows the following, in order:

1. R1 and R3 advertise 10.1.2.0/24 as an E2 route, metric 20. R4 uses the route through R3, because R4's cost to reach ASBR R3 is lower than its cost to reach ASBR R1.

2. After changing R1 to advertise redistributed routes into OSPF as E1 routes, R4 uses the E1 routes through R1, even though the metric is larger than the E2 route through R3.

3. R4 uses it higher-metric intra-area route to 10.1.5.0/24 through R5. Then, the R4-R5 link fails, causing R4 to use the OSPF external E2 route to 10.1.5.0/24—the route that leads through the RIP domain and back into OSPF via the R3-R2-R1-R5 path.

Example 10-7 *Demonstration of the Other Decision Criteria for Choosing the Best Routes*

```
! R4 has E2 routes to all the subnets in the RIP domain, and they all point to R3.
R4# sh ip route ospf
10.0.0.0/24 is subnetted, 10 subnets
O       10.1.15.0 [110/128] via 10.1.45.5, 00:03:23, Serial0/0/0.5
O E2    10.1.12.0 [110/20] via 10.1.34.3, 00:03:23, Serial0/0/0.3
O E2    10.1.3.0 [110/20] via 10.1.34.3, 00:03:23, Serial0/0/0.3
O E2    10.1.2.0 [110/20] via 10.1.34.3, 00:03:23, Serial0/0/0.3
O E2    10.1.1.0 [110/20] via 10.1.34.3, 00:03:23, Serial0/0/0.3
O       10.1.5.0 [110/65] via 10.1.45.5, 00:03:23, Serial0/0/0.5
O E2    10.1.23.0 [110/20] via 10.1.34.3, 00:03:23, Serial0/0/0.3
! R4 chose the routes through R3 instead of R1 due to the lower cost to R3.
R4# show ip ospf border-routers
OSPF Process 1 internal Routing Table
Codes: i - Intra-area route, I - Inter-area route
```

continues

Example 10-7 *Demonstration of the Other Decision Criteria for Choosing the Best Routes (Continued)*

```
i 1.1.1.1 [128] via 10.1.45.5, Serial0/0/0.5, ASBR, Area 0, SPF 13
i 3.3.3.3 [64] via 10.1.34.3, Serial0/0/0.3, ASBR, Area 0, SPF 13
! (Not Shown): R1 is changed to redistribute RIP routes as E1 routes by
! adding the metric-type 1 option on the redistribute command on R1.
! R4 picks routes through R1 because they are E1 routes, even though the metric
! (148) is higher than the routes through R3 (cost 20)
R4# show ip route ospf
10.0.0.0/24 is subnetted, 10 subnets
O E1    10.1.2.0 [110/148] via 10.1.45.5, 00:00:11, Serial0/0/0.5
! lines omitted for brevity
! R4's route to 10.1.5.0/24 below is intra-area, metric 65
R4# show ip route | incl 10.1.5.0
O       10.1.5.0 [110/65] via 10.1.45.5, 00:04:48, Serial0/0/0.5
! (Not Shown): R4 shuts down link to R5
! R4's new route to 10.1.5.0/24 is E2, learned from R3, with metric 20
R4# show ip route | incl 10.1.5.0\
O E2    10.1.5.0 [110/20] via 10.1.34.3, 00:10:52, Serial0/0/0.3
```

Route Summarization

Route summarization creates a single route whose numeric range, as implied by the prefix/prefix length, is larger than the one or more smaller component routes. For example, 10.1.0.0/16 is a summary route that includes component subnets 10.1.1.0/24, 10.1.4.132/30, and any other subnets with the range 10.1.0.0 through 10.1.255.255.

> **NOTE** I use the term *component route* to refer to a route whose range of IP addresses is a subset of the range specified by a summary route; however, I have not seen this term in other reference materials from Cisco.

The following list details some of the key features that the three IGPs covered in this book have in common with regard to how route summarization works (by default):

- The advertised summary is assigned the same metric as the currently lowest-metric component subnet.

- The router does not advertise the component subnets.

- The router does not advertise the summary when its routing table does not have any of the component subnets.

- The summarizing router creates a local route to the summary, with destination null0, to prevent routing loops.

- Summary routes reduce the size of routing tables and topology databases, indirectly improving convergence.

- Summary routes decrease the amount of specific information in routing tables, sometimes causing suboptimal routing.

Figure 10-7 depicts the suboptimal-routing side effect when using route summarization. It also depicts the effect of using a summary to null0 on the summarizing router.

Figure 10-7 *Route Summarization Suboptimal Routing and Routing to Null0*

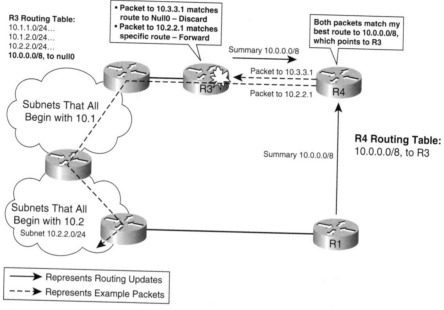

In Figure 10-7, R4 learned two paths to summary route 10.0.0.0/8, and picked the route through R3 based on the metric. Because R4 does not have a route for 10.2.2.0/24, R4 then sends any packets to that subnet based on its route to network 10.0.0.0/8, through R3. So, although subnets like 10.2.2.0/24 may be topologically closer to R4 through R1, R4 sends the packets via the scenic, suboptimal route through R3.

Also note that R4's summary route to 10.0.0.0/8 matches packets for which the component subnet does not exist anywhere in the network. In that case, routers like R4 forward the packets based on the larger summary, but once the packet reaches the router that created the summary, the packet is discarded by the summarizing router due to its null route. For instance, Figure 10-7 shows R4 forwarding a packet destined to 10.3.3.1 to R3. R3 does not have a more specific route than its route to 10.0.0.0/8, with next-hop interface null0. As a result, R3 discards the packet.

The sections that follow provide a few details about summarization with each routing protocol.

EIGRP Route Summarization

EIGRP provides the easiest and most straightforward rules for summarizing routes as compared with RIPv2, OSPF, and IS-IS. To summarize routes, the **ip summary-address eigrp** *as-number network-address subnet-mask* [*admin-distance*] command is placed under an interface. If any of the component routes are in that router's routing table, EIGRP advertises the summary route *out* that interface. The summary is defined by the *network-address subnet-mask* parameters.

One of the more interesting features of the EIGRP summary is the ability to set the AD of the summary route. The AD is not advertised with the route; the summarizing router, however, uses the configured AD to determine whether the null route for the summary should be put into its routing table. The EIGRP AD for summary routes defaults to 5.

OSPF Route Summarization

All OSPF routers in the same area must have identical LSDBs after flooding is complete. As a result, all routers in the same OSPF area must have the same summary routes, and must be missing the same component subnets of each summary. To make that happen, OSPF allows route summarization only as routes are injected into an area, either by an ABR (inter-area routes) or by an ASBR (external routes).

OSPF uses two different configuration commands to create the summary routes, depending on whether the summary is for inter-area or external routes. Table 10-9 lists the two commands. Both commands are configured under **router ospf**.

Table 10-9 *OSPF Route Summarization Commands*

Where used	Command
ASBR	**summary-address** {{*ip-address mask*}	{*prefix mask*}} [**not-advertise**] [**tag** *tag*]
ABR	**area** *area-id* **range** *ip-address mask* [**advertise**	**not-advertise**] [**cost** *cost*]

The commands have a couple of important attributes. First, the **area range** command specifies an area; this area is the area in which the component subnets reside, with the summary being advertised into *all other areas*. Also, the **area range** command can set the cost for the summary route, instead of using the lowest cost of all component routes. Also, the **not-advertise** keyword can essentially be used to filter the subnets implied by the summary, as covered in Chapter 9, "OSPF."

The **summary-address** command summarizes external routes as they are injected into OSPF as an ASBR. The cost can be assigned, and the routes can be filtered using the **not-advertise** keyword.

Default Routes

Routers forward packets using a default route when there are no specific routes that match a packet's destination IP address in the IP routing table. Routing protocols can advertise default routes, with each router choosing the best default route to list as that router's *gateway of last resort*. This section covers how a router can create a default route and then cause an IGP to advertise the default route.

In addition to the advertisement of default routes, each router may use one of two options for how the default route is used. As described in Chapter 6, "IP Forwarding (Routing)," each router's configuration includes either the (default) **ip classless** command or the **no ip classless** command. With **ip classless**, if a packet's destination does not match a specific route in the IP routing table, the router uses the default route. With **no ip classless**, the router first checks to see if any part of the destination address's classful network is in the routing table. If so, that router will not use the default route for forwarding that packet.

> **NOTE**   The topic of default routing requires discussion of the configuration on one router, plus configuration of the other routers using the same IGP. For this section, I will call the router with the default routing configuration the "local" router, and other routers using the same IGP "other" routers.

Cisco IOS supports five basic methods of advertising default routes with IGPs, four of which are covered here. One method for advertising a default route is for one routing protocol to redistribute another routing protocol's default route. Because route redistribution has already been covered heavily, this section of the chapter covers other methods. Of the other four methods, not all are supported by all IGPs, as you can see in Table 10-10.

Table 10-10 *Four Methods for Learning Default Routes*

Feature	RIP	EIGRP	OSPF
Static route to 0.0.0.0, with the **redistribute static** command	Yes	Yes	No
The **default-information originate** command	Yes	No	Yes
The **ip default-network** command	Yes	Yes	No
Using summary routes	No	Yes	No

Interestingly, when a router learns of multiple default routes, using any of these methods, it will use the usual process for choosing the best route: administrative distance, route type (per Table 10-9, earlier in this chapter), and lowest metric, in that order.

> **NOTE** Table 10-10 has details that may be difficult to memorize. To make it easier, you could start by ignoring the use of summary static routes, because it is not recommended by Cisco. Then, note that RIP supports the other three methods, whereas EIGRP supports two methods and OSPF supports only one—with EIGRP and OSPF not supporting any of the same options.

Figure 10-8 shows a sample network used with all the default route examples, in which R1 is the local router that configures the default routing commands.

Figure 10-8 *Sample Network for Default Route Examples*

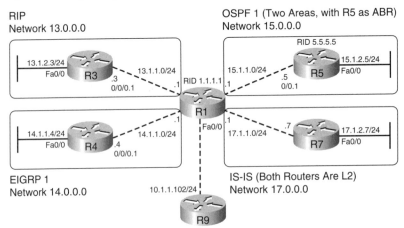

Using Static Routes to 0.0.0.0, with redistribute static

Routers consider a route to 0.0.0.0/0 as a default route. RIP and EIGRP support redistribution of static routes, including such a default static route. The rules and conditions for redistributing static defaults into RIP and EIGRP are as follows:

- The static **ip route 0.0.0.0 0.0.0.0** and **redistribute static** commands need to be configured on the same local router.

- The metric must be defaulted or set, using the same methods covered earlier in this chapter.

- The **redistribute** command can refer to a route map, which examines all static routes (not just the default).

- EIGRP treats the default route as an external route by default, with default AD 170.

- This method is not supported by OSPF.

Example 10-8 shows how R1 can inject defaults via RIP to R3 and via EIGRP to R4. The EIGRP configuration refers to a route map that examines all static routes, matching only static default routes. If other static routes existed, EIGRP would not advertise those routes based on the route map.

Example 10-8   *Static Default Route with Route Redistribution*

```
! R1 Config—note that ip classless is configured, but it does not impact the
! advertisement of the static route at all.
router eigrp 1
 redistribute static route-map just-default
 network 10.0.0.0
 network 14.0.0.0
 default-metric 1544 10 1 1 1
!
router rip
 version 2
 redistribute static
 network 13.0.0.0
 default-metric 1
!
ip classless
! The static route is configured next, followed by the prefix list that matches
! the default route, and the route map that refers to the prefix list.
ip route 0.0.0.0 0.0.0.0 10.1.1.102
!
ip prefix-list zero-prefix seq 5 permit 0.0.0.0/0
!
route-map just-default permit 10
 match ip address prefix-list zero-prefix
!
```

continues

Example 10-8 *Static Default Route with Route Redistribution (Continued)*

```
route-map just-default deny 20
! Next, R3, the RIP router, lists R1 (13.1.1.1) as its gateway of last resort,
! based on the RIP route to 0.0.0.0/0, next hop 13.1.1.1.
R3# sh ip route
! Lines omitted for brevity
Gateway of last resort is 13.1.1.1 to network 0.0.0.0


     13.0.0.0/24 is subnetted, 2 subnets
C       13.1.1.0 is directly connected, Serial0/0/0.1
C       13.1.2.0 is directly connected, FastEthernet0/0
R*   0.0.0.0/0 [120/1] via 13.1.1.1, 00:00:12, Serial0/0/0.1
! Next, R4, the EIGRP router, lists R1 (14.1.1.1) as its gateway of last resort,
! based on the EIGRP route to 0.0.0.0/0, next hop 14.1.1.1. Note that the default
! points to 0.0.0.0/0, AD 170, as it is an external route, due to the EX listed
! in the output of the show ip route command.
R4# sh ip route
! lines omitted for brevity
Gateway of last resort is 14.1.1.1 to network 0.0.0.0


D    10.0.0.0/8 [90/2172416] via 14.1.1.1, 00:01:30, Serial0/0/0.1
     14.0.0.0/24 is subnetted, 2 subnets
C       14.1.2.0 is directly connected, FastEthernet0/0
C       14.1.1.0 is directly connected, Serial0/0/0.1
D*EX 0.0.0.0/0 [170/2172416] via 14.1.1.1, 00:01:30, Serial0/0/0.1
```

Using the default-information originate Command

OSPF does not support redistribution of statically defined default routes. Instead, OSPF requires the **default-information originate** router subcommand, which essentially tells OSPF to redistribute any default routes found in the routing table, either static routes or routes from another routing protocol. The following list summarizes the default routing features when using the **default-information originate** command with OSPF:

- Redistributes any default route (0.0.0.0/0) in the routing table.

- The command can set the metric and metric type directly, with OSPF defaulting to cost 1 and type E2.

- OSPF allows the use of the **always** keyword, which means a default is sourced regardless of whether a default route is in the routing table.

- Not supported by EIGRP.

- Supported by RIP, with some differences. (Refer to the text following Example 10-9 for an explanation of the differences.)

Example 10-9 shows an example of using the **default-information originate** command with OSPF. In this case, R1 has learned a route to 0.0.0.0/0 via BGP from R9 in Figure 10-8.

Example 10-9 *Static Default Route with Route Redistribution*

```
router ospf 1
 network 15.0.0.0 0.255.255.255 area 0
 default-information originate
! R5 has a default route, defaulting to type E2, cost 1. It as advertised as a
! type 5 LSA.
R5# show ip route ospf
O*E2 0.0.0.0/0 [110/1] via 15.1.1.1, 00:18:07, Serial0/0.1
R5# sh ip ospf data | begin Type-5
                Type-5 AS External Link States

Link ID         ADV Router     Age       Seq#       Checksum Tag
0.0.0.0         1.1.1.1        1257      0x80000001 0x008C12 1
```

As mentioned earlier, RIP does support the **default-information originate** command; however, the command behaves slightly differently in RIP than it does in OSPF. With RIP, this command creates and advertises a default route if either no default route exists or a default route was learned from another routing protocol. However, if a static route to 0.0.0.0/0 is in the local routing table, the **default-information originate** command does *not* cause RIP to inject a default—the reason behind this behavior is that RIP already supports redistribution of static routes, so **redistribute static** should be used in that case.

Using the ip default-network Command

RIP and EIGRP can inject default routes by using the **ip default-network** command. To do so, the following must be true on the local router:

- The local router must configure the **ip default-network** *net-number* command, with *net-number* being a classful network number.

- The classful network must be in the local router's IP routing table, via any means.

- For EIGRP only, the classful network must be advertised by the local router into EIGRP, again through any means.

- This method is not supported by OSPF.

When using the **ip default-network** command, RIP and EIGRP differ in how they advertise the default. RIP advertises a route to 0.0.0.0/0, but EIGRP flags its route to the classful network as a candidate default route. Because EIGRP flags these routes as candidates, EIGRP must then also be advertising those classful networks. However, because RIP does not flag the classful network as a candidate default route, RIP does not actually have to advertise the classful network referenced in the **ip default-network** command.

Example 10-10 shows the key difference between RIP and EIGRP with regard to the **ip default-network** command. In this case, R1 will advertise about classful network 10.0.0.0 using EIGRP due to the **auto-summary** command.

Example 10-10 *Static Default Route with Route Redistribution*

```
! EIGRP will advertise classful network 10.0.0.0/8 due to its network command,
! matching R1's fa0/0 interface, and the auto-summary command. Also, R1 must have
! a route to classful network 10.0.0.0/8, in this case due to a static route.
! RIP will not advertise classful network 10.0.0.0/8, but it will still be able
! to inject a default route based on the ip default-network command.
router eigrp 1
 network 10.0.0.0
 network 14.0.0.0
 auto-summary
!
router rip
 version 2
 network 13.0.0.0
!
ip classless
ip default-network 10.0.0.0
ip route 10.0.0.0 255.0.0.0 10.1.1.102
! On R3, RIP learns a route to 0.0.0.0/0 as its default.
R3# show ip route rip
R*    0.0.0.0/0 [120/1] via 13.1.1.1, 00:00:19, Serial0/0/0.1
! On R4, note that EIGRP learned a route to 10.0.0.0/8, shown with a * that
! flags the route as a candidate default route.
R4# show ip route
! lines omitted for brevity
         ia - IS-IS inter area, * - candidate default, U - per-user static route
         o - ODR, P - periodic downloaded static route

Gateway of last resort is 14.1.1.1 to network 10.0.0.0

D*    10.0.0.0/8 [90/2172416] via 14.1.1.1, 00:05:35, Serial0/0/0.1
         14.0.0.0/24 is subnetted, 2 subnets
C        14.1.2.0 is directly connected, FastEthernet0/0
C        14.1.1.0 is directly connected, Serial0/0/0.1
```

Using Route Summarization to Create Default Routes

Generally speaking, route summarization combines smaller address ranges into a small number of larger address ranges. From that perspective, 0.0.0.0/0 is the largest possible summary, because it includes all possible IPv4 addresses. And, as it turns out, EIGRP route summarization supports summarizing the 0.0.0.0/0 supernet, effectively creating a default route.

Because route summarization causes a null route to be created for the summary, some Cisco documentation advises against using route summarization to create a default route. For example, in Figure 10-8, imagine that R9 is owned by this network's ISP, and R1 learns a default route (0.0.0.0/0) via EBGP from R9. However, when R1 configures an EIGRP default route using route summarization, R1 will also create a local route to 0.0.0.0/0 as well, but with destination null0. The EBGP route has a higher AD (20) than the EIGRP summary route to null0 (AD 5), so R1 will now replace its BGP-learned default route with the summary route to null0—preventing R1 from being able to send packets to the Internet.

Route summarization can still be used to create default routes with the proper precautions. The following list details a few of the requirements and options:

■ The local router creates a local summary route, destination null0, using AD 5 (EIGRP), when deciding if its route is the best one to add to the local routing table.

■ EIGRP advertises the summary to other routers as AD 90 (internal).

■ This method is not supported by RIP and OSPF.

■ To overcome the caveat of EIGRP's default route being set to null by having a low AD, set the AD higher (as needed) with the **ip summary-address** command.

Example 10-11 lists a sample configuration on R1 again, this time creating summary routes to 0.0.0.0/0 for EIGRP.

Example 10-11   *EIGRP and IS-IS Configuration for Creating Default Summary Routes*

```
! EIGRP route summarization is done under s0/0/0.4, the subnet connected to R4. In this
! example, the AD was changed to 7 (default 5) just to show how to change the AD. To
! avoid the problem with the default route to null0 on R1, the AD should have been set
! higher than the default learned via BGP.
interface Serial0/0/0.4 point-to-point
 ip address 14.1.1.1 255.255.255.0
 ip summary-address eigrp 1 0.0.0.0 0.0.0.0 7
! In this example, R1 has two sources for a local route to 0.0.0.0/0: EIGRP
! (AD 7, per the ip summary-address command), and BGP from R9
! (AD 20). R1 installs the EIGRP route based on the lowest AD.
R1# show ip route eigrp
        14.0.0.0/8 is variably subnetted, 3 subnets, 2 masks
D        14.1.2.0/24 [90/2172416] via 14.1.1.4, 00:01:03, Serial0/0/0.4
D        14.0.0.0/8 is a summary, 05:53:19, Null0
D*   0.0.0.0/0 is a summary, 00:01:08, Null0
! Next, R4's EIGRP route shows AD 90, instead of the AD 7 configured at R1. AD is
! a local parameter—R4 uses its default AD of 90 for internal routes.
R4# show ip route eigrp
D*   0.0.0.0/0 [90/2172416] via 14.1.1.1, 00:01:14, Serial0/0/0.1
```

Foundation Summary

This section lists additional details and facts to round out the coverage of the topics in this chapter. Unlike most of the Cisco Press *Exam Certification Guides*, this "Foundation Summary" does not repeat information presented in the "Foundation Topics" section of the chapter. Please take the time to read and study the details in the "Foundation Topics" section of the chapter, as well as review items noted with a Key Topic icon.

Table 10-11 lists some of the most relevant Cisco IOS commands related to the topics in this chapter. Also refer to Tables 10-2 and 10-3 for the **match** and **set** commands.

Table 10-11 *Command Reference for Chapter 10*

Command	Command Mode and Description
redistribute *protocol* [*process-id*] {**level-1** | **level-1-2** | **level-2**} [*as-number*] [**metric** *metric-value*] [**metric-type** *type-value*] [**match** {**internal** | **external 1** | **external 2**}] [**tag** *tag-value*] [**route-map** *map-tag*] [**subnets**]	Router config mode; defines the routing protocol from which to take routes, several matching parameters, and several things that can be marked on the redistributed routes.
ip prefix-list *list-name* [**seq** *seq-value*] {**deny** *network/length* | **permit** *network/length*} [**ge** *ge-value*] [**le** *le-value*]	Global config mode; defines members of a prefix list, which match a prefix (subnet) and prefix length (subnet mask).
ip prefix-list *list-name* *sequence-number* **description** *text*	Global config; sets a description to a line in a prefix list.
distance {*ip-address* {*wildcard-mask*}} [*ip-standard-list*] [*ip-extended-list*]	Router config mode; identifies the route source, and an optional ACL to define a subnet of routes, for which this router's AD is changed. Influences the selection of routes by selectively overriding default AD.
distance eigrp *internal-distance external-distance*	EIGRP config; sets the AD for all internal and external routes.
distance ospf {[**intra-area** *dist1*] [**inter-area** *dist2*] [**external** *dist3*]}	OSPF config; sets the AD for all intra-area, interarea, and external routes.
ip summary-address eigrp *as-number network-address subnet-mask* [*admin-distance*]	Interface mode; configures an EIGRP route summary.
ip summary-address rip *ip-address ip-network-mask*	Interface mode; configures a RIP route summary.
area *area-id* **range** *ip-address mask* [**advertise** | **not-advertise**] [**cost** *cost*]	OSPF mode; configures an OSPF summary between areas.
summary-address *address mask* {**level-1** | **level-1-2** | **level-2**}	IS-IS mode; configures an IP summary route.

Table 10-11 *Command Reference for Chapter 10 (Continued)*

Command	Command Mode and Description
summary-address {{*ip-address mask*} | {*prefix mask*}} [**not-advertise**] [**tag** *tag*]	OSPF mode; configures an OSPF summary of external routes.
ip default-network *network-number*	Global config; sets a network from which to derive default routes.
default-information originate [**route-map** *map-name*]	IS-IS config; tells IS-IS to advertise a default route if it is in the routing table.
default-information originate [**always**] [**metric** *metric-value*] [**metric-type** *type-value*] [**route-map** *map-name*]	OSPF config; tells OSPF to advertise a default route, either if it is in the routing table or always.
ip route *prefix mask* {*ip-address* | *interface-type interface-number* [*ip-address*]} [*distance*] [*name*] [**permanent**] [**tag** *tag*]	Global config; used to create static IP routes, including static routes to 0.0.0.0 0.0.0.0, which denotes a default route.

Memory Builders

The CCIE Routing and Switching written exam, like all Cisco CCIE written exams, covers a fairly broad set of topics. This section provides some basic tools to help you exercise your memory about some of the broader topics covered in this chapter.

Fill in Key Tables from Memory

Appendix E, "Key Tables for CCIE Study," on the CD in the back of this book contains empty sets of some of the key summary tables in each chapter. Print Appendix E, refer to this chapter's tables in it, and fill in the tables from memory. Refer to Appendix F, "Solutions for Key Tables for CCIE Study," on the CD to check your answers.

Definitions

Next, take a few moments to write down the definitions for the following terms:

> default route, route redistribution, external route, aggregate route, route map, IP prefix list, summary route, component route, gateway of last resort

Refer to the glossary to check your answers.

Further Reading

Routing TCP/IP, Volume I, Second Edition, by Jeff Doyle and Jennifer DeHaven Carroll

CCIE Practical Studies, Volume II, by Karl Solie and Leah Lynch

Blueprint topics covered in this chapter:

This chapter covers the following subtopics from the Cisco CCIE Routing and Switching written exam blueprint. Refer to the full blueprint in Table I-1 in the Introduction for more details on the topics covered in each chapter and their context within the blueprint.

- Protocol on Which BGP Peers Communicate

- Next Hop

- Peering

- Troubleshooting a BGP Route That Will Not Install in the Routing Table

- Routing Information Base (RIB) and Routing Protocol Interaction

CHAPTER 11

BGP

This chapter covers what might be the single most important topic on both the CCIE Routing and Switching written and lab exams—Border Gateway Protocol (BGP) Version 4. This chapter focuses on how BGP accomplishes its fundamental tasks:

1. Forming neighbor relationships

2. Injecting routes into BGP from some other source

3. Exchanging those routes with other routers

4. Placing routes into IP routing tables

All of these BGP topics have close analogies with those of BGP's IGP cousins, but of course there are many differences in the details.

This chapter focuses on how BGP performs its central role as a routing protocol.

"Do I Know This Already?" Quiz

Table 11-1 outlines the major headings in this chapter and the corresponding "Do I Know This Already?" quiz questions.

Table 11-1 *"Do I Know This Already?" Foundation Topics Section-to-Question Mapping*

Foundation Topics Section	Questions Covered in This Section	Score
Building BGP Neighbor Relationships	1–3	
Building the BGP Table	4–8	
Building the IP Routing Table	9–12	
Total Score		

In order to best use this pre-chapter assessment, remember to score yourself strictly. You can find the answers in Appendix A, "Answers to the 'Do I Know This Already?' Quizzes."

1. Into which of the following neighbor states must a neighbor stabilize before BGP Update messages may be sent?

    a. Active

    b. Idle

    c. Connected

    d. Established

2. BGP neighbors check several parameters before the neighbor relationship can be completed. Which of the following is not checked?

    a. That the neighbor's router ID is not duplicated with other routers

    b. That the **neighbor** command on one router matches the update source IP address on the other router

    c. If eBGP, that the **neighbor** command points to an IP address in a connected network

    d. That a router's **neighbor remote-as** command refers to the same autonomous system number (ASN) as in the other router's **router bgp** command (assuming confederations are not used)

3. A group of BGP routers, some with iBGP and some with eBGP connections, all use loopback IP addresses to refer to each other in their **neighbor** commands. Which of the following statements are false regarding the configuration of these peers?

    a. IBGP peers require a **neighbor** *ip-address* **ibgp-multihop** command for the peer to become established.

    b. eBGP peers require a **neighbor** *ip-address* **ebgp-multihop** command for the peer to become established.

    c. eBGP and iBGP peers cannot be placed into the same peer group.

    d. For eBGP peers, a router's BGP router ID must be equal to the IP address listed in the eBGP neighbor's **neighbor** command.

4. A router has routes in the IP routing table for 20.0.0.0/8, 20.1.0.0/16, and 20.1.2.0/24. BGP on this router is configured with the **no auto-summary** command. Which of the following is true when using the BGP **network** command to cause these routes to be injected into the BGP table?

    a. The **network 20.0.0.0** command would cause all three routes to be added to the BGP table.

    b. The **network 20.0.0.0 mask 255.0.0.0** command would cause all three routes to be added to the BGP table.

    c. The **network 20.1.0.0 mask 255.255.0.0** command would cause 20.1.0.0/16 and 20.1.2.0/24 to be added to the BGP table.

    d. The **network 20.0.0.0** command would cause only 20.0.0.0/8 to be added to the BGP table.

5. A router has configured redistribution of EIGRP routes into BGP using the command **redistribute eigrp 1 route-map fred**. This router's BGP configuration includes the **no auto-summary** command. Which of the following are true?

    a. **route-map fred** can consider for redistribution routes listed in the IP routing table as EIGRP-learned routes.

    b. **route-map fred** can consider for redistribution routes in the IP routing table listed as connected routes, but only if those interfaces are matched by EIGRP 1's **network** commands.

    c. **route-map fred** can consider for redistribution routes that are listed in the EIGRP topology table as successor routes but that are not in the IP routing table because a lower administrative distance (AD) route from a competing routing protocol exists.

    d. **route-map fred** can consider for redistribution routes listed in the IP routing table as EIGRP-learned routes, but only if those routes also have at least one feasible successor route.

6. Using BGP, R1 has learned its best route to 9.1.0.0/16 from R3. R1 has a neighbor connection to R2, over a point-to-point serial link using subnet 8.1.1.4/30. R1 has **auto-summary** configured. Which of the following is true regarding what R1 advertises to R2?

    a. R1 advertises only 9.0.0.0/8 to R2, and not 9.1.0.0/16.

    b. If the **aggregate-address 9.0.0.0 255.0.0.0** BGP subcommand is configured, R1 advertises only 9.0.0.0/8 to R2, and not 9.1.0.0/16.

    c. If the **network 9.0.0.0 mask 255.0.0.0** BGP subcommand is configured, R1 advertises only 9.0.0.0/8 to R2, and not 9.1.0.0/16.

    d. None of the other answers is correct.

7. Which of the following statements are false regarding what routes a BGP router can advertise to a neighbor? (Assume no confederations or route reflectors are in use.)

   a. To advertise a route to an eBGP peer, the route cannot have been learned from an iBGP peer.

   b. To advertise a route to an iBGP peer, the route must have been learned from an eBGP peer.

   c. The NEXT_HOP IP address must respond to a ping command.

   d. Do not advertise routes if the neighboring router's AS is in the AS_PATH.

   e. The route must be listed as **valid** in the output of the **show ip bgp** command, but it does not have to be listed as **best**.

8. Several different routes were injected into BGP via various methods on R1. Those routes were then advertised via iBGP to R2. R2 summarized the routes using the **aggregate-address summary-only** command, and then advertised via eBGP to R3. Which of the following are true about the ORIGIN path attribute of these routes?

   a. The routes injected using the **network** command on R1 have an ORIGIN value of IGP.

   b. The routes injected using the **redistribute ospf** command on R1 have an ORIGIN value of IGP.

   c. The routes injected using the **redistribute** command on R1 have an ORIGIN value of EGP.

   d. The routes injected using the **redistribute static** command on R1 have an ORIGIN value of incomplete.

   e. If the **as-set** option was not used, the summary route created on R2 has an ORIGIN code of IGP.

9. Which of the following statements is true regarding the use of BGP synchronization?

   a. With BGP synchronization enabled, a router can add an iBGP-learned route to its IP routing table only if that same prefix is also learned via eBGP.

   b. With BGP synchronization enabled, a router cannot consider an iBGP-learned route as a "best" route to that prefix unless the NEXT_HOP IP address matches an IGP route in the IP routing table.

   c. BGP synchronization can be safely disabled when the routers inside a single AS either create a full mesh of BGP peers or create a hub-and-spoke to the router that learns the prefix via eBGP.

   d. None of the other answers is correct.

10. Which of the following statements are true regarding the operation of BGP confederations?

   a. Confederation eBGP connections act like normal (nonconfederation) eBGP connections with regard to the need for the **neighbor ebgp-multihop** command for nonadjacent neighbor IP addresses.

   b. iBGP-learned routes are advertised over confederation eBGP connections.

   c. A full mesh of iBGP peers inside a confederation sub-AS is not required.

   d. None of the other answers is correct.

11. R1 is BGP peered to R2, R3, R4, and R5 inside ASN 1, with no other peer connections inside the AS. R1 is a route reflector, serving R2 and R3 only. Each router also has an eBGP connection, through which it learns the following routes: 1.0.0.0/8 by R1, 2.0.0.0/8 by R2, 3.0.0.0/8 by R3, 4.0.0.0 by R4, and 5.0.0.0/8 by R5. Which of the following are true regarding the propagation of these routes?

   a. NLRI 1.0.0.0/8 is forwarded by R1 to each of the other routers.

   b. NLRI 2.0.0.0/8 is sent by R2 to R1, with R1 forwarding only to R3.

   c. NLRI 3.0.0.0/8 is sent by R3 to R1, with R1 forwarding to R2, R4, and R5.

   d. NLRI 4.0.0.0/8 is sent by R4 to R1, but R1 does not forward the information to R2 or R3.

   e. NLRI 5.0.0.0/8 is sent by R5 to R1; R1 reflects the route to R2 and R3, but not to R4.

12. R1 is in confederation ASN 65001; R2 and R3 are in confederation ASN 65023. R1 is peered to R2, and R2 is peered to R3. These three routers are perceived to be in AS 1 by eBGP peers. Which of the following is true regarding the configuration of these routers?

   a. Each of the three routers has a **router bgp 1** command.

   b. Both R2 and R3 need a **bgp confederation peers 65001** BGP subcommand.

   c. R1 needs a **bgp confederation identifier 1** BGP subcommand.

   d. Both R2 and R3 need a **bgp confederation identifier 65023** BGP subcommand.

Foundation Topics

Like Interior Gateway Protocols (IGPs), BGP exchanges topology information in order for routers to eventually learn the best routes to a set of IP prefixes. Unlike IGPs, BGP does not use a metric to select the best route among alternate routes to the same destination. Instead, BGP uses several BGP *path attributes (PAs)* and an involved decision process when choosing between multiple possible routes to the same subnet.

BGP uses the BGP *autonomous system path (AS_PATH)* PA as its default metric mechanism when none of the other PAs has been overly set and configured. Generally speaking, BGP uses PAs to describe the characteristics of a route; this introduces and explains a wide variety of BGP PAs. The AS_PATH attribute lists the path, as defined by a sequence of *autonomous system numbers (ASNs)* through which a packet must pass to reach a prefix. Figure 11-1 shows an example.

Figure 11-1 *BGP AS_PATHs and Path Vector Logic*

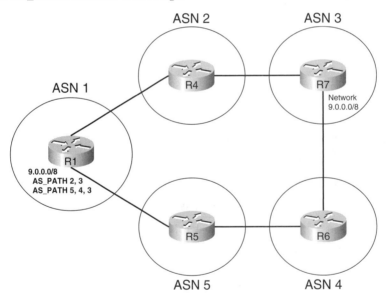

Figure 11-1 shows a classic case of how BGP uses *path vector* logic to choose routes. In the figure, R1 learns of two AS_PATHs by which to reach 9.0.0.0/8—through ASNs 2-3 and through ASNs 5-4-3. If none of the routers has used routing policies to influence other PAs that influence BGP's choice of which route is best, R1 will choose the shortest AS_PATH—in this case, AS_PATH 2-3. In effect, BGP treats the AS_PATH as a vector, and the length of the vector (the number of ASNs in the path) determines the best route. With BGP, the term *route* still refers to traditional hop-by-hop IP routes, but the term *path* refers to the sequence of autonomous systems used to reach a particular destination.

This chapter follows a similar sequence as several of the IGP chapters. First, the text focuses on neighbor relationships, followed by how BGP exchanges routing information with its neighbors. The chapter ends with a section covering how BGP adds IP routes to a router's IP routing table based on the BGP topology table.

Building BGP Neighbor Relationships

BGP neighbors form a TCP connection with each neighbor, sending BGP messages over the connections—culminating in *BGP Update* messages that contain the routing information. Each router explicitly configures its neighbors' IP addresses, using these definitions to tell a router with which IP addresses to attempt a TCP connection. Also, if a router receives a TCP connection request (to BGP port 179) from a source IP address that is not configured as a BGP neighbor, the router rejects the request.

After the TCP connection is established, BGP begins with BGP *Open* messages. Once a pair of BGP Open messages has been exchanged, the neighbors have reached the *established* state, which is the stable state of two working BGP peers. At this point, BGP Update messages can be exchanged.

This section examines many of the details about protocols and configuration for BGP neighbor formation. If you are already familiar with BGP, Table 11-2 summarizes some of the key facts found in this section.

Table 11-2 *BGP Neighbor Summary Table*

BGP Feature	Description and Values
TCP port	179
Setting the keepalive interval and hold time (using the **bgp timers** *keepalive holdtime* router subcommand or **neighbor timers** command, per neighbor)	Default to 60 and 180 seconds; define time between keepalives and time for which silence means the neighbor has failed
What makes a neighbor internal BGP (iBGP)?	Neighbor is in the same AS
What makes a neighbor external BGP (eBGP)?	Neighbor is in another AS
How is the BGP router ID (RID) determined?	In order: The **bgp router-id** command The highest IP of an up/up loopback at the time that the BGP process starts The highest IP of another up/up interface at the time that the BGP process starts.

continues

Table 11-2 *BGP Neighbor Summary Table (Continued)*

BGP Feature	Description and Values
How is the source IP address used to reach a neighbor determined?	Defined with the **neighbor update-source** command; or, by default, uses the outgoing interface IP address for the route used to reach the neighbor
How is the destination IP address used to reach a neighbor determined?	Explicitly defined on the **neighbor** command
Auto-summary*	Off by default, enabled with **auto-summary** router subcommand
Neighbor authentication	MD5 only, using the **neighbor password** command

* Cisco changed the IOS default for BGP **auto-summary** to be disabled as of Cisco IOS Software Release 12.3.

Internal BGP Neighbors

A BGP router considers each neighbor to be either an *internal BGP (iBGP)* peer or an *external BGP (eBGP)* peer. Each BGP router resides in a single AS, so neighbor relationships are either with other routers in the same AS (iBGP neighbors) or with routers in other autonomous systems (eBGP neighbors). The two types of neighbors differ only slightly in regard to forming neighbor relationships, with more significant differences in how the type of neighbor (iBGP or eBGP) impacts the BGP update process and the addition of routes to the routing tables.

iBGP peers often use loopback interface IP addresses for BGP peering to achieve higher availability. Inside a single AS, the physical topology often has at least two routes between each pair of routers. If BGP peers use an interface IP address for their TCP connections, and that interface fails, there still might be a route between the two routers, but the underlying BGP TCP connection will fail. Any time two BGP peers have more than one route through which they can reach the other router, peering using loopbacks makes the most sense.

Several examples that follow demonstrate BGP neighbor configuration and protocols, beginning with Example 11-1. The example shows some basic BGP configuration for iBGP peers R1, R2, and R3 in AS 123, with the following features, based on Figure 11-2.

Figure 11-2   *Sample Network for BGP Neighbor Configuration*

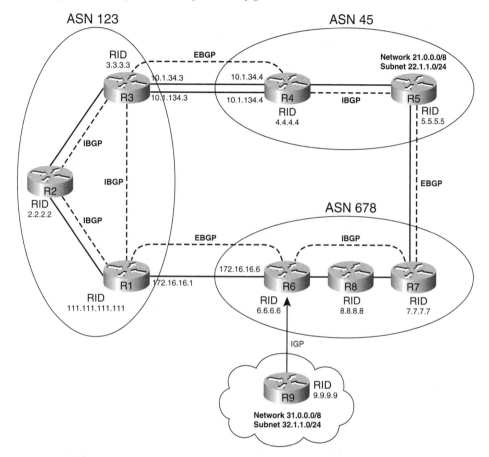

- The three routers in ASN 123 will form iBGP neighbor relationships with each other (full mesh).

- R1 will use the **bgp router-id** command to configure its RID, rather than use a loopback.

- R3 uses a **peer-group** configuration for neighbors R1 and R2. This allows fewer configuration commands, and improves processing efficiency by having to prepare only one set of outbound Update packets for the peer group. (Identical Updates are sent to all peers in the peer group.)

- The R1-R3 relationship uses BGP MD5 authentication, which is the only type of BGP authentication supported in Cisco IOS.

Example 11-1 *Basic iBGP Configuration of Neighbors*

```
! R1 Config—R1 correctly sets its update-source to 1.1.1.1 for both R2 and R3,
! in order to match the R2 and R3 neighbor commands. The first three highlighted
! commands below were not typed, but added automatically as defaults by IOS 12.3
!—in fact, IOS 12.3 docs imply that the defaults of sync and auto-summary at
! IOS 12.2 has changed to no sync and no auto-summary as of IOS 12.3. Also, R1
! knows that neighbors 2.2.2.2 and 3.3.3.3 are iBGP because their remote-as values
! match R1's router BGP command.
interface Loopback1
 ip address 1.1.1.1 255.255.255.255
!
router bgp 123
 no synchronization
 bgp router-id 111.111.111.111
 bgp log-neighbor-changes
 neighbor 2.2.2.2 remote-as 123
 neighbor 2.2.2.2 update-source Loopback1
 neighbor 3.3.3.3 remote-as 123
 neighbor 3.3.3.3 password secret-pw
 neighbor 3.3.3.3 update-source Loopback1
 no auto-summary
```

```
! R3 Config—R3 uses a peer group called "my-as" for combining commands related
! to R1 and R2. Note that not all parameters must be in the peer group: R3-R2 does
! not use authentication, but R3-R1 does, so the neighbor password command was
! not placed inside the peer group, but instead on a neighbor 1.1.1.1 command.
interface Loopback1
 ip address 3.3.3.3 255.255.255.255
!
router bgp 123
 no synchronization
 bgp log-neighbor-changes
 neighbor my-as peer-group
 neighbor my-as remote-as 123
 neighbor my-as update-source Loopback1
 neighbor 1.1.1.1 peer-group my-as
 neighbor 1.1.1.1 password secret-pw
 neighbor 2.2.2.2 peer-group my-as
 no auto-summary
```

```
! Next, R1 has two established peers, but the fact that the status is "established"
! is implied by not having the state listed on the right side of the output, under
! the heading State/PfxRcd. Once established, that column lists the number of
! prefixes learned via BGP Updates received from each peer. Note also R1's
! configured RID, and the fact that it is not used as the update source.
R1# show ip bgp summary
BGP router identifier 111.111.111.111, local AS number 123
BGP table version is 1, main routing table version 1

Neighbor        V    AS MsgRcvd MsgSent   TblVer  InQ OutQ Up/Down  State/PfxRcd
2.2.2.2         4   123      59      59        0    0    0 00:56:52            0
3.3.3.3         4   123      64      64        0    0    0 00:11:14            0
```

A few features in Example 11-1 are particularly important. First, note that the configuration does not overtly define peers as iBGP or eBGP. Instead, each router examines its own ASN as defined on the **router bgp** command, and compares that value to the neighbor's ASN listed in the **neighbor remote-as** command. If they match, the peer is iBGP; if not, the peer is eBGP.

R3 in Example 11-1 shows how to use the **peer-group** construct to reduce the number of configuration commands. BGP peer groups do not allow any new BGP configuration settings; they simply allow you to group BGP neighbor configuration settings into a group, and then apply that set of settings to a neighbor using the **neighbor peer-group** command. Additionally, BGP builds one set of Update messages for the peer group, applying routing policies for the entire group—rather than one router at a time—thereby reducing some BGP processing and memory overhead.

External BGP Neighbors

The physical topology between eBGP peers is often a single link, mainly because the connection is between different companies in different autonomous systems. As a result, eBGP peering can simply use the interface IP addresses for redundancy, because if the link fails, the TCP connection will fail because there is no longer an IP route between the peers. For instance, in Figure 11-2, the R1-R6 eBGP peering uses interface IP addresses defined in the **neighbor** commands.

When IP redundancy exists between two eBGP peers, the eBGP **neighbor** commands should use loopback IP addresses to take advantage of that redundancy. For example, two parallel links exist between R3 and R4. With **neighbor** commands that reference loopback addresses, either of these links could fail, but the TCP connection would remain. Example 11-2 shows additional configuration for the network in Figure 11-2, showing the use of loopbacks between R3 and R4, and interface addresses between R1 and R6.

Example 11-2 *Basic eBGP Configuration of Neighbors*

```
! R1 Config—This example shows only commands added since Example 11-1.
router bgp 123
 neighbor 172.16.16.6 remote-as 678
! R1 does not have a neighbor 172.16.16.6 update-source command configured. R1
! uses its s0/0/0.6 IP address, 172.16.16.1, because R1's route to 172.16.16.6
! uses s0/0/0.6 as the outgoing interface, as seen below.
R1# show ip route 172.1.16.6
Routing entry for 172.16.16.0/24
  Known via "connected", distance 0, metric 0 (connected, via interface)
  Routing Descriptor Blocks:
  * directly connected, via Serial0/0/0.6
      Route metric is 0, traffic share count is 1
R1# show ip int brief | include 0/0/0.6
Serial0/0/0.6                  172.16.16.1       YES manual up              up
```

continues

Example 11-2 *Basic eBGP Configuration of Neighbors (Continued)*

```
! R3 Config—Because R3 refers to R4's loopback (4.4.4.4), and R4 is an eBGP
! peer, R3 and R4 have added the neighbor ebgp-multihop command to set TTL to 2.
! R3's update source must be identified as its loopback in order to match
! R4's neighbor 3.3.3.3 commands.
router bgp 123
 neighbor 4.4.4.4 remote-as 45
 neighbor 4.4.4.4 update-source loopback1
 neighbor 4.4.4.4 ebgp-multihop 2
! R3 now has three working neighbors. Also note the three TCP connections, one for
! each BGP peer. Note that because R3 is listed using a dynamic port number, and
! R4 as using port 179, R3 actually initiated the TCP connection to R4.
R3# show ip bgp summary
BGP router identifier 3.3.3.3, local AS number 123
BGP table version is 1, main routing table version 1

Neighbor        V    AS MsgRcvd MsgSent   TblVer  InQ OutQ Up/Down  State/PfxRcd
1.1.1.1         4   123     247     247        0    0    0 03:14:49           0
2.2.2.2         4   123     263     263        0    0    0 03:15:07           0
4.4.4.4         4    45      17      17        0    0    0 00:00:11           0
R3# show tcp brief
TCB       Local Address        Foreign Address         (state)
649DD08C  3.3.3.3.179          2.2.2.2.43521           ESTAB
649DD550  3.3.3.3.179          1.1.1.1.27222           ESTAB
647D928C  3.3.3.3.21449        4.4.4.4.179             ESTAB
```

The eBGP configurations differ from iBGP configuration in a couple of small ways. First, the **neighbor remote-as** commands refer to a different AS than does the **router bgp** command, which implies that the peer is an eBGP peer. Second, R3 had to configure the **neighbor 4.4.4.4 ebgp-multihop 2** command (and R4 with a similar command) or the peer connection would not have formed. For eBGP connections, Cisco IOS defaults the IP packet's TTL field to a value of 1, based on the assumption that the interface IP addresses will be used for peering (like R1-R6 in Example 11-2). In this example, if R3 had not used multihop, it would have sent packets to R4 with TTL 1. R4 would have received the packet (TTL 1 at that point), then attempt to route the packet to its loopback interface—a process that would decrement the TTL to 0, causing R4 to drop the packet. So, even though the router is only one hop away, think of the loopback as being on the other side of the router, requiring that extra hop.

Checks Before Becoming BGP Neighbors

Similar to IGPs, BGP checks certain requirements before another router may become a neighbor, reaching the BGP established state. Most of the settings are straightforward; the only tricky part relates to the use of IP addresses. The following list describes the checks that BGP performs when forming neighbor relationships:

1. The router must receive a TCP connection request with a source address that the router finds in a BGP **neighbor** command.

2.   A router's ASN (on the **router bgp** *asn* command) must match the neighboring router's reference to that ASN with its **neighbor remote-as** *asn* command. (This requirement is not true of confederation configurations.)

3.   The BGP RIDs of the two routers must not be the same.

4.   If configured, MD5 authentication must pass.

Figure 11-3 shows the first three items in the list graphically, with R3 initiating a BGP TCP connection to R1. The circled numbers 1, 2, and 3 in the figure correspond to the item numbers in the previous list. Note that R1's check at Step 2 uses the **neighbor** command R1 identified as part of Step 1.

Figure 11-3 *BGP Neighbor Parameter Checking*

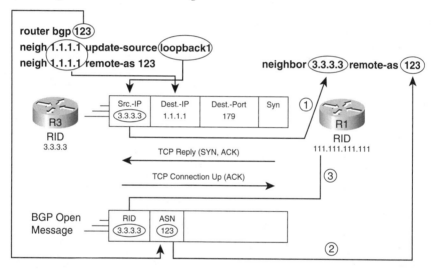

Note: R3's Loopback IP Address is 3.3.3.3

In Figure 11-3, R3 initiates a TCP connection with its update source IP address (3.3.3.3) as the source address of the packet. The first check occurs when R1 receives the first packet, looks at the source IP address of the packet (3.3.3.3), and finds that address in a **neighbor** command. The second check has R1 comparing R3's stated ASN (in R3's BGP Open message) to R1's **neighbor** command it identified at Step 1. Step 3 checks to ensure the BGP RIDs are unique, with the BGP Open message stating the sender's BGP RID.

While the check at Step 1 might seem intuitive, interestingly, the reverse bit of logic does not have to be true for the neighbors to come up. For instance, if R1 did not have a **neighbor 3.3.3.3 update-source 1.1.1.1** command, the process shown in Figure 11-3 would still work. Succinctly put, only one of the two routers' update source IP addresses needs to be in the other router's **neighbor** command for the neighbor to come up. Examples 11-1 and 11-2 showed the correct update source on both routers, and that makes good sense, but it works with only one of the two.

BGP uses a *keepalive timer* to define how often that router sends BGP keepalive messages, and a *Hold* timer to define how long a router will wait without receiving a keepalive message before resetting a neighbor connection. The Open message includes each router's stated keepalive timer. If they do not match, each router uses the lower of the values for each of the two timers, respectively. *Mismatched settings do not prevent the routers from becoming neighbors.*

BGP Messages and Neighbor States

The desired state for BGP neighbors is the established state. In that state, the routers have formed a TCP connection, and they have exchanged Open messages, with the parameter checks having passed. At this point, topology information can be exchanged using Update messages. Table 11-3 lists the BGP neighbor states, along with some of their characteristics. Note that if the IP addresses mismatch, the neighbors settle into an active state.

Table 11-3 *BGP Neighbor States*

State	Listen for TCP?	Initiate TCP?	TCP Up?	Open Sent?	Open Received?	Neighbor Up?
Idle	No					
Connect	Yes					
Active	Yes	Yes				
Open sent	Yes	Yes	Yes	Yes		
Open confirm	Yes	Yes	Yes	Yes	Yes	
Established	Yes	Yes	Yes	Yes	Yes	Yes

BGP Message Types

BGP uses four basic messages. Table 11-4 lists the message types and provides a brief description of each.

Table 11-4 *BGP Message Types*

Message	Purpose
Open	Used to establish a neighbor relationship and exchange basic parameters.
Keepalive	Used to maintain the neighbor relationship, with nonreceipt of a keepalive message within the negotiated Hold timer causing BGP to bring down the neighbor connection. (The timers can be configured with the **bgp timers** *keepalive holdtime* subcommand or the **neighbor** [*ip-address | peer-group-name*] **timers** *keepalive holdtime* BGP subcommand.)

Table 11-4 *BGP Message Types (Continued)*

Message	Purpose
Update	Used to exchange routing information, as covered more fully in the next section.
Notification	Used when BGP errors occur; causes a reset to the neighbor relationship when sent.

Purposefully Resetting BGP Peer Connections

Example 11-3 shows how to reset neighbor connections by using the **neighbor shutdown** command and, along the way, shows the various BGP neighbor states. The example uses routers R1 and R6 from Figure 11-2, as configured in Example 11-2.

Example 11-3 *Examples of Neighbor States*

```
! R1 shuts down R6's peer connection. debug ip bgp shows moving to a down state,
! which shows as "Idle (Admin)" under show ip bgp summary.
R1# debug ip bgp
BGP debugging is on for address family: BGP IPv4
R1# conf t
Enter configuration commands, one per line.  End with CNTL/Z.
R1(config)# router bgp 123
R1(config-router)# neigh 10.1.16.6 shutdown
R1#
*Mar  4 21:01:45.946: BGP: 10.1.16.6 went from Established to Idle
*Mar  4 21:01:45.946: %BGP-5-ADJCHANGE: neighbor 10.1.16.6 Down Admin. shutdown
*Mar  4 21:01:45.946: BGP: 10.1.16.6 closing
R1# show ip bgp summary ¦ include 10.1.16.6
10.1.16.6    4    678    353    353     0   0   0 00:00:06 Idle (Admin)
! Next, the no neighbor shutdown command reverses the admin state. The various
! debug messages (with some omitted) list the various states. Also note that the
! final message is the one log message in this example that occurs due to the
! default configuration of bgp log-neighbor-changes. The rest are the result of
! a debug ip bgp command.
R1# conf t
Enter configuration commands, one per line.  End with CNTL/Z.
R1(config)# router bgp 123
R1(config-router)# no neigh 10.1.16.6 shutdown
*Mar  4 21:02:16.958: BGP: 10.1.16.6 went from Idle to Active
*Mar  4 21:02:16.958: BGP: 10.1.16.6 open active, delay 15571ms
*Mar  4 21:02:29.378: BGP: 10.1.16.6 went from Idle to Connect
*Mar  4 21:02:29.382: BGP: 10.1.16.6 rcv message type 1, length (excl. header) 26
*Mar  4 21:02:29.382: BGP: 10.1.16.6 rcv OPEN, version 4, holdtime 180 seconds
*Mar  4 21:02:29.382: BGP: 10.1.16.6 went from Connect to OpenSent
*Mar  4 21:02:29.382: BGP: 10.1.16.6 sending OPEN, version 4, my as: 123, holdtime 180
  seconds
*Mar  4 21:02:29.382: BGP: 10.1.16.6 rcv OPEN w/ OPTION parameter len: 16
BGP: 10.1.16.6 rcvd OPEN w/ remote AS 678
```

continues

Example 11-3 *Examples of Neighbor States (Continued)*

```
*Mar  4 21:02:29.382: BGP: 10.1.16.6 went from OpenSent to OpenConfirm
*Mar  4 21:02:29.382: BGP: 10.1.16.6 send message type 1, length (incl. header) 45
*Mar  4 21:02:29.394: BGP: 10.1.16.6 went from OpenConfirm to Established
*Mar  4 21:02:29.398: %BGP-5-ADJCHANGE: neighbor 10.1.16.6 Up
```

All BGP neighbors can be reset with the **clear ip bgp *** exec command, which, like the **neighbor shutdown** command, resets the neighbor connection, closes the TCP connection to that neighbor, and removes all entries from the BGP table learned from that neighbor. The **clear** command will be shown in the rest of the chapter as needed, including in coverage of how to clear just some neighbors.

> **NOTE** The **clear** command can also be used to implement routing policy changes without resetting the neighbor completely, using a feature called *soft reconfiguration*. This feature is not covered in detail in this book.

Building the BGP Table

The BGP *topology table*, also called the BGP *Routing Information Base (RIB)*, holds the *network layer reachability information* (NLRI) learned by BGP, as well as the associated PAs. An NLRI is simply an IP prefix and prefix length. This section focuses on the process of how BGP injects NLRI into a router's BGP table, followed by how routers advertise their associated PAs and NLRI to neighbors.

> **NOTE** Technically, BGP does not advertise routes; rather, it advertises PAs plus a set of NLRI that shares the same PA values. However, most people simply refer to NLRI as *BGP prefixes* or *BGP routes*. This book uses all three terms. However, because there is a distinction between a BGP route in the BGP table and an IP route in the IP routing table, the text takes care to refer to the BGP table or IP routing table to distinguish the two tables.

Injecting Routes/Prefixes into the BGP Table

Unsurprisingly, an individual BGP router adds entries to its local BGP table by using the same general methods used by IGPs: by using the **network** command, by hearing the topology information via an Update message from a neighbor, or by redistributing from another routing protocol. The next few sections show examples of how a local BGP router adds routes to the BGP table by methods other than learning them from a BGP neighbor.

BGP network Command

This section, and the next section, assumes the BGP **no auto-summary** command has been configured. Note that as of the Cisco IOS Software Release 12.3 Mainline, **no auto-summary** is the default; earlier releases defaulted to use **auto-summary**. Following that, the section, "The Impact of

Auto-Summary on Redistributed Routes and the **network** Command," discusses the impact of the **auto-summary** command on both the **network** command and the **redistribute** command.

The BGP **network** router subcommand differs significantly from the **network** command used by IGPs. The BGP **network** command instructs that router's BGP process to do the following:

Look for a route in the router's current IP routing table that exactly matches the parameters of the **network** command; if the IP route exists, put the equivalent NLRI into the local BGP table.

With this logic, connected routes, static routes, or IGP routes could be taken from the IP routing table and placed into the BGP table for later advertisement. When the router removes that route from its IP routing table, BGP then removes the NLRI from the BGP table, and notifies neighbors that the route has been withdrawn.

Note that the IP route must be matched exactly when the **no auto-summary** command is configured or used by default.

Table 11-5 lists a few of the key features of the BGP **network** command, whose generic syntax is:

```
network {network-number [mask network-mask]} [route-map map-tag]
```

Table 11-5 *Key Features of the BGP* **network** *Command*

Feature	Implication
No mask is configured	Assumes the default classful mask.
Matching logic with **no auto-summary** configured	An IP route must match both the prefix and prefix length (mask).
Matching logic with **auto-summary** configured	If the **network** command lists a classful network, it matches if any subnets of the classful network exist.
NEXT_HOP of BGP route added to the BGP table*	Uses next hop of IP route.
Maximum number injected by the **network** command into one BGP process	200
Purpose of the **route-map** option on the **network** command	Can be used to filter routes and manipulate PAs, including NEXT_HOP*.

*NEXT_HOP is a BGP PA that denotes the next-hop IP address that should be used to reach the NLRI.

Example 11-4 shows an example **network** command as implemented on R5 of Figure 11-4 (R5's BGP neighbors have been shut down so that the BGP table shows only BGP table entries created by the **network** commands on R5). In Example 11-4, R5 uses two **network** commands to add 21.0.0.0/8 and 22.1.1.0/24 to its BGP table.

Figure 11-4 *Sample BGP Network, with IP Addresses*

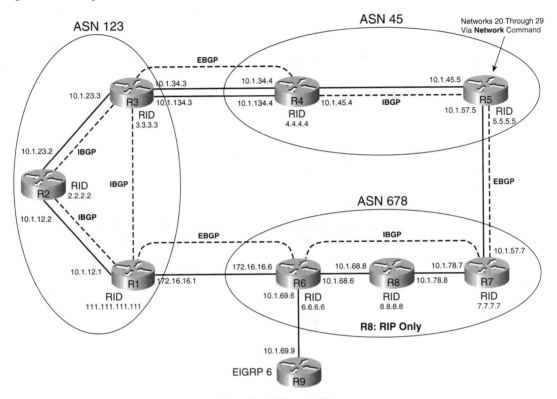

Example 11-4 *Examples of Populating the BGP Table via the* **network** *Command*

```
! On R5, the network commands specifically match prefixes 21.0.0.0/8 and 22.1.1.0/24. The
! omission of the mask on the first command implies the associated classful mask
! of 255.0.0.0, as the IP address listed (21.0.0.0) is a class A address.
router bgp 45
 no synchronization
 bgp log-neighbor-changes
 network 21.0.0.0
 network 22.1.1.0 mask 255.255.255.0
! The neighbor commands are not shown, as they are not pertinent to the topics
! covered in this example.
! Next, the two routes matched by the network commands are indeed in the IP
! routing table. Note that the route to 21.0.0.0/8 is a connected route, and the
! route to 22.1.1.0/24 is a static route.
R5# show ip route | incl 21 | 22
```

Example 11-4 *Examples of Populating the BGP Table via the* **network** *Command (Continued)*

```
C    21.0.0.0/8 is directly connected, Loopback20
     22.0.0.0/24 is subnetted, 1 subnets
S       22.1.1.0 [1/0] via 10.1.5.9
! Below, the prefixes have been added to the BGP table. Note that the NEXT_HOP
! PA has been set to 0.0.0.0 for the route (21.0.0.0/8) that was taken from a
! connected route, with the NEXT_HOP for 22.1.1.0/24 matching the IP route.
R5# show ip bgp
BGP table version is 38, local router ID is 5.5.5.5
Status codes: s suppressed, d damped, h history, * valid, > best, i - internal,
              r RIB-failure, S Stale
Origin codes: i - IGP, e - EGP, ? - incomplete

   Network          Next Hop          Metric LocPrf Weight Path
*> 21.0.0.0         0.0.0.0                0         32768 i
*> 22.1.1.0/24      10.1.5.9               0         32768 i
```

Redistributing from an IGP, Static, or Connected Route

The BGP **redistribute** subcommand can redistribute static, connected, and IGP-learned routes. The mechanics of the BGP **redistribute** command work very similarly with redistribution as covered in Chapter 10, "IGP Route Redistribution, Route Summarization, and Default Routing"; however, this section covers a few nuances that are unique to BGP.

BGP does not use the concept of calculating a metric for each alternate route to reach a particular prefix. Instead, BGP uses a step-wise decision process that examines various PAs to determine the best route. As a result, redistribution into BGP does not require any consideration of setting metrics. However, a router might need to apply a route map to the redistribution function to manipulate PAs, which in turn affects the BGP decision process. If a metric is assigned to a route injected into BGP, BGP assigns that metric value to the BGP *Multi-Exit Discriminator (MED)* PA, which is commonly referred to as *metric*.

> **NOTE** Although this point is not unique to BGP, keep in mind that redistribution from an IGP causes two types of routes to be taken from the routing table—those learned by the routing protocol, and those connected routes for which that routing protocol matches with a **network** command.

Example 11-5 shows R6 (from Figure 11-4) filling its BGP table through route redistribution from Enhanced IGRP (EIGRP) process 6 (as configured in Example 11-5 with the **router eigrp 6** command) and redistributing a single static route. EIGRP on R6 learns routes only for networks 30 through 39. The goals of this example are as follows:

■ Redistribute EIGRP routes for networks 31 and 32

- Redistribute the static route to network 34, and set the MED (metric) to 9

- Do not accidentally redistribute the connected routes that are matched by EIGRP's **network** commands

- Use the Cisco IOS 12.3 default setting of **no auto-summary**

Example 11-5 shows the mistake of accidentally redistributing additional routes—the connected subnets of network 10.0.0.0 matched by EIGRP **network** commands. Later in the example, a route map is added to prevent the problem.

Example 11-5 *Example of Populating the BGP Table via Redistribution*

```
! R6 redistributes EIGRP 6 routes and static routes below, setting the metric on
! redistributed static routes to 9. Note that EIGRP 6 matches subnets 10.1.68.0/24
! and 10.1.69.0/24 with its network command.
router bgp 678
 redistribute static metric 9
 redistribute eigrp 6
!
router eigrp 6
 network 10.0.0.0
!
ip route 34.0.0.0 255.0.0.0 null0
! Commands unrelated to populating the local BGP table are omitted.
! R6 has met the goal of injecting 31 and 32 from EIGRP, and 34 from static.
! It also accidentally picked up two subnets of 10.0.0.0/8 because EIGRP's network
! 10.0.0.0 command matched these connected subnets.
R6# show ip bgp
BGP table version is 1, local router ID is 6.6.6.6
Status codes: s suppressed, d damped, h history, * valid, > best, i - internal,
              r RIB-failure, S Stale
Origin codes: i - IGP, e - EGP, ? - incomplete
   Network          Next Hop          Metric LocPrf Weight Path
*> 10.1.68.0/24     0.0.0.0                0          32768 ?
*> 10.1.69.0/24     0.0.0.0                0          32768 ?
*> 31.0.0.0         10.1.69.9         156160          32768 ?
*> 32.1.1.0/24      10.1.69.9         156160          32768 ?
*> 34.0.0.0/24      0.0.0.0                9          32768 ?
! Below, note the metrics for the two EIGRP routes. The show ip bgp command output
! above shows how BGP assigned the MED (metric) that same value.
R6# show ip route eigrp
     32.0.0.0/24 is subnetted, 1 subnets
D       32.1.1.0 [90/156160] via 10.1.69.9, 00:12:17, FastEthernet0/0
D     31.0.0.0/8 [90/156160] via 10.1.69.9, 00:12:17, FastEthernet0/0
! Below, the redistribute eigrp command has been changed to the following, using
! a route map to only allow routes in networks in the 30s.
redist eigrp 6 route-map just-30-something
```

Example 11-5 *Example of Populating the BGP Table via Redistribution (Continued)*

```
! The route map and ACLs used for the filtering are shown next. As a result, the
! two subnets of 10.0.0.0/8 will not be redistributed into the BGP table.
R6# show route-map
route-map just-30-something, permit, sequence 10
  Match clauses:
    ip address (access-lists): permit-30-39
  Set clauses:
  Policy routing matches: 0 packets, 0 bytes
R6# show access-list
Standard IP access list permit-30-39
    10 permit 32.0.0.0, wildcard bits 7.255.255.255 (1538 matches)
    20 permit 30.0.0.0, wildcard bits 1.255.255.255 (1130 matches)
```

Also note that the NEXT_HOP PA for each route either matches the next hop of the redistributed route or is 0.0.0.0 for connected routes and routes to null0.

Impact of Auto-Summary on Redistributed Routes and the network Command

As it does with IGPs, the BGP **auto-summary** command causes a classful summary route to be created if any component subnet of that summary exists. However, unlike IGPs, the BGP **auto-summary** router subcommand causes BGP to summarize only those routes *injected due to redistribution on that router*. BGP **auto-summary** does not look for classful network boundaries in the topology, and it does not look at routes already in the BGP table. It simply looks for routes injected into the BGP due to the **redistribute** and **network** commands on that same router.

The logic differs slightly based on whether the route is injected with the **redistribute** command or the **network** command. The logic for the two commands is summarized as follows:

- **redistribute**—When the redistribution process would normally inject subnets of a classful network, do not inject the subnets into the routing table, but instead inject the classful network.

- **network**—For **network** commands that list a classful network number and no mask parameter, inject the classful network if at least one subnet of that classful network exists in the IP routing table.

While the preceding definitions are concise for study purposes, a few points deserve further emphasis and explanation. First, for redistribution, the **auto-summary** command causes the redistribution process to inject only classful networks into the local BGP table, and no subnets. The **network** command, with **auto-summary** configured, still injects subnets based on the same logic already described in this chapter. In addition to that logic, if a **network** command matches the classful **network** number, BGP injects the classful **network**, as long as at least any one subnet of that classful network exists in the IP routing table.

Example 11-6 shows an example that points out the impact of the **auto-summary** command. The example follows these steps on router R5 from Figure 11-2:

1. 10.15.0.0/16 is injected into BGP due to the **redistribute** command.

2. Auto-summary is configured, BGP is cleared, and now only 10.0.0.0/8 is in the BGP table.

3. Auto-summary and redistribution are disabled.

4. The **network 10.0.0.0** command, **network 10.12.0.0 mask 255.254.0.0** command, and **network 10.14.0.0 mask 255.255.0.0** command are configured. Only the last of these three commands exactly matches a current route, so only that route is injected into BGP.

5. Auto-summary is enabled, causing 10.0.0.0/8 to be injected, as well as the original 10.14.0.0/16 route.

Example 11-6 *Auto-Summary Impact on Routing Tables*

```
! R5 has shut down all neighbor connections, so the output of show ip bgp only shows
! routes injected on R5.
! Step 1 is below. Only 10.15.0.0/16 is injected by the current configuration. Note that
! the unrelated lines of output have been removed, and route-map only15 only
! matches 10.15.0.0/16.
R5# show run | be router bgp
router bgp 5
 no synchronization
 redistribute connected route-map only15
 no auto-summary
! Below, note the absence of 10.0.0.0/8 as a route, and the presence of 10.15.0.0/16,
! as well as the rest of the routes used in the upcoming steps.
R5# show ip route 10.0.0.0
Routing entry for 10.0.0.0/8, 4 known subnets
  Attached (4 connections)
  Redistributing via eigrp 99, bgp 5
  Advertised by bgp 5 route-map only15
C       10.14.0.0/16 is directly connected, Loopback10
C       10.15.0.0/16 is directly connected, Loopback10
C       10.12.0.0/16 is directly connected, Loopback10
C       10.13.0.0/16 is directly connected, Loopback10
! Only 10.15.0.0/16 is injected into BGP.
R5# show ip bgp
BGP table version is 2, local router ID is 5.5.5.5
Status codes: s suppressed, d damped, h history, * valid, > best, i - internal,
              r RIB-failure, S Stale
Origin codes: i - IGP, e - EGP, ? - incomplete

   Network          Next Hop          Metric LocPrf Weight Path
*> 10.15.0.0/16     0.0.0.0                0         32768 ?
! Next, step 2, where auto-summary is enabled. Now, 10.15.0.0/16 is no longer
```

Example 11-6 *Auto-Summary Impact on Routing Tables (Continued)*

```
! injected into BGP, but classful 10.0.0.0/8 is.
R5# conf t
Enter configuration commands, one per line.  End with CNTL/Z.
R5(config)# router bgp 5
R5(config-router)# auto-summary
R5(config-router)# ^Z
R5# clear ip bgp *
R5# show ip bgp
BGP table version is 2, local router ID is 5.5.5.5
Status codes: s suppressed, d damped, h history, * valid, > best, i - internal,
              r RIB-failure, S Stale
Origin codes: i - IGP, e - EGP, ? - incomplete

   Network          Next Hop            Metric LocPrf Weight Path
*> 10.0.0.0         0.0.0.0                  0         32768 ?
! Now, at step 3, no auto-summary disables automatic summarization, redistribution is
! disabled, and at step 4, the network commands are added. Note that 10.12.0.0/15 is
! not injected, as there is no exact match, nor is 10.0.0.0/8, as there is no exact
! match. However, 10.14.0.0/16 is injected due to the exact match of the prefix and
! prefix length.
R5# conf t
Enter configuration commands, one per line.  End with CNTL/Z.
R5(config)# router bgp 5
R5(config-router)# no auto-summary
R5(config-router)# no redist conn route-map only15
R5(config-router)# no redist connected
R5(config-router)# network 10.0.0.0
R5(config-router)# network 10.12.0.0 mask 255.254.0.0
R5(config-router)# network 10.14.0.0 mask 255.255.0.0
R5(config-router)# ^Z
R5# clear ip bgp *
R5# sh ip bgp ¦ begin network
   Network          Next Hop            Metric LocPrf Weight Path
*> 10.14.0.0/16     0.0.0.0                  0         32768 i
! Finally, auto-summary is re-enabled (not shown in the example).
! 10.14.0.0/16 is still an exact match, so it is
! still injected. 10.0.0.0/8 is also injected because of the network 10.0.0.0 command.
R5# sh ip bgp | begin network
   Network          Next Hop            Metric LocPrf Weight Path
*  10.0.0.0         0.0.0.0                  0         32768 i
*  10.14.0.0/16     0.0.0.0                  0         32768 i
```

Manual Summaries and the AS_PATH Path Attribute

As covered in the last several pages, a router can add entries to its BGP table using the **network** command and route redistribution. Additionally, BGP can use manual route summarization to advertise summary routes to neighboring routers, causing the neighboring routers to learn additional BGP routes. BGP manual summarization with the **aggregate-address** command differs significantly from using the **auto-summary** command. It can summarize based on any routes in the BGP table, creating a summary of any prefix length. It does not always suppress the advertisement of the component subnets, although it can be configured to do so.

The aggregate route must include the AS_PATH PA, just like it is required for every other NLRI in the BGP table. However, to fully understand what this command does, you need to take a closer look at the AS_PATH PA.

The AS_PATH PA consists of up to four different components, called segments, as follows:

- AS_SEQ (short for AS Sequence)

- AS_SET

- AS_CONFED_SEQ (short for AS Confederation Sequence)

- AS_CONFED_SET

The most commonly used segment is called AS_SEQ. AS_SEQ is the idea of AS_PATH as shown back in Figure 11-1, with the PA representing all ASNs, in order, through which the route has been advertised.

However, the **aggregate-address** command can create a summary route for which the AS_SEQ must be null. When the component subnets of the summary route have differing AS_SEQ values, the router simply can't create an accurate representation of AS_SEQ, so it uses a null AS_SEQ. However, this action introduces the possibility of creating routing loops, because the contents of AS_PATH, specifically AS_SEQ, are used to prevent a route from being re-advertised to an AS that has already heard about the route.

The AS_PATH AS_SET segment solves the problem when the summary route has a null AS_SEQ. The AS_SET segment holds an unordered list of all the ASNs in all the component subnets' AS_SEQ segments.

Example 11-7 shows an example in which the router does use a null AS_SEQ for a summary route, and then the same summary with the **as-set** option creating the AS_SET segment.

> **NOTE** AS_PATH includes the AS_CONFED_SEQ and AS_CONFED_SET segments as well, which are covered later, in the section "Confederations."

The following list summarizes the actions taken by the **aggregate-address** command when it creates a summary route:

**Key
Topic**

■ It does not create the summary if the BGP table does not currently have any routes for NLRI inside the summary.

■ If all the component subnets are withdrawn from the aggregating router's BGP table, it also then withdraws the aggregate. (In other words, the router tells its neighbors that the aggregate route is no longer valid.)

■ It sets the NEXT_HOP address of the summary, as listed in the local BGP table, as 0.0.0.0.

■ It sets the NEXT_HOP address of the summary route, as advertised to neighbors, to the router's update source IP address for each neighbor, respectively.

■ If the component subnets inside the summary all have the same AS_SEQ, it sets the new summary route's AS_SEQ to be exactly like the AS_SEQ of the component subnets.

■ If the AS_SEQ of the component subnets differs in any way, it sets the AS_SEQ of the new summary route to null.

■ When the **as-set** option has been configured, the router creates an AS_SET segment for the aggregate route, but only if the summary route's AS_SEQ is null.

■ As usual, if the summary is advertised to an eBGP peer, the router prepends its own ASN to the AS_SEQ before sending the Update.

■ It suppresses the advertisement of all component subnets if the **summary-only** keyword is used; advertises all of them if the **summary-only** keyword is omitted; or advertises a subset if the **suppress-map** option is configured.

Example 11-7 shows R3 from Figure 11-4 summarizing 23.0.0.0/8. R3 advertises the summary with ASN 123 as the only AS in the AS_SEQ, because some component subnets have AS_PATHS of 45, and others have 678 45. As a result, R3 uses a null AS_SEQ for the aggregate. The example goes on to show the impact of the **as-set** option.

Example 11-7 *Route Aggregation and the* **as-set** *Option*

```
! Note that R3's routes to network 23 all have the same AS_PATH except one new
! prefix, which has an AS_PATH that includes ASN 678. As a result, R3 will
! create a null AS_SEQ for the summary route.
R3# show ip bgp | include 23
*> 23.3.0.0/20      4.4.4.4                            0 45 i
*> 23.3.16.0/20     4.4.4.4                            0 45 i
*> 23.3.32.0/19     4.4.4.4                            0 45 i
```

continues

Example 11-7 *Route Aggregation and the **as-set** Option (Continued)*

```
*> 23.3.64.0/18    4.4.4.4                         0 45 i
*> 23.3.128.0/17   4.4.4.4                         0 45 i
*> 23.4.0.0/16     4.4.4.4                         0 45 678 i
! The following command is now added to R3's BGP configuration:
aggregate-address 23.0.0.0 255.0.0.0 summary-only
! Note: R3 will not have a BGP table entry for 23.0.0.0/8; however, R3 will
! advertise this summary to its peers, because at least one component subnet
! exists.
! R1 has learned the prefix, NEXT_HOP 3.3.3.3 (R3's update source IP address for
! R1), but the AS_PATH is now null because R1 is in the same AS as R3.
! (Had R3-R1 been an eBGP peering, R3 would have prepended its own ASN.)
! Note that the next command is on R1 R1 R1 R1.
R1# sh ip bgp | begin Network
   Network         Next Hop          Metric LocPrf Weight Path
*>i21.0.0.0        3.3.3.3                0    100      0 45 i
*>i23.0.0.0        3.3.3.3                0    100      0 i
! Next, R1 displays the AGGREGATOR PA, which identifies R3 (3.3.3.3) and its AS
! (123) as the aggregation point at which information is lost. Also, the phrase
! "atomic-aggregate" refers to the fact that the ATOMIC_AGGREGATE PA has also
! been set; this PA simply states that this NLRI is a summary.
R1# show ip bgp 23.0.0.0
BGP routing table entry for 23.0.0.0/8, version 45
Paths: (1 available, best #1, table Default-IP-Routing-Table)
Flag: 0x800
  Advertised to update-groups:
     2
  Local, (aggregated by 123 3.3.3.3), (received & used)
     3.3.3.3 (metric 2302976) from 3.3.3.3 (3.3.3.3)
        Origin IGP, metric 0, localpref 100, valid, internal, atomic-aggregate, best
! R6, in AS 678, receives the summary route from R1, but the lack of information
! in the current AS_PATH allows R6 to learn of the route, possibly causing
! a routing loop. (Remember, one of the component subnets, 23.4.0.0/16, came from
! ASN 678.)
R6# sh ip bgp nei 172.16.16.1 received-routes | begin Network
   Network         Next Hop          Metric LocPrf Weight Path
*> 21.0.0.0        172.16.16.1                            0 123 45 i
*> 23.0.0.0        172.16.16.1                            0 123 i
! The R3 configuration is changed as shown next to use the as-set option.
R3# aggregate-address 23.0.0.0 255.0.0.0 summary-only as-set
! R1 now has the AS_SET component of the AS_PATH PA, which includes an unordered
! list of all autonomous systems from all the component subnets' AS_PATHs on R3.
R1# sh ip bgp | begin Network
   Network         Next Hop          Metric LocPrf Weight Path
*>i21.0.0.0        3.3.3.3                0    100      0 45 i
*>i23.0.0.0        3.3.3.3                0    100      0 {45,678} i
```

Example 11-7 *Route Aggregation and the* **as-set** *Option (Continued)*

```
! Now R6 does not receive the 23.0.0.0 prefix due to R1's check of the AS_SET PA,
! noticing that ASN 678 is in the AS_SET and is also R6's ASN.
R6# sh ip bgp nei 172.16.16.1 received-routes | begin Network
   Network          Next Hop          Metric LocPrf Weight Path
*> 21.0.0.0         172.16.16.1              0 123 45 i
```

> **NOTE**   Summary routes can also be added via another method. First, the router would create a static route, typically with destination of interface null0. Then, the prefix/length can be matched with the **network** command to inject the summary. This method does not filter any of the component subnets.

Table 11-6 summarizes the key points regarding summarization using the **aggregate-address**, **auto-summary**, and **network** commands.

Table 11-6 *Summary: Injecting Summary Routes in BGP*

Command	Component Subnets Removed	Routes It Can Summarize
auto-summary (with redistribution)	All	Only those injected into BGP on that router using the **redistribute** command
aggregate-address	All, none, or a subset	Any prefixes already in the BGP table
auto-summary (with the **network** command)	None	Only those injected into BGP on that router using the **network** command

Adding Default Routes to BGP

The final method covered in this chapter for adding routes to a BGP table is to inject default routes into BGP. Default routes can be injected into BGP in one of three ways:

- By injecting the default using the **network** command

- By injecting the default using the **redistribute** command

- By injecting a default route into BGP using the **neighbor** *neighbor-id* **default-information** [**route-map** *route-map-name*] BGP subcommand

When injecting a default route into BGP using the **network** command, a route to 0.0.0.0/0 must exist in the local routing table, and the **network 0.0.0.0** command is required. The default IP route can be learned via any means, but if it is removed from the IP routing table, BGP removes the default route from the BGP table.

Injecting a default route through redistribution requires an additional configuration command—**default-information originate**. The default route must first exist in the IP routing table; for instance, a static default route to null0 could be created. Then, the **redistribute static** command could be used to redistribute that static default route. However, in the special case of the default route, Cisco IOS also requires the **default-information originate** BGP subcommand.

Injecting a default route into BGP by using the **neighbor** *neighbor-id* **default-information** [**route-map** *route-map-name*] BGP subcommand does not add a default route to the local BGP table; instead, it causes the advertisement of a default to the specified neighbor. In fact, this method does not even check for the existence of a default route in the IP routing table by default, but it can. With the **route-map** option, the referenced route map examines the entries in the IP routing table (not the BGP table); if a route map **permit** clause is matched, then the default route is advertised to the neighbor. Example 11-8 shows just such an example on R1, with **route-map check-default** checking for the existence of a default route before R1 would originate a default route to R3.

Example 11-8 *Originating a Default Route to a Neighbor with the* **neighbor default-originate** *Command*

```
! The pertinent parts of the R1 configuration are listed next, with the route map
! matching an IP route to 0.0.0.0/0 with a permit action, enabling the
! advertisement of a default route to neighbor 3.3.3.3 (R3).
router bgp 123
 neighbor 3.3.3.3 remote-as 123
 neighbor 3.3.3.3 update-source Loopback1
 neighbor 3.3.3.3 default-originate route-map check-default
!
ip route 0.0.0.0 0.0.0.0 Null0
!
ip prefix-list def-route seq 5 permit 0.0.0.0/0
!
route-map check-default permit 10
 match ip address prefix-list def-route
! R1 indeed has a default route, as seen below.
R1# show ip route | include 0.0.0.0/0
S*    0.0.0.0/0 is directly connected, Null0

! R3 now learns a default route from R1, as seen below.
R3# show ip bgp | begin Network
   Network          Next Hop            Metric LocPrf Weight Path
*>i0.0.0.0          1.1.1.1                    100       0 i
```

ORIGIN Path Attribute

Depending on the method used to inject a route into a local BGP table, BGP assigns one of three BGP ORIGIN PA codes: IGP, EGP, or incomplete. The ORIGIN PA provides a general descriptor as to how a particular NLRI was first injected into a router's BGP table. The **show ip bgp** command includes the three possible values in the legend at the top of the command output, listing the actual ORIGIN code for each BGP route at the far right of each output line. Table 11-7 lists the three ORIGIN code names, the single-letter abbreviation used by Cisco IOS, and the reasons why a route is assigned a particular code.

The ORIGIN codes and meanings hide a few concepts that many people find counterintuitive. First, routes redistributed into BGP from an IGP actually have an ORIGIN code of incomplete. Also, do not confuse EGP with eBGP; an ORIGIN of EGP refers to Exterior Gateway Protocol, the very old and deprecated predecessor to BGP. In practice, the EGP ORIGIN code should not be seen today.

Table 11-7 *BGP ORIGIN Codes*

ORIGIN Code	Cisco IOS Notation	Used for Routes Injected Due to the Following Commands
IGP	i	**network**, **aggregate-address** (in some cases), and **neighbor default-originate** commands
EGP	e	Exterior Gateway Protocol (EGP). No specific commands apply.
Incomplete	?	**redistribute**, **aggregate-address** (in some cases), and **default-information originate** command

The rules regarding the ORIGIN codes used for summary routes created with the **aggregate-address** command can also be a bit surprising. The rules are summarized as follows:

- If the **as-set** option is not used, the aggregate route uses ORIGIN code **i**.

- If the **as-set** option is used, and all component subnets being summarized use ORIGIN code **i**, the aggregate has ORIGIN code **i**.

- If the **as-set** option is used, and at least one of the component subnets has an ORIGIN code **?**, the aggregate has ORIGIN code **?**.

> **NOTE**   The BGP ORIGIN PA provides a minor descriptor for the origin of a BGP table entry, which is used as part of the BGP decision process.

Advertising BGP Routes to Neighbors

The previous section focused on the tools that BGP can use to inject routes into a local router's BGP table. BGP routers take routes from the local BGP table and advertise a subset of those routes to their BGP neighbors. This section continues focusing on the BGP table because the BGP route advertisement process takes routes from the BGP table and sends them to neighboring routers, where the routes are added to the neighbors' BGP tables. Later, the final major section in the chapter, "Building the IP Routing Table," focuses on the rules regarding how BGP places routes into the IP routing table.

BGP Update Message

Once a BGP table has a list of routes, paths, and prefixes, the router needs to advertise the information to neighboring routers. To do so, a router sends BGP Update messages to its neighbors. Figure 11-5 shows the general format of the BGP Update message.

Figure 11-5 *BGP Update Message Format*

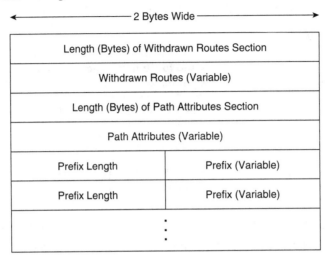

Each Update message has three main parts:

■ The Withdrawn Routes field enables BGP to inform its neighbors about failed routes.

■ The Path Attributes field lists the PAs for each route. NEXT_HOP and AS_PATH are sample values for this field.

■ The Prefix and Prefix Length fields define each individual NLRI.

The central concept in an individual Update message is the set of PAs. Then, all the prefixes (NLRIs) that share the exact same set of PAs and PA values are included at the end of the Update message. If a router needs to advertise a set of NLRIs, and each NLRI has a different setting for at least one PA, then separate Update messages will be required for each NLRI. However, when many routes share the same PAs—typical of prefixes owned by a particular ISP, for instance— multiple NLRIs are included in a single Update. This reduces router CPU load and uses less link bandwidth.

Determining the Contents of Updates

A router builds the contents of its Update messages based on the contents of its BGP table. However, the router must choose which subset of its BGP table entries to advertise to each neighbor, with the set likely varying from neighbor to neighbor. Table 11-8 summarizes the rules about which routes BGP does *not* include in routing updates to each neighbor; each rule is described more fully following the table.

Table 11-8 *Summary of Rules Regarding Which Routes BGP Does Not Include in an Update*

iBGP and/or eBGP	Routes Not Taken from the BGP Table
Both	Routes that are not considered "best"
Both	Routes matched by a **deny** clause in an outbound BGP filter
iBGP	iBGP-learned routes[*]
eBGP	Routes whose AS_PATH includes the ASN of the eBGP peer to which a BGP Update will be sent

[*]This rule is relaxed or changed as a result of using route reflectors or confederations.

BGP only advertises a route to reach a particular subnet (NLRI) if that route is considered to be the best route. If a BGP router learns of only one route to reach a particular prefix, the decision process is very simple. However, when choosing between multiple paths to reach the same prefix, BGP determines the best route based on a lengthy BGP decision process, which is outside the scope of this book. Assuming that none of the routers has configured any routing policies that impact the decision process, the decision tree reduces to a four-step process that is mainly comprised of tie-breakers, as follows:

1. Choose the route with the shortest AS_PATH.

2. If AS_PATH length is a tie, prefer a single eBGP-learned route over one or more iBGP routes.

3. If the best route has not yet been chosen, choose the route with the lowest IGP metric to the NEXT_HOP of the routes.

4. If the IGP metric ties, choose the iBGP-learned route with the lowest BGP RID of the advertising router.

Additionally, BGP rules out some routes from being considered best based on the value of the NEXT_HOP PA. For a route to be a candidate to be considered best, the NEXT_HOP must be either:

■ 0.0.0.0, as the result of the route being injected on the local router.

■ Reachable according to that router's current IP routing table. In other words, the NEXT_HOP IP address must match a route in the routing table.

Because the NEXT_HOP PA is so important with regard to BGP's choice of its best path to reach each NLRI, this section summarizes the logic and provides several examples. The logic is separated into two parts based on whether the route is being advertised to an iBGP or eBGP peer. By default, when sending to an eBGP peer, the NEXT_HOP is changed to an IP address on the advertising router—specifically, to the same IP address the router used as the source IP address of the BGP Update message, for each respective neighbor. When sending to an iBGP peer, the default action is to leave the NEXT_HOP PA unchanged. Both of these default behaviors can be changed via the commands listed in Table 11-9.

Table 11-9 *Conditions for Changing the NEXT_HOP PA*

Type of Neighbor	Default Action for Advertised Routes	Command to Switch to Other Behavior
iBGP	Do not change the NEXT_HOP	**neighbor... next-hop-self**
eBGP	Change the NEXT_HOP to the update source IP address	**neighbor... next-hop-unchanged**

Note that the NEXT_HOP PA cannot be set via a route map; the only way to change the NEXT_HOP PA is through the methods listed in Table 11-9.

Example: Impact of the Decision Process and NEXT_HOP on BGP Updates

The next several examples together show a sequence of events regarding the propagation of network 31.0.0.0/8 by BGP throughout the network of Figure 11-4. R6 originated the routes in the 30s (as in Example 11-4) by redistributing EIGRP routes learned from R9. The purpose of this series of examples is to explain how BGP chooses which routes to include in Updates under various conditions.

The first example, Example 11-9, focuses on the commands used to examine what R6 sends to R1, what R1 receives, and the resulting entries in R1's BGP table. The second example, Example 11-10, then examines those same routes propagated from R1 to R3, including problems related to R1's default behavior of not changing the NEXT_HOP PA of those routes. Finally, Example 11-11 shows the solution of R1's use of the **neighbor 3.3.3.3 next-hop-self** command, and the impact that has on the contents of the BGP Updates in AS 123.

Example 11-9 *R6 Sending the 30s Networks to R1 Using BGP*

```
! R6 has injected the three routes listed below; they were not learned from
! another BGP neighbor. Note all three show up as >, meaning they are the best
! (and only in this case) routes to the destination NLRIs.
R6# show ip bgp
BGP table version is 5, local router ID is 6.6.6.6
Status codes: s suppressed, d damped, h history, * valid, > best, i - internal,
              r RIB-failure, S Stale
Origin codes: i - IGP, e - EGP, ? - incomplete

   Network          Next Hop            Metric LocPrf Weight Path
*> 31.0.0.0         10.1.69.9            156160         32768 ?
*> 32.0.0.0         0.0.0.0                             32768 i
*> 32.1.1.0/24      10.1.69.9            156160         32768 ?
! R6 now lists the routes it advertises to R1—sort of. This command lists R6's
! BGP table entries that are intended to be sent, but R6 can (and will in this
! case) change the information before advertising to R1. Pay particular attention
! to the Next Hop column, versus upcoming commands on R1. In effect, this command
shows R6's current BGP table entries that will be sent to R1, but it shows them
```

Example 11-9 *R6 Sending the 30s Networks to R1 Using BGP (Continued)*

```
before R6 makes any changes, including NEXT_HOP.
R6# show ip bgp neighbor 172.16.16.1 advertised-routes
BGP table version is 5, local router ID is 6.6.6.6
Status codes: s suppressed, d damped, h history, * valid, > best, i - internal,
              r RIB-failure, S Stale
Origin codes: i - IGP, e - EGP, ? - incomplete

   Network          Next Hop          Metric LocPrf Weight Path
*> 31.0.0.0         10.1.69.9         156160         32768 ?
*> 32.0.0.0         0.0.0.0                          32768 i
*> 32.1.1.0/24      10.1.69.9         156160         32768 ?
Total number of prefixes 3
```
```
! The next command (R1) lists the info in the received BGP update from R6. Note
! that the NEXT_HOP is different; R6 changed the NEXT_HOP before sending the
! update, because it has an eBGP peer connection to R1, and eBGP defaults to set
! NEXT_HOP to itself. As R6 was using 172.16.16.6 as the IP address from which to
! send BGP messages to R1, R6 set NEXT_HOP to that number. Also note that R1 lists
! the neighboring AS (678) in the Path column at the end, signifying the AS_PATH
! for the route.
R1# show ip bgp neighbor 172.16.16.6 received-routes
BGP table version is 7, local router ID is 111.111.111.111
Status codes: s suppressed, d damped, h history, * valid, > best, i - internal,
              r RIB-failure, S Stale
Origin codes: i - IGP, e - EGP, ? - incomplete

   Network          Next Hop          Metric LocPrf Weight Path
*> 31.0.0.0         172.16.16.6       156160             0 678 ?
*> 32.0.0.0         172.16.16.6            0             0 678 i
*> 32.1.1.0/24      172.16.16.6       156160             0 678 ?
Total number of prefixes 3
! The show ip bgp summary command lists the state of the neighbor until the
! neighbor becomes established; at that point, the State/PfxRcd column lists the number
! of NLRIs (prefixes) received (and still valid) from that neighbor.
R1# show ip bgp summary | begin Neighbor
Neighbor        V    AS MsgRcvd MsgSent   TblVer  InQ OutQ Up/Down  State/PfxRcd
2.2.2.2         4   123      55      57        7    0    0 00:52:30           0
3.3.3.3         4   123      57      57        7    0    0 00:52:28           3
172.16.16.6     4   678      53      51        7    0    0 00:48:50           3
! R1 has also learned of these prefixes from R3, as seen below. The routes through
! R6 have one AS in the AS_PATH, and the routes through R3 have two autonomous systems, so the
! routes through R6 are best. Also, the iBGP routes have an "i" for "internal"
! just before the prefix.
R1# show ip bgp
BGP table version is 7, local router ID is 111.111.111.111
Status codes: s suppressed, d damped, h history, * valid, > best, i - internal,
              r RIB-failure, S Stale
```

continues

Example 11-9 *R6 Sending the 30s Networks to R1 Using BGP (Continued)*

```
Origin codes: i - IGP, e - EGP, ? - incomplete

   Network          Next Hop          Metric LocPrf Weight Path
* i31.0.0.0         3.3.3.3               0    100      0 45 678 ?
*>                  172.16.16.6      156160               0 678 ?
* i32.0.0.0         3.3.3.3               0    100      0 45 678 i
*>                  172.16.16.6           0               0 678 i
* i32.1.1.0/24      3.3.3.3               0    100      0 45 678 ?
*>                  172.16.16.6      156160               0 678 ?
```

Example 11-9 showed examples of how you can view the contents of the actual Updates sent to neighbors (using the **show ip bgp neighbor advertised-routes** command) and the contents of Updates received from a neighbor (using the **show ip bgp neighbor received-routes** command). RFC 1771 suggests that the BGP RIB can be separated into components for received Updates from each neighbor and sent Updates for each neighbor. Most implementations (including Cisco IOS) keep a single RIB, with notations as to which entries were sent and received to and from each neighbor.

> **NOTE**   For the **received-routes** option to work, the router on which the command is used must have the **neighbor** *neighbor-id* **soft-reconfiguration inbound** BGP subcommand configured for the other neighbor.

These **show ip bgp neighbor** commands with the **advertised-routes** option list the BGP table entries that will be advertised to that neighbor. However, note that any changes to the PAs inside each entry are not shown in the command output. For example, the **show ip bgp neighbor 172.16.16.1 advertised-routes** command on R6 listed the NEXT_HOP for 31/8 as 10.1.69.9, which is true of that entry in R6's BGP table. R6 then changes the NEXT_HOP PA before sending the actual Update, with a NEXT_HOP of 172.16.16.6.

By the end of Example 11-9, R1 knows of both paths to each of the three prefixes in the 30s (AS_PATH 678 and 45-678), but has chosen the shortest AS_PATH (through R6) as the best path in each case. Note that the > in the **show ip bgp** output designates the routes as R1's best routes. Next, Example 11-10 shows some possibly surprising results on R3 related to its choices of best routes.

Example 11-10 *Examining the BGP Table on R3*

```
! R1 now updates R3 with R1's "best" routes
R1# show ip bgp neighbor 3.3.3.3 advertised-routes | begin Network
   Network          Next Hop          Metric LocPrf Weight Path
*> 31.0.0.0         172.16.16.6      156160               0 678 ?
*> 32.0.0.0         172.16.16.6           0               0 678 i
*> 32.1.1.0/24      172.16.16.6      156160               0 678 ?
```

Example 11-10 *Examining the BGP Table on R3 (Continued)*

```
Total number of prefixes 3
! R3 received the routes, but R3's best routes to each prefix point back to
! R4 in AS 45, with AS_PATH 45-678, which is a longer path. The route through R1
! cannot be "best" because the NEXT_HOP was sent unchanged by iBGP neighbor R1.
R3# show ip bgp
BGP table version is 7, local router ID is 3.3.3.3
Status codes: s suppressed, d damped, h history, * valid, > best, i - internal,
              r RIB-failure, S Stale
Origin codes: i - IGP, e - EGP, ? - incomplete

   Network          Next Hop            Metric LocPrf Weight Path
*> 31.0.0.0         4.4.4.4                              0 45 678 ?
*  i                172.16.16.6         156160    100    0 678 ?
*> 32.0.0.0         4.4.4.4                              0 45 678 i
*  i                172.16.16.6              0    100    0 678 i
*> 32.1.1.0/24      4.4.4.4                              0 45 678 ?
*  i                172.16.16.6         156160    100    0 678 ?
! Proof that R3 cannot reach the next-hop IP address is shown next.
R3# ping 172.16.16.6

Type escape sequence to abort.
Sending 5, 100-byte ICMP Echos to 172.16.16.6, timeout is 2 seconds:
.....
Success rate is 0 percent (0/5)
```

Example 11-10 points out a quirk with some terminology in the **show ip bgp** command output, as well as an important design choice with BGP. First, the command output lists * as meaning valid; however, that designation simply means that the route is a candidate for use. Before the route can be actually used and added to the IP routing table, the NEXT_HOP must also be reachable. In some cases, routes that the **show ip bgp** command considers "valid" might not be usable routes, with Example 11-10 showing just such an example.

Each BGP route's NEXT_HOP must be reachable for a route to be truly valid. With all default settings, an iBGP-learned route has a NEXT_HOP IP address of the last eBGP router to advertise the route. For example, R3's route to 31.0.0.0/8 through R1 lists R6's IP address (172.16.16.6) in the NEXT_HOP field. Unfortunately, R3 does not have a route for 172.16.16.6, so that route cannot be considered "best" by BGP.

There are two easy choices to solve the problem:

- Make the eBGP neighbor's IP address reachable by advertising that subnet into the IGP.

- Use the **next-hop-self** option on the **neighbor** command that points to iBGP peers.

The first option typically can be easily implemented. Because many eBGP neighbors use interface IP addresses on their **neighbor** commands, the NEXT_HOP exists in a subnet directly connected to the AS. For example, R1 is directly connected to 172.16.16.0/24, so R1 could simply advertise that connected subnet into the IGP inside the AS.

However, this option might be problematic when loopback addresses are used for BGP neighbors. For example, if R1 had been configured to refer to R6's 6.6.6.6 loopback IP address, and it was working, R1 must have a route to reach 6.6.6.6. However, it is less likely that R1 would already be advertising a route to reach 6.6.6.6 into ASN 123.

The second option causes the router to change the NEXT_HOP PA to one of its own IP addresses—an address that is more likely to already be in the neighbor's IP routing table, which works well even if using loopbacks with an eBGP peer. Example 11-11 points out such a case, with R1 using the **neighbor next-hop-self** command, advertising itself (1.1.1.1) as the NEXT_HOP. As a result, R3 changes its choice of best routes, because R3 has a route to reach 1.1.1.1, overcoming the "NEXT_HOP unreachable" problem.

Example 11-11 points out how an iBGP peer can set NEXT_HOP to itself. However, it's also a good example of how BGP decides when to advertise routes to iBGP peers. The example follows this sequence, with the command output showing evidence of these events:

1. The example begins like the end of Example 11-10, with R1 advertising routes with R6 as the next hop, and with R3 not being able to use those routes as best routes.

2. Because R3's best routes are eBGP routes (through R4), R3 is allowed to advertise those routes to R2.

3. R1 then changes its configuration to use NEXT_HOP SELF.

4. R3 is now able to treat the routes learned from R1 as R3's best routes.

5. R3 can no longer advertise its best routes to these networks to R2, because the new best routes are iBGP routes.

Example 11-11 *R3 Advertises the 30s Networks to R2, and Then R3 Withdraws the Routes*

```
! (Step 1): At this point, R3 still believes its best route to all three prefixes
! in the 30s is through R4; as those are eBGP routes, R3 advertises all three
! routes to iBGP peer R2, as seen next.
R3# show ip bgp neighbor 2.2.2.2 advertised-routes
BGP table version is 7, local router ID is 3.3.3.3
Status codes: s suppressed, d damped, h history, * valid, > best, i - internal,
              r RIB-failure, S Stale
Origin codes: i - IGP, e - EGP, ? - incomplete
```

Example 11-11 *R3 Advertises the 30s Networks to R2, and Then R3 Withdraws the Routes (Continued)*

```
  Network          Next Hop           Metric LocPrf Weight Path
*> 31.0.0.0        4.4.4.4                              0 45 678 ?
*> 32.0.0.0        4.4.4.4                              0 45 678 i
*> 32.1.1.0/24     4.4.4.4                              0 45 678 ?
Total number of prefixes 3
```

```
! (Step 2) R2 lists the number of prefixes learned from R3 next (3).
R2# show ip bgp summary | begin Neighbor
Neighbor       V    AS MsgRcvd MsgSent   TblVer  InQ OutQ Up/Down   State/PfxRcd
1.1.1.1        4   123     212     210        7    0    0 03:27:59             3
3.3.3.3        4   123     213     211        7    0    0 03:28:00             3
```

```
! (Step 3) R1 now changes to use next-hop-self to peer R3.
R1# conf t
Enter configuration commands, one per line.  End with CNTL/Z.
R1(config)# router bgp 123
R1(config-router)# neigh 3.3.3.3 next-hop-self
```

```
! (Step 4) R3 now lists the routes through R1 as best, because the new
! NEXT_HOP is R1's update source IP address, 1.1.1.1, which is reachable by R3.
R3# show ip bgp
BGP table version is 10, local router ID is 3.3.3.3
Status codes: s suppressed, d damped, h history, * valid, > best, i - internal,
              r RIB-failure, S Stale
Origin codes: i - IGP, e - EGP, ? - incomplete

  Network          Next Hop           Metric LocPrf Weight Path
*  31.0.0.0        4.4.4.4                              0 45 678 ?
*>i                1.1.1.1             156160    100    0 678 ?
*  32.0.0.0        4.4.4.4                              0 45 678 i
*>i                1.1.1.1                  0    100    0 678 i
*  32.1.1.0/24     4.4.4.4                              0 45 678 ?
*>i                1.1.1.1             156160    100    0 678 ?
```

```
! (Step 5) First, note above that all three "best" routes are iBGP routes, as noted by the "i"
! immediately before the prefix. R3 only advertises "best" routes, with the added
! requirement that it must not advertise iBGP routes to other iBGP peers. As a
! result, R3 has withdrawn the routes that had formerly been sent to R2.
R3# show ip bgp neighbor 2.2.2.2 advertised-routes

Total number of prefixes 0
```

```
! The next command confirms on R2 that it no longer has any prefixes learned from
! R3.
R2# show ip bgp summary | begin Neighbor
Neighbor       V    AS MsgRcvd MsgSent   TblVer  InQ OutQ Up/Down   State/PfxRcd
1.1.1.1        4   123     213     211        7    0    0 03:28:44             3
3.3.3.3        4   123     214     211        7    0    0 03:28:46             0
```

Summary of Rules for Routes Advertised in BGP Updates

The following list summarizes the rules dictating which routes a BGP router sends in its Update messages:

- Send only the best route listed in the BGP table.

- To iBGP neighbors, do not advertise paths learned from other iBGP neighbors.

- To eBGP neighbors, do not advertise paths for which the neighbor's AS is already in the AS_PATH PA.

- Do not advertise suppressed or dampened routes.

- Do not advertise routes filtered via configuration.

The first two rules have been covered in some depth in this section. The remaining rules are outside the scope of this book.

Building the IP Routing Table

So far, this chapter has explained how to form BGP neighbor relationships, how to inject routes into the BGP table, and how BGP routers choose which routes to propagate to neighboring routers. Part of that logic relates to how the BGP decision process selects a router's best route to each prefix, with the added restriction that the NEXT_HOP must be reachable before the route can be considered as a best route.

This section completes the last step in BGP's ultimate goal—adding the appropriate routes to the IP routing table. In its simplest form, BGP takes the already identified best BGP routes for each prefix and adds those routes to the IP routing table. However, there are some additional restrictions, mainly related to administrative distance (AD) (for eBGP and iBGP routes) and BGP synchronization (iBGP routes only). The sections that follow detail the exceptions.

Adding eBGP Routes to the IP Routing Table

Cisco IOS software uses simple logic when determining which eBGP routes to add to the IP routing table. The only two requirements are as follows:

- The eBGP route in the BGP table is considered to be a "best" route.

- If the same prefix has been learned via another IGP or via static routes, the AD for BGP external routes must be lower than the ADs for other routing source(s).

By default, Cisco IOS considers eBGP routes to have AD 20, which gives eBGP routes a better (lower) AD than any other dynamic routing protocol's default AD (except for the AD 5 of EIGRP summary routes). The rationale behind the default is that eBGP-learned routes should never be prefixes from within an AS. Under normal conditions, eBGP-learned prefixes should seldom be seen as IGP-learned routes as well, but when they are, the BGP route would win by default.

BGP sets the AD differently for eBGP routes, iBGP routes, and for local (locally injected) routes—with defaults of 20, 200, and 200, respectively. These values can be overridden in two ways, both consistent with the coverage of AD in Chapter 10:

■ By using the **distance bgp** *external-distance internal-distance local-distance* BGP subcommand, which allows the simple setting of AD for eBGP-learned prefixes, iBGP-learned prefixes, and prefixes injected locally, respectively.

■ By changing the AD using the **distance** {*ip-address* {*wildcard-mask*}} [*ip-standard-list* | *ip-extended-list*] BGP subcommand

Similar commands were covered in the Chapter 10 section "Preventing Suboptimal Routes by Setting the Administrative Distance." With BGP, the IP address and wildcard mask refer to the IP address used on the **neighbor** command for that particular neighbor, not the BGP RID or NEXT_HOP of the route. The ACL examines the BGP routes received from the neighbor, assigning the specified AD for any routes matching the ACL with a permit action.

Finally, a quick note is needed about the actual IP route added to the IP routing table. The route contains the exact same prefix, prefix length, and next-hop IP address as listed in the BGP table—even if the NEXT_HOP PA is an IP address that is not in a connected network. As a result, the IP forwarding process may require a recursive route lookup. Example 11-12 shows such a case on R3, where the three BGP routes each list a next hop of 1.1.1.1, which happens to be a loopback interface on R1. As you can see from Figure 11-4, R3 and R1 have no interfaces in common. The route to 1.1.1.1 lists the actual next-hop IP address to which a packet would be forwarded.

Example 11-12   *R3 Routes with Next-Hop 1.1.1.1, Requiring Recursive Route Lookup*

```
! Packets forwarded to 31.0.0.0/8 match the last route, with next-hop 1.1.1.1; R3
! then finds the route that matches destination 1.1.1.1 (the first route), finding
! the appropriate next-hop IP address and outgoing interface.
R3# show ip route | incl 1.1.1.1
D        1.1.1.1 [90/2809856] via 10.1.23.2, 04:01:44, Serial0/0/1
B        32.1.1.0/24 [200/156160] via 1.1.1.1, 00:01:00
B        32.0.0.0/8 [200/0] via 1.1.1.1, 00:01:00
B        31.0.0.0/8 [200/156160] via 1.1.1.1, 00:01:00
```

Backdoor Routes

Having a low default AD (20) for eBGP routes can cause a problem in some topologies. Figure 11-6 shows a typical case, in which Enterprise 1 uses its eBGP route to reach network 99.0.0.0 in Enterprise 2. However, the two enterprises want to use the OSPF-learned route via the leased line between the two companies.

Figure 11-6 *The Need for BGP Backdoor Routes*

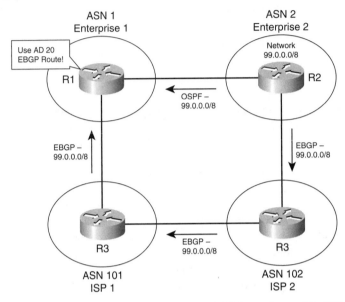

R1 uses its eBGP route to reach 99.0.0.0 because eBGP has a lower AD (20) than OSPF (110). One solution would be to configure the **distance** command to lower the AD of the OSPF-learned route. However, BGP offers an elegant solution to this particular problem through the use of the **network backdoor** command. In this case, if R1 configures the **network 99.0.0.0 backdoor** router BGP subcommand, the following would occur:

- R1 would use the local AD (default 200) for the eBGP-learned route to network 99.0.0.0.

- R1 does not advertise 99.0.0.0 with BGP.

Given that logic, R1 can use a **network backdoor** command for each prefix for which R1 needs to use the private link to reach Enterprise 2. If the OSPF route to each prefix is up and working, R1 uses the OSPF (AD 110) route over the eBGP-learned (AD 200) route through the Internet. If the OSPF route is lost, the two companies can still communicate through the Internet.

Adding iBGP Routes to the IP Routing Table

Cisco IOS has the same two requirements for adding iBGP routes to the IP routing table as it does for eBGP routes:

- The route must be the best BGP route.

- The route must be the best route (according to the AD) in comparison with other routing sources.

Additionally, for iBGP-learned routes, IOS considers the concept of *BGP synchronization.*

With BGP synchronization (often called *sync*) disabled using the **no synchronization** command, BGP uses the same logic for iBGP routes as it does for eBGP routes regarding which routes to add to the IP routing table. However, enabling BGP sync (with the **synchronization** BGP subcommand) prevents a couple of problems related to IP routing. Figure 11-7 shows the details of just such a problem. In this case, sync was inappropriately disabled in ASN 678, creating a black hole.

Figure 11-7   *Problem: Routing Black Hole Due to Not Using BGP Sync*

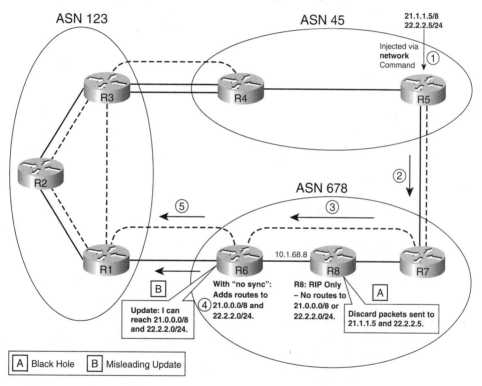

The following list takes a sequential view of what occurs within BGP in Figure 11-7:

1. R5 adds two prefixes (21.0.0.0/8 and 22.2.2.0/24) into its BGP table using two **network** commands.

2. R5 advertises the prefixes to R7, but does not redistribute the routes into its IGP.

3. R7 advertises the prefixes to R6.

4. R6, with synchronization disabled, considers the routes as "best," so R6 adds the routes to its routing table.

5. R6 also advertises the two prefixes to R1.

Two related problems (labeled A and B in the figure) actually occur in this case. The routing *black hole* occurs because R8 does not have a route to either of the prefixes advertised by BGP. R8 is not running BGP—a common occurrence for a router that does not directly connect to an eBGP peer. R7 did not redistribute those two prefixes into the IGP; as a result, R8 cannot route packets for those prefixes. R6, and possibly routers in AS 123, try to forward packets destined to the two prefixes through AS 678, but R8 discards the packets—hence the black hole.

The second related problem, labeled B, occurs at Step 5. R6 exacerbated the routing black-hole problem by advertising to another AS (AS 123) that it could reach the prefixes. R6 considers its routes to 21.0.0.0/8 and 22.2.2.0/24 as "best" routes in its BGP table, so R6 then advertises those routes to R1. Depending on the topology and PA settings, R1 could have considered these routes as its best routes—thereby sending packets destined for those prefixes into AS 678. (Assuming the configuration as shown in the previous examples, R1 would actually believe the 1 AS_PATH through R3 to AS 45 as the best path.)

The solutions to these problems are varied, but all the solutions result in the internal routers (for example, R8) learning the routes to these prefixes, thereby removing the black hole and removing the negative effect of advertising the route. The original solution to this problem involves the use of BGP synchronization, along with redistributing BGP routes into the IGP. However, two later solutions provide better options today:

■ BGP route reflectors

■ BGP confederations

The next several sections cover all of these options.

Using Sync and Redistributing Routes

BGP synchronization is best understood when considered in the context in which it was intended to be used—namely, in conjunction with the redistribution of BGP routes into the IGP. This method is seldom used by ISPs today, mainly because of the large number of routes that would be injected into the IGP. However, using BGP sync in conjunction with redistribution solves both problems related to the routing black hole.

The key to understanding BGP sync is to know that redistribution solves the routing black-hole problem, and sync solves the problem of advertising a black-hole route to another AS. For example, to solve the routing black-hole problem, R7 redistributes the two prefixes into RIP (from Figure 11-7). R8 then has routes to those prefixes, solving the black-hole problem.

Sync logic on R6 controls the second part of the overall problem, regulating the conditions under which R6 advertises the prefixes to other eBGP peers (like R1). Sync works by controlling whether a BGP table entry can be considered "best"; keep in mind that a route in the BGP table must be considered to be "best" before it can be advertised to another BGP peer. The BGP sync logic controls that decision as follows:

Do not consider an iBGP route in the BGP table as "best" unless the exact prefix was learned via an IGP and is currently in the routing table.

Sync logic essentially gives a router a method to know whether the non-BGP routers inside the AS should have the ability to route packets to the prefix. Note that the route must be IGP-learned because a static route on R6 would not imply anything about what other routers (like R8) might or might not have learned. For example, using Figure 11-7 again, once R6 learns the prefixes via RIP, RIP will place the routes in its IP routing table. At that point, the sync logic on R6 can consider those same BGP-learned prefixes in the BGP table as candidates to be best routes. If chosen as best, R6 can then advertise the BGP routes to R1.

Example 11-13 shows the black hole occurring from R6's perspective, with sync disabled on R6 using the **no synchronization** BGP subcommand. Following that, the example shows R6's behavior once R7 has begun redistributing BGP routes into RIP, with sync enabled on R6.

Example 11-13 *Comparing the Black Hole (No Sync) and Solution (Sync)*

```
! R6 has a "best" BGP route to 21.0.0.0/8 through R7 (7.7.7.7), but a trace
! command shows that the packets are discarded by R8 (10.1.68.8).
R6# show ip bgp | begin Network
   Network          Next Hop          Metric LocPrf Weight Path
*  21.0.0.0         172.16.16.1                        0 123 45 i
*>i                 7.7.7.7                 0    100    0 45 i
*  22.2.2.0/24      172.16.16.1                        0 123 45 i
*>i                 7.7.7.7                 0    100    0 45 i
R6# trace 21.1.1.5
Type escape sequence to abort.
Tracing the route to 21.1.1.5

  1 10.1.68.8 20 msec 20 msec 20 msec
  2 10.1.68.8 !H  *  !H
! R7 is now configured to redistribute BGP into RIP.
R7# conf t
Enter configuration commands, one per line.  End with CNTL/Z.
R7(config)# router rip
R7(config-router)# redist bgp 678 metric 3
! Next, R6 switches to use sync, and the BGP process is cleared.
R6# conf t
Enter configuration commands, one per line.  End with CNTL/Z.
R6(config)# router bgp 678
R6(config-router)# synchronization
R6(config-router)# ^Z
R6# clear ip bgp *
```

continues

Example 11-13 *Comparing the Black Hole (No Sync) and Solution (Sync) (Continued)*

```
! R6's BGP table entries now show "RIB-failure," a status code that can mean
! (as of some 12.2T IOS releases) that the prefix is known via an IGP. 21.0.0.0/8
! is shown to be included as a RIP route in R6's routing table. Note also that R6
! considers the BGP routes through R7 as the "best" routes; these are still
! advertised to R1.
R6# show ip bgp
BGP table version is 5, local router ID is 6.6.6.6
Status codes: s suppressed, d damped, h history, * valid, > best, i - internal,
              r RIB-failure, S Stale
Origin codes: i - IGP, e - EGP, ? - incomplete

   Network          Next Hop         Metric LocPrf Weight Path
r  21.0.0.0         172.16.16.1                      0 123 45 i
r>i                 7.7.7.7               0    100    0 45 i
r  22.2.2.0/24      172.16.16.1                      0 123 45 i
r>i                 7.7.7.7               0    100    0 45 i
R6# show ip route ¦ incl 21.0.0.0
R     21.0.0.0/8 [120/4] via 10.1.68.8, 00:00:15, Serial0/0.8
! R6 considers the routes through R7 as the "best" routes; these are still
! advertised to R1, even though they are in a "RIB-failure" state.
R6# show ip bgp neighbor 172.16.16.1 advertised-routes ¦ begin Network
   Network          Next Hop         Metric LocPrf Weight Path
r>i21.0.0.0         7.7.7.7               0    100    0 45 i
r>i22.2.2.0/24      7.7.7.7               0    100    0 45 i
```

> **NOTE** Sync includes an additional odd requirement when OSPF is used as the IGP. If the OSPF RID of the router advertising the prefix is a different number than the BGP router advertising that same prefix, then sync still does not allow BGP to consider the route to be the best route. OSPF and BGP use the same priorities and logic to choose their RIDs; however, when using sync, it makes sense to explicitly configure the RID for OSPF and BGP to be the same value on the router that redistributes from BGP into OSPF.

Disabling Sync and Using BGP on All Routers in an AS

A second method to overcome the black-hole issue is to simply use BGP to advertise all the BGP-learned prefixes to all routers in the AS. Because all routers know the prefixes, sync can be disabled safely. The downside is the introduction of BGP onto all routers, and the addition of iBGP neighbor connections between each pair of routers. (In an AS with *N* routers, N(N–1)/2 neighbor connections will be required.) With large autonomous systems, BGP performance and convergence time can degrade as a result of the large number of peers.

BGP needs the full mesh of iBGP peers inside an AS because BGP does not advertise iBGP routes (routes learned from one iBGP peer) to another iBGP peer. This additional restriction helps prevent routing loops, but it then requires a full mesh of iBGP peers—otherwise, only a subset of the iBGP peers would learn each prefix.

BGP offers two tools (confederations and route reflectors) that reduce the number of peer connections inside an AS, prevent loops, and allow all routers to learn about all prefixes. These two tools are covered next.

Confederations

An AS using BGP confederations, as defined in RFC 3065, separates each router in the AS into one of several confederation sub-autonomous systems (sub-autonomous systems). Peers inside the same sub-AS are considered to be *confederation iBGP peers*, and routers in different sub-autonomous systems are considered to be *confederation eBGP peers*.

Confederations propagate routes to all routers, without a full mesh of peers inside the entire AS. To do so, confederation eBGP peer connections act like true eBGP peers in some respects. In a single sub-AS, the confederation iBGP peers must be fully meshed, because they act exactly like normal iBGP peers—in other words, they do not advertise iBGP routes to each other. However, confederation eBGP peers act like eBGP peers in that they can advertise iBGP routes learned inside their confederation sub-AS into another confederation sub-AS.

Confederations prevent loops inside a confederation AS by using the AS_PATH PA. BGP routers in a confederation add the sub-autonomous systems into the AS_PATH as part of an AS_PATH segment called the AS_CONFED _SEQ. (The AS_PATH consists of up to four different components, called segments—AS_SEQ, AS_SET, AS_CONFED_ SEQ, and AS_CONFED_SET; see the earlier section titled "Manual Summaries and the AS_PATH Path Attribute" for more information on AS_SEQ and AS_SET.)

> **NOTE**   The terms *AS* and *sub-AS* refer to the concept of an autonomous system and sub-autonomous system. *ASN* and *sub-ASN* refer to the actual AS numbers used.

Just as the AS_SEQ and AS_SET components help prevent loops between autonomous systems, AS_CONFED_SEQ and AS_CONFED_SET help prevent loops within confederation autonomous systems. Before confederation eBGP peers can advertise an iBGP route into another sub-AS, the router must make sure the destination sub-AS is not already in the AS_PATH AS_CONFED_SEQ segment. For example, in Figure 11-8, the routers in sub-ASN 65001 learn some routes and then advertise those routes to sub-ASNs 65002 and 65003. Routers in these two sub-ASNs advertise the routes to each other. However, they never re-advertise the routes back to routers in sub-ASN 65001 due to AS_CONFED_SEQ, as shown in parentheses inside the figure.

Figure 11-8 *AS_PATH Changes in a Confederation*

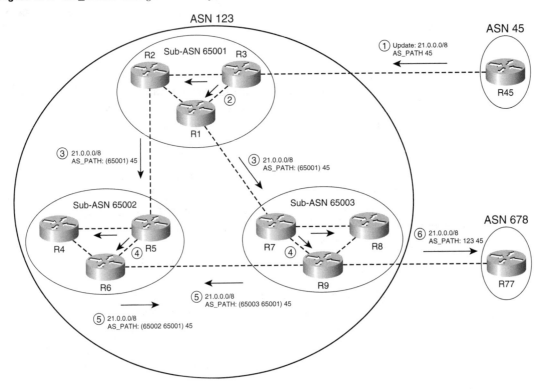

Figure 11-8 depicts a detailed example, with the steps in the following list matching the steps outlined in circled numbers in the figure:

1. 21.0.0.0/8 is injected by R45 and advertised via eBGP to AS 123. This route has an AS_PATH of 45.

2. R3 advertises the prefix via its two iBGP connections; however, due to iBGP rules inside the sub-AS, R1 and R2 do not attempt to advertise this prefix to each other.

3. Routers in sub-AS 65001 use eBGP-like logic to advertise 21.0.0.0/8 to their confederation eBGP peers, but first they inject their own sub-AS into the AS_PATH AS_CONFED_SEQ segment. (This part of the AS_PATH is displayed inside parentheses in the output of the **show ip bgp** command, as shown in the figure.)

4. The same process as in Step 2 occurs in the other two sub-autonomous systems, respectively.

5. R6 and R9 advertise the route to each other after adding their respective ASNs to the AS_CONFED_SEQ.

6. R9 advertises the prefix via a true eBGP connection after removing the sub-AS portion of the AS_PATH.

By the end of these steps, all the routers inside ASN 123 have learned of the 21.0.0.0/8 prefix. Also, ASN 678 (R77 in this case) learned of a route for that same prefix—a route that would work and would not have the black-hole effect. In fact, from ASN 678's perspective, it sees a route that appears to be through ASNs 123 and 45. Also note that routers in sub-AS 65002 and 65003 will not advertise the prefix back into sub-AS 65001 because AS 65001 is already in the confederation AS_PATH.

The choice of values for sub-ASNs 65001, 65002, and 65003 is not coincidental in this case. ASNs 64512 through 65535 are *private ASNs*, meant for use in cases where the ASN will not be advertised to the Internet or other autonomous systems. By using private ASNs, a confederation can hopefully avoid the following type of problem. Imagine that sub-AS 65003 instead used ASN 45. The AS_PATH loop check examines the entire AS_PATH. As a result, the prefixes shown in Figure 11-8 would never be advertised to sub-AS 45, and in turn would not be advertised to ASN 678. Using private ASNs would prevent this problem.

The following list summarizes the key points regarding confederations:

- Inside a sub-AS, full mesh is required, because full iBGP rules are in effect.

- The confederation eBGP connections act like normal eBGP connections in that iBGP routes are advertised—as long as the AS_PATH implies that such an advertisement would not cause a loop.

- Confederation eBGP connections also act like normal eBGP connections regarding Time to Live (TTL), because all packets use a TTL of 1 by default. (TTL can be changed with the **neighbor ebgp-multihop** command.)

- Confederation eBGP connections act like iBGP connections in every other regard—for example, the NEXT_HOP is not changed by default.

- Confederation ASNs are not considered part of the length of the AS_PATH when a router chooses the best routes based on the shortest AS_PATH.

- Confederation routers remove the confederation ASNs from the AS_PATH in Updates sent outside the confederation; therefore, other routers do not know that a confederation was used.

Configuring Confederations

Configuring confederations requires only a few additional commands beyond those already covered in this chapter. However, migrating to use confederations can be quite painful. The problem is that the true ASN will no longer be configured on the **router bgp** command, but instead on the **bgp confederation identifier** BGP subcommand. So, BGP will simply be out of service on one or more routers while the migration occurs. Table 11-10 lists the key confederation commands, and their purpose.

Table 11-10 *BGP Subcommands Used for Confederations*

Purpose	Command
Define a router's sub-AS	**router bgp** *sub-as*
Define the true AS	**bgp confederation identifier** *asn*
To identify a neighboring AS as another sub-AS	**bgp confederation peers** *sub-asn*

Example 11-14 shows a simple configuration for the topology in Figure 11-9.

Figure 11-9 *Internetwork Topology with Confederations in ASN 123*

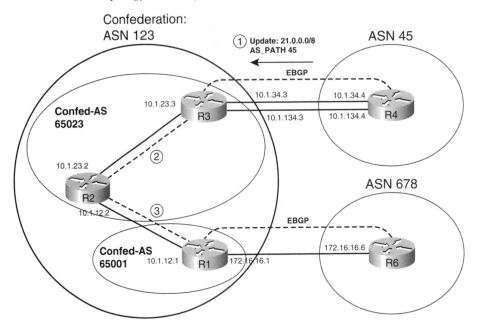

In this internetwork topology, R1 is in sub-AS 65001, with R2 and R3 in sub-AS 65023. In this case, R1 and R3 will not be neighbors. The following list outlines the sequence of events to propagate a prefix:

1. R3 will learn prefix 21.0.0.0/8 via eBGP from AS 45 (R4).

2. R3 will advertise the prefix via iBGP to R2.

3. R2 will advertise the prefix via confederation eBGP to R1.

Example 11-14 *Confederation Inside AS 123*

```
! R1 Configuration. Note the sub-AS in the router bgp command, and the true AS in
! the bgp confederation identifier command. Also note the neighbor ebgp-multihop
! command for confederation eBGP peer R2, as they are using loopbacks. Also, sync
```

Example 11-14 *Confederation Inside AS 123 (Continued)*

```
! is not needed now that the confederation has been created.
router bgp 65001
 no synchronization
 bgp router-id 111.111.111.111
 bgp confederation identifier 123
 bgp confederation peers 65023
 neighbor 2.2.2.2 remote-as 65023
 neighbor 2.2.2.2 ebgp-multihop 2
 neighbor 2.2.2.2 update-source Loopback1
 neighbor 2.2.2.2 next-hop-self
 neighbor 172.16.16.6 remote-as 678
! R2 Configuration. Note the bgp confederation peers 65023 command. Without it,
! R2 would think that neighbor 1.1.1.1 was a true eBGP connection, and remove
! the confederation AS_PATH entries before advertising to R1.
router bgp 65023
 no synchronization
 bgp confederation identifier 123
 bgp confederation peers 65001
 neighbor 1.1.1.1 remote-as 65001
 neighbor 1.1.1.1 ebgp-multihop 2
 neighbor 1.1.1.1 update-source Loopback1
 neighbor 3.3.3.3 remote-as 65023
 neighbor 3.3.3.3 update-source Loopback1
! R3 Configuration. Note that R3 does not need a bgp confederation peers command,
! as it does not have any confederation eBGP peers.
router bgp 65023
 no synchronization
 bgp log-neighbor-changes
 bgp confederation identifier 123
 neighbor 2.2.2.2 remote-as 65023
 neighbor 2.2.2.2 update-source Loopback1
 neighbor 2.2.2.2 next-hop-self
 neighbor 4.4.4.4 remote-as 45
 neighbor 4.4.4.4 ebgp-multihop 2
 neighbor 4.4.4.4 update-source Loopback1
! R1 has received the 21.0.0.0/8 prefix, with sub-AS 65023 shown in parentheses,
! and true AS 45 shown outside the parentheses. R1 has also learned the same
! prefix via AS 678 and R6. The route through the sub-AS is best because it is the
! shortest AS_PATH; the shortest AS_PATH logic ignores the confederation sub-autonmous systems.
R1# show ip bgp | begin Network
   Network          Next Hop         Metric LocPrf Weight Path
*> 21.0.0.0          3.3.3.3               0    100      0 (65023) 45 i
*                    172.16.16.6                         0 678 45 i
*> 22.2.2.0/24       3.3.3.3               0    100      0 (65023) 45 i
*                    172.16.16.6                         0 678 45 i
```

continues

Example 11-14 *Confederation Inside AS 123 (Continued)*

```
! R6 shows its received update from R1, showing the removed sub-AS, and the
! inclusion of the true AS, AS 123.
R6# show ip bgp neighbor 172.16.16.1 received-routes | begin Network
   Network          Next Hop          Metric LocPrf Weight Path
r   21.0.0.0         172.16.16.1                        0 123 45 i
r   22.2.2.0/24      172.16.16.1                        0 123 45 i
```

Route Reflectors

Route reflectors (RRs) achieve the same result as confederations—they remove the need for a full mesh of iBGP peers, allow all iBGP routes to be learned by all iBGP routers in the AS, and prevent loops. In an iBGP design using RRs, a partial mesh of iBGP peers is defined. Some routers are configured as RR servers; these servers are allowed to learn iBGP routes from their clients and then advertise them to other iBGP peers. The example in Figure 11-10 shows the key terms and some of the core logic used by an RR; note that only the RR server itself uses different logic, with clients and nonclients acting as normal iBGP peers.

Figure 11-10 *Basic Flow Using a Single RR, Four Clients, and Two Nonclients*

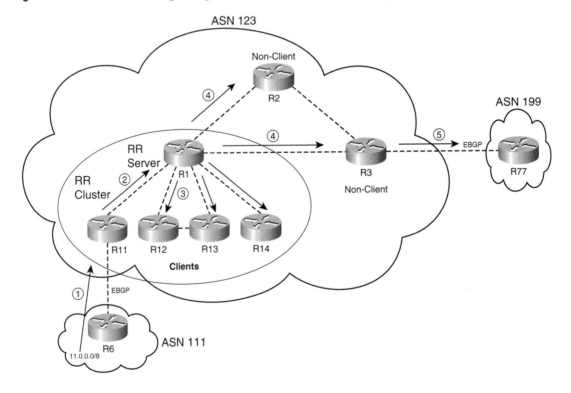

Figure 11-10 shows how prefix 11.0.0.0/8 is propagated through the AS, using the following steps:

1. R11 learns 11.0.0.0/8 using eBGP.

2. R11 uses normal iBGP rules and sends an Update to R1.

3. R1 reflects the routes by sending Updates to all other clients.

4. R1 also reflects the routes to all non-clients.

5. Nonclients use non-RR rules, sending an Update over eBGP to R77.

Only the router acting as the RR uses modified rules; the other routers (clients and non-clients) are not even aware of the RR, nor do they change their operating rules. Table 11-11 summarizes the rules for RR operation, which vary based on from what type of BGP peer the RR receives the prefix. The table lists the sources from which a prefix can be learned, and the types of other routers to which the RR will reflect the prefix information.

Table 11-11 *Types of Neighbors to Which Prefixes Are Reflected*

Location from Which a Prefix Is Learned	Are Routes Advertised to Clients?	Are Routes Advertised to Non-clients?
Client	Yes	Yes
Non-client	Yes	No
eBGP	Yes	Yes

The one case in which the RR does not reflect routes is when the RR receives a route from a nonclient, with the RR not reflecting that route to other nonclients. The perspective behind that logic is that RRs act like normal iBGP peers with nonclients and with eBGP neighbors—in other words, the RR does not forward iBGP-learned routes to other nonclient iBGP peers. The difference in how the RR behaves relates to when a client sends the RR a prefix, or when the RR decides to reflect a prefix to the clients.

One (or more) RR servers, and their clients, create a single RR cluster. A BGP design using RRs can consist of:

- Clusters with multiple RRs in a cluster

- Multiple clusters, although using multiple clusters makes sense only when physical redundancy exists as well.

With multiple clusters, at least one RR from a cluster must be peered with at least one RR in each of the other clusters. Typically, all RRs are peered directly, creating a full mesh of RR iBGP peers among RRs. Also, if some routers are nonclients, they should be included in the full mesh of RRs.

Figure 11-11 shows the concept, with each RR fully meshed with the other RRs in other clusters, as well as with the nonclient.

Figure 11-11 *Multiple RR Clusters with Full Mesh Among RRs and Nonclients*

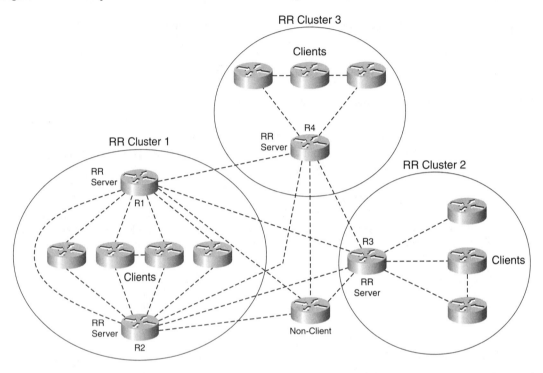

If you consider the logic summary in Table 11-11 compared to Figure 11-11, it appears that routing loops are not only possible but probable with this design. However, the RR feature uses several tools to prevent loops, as follows:

- **CLUSTER_LIST**—RRs add their *cluster ID* into a BGP PA called the CLUSTER_LIST before sending an Update. When receiving a BGP Update, RRs discard received prefixes for which their cluster ID already appears. As with AS_PATH for confederations, this prevents RRs from looping advertisements between clusters.

- **ORIGINATOR_ID**—This PA lists the RID of the first iBGP peer to advertise the route into the AS. If a router sees its own BGP ID as the ORIGINATOR_ID in a received route, it does not use or propagate the route.

- **Only advertise the best routes**—RRs reflect routes only if the RR considers the route to be a "best" route in its own BGP table. This further limits the routes reflected by the RR. (It also has a positive effect compared with confederations in that an average router sees fewer, typically useless, redundant routes.)

Example 11-15 shows a simple example of using RRs. Figure 11-12 shows the modified AS 123 from the network of Figure 11-4, now with four routers. The design uses two clusters, with two RRs (R9 and R2) and two clients (R1 and R3). The following list outlines the sequence of events to propagate a prefix, as shown in Figure 11-12:

1. R3 learns prefix 21.0.0.0/8 via eBGP from AS 45 (R4).

2. R3 advertises the prefix via iBGP to R2 using normal logic.

3. R2, an RR, receiving a prefix from an RR client, reflects the route via iBGP to R9—a nonclient as far as R2 is concerned.

4. R9, an RR, receiving an iBGP route from a nonclient, reflects the route to R1, its RR client.

Figure 11-12   *Modified AS 123 Used in RR Example 11-15*

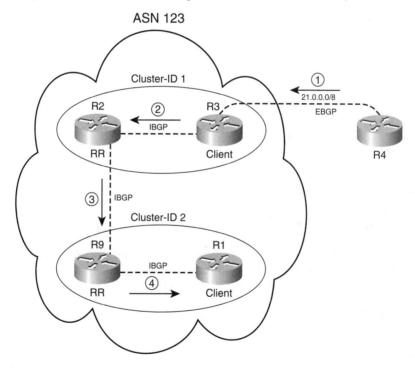

Example 11-15   *RR Configuration for AS 123, Two RRs, and Two Clients*

```
! R3 Configuration. The RR client has no overt signs of being a client; the
! process is completely hidden from all routers except RRs. Also, do not forget
! that one of the main motivations for using RRs is to allow sync to be disabled.
router bgp 123
 no synchronization
 neighbor 2.2.2.2 remote-as 123
```

continues

Example 11-15 *RR Configuration for AS 123, Two RRs, and Two Clients (Continued)*

```
 neighbor 2.2.2.2 update-source Loopback1
 neighbor 2.2.2.2 next-hop-self
 neighbor 4.4.4.4 remote-as 45
 neighbor 4.4.4.4 ebgp-multihop 255
 neighbor 4.4.4.4 update-source Loopback1
! R2 Configuration. The cluster ID would default to R2's BGP RID, but it has been
! manually set to "1," which will be listed as "0.0.0.1" in command output. R2
! designates 3.3.3.3 (R3) as a client.
router bgp 123
 no synchronization
 bgp cluster-id 1
 neighbor 3.3.3.3 remote-as 123
 neighbor 3.3.3.3 update-source Loopback1
 neighbor 3.3.3.3 route-reflector-client
 neighbor 9.9.9.9 remote-as 123
 neighbor 9.9.9.9 update-source Loopback1
! R9 Configuration. The configuration is similar to R2, but with a different
! cluster ID.
router bgp 123
 no synchronization
 bgp router-id 9.9.9.9
 bgp cluster-id 2
 neighbor 1.1.1.1 remote-as 123
 neighbor 1.1.1.1 update-source Loopback2
 neighbor 1.1.1.1 route-reflector-client
 neighbor 2.2.2.2 remote-as 123
 neighbor 2.2.2.2 update-source Loopback2
 no auto-summary
! The R1 configuration is omitted, as it contains no specific RR configuration,
! as is the case with all RR clients.
! The 21.0.0.0/8 prefix has been learned by R3, forwarded over iBGP as normal to
! R2. Then, R2 reflected the prefix to its only other peer, R9. The show ip bgp
! 21.0.0.0 command shows the current AS_PATH (45); the iBGP originator of the
! route (3.3.3.3), and the iBGP neighbor from which it was learned ("from
! 2.2.2.2"); and the cluster list, which currently has R2's cluster (0.0.0.1).
! The next output is from R9.
R9# show ip bgp 21.0.0.0
BGP routing table entry for 21.0.0.0/8, version 3
Paths: (1 available, best #1, table Default-IP-Routing-Table)
Flag: 0x820
  Advertised to update-groups:
     2
  45
    3.3.3.3 (metric 2300416) from 2.2.2.2 (2.2.2.2)
      Origin IGP, metric 0, localpref 100, valid, internal, best
      Originator: 3.3.3.3, Cluster list: 0.0.0.1
```

Example 11-15 *RR Configuration for AS 123, Two RRs, and Two Clients (Continued)*

```
! RR R9 reflected the prefix to its client (R1), as seen next. Note the changes
! compared to R9's output, with iBGP route being learned from R9 ("from 9.9.9.9"),
! and the cluster list now including cluster 0.0.0.2, as added by R9.
R1# sho ip bgp 21.0.0.0
BGP routing table entry for 21.0.0.0/8, version 20
Paths: (1 available, best #1, table Default-IP-Routing-Table)
  Not advertised to any peer
  45
    3.3.3.3 (metric 2302976) from 9.9.9.9 (9.9.9.9)
      Origin IGP, metric 0, localpref 100, valid, internal, best
      Originator: 3.3.3.3, Cluster list: 0.0.0.2, 0.0.0.1
```

Foundation Summary

This section lists additional details and facts to round out the coverage of the topics in this chapter. Unlike most of the Cisco Press *Exam Certification Guides*, this "Foundation Summary" does not repeat information presented in the "Foundation Topics" section of the chapter. Please take the time to read and study the details in the "Foundation Topics" section of the chapter, as well as review items noted with a Key Topic icon.

Table 11-12 lists some of the key RFCs for BGP.

Table 11-12 *Protocols and Standards for Chapter 12*

Topic	Standard
BGP-4	RFC 1771
BGP Confederations	RFC 3065
BGP Route Reflection	RFC 2796
MD5 Authentication	RFC 2385

Table 11-13 lists the BGP path attributes mentioned in this chapter, and describes their purpose.

Table 11-13 *BGP PAs*

Path Attribute	Description	Characteristics
AS_PATH	Lists ASNs through which the route has been advertised	Well known Mandatory
NEXT_HOP	Lists the next-hop IP address used to reach an NLRI	Well known Mandatory
AGGREGATOR	Lists the RID and ASN of the router that created a summary NLRI	Optional Transitive
ATOMIC_AGGREGATE	Tags a summary NLRI as being a summary	Well known Discretionary
ORIGIN	Value implying from where the route was taken for injection into BGP; **i**(IGP), **e** (EGP), or **?** (incomplete information)	Well known Mandatory

Table 11-13   *BGP PAs (Continued)*

Path Attribute	Description	Characteristics
ORIGINATOR_ID	Used by RRs to denote the RID of the iBGP neighbor that injected the NLRI into the AS	Optional Nontransitive
CLUSTER_LIST	Used by RRs to list the RR cluster IDs in order to prevent loops	Optional Nontransitive

Table 11-14 lists and describes the methodes to introduce entries into the BGP table.

Table 11-14   *Summary: Methods to Introduce Entries into the BGP Table*

Key
Topic

Method	Summary Description
network command	Advertises a route into BGP. Depends on the existence of the configured network/subnet in the IP routing table.
Redistribution	Takes IGP, static, or connected routes; metric (MED) assignment is not required.
Manual summarization	Requires at least one component subnet in the BGP table; options for keeping all component subnets, suppressing all from advertisement, or suppressing a subset from being advertised.
default-information originate	Requires a default route in the IP routing table, plus the **redistribute** command.
neighbor default-originate	With the optional route map, requires the route map to match the IP routing table with a permit action before advertising a default route. Without the route map, the default is always advertised.

Table 11-15 lists some of the most popular Cisco IOS commands related to the topics in this chapter.

Table 11-15   *Command Reference for Chapter 11*

Command	Command Mode and Description
aggregate-address *address mask* [**as-set**] [**summary-only**] [**suppress-map** *map-name*] [**advertise-map** *map-name*] [**attribute-map** *map-name*]	BGP mode; summarizes BGP routes, suppressing all/none/some of the component subnets
auto-summary	BGP mode; enables automatic summarization to classful boundaries of locally injected routes

continues

Table 11-15 *Command Reference for Chapter 11 (Continued)*

Command	Command Mode and Description
bgp client-to-client reflection	BGP mode; on by default, tells a RR server to reflect routes learned from a client to other clients
bgp cluster-id *cluster-id*	BGP mode; defines a nondefault RR cluster ID to a RR server
bgp confederation identifier *as-number*	BGP mode; for confederations, defines the ASN used for the entire AS as seen by other autonmous systems
bgp confederation peers *as-number* [*... as-number*]	BGP mode; for confederations, identifies which neighboring ASNs are in other confederation sub-autonmous systems
bgp log-neighbor-changes	BGP mode; on by default, it tells BGP to create log messages for significant changes in BGP operation
bgp router-id *ip-address*	BGP mode; defines the BGP router ID.
default-information originate	BGP mode; required to allow a static default route to be redistributed into BGP
default-metric *number*	BGP mode; sets the default metric assigned to routes redistributed into BGP; normally defaults to the IGP metric for each route
distance bgp *external-distance internal-distance local-distance*	BGP mode; defines the administrative distance for eBGP, iBGP, and locally injected BGP routes
neighbor {*ip-address* | *peer-group-name*} **default-originate** [**route-map** *map-name*]	BGP mode; tells the router to add a default route to the BGP Update sent to this neighbor, under the conditions set in the optional route map
neighbor {*ip-address* | *peer-group-name*} **description** *text*	BGP mode; adds a descriptive text reference in the BGP configuration
neighbor {*ip-address* | *peer-group-name*} **ebgp-multihop** [*ttl*]	BGP mode; for eBGP peers, sets the TTL in packets sent to this peer to something larger than the default of 1
neighbor *ip-address* | *peer-group-name* **next-hop-self**	BGP mode; causes IOS to reset the NEXT_HOP PA to the IP address used as the source address of Updates sent to this neighbor
neighbor {*ip-address* | *peer-group-name*} **password** *string*	BGP mode; defines the key used in an MD5 hash of all BGP messages to this neighbor
neighbor *ip-address* **peer-group** *peer-group-name*	BGP mode; associates a neighbor's IP address as part of a peer group

Table 11-15 *Command Reference for Chapter 11 (Continued)*

Command	Command Mode and Description
neighbor *peer-group-name* **peer-group**	BGP mode; defines the name of a peer group
neighbor {*ip-address* | *peer-group-name*} **remote-as** *as-number*	BGP mode; defines the AS of the neighbor
neighbor {*ip-address* | *peer-group-name*} **shutdown**	BGP mode; administratively shuts down a neighbor, stopping the TCP connection
neighbor [*ip-address* | *peer-group-name*] **timers** *keepalive holdtime*	BGP mode; sets the two BGP timers, just for this neighbor
neighbor {*ip-address* | *ipv6-address* | *peer-group-name*} **update-source** *interface-type interface-number*	BGP mode; defines the source IP address used for BGP messages sent to this neighbor
network {*network-number* [**mask** *network-mask*] [**route-map** *map-tag*]	BGP mode; causes IOS to add the defined prefix to the BGP table if it exists in the IP routing table
router bgp *as-number*	Global command; defines the ASN and puts the user in BGP mode
synchronization	BGP mode; enables BGP synchronization
timers bgp *keepalive holdtime*	BGP mode; defines BGP timers for all neighbors
show ip bgp [*network*] [*network-mask*] [**longer-prefixes**] [**prefix-list** *prefix-list-name* | **route-map** *route-map-name*] [**shorter prefixes mask-length**]	Exec mode; lists details of a router's BGP table
show ip bgp injected-paths	Exec mode; lists routes locally injected into BGP
show ip bgp neighbors [*neighbor-address*] [**received-routes** | **routes** | **advertised-routes** | {**paths** *regexp*} | **dampened-routes** | received prefix-filter]]	Exec mode; lists information about routes sent and received to particular neighbors
show ip bgp peer-group [*peer-group-name*] [**summary**]	Exec mode; lists details about a particular peer group
show ip bgp summary	Exec mode; lists basic statistics for each BGP peer

Memory Builders

The CCIE Routing and Switching written exam, like all Cisco CCIE written exams, covers a fairly broad set of topics. This section provides some basic tools to help you exercise your memory about some of the broader topics covered in this chapter.

Fill in Key Tables from Memory

Appendix E, "Key Tables for CCIE Study," on the CD in the back of this book contains empty sets of some of the key summary tables in each chapter. Print Appendix E, refer to this chapter's tables in it, and fill in the tables from memory. Refer to Appendix F, "Solutions for Key Tables for CCIE Study," on the CD to check your answers.

Definitions

Next, take a few moments to write down the definitions for the following terms:

path attribute, BGP table, BGP Update, established, iBGP, eBGP, EGP, BGP, peer group, eBGP multihop, autonomous system, AS number, AS_PATH, ORIGIN, NLRI, NEXT_HOP, MULTI_EXIT_DISC, LOCAL_PREF, routing black hole, synchronization, confederation, route reflector, confederation identifier, sub-AS, route reflector server, route reflector client, route reflector nonclient, confederation AS, confederation eBGP, weight

Refer to the glossary to check your answers.

Further Reading

Routing TCP/IP, Volume II, by Jeff Doyle and Jennifer DeHaven Carrol

Cisco BGP-4 Command and Configuration Handbook, by William R. Parkhurst

Internet Routing Architectures, by Bassam Halabi

Troubleshooting IP Routing Protocols, by Zaheer Aziz, Johnson Liu, Abe Martey, and Faraz Shamim

Most every reference reached from Cisco's BGP support page at http://www.cisco.com/en/US/partner/tech/tk365/tk80/tsd_technology_support_sub-protocol_home.html. Requires a CCO username/password.

Part IV: QoS

Blueprint topics covered in this chapter:

This chapter covers the following subtopics from the Cisco CCIE Routing and Switching written exam blueprint. Refer to the full blueprint in Table I-1 in the Introduction for more details on the topics covered in each chapter and their context within the blueprint.

- Modular QoS CLI (MQC)

- Marking

- Policy Routing

CHAPTER 12

Classification and Marking

The goal of classification and marking tools is to simplify the classification process of other QoS tools by performing complicated classification steps as few times as possible. For instance, a classification and marking tool might examine the source IP address of packets, incoming Class of Service (CoS) settings, and possibly TCP or UDP port numbers. Packets matching all those fields may have their IP Precedence (IPP) or DiffServ Code Points (DSCPs) field marked with a particular value. Later, other QoS tools—on the same router/switch or a different one—can simply look for the marked field when making a QoS decision, rather than having to perform the detailed classification again before taking the desired QoS action.

"Do I Know This Already?" Quiz

Table 12-1 outlines the major headings in this chapter and the corresponding "Do I Know This Already?" quiz questions.

Table 12-1 *"Do I Know This Already?" Foundation Topics Section-to-Question Mapping*

Foundation Topics Section	Questions Covered in This Section	Score
Fields that Can Be Marked for QoS Purposes	1–4	
Cisco Modular QoS CLI	5–7	
Classification and Marking Tools	8–10	
Total Score		

In order to best use this pre-chapter assessment, remember to score yourself strictly. You can find the answers in Appendix A, "Answers to the 'Do I Know This Already?' Quizzes."

1. According to the DiffServ RFCs, which PHB defines a set of three DSCPs in each service class, with different drop characteristics for each of the three DSCP values?

   a. Expedited Forwarding

   b. Class Selector

   c. Assured Forwarding

   d. Multi-class-multi-drop

2. Which of the following are true about the location of DSCP in the IP header?

   a. High-order 6 bits of ToS byte/DS field

   b. Low-order 6 bits of ToS byte

   c. Middle 6 bits of ToS byte

   d. Its first 3 bits overlap with IP Precedence

   e. Its last 3 bits overlap with IP Precedence

3. Imagine that a packet is marked with DSCP CS3. Later, a QoS tool classifies the packet. Which of the following classification criteria would match the packet, assuming the marking had not been changed from the original CS3 marking?

   a. Match on DSCP CS3

   b. Match on precedence 3

   c. Match on DSCP AF32

   d. Match on DSCP AF31

   e. Match on DSCP decimal 24

4. Imagine that a packet is marked with AF31. Later, a QoS tool classifies the packet. Which of the following classification criteria would match the packet, assuming the marking had not been changed from the original AF31 marking?

   a. Match on DSCP CS3

   b. Match on precedence 3

   c. Match on DSCP 24

   d. Match on DSCP 26

   e. Match on DSCP 28

5. Examine the following output from a router that shows a user adding configuration to a router. Which of the following statements is true about the configuration?

```
Router(config)# class-map fred
Router(config-cmap)# match dscp EF
Router(config-cmap)# match access-group 101
```

   a. Packets that match both DSCP EF and ACL 101 will match the class.

   b. Packets that match either DSCP EF or ACL 101 will match the class.

   c. Packets that match ACL 101 will match the class, because the second **match** command replaces the first.

   d. Packets will only match DSCP EF because the first match exits the class map.

6. Router R1 is configured with the following three class maps. Which class map(s) would match an incoming frame whose CoS field is set to 3, IP Precedence is set to 2, and DSCP is set to AF21?

```
class-map match-all c1
 match cos 3 4
class-map match-any c2
 match cos 2 3
 match cos 1
class-map match-all c3
 match cos 3 4
 match cos 2
```

   a. c1

   b. c2

   c. c3

   d. All of these answers are correct.

7. Examine the following example of commands typed in configuration mode to create a class map. Assuming that the **class fred** command was used inside a policy map, and the policy map was enabled on an interface, which of the following would be true with regard to packets classified by the class map?

```
Router(config)# class-map fred
Router(config-cmap)# match ip dscp ef
Router(config-cmap)# match ip dscp af31
```

   a. Match packets with both DSCP EF and AF31

   b. Match packets with either DSCP EF or AF31

   c. Match all packets that are neither EF or AF31

   d. Match no packets

   e. Match packets with precedence values of 3 and 5

8. The **service-policy output fred** command is found in router R1's configuration under Frame Relay subinterface s0/0.1. Which of the following could be true about this CB Marking policy map?

   a. The policy map can classify packets using class maps that match based on the DE bit.

   b. The policy map can refer to class maps that match based on DSCP.

   c. The policy map can set CoS.

   d. The policy map can set CLP.

   e. The policy map can set DE.

9. Which of the following is true regarding the listed configuration steps?

   ```
   Router(config)# class-map barney
   Router(config-cmap)# match protocol http url "this-here.jpg"
   Router(config-cmap)# policy-map fred
   Router(config-pmap)# class barney
   Router(config-pmap-c)# set dscp af21
   Router(config-pmap-c)# interface fa0/0
   Router(config-if)# service-policy output fred
   ```

   a. If not already configured, the **ip cef** global command is required.

   b. The configuration does not use NBAR because the **match nbar** command was not used.

   c. The **service-policy** command would be rejected because **match protocol** is not allowed as an output function.

   d. None of these answers is correct.

10. In which mode can the **qos pre-classify** command be issued on a router?

    a. In crypto map configuration mode

    b. In GRE tunnel configuration mode

    c. In point-to-point subinterface configuration mode

    d. Only in physical interface configuration mode

    e. In class map configuration mode

    f. In global configuration mode

Foundation Topics

This chapter has three major sections. The chapter begins by examining the fields that can be marked by the classification and marking (C&M) tools. Next, the chapter covers the mechanics of the Cisco IOS Modular QoS CLI (MQC), which is used by all the IOS QoS tools that begin with the words "Class-Based." Finally, the C&M tools are covered, with most of the content focused on the most important C&M tool, Class-Based Marking (CB Marking).

Fields That Can Be Marked for QoS Purposes

The IP header, LAN trunking headers, Frame Relay header, and ATM cell header all have at least one field that can be used to perform some form of QoS marking. This section lists and defines those fields, with the most significant coverage focused on the IP header IP Precedence (IPP) and Differentiated Services Code Point (DSCP) fields.

IP Precedence and DSCP Compared

The IP header is defined in RFC 791, including a 1-byte field called the Type of Service (ToS) byte. The ToS byte was intended to be used as a field to mark a packet for treatment with QoS tools. The ToS byte itself was further subdivided, with the high-order 3 bits defined as the *IP Precedence (IPP)* field. The complete list of values from the ToS byte's original IPP 3-bit field, and the corresponding names, is provided in Table 12-2.

Table 12-2 *IP Precedence Values and Names*

Name	Decimal Value	Binary Value
Routine	Precedence 0	**000**
Priority	Precedence 1	**001**
Immediate	Precedence 2	**010**
Flash	Precedence 3	**011**
Flash Override	Precedence 4	**100**
Critic/Critical	Precedence 5	**101**
Internetwork Control	Precedence 6	**110**
Network Control	Precedence 7	**111**

Bits 3 through 6 of the ToS byte included flag fields that were toggled on or off to imply a particular QoS service. The final bit (bit 7) was not defined in RFC 791. The flags were not used very often, so in effect, the ToS byte's main purpose was to hold the 3-bit IPP field.

A series of RFCs collectively called *Differentiated Services (DiffServ)* came along later. DiffServ needed more than 3 bits to mark packets, so DiffServ standardized a redefinition of the ToS byte. The ToS byte itself was renamed the *Differentiated Services (DS) field*, and IPP was replaced with a 6-bit field (high-order bits 0–5) called the *Differentiated Services Code Point (DSCP)* field. Later, RFC 3168 defined the low-order 2 bits of the DS field for use with the QoS *Explicit Congestion Notification (ECN)* feature. Figure 12-1 shows the ToS byte's format with the pre-DiffServ and post-DiffServ definition of the field.

Figure 12-1 *IP ToS Byte and DS Field Compared*

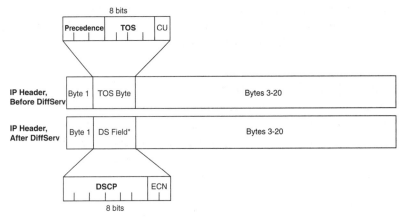

C&M tools often mark DSCP or IPP because the IP packet remains intact as it is forwarded throughout an IP network. The other possible marking fields reside inside Layer 2 headers, which means the headers are discarded when forwarded by a Layer 3 process. Thus, the latter cannot be used to carry QoS markings beyond the current hop.

DSCP Settings and Terminology

Several DiffServ RFCs suggest a set of values to use in the DSCP field and an implied meaning for those settings. For instance, RFC 2598 defines a DSCP of decimal 46, with a name *Expedited Forwarding (EF)*. According to that RFC, packets marked as EF should be given queuing preference so that they experience minimal latency, but the packets should be policed to prevent them from taking over a link and preventing any other types of traffic from exiting an interface during periods when this high-priority traffic reaches or exceeds the interface bandwidth. These suggested settings, and the associated QoS behavior recommended when using each setting, are called *Per-Hop Behaviors (PHBs)* by DiffServ. (The particular example listed in this paragraph is called the Expedited Forwarding PHB.)

Class Selector PHB and DSCP Values

IPP overlaps with the first 3 bits of the DSCP field because the DS field is simply a redefinition of the original ToS byte in the IP header. Because of this overlap, RFC 2475 defines a set of DSCP values and PHBs, called *Class Selector (CS)* PHBs, that provide backward compatibility with IPP. A C&M feature can set a CS DSCP value, and if another router or switch just looks at the IPP field, the value will make sense from an IPP perspective. Table 12-3 lists the CS DSCP names and values, and the corresponding IPP values and names.

Table 12-3 *Default and Class Selector DSCP Values*

DSCP Class Selector Names	Binary DSCP Values	IPP Binary Values	IPP Names
Default/CS0*	**000**000	000	Routine
CS1	**001**000	001	Priority
CS2	**010**000	010	Immediate
CS3	**011**000	011	Flash
CS4	**100**000	100	Flash Override
CS5	**101**000	101	Critic/Critical
CS6	**110**000	110	Internetwork Control
CS7	**111**000	111	Network Control

*The terms "CS0" and "Default" both refer to a binary DSCP of 000000, but most Cisco IOS commands allow only the keyword "default" to represent this value.

Besides defining eight DSCP values and their text names, the CS PHB also suggests a simple set of QoS actions that should be taken based on the CS values. The CS PHB simply states that packets with larger CS DSCPs should be given better queuing preference than packets with lower CS DSCPs.

Assured Forwarding PHB and DSCP Values

The *Assured Forwarding (AF)* PHB (RFC 2597) defines four classes for queuing purposes, along with three levels of drop probability inside each queue. To mark packets and distinguish into which of four queues a packet should be placed, along with one of three drop priorities inside each queue, the AF PHB defines 12 DSCP values and their meanings. The names of the AF DSCPs conform to the following format:

AF*xy*

where *x* implies one of four queues (values 1 through 4), and *y* implies one of three drop priorities (values 1 through 3).

The AF PHB suggests that the higher the value of *x* in the DSCP name AF*xy*, the better the queuing treatment a packet should get. For example, packets with AF11 DSCPs should get worse queuing treatment than packets with AF23 DSCP values. Additionally, the AF PHB suggests that the higher the value of *y* in the DSCP name AF*xy*, the worse the drop treatment for those packets. (Treating a packet worse for drop purposes means that the packet has a higher probability of being dropped.) For example, packets with AF11 DSCPs should get better drop treatment than packets with AF23 DSCP values. Table 12-4 lists the names of the DSCP values, the queuing classes, and the implied drop likelihood.

Table 12-4   *Assured Forwarding DSCP Values—Names, Binary Values, and Decimal Values*

Queue Class	Low Drop Probability	Medium Drop Probability	High Drop Probability
	Name/Decimal/Binary	Name/Decimal/Binary	Name/Decimal/Binary
1	AF11 / 10 / 001010	AF12 / 12 / 001100	AF13 / 14 / 001110
2	AF21 / 18 / 010010	AF22 / 20 / 010100	AF23 / 22 / 010110
4	AF31 / 26 / 011010	AF32 / 28 / 011100	AF33 / 30 / 011110
5	AF41 / 34 / 100010	AF42 / 36 / 100100	AF43 / 38 / 100110

The text AF PHB names do not follow the "bigger-is-better" logic in all cases. For example, the name AF11 represents a decimal value of 10, and the name AF13 represents a decimal DSCP of 14. However, AF11 is "better" than AF13, because AF11 and AF13 are in the same queuing class, but AF11 has a lower probability of being dropped than AF13.

The binary version of the AF DSCP values shows the patterns of the values. The first 3 bits of the binary DSCP values imply the queuing class (bits 0 through 2), and the next 2 bits (bits 3 and 4) imply the drop preference. As a result, queuing tools that operate only on IPP can still react to the AF DSCP values, essentially making the AF DSCPs backward compatible with non-DiffServ nodes for queuing purposes.

NOTE   To convert from the AF name to the decimal equivalent, you can use a simple formula. If you think of the AF values as AF*xy*, the formula is:

$8x + 2y$ = decimal value

For example, AF41 gives you a formula of $(8 * 4) + (2 * 1) = 34$.

Expedited Forwarding PHB and DSCP Values

RFC 2598 defines the *Expedited Forwarding (EF)* PHB, which was described briefly in the introduction to this section. This RFC defines a very simple pair of PHB actions:

■   Queue EF packets so that they get scheduled quickly, to give them low latency.

■ Police the EF packets so that they do not consume all bandwidth on the link or starve other queues.

The DSCP value defined for EF is named EF, with decimal value 46, binary value 101110.

Non-IP Header Marking Fields

As IP packets pass through an internetwork, the packet is encapsulated in a variety of other headers. In several cases, these other headers have QoS fields that can be used for classification and marking.

Ethernet LAN Class of Service

Ethernet supports a 3-bit QoS marking field, but the field only exists when the Ethernet header includes either an 802.1Q or ISL trunking header. IEEE 802.1Q defines its QoS field as the 3 most-significant bits of the 2-byte *Tag Control* field, calling the field the *user-priority bits*. ISL defines the 3 least-significant bits from the 1-byte *User* field, calling this field the *Class of Service (CoS)*. Generally speaking, most people (and most IOS commands) refer to these fields as *CoS*, regardless of the type of trunking. Figure 12-2 shows the general location of the CoS field inside ISL and 802.1P headers.

Figure 12-2 *LAN CoS Fields*

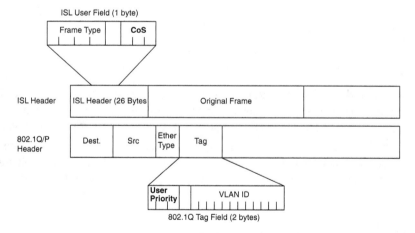

WAN Marking Fields

Frame Relay and ATM support a single bit that can be set for QoS purposes, but these single bits are intended for a very strict use related to drop probability. Frames or cells with these bits set to 1 are considered to be better candidates to be dropped than frames or cells without the bit set to 1. Named the Frame Relay *Discard Eligibility (DE)* bit and the ATM *Cell Loss Priority (CLP)* bit, these bits can be set by a router, or by an ATM or Frame Relay switch. Router and switch drop features can then be configured to more aggressively drop frames and cells that have the DE or CLP bit set, respectively.

MPLS defines a 3-bit field called the *MPLS Experimental (EXP)* bit that is intended for general QoS marking. Often, C&M tools are used on the edge of MPLS networks to remap DSCP or IPP values to MPLS Experimental bit values to provide QoS inside the MPLS network.

Locations for Marking and Matching

Figure 12-3 shows a sample network, with notes about the locations of the QoS fields.

Figure 12-3 *Sample Network Showing Non-IP Markable QoS Fields*

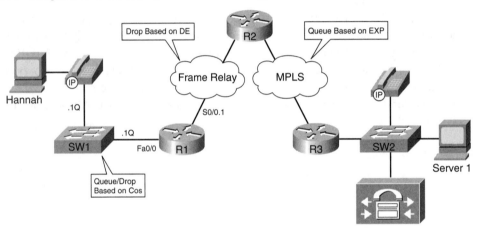

In such a network, the IPP and DSCP inside the IP packet remain intact from end to end. However, some devices may not be able to look at the IPP or DSCP fields, and some may find it more convenient to look at some other header field. For instance, an MPLS Label Switch Router (LSR) inside the MPLS cloud may be configured to make QoS decisions based on the 3-bit MPLS EXP field in the MPLS label, but unable to look at the encapsulated IP header and DSCP field. In such cases, QoS tools may need to be configured on edge devices to look at the DSCP and then mark a different field.

The non-IP header markable fields exist in only parts of the network. As a result, those fields can be used for classification or marking only on the appropriate interfaces. The rules for where these fields (CoS, DE, CLP, EXP) can be used are as follows:

■ **For classification**—On ingress only, and only if the interface supports that particular header field

■ **For marking**—On egress only, and only if the interface supports that particular header field

For example, if CB Marking were to be configured on R1's fa0/0.1 802.1Q subinterface, it could classify incoming frames based on their CoS values, and mark outgoing frames with a CoS value. However, on ingress, it could not mark CoS, and on egress, it could not classify based on CoS. Similarly, on that same fa0/0.1 subinterface, CB Marking could neither classify nor mark based on a DE bit, CLP bit, or MPLS EXP bits, because these headers never exist on Ethernet interfaces.

Table 12-5 summarizes the QoS marking fields.

Table 12-5 *Marking Field Summary*

Field	Location	Length
IP Precedence (IPP)	IP header	3 bits
IP DSCP	IP header	6 bits
DS field	IP header	1 byte
ToS byte	IP header	1 byte
CoS	ISL and 802.1Q header	3 bits
Discard Eligible (DE)	Frame Relay header	1 bit
Cell Loss Priority (CLP)	ATM cell header	1 bit
MPLS Experimental	MPLS header	3 bits

Cisco Modular QoS CLI

For many years and over many IOS releases, Cisco added QoS features and functions, each of which used its own separate set of configuration and exec commands. Eventually, the number of different QoS tools and different QoS commands got so large that QoS configuration became a big chore. Cisco created the *Modular QoS CLI (MQC)* to help resolve these problems, by defining a common set of configuration commands to configure many QoS features in a router or switch.

MQC is not a totally new CLI, different from IOS configuration mode, for configuring QoS. Rather, it is a method of categorizing IOS classification, marking, and related actions into logical groupings to unify the command-line interface. MQC defines a new set of configuration commands—commands that are typed in using the same IOS CLI, in configuration mode. However, once you understand MQC, you typically need to learn only one new command to know how to configure any additional MQC-based QoS tools. You can identify MQC-based tools by the name of the tool; they all begin with the phrase "Class-Based" (abbreviated CB for this discussion). These tools include CB Marking, CB Weighted Fair Queuing (CBWFQ), CB Policing, CB Shaping, and CB Header Compression.

Mechanics of MQC

MQC separates the classification function of a QoS tool from the action (PHB) that the QoS tool wants to perform. To do so, there are three major commands with MQC, with several subordinate commands:

- The **class-map** command defines the matching parameters for classifying packets into service classes.

- The PHB actions (marking, queuing, and so on) are configured under a **policy-map** command.

- The policy map is enabled on an interface by using a **service-policy** command.

Figure 12-4 shows the general flow of commands.

Figure 12-4 *MQC Commands and Their Correlation*

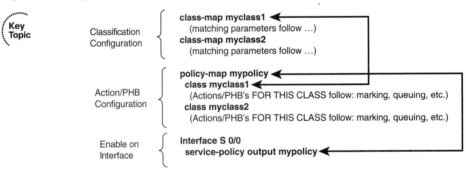

In Figure 12-4, the network's QoS policy calls for treating packets in one of two categories, called *QoS service classes*. (The actual types of packets that are placed into each class are not shown, to keep the focus on the general flow of how the main commands work together.) Classifying packets into two classes calls for the use of two **class-map** commands. Each **class-map** command would be followed by a **match** subcommand, which defines the actual parameters that are compared to the frame/packet header contents to match packets for classification.

For each class, some QoS action (PHB) needs to be performed; this action is configured using the **policy-map** command. Under a single policy map, multiple classes can be referenced; in Figure 12-4, the two classes myclass1 and myclass2. Inside the single policy called mypolicy, under each of the two classes myclass1 and myclass2, you can configure separate QoS actions. For instance, you could apply different markings to packets in myclass1 and myclass2 at this point. Finally, when the **service-policy** command is applied to an interface, the QoS features are enabled either inbound or outbound on that interface.

The next section takes a much closer look at packet classification using class maps. Most of the discussion of policy maps will be included when specifically covering CB Marking configuration later in the chapter.

Classification Using Class Maps

MQC-based tools classify packets using the **match** subcommand inside an MQC class map. The following list details the rules surrounding how class maps work for matching and classifying packets:

- The **match** command has many options for matching packets, including QoS fields, ACLs, and MAC addresses. (See Table 12-10 in the "Foundation Summary" section for a reference.)

- Class-map names are case sensitive.

- The **match protocol** command means that IOS uses Network Based Application Recognition (NBAR) to perform that match.

- The **match any** command matches any packet—in other words, any and all packets.

Example 12-1 shows a simple CB Marking configuration, with comments focused on the classification configuration. Note that the names and logic match Figure 12-4.

Example 12-1 *Basic CB Marking Example*

```
! CEF is required for CB Marking. Without it, the class map and policy map
! configuration would be allowed, but the service-policy command would be rejected.
ip cef
! The first class map matches all UDP/RTP packets with UDP ports between 16384 and
! 32767 (the 2nd number is added to the first to get the end of the range.) The
! second class map matches any and all packets.
class-map match-all msclass1
  match ip rtp 16384 16383
class-map match-all myclass2
  match any
! The policy map calls each of the two class maps for matching. The set command
! implies that the PHB is marking, meaning that this is a CB Marking config.
policy-map mypolicy
  class myclass1
   set dscp EF
  class myclass2
   set dscp default
! The policy map processes packets leaving interface fa0/0.
interface Fastethernet0/0
 service-policy output mypolicy
```

With Example 12-1, each packet leaving interface fa0/0 will match one of the two classes. Because the policy map uses a **set dscp** command in each class, and all packets happen to match either myclass1 or myclass2, each packet will leave the interface marked either with DSCP EF (decimal 46) or default (decimal 0). (If the matching logic was different and some packets match neither myclass1 nor myclass2, those packets would not be marked, and would retain their existing DSCP values.)

Using Multiple match Commands

In some cases, a class map may need to examine multiple items in a packet to decide whether the packet should be part of that class. Class maps can use multiple **match** commands, and even nest class maps inside other class maps, to achieve the desired combination of logic. The following list summarizes the key points regarding these more complex matching options:

- Up to four (CoS and IPP) or eight (DSCP) values can be listed on a single **match cos**, **match precedence**, or **match dscp** command, respectively. If any of the values are found in the packet, the statement is matched.

- If a class map has multiple **match** commands in it, the **match-any** or **match-all** (default) parameter on the **class-map** command defines whether a logical OR or a logical AND (default) is used between the **match** commands, respectively.

- The **match class** *name* command refers to another class map by name, nesting the named class map's matching logic; the **match class** *name* command is considered to match if the referenced **class-map** also results in a match.

Example 12-2 shows several examples of this more complicated matching logic, with notations inside the example of what must be true for a class map to match a packet.

Example 12-2 *Complex Matching with Class Maps*

```
! class-map example1 uses match-all logic (default), so this class map matches
! packets that are permitted by ACL 102, and that also have an IP precedence of 5.
class-map match-all example1
  match access-group 102
  match precedence 5
! class-map example2 uses match-any logic, so this class map matches packets that
! are permitted by ACL 102, or have DSCP AF21, or both.
class-map match-any example2
  match access-group 102
  match dscp AF21
! class-map example3 matches no packets, due to a common mistake—the two match
! commands use a logical AND between them due to the default match-all argument, meaning
! that a single packet must have DSCP 0 and DSCP 1, which is impossible. class-map example4
! shows how to correctly match either DSCP 0 or 1.
class-map match-all example3
  match dscp 0
  match dscp 1
!
class-map match-any example4
  match dscp 0 1
! class-map i-am-nesting refers to class-map i-am-nested through the match class
! i-am-nested command. The logic is explained after the example.
class-map match-all i-am-nested
  match access-group 102
```

Example 12-2   *Complex Matching with Class Maps (Continued)*

```
   match precedence 5
!
class-map match-any i-am-nesting
   match class i-am-nested
   match cos 5
```

The trickiest part of Example 12-2 is how the class maps can be nested, as shown at the end. **class-map i-am-nesting** uses OR logic between its two **match** commands, meaning "I will match if the CoS is 5, or if **class-map i-am-nested** matches the packet, or both." When combined with the match-all logic of the **i-am-nested** class map, the logic matches the following packets/frames:

> Packets that are permitted by ACL 102, AND marked with precedence 5
> or
> frames with CoS 5

Classification Using NBAR

NBAR classifies packets that are normally difficult to classify. For instance, some applications use dynamic port numbers, so a statically configured **match** command, matching a particular UDP or TCP port number, simply could not classify the traffic. NBAR can look past the UDP and TCP header, and refer to the host name, URL, or MIME type in HTTP requests. (This deeper examination of the packet contents is sometimes called *deep packet inspection*.) NBAR can also look past the TCP and UDP headers to recognize application-specific information. For instance, NBAR allows recognition of different Citrix application types, and allows searching for a portion of a URL string.

NBAR itself can be used for a couple of different purposes. Independent of QoS features, NBAR can be configured to keep counters of traffic types and traffic volume for each type. For QoS, NBAR can be used by CB Marking to match difficult-to-match packets. Whenever the MQC **match protocol** command is used, IOS is using NBAR to match the packets. Table 12-6 lists some of the more popular uses of the **match protocol** command and NBAR.

Table 12-6   *Popular Fields Matchable by CB Marking Using NBAR*

Field	Comments
RTP audio versus video	RTP uses even-numbered UDP ports from 16,384 to 32,768. The odd-numbered port numbers are used by RTCP for call control traffic. NBAR allows matching the even-numbered ports only, for classification of voice payload into a different service class from that used for voice signaling.
Citrix applications	NBAR can recognize different types of published Citrix applications.

continues

Table 12-6 *Popular Fields Matchable by CB Marking Using NBAR (Continued)*

Field	Comments
Host name, URL string, MIME type	NBAR can also match URL strings, including the host name and the MIME type, using regular expressions for matching logic.
Peer-to-peer applications	NBAR can find file-sharing applications like KaZaa, Morpheus, Grokster, and Gnutella.

Classification and Marking Tools

The final major section of this chapter covers CB Marking, with a brief mention of a few other, less popular marking tools.

Class-Based Marking (CB Marking) Configuration

As with the other QoS tools whose names begin with the phrase "Class-Based," you will use MQC commands to configure CB Marking. The following list highlights the key points regarding CB Marking configuration and logic:

- CB Marking requires CEF (enabled using the **ip cef** global command).

- Packets are classified based on the logic in MQC class maps.

- An MQC policy map refers to one or more class maps using the **class** *class-map-name* command; packets classified into that class are then marked.

- CB Marking is enabled for packets either entering or exiting an interface using the MQC **service-policy in | out** *policy-map-name* interface subcommand.

- A CB Marking policy map is processed sequentially; once a packet has matched a class, it is marked based on the **set** command(s) defined for that class.

- You can configure multiple **set** commands in one class to set multiple fields; for example, to set both DSCP and CoS.

- Packets that do not explicitly match a defined class are considered to have matched a special class called *class-default*.

- For any class inside the policy map for which there is no set command, packets in that class are not marked.

Table 12-7 lists the syntax of the CB Marking **set** command, showing the familiar fields that can be set by CB Marking. Table 12-8 lists the key **show** commands available for CB Marking.

Table 12-7 **set** *Configuration Command Reference for CB Marking*

Command	Function
set [ip] precedence *ip-precedence-value*	Marks the value for IP Precedence for IPv4 and IPv6 packets if the **ip** parameter is omitted; sets only IPv4 packets if the **ip** parameter is included
set [ip] dscp *ip-dscp-value*	Marks the value for IP DSCP for IPv4 and IPv6 packets if the **ip** parameter is omitted; sets only IPv4 packets if the **ip** parameter is included
set cos *cos-value*	Marks the value for CoS
set qos-group *group-id*	Marks the group identifier for the QoS group
set atm-clp	Sets the ATM CLP bit
set fr-de	Sets the Frame Relay DE bit

Table 12-8 *EXEC Command Reference for CB Marking*

Command	Function
show policy-map *policy-map-name*	Lists configuration information about a policy map
show policy-map *interface-spec* [*input* | *output*] [**class** *class-name*]	Lists statistical information about the behavior of a policy map when enabled on an interface

CB Marking Example

The first CB Marking example uses the network shown in Figure 12-5. Traffic was generated in the network to make the **show** commands more meaningful. Two G.711 voice calls were completed between R4 and R1 using *Foreign Exchange Station (FXS)* cards on these two routers, with *Voice Activity Detection (VAD)* disabled. Client1 performed an FTP get of a large file from Server1, and downloaded two large HTTP objects, named important.jpg and not-so.jpg. Finally, Client1 and Server1 held a Microsoft NetMeeting conference, using G.723 for the audio and H.263 for the video.

Figure 12-5 *Sample Network for CB Marking Examples*

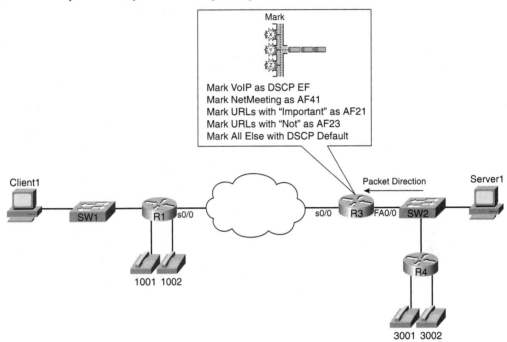

The following criteria define the requirements for marking the various types of traffic for Example 12-3:

■ VoIP payload is marked with DSCP EF.

■ NetMeeting video traffic is marked with DSCP AF41.

■ Any HTTP traffic whose URL contains the string "important" anywhere in the URL is marked with AF21.

■ Any HTTP traffic whose URL contains the string "not-so" anywhere in the URL is marked with AF23.

■ All other traffic is marked with DSCP Default (0).

Example 12-3 lists the annotated configuration, including the appropriate **show** commands.

Example 12-3 *CB Marking Example 1, with **show** Command Output*

```
ip cef
! Class map voip-rtp uses NBAR to match all RTP audio payload, but not the video
! or the signaling.
class-map voip-rtp
 match protocol rtp audio
```

Example 12-3 *CB Marking Example 1, with* **show** *Command Output (Continued)*

```
! Class map http-impo matches all packets related to downloading objects whose
! name contains the string "important," with any text around it. Similar logic
! is used for class-map http-not.
class-map http-impo
 match protocol http url "*important*"
!
class-map http-not
 match protocol http url "*not-so*"
! Class map NetMeet matches two RTP subtypes—one for G.723 audio (type 4) and
! one for H.263 video (type 34). Note the match-any logic so that if either is
! true, a match occurs for this class map.
class-map match-any NetMeet
 match protocol rtp payload-type 4
 match protocol rtp payload-type 34
! policy-map laundry-list calls each of the class maps. Note that the order
! listed here is the order in which the class commands were added to the policy
! map.
policy-map laundry-list
 class voip-rtp
  set ip dscp EF
 class NetMeet
  set ip dscp AF41
 class http-impo
  set ip dscp AF21
 class http-not
  set ip dscp AF23
 class class-default
  set ip DSCP default
! Above, the command class class-default is only required if some nondefault action
! needs to be taken for packets that are not explicitly matched by another class.
! In this case, packets not matched by any other class fall into the class-default
! class, and are marked with DSCP Default (decimal 0). Without these two commands,
! packets in this class would remain unchanged.
!!!!!!!!!!!!!!!!!!!!!!!!!!!!!!!!!!!!!!!!!!!!!!!!!!!!!!!!!!!!!!!!!!!!!!!!!!!!!!!!!!!!!!!!
! Below, the policy map is enabled for input packets on fa0/0.
 interface Fastethernet 0/0
 service-policy input laundry-list
! The command show policy-map laundry-list simply restates the configuration.
R3# show policy-map laundry-list
  Policy Map laundry-list
    Class voip-rtp
      set ip dscp 46
    Class NetMeet
      set ip dscp 34
    Class http-impo
      set ip dscp 18
    Class http-not
```

continues

Example 12-3 *CB Marking Example 1, with* **show** *Command Output (Continued)*

```
    set ip dscp 22
  Class class-default
    set ip dscp 0
! The command show policy-map interface lists statistics related to MQC features.
! Several stanzas of output were omitted for brevity.
R3# show policy-map interface fastethernet 0/0 input
 Fastethernet0/0

  Service-policy input:    laundry-list

    Class-map: voip-rtp (match-all)
      35268 packets, 2609832 bytes
      5 minute offered rate    59000 bps, drop rate 0 bps
      Match: protocol rtp audio
      QoS Set
        ip dscp 46
            Packets marked 35268

    Class-map: NetMeet (match-any)
      817 packets, 328768 bytes
      5 minute offered rate    19000 bps, drop rate 0 bps
      Match: protocol rtp payload-type 4
            protocol rtp payload-type 34
      QoS Set
        ip dscp 34
            Packets marked 817

! omitting stanza of output for class http-impo
! omitting stanza of output for class http-not

    Class-map: class-default (match-all)
      33216 packets, 43649458 bytes
      5 minute offered rate    747000 bps, drop rate 0 bps
      Match: any
      QoS Set
        ip dscp 0
Packets marked 33301
```

Example 12-3 includes several different classification options using the **match** command, including the matching of Microsoft NetMeeting traffic. NetMeeting uses RTP for the video flows, and by default uses G.723 for audio and H.323 for video. To match both the audio and video for NetMeeting, a class map that matches either of the two RTP payload subtypes for G.723 and H.263 is needed. So, class map **NetMeet** uses match-any logic, and matches on RTP payload types 4 (G.723) and 34 (H.263). (For more background information on RTP payload types, refer to http://www.cisco.com/en/US/products/ps6616/products_white_paper09186a0080110040.shtml.)

The **show policy-map interface** command provides statistical information about the number of packets and bytes that have matched each class in the policy maps. The generic syntax is as follows:

```
show policy-map interface interface-name [vc [vpi/] vci] [dlci dlci] [input | output]
[class class-name]
```

The end of Example 12-3 shows a sample of the command, which lists statistics for marking. If other MQC-based QoS features were configured, statistics for those features would also be displayed. As you see from the generic command, the **show policy-map interface** command allows you to select just one interface, either input or output, and even select a single class inside a single policy map for display.

The **load-interval** interface subcommand can also be useful when looking at any QoS tool's statistics. The **load-interval** command defines the time interval over which IOS measures packet and bit rates on an interface. With a lower load interval, the statistics change more quickly; with a larger load interval, the statistics change more slowly. The default setting is 5 minutes, and it can be lowered to 30 seconds.

Example 12-3 also shows a common oversight with QoS configuration. Note that the first class in **policy-map laundry-list** is **class voip-rtp**. Because that class map matches all RTP audio, it matches the Microsoft NetMeeting audio stream as well, so the NetMeeting audio is not matched by class **NetMeet** that follows. If the first two classes (**voip-rtp** and **NetMeet**) called in the policy map had been reversed, then the NetMeeting audio would have been correctly matched in the **NetMeet** class, and all other audio would have been marked as part of the **voip-rtp** class.

CB Marking of CoS and DSCP

Example 12-4 shows how a router might be configured for CB Marking when an attached LAN switch is performing QoS based on CoS. In this case, R3 looks at frames coming in its fa0/0 interface, marking the DSCP values based on the incoming CoS settings. Additionally, R3 looks at the DSCP settings for packets exiting its fa0/0 interface toward the switch, setting the CoS values in the 802.1Q header. The actual values used on R3's fa0/0 interface for classification and marking are as follows:

- Frames entering with CoS 5 will be marked with DSCP EF.

- Frames entering with CoS 1 will be marked with DSCP AF11.

- Frames entering with any other CoS will be marked DSCP 0.

- Packets exiting with DSCP EF will be marked with CoS 5.

- Packets exiting with DSCP AF11 will be marked with CoS 1.

- Packets exiting with any other DSCP will be marked with CoS 0.

Example 12-4 *Marking DSCP Based on Incoming CoS, and Vice Versa*

```
! The class maps each simply match a single CoS or DSCP value.
class-map cos1
 match cos 1
!
class-map cos5
 match cos 5
!
class-map AF11
 match dscp af11
!
class-map EF
 match dscp EF
! This policy map will map incoming CoS to a DSCP value
policy-map map-cos-to-dscp
 class cos1
  set DSCP af11
 class cos5
  set ip DSCP EF
 class class-default
   set ip dscp default
! This policy map will map incoming DSCP to outgoing CoS. Note that the DSCP
! value is not changed.
policy-map map-dscp-to-cos
 class AF11
  set cos 1
 class EF
  set cos 5
 class class-default
   set cos 0
!!!!!!!!!!!!!!!!!!!!!!!!!!!!!!!!!!!!!!!!!!!!!!!!!!!!!!!!!!!!!!!!!!!!!!!!!!!!!!!!!!!!
! The policy maps are applied to an 802.1q subinterface.
interface FastEthernet0/0.1
 encapsulation dot1Q 102
 service-policy input map-cos-to-dscp
 service-policy output map-dscp-to-cos
!
interface FastEthernet0/0.2
 encapsulation dot1Q 2 native
```

The QoS policy requires two policy maps in this example. Policy map **map-cos-to-dscp** matches CoS values for frames entering R3's fa0/0.1 interface, and marks DSCP values, for packets flowing right to left in Figure 12-5. Therefore, the policy map is enabled on input of R3's fa0/0.1 interface. Policy map **map-dscp-to-cos** matches DSCP values for packets exiting R3's fa0/0.1 interface, and marks the corresponding CoS value. Therefore, the policy map was enabled on the output of R3's fa0/0.1 interface. Neither policy map could be applied on the WAN interface, because only interfaces configured for 802.1Q accept **service-policy** commands that reference policy maps that either classify or mark based on CoS.

Note that you cannot enable a **policy-map** that refers to CoS on interface fa0/0.2 in this example. That subinterface is in the native VLAN, meaning that no 802.1Q header is used.

Network-Based Application Recognition

CB Marking can make use of NBAR's powerful classification capabilities via the **match protocol** subcommand. Example 12-5 shows a configuration for CB Marking and NBAR in which the following requirements are met:

- Any HTTP traffic whose URL contains the string "important" anywhere in the URL is marked with AF21.

- Any HTTP traffic whose URL contains the string "not-so" anywhere in the URL is marked with DSCP default.

- All other traffic is marked with AF11.

Example 12-5 shows the configuration, along with a few NBAR-related **show** commands.

Example 12-5 *CB Marking Based on URLs, Using NBAR for Classification*

```
ip cef
! The "*" in the url string is a wildcard meaning "0 or more characters."
class-map http-impo
    match protocol http url "*important*"
class-map http-not
    match protocol http url "*not-so*"
! The policy map lists the three classes in order, setting the DSCP values.
policy-map http
 class http-impo
  set dscp AF21
!
 class http-not
  set dscp default
!
 class class-default
  set DSCP AF11
! The ip nbar protocol discovery command may or may not be required—see the notes
! following this example.
interface fastethernet 0/0
 ip nbar protocol-discovery
 service-policy input http
! The show ip nbar command only displays statistics if the ip nbar
! protocol-discovery command is applied to an interface. These statistics are
```

continues

Example 12-5 *CB Marking Based on URLs, Using NBAR for Classification (Continued)*

```
! independent of those created by CB Marking. This example shows several of
! the large number of options on the command.
R3# show ip nbar protocol-discovery interface fastethernet 0/0 stats packet-count top-n 5
 FastEthernet0/0
                           Input                   Output
    Protocol               Packet Count            Packet Count
 ----------------------- ----------------------- -----------------------
    http                   721                     428
    eigrp                  635                     0
    netbios                199                     0
    icmp                   1                       1
    bgp                    0                       0
    unknown                46058                   63
    Total                  47614                   492
```

NOTE   Before the 12.2T/12.3 IOS releases, the **ip nbar protocol-discovery** command was required on an interface before using a **service-policy** command that used NBAR matching. With 12.2T/12.3 train releases, this command is no longer required.

The use of the **match protocol** command implies that NBAR will be used to match the packet.

Unlike most other IOS features, you can upgrade NBAR without changing to a later IOS version. Cisco uses a feature called *Packet Description Language Modules (PDLMs)* to define new protocols that NBAR should match. When Cisco decides to add one or more new protocols to the list of protocols that NBAR should recognize, it creates and compiles a PDLM. You can then download the PDLM from Cisco, copy it into Flash memory, and add the **ip nbar pdlm** *pdlm-name* command to the configuration, where *pdlm-name* is the name of the PDLM file in Flash memory. NBAR can then classify based on the protocol information from the new PDLM.

CB Marking Design Choices

The intent of CB Marking is to simplify the work required of other QoS tools by marking packets of the same class with the same QoS marking. For other QoS tools to take advantage of those markings, packets should generally be marked as close to the ingress point of the packet as possible. However, the earliest possible point may not be a trusted device. For instance, in Figure 12-5 (the figure upon which Examples 12-3 and 12-4 are based), Server1 could set its own DSCP and even CoS if its NIC supported trunking. However, trusting the server administrator may or may not be desirable. So, the following rule summarizes how to choose the best location to perform marking:

Mark as close to the ingress edge of the network as possible, but not so close to the edge that the marking is made by an untrusted device.

Cisco QoS design guide documents make recommendations not only as to where to perform marking, but also as to which CoS, IPP, and DSCP values to set for certain types of traffic. Table 12-9 summarizes those recommendations.

Table 12-9 *RFC-Recommended Values for Marking*

Type of Traffic	CoS	IPP	DSCP
Voice payload	5	5	EF
Video payload	4	4	AF41
Voice/video signaling	3	3	CS3
Mission-critical data	3	3	AF31, AF32, AF33
Transactional data	2	2	AF21, AF22, AF23
Bulk data	1	1	AF11, AF12, AF13
Best effort	0	0	BE
Scavenger (less than best effort)	0	0	2, 4,6

Also note that Cisco recommends not to use more than four or five different service classes for data traffic. By using more classes, the difference in behavior between the various classes tends to blur. For the same reason, do not give too many data service classes high-priority service.

Marking Using Policers

Traffic policers measure the traffic rate for data entering or exiting an interface, with the goal of determining if a configured *traffic contract* has been exceeded. The contract has two components: a *traffic rate*, configured in bits/second, and a *burst size*, configured as a number of bytes. If the traffic is within the contract, all packets are considered to have *conformed* to the contract. However, if the rate or burst exceeds the contract, then some packets are considered to have *exceeded* the contract. QoS actions can be taken on both categories of traffic.

The simplest form of policing enforces the traffic contract strictly by forwarding conforming packets and discarding packets that exceed the contract. However, both IOS policers allow a compromise action in which the policer *marks down* packets instead of dropping them. To mark down the packet, the policer re-marks a QoS field, typically IPP or DSCP, with a value that makes the packet more likely to be discarded downstream. For instance, a policer could re-mark AF11 packets that exceed a contract with a new DSCP value of AF13, but not discard the packet. By doing so, the packet still passes through the router, but if the packet experiences congestion later in its travels, it is more likely to be discarded than it would have otherwise been. (Remember, DiffServ suggests that AF13 is more likely to be discarded than AF11 traffic.)

When marking requirements can be performed by using CB Marking, CB Marking should be used instead of either policer. However, if a requirement exists to mark packets based on whether they conform to a traffic contract, marking with policers must be used. Chapter 14, "Shaping and Policing," covers CB policing, with an example of the syntax it uses for marking packets.

QoS Pre-Classification

With unencrypted, unencapsulated traffic, routers can match and mark QoS values, and perform ingress and egress actions based on markings, by inspecting the IP headers. However, what happens if the traffic is encrypted? If we encapsulate traffic inside a VPN tunnel, the original headers and packet contents are unavailable for inspection. The only thing we have to work with is the ToS byte of the original packet, which is automatically copied to the tunnel header (in IPsec transport mode, in tunnel mode, and in GRE tunnels) when the packet is encapsulated. But features like NBAR are broken when we are dealing with encapsulated traffic.

The issue that arises from this inherent behavior of tunnel encapsulation is the inability of a router to take egress QoS actions based on encrypted traffic. To mitigate this limitation, Cisco IOS includes a feature called QoS pre-classification. This feature can be enabled on VPN endpoint routers to permit the router to make egress QoS decisions based on the original traffic, before encapsulation, rather than just the encapsulating tunnel header. QoS pre-classification works by keeping the original, unencrypted traffic in memory until the egress QoS actions are taken.

You can enable QoS pre-classification in tunnel interface configuration mode, virtual-template configuration mode, or crypto map configuration mode by issuing the **qos pre-classify** command. You can view the effects of pre-classification using several **show** commands, which include **show interface** and **show crypto-map**.

Table 12-10 lists the modes in which you apply the **qos pre-classify** command.

Table 12-10 *Where to Use the* **qos pre-classify** *Command*

Configuration Command Under Which qos pre-classify Is Configured	VPN Type
interface tunnel	GRE and IPIP
interface virtual-template	L2F and L2TP
crypto map	IPsec

Policy Routing for Marking

Policy routing provides the capability to route a packet based on information in the packet besides the destination IP address. The policy routing configuration uses route maps to classify packets. The **route-map** clauses include **set** commands that define the route (based on setting a next-hop IP address or outgoing interface).

Policy routing can also mark the IPP field, or the entire ToS byte, using the **set** command in a route map. When using policy routing for marking purposes, the following logic sequence is used:

1. Packets are examined as they enter an interface.

2. A route map is used to match subsets of the packets.

3. Mark either the IPP or entire ToS byte using the **set** command.

4. The traditional policy routing function of using the **set** command to define the route may also be configured, but it is not required.

Policy routing should be used to mark packets only in cases where CB Marking is not available, or when a router needs to both use policy routing and mark packets entering the same interface. Refer to Chapter 6, "IP Forwarding (Routing)," for a review of policy routing configuration, and note the syntax of the **set** commands for marking, listed in Table 6-5.

Foundation Summary

This section lists additional details and facts to round out the coverage of the topics in this chapter. Unlike most of the Cisco Press *Exam Certification Guides*, this "Foundation Summary" does not repeat information presented in the "Foundation Topics" section of the chapter. Please take the time to read and study the details in the "Foundation Topics" section of the chapter, as well as review items noted with a Key Topic icon.

Table 12-11 lists the various **match** commands that can be used for MQC tools like CB Marking.

Table 12-11 **match** *Configuration Command Reference for MQC Tools*

Command	Function
match [ip] precedence *precedence-value* [*precedence-value precedence-value precedence-value*]	Matches precedence in IPv4 packets when the **ip** parameter is included; matches IPv4 and IPv6 packets when **ip** parameter is missing.
match access-group {*access-group* | **name** *access-group-name*}	Matches an ACL by number or name.
match any	Matches all packets.
match class-map *class-map-name*	Matches based on another class map.
match cos *cos-value* [*cos-value cos-value cos-value*]	Matches a CoS value.
match destination-address mac *address*	Matches a destination MAC address.
match fr-dlci *dlci-number*	Matches a particular Frame Relay DLCI.
match input-interface *interface-name*	Matches an ingress interface.
match ip dscp *ip-dscp-value* [*ip-dscp-value ip-dscp- value ip-dscp-value ip-dscp-value ip-dscp-value ip- dscp-value ip-dscp-value*]	Matches DSCP in IPv4 packets when the **ip** parameter is included; matches IPv4 and IPv6 packets when the **ip** parameter is missing.
match ip rtp *starting-port-number port-range*	Matches the RTP's UDP port-number range, even values only.
match mpls experimental *number*	Matches an MPLS Experimental value.
match mpls experimental topmost *value*	When multiple labels are in use, matches the MPLS EXP field in the topmost label.

continues

Table 12-11   **match** *Configuration Command Reference for MQC Tools (Continued)*

Command	Function
match not *match-criteria*	Reverses the matching logic. In other words, things matched by the matching criteria do *not* match the class map.
match packet length {**max** *maximum-length-value* [**min** *minimum-length-value*] | **min** *minimum-length-value* [**max** *maximum-length-value*]}	Matches packets based on the minimum length, maximum length, or both.
match protocol citrix app *application-name-string*	Matches NBAR Citrix applications.
match protocol http [**url** *url-string* | **host** *hostname- string* | **mime** *MIME-type*]	Matches a host name, URL string, or MIME type.
match protocol *protocol-name*	Matches NBAR protocol types.
match protocol rtp [**audio** | **video** | **payload-type** *payload-string*]	Matches RTP audio or video payload, based on the payload type. Also allows explicitly specifying payload types.
match qos-group *qos-group-value*	Matches a QoS group.
match source-address mac *address-destination*	Matches a source MAC address.

Table 12-12 lists the RFCs related to DiffServ.

Table 12-12   *DiffServ RFCs*

RFC	Title	Comments
2474	Definition of the Differentiated Services Field (DS Field) in the IPv4 and IPv6 Headers	Contains the details of the 6-bit DSCP field in IP header
2475	An Architecture for Differentiated Service	The core DiffServ conceptual document
2597	Assured Forwarding PHB Group	Defines a set of 12 DSCP values and a convention for their use
2598	An Expedited Forwarding PHB	Defines a single DSCP value as a convention for use as a low-latency class
3260	New Terminology and Clarifications for DiffServ	Clarifies, but does not supersede, existing DiffServ RFCs

Memory Builders

The CCIE Routing and Switching written exam, like all Cisco CCIE written exams, covers a fairly broad set of topics. This section provides some basic tools to help you exercise your memory about some of the broader topics covered in this chapter.

Fill in Key Tables from Memory

Appendix E, "Key Tables for CCIE Study," on the CD in the back of this book contains empty sets of some of the key summary tables in each chapter. Print Appendix E, refer to this chapter's tables in it, and fill in the tables from memory. Refer to Appendix F, "Solutions for Key Tables for CCIE Study," on the CD to check your answers.

Definitions

Next, take a few moments to write down the definitions for the following terms:

IP Precedence, ToS byte, Differentiated Services, DS field, Per-Hop Behavior, Assured Forwarding, Expedited Forwarding, Class Selector, Class of Service, Differentiated Services Code Point, User Priority, Discard Eligible, Cell Loss Priority, MPLS Experimental bits, class map, policy map, service policy, Modular QoS CLI, Class-Based Marking, Network Based Application Recognition, QoS preclassification

Refer to the glossary to check your answers.

Further Reading

Cisco QoS Exam Certification Guide, by Wendell Odom and Michael Cavanaugh

The *Enterprise QoS SRND Guide*, posted at http://www.cisco.com/en/US/netsol/ns656/networking_solutions_program_home.html, provides great background and details for real-life QoS deployments.

Blueprint topics covered in this chapter:

This chapter covers the following subtopics from the Cisco CCIE Routing and Switching written exam blueprint. Refer to the full blueprint in Table I-1 in the Introduction for more details on the topics covered in each chapter and their context within the blueprint.

- Class-Based Weighted Fair Queuing (CBWFQ)

- Random Early Detection (RED)

- Modified Deficit Round-Robin (MDRR)

CHAPTER 13

Congestion Management and Avoidance

Congestion management, commonly called *queuing*, refers to how a router or switch manages packets or frames while they wait to exit a device. With routers, the waiting occurs when IP forwarding has been completed, so the queuing is always considered to be output queuing. LAN switches often support both output queuing and input queuing, where input queuing is used for received frames that are waiting to be switched to the switch's output interfaces.

Congestion avoidance refers to the logic used when deciding if and when packets should be dropped as a queuing system becomes more congested. This chapter covers a wide variety of Cisco IOS queuing tools, along with the most pervasive congestion avoidance tool, namely weighted random early detection (WRED).

"Do I Know This Already?" Quiz

Table 13-1 outlines the major headings in this chapter and the corresponding "Do I Know This Already?" quiz questions.

Table 13-1 *"Do I Know This Already?" Foundation Topics Section-to-Question Mapping*

Foundation Topics Section	Questions Covered in This Section	Score
Cisco Router Queuing Concepts	1	
Queuing Tools: CBWFQ and LLQ	2–3	
Weighted Random Early Detection	4–5	
Modified Deficit Round-Robin	6	
LAN Switch Congestion Management and Avoidance	7–8	
Total Score		

In order to best use this pre-chapter assessment, remember to score yourself strictly. You can find the answers in Appendix A, "Answers to the 'Do I Know This Already?' Quizzes."

1. What is the main benefit of the hardware queue on a Cisco router interface?

   a. Prioritizes latency-sensitive packets so that they are always scheduled next

   b. Reserves a minimum amount of bandwidth for particular classes of traffic

   c. Provides a queue in which to hold a packet so that, as soon as the interface is available to send another packet, the packet can be sent without requiring an interrupt to the router CPU

   d. Allows configuration of a percentage of the remaining link bandwidth, after allocating bandwidth to the LLQ and the class-default queue

2. Examine the following configuration snippet. If a new class, called class3, is added to the policy map, which of the following commands could be used to reserve 25 kbps of bandwidth for the class?

   ```
   policy-map fred
    class class1
     priority 20
    class class2
     bandwidth 30
    !
    interface serial 0/0
     bandwidth 100
     service-policy output fred
   ```

   a. **priority 25**

   b. **bandwidth 25**

   c. **bandwidth percent 25**

   d. **bandwidth remaining-percent 25**

3. Examine the following configuration snippet. How much bandwidth does Cisco IOS assign to class2?

   ```
   policy-map fred
    class class1
     priority percent 20
    class class2
     bandwidth remaining percent 20
    interface serial 0/0
     bandwidth 100
     service-policy output fred
   ```

   a. 10 kbps

   b. 11 kbps

   c. 20 kbps

   d. 21 kbps

   e. Not enough information to tell

4. Which of the following impacts the percentage of packet discards when using WRED, when the current average queue depth is between the minimum and maximum thresholds?

   a. The **bandwidth** command setting on the interface

   b. The mark probability denominator (MPD)

   c. The exponential weighting constant

   d. The congestive discard threshold

5. Which of the following commands, under an interface like s0/0, would enable WRED and tell it to use IP Precedence (IPP) when choosing its default traffic profiles?

   a. **random-detect**

   b. **random-detect precedence-based**

   c. **random-detect dscp-based**

   d. **random-detect precedence 1 20 30 40**

6. On a Catalyst 3550 switch, interface fa0/1 has been configured for WRR scheduling, and fa0/2 has been configured for WRR scheduling with an expedite queue. Which of the following is true regarding interface fa0/2?

   a. It must be configured with the **priority-queue out** command.

   b. The last parameter (*w4*) of the **wrr-queue bandwidth** *w1 w2 w3 w4* command must be 0.

   c. Only CoS 5 frames can be placed into queue 1, the expedite queue.

   d. Only DSCP EF frames can be placed into queue 4, the expedite queue.

7. In modified deficit round-robin, what is the function of QV?

   a. Sets the ratio of bandwidth to be sent from each queue on each pass through the queues

   b. Sets the absolute bandwidth for each queue on each pass through the queues

   c. Sets the number of bytes removed from each queue on each pass through the queues

   d. Identifies the MDRR priority queue

8. The Cisco 3560 switch uses SRR and WTD for its queuing and congestion management methods. How many ingress queues and egress queues can be configured on each port of a 3560 switch, and how many priority queues are configurable on ingress and egress?

   a. One ingress queue, four egress queues; one priority queue on each side

   b. One ingress queue, four egress queues; one priority queue on the egress side

   c. Two ingress queues, four egress queues; one priority queue on the egress side

   d. Two ingress queues, four egress queues; one priority queue on each side

Cisco Router Queuing Concepts

Cisco routers can be configured to perform *fancy queuing* for packets that are waiting to exit an interface. For instance, if a router receives 5 Mbps of traffic every second for the next several seconds, and all that traffic needs to exit a T1 serial link, the router can't forward all the traffic. So, the router places the packets into one or more *software queues*, which can then be managed—thus impacting which packets get to leave next and which packets might be discarded.

Software Queues and Hardware Queues

Although many network engineers already understand queuing, many overlook some of the details behind the concepts of a hardware queue and a software queue associated with each physical interface. The queues created on an interface by the popularly known queuing tools are called *software queues*, as these queues are implemented in software. However, when the queuing scheduler picks the next packet to take from the software queues, the packet does not move directly out the interface. Instead, the router moves the packet from the interface software queue to a small hardware FIFO (first-in, first-out) queue on each interface. Cisco calls this separate, final queue either the *transmit queue* (TX queue) or *transmit ring* (TX ring), depending on the model of the router; generically, these queues are called *hardware queues*.

Hardware queues provide the following features:

- When an interface finishes sending a packet, the next packet from the hardware queue can be encoded and sent out the interface, without requiring a software interrupt to the CPU—ensuring full use of interface bandwidth.

- Always use FIFO logic.

- Cannot be affected by IOS queuing tools.

- IOS automatically shrinks the length of the hardware queue to a smaller length than the default when a queuing tool is present.

- Short hardware queue lengths mean packets are more likely to be in the controllable software queues, giving the software queuing more control of the traffic leaving the interface.

The only function of a hardware queue that can be manipulated is the length of the queue. Example 13-1 shows how to see the current length of the queue and how to change the length.

Example 13-1 *TX Queue Length: Finding and Changing the Length*

```
! The example begins with only FIFO queuing on the interface. For this
! router, it defaults to a TX queue length 16.
R3# show controllers serial 0/0
Interface Serial0/0
! about 30 lines omitted for brevity
tx_limited=0(16)
! lines omitted for brevity
! Next, the TX ring is set to length 1.
! (The smallest recommended value is 2.)
R3# conf t
Enter configuration commands, one per line.  End with CNTL/Z.
R3(config)# int s 0/0
R3(config-if)# tx-ring-limit 1
R3(config-if)# ^Z
```

Queuing on Interfaces Versus Subinterfaces and Virtual Circuits

IOS queuing tools can create and manage software queues associated with a physical interface, and then the packets drain into the hardware queue associated with the interface. Additionally, queuing tools can be used in conjunction with traffic shaping. Traffic-shaping tools delay packets to ensure that a class of packets does not exceed a defined traffic rate. While delaying the packets, the shaping function queues the packets—by default in a FIFO queue. Depending on the type of shaping tool in use, various queuing tools can be configured to manage the packets delayed by the shaping tool.

Chapter 14, "Shaping and Policing," covers traffic shaping, including how to use queuing tools with shapers. The queuing coverage in this chapter focuses on the implementation of software queuing tools directly on the physical interface.

Comparing Queuing Tools

Cisco IOS provides a wide variety of queuing tools. The upcoming sections of this chapter describe several different IOS queuing tools, with a brief summary ending the section on queuing. Table 13-2 summarizes the main characteristics of different queuing tools that you will want to keep in mind while comparing each successive queuing tool.

Table 13-2 *Key Comparison Points for Queuing Tools*

Key
Topic

Feature	Definition
Classification	The ability to look at packet headers to choose the right queue for each packet
Drop policy	The rules used to choose which packets to drop as queues begin to fill

continues

Table 13-2 *Key Comparison Points for Queuing Tools (Continued)*

Feature	Definition
Scheduling	The logic used to determine which packet should be dequeued next
Maximum number of queues	The number of unique classes of packets for a queuing tool
Maximum queue length	The maximum number of packets in a single queue

Queuing Tools: CBWFQ and LLQ

This section hits the highlights of the modern queuing tools in Cisco IOS and covers detailed configuration for the more popular tools—specifically class-based weighted fair queuing (CBWFQ) and low-latency queuing (LLQ). Because the CCIE Routing and Switching exam blueprint no longer includes the priority queuing (PQ) and custom queuing (CQ) legacy queuing methods, they are not covered in this book. Furthermore, WFQ is covered only in the context of CBWFQ and not as a standalone feature.

Cisco created CBWFQ and LLQ using some of the best concepts from the legacy queuing methods PQ and CQ, as well as WFQ, while adding several additional features. CBWFQ reserves bandwidth for each queue, and provides the ability to use WFQ concepts for packets in the default (class-default) queue. LLQ adds to CBWFQ the concept of a priority queue, but unlike legacy PQ, LLQ prevents the high-priority queue from starving other queues. Additionally, both CBWFQ and LLQ use MQC for configuration, which means that they have robust classification options, including NBAR.

CBWFQ and LLQ use almost identical configuration; the one major difference is whether the **bandwidth** command (CBWFQ) or the **priority** command (LLQ) is used to configure the tool. Because both tools use MQC, both use class maps for classification and policy maps to create a set of classes to be used on an interface. The classes defined in the policy map each define a single queue; as a result, the terms *queue* and *class* are often used interchangeably when working with LLQ and CBWFQ.

CBWFQ and LLQ support 64 queues/classes. The maximum queue length can be changed, with the maximum possible value and the default length varying based on the model of router and the amount of memory installed. They both also have one special queue called the *class-default queue*. This queue exists even if it is not configured. If a packet does not match any of the explicitly configured classes in a policy map, IOS places the packet into the class-default class/queue. CBWFQ settings can be configured for the class-default queue.

The sections that follow cover the details of CBWFQ and then LLQ.

CBWFQ Basic Features and Configuration

The CBWFQ scheduler guarantees a minimum percentage of a link's bandwidth to each class/ queue. If all queues have a large number of packets, each queue gets the percentage bandwidth implied by the configuration. However, if some queues are empty and do not need their bandwidth for a short period, the bandwidth is proportionally allocated across the other classes. (Cisco does not publish the details of how CBWFQ achieves these functions.)

Table 13-3 summarizes some of the key features of CBWFQ.

Table 13-3   *CBWFQ Functions and Features*

CBWFQ Feature	Description
Classification	Classifies based on anything that MQC commands can match
Drop policy	Tail drop or WRED, configurable per queue
Number of queues	64
Maximum queue length	Varies based on router model and memory
Scheduling inside a single queue	FIFO on 63 queues; FIFO or WFQ on class-default queue[1]
Scheduling among all queues	Result of the scheduler provides a percentage of guaranteed bandwidth to each queue

[1] Cisco 7500 series routers support FIFO or WFQ in all the CBWFQ queues.

Table 13-4 lists the key CBWFQ commands that were not covered in Chapter 12, "Classification and Marking."

Table 13-4   *Command Reference for CBWFQ*

Command	Mode and Function
bandwidth {*bandwidth-kbps* | **percent** *percent*}	Class subcommand; sets literal or percentage bandwidth for the class
bandwidth {**remaining percent** *percent*}	Class subcommand; sets percentage of remaining bandwidth for the class
queue-limit *queue-limit*	Class subcommand; sets the maximum length of a CBWFQ queue
fair-queue [**queue-limit** *queue-value*]	Class subcommand; enables WFQ in the class (class-default only)
max-reserved-bandwidth *percent*	Interface subcommand; defines the percentage of link bandwidth that can be reserved for CBWFQ queues besides class-default (default: 75 percent)

Example 13-2 shows a simple CBWFQ configuration that uses the class-default queue. The configuration was created on R3 in Figure 13-1, using the following requirements:

■ All VoIP payload traffic is placed in a queue.

■ All other traffic is placed in another queue.

■ Give the VoIP traffic 50 percent of the bandwidth.

■ WFQ should be used on the non-VoIP traffic.

Figure 13-1 *Network Used with CBWFQ and LLQ Configuration Examples*

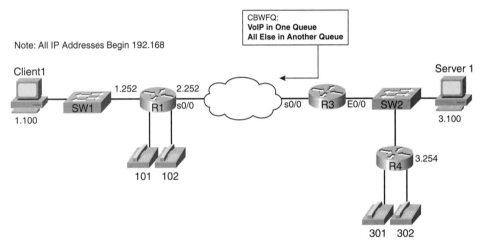

Example 13-2 *CBWFQ with VoIP in One Queue, Everything Else in Class-Default*

```
! The class map matches on UDP/RTP header and RTP port numbers.
class-map match-all voip-rtp
  match ip rtp 16384 16383
! Next, the policy map uses the bandwidth command to reserve 64 kbps for the class
! voip-rtp. Class-default gets some of the leftover bandwidth by default.
policy-map queue-voip
  class voip-rtp
   bandwidth 64
  class class-default
   fair-queue
! The interface's bandwidth 128 command is used as the basis for the limit on the
! amount of bandwidth that can be allocated in the policy map queue-voip.
! The load-interval command sets how often counters are updated. Also, note
! that the policy-map is enabled for output; input is not allowed on routers for
! policy maps that perform queuing.
interface Serial0/0
```

Example 13-2 *CBWFQ with VoIP in One Queue, Everything Else in Class-Default (Continued)*

```
encapsulation frame-relay
load-interval 30
bandwidth 128
service-policy output queue-voip
! This command lists counters, reserved bandwidth, maximum queue length (listed
! as max threshold), and a reminder that WFQ is used in the class-default queue.
R3# show policy-map int s 0/0
 Serial0/0

  Service-policy output:    queue-voip


    Class-map: voip-rtp (match-all)
       136435 packets, 8731840 bytes
       30 second offered rate 51000 bps, drop rate 0 bps
      Match:    ip rtp 16384 16383
      Weighted Fair Queueing
        Output Queue: Conversation 265
        Bandwidth 64 (kbps) Max Threshold 64 (packets)
        (pkts matched/bytes matched) 48550/3107200
        (depth/total drops/no-buffer drops) 14/0/0


    Class-map: class-default (match-any)
       1958 packets, 1122560 bytes
       30 second offered rate 59000 bps, drop rate 0 bps
      Match: any
      Weighted Fair Queueing
        Flow Based Fair Queueing
        Maximum Number of Hashed Queues 256
        (total queued/total drops/no-buffer drops) 15/0/0
! This command just lists the configuration in a concise manner.
R3# show policy-map
  Policy Map queue-voip
    Class voip-rtp
      Weighted Fair Queueing
            Bandwidth 64 (kbps) Max Threshold 64 (packets)
    Class class-default
      Weighted Fair Queueing
Flow based Fair Queueing Max Threshold 64 (packets)
```

Defining and Limiting CBWFQ Bandwidth

Cisco IOS checks a CBWFQ policy map to ensure that it does not allocate too much bandwidth. IOS performs the check when the **service-policy output** command is added; if the policy map defines too much bandwidth for that interface, the **service-policy** command is rejected. IOS defines the allowed bandwidth based on two interface subcommands: the **bandwidth** command and the reserved bandwidth implied by the **max-reserved-bandwidth** command (abbreviated hereafter as **int-bw** and **max-res,** respectively). The nonreservable bandwidth is meant for overhead traffic, much like CQ's system queue.

IOS allows a policy map to allocate bandwidth based on the product of **int-bw** and **max-res**. In other words, with a default max-res setting of 75 (75 percent), on an interface with **int-bw** of 256 (256 kbps), the policy map could allocate at most 192 kbps of bandwidth with its various **bandwidth** commands. Example 13-3 shows a simple example with a policy map that contains one class that has 64 kbps configured. The **service-policy** command is rejected on an interface whose bandwidth is set to 64 kbps.

Example 13-3   *CBWFQ Rejected Due to Request for Too Much Bandwidth*

```
! max-res was defaulted to 75, so only 75% of 64 kbps, or 48 kbps,
! is available. Note that the 48 kbps is mentioned in the error message.
R3(config-cmap)# policy-map explicit-bw
R3(config-pmap)# class class1
R3(config-pmap-c)# bandwidth 64
R3(config-pmap-c)# int s 0/1
R3(config-if)# bandwidth 64
R3(config-if)# service-policy output explicit-bw
I/f Serial0/1 class class1 requested bandwidth 64 (kbps), available only 48 (kbps)
```

To overcome such problems, the engineer can simply pay attention to details and ensure that the policy map's configured **bandwidth** commands do not total more than **max-res** × **int-bw**. Alternatively, **max-res** can be defined to a higher number, up to a value of 100; however, Cisco does not recommend changing **max-res**.

The bandwidths can also be defined as percentages using either the **bandwidth percent** or **bandwidth remaining percent** command. By using percentages, it is easier to ensure that a policy map does not attempt to allocate too much bandwidth.

The two percentage-based **bandwidth** command options work in slightly different ways. Figure 13-2 shows the concept for each.

Figure 13-2 *Bandwidth Percent and Bandwidth Remaining Percent Concepts*

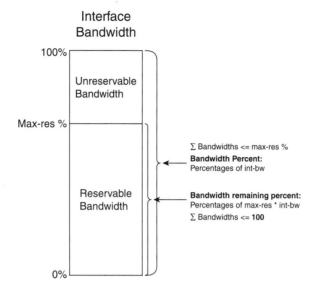

The **bandwidth percent** *bw-percent* command sets a class's reserved bandwidth as a percentage of **int-bw**. For instance, in Example 13-2, if the **bandwidth percent 50** command had been used instead of **bandwidth 64**, the voip-rtp class would have used 50% × 128 kbps, or 64 kbps. IOS checks all the **bandwidth percent** commands in a single policy map to ensure that the total does not exceed the **max-res** setting for the interface—in other words, with a default setting for **max-res**, all the **bandwidth percent** commands in a single policy map cannot total more than 75.

The **bandwidth remaining percent** *bw-percent* command sets a class's reserved bandwidth as a percentage of remaining bandwidth. *Remaining bandwidth* is the reservable bandwidth, calculated as **int-bw** × **max-res**. This method allows a policy map to allocate percentages that total 100 12(100 percent). Using Example 13-2 again, the remaining bandwidth would be 75% × 128 kbps, or
96 kbps, and the command **bandwidth remaining percent 50** would allocate 48 kbps for a class.

> **NOTE**   Using the **bandwidth remaining percent** command is particularly useful with LLQ and will be explained in that context later in the chapter. The reason is that the remaining bandwidth calculation is changed by the addition of LLQ.

Note that in a single policy map, only one of the three variations of the **bandwidth** command can be used. Table 13-5 summarizes the three methods for reserving bandwidth with CBWFQ.

Table 13-5 *Reference for CBWFQ Bandwidth Reservation*

Method	Amount of Bandwidth Reserved by the bandwidth Command	The Sum of Values in a Single Policy Map Must Be <= …
Explicit bandwidth	As listed in commands	**max-res** × **int-bw**
Percent	A percentage of the **int-bw**	**max-res** setting
Remaining percent	A percentage of the reservable bandwidth (**int-bw** × **max-res**)	100

Low-Latency Queuing

Low-latency queuing sounds like the best queuing tool possible, just based on the name. What packet wouldn't want to experience low latency? As it turns out, for delay (latency) sensitive traffic, LLQ is indeed the queuing tool of choice. LLQ looks and acts just like CBWFQ in most regards, except it adds the capability for some queues to be configured as low-latency queues. LLQ schedules these specific queues as strict-priority queues. In other words, LLQ always services packets in these priority queues first.

LLQ lingo can sometimes be used in a couple of different ways. With a single policy map that has at least one low-latency queue, the policy map might be considered to be implementing LLQ, while at the same time, that one low-latency queue is often called "the LLQ." Sometimes, a single low-latency queue is even called "the PQ" as a reference to the legacy PQ-like behavior, or even a "priority queue."

While LLQ adds a low-latency queue to CBWFQ, it also prevents the queue starvation that occurs with legacy PQ. LLQ actually *polices* the PQ based on the configured bandwidth. In effect, the bandwidth given to an LLQ priority queue is both the guaranteed minimum and policed maximum. (You may recall from Chapter 12, that the DiffServ Expedited Forwarding PHB formally defines the priority queuing and policing PHBs.) As a result, the packets that make it out of the queue experience low latency, but some may be discarded to prevent starving the other queues.

Figure 13-3 depicts the scheduler logic for LLQ. Note that the PQ logic is shown, but with the policer check as well.

Figure 13-3 *LLQ Scheduler Logic*

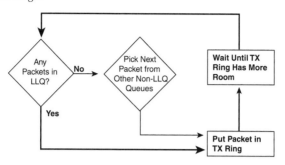

LLQ configuration requires one more command in addition to the commands used for CBWFQ configuration. Instead of using the **bandwidth** command on a class, use the **priority** command:

```
priority {bandwidth-kbps | percent percentage} [burst]
```

This **class** subcommand enables LLQ in the class, reserves bandwidth, and enables the policing function. You can also configure the burst size for the policer with this command, but the default setting of 20 percent of the configured bandwidth is typically a reasonable choice.

Example 13-4 shows a sample LLQ configuration, using the following criteria. Like Example 13-2, the LLQ policy is applied to R3's s0/0 interface from Figure 13-1:

- R3's s0/0 bandwidth is 128 kbps.

- Packets will already have been marked with good DSCP values.

- VoIP payload is already marked DSCP EF and should be LLQed with 58 kbps of bandwidth.

- AF41, AF21, and AF23 traffic should get 22, 20, and 8 kbps, respectively.

- All other traffic should be placed into class class-default, which should use WRED and WFQ.

Example 13-4 *LLQ for EF, CBWFQ for AF41, AF21, AF23, and All Else*

```
! The class maps used by the queue-on-dscp are not shown, but the names imply what
! each class map has been configured to match. Note the priority 58 command makes
! class dscp-ef an LLQ.
policy-map queue-on-dscp
  class dscp-ef
    priority 58
  class dscp-af41
    bandwidth 22
  class dscp-af21
    bandwidth 20
    random-detect dscp-based
```

continues

Example 13-4 *LLQ for EF, CBWFQ for AF41, AF21, AF23, and All Else (Continued)*

```
  class dscp-af23
   bandwidth 8
   random-detect dscp-based
  class class-default
   fair-queue
   random-detect dscp-based
! max-res has to be raised or the policy map would be rejected.
interface Serial0/0
 bandwidth 128
 encapsulation frame-relay
 load-interval 30
 max-reserved-bandwidth 85
 service-policy output queue-on-dscp
! Below, for class dscp-ef, note the phrase "strict priority," as well as the
! computed policing burst of 1450 bytes (20% of 58 kbps and divided by 8 to convert
! the value to a number of bytes.)
R3# show policy-map queue-on-dscp
    Policy Map queue-on-dscp
     Class dscp-ef
      Weighted Fair Queueing
           Strict Priority
           Bandwidth 58 (kbps) Burst 1450 (Bytes)
! lines omitted for brevity
! Note the statistics below. Any packets dropped due to the policer would show
! up in the last line below.
R3# show policy-map interface s 0/0 output class dscp-ef
 Serial0/0
  Service-policy output: queue-on-dscp
    Class-map: dscp-ef (match-all)
      227428 packets, 14555392 bytes
      30 second offered rate 52000 bps, drop rate 0 bps
      Match: ip dscp ef
      Weighted Fair Queueing
        Strict Priority
        Output Queue: Conversation 40
        Bandwidth 58 (kbps) Burst 1450 (Bytes)
        (pkts matched/bytes matched) 12194/780416
 (total drops/bytes drops) 0/0
```

Defining and Limiting LLQ Bandwidth

The LLQ **priority** command provides two syntax options for defining the bandwidth of an LLQ—a simple explicit amount or bandwidth as a percentage of interface bandwidth. (There is no remaining bandwidth equivalent for the **priority** command.) However, unlike the **bandwidth** command, both the explicit and percentage versions of the **priority** command can be used inside the same policy map.

IOS still limits the amount of bandwidth in an LLQ policy map, with the actual bandwidth from both LLQ classes (with **priority** commands) and non-LLQ classes (with **bandwidth** commands) not being allowed to exceed **max-res** × **int-bw**. Although the math is easy, the details can get confusing, especially because a single policy map could have one queue configured with **priority** *bw*, another with **priority percent** *bw*, and others with one of the three versions of the **bandwidth** command. Figure 13-4 shows an example with three versions of the commands.

The figure shows both versions of the **priority** command. Class3 has an explicit **priority 32** command, which reserves 32 kbps. Class2 has a **priority percent 25** command, which, when applied to the interface bandwidth (256 kbps), gives class2 64 kbps.

Figure 13-4 *Priority, Priority Percent, and Bandwidth Remaining Percent*

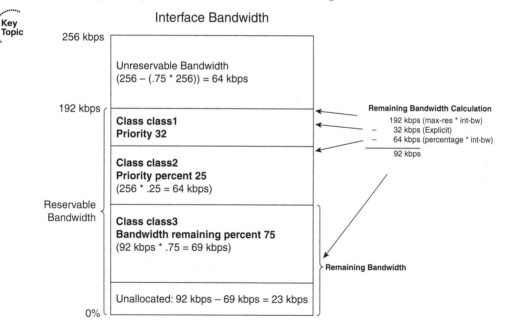

The most interesting part of Figure 13-4 is how IOS views the remaining-bandwidth concept when **priority** queues are configured. IOS subtracts the bandwidth reserved by the priority commands as well. As a result, a policy map can essentially allocate non-priority classes based on percentages of the leftover (remaining) bandwidth, with those values totaling 100 (100 percent).

LLQ with More Than One Priority Queue

LLQ allows multiple queues/classes to be configured as priority queues. This begs the question, "Which queue gets scheduled first?" As it turns out, LLQ actually places the packets from multiple

LLQs into a single internal LLQ. So, packets in the different configured priority queues still get scheduled ahead of non-priority queues, but they are serviced based on their arrival time for all packets in any of the priority queues.

So why use multiple priority queues? The answer is *policing*. By policing traffic in one class at one speed, and traffic in another class at another speed, you get more granularity for the policing function of LLQ. For instance, if you are planning for video and voice, you can place each into a separate LLQ and get low-latency performance for both types of traffic, but at the same time prevent video traffic from consuming the bandwidth engineered for voice and vice versa.

Miscellaneous CBWFQ/LLQ Topics

CBWFQ and LLQ allow a policy map to either allocate bandwidth to the class-default class, or not. When a **bandwidth** command is configured under **class class-default**, the class is indeed reserved that minimum bandwidth. (IOS will not allow the **priority** command in **class-default**.) When **class class-default** does not have a **bandwidth** command, IOS internally allocates any unassigned bandwidth among all classes. As a result, **class class-default** might not get much bandwidth unless the class is configured a minimum amount of bandwidth using the **bandwidth** command.

This chapter's coverage of guaranteed bandwidth allocation is based on the configuration commands. In practice, a policy map might not have packets in all queues at the same time. In that case, the queues get more than their reserved bandwidth. IOS allocates the extra bandwidth proportionally to each active class's bandwidth reservation.

Finally, IOS uses queuing only when congestion occurs. IOS considers congestion to be occurring when the hardware queue is full; that generally happens when the offered load of traffic is far less than the clock rate of the link. So, a router could have a **service-policy out** command on an interface, with LLQ configured, but the LLQ logic would be used only when the hardware queue is full.

Queuing Summary

Table 13-6 summarizes some of the key points regarding the IOS queuing tools covered in this chapter.

Table 13-6 *Queuing Protocol Comparison*

Key Topic

Feature	CBWFQ	LLQ
Includes a strict-priority queue	No	Yes
Polices priority queues to prevent starvation	No	Yes
Reserves bandwidth per queue	Yes	Yes
Includes robust set of classification fields	Yes	Yes
Classifies based on flows	Yes[1]	Yes[1]
Supports RSVP	Yes	Yes
Maximum number of queues	64	64

[1] WFQ can be used in the class-default queue or in all CBWFQ queues in 7500 series routers.

Weighted Random Early Detection

When a queue is full, IOS has no place to put newly arriving packets, so it discards them. This phenomenon is called *tail drop*. Often, when a queue fills, several packets are tail dropped at a time, given the bursty nature of data packets.

Tail drop can have an overall negative effect on network traffic, particularly TCP traffic. When packets are lost, for whatever reason, TCP senders slow down their rate of sending data. When tail drops occur and multiple packets are lost, the TCP connections slow down even more. Also, most networks send a much higher percentage of TCP traffic than UDP traffic, meaning that the overall network load tends to drop after multiple packets are tail dropped.

Interestingly, overall throughput can be improved by discarding a few packets as a queue begins to fill, rather than waiting for the larger impact of tail drops. Cisco created *weighted random early detection (WRED)* specifically for the purpose of monitoring queue length and discarding a percentage of the packets in the queue to improve overall network performance. As a queue gets longer and longer, WRED begins to discard more packets, hoping that a small reduction in offered load that follows may be just enough to prevent the queue from filling.

WRED uses several numeric settings when making its decisions. First, WRED uses the measured *average queue depth* when deciding if a queue has filled enough to begin discarding packets. WRED then compares the average depth to a minimum and maximum queue threshold, performing different discard actions depending on the outcome. Table 13-7 lists the actions.

When the average queue depth is very low or very high, the actions are somewhat obvious, although the term full drop in Table 13-7 may be a bit of a surprise. When the average depth rises above the maximum threshold, WRED discards all new packets. Although this action might seem like tail drop, technically it is not, because the actual queue might not be full. So, to make this fine distinction, WRED calls this action category *full drop*.

Table 13-7 *WRED Discard Categories*

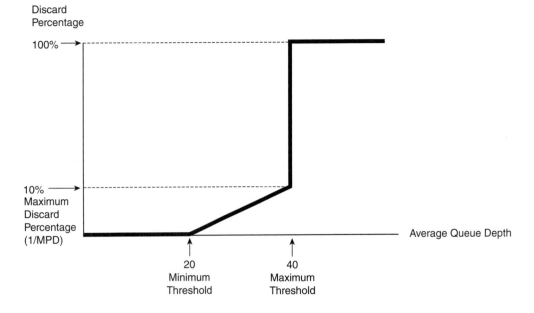

Average Queue Depth Versus Thresholds	Action	WRED Name for Action
Average < minimum threshold	No packets dropped.	No drop
Minimum threshold < average depth < maximum threshold	A percentage of packets dropped. Drop percentage increases from 0 to a maximum percent as the average depth moves from the minimum threshold to the maximum.	Random drop
Average depth > maximum threshold	All new packets discarded; similar to tail drop.	Full drop

When the average queue depth is between the two thresholds, WRED discards a percentage of packets. The percentage grows linearly as the average queue depth grows from the minimum threshold to the maximum, as depicted in Figure 13-5 (which shows WRED's default settings for IPP 0 traffic).

Figure 13-5 *WRED Discard Logic with Defaults for IPP 0*

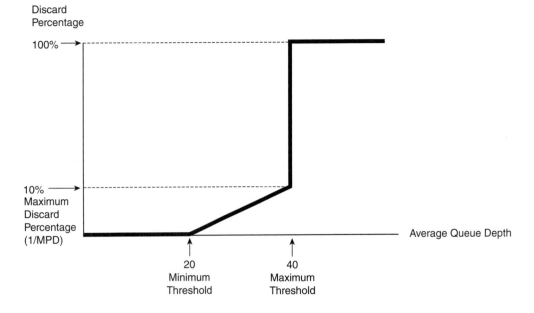

The last of the WRED numeric settings that affect its logic is the *mark probability denominator (MPD)*, from which the maximum percentage of 10 percent is derived in Figure 13-5. IOS calculates the discard percentage used at the maximum threshold based on the simple formula 1/MPD. In the figure, an MPD of 10 yields a calculated value of 1/10, meaning the discard rate grows from 0 percent to 10 percent as the average queue depth grows from the minimum threshold to the maximum. Also, when WRED discards packets, it randomly chooses the packets to discard.

How WRED Weights Packets

WRED gives preference to packets with certain IPP or DSCP values. To do so, WRED uses different traffic profiles for packets with different IPP and DSCP values. A WRED *traffic profile* consists of a setting for three key WRED variables: the minimum threshold, the maximum threshold, and the MPD. Figure 13-6 shows just such a case, with two WRED traffic profiles (for IPP 0 and IPP 3).

As Figure 13-6 illustrates, IPP 3's minimum threshold was higher than for IPP 0. As a result, IPP 0 traffic will be discarded earlier than IPP 3 packets. Also, the MPD is higher for IPP 3, resulting in a lower discard percentage (based on the formula discard percentage = 1/MPD).

Figure 13-6 *Example WRED Profiles for Precedences 0 and 3*

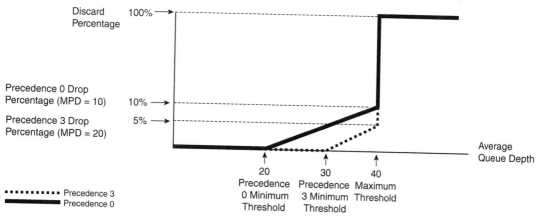

Table 13-8 lists the IOS default WRED profile settings for various DSCP values. You may recall from Chapter 12 that Assured Forwarding DSCPs whose names end in 1 (for example, AF21) should get better WRED treatment than those settings that end in 2 (for example, AF32). The IOS defaults listed in Table 13-8 achieve that goal by setting lower minimum thresholds for the appropriate AF DSCPs.

Table 13-8 *Cisco IOS Software Default WRED Profiles for DSCP-Based WRED*

DSCP	Minimum Threshold	Maximum Threshold	MPD	1/MPD
AFx1	33	40	10	10%
AFx2	28	40	10	10%
AFx3	24	40	10	10%
EF	37	40	10	10%

WRED Configuration

Because WRED manages drops based on queue depth, WRED must be configured alongside a particular queue. However, most queuing mechanisms do not support WRED; as a result, WRED can be configured only in the following locations:

- On a physical interface (with FIFO queuing)

- For a non-LLQ class inside a CBWFQ policy map

- For an ATM VC

To use WRED directly on a physical interface, IOS actually disables all other queuing mechanisms and creates a single FIFO queue. WRED then manages the queue with regard to drops. For CBWFQ, WRED is configured in a class inside a policy map, in the same location as the **bandwidth** and **priority** commands discussed earlier in this chapter.

The **random-detect** command enables WRED, either under a physical interface or under a **class** in a policy map. This command enables WRED to use IPP, and not DSCP. The **random-detect dscp-based** command both enables WRED and tells it to use DSCP for determining the traffic profile for a packet.

To change WRED configuration from the default WRED profile for a particular IPP or DSCP, use the following commands, in the same location as the other **random-detect** command:

```
random-detect precedence precedence min-threshold max-threshold [mark-prob-
  denominator]
random-detect dscp dscpvalue min-threshold max-threshold [mark-probability-
  denominator]
```

Finally, calculation of the rolling average queue depth can be affected through configuring a parameter called the *exponential weighting constant*. A low exponential weighting constant means that the old average is a small part of the calculation, resulting in a more quickly changing average.

The setting can be changed with the following command, although changing it is not recommended:

```
random-detect exponential-weighting-constant exponent
```

Note that earlier, Example 13-4 showed basic WRED configuration inside some classes of a CBWFQ configuration.

Modified Deficit Round-Robin

MDRR is a queuing feature implemented only in the Cisco 12000 series router family. Because the 12000 series does not support CBWFQ and LLQ, MDRR serves in place of these features. Its main claims to fame are better fairness than legacy queuing methods such as priority queuing and custom queuing, and that it supports a priority queue (like LLQ). For the CCIE Routing and Switching qualifying exam, you need to understand how MDRR works at the conceptual level, but you don't need to know how to configure it.

MDRR allows classifying traffic into seven round-robin queues (0–6), with one additional priority queue. When no packets are placed into the priority queue, MDRR normally services its queues in a round-robin approach, cycling through each queue once per cycle. With packets in the priority queue, MDRR has two options for how to include the priority queue in the queue service algorithm:

■ Strict priority mode

■ Alternate mode

Strict priority mode serves the priority queue whenever traffic is present in that queue. The benefit is, of course, that this traffic gets the first service regardless of what is going on in the other queues. The downside is that it may lead to queue starvation in other queues if there is always traffic in the priority queue. In this mode, the priority queue also can get more than the configured bandwidth percentage, because this queue is served more than once per cycle.

By contrast, alternate mode serves the priority queue in between serving each of the other queues. Let's say that five queues are configured: 0, 1, 2, 3, and the priority queue (P). Assuming that there is always traffic in each queue, here is how it would be processed: 0, P, 1, P, 2, P, 3, P, and so on. The result is that queue starvation in non-priority queues does not occur, because each queue is being served. The drawback of this mode is that it can cause jitter and additional latency for the traffic in the priority queue, compared to strict priority mode.

Two terms in MDRR, unique to this queuing method, help to differentiate MDRR from other queuing tools:

- Quantum value (QV)

- Deficit

MDRR supports two types of scheduling, one of which uses the same general algorithm as the legacy CQ feature in Cisco IOS routers (other than the 12000 series). MDRR removes packets from a queue until the quantum value (QV) for that queue has been removed. The QV quantifies a number of bytes and is used much like the byte count is used by the CQ scheduler. MDRR repeats the process for every queue, in order from 0 through 7, and then repeats this round-robin process. The end result is that each queue gets some percentage bandwidth of the link.

MDRR deals with the CQ scheduler's problem by treating any "extra" bytes sent during a cycle as a "deficit." If too many bytes were taken from a queue, next time around through the queues, the number of extra bytes sent by MDRR is subtracted from the QV. In effect, if more than the QV is sent from a queue in one pass, that many fewer bytes are taken in the next pass. As a result, averaged over many passes through the cycle, the MDRR scheduler provides an exact bandwidth reservation.

Figure 13-7 shows an example of how MDRR works. In this case, MDRR is using only two queues, with QVs of 1500 and 3000, respectively, and with all packets at 1000 bytes in length.

Figure 13-7 *MDRR: Making Up Deficits*

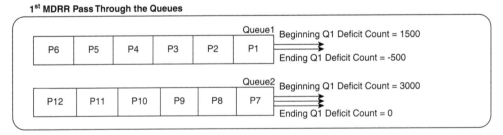

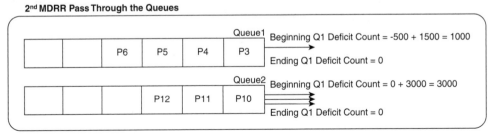

Some discussion of how to interpret Figure 13-7 may help you digest what is going on. The figure shows the action during the first round-robin pass in the top half of the figure, and the action during the second pass in the lower half of the figure. The example begins with six packets (labeled P1 through P6) in queue 1, and six packets (labeled P7 through P12) in queue 2. Each arrowed line to the right sides of the queues, pointing to the right, represents the choice by MDRR to send a single packet.

When a queue first fills, the queue's deficit counter (DC) is set to the QV for that queue, which is 1500 for queue 1 and 3000 for queue 2. In Figure 13-7, MDRR begins by taking one packet from queue 1, decrementing the DC to 500, and deciding that the DC is still greater than 0. Therefore, MDRR takes a second packet from queue 1, decrementing the DC to –500. MDRR then moves on to queue 2, taking three packets, after which the deficit counter (DC) for queue 2 has decremented to 0.

That concludes the first round-robin pass through the queues. MDRR has taken 2000 bytes from queue 1 and 3000 bytes from queue 2, giving the queues 40 percent and 60 percent of link bandwidth, respectively.

In the second round-robin pass, shown in the lower half of Figure 13-7, the process begins by MDRR adding the QV for each queue to the DC for each queue. Queue 1's DC becomes 1500 + (–500), or 1000, to begin the second pass. During this pass, MDRR takes P3 from queue 1, decrements DC to 0, and then moves on to queue 2. After taking three more packets from queue 3, decrementing queue 2's DC to 0, MDRR completes the second pass. Over these two round-robin passes, MDRR has taken 3000 bytes from queue 1 and 6000 bytes from queue 2— which is the same ratio as the ratio between the QVs. In other words, MDRR has exactly achieved the configured bandwidth ratio between the two queues.

The deficit feature of MDRR provides a means that, over time, gives each queue a guaranteed bandwidth based on the following formula:

$$\frac{\text{QV for Queue X}}{\text{Sum of All QVs}}$$

For additional examples of the operation of the MDRR deficit feature, refer to http://www.cisco.com/warp/public/63/toc_18841.html. Alternatively, you can go to Cisco.com and search for "Understanding and Configuring MDRR and WRED on the Cisco 12000 Series Internet Router."

LAN Switch Congestion Management and Avoidance

The final section of this chapter looks at the ingress and egress queuing, SRR, WTD, and WRED features on Cisco 3550 and 3560 switches.

Cisco 3550 and 3560 Switch Ingress Queueing

Cisco 3550 and 3560 switches perform both ingress and egress queuing. The 3550 uses a single FIFO ingress queue as a place to hold frames waiting to be forwarded to the egress interface, so the details are not terribly interesting. The 3560, on the other hand, has two ingress queues, one of which can be configured as a priority queue. This section addresses the details of these features.

The 3560 packet scheduler uses a method called *shared round-robin (SRR)* to control the rates at which packets are sent. On ingress queues, SRR performs sharing. In shared mode, SRR shares the bandwidth among the queues according to the weights that you configure. The weights are relative rather than absolute—only the ratios affect the frequency of dequeuing. SRR's shared operation is much like CBWFQ configured for percentages rather than bandwidth.

To configure ingress queuing, you first allocate the ratio by which to divide the ingress buffers to the two queues using the **mls qos srr-queue input buffers** *percentage1 percentage2* command. Then, you configure the bandwidth percentage for each queue, which sets the frequency at which the scheduler takes packets from the two buffers, using the **mls qos srr-queue input bandwidth** *weight1 weight2* command. (Although the command uses the **bandwidth** keyword, the parameters are just relative weightings and do not represent any particular bit rate.) These two commands, together, determine how much data the switch can buffer and send before it begins dropping packets.

Either of the two ingress queues can be configured as a priority queue. You would usually use a priority queue for voice traffic to ensure that it is forwarded ahead of other traffic to reduce latency for the voice traffic. To enable ingress priority queuing, use the **mls qos srr-queue input priority-queue** *queue-id bandwidth weight* command. The *weight* parameter defines the percentage of the link's bandwidth that can be consumed by the priority queue when there is competing traffic in the non-priority queue.

For example, consider a case with queue 2 as the priority queue, with a configured bandwidth of 40 percent. If frames have been coming in only queue 1 for a while and then some frames arrive in queue 2, the scheduler would finish servicing the current frame from queue 1 but then immediately start servicing queue 2, trying to empty queue 2. However, to prevent starvation, if both queues contain frames over a period of time, the scheduler would limit the overall bandwidth to the (configured) 40 percent for queue 2 to prevent queue starvation of queue 1.

The ingress queues in the 3560 use a method called *weighted tail drop*, or WTD, to set discard thresholds for each queue. (WTD is discussed later, in the section "Cisco 3560 Congestion Avoidance.")

Cisco 3550 Switch Egress Queuing

For egress, the 3550 supports four queues per interface, with classification into the queues based on CoS. Scheduling is based on weighted round-robin (WRR) logic, with an optional expedited (priority) queue.

The Cisco 3550 uses a relatively simple classification scheme, assuming you consider only what happens when the forwarding decision has been made. These switches make most internal QoS decisions based on an *internal DSCP* setting. The internal DSCP has been determined when the frame is forwarded. So, when a frame has been assigned an internal DSCP and an egress interface, the following logic determines into which of the four interface output queues the frame is placed:

1. The frame's internal DSCP is compared to a global DSCP-to-CoS map to determine a CoS value.

2. The per-interface CoS-to-queue map determines the queue for a frame based on the assigned CoS.

WRR scheduling works by taking a number of frames from each queue as it cycles through the queues. The **wrr-queue bandwidth** command defines the proportion of the number of frames taken in each cycle, not the number of frames taken in each cycle. For example, the **wrr-queue bandwidth 10 20 30 40** and **wrr-queue bandwidth 1 2 3 4** commands configure the same proportions and are equivalent. The switch is not concerned about allocating bandwidth; in fact, because frames vary in length, switch WRR logic does not even indirectly define a reserved minimum bandwidth percentage. However, it does empty the queue slots as defined so that there is then more space to temporarily store subsequent frames.

The 3550 can be configured to treat egress queue 4 on an interface as a PQ (also called an expedite queue). To do so, the interface subcommand **priority-queue out** is configured under the interface. On the 3550, only queue 4 can become the PQ. If the priority queue is configured, the switch still applies WRR scheduling to queues 1 through 3, with the scheduler always servicing the PQ next each time the scheduler looks for the next frame, assuming a new frame has made it to the PQ.

Example 13-5 shows Cisco 3550 egress queuing configuration. By default, the global DSCP-to-CoS map maps the first eight DSCP values to CoS 0, the next eight to CoS 1, and so on. Also, the default per-interface CoS-to-queue mapping maps the first two CoS values to queue 1, the next two to queue 2, and so on. For this example, to show how some of the commands work, the following nondefault criteria are used:

■   The global DSCP-to-CoS map is changed so that DSCPs 60–63 are mapped to CoS 1.

■   Interface gi0/1's CoS-to-queue map is changed so that CoS 5 is mapped to queue 4, and CoS 6 and 7 are mapped to queue 3.

- The gi0/1 bandwidth ratios are set to 10, 15, 25, and 150.

- Later, the expedite queue is enabled, giving queues 1, 2, and 3 approximately 20 percent, 30 percent, and 50 percent, respectively, of the bandwidth not consumed by priority queue 4.

Example 13-5 *Cisco 3550 Egress Queuing Example*

```
! For the global DSCP-to-CoS map, up to eight DSCPs can be mapped in a single command,
! as seen below. The show mls qos map dscp-cos command shows a grid, with the
! DSCP's decimal first digit on the left-side column, and the 2nd digit across the
! top.
S1(config)# mls qos map dscp-cos 60 61 62 63 to 1
S1# sh mls qos map dscp-cos
   Dscp-cos map:
      d1 :  d2 0  1  2  3  4  5  6  7  8  9
      ---------------------------------------
       0 :    00 00 00 00 00 00 00 00 01 01
       1 :    01 01 01 01 01 01 02 02 02 02
       2 :    02 02 02 02 03 03 03 03 03 03
       3 :    03 03 04 04 04 04 04 04 04 04
       4 :    05 05 05 05 05 05 05 05 06 06
       5 :    06 06 06 06 06 06 07 07 07 07
       6 :    01 01 01 01
! Next, queue 4 is assigned CoS 5, queue 3 is assigned CoSs 6 and 7. Note that
! the wrr-queue cos-map 3 6 7 command does not remove other CoS values from queue
! 3, but just assigns CoSs 6 and 7 to queue 3. The non-highlighted CoS values in
! the show mls qos int gi 0/1 queue command reflect default settings.
S1(config)# int gi 0/1
S1(config-if)# wrr-queue cos-map 4 5
S1(config-if)# wrr-queue cos-map 3 6 7
S1(config-if)# do show mls qos int gi 0/1 queue | begin Cos-queue
Cos-queue map:
cos-qid
 0-1
 1-1
 2-2
 3-2
 4-3
 5-4
 6-3
 7-3
! Next, the ratios used by the WRR scheduler are defined. Note that the show
! command lists the exact weights, and that it lists "dis" beside the phrase
! "Egress Expedite Queue," meaning that the PQ is not yet enabled. Note also that
! the four weights must be values between 1 and 65,536, inclusive.
S1(config)# int gi 0/1
S1(config-if)# wrr-queue bandwidth 10 15 25 150
S1(config-if)# do sh mls qos int gi 0/1 queue
GigabitEthernet0/1
```

Example 13-5 *Cisco 3550 Egress Queuing Example (Continued)*

```
Egress expedite queue: dis
wrr bandwidth weights:
qid-weights
 110
 215
 325
 4150
! Finally, the PQ is enabled.
S1(config-if)# priority-queue out
S1(config-if)# do sh mls qos int gi 0/1 queue
GigabitEthernet0/1
Egress expedite queue: ena
wrr bandwidth weights:
qid-weights
 1-10
 2-15
 3-25
 4-150    when expedite queue is disabled
! Lines omitted for brevity
```

Cisco 3560 Switch Egress Queuing

Cisco 3560 egress queuing improves on the core concepts of 3550 egress queuing by adding a couple of key features. First, 3560 egress queuing creates a mechanism to prevent queue starvation of the non-PQ queues—a potential issue with the 3550 egress scheduling logic. Second, 3560 queuing adds a shaping feature that slows down egress traffic, which helps prevent some types of DoS attacks and provides the means to implement subrate speed for Metro Ethernet implementations.

First, it helps to know a few details about the basic egress queuing system on the 3560. Like the 3550, there are four egress queues per interface. Also like the 3550, one queue can be configured as an expedite queue, although it must be queue 1 (instead of queue 4 on the 3550). The classification logic is the same, with the egress queue being determined indirectly by the internal DSCP, with the internal DSCP being compared to the DSCP-to-CoS map and the resulting CoS being compared to the Cos-to-queue map—just like it is in the 3550.

This section focuses on the scheduler, assuming that frames have been classified and placed into the four output queues. In particular, the 3560 has two options for the scheduler, both using the acronym SRR: shared round-robin and shaped round-robin. The key differences between the two schedulers is that while both help to prevent queue starvation when a priority queue exists, the shaped option also rate-limits (shapes) the queues so that they do not exceed the configured percentage of the link's bandwidth.

To see the similarities and differences, it is helpful to think about both options without a PQ and with two scenarios: first, with all four queues holding plenty of frames, and second, with only one queue holding frames.

In the first case, with all four output queues holding several frames, both shared and shaped modes work the same. Both use the configuration of weights for each queue, with the queues serviced proportionally based on the weights. The following two commands configure the weights, depending on which type of scheduling is desired on the interface:

> **srr-queue bandwidth share** *weight1 weight2 weight3 weight4*
> **srr-queue bandwidth shape** *weight1 weight2 weight3 weight4*

For example, with the default weights of 25 for each queue in shared mode, still assuming that all four queues contain frames, the switch would service each queue equally.

The two schedulers' operations differ, however, when the queues are not all full. Consider a second scenario, with frames only in one queue with a weight of 25 (default) in that queue. With shared scheduling, the switch would keep servicing this single queue with that queue getting all of the link's bandwidth. However, with shaped scheduling, the switch would purposefully wait to service the queue, not sending any data out the interface so that the queue would receive only its configured percentage of link bandwidth—25 percent in this scenario.

Next, consider the inclusion of queue 1 as the priority queue. First, consider a case where queues 2, 3, and 4 all have frames, queue 1 has no frames, and then some frames arrive in the egress PQ. The switch completes its servicing of the current frame but then transitions over to serve the PQ. However, instead of starving the other queues, while all the queues have frames waiting to exit the queues, the scheduler limits the bandwidth used for the PQ to the configured bandwidth. However, this limiting queues the excess rather than discarding the excess. (In this scenario, the behavior is the same in both shaped and shared mode.)

Finally, to see the differences between shared and shaped modes, imagine that the PQ still has many frames to send, but queues 2, 3, and 4 are now empty. In shared mode, the PQ would send at full line rate. In shaped mode, the switch would simply not service the PQ part of the time so that its overall rate would be the bandwidth configured for that queue.

Hopefully, these examples help demonstrate some of the similarities and differences between the SRR scheduler in shaped and shared modes. The following list summarizes the key points:

- Both shared and shaped mode scheduling attempt to service the queues in proportion to their configured bandwidths when more than one queue holds frames.

- Both shared and shaped mode schedulers service the PQ as soon as possible if at first the PQ is empty but then frames arrive in the PQ.

- Both shared and shaped mode schedulers prevent the PQ from exceeding its configured bandwidth when all the other queues have frames waiting to be sent.

- The shaped scheduler never allows any queue, PQ or non-PQ, to exceed its configured percentage of link bandwidth, even if that means that link sits idle.

> **NOTE**   The 3560 supports the ability to configure shared mode scheduling on some queues, and shaped mode on others, on a single interface. The only difference in operation is that the queues in shaped mode never exceed their configured bandwidth setting.

Cisco 3550 Congestion Avoidance

Catalyst 3550 Gigabit interfaces support a mutually exclusive choice of either WRED or tail-drop logic for managing drops in egress queues. The 3550 Fast Ethernet interfaces do not use WRED or tail drop, but rather use a switch-specific method of managing internal buffers (which is not covered in this book).

Cisco 3550 WRED has the same overall strategy as WRED as implemented in Cisco routers but with many differences in implementation details. The key features of Cisco 3550 WRED are as follows, with Figure 13-8 depicting the main concepts:

- Each egress queue has two WRED thresholds.

- Thresholds are defined as percentages of the queue length.

- The thresholds can be set differently for each egress queue on each interface.

- When the actual queue depth is below the threshold, WRED does not discard packets (no drop).

- When the actual queue depth exceeds a threshold, WRED discards a percentage of packets; the percentage ranges linearly from 0 to 100 percent, as the queue depth grows from the threshold to 100 percent full.

Figure 13-8 *Cisco 3550 WRED Logic and Commands*

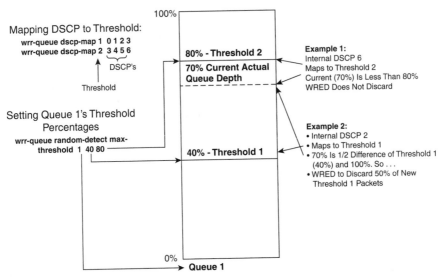

Figure 13-8 shows WRED configuration and logic once a particular egress queue has been chosen. In the figure, a frame has been assigned to egress queue 1. Before enqueuing the frame, WRED finds the frame's internal DSCP in the DSCP-to-threshold map, as configured with the **wrr-queue dscp-map** interface subcommand. That mapping identifies the WRED threshold to use (either threshold 1 or 2). The default DSCP map maps all 64 DSCP values to WRED threshold 1, so to use threshold 2, the map must be configured.

The existence of a single **wrr-queue random-detect** command under an interface both enables WRED on the interface for all queues and disables the default tail-drop logic for each queue. If only one interface egress queue has a **wrr-queue random-detect** command, the other three egress queues do use WRED. However, WRED defaults to use thresholds of 100 percent, meaning that queues that have no specifically configured thresholds behave as if tail drop were used. To enable WRED-like behavior, each queue needs to have nondefault thresholds configured.

The Cisco 3550 uses tail drop by default, but with some interesting optional features. You can configure tail drop at levels less than a 100-percent-full queue, with two thresholds as configured with the **wrr-queue threshold** interface subcommand. Along with the DSCP map (configured with the **wrr-queue dscp-map** command), frames with one set of DSCP values will all be discarded once the queue reaches the defined depth. Frames of the other DSCPs are discarded at a second threshold. In effect, this configuration provides for differentiated tail drop, discarding all packets at one lower threshold.

Cisco 3560 Congestion Avoidance

The 3560 uses a different method for congestion avoidance, known as *weighted tail drop*, or WTD. WTD creates three thresholds per queue into which traffic can be divided, based on CoS value, for tail drop when the associated queue reaches a particular percentage. For example, you can configure a queue so that it drops traffic with CoS values of 0–3 when the queue reaches 40 percent full, then drops traffic with CoS 4 and 5 at 60 percent full, and finally drops CoS 6 and 7 traffic only when the queue is 100 percent full. Figure 13-9 shows this behavior.

Figure 13-9 *WTD Configuration in Graphical Form*

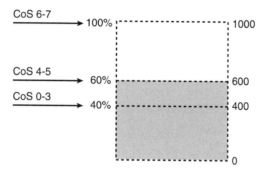

NOTE   Figure 13-9 is redrawn from Figure 31-6 in "Configuring QoS" at http://www.ciscosystems.com/en/US/products/hw/switches/ps5528/products_configuration_guide_chapter09186a00802113d0.html#wp1284809.

Because WTD is configurable separately for all six queues in the 3560 (two ingress, four egress), a great deal of granularity is possible in 3560 configuration (maybe even *too* much!).

Comparisons Between Cisco 3550 and 3560 Switches

Cisco includes the 3550 and 3560 series switches in the CCIE Routing and Switching lab exam. Cisco is not specific about any particular switch models to expect on the CCIE Routing and Switching written exam. As a result, it is useful to compare the QoS features of the two switches that you may encounter in the lab exam. Table 13-9 summarizes the key differences. (The comparisons listed here assume the Enhanced software image is used on both models of switches.)

Table 13-9   *Comparison of Cisco 3550 and 3560 Queuing Options*

Feature Description	3550	3560
Number of ingress queues	1	2
Number of egress queues	4	4
Queue number of expedite queue	4	Configurable

continues

Table 13-9 *Comparison of Cisco 3550 and 3560 Queuing Options (Continued)*

Feature Description	3550	3560
Granularity for setting queue weights	Interface	Interface
Frames classified into queues based on…	CoS	CoS
Granularity for CoS-to-queue mapping	Interface	Interface
Expedite queue enabled via **priority-queue out** interface subcommand	Yes	Yes
Ingress policers per port Fast Ethernet/Gigabit Ethernet	8/128	64/64
QoS egress method	Policing	Shaping or policing
Congestion avoidance method/number of thresholds per queue	WRR/2	WTD/3
Default scheduler	WRR	SRR
Drop strategy	WRED	WTD

Foundation Summary

Please take the time to read and study the details in the "Foundation Topics" section of the chapter, as well as review the items in the "Foundation Topics" section noted with a Key Topic icon.

Memory Builders

The CCIE Routing and Switching written exam, like all Cisco CCIE written exams, covers a fairly broad set of topics. This section provides some basic tools to help you exercise your memory about some of the broader topics covered in this chapter.

Fill in Key Tables from Memory

Appendix E, "Key Tables for CCIE Study," on the CD in the back of this book contains empty sets of some of the key summary tables in each chapter. Print Appendix E, refer to this chapter's tables in it, and fill in the tables from memory. Refer to Appendix F, "Solutions for Key Tables for CCIE Study," on the CD to check your answers.

Definitions

Next, take a few moments to write down the definitions for the following terms:

class-based weighted fair queuing, low-latency queuing, weighted round-robin, modified deficit round-robin, shared round-robin, shared mode, shaped mode, WTD, WRR, quantum value, alternate mode, tail drop, full drop, priority queue, sequence number, finish time, modified tail drop, scheduler, queue starvation, strict priority, software queue, hardware queue, remaining bandwidth, maximum reserved bandwidth, actual queue depth, average queue depth, minimum threshold, maximum threshold, mark probability denominator, exponential weighting constant, expedite queue, DSCP-to-CoS map, DSCP-to-threshold map, internal DSCP, differentiated tail drop

Refer to the glossary to check your answers.

Further Reading

Cisco QoS Exam Certification Guide, Second Edition, by Wendell Odom and Michael Cavanaugh.

Cisco Catalyst QoS: Quality of Service in Campus Networks, by Mike Flanagan, Richard Froom, and Kevin Turek.

Cisco.com includes a great deal more information on the very detailed aspects of 3560 QoS configuration, including SRR and WTD, at http://www.ciscosystems.com/en/US/products/hw/switches/ps5528/products_configuration_guide_chapter09186a00802113d0.html.

Blueprint topics covered in this chapter:

This chapter covers the following subtopics from the Cisco CCIE Routing and Switching written exam blueprint. Refer to the full blueprint in Table I-1 in the Introduction for more details on the topics covered in each chapter and their context within the blueprint.

- Marking

- Shaping

- Policing

- Class-based Weighted Fair Queuing (CBWFQ)

Shaping and Policing

Traffic-shaping tools delay packets exiting a router so that the overall bit rate does not exceed a defined shaping rate. This chapter covers the concepts behind traffic shaping, as well as two Cisco IOS shapers, namely Frame Relay Traffic Shaping (FRTS) and Class-Based Shaping (CB Shaping).

Traffic policers measure bit rates for packets either entering or exiting an interface. If the defined rate is exceeded, the policer either discards enough packets so that the rate is not exceeded, or marks some packets such that the packets are more likely to be discarded later. This chapter covers the concepts and configuration behind Class-Based Policing (CB Policing), with a brief mention of committed access rate (CAR).

"Do I Know This Already?" Quiz

Table 14-1 outlines the major headings in this chapter and the corresponding "Do I Know This Already?" quiz questions.

Table 14-1 *"Do I Know This Already?" Foundation Topics Section-to-Question Mapping*

Foundation Topics Section	Questions Covered in This Section	Score
Traffic-Shaping Concepts	1–2	
Class-Based Shaping Configuration	3–5	
Frame Relay Traffic Shaping Configuration	6–7	
Policing Concepts and Configuration	8–10	
Total Score		

In order to best use this pre-chapter assessment, remember to score yourself strictly. You can find the answers in Appendix A, "Answers to the 'Do I Know This Already?' Quizzes."

1. When does Class-Based Shaping add tokens to its token bucket, and how many tokens does it add when Bc and Be are both set to something larger than 0?

   a. Upon the arrival of each packet, a pro-rated portion of Bc is added to the token bucket.

   b. Upon the arrival of each packet, a pro-rated portion of Bc + Be is added to the token bucket.

   c. At the beginning of each time interval, Bc worth of tokens are added to the token bucket.

   d. At the beginning of each time interval, Bc + Be worth of tokens are added to the token bucket.

   e. None of the answers is correct.

2. If shaping was configured with a rate of 128 kbps and a Bc of 3200 bits, what value would be calculated for Tc?

   a. 125 ms

   b. 125 sec

   c. 25 ms

   d. 25 sec

   e. Shaping doesn't use a Tc.

   f. Not enough information is provided to tell.

3. Which of the following commands, when typed in the correct configuration mode, enables CB Shaping at 128 kbps, with no excess burst?

   a. **shape average 128000 8000 0**

   b. **shape average 128 8000 0**

   c. **shape average 128000**

   d. **shape peak 128000 8000 0**

   e. **shape peak 128 8000 0**

   f. **shape peak 128000**

4. Examine the following configuration, noting the locations of the comment lines labeled point 1, point 2, and so on. Assume that a correctly configured policy map that implements CBWFQ, called **queue-it**, is also configured but not shown. To enable CBWFQ for the packets queued by CB Shaping, what command is required, and at what point in the configuration is the command required?

```
policy-map shape-question
! point 1
 class class-default
```

```
! point 2
  shape average 256000 5120
! point 3
interface serial 0/0
! point 4
  service-policy output shape-question
! point 5
interface s0/0.1 point-to-point
! point 6
  ip address 1.1.1.1
! point 7
  frame-relay interface-dlci 101
! point 8
```

   a. **service-policy queue-it**, at point 1

   b. **service-policy queue-it**, at point 3

   c. **service-policy queue-it**, at point 5

   d. **shape queue service-policy queue-it**, at point 1

   e. **shape queue service-policy queue-it**, at point 3

   f. **shape queue service-policy queue-it**, at point 6

5. Using the same configuration snippet as in the previous question, what command would list the calculated Tc value, and what would that value be?

   a. **show policy-map**, Tc = 125 ms

   b. **show policy-map**, Tc = 20 ms

   c. **show policy-map**, Tc = 10 ms

   d. **show policy-map interface s0/0**, Tc = 125 ms

   e. **show policy-map interface s0/0**, Tc = 20 ms

   f. **show policy-map interface s0/0**, Tc = 10 ms

6. Assume that several **map-class frame-relay** commands exist in addition to the following configuration. The map classes are named C1, C2, and C3. Which VC use the settings in map class C2?

```
interface s0/0
 encapsulation frame-relay
 frame-relay traffic-shaping
 frame-relay class C2
!
interface s0/0.1 point-to-point
 frame-relay class C1
 frame-relay interface-dlci 101
interface s0/0.3 multipoint
  frame-relay interface-dlci 103
  frame-relay interface-dlci 203
    class C3
```

    a. The VC with DLCI 101.

    b. The VC with DLCI 103.

    c. The VC with DLCI 203.

    d. None of the answers is correct.

7. Which of the following FRTS commands, in the same FRTS map class, sets the shaping rate to 128 kbps, with a shaping time interval of 62.5 ms?

    a. **frame-relay traffic-rate 128**

    b. **frame-relay traffic-rate 128000**

    c. **frame-relay cir 128, frame-relay Bc 8000**

    d. **frame-relay cir 128000, frame-relay Bc 8000**

8. Which of the following are true about policers in general, but not true about shapers?

    a. Monitor traffic rates using the concept of a token bucket

    b. Can discard traffic that exceeds a defined traffic rate

    c. Can delay packets by queuing to avoid exceeding a traffic rate

    d. Can re-mark a packet

9. Which of the following commands, when typed in the correct configuration mode, enables CB Policing at 128 kbps, with no excess burst?

    a. **police 128000 conform-action transmit exceed-action transmit violate-action drop**

    b. **police 128 conform-action transmit exceed-action transmit violate-action drop**

    c. **police 128000 conform-action transmit exceed-action drop**

    d. **police 128 conform-action transmit exceed-action drop**

    e. **police 128k conform-action transmit exceed-action drop**

10. Which of the following features of CB Policing are not supported by CAR?

    a. The capability to categorize packets as conforming, exceeding, and violating a traffic contract

    b. The capability to police all traffic at one rate, and subsets of that same traffic at other rates

    c. The capability to configure policing using MQC commands

    d. The capability to police input or output packets on an interface

Foundation Topics

Traffic-Shaping Concepts

Traffic shaping prevents the bit rate of the packets exiting an interface from exceeding a configured shaping rate. To do so, the shaper monitors the bit rate at which data is being sent. If the configured rate is exceeded, the shaper delays packets, holding the packets in a *shaping queue*. The shaper then releases packets from the queue such that, over time, the overall bit rate does not exceed the shaping rate.

Traffic shaping solves two general types of problems that can occur in multi-access networks. First, if a service provider purposefully discards any traffic on a VC when the traffic rate exceeds the committed information rate (CIR), then it makes sense for the router to not send traffic faster than the CIR.

Egress blocking is the second type of problem for which shaping provides some relief. *Egress blocking* occurs when a router sends data into a Frame Relay or ATM service, and the egress Frame Relay or ATM switch has to queue the data before it can be sent out to the router on the other end of the VC. For example, when a T1-connected router sends data, it must be sent at T1 speed. If the router on the other end of the VC has a link clocked at 256 kbps, the frames/cells will start to back up in the output queue of the egress switch. Likewise, if that same T1 site has VCs to 20 remote sites, and each remote site uses a 256-kbps link, then when all 20 remote sites send at about the same time, frames/cells will be queued, waiting to exit the WAN egress switch to the T1 router. In this case, shaping can be used to essentially prevent egress queuing, moving the packets back into a queue in the router, where they can then be manipulated with fancy queuing tools.

Shaping Terminology

Routers can send bits out an interface only at the physical clock rate. To average sending at a lower rate, the router has to alternate between sending packets and being silent. For instance, to average sending at a packet rate of half the physical link speed, the router should send packets half of the time, and not send packets the other half of the time. Over time, it looks like a staccato series of sending and silence. Figure 14-1 shows a graph of what happens when a router has a link with a clock rate of 128 kbps and a shaper configured to shape traffic to 64 kbps.

Figure 14-1 shows the sending rate and implies quite a bit about how Cisco IOS implements shaping. A shaper sets a static time interval, called *Tc*. Then, it calculates the number of bits that can be sent in the Tc interval such that, over time, the number of bits/second sent matches the shaping rate.

Figure 14-1 *Mechanics of Traffic Shaping—128-kbps Access Rate, 64-kbps Shaped Rate*

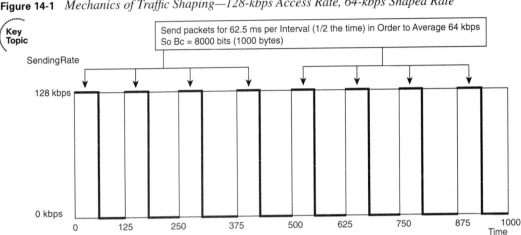

The number of bits that can be sent in each Tc is called the *committed burst (Bc)*. In Figure 14-1, an 8000-bit Bc can be sent in every 125-ms Tc to achieve a 64-kbps average rate. In other words, with a Tc of 125 ms, there will be eight Tc intervals per second. If Bc bits (8000) are sent each Tc, then eight sets of 8000 bits will be sent each second, resulting in a rate of 64,000 bps.

Because the bits must be encoded on the link at the clock rate, the 8000 bits in each interval require only 62.5 ms (8000/128,000) to exit the interface onto the link. The graph shows the results: the interface sends at the line rate (access rate) for 62.5 ms, and then waits for 62.5 ms, while packets sit in the shaping queue.

Table 14-2 lists the terminology related to this shaping model. Note in particular that the term *CIR* refers to the traffic rate for a VC based on a business contract, and *shaping rate* refers to the rate configured for a shaper on a router.

Table 14-2 *Shaping Terminology*

Term	Definition
Tc	Time interval, measured in milliseconds, over which the committed burst (Bc) can be sent. With many shaping tools, Tc = Bc/CIR.
Bc	Committed burst size, measured in bits. This is the amount of traffic that can be sent during the Tc interval. Typically defined in the traffic contract.
CIR	Committed information rate, in bits per second, which defines the rate of a VC according to the business contract.
Shaped rate	The rate, in bits per second, to which a particular configuration wants to shape the traffic. It may or may not be set to the CIR.
Be	Excess burst size, in bits. This is the number of bits beyond Bc that can be sent after a period of inactivity.

Shaping with an Excess Burst

To accommodate bursty data traffic, shapers implement a concept by which, after a period in which an interface sends relatively little data compared to its CIR, more than Bc bits can be sent in one or more time intervals. This concept is called *excess burst (Be)*. When using a Be, the shaper can allow, in addition to the Bc bits per Tc, Be extra bits to be sent. Depending on the settings, it may take one time interval to send the extra bits, or it may require multiple time intervals. Figure 14-2 shows a graph of the same example in Figure 14-1, but with a Be also equal to 8000 bits. In this case, the Be extra bits are all sent in the first time interval after the relative inactivity.

Figure 14-2 *Bc and Be, After a Period of Inactivity*

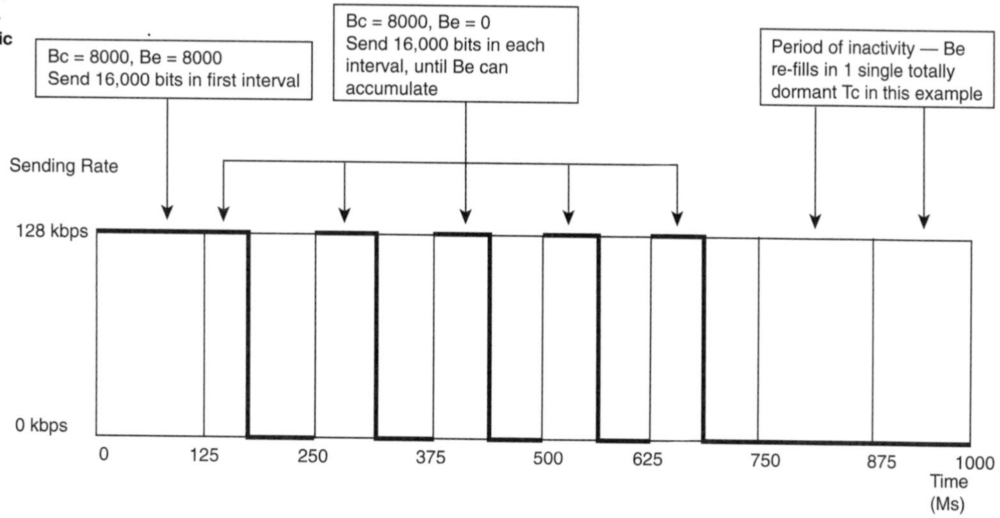

In the first interval, traffic shaping can send a total of 16,000 bits (Bc + Be bits). On a 128-kbps link, assuming a 125-ms Tc, all 125 ms is required to send 16,000 bits. In this particular case, after a period of inactivity, R1 sends continuously for the entire first interval. In the second interval, the shaper allows the usual Bc bits to be sent. In effect, with these settings, the shaper allows 192.5 ms of consecutive sending after a period of low activity.

Underlying Mechanics of Shaping

Shapers apply a simple formula to the Tc, Bc, and shaping rate parameters:

Tc = Bc/shaping rate

For example, in Figures 14-1 and 14-2, if the shaping rate (64 kbps) and the Bc (8000 bits) were both configured, the shaper would then calculate the Tc as 8000/64,000 = 0.125 seconds. Alternatively, if the rate and Tc had been configured, the shaper would have calculated Bc as Bc = rate * Tc (a simple derivation of the formula listed earlier), or 64 kbps * 0.125 ms = 8000 bits. (Both CB Shaping and FRTS use default values in some cases, as described in the configuration sections of this chapter.)

Traffic shaping uses a *token bucket* model to manage the shaping process. First, consider the case in which the shaper is not using Be. Imagine a bucket of size Bc, with the bucket filled with tokens at the beginning of each Tc. Each token lets the shaper buy the right to send 1 bit. So, at the beginning of each Tc, the shaper has the ability to release Bc worth of bits.

Shapers perform two main actions related to the bucket:

1. Refill the bucket with new tokens at the beginning of each Tc.

2. Spend tokens to gain the right to forward packets.

Step 1 describes how the bucket is filled with Bc tokens to start each interval. Figure 14-3 shows a visual representation of the process. Note that if some of the tokens from the previous time interval are still in the bucket, some of the new tokens spill over the side of the bucket and are wasted.

Figure 14-3 *Mechanics of Filling the Shaping Token Bucket*

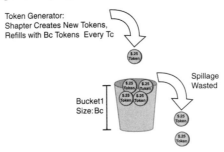

Step 2 describes how the shaper spends the tokens. The shaper has to take tokens from the bucket equal to the number of bits in a packet in order to release that packet for transmission. For example, if the packet is 1000 bits long, the shaper must remove 1000 tokens from the bucket to send that packet. When traffic shaping tries to send a packet, and the bucket does not have enough tokens in it to buy the right to send the packet, traffic shaping must wait until the next interval, when the token bucket is refilled.

Traffic shaping implements Be by making the single token bucket bigger, with no other changes to the token-bucket model. In other words, only Bc tokens are added each Tc, and tokens must still be consumed in order to send packets. The key difference using Be (versus not using Be) is that when some of the tokens are left in the bucket at the end of the time interval, and Bc tokens are added at the beginning of the next interval, more than Bc tokens are in the bucket—therefore allowing a larger burst of bits in this new interval.

Traffic-Shaping Adaptation on Frame Relay Networks

A shaper used with Frame Relay can be configured to vary the shaping rate over time based on the presence or absence of congestion. When there is no congestion, the shaper uses the shaping rate, but when congestion occurs, it lowers the shaping rate, eventually reaching a *minimum shaping rate*. The minimum rate can be configured, or default to 50 percent of the shaping rate. This lower rate is typically called either the *minimum information rate (MIR)* or the *mincir*.

To lower the rate, shapers must notice congestion via one of two methods:

- Receipt of a frame with the *Backward Explicit Congestion Notification (BECN)* bit set

- Receipt of a Cisco-proprietary *ForeSight* congestion message

Each time a BECN or ForeSight message is received, the shaper slows down by 25 percent of the maximum rate. To slow down, CB Shaping simply decreases Bc and Be by 25 percent, keeping the Tc value the same. If more BECNs or ForeSight messages are received, the Bc and Be settings are ratcheted down another 25 percent, until they bottom out at values that match the mincir. The rate grows again after 16 consecutive Tc values without a BECN or ForeSight congestion message. At that point, the shaping rate grows by $\frac{1}{16}$ of the shaping rate during each Tc, in this case by increasing the actual Bc and Be values used, until the maximum rate is reached again.

Class-Based Shaping Configuration

Class-Based Shaping (CB Shaping) implements all the core concepts described so far in this chapter, plus several other important features. First, it allows for several Cisco IOS queuing tools to be applied to the packets delayed by the shaping process. At the same time, it allows for fancy queuing tools to be used on the interface software queues. It also allows for classification of packets, so that some types of packets can be shaped at one rate, a second type of packet can be shaped at another rate, while allowing a third class of packets to not be shaped at all.

The only new MQC command required to configure CB Shaping is the **shape** command. The "Foundation Summary" section provides a CB Shaping command reference, in Table 14-9:

```
shape [average | peak] mean-rate [[burst-size] [excess-burst-size]]
```

CB Shaping can be implemented for output packets only, and it can be associated with either a physical interface or a subinterface.

To enable CB Shaping, the **service-policy output** command is configured under either the interface or the subinterface, with the referenced policy map including the **shape** command.

Example 14-1 shows a simple CB Shaping configuration that uses the following criteria:

■ Interface clock rate is 128 kbps.

■ Shape all traffic at a 64-kbps rate.

■ Use the default setting for Tc.

■ Shape traffic exiting subinterface s0/0.1.

■ The software queuing on s0/0 will use WFQ (the default).

■ The shaping queue will use FIFO (the default).

Example 14-1 *CB Shaping of All Traffic Exiting S0/0.1 at 64 kbps*

```
! Policy map shape-all places all traffic into the class-default class, matching
! all packets. All packets will be shaped to an average of 64 kbps. Note the
! units are in bits/second, so 64000 means 64 kbps.
policy-map shape-all
  class class-default
    shape average 64000
! The physical interface will not show the fair-queue command, but it is
! configured by default, implementing WFQ for interface s0/0 software queuing.
interface serial0/0
 bandwidth 128
! Below, CB Shaping has been enabled for all packets forwarded out s0/0.1.
interface serial0/0.1
  service-policy output shape-all
! Refer to the text after this example for more explanations of this next command.
R3# show policy-map interface s0/0.1
 Serial0/0.1
  Service-policy output: shape-all

    Class-map: class-default (match-any)
      7718 packets, 837830 bytes
      30 second offered rate 69000 bps, drop rate 5000 bps
      Match: any
      Traffic Shaping
```

Target/Average Rate	Byte Limit	Sustain bits/int	Excess bits/int	Interval (ms)	Increment (bytes)
64000/64000	2000	8000	8000	125	1000

Adapt Active	Queue Depth	Packets	Bytes	Packets Delayed	Bytes Delayed	Shaping Active
—	56	6393	692696	6335	684964	yes

The configuration itself is relatively straightforward. The **shape-all** policy map matches all packets in a single class (class-default) and is enabled on s0/0.1. So, all packets exiting s0/0.1 will be shaped to the defined rate of 64 kbps.

The output of the **show policy-map interface s0/0.1** command shows the settings for all the familiar shaping concepts, but it uses slightly different terminology. CB Shaping defaults to a Bc and Be of 8000 bits each, listed under the columns **Sustain bits/int** (with "int" meaning "interval," or Tc) and **Excess bits/int**, respectively. The heading **Byte Limit** represents the size of the token bucket—the sum of Bc and Be, but listed as a number of bytes (2000 bytes in this case) instead of bits. The last column in that same part of the command output, **Increment (bytes)**, indicates how many bytes' worth of tokens are replenished each Tc. This value is equal to Bc (8000 bits), but the output is listed as a number of bytes (1000 bytes).

The CB Shaping **shape** command requires the shaping rate to be set. However, Bc and Be can be omitted, and Tc cannot be set directly. As a result, CB Shaping calculates some or all of these settings. CB Shaping calculates the values differently based on whether the shaping rate exceeds 320 kbps. Table 14-3 summarizes the rules.

Table 14-3   *CB Shaping Calculation of Default Variable Settings*

Variable	Rate <= 320 kbps	Rate > 320 kbps
Bc	8000 bits	Bc = shaping rate * Tc
Be	Be = Bc = 8000	Be = Bc
Tc	Tc = Bc/shaping rate	25 ms

Tuning Shaping for Voice Using LLQ and a Small Tc

Example 14-1 in the previous section shows default settings for queuing for the interface software queues (WFQ) and for the shaping queue (FIFO). Example 14-2 shows an alternative configuration that works better for voice traffic by using LLQ for the shaped traffic. Also, the configuration forces the Tc down to 10 ms, which means that each packet will experience only a short delay waiting for the beginning of the next Tc. By keeping Tc to a small value, the LLQ logic applied to the shaped packets does not have to wait nearly as long to release packets from the PQ, as compared with the default Tc settings.

The revised requirements, as compared with Example 14-1, are as follows:

■   Enable LLQ to support a single G.729 voice call.

■   Shape to 96 kbps—less than the clock rate (128 kbps), but more than the CIR of the VC.

■   Tune Tc to 10 ms.

Example 14-2 *CB Shaping on R3, 96-kbps Shape Rate, with LLQ for Shaping Queues*

```
class-map match-all voip-rtp
  match ip rtp 16384 16383
! queue-voip implements a PQ for VoIP traffic, and uses WFQ in the default class.
policy-map queue-voip
  class voip-rtp
   priority 32
  class class-default
   fair-queue
! shape-all shapes all traffic to 96 kbps, with Bc of 960. Tc is calculated as
! 960/96000 or 10 ms. Also note the service-policy queue-voip command. This applies
! policy map queue-voip to all packets shaped by the shape command.
policy-map shape-all
  class class-default
   shape average 96000 960
   service-policy queue-voip
!
interface serial0/0.1
 service-policy output shape-all
! Note the Interval is now listed as 10 ms. Also, note the detailed stats for LLQ
! are also listed at the end of the command.
R3# show policy-map interface serial 0/0.1
 Serial0/0.1

  Service-policy output: shape-all

    Class-map: class-default (match-any)
      5189 packets, 927835 bytes
      30 second offered rate 91000 bps, drop rate 0 bps
      Match: any
      Traffic Shaping
          Target/Average   Byte    Sustain    Excess    Interval  Increment
            Rate           Limit   bits/int   bits/int  (ms)      (bytes)
          96000/96000      1200      960        960       10        120


          Adapt  Queue   Packets   Bytes    Packets  Bytes    Shaping
          Active Depth                      Delayed  Delayed  Active
          —       17      5172      910975   4002     831630   yes


      Service-policy : queue-voip
        Class-map: voip-rtp (match-all)
          4623 packets, 295872 bytes
          30 second offered rate 25000 bps, drop rate 0 bps
          Match: ip rtp 16384 16383
          Weighted Fair Queueing
            Strict Priority
            Output Queue: Conversation 24
            Bandwidth 32 (kbps) Burst 800 (Bytes)
```

Example 14-2 *CB Shaping on R3, 96-kbps Shape Rate, with LLQ for Shaping Queues (Continued)*

```
                (pkts matched/bytes matched) 3528/225792
                (total drops/bytes drops) 0/0

        Class-map: class-default (match-any)
           566 packets, 631963 bytes
           30 second offered rate 65000 bps, drop rate 0 bps
           Match: any
           Weighted Fair Queueing
              Flow Based Fair Queueing
              Maximum Number of Hashed Queues 16
 (total queued/total drops/no-buffer drops) 17/0/0
```

Example 14-2 shows how to use LLQ against the packets shaped by CB Shaping by calling an LLQ policy map with the **service-policy** command. Note the command syntax (**service-policy queue-voip**) does not include the **output** keyword; the output direction is implied. Figure 14-4 shows the general idea behind what is happening in the configuration.

Figure 14-4 *Interaction Between Shaping Policy Map* **shape-all** *and Queuing Policy Map* **queue-voip**

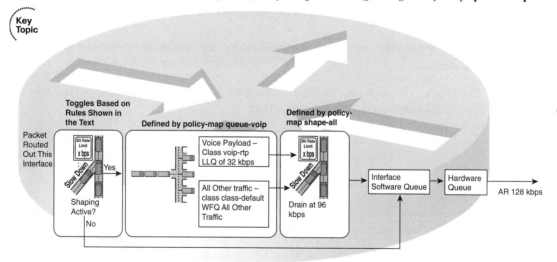

Scanning Figure 14-4 from left to right, CB Shaping must make the first decision after a packet has been routed out the subinterface. CB Shaping first needs to decide if shaping is active; if it is, CB Shaping should put the packet into a shaping queue. If it is not active, the packet can move right on to the appropriate interface software queue. Shaping becomes active when a single packet exceeds the traffic contract; shaping only becomes inactive again when all the shaping queues are drained.

Assuming that a packet needs to be delayed by CB Shaping, the LLQ logic of **policy-map queue-voip** determines into which of the two shaping queues the packet should be placed. Later, when CB Shaping decides to release the next packet (typically when the next Tc begins), LLQ determines which packets are taken next. This example has only two queues, one of which is an LLQ, so packets are always taken from the LLQ if any are present in that queue.

When a packet leaves one of the two shaping queues, it drains into the interface software queues. For routers with many VCs on the same physical interface, the VCs compete for the available interface bandwidth. Examples 14-1 and 14-2 both defaulted to use WFQ on the interface. However, LLQ or CBWFQ could have been used on the interface in addition to its use on the shaping function, simply by adding a **service-policy output policy-map-name** command under s0/0.

> **NOTE** When one policy map refers to another, as in Example 14-2, the configurations are sometimes called "hierarchical" policy maps. Other times, they are called "nested" policy maps. Or, you can just think of it as how CBWFQ and LLQ can be configured for the shaping queues.

Configuring Shaping by Bandwidth Percent

The **shape** command allows the shaping rate to be stated as a percentage of the setting of the interface or subinterface **bandwidth** setting. Configuring based on a simple percentage of the bandwidth command setting seems obvious at first. However, you should keep in mind the following facts when configuring the **shape** command based on percentage of interface bandwidth:

- The **shape percent** command uses the bandwidth of the interface or subinterface under which it is enabled.

- Subinterfaces do not inherit the bandwidth setting of the physical interface, so if it not set via the **bandwidth** command, it defaults to 1544.

- The Bc and Be values are configured as a number of milliseconds; the values are calculated as the number of bits that can be sent at the configured shaping rate, in the configured time period.

- Tc is set to the configured Bc value, which is in milliseconds.

Example 14-3 shows a brief example of CB Shaping configuration using percentages, including explanations of the points from the preceding list.

Example 14-3 *Shaping Based on Percent*

```
! With s0/0.1 bandwidth of 128, the rate is 50% * 128, or 64 kbps. At 64 kbps, 8000
! bits can be sent in the configured 125-ms time interval (64000 * 0.125 = 8000).
! Note that the ms parameter in the shape command is required after the Bc
! (shown) or Be (not shown), otherwise the command is rejected. Not shown: The
! Tc was set to 125 ms, the exact value configured for Bc.
policy-map percent-test
  class class-default
    shape average percent 50 125 ms
interface Serial0/1
 bandwidth 128
 service-policy output percent-test
```

CB Shaping to a Peak Rate

The **shape average** command has been used in all the examples so far. However, the command **shape peak** *mean-rate* is also allowed, which implements slightly different behavior as compared with **shape average** for the same configured rate. The key actions of the **shape peak** *mean-rate* command are summarized as follows:

- It calculates (or defaults) Bc, Be, and Tc the same way as the **shape average** command.

- It refills Bc + Be tokens (instead of just Bc tokens) into the token bucket for each time interval.

This logic means that CB Shaping gets the right to send the committed burst, and the excess burst, every time period. As a result, the actual shaping rate is as follows:

$$\text{Shaping\_rate} = \text{configured\_rate} \ (1 + Be/Bc)$$

For instance, the **shape peak 64000** command, with Bc and Be defaulted to 8000 bits each, results in an actual shaping rate of 128 kbps, based on the following formula:

$$64 \ (1 + 8000/8000) = 128$$

Adaptive Shaping

Adaptive shaping configuration requires only a minor amount of effort compared to the topics covered so far. To configure it, just add the **shape adaptive** *min-rate* command under the **shape** command. Example 14-4 shows a short example.

Example 14-4 *Adaptive CB Shaping Configuration*

```
policy-map shape-all
  class class-default
   shape average 96000 9600 ms
   shape adaptive 32000
```

Frame Relay Traffic Shaping Configuration

Frame Relay Traffic Shaping (FRTS) differs from CB Shaping in several significant ways, although the underlying token-bucket mechanics are identical. The following list highlights some of the key similarities and differences:

- FRTS can be used only on Frame Relay interfaces, whereas CB Shaping can be used with any underlying data link protocol.

- Like CB Shaping, FRTS allows a large number of IOS queuing tools to be used instead of a single FIFO shaping queue.

- Unlike CB Shaping, FRTS does not allow any fancy queuing tools to be enabled on the physical interface concurrent with FRTS.

- FRTS *always* shapes the traffic on each VC separately.

- FRTS cannot classify traffic in order to shape a subset of traffic on a particular VC.

- Unlike CB Shaping, FRTS can dynamically learn the CIR, Bc, and Be values configured on the Frame Relay switch by using the *Enhanced Local Management Interface (ELMI)* feature.

Prior to Cisco IOS version 12.2(13)T, MQC did not support FRTS, making FRTS configuration significantly different from that of CB Shaping. Later IOS releases support the configuration of FRTS using MQC. Some specifics of MQC-based FRTS are included in this section. In the non-MQC configuration, which is detailed first, FRTS organizes a set of shaping parameters (rate, Bc, and so on) into a named Frame Relay map class, using the **map-class frame-relay** command. The **frame-relay class** command and the **class** command then refer to those map classes, defining the shaping parameters to use for each Frame Relay VC. Figure 14-5 shows several examples of how these commands work together.

Figure 14-5 *Assignment of Map Classes to DLCIs with FRTS*

Key
Topic

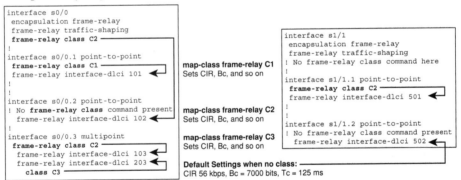

As Figure 14-5 illustrates, FRTS uses the map class referenced by the **class** command under the **frame-relay interface-dlci** command, if it exists (example: DLCI 203). If not, FRTS assigns the map class based on the subinterface's **frame-relay class** command (example: DLCI 103). Otherwise, FRTS looks for the setting on the physical interface (example: DLCI 102). If FRTS still has not found a reference to a map class, it uses default settings for that VC (example: DLCI 502). (Beware of enabling FRTS and not setting a VC's shaping parameters, especially if you want to get more than 56 kbps out of that VC!) These rules can be summarized as follows:

Key
Topic

- If the **class** *map-class-name* command is configured under the **interface-dlci** command, that map class defines the FRTS parameters for that VC.

- If not, if the **frame-relay class** *map-class-name* command is configured under the subinterface, that map class defines the FRTS parameters for the remaining underlying VCs.

- If not, if the **frame-relay class** *map-class-name* command is configured under the physical interface, that map class defines the FRTS parameters for the remaining underlying VCs.

- If not, FRTS uses the default settings of shaping at 56 kbps, Bc = 7000 bits, and Tc = 125 ms.

FRTS Configuration Using the traffic-rate Command

FRTS uses two main styles of configuration for the shaping parameters. The **frame-relay traffic-rate** *average* [*peak*] command configures the average and peak rate, with Cisco IOS calculating Bc and Be with an assumed Tc of 125 ms. This method is simpler to configure, but offers no ability to tune Tc or set Bc and Be.

Example 14-5 uses FRTS to implement the same requirements as the first CB Shaping example shown in Example 14-1, except that it uses FIFO queuing for the interface software queues.

Example 14-5 *FRTS Configuration, 64 kbps, with the* **frame-relay traffic-rate** *Command*

```
! The frame-relay traffic-shaping command enables FRTS for all VCs on s0/0. The
! frame-relay class shape-all-64 command refers to a map class.
interface Serial0/0
 encapsulation frame-relay
 frame-relay traffic-shaping
!
interface Serial0/0.1 point-to-point
 frame-relay class shape-all-64
 frame-relay interface-dlci 101
! lines omitted for brevity
! Above, note that the frame-relay class shape-all-64 command could have been
! listed under S0/0 instead, with the same results, as only one VC exists on the
! interface. Alternately, the class shape-all-64 command could have been used
! under the frame-relay interface-dlci 101 command.
! Next, The traffic-rate command sets the peak equal to the average, which results
! in a Be of 0.
map-class frame-relay shape-all-64
 frame-relay traffic-rate 64000 64000
! The show frame pvc command, with no DLCI listed, does not list FRTS info, but
! it does show FRTS info when the specific DLCI is given. The word "fifo" refers
! to the shaping queue.
R3# show frame-relay pvc 101
PVC Statistics for interface Serial0/0 (Frame Relay DTE)
DLCI = 101, DLCI USAGE = LOCAL, PVC STATUS = ACTIVE, INTERFACE = Serial0/0.1
! lines omitted for brevity
 shaping active
 traffic shaping drops 2774
 Queueing strategy: fifo
 Output queue 3/40, 678 drop, 3777 dequeued
! The next command shows the default 125-ms Tc, the calculated Bc = Tc * CIR,
```

Example 14-5 *FRTS Configuration, 64 kbps, with the* **frame-relay traffic-rate** *Command (Continued)*

```
! and it uses the same text in the headings as in the CB Shaping examples.
R3# show traffic-shape
Interface   Se0/0.1
         Access Target   Byte   Sustain   Excess   Interval  Increment Adapt
VC       List   Rate     Limit  bits/int  bits/int (ms)      (bytes)   Active
101             64000    1000   64000     0        125       1000      —
! This command lists basic stats for FRTS. The "fcfs" refers to the shaping queue
! as well, meaning "first come first served," which means the same thing as "fifo."
R3# show traffic-shape queue
Traffic queued in shaping queue on Serial0/0.1 dlci 101
  Queueing strategy: fcfs
  Queueing Stats: 23/40/959 (size/max total/drops)
! lines omitted for brevity
```

To use the **frame-relay traffic-rate** command to use a Be, the peak rate must be configured, and it must be more than the average rate. This command causes FRTS to calculate Be based on this formula:

$$Be = Tc * (PIR - CIR)$$

Key Topic

In Example 14-5, Be = 0.125 * (64,000 – 64,000) = 0, as shown in the output of the **show traffic-shape** command in the example. However, if the **frame-relay traffic-rate 64000 96000** command had been used, the Be would be .125 (96,000 – 64,000) = 4000.

Setting FRTS Parameters Explicitly

The **frame-relay cir**, **frame-relay Bc**, and **frame-relay Be** commands can be used to directly set FRTS parameters in an FRTS map class, instead of setting the Bc, Be, and Tc values indirectly using the **frame-relay traffic-rate** command. Example 14-6 shows two new map classes on the same router configured in Example 14-5. These new map classes use these additional commands to set FRTS parameters explicitly, which is particularly useful for tuning FRTS to use a small Tc.

Example 14-6 *FRTS Configuration by Setting CIR and BC to Manipulate Tc*

```
! map-class shape-all-64-long sets CIR and Bc directly, defaulting Be to 0, with
! Tc calculated via Tc = Bc/CIR
map-class frame-relay shape-all-64-long
 frame-relay cir 64000
 frame-relay bc 8000
! All VCs on s0/0.1 that do not have class commands will use shape-all-64-long.
R3(config)# interface serial 0/0.1
R3(config-subif)# frame class shape-all-64-long
R3(config-subif)# ^Z
! This command confirms the configured rate, with the Tc calculated as Bc/rate, or
```

Example 14-6 *FRTS Configuration by Setting CIR and BC to Manipulate Tc (Continued)*

```
! in this case, 8000/64000. Note the default Be of 0 is also listed.
R3# show traffic-shape
Interface   Se0/0.1
        Access Target   Byte    Sustain  Excess    Interval  Increment Adapt
VC      List   Rate     Limit   bits/int bits/int  (ms)      (bytes)   Active
101            64000    1000    8000     0         125       1000      -
! The next commands create another map class, with the Bc set to 1/100th
! of the shaping rate (10 ms).
R3(config)# map-class frame-relay shape-all-64-shortTC
R3(config-map-class)# frame-relay cir 64000
R3(config-map-class)# frame-relay bc 640
R3(config-map-class)# int s 0/0.1
R3(config-subif)# frame class shape-all-64-shortTC
R3# show traffic-shape
Interface   Se0/0.1
        Access Target   Byte    Sustain  Excess    Interval  Increment Adapt
VC      List   Rate     Limit   bits/int bits/int  (ms)      (bytes)   Active
101            64000    80      640      0         10        80        -
```

FRTS Configuration Using LLQ

FRTS supports a variety of queuing tools for managing packets it queues. The queuing tool is enabled via a command in the map class. Example 14-7 shows just such an example, with a new map class. The requirements implemented in this example are as follows:

- Shape traffic on the two VCs (101 and 102) on s0/0 with the same settings for shaping.

- Use LLQ only on the VC with DLCI 101.

- Set Be to 0, and tune Tc to 10 ms.

Note that the example does not show the configuration for policy map **queue-voip**. Its full configuration can be seen back in Example 14-2.

Example 14-7 *FRTS to Two Sites, with LLQ Used to Shape the Queue to Site 1*

```
R3# show running-config
! FRTS is first enabled, and class shape-all-96 is set up to filter down to the
! remaining VCs, assuming no other frame-relay class or class subcommands are applied
! to them.
interface Serial0/0
 encapsulation frame-relay
 frame-relay class shape-all-96
 frame-relay traffic-shaping
! DLCI 101 will use class shape-with-LLQ based on the next few commands.
interface Serial0/0.1 point-to-point
```

continues

Example 14-7 *FRTS to Two Sites, with LLQ Used to Shape the Queue to Site 1 (Continued)*

```
 frame-relay class shape-with-LLQ
 frame-relay interface-dlci 101
! DLCI 102 will use class shape-all-96 because it is configured under s0/0.
interface Serial0/0.2 point-to-point
 frame-relay interface-dlci 102
! The only difference between the two map classes is the service-policy output
! voip-and-allelse command, which enables LLQ in the shape-with-LLQ class.
map-class frame-relay shape-all-96
 frame-relay cir 96000
 frame-relay bc 960
 frame-relay be 0
!
map-class frame-relay shape-with-LLQ
 frame-relay cir 96000
 frame-relay bc 960
 frame-relay be 0
 service-policy output queue-voip
! The show policy-map interface command does not show any LLQ stats with FRTS.
! Instead, the show frame-relay pvc DLCI command is required, with output similar
! to the show policy-map interface command.
R3# show frame-relay pvc 101
PVC Statistics for interface Serial0/0 (Frame Relay DTE)
DLCI = 101, DLCI USAGE = LOCAL, PVC STATUS = ACTIVE, INTERFACE = Serial0/0.1
! lines omitted for brevity
  shaping active
  traffic shaping drops 0
  service policy queue-voip
 Serial0/0.1: DLCI 101 -

   Service-policy output: queue-voip
     Class-map: voip-rtp (match-all)
       5101 packets, 326464 bytes
       30 second offered rate 25000 bps, drop rate 0 bps
       Match: ip rtp 16384 16383
       Weighted Fair Queueing
        Strict Priority
! lines omitted for brevity
```

FRTS Adaptive Shaping

Adding FRTS adaptive shaping configuration to an existing FRTS configuration is relatively simple. To enable it, do the following:

Key Topic

1. Add either a **frame-relay adaptive-shaping becn** or **frame-relay adaptive-shaping foresight** command into the appropriate map class.

2. To set the minimum to something other than the default of 50 percent of the shaping rate, add the **frame-relay mincir** *rate* command in the map class.

FRTS with MQC

MQC-based FRTS is another method of configuring the same behaviors that you can configure with the legacy FRTS commands. FRTS integration into the MQC represents the continuing migration toward MQC for its modular characteristics, rather than the many separate tools that MQC replaces, to make configuring QoS features easier.

Configuring MQC-based FRTS requires knowledge of a few key rules:

- You must create a default class in the FRTS service policy, under which all FRTS commands are applied.

- If FRTS and fragmentation are both applied to a PVC using the MQC commands, the interface will use a dual FIFO queue. One of the queues will carry high-priority voice traffic and control traffic; the other queue will carry all other traffic.

- If you are using nested policy maps, and you are using CBWFQ, the shaping rate configured in the parent policy map represents the total bandwidth available to the child policy map.

- If the **shape average** and **shape adaptive** commands are both configured, the available bandwidth is based on the bandwidth configured for the **shape adaptive** command.

- The **frame-relay ip rtp priority** command is not supported in MQC, because LLQ replaces this function in MQC.

See the "Further Reading" section at the end of the chapter for a reference to additional information on, and examples of, configuring MQC-based FRTS.

Policing Concepts and Configuration

Class-Based Policing (CB Policing) performs different internal processing than the older, alternative policer in Cisco router IOS, namely committed access rate (CAR). This section focuses on CB Policing, starting with concepts and then covering configuration details.

CB Policing Concepts

CB Policing is enabled for packets either entering or exiting an interface, or those entering or exiting a subinterface. It monitors, or *meters*, the bit rate of the combined packets; when a packet pushes the metered rate past the configured policing rate, the policer takes action against that packet. The most aggressive action is to discard the packet. Alternately, the policer can simply re-mark a field in the packet. This second option allows the packets through, but if congestion occurs at later places during a marked-down packet's journey, it is more likely to be discarded.

Table 14-4 lists the keywords used to imply the policer's actions.

Table 14-4 *Policing Actions Used CB Policing*

Command Option	Mode and Function
drop	Drops the packet
set-dscp-transmit	Sets the DSCP and transmits the packet
set-prec-transmit	Sets the IP Precedence (0 to 7) and sends the packet
set-qos-transmit	Sets the QoS Group ID (1 to 99) and sends the packet
set-clp-transmit	Sets the ATM CLP bit (ATM interfaces only) and sends the packet
set-fr-de	Sets the Frame Relay DE bit (Frame Relay interfaces only) and sends the packet
transmit	Sends the packet

CB Policing categorizes packets into two or three categories, depending on the style of policing, and then applies one of these actions to each category of packet. The categories are *conforming* packets, *exceeding* packets, and *violating* packets. The CB Policing logic that dictates when packets are placed into a particular category varies based on the type of policing. The next three sections outline the types of CB Policing logic.

Single-Rate, Two-Color Policing (One Bucket)

Single-rate, two-color policing is the simplest option for CB Policing. This method uses a single policing rate with no excess burst. The policer will then use only two categories (*conform* and *exceed*), defining a different action on packets of each type. (Typically, the conform action is to transmit the packet, with the exceed action either being to drop the packet or mark it down.)

While this type of policing logic is often called *single-rate, two-color* policing, it is sometimes called *single-bucket two-color* policing because it uses a single token bucket for internal processing. Like shaping's use of token buckets, the policer's main logic relates to filling the bucket with tokens, and then spending the tokens. Over time, the policer refills the bucket according to the policing rate. For instance, policing at 96 kbps, over the course of 1 second, adds 12,000 tokens to the bucket. (A token represents a byte with policers, so 12,000 tokens is 96,000 bits' worth of tokens.)

CB Policing does not refill the bucket based on a time interval. Instead, CB Policing reacts to the arrival of a packet by replenishing a prorated number of tokens into the bucket. The number of tokens is defined by the following formula:

$$\frac{(Current\_packet\_arrival\_time - Previous\_packet\_arrival\_time) * Police\_rate}{8}$$

NOTE Note that a token represents the right to send 1 byte, so the formula includes the division by 8 to convert the units to bytes instead of bits.

The idea behind the formula is simple—essentially, a small number of tokens are replenished before each packet is policed; the end result is that tokens are replenished at the policing rate. For example, for a police rate of 128 kbps, the policer should replenish 16,000 tokens per second. If 1 second has elapsed since the previous packet arrived, CB Policing would replenish the bucket with 16,000 tokens. If 0.1 second has passed since the previous packet had arrived, CB Policing would replenish the bucket with 0.1 second's worth of tokens, or 1600 tokens. If 0.01 second had passed, CB Policing would replenish 160 tokens at that time.

The policer then considers whether it should categorize the newly arrived packet as either conforming or exceeding the traffic contract. The policer compares the number of bytes in the packet (represented here as Xp, with "p" meaning "packet") to the number of tokens the token bucket (represented here as Xb, with "b" meaning "bucket"). Table 14-5 shows the decision logic, along with whether the policer spends/removes tokens from the bucket.

Table 14-5 *Single-Rate, Two-Color Policing Logic for Categorizing Packets*

Category	Requirements	Tokens Drained from Bucket
Conform	If $Xp <= Xb$	Xp tokens
Exceed	If $Xp > Xb$	None

As long as the overall bit rate does not exceed the policing rate, the packets will all conform. However, if the rate is exceeded, then as tokens are removed for each conforming packet, the bucket will eventually empty—causing some packets to exceed the contract. Over time, tokens are added back to the bucket, so some packets will conform. Once the bit rate lowers below the policing rate, all packets will again conform to the contract.

Single-Rate, Three-Color Policer (Two Buckets)

When you want the policer to police at a particular rate, but to also support a Be, the policer uses two token buckets. It also uses all three categories for packets—conform, exceed, and violate. Combining those concepts together, such policing is typically called *single-rate, three-color policing*.

As before, CB Policing fills the buckets in reaction to packet arrival. (For lack of a better set of terms, this discussions calls the first bucket the Bc bucket, because it is Bc in size, and the other one the Be bucket, because it is Be in size.) CB Policing fills the Bc bucket just like a single-bucket model. However, if the Bc bucket has any tokens left in it, some will spill; these tokens then fill the Be bucket. Figure 14-6 shows the basic process.

After filling the buckets, the policer then determines the category for the newly arrived packet, as shown in Table 14-6. In this case, Xbc is the number of tokens in the Bc bucket, and Xbe is the number in the Be bucket.

Figure 14-6 *Refilling Dual Token Buckets with CB Policing*

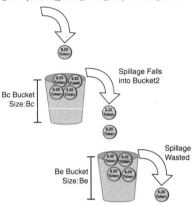

Table 14-6 *Single-Rate Three-Color Policing Logic for Categorizing Packets*

Category	Requirements	Tokens Drained from Bucket
Conform	$Xp <= Xbc$	Xp tokens from the Bc bucket
Exceed	$Xp > Xbc$ and $Xp <= Xbe$	Xp tokens from the Be bucket
Violate	$Xp > Xbc$ and $Xp > Xbe$	None

Two-Rate, Three-Color Policer (Two Buckets)

The third main option for CB Policing uses two separate policing rates. The lower rate is the previously discussed committed information rate (CIR), and the higher, second rate is called the *peak information rate (PIR)*. Packets that fall under the CIR conform to the traffic contract. Packets that exceed the CIR, but fall below PIR, are considered to exceed the contract. Finally, packets beyond the PIR are considered to violate the contract.

The key difference between the single-rate and dual-rate three-color policers is that the dual-rate method essentially allows sustained excess bursting. With a single-rate, three-color policer, an excess burst exists, but the burst is sustained only until the Be bucket empties. A period of relatively low activity has to occur to refill the Be bucket. With the dual-rate method, the Be bucket does not rely on spillage when filling the Bc bucket, as depicted in Figure 14-7. (Note that these buckets are sometimes called the CIR and PIR buckets with dual-rate policing.)

The refilling of the two buckets based on two different rates is very important. For example, imagine you set a CIR of 128 kbps (16 kilobytes/second), and a PIR of 256 kbps (32 kBps). If 0.1 second passed before the next packet arrived, then the CIR bucket would be replenished with 1600 tokens (1/10 of 1 second's worth of tokens, in bytes), while the PIR bucket would be replenished with 3200 tokens. So, there are more tokens to use in the PIR bucket, as compared to the CIR bucket.

Figure 14-7 *Refilling CIR and PIR Dual Token Buckets*

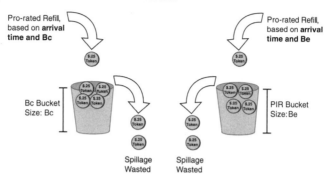

Next, the policer categorizes the packet. The only difference in logic as compared with the single-rate, three-color policer is highlighted in Table 14-7, specifically related to how tokens are consumed for conforming packets.

Table 14-7 *Two-Rate, Three-Color Policing Logic for Categorizing Packets*

Category	Requirements	Tokens Drained from Bucket
Conform	$Xp <= Xbc$	Xp tokens from the Bc bucket AND Xp tokens from the Be bucket
Exceed	$Xp > Xbc$ and $Xp <= Xbe$	Xp tokens from the Be bucket
Violate	$Xp > Xbc$ and $Xp > Xbe$	None

While Table 14-7 does outline each detail, the underlying logic might not be obvious from the table. In effect, by filling the Be bucket based on the higher PIR, but also draining tokens from the Be bucket for packets that conform to the lower CIR, the Be bucket has tokens that represent the difference between the two rates.

Class-Based Policing Configuration

CB Policing uses the familiar MQC commands for configuration. As a result, a policy map can police all packets using the convenient class-default class, or it can separate traffic into classes, apply different policing parameters to different classes of traffic, or even simply not police some classes.

The **police** command configures CB Policing inside a policy map. On the **police** command, you define the policing rate in bps, the Bc in bytes, and the Be in bytes, along with the actions for each category:

```
police bps burst-normal burst-max conform-action action exceed-action action
   [violate-action action]
```

Single-Rate, Three-Color Policing of All Traffic

Example 14-8 shows how to police all traffic, with criteria as follows:

■ Create a single-rate, three-color policing configuration.

■ All traffic policed at 96 kbps at ingress.

■ Bc of 1 second's worth of traffic is allowed.

■ Be of 0.5 second's worth of traffic is allowed.

■ The conform, exceed, and violate actions should be to forward, mark down to DSCP 0, and discard, respectively.

Example 14-8 *Single-Rate, Three-Color CB Policing at 96 kbps*

```
! The police command sets the rate (in bps), Bc and Be (in bytes), and the three
! actions.
policy-map police-all
  class class-default
! note: the police command wraps around to a second line.
  police cir 96000 bc 12000 be 6000 conform-action transmit exceed-action set-dscp-
  transmit 0 violate-action drop
!
interface Serial1/0
 encapsulation frame-relay
 service-policy input police-all
! The show command below lists statistics for each of the three categories.
ISP-edge# show  policy-map  interface s 1/0
 Serial1/0
  Service-policy input: police-all

    Class-map: class-default (match-any)
      8375 packets, 1446373 bytes
      30 second offered rate 113000 bps, drop rate 15000 bps
      Match: any
      police:
        cir 96000 bps, conform-burst 12000, excess-burst 6000
        conformed 8077 packets, 1224913 bytes; action: transmit
        exceeded 29 packets, 17948 bytes; action: set-dscp-transmit 0
        violated 269 packets, 203512 bytes; action: drop
        conformed 95000 bps, exceed 0 bps violate 20000 bps
```

The **police** command defines a single rate, but the fact that it is a three-color policing configuration, and not a two-color configuration, is not obvious at first glance. To configure a single-rate, three-color policer, you need to configure a violate action or explicitly set Be to something larger than 0.

Policing a Subset of the Traffic

One of the advantages of CB Policing is the ability to perform policing per class. Example 14-9 shows CB Policing with HTTP traffic classified and policed differently than the rest of the traffic, with the following criteria:

- Police web traffic at 80 kbps at ingress to the ISP-edge router. Transmit conforming and exceeding traffic, but discard violating traffic.

- Police all other traffic at 16 kbps at ingress to the ISP-edge router. Mark down exceeding and violating traffic to DSCP 0.

- For both classes, set Bc and Be to 1 second's worth and .5 second's worth of traffic, respectively.

Example 14-9 *CB Policing 80 kbps for Web Traffic, 16 kbps for the Rest with Markdown to Be, at ISP-Edge Router*

```
class-map match-all match-web
  match protocol http
! The new policy map uses the new class to match http, and class-default to
! match all other traffic.
policy-map police-web
  class match-web
    police cir 80000 bc 10000 be 5000 conform-action transmit exceed-action transmit
violate-action drop
  class class-default
    police cir 16000 bc 2000 be 1000 conform-action transmit exceed-action
transmit violate-action set-dscp-transmit 0
!
interface Serial1/0
 encapsulation frame-relay
 service-policy input police-web
```

Key
Topic

CB Policing Defaults for Bc and Be

If you do not configure a Bc value on the **police** command, then CB Policing configures a default value equivalent to the bytes that could be sent in $1/4$ second at the defined policing rate. The formula is as follows:

$$Bc = \frac{(CIR * 0.25 \text{ second})}{8 \text{ bits/byte}} = \frac{CIR}{32}$$

The only part that may not be obvious is the division by 8 on the left—that is simply for the conversion from bits to bytes. The math reduces to CIR/32. Also, if the formula yields a number less than 1500, CB Policing uses a Bc of 1500.

If the **police** command does not include a Be value, the default Be setting depends on the type of policing. Table 14-8 summarizes the details.

Table 14-8 *Setting CB Policing Bc and Be Defaults*

Type of Policing Configuration	Telltale Signs in the police Command	Defaults
Single rate, two color	No **violate-action** configured	Bc = CIR/32; Be = 0
Single rate, three color	**violate-action** is configured	Bc = CIR/32; Be = Bc
Dual rate, three color	PIR is configured	Bc = CIR/32; Be = PIR/32

Configuring Dual-Rate Policing

Dual-rate CB Policing requires the same MQC commands, but with slightly different syntax on the **police** command, as shown here:

```
police {cir cir} [bc conform-burst] {pir pir} [be peak-burst]
    [conform-action action [exceed-action action [violate-action action]]]
```

Note that the syntax of this command requires configuration of both the CIR and a PIR because the curly brackets mean that the parameter is required. The command includes a place to set the Bc value and the Be value as well, plus the same set of options for conform, exceed, and violate actions. For example, if you wanted to perform dual-rate policing, with a CIR of 96 kbps and a PIR of 128 kbps, you would simply use a command like **police cir 96000 pir 128000**, with optional setting of Bc and Be, plus the settings for the actions for each of the three categories.

Multi-Action Policing

When CB Policing re-marks packets instead of discarding them, the design might call for marking more than one field in a packet. For instance, when transmitting into a Frame Relay cloud, it might be useful to mark both DSCP and FR DE when a packet violates the contract. Marking multiple fields in the same packet with CB Policing is called *multi-action policing*.

The **police** command uses a slightly different syntax to implement multi-action policing. By omitting the actions from the command, the **police** command places the user into a policing subconfiguration mode in which the actions can be added via separate commands (the **conform-action**, **exceed-action**, and **violate-action** commands). To configure multiple actions, one of these three **action** commands would be used more than once, as shown in Example 14-10, which marks DSCP 0 and sets FR DE for packets that violate the traffic contract.

Example 14-10 *Multi-Action Policing*

```
R3# conf t
Enter configuration commands, one per line.  End with CNTL/Z.
R3(config)# policy-map testpol1
R3(config-pmap)# class class-default
! This command implements dual-rate policing as well, but it is not required
R3(config-pmap-c)# police 128000 256000
R3(config-pmap-c-police)# conform-action transmit
R3(config-pmap-c-police)# exceed-action transmit
R3(config-pmap-c-police)# violate-action set-dscp-transmit 0
R3(config-pmap-c-police)# violate-action set-frde-transmit
```

Policing by Percentage

As it does with the **shape** command, Cisco IOS supports configuring policing rates as a percentage of link bandwidth. The Bc and Be values are configured as a number of milliseconds, from which IOS calculates the actual Bc and Be values based on how many bits can be sent in that many milliseconds. Example 14-11 shows an example of a dual-rate policing configuration using the **percentage** option.

Example 14-11 *Configuring Percentage-Based Policing*

```
R3# show running-config
! Portions omitted for Brevity
 policy-map test-pol6
  class class-default
   police cir percent 25 bc 500 ms pir percent 50 be 500 ms conform transmit exceed transmit
     violate drop
!
interface serial0/0
 bandwidth 256
 service-policy output test-pol6
! The output below shows the configured percentage for the rate and the time for
! Bc and Be, with the calculated values immediately below.
R3# show policy-map interface s0/0
! lines omitted for brevity
      police:
           cir 25 % bc 500 ms
           cir 64000 bps, bc 4000 bytes
           pir 50 % be 500 ms
           pir 128000 bps, be 8000 bytes
! lines omitted
```

Committed Access Rate

CAR implements single-rate, two-color policing. As compared with that same option in CB Policing, CAR and CB Policing have many similarities. They both can police traffic either entering or exiting an interface or subinterface; they can both police subsets of that traffic based on classification logic; and they both set the rate in bps, with Bc and Be configured as a number of bytes.

CAR differs from CB Policing regarding four main features, as follows:

- CAR uses the **rate-limit** command, which is not part of the MQC set of commands.

- CAR has a feature called *cascaded* or *nested* **rate-limit** commands, which allows multiple **rate-limit** commands on an interface to process the same packet.

- CAR does support Be; however, even in this case, it still supports only conform and exceed categories, and never supports a third (violate) category.

- When CAR has a Be configured, the internal logic used to determine which packets conform and exceed differs as compared with CB Policing.

CAR puts most parameters on the **rate-limit** command, which is added under an interface or subinterface:

```
rate-limit {input | output} [access-group [rate-limit] acl-index] bps burst-normal
    burst-max conform-action conform-action exceed-action exceed-action
```

Example 14-12 shows an example CAR configuration for perspective. The criteria for the CAR configuration in Example 14-12 are as follows:

- All traffic policed at 96 kbps at ingress to the ISP-edge router.

- Bc of 1 second's worth of traffic is allowed.

- Be of 0.5 second's worth of traffic is allowed.

- Traffic that exceeds the contract is discarded.

- Traffic that conforms to the contract is forwarded with Precedence reset to 0.

Example 14-12 *CAR at 96 kbps at ISP-Edge Router*

```
! The rate-limit command omits the access-group option, meaning that it has no matching
! parameters, so all packets are considered to match the command. The rest of the
! options simply match the requirements.
interface Serial1/0.1 point-to-point
ip address 192.168.2.251 255.255.255.0
! note: the rate-limit command wraps around to a second line.
 rate-limit input 96000 12000 18000 conform-action set-prec-transmit 0
   exceed-action drop
 frame-relay interface-dlci 103
! The output below confirms the parameters, including matching all traffic.
ISP-edge# show interfaces s 1/0.1 rate-limit
  Input
    matches: all traffic
      params:  96000 bps, 12000 limit, 18000 extended limit
```

Example 14-12 *CAR at 96 kbps at ISP-Edge Router*

```
            conformed 2290 packets, 430018 bytes; action: set-prec-transmit 0
            exceeded 230 packets, 67681 bytes; action: drop
            last packet: 0ms ago, current burst: 13428 bytes
 last cleared 00:02:16 ago, conformed 25000 bps, exceeded 3000 bps
```

To classify traffic, CAR requires the use of either a normal ACL or a *rate-limit ACL*. A rate-limit ACL can match MPLS Experimental bits, IP Precedence, or MAC Address. For other fields, an IP ACL must be used. Example 14-13 shows an example in which CAR polices three different subsets of traffic using ACLs for matching the traffic, as well as limiting the overall traffic rate. The criteria for this example are as follows (Note that CAR allows only policing rates that are multiples of 8 kbps):

■ Police all traffic on the interface at 496 kbps; but before sending this traffic on its way....

■ Police all web traffic at 400 kbps.

■ Police all FTP traffic at 160 kbps.

■ Police all VoIP traffic at 200 kbps.

■ Choose Bc and Be so that Bc has 1 second's worth of traffic, and Be provides no additional burst capability over Bc.

Example 14-13 *Cascaded CAR* **rate-limit** *Commands, with Subclassifications*

```
! ACL 101 matches all HTTP traffic
! ACL 102 matches all FTP traffic
! ACL 103 matches all VoIP traffic
interface s 0/0
rate-limit input 496000 62000 62000 conform-action continue exceed-action drop
rate-limit input access-group 101 400000 50000 50000 conform-action transmit exceed-action
drop
rate-limit input access-group 102 160000 20000 20000 conform-action transmit exceed-action
drop
rate-limit input access-group 103 200000 25000 25000 conform-action transmit exceed-action
drop
```

The CAR configuration refers to IP ACLs in order to classify the traffic, using three different IP ACLs in this case. ACL 101 matches all web traffic; ACL 102 matches all FTP traffic; and ACL 103 matches all VoIP traffic.

Under subinterface s1/0.1, four **rate-limit** commands are used. The first sets the rate for all traffic, dropping traffic that exceeds 496 kbps. However, the conform action is "continue." This means that packets conforming to this statement will be compared to the next **rate-limit** statements, and when matching a statement, some other action will be taken. For instance, web traffic matches the second **rate-limit** command, with a resulting action of either transmit or drop. VoIP traffic would be compared with the next three **rate-limit** commands before matching the last one. As a result, all traffic is limited to 496 kbps, and three particular subsets of traffic are prevented from taking all the bandwidth.

CB Policing can achieve the same effect of policing subsets of traffic by using nested policy maps.

Foundation Summary

This section lists additional details and facts to round out the coverage of the topics in this chapter. Unlike most of the Cisco Press *Exam Certification Guides*, this "Foundation Summary" does not repeat information presented in the "Foundation Topics" section of the chapter. Please take the time to read and study the details in the "Foundation Topics" section of the chapter, as well as review items noted with a Key Topic icon.

Table 14-9 lists commands related to CB Shaping.

Table 14-9 *Class-Based Shaping Command Reference*

Command	Mode and Function
shape [**average**	**peak**] *mean-rate* [[*burst-size*] [*excess-burst-size*]]	Class configuration mode; enables shaping for the class
shape [**average**	**peak**] **percent** *percent* [[*burst- size*] [*excess-burst-size*]]	Enables shaping based on percentage of bandwidth
shape adaptive *min-rate*	Enables the minimum rate for adaptive shaping
shape fecn-adapt	Causes reflection of BECN bits after receipt of an FECN
service-policy {**input**	**output**} *policy- map-name*	Interface or subinterface configuration mode; enables CB Shaping on the interface
shape max-buffers *number-of-buffers*	Sets the maximum queue length for the default FIFO shaping queue
show policy-map *policy-map-name*	Lists configuration information about all MQC-based QoS tools
show policy-map *interface-spec* [**input**	**output**] [**class** *class-name*]	Lists statistical information about the behavior of all MQC-based QoS tools

Table 14-10 lists commands related to FRTS.

Table 14-10 *FRTS Command Reference*

Command	Mode and Function
frame-relay traffic-shaping	Interface subcommand; enables FRTS on the interface
class *name*	Used under the **interface-dlci** to point to a map class
frame-relay class *name*	Used under an interface or subinterface to point to a map class
map-class frame-relay *map-class-name*	Global command to name map class, with subcommands detailing a set of shaping parameters
service-policy output *policy-map-name*	Used in a map class to enable LLQ or CBWFQ
frame-relay traffic-rate *average* [*peak*]	Used in a map class to define shaping rates
frame-relay bc out *bits*	Used in a map class to explicitly set Bc
frame-relay be out *bits*	Used in a map class to explicitly set Be
frame-relay cir out *bps*	Used in a map class to explicitly set CIR
frame-relay adaptive-shaping {**becn** | **foresight**}	Used in a map class to both enable adaptive shaping and define what causes FRTS to slow down
frame-relay mincir out *bps*	Used in a map class to define how far adaptive shaping will lower the rate
frame-relay tc *milliseconds*	Used in a map class to explicitly set Tc
frame-relay qos-autosense	Interface command telling the router to use ELMI to discover the CIR, Bc, and Be from the switch
shape adaptive *mean-rate-lower-bound*	Policy-map configuration command used to estimate the available bandwidth using BECN messages; shapes traffic to no less than the configured *mean-rate-lower-bound* parameter
shape fecn-adapt	Policy-map configuration command that reflects FECN messages as BECN messages to the Frame Relay switch
show frame-relay pvc [**interface** *interface*] [*dlci*]	Shows PVC statistics, including shaping statistics
show traffic-shape [*interface-type interface-number*]	Shows information about FRTS configuration per VC
show traffic-shape queue [*interface-number* [**dlci** *dlci-number*]]	Shows information about the queuing tool used with the shaping queue
show traffic-shape statistics [*interface-type interface-number*]	Shows traffic-shaping statistics

Table 14-11 provides a command reference for CB Policing.

Table 14-11 *Class-Based Policing Command Reference*

Command	Mode and Function
police *bps burst-normal burst-max* **conform-action** *action* **exceed-action** *action* [**violate-action** *action*]	**policy-map** class subcommand; enables policing for the class
police cir percent *percent* [**bc** *conform-burst-in-msec*] [**pir percent** *percent*] [**be** *peak-burst-in-msec*] [**conform-action** *action* [**exceed-action** *action* [**violate-action** *action*]]]	**policy-map** class subcommand; enables policing using percentages of bandwidth
police {**cir** *cir*} [**bc** *conform-burst*] {**pir** *pir*} [**be** *peak-burst*] [**conform-action** *action* [**exceed-action** *action* [**violate-action** *action*]]]	**policy-map** class subcommand; enables dual-rate policing
service-policy {**input**	**output**} *policy-map-name*	Enables CB Policing on an interface or subinterface

Memory Builders

The CCIE Routing and Switching written exam, like all Cisco CCIE written exams, covers a fairly broad set of topics. This section provides some basic tools to help you exercise your memory about some of the broader topics covered in this chapter.

Fill in Key Tables from Memory

Appendix E, "Key Tables for CCIE Study," on the CD in the back of this book contains empty sets of some of the key summary tables in each chapter. Print Appendix E, refer to this chapter's tables in it, and fill in the tables from memory. Refer to Appendix F, "Solutions for Key Tables for CCIE Study," on the CD to check your answers.

Definitions

Next, take a few moments to write down the definitions for the following terms:

Tc, Bc, Be, CIR, shaping rate, policing rate, token bucket, Bc bucket, Be bucket, adaptive shaping, BECN, ForeSight, ELMI, mincir, map class, marking down, single-rate two-color policer, single-rate three-color policer, dual-rate three-color policer, conform, exceed, violate, traffic contract, dual token bucket, PIR, nested policy maps, multi-action policing

Refer to the glossary to check your answers.

Further Reading

Cisco QoS Exam Certification Guide, by Wendell Odom and Michael Cavanaugh

"MQC-Based Frame Relay Traffic Shaping," http://www.cisco.com/en/US/products/sw/iosswrel/ps1839/products_feature_guide09186a0080110bc6.html

Part V: Wide-Area Networks

Chapter 15: Frame Relay

Blueprint topics covered in this chapter:

This chapter covers the following subtopics from the Cisco CCIE Routing and Switching written exam blueprint. Refer to the full blueprint in Table I-1 in the Introduction for more details on the topics covered in each chapter and their context within the blueprint.

- Frame Relay

- Local Management Interface (LMI)

- Traffic Shaping

- Hub and Spoke Routers

- Discard Eligible (DE) Bit

Frame Relay

This chapter covers the details of Frame Relay.

"Do I Know This Already?" Quiz

Table 15-1 outlines the major sections in this chapter and the corresponding "Do I Know This Already?" quiz questions.

Table 15-1 *"Do I Know This Already?" Foundation Topics Section-to-Question Mapping*

Foundation Topics Section	Questions Covered in This Section	Score
Frame Relay Concepts	1–4	
Frame Relay Configuration	5–7	
Total Score		

In order to best use this pre-chapter assessment, remember to score yourself strictly. You can find the answers in Appendix A, "Answers to the 'Do I Know This Already?' Quizzes."

1. Which of the following is true about both the ANSI and ITU options for Frame Relay LMI settings in a Cisco router, but not for the LMI option called **cisco**?

   a. They use DLCI 1023 for LMI functions.

   b. They use DLCI 0 for LMI functions.

   c. They include support for a maximum of 1022 DLCIs on a single access link.

   d. They include support for a maximum of 992 DLCIs on a single access link.

   e. They can be autosensed by a Cisco router.

2. R1 sends a Frame Relay frame over a PVC to R2. When R2 receives the frame, the frame has the DE and FECN bits set, but not the BECN bit. Which of the following statements accurately describes how R2 could have reacted to this frame, or how R1 might have impacted the contents of the frame?

   a. R2 would lower its shaping rate on the PVC assuming R2 has configured adaptive shaping.

   b. R2 could discard the received frame because of the DE setting.

   c. R2 could set BECN in the next frame it sends to R1, assuming FECN reflection is configured.

   d. R1 could have set the FECN bit before sending the frame if R1 had configured outbound policing with the policer marking FECN for out-of-contract frames.

3. Which of the following statements are true regarding Frame Relay encapsulation?

   a. Encapsulation type *cisco* can be configured using the **encapsulation cisco** interface sub-command.

   b. Encapsulation type *ietf* can be configured using the **encapsulation frame-relay** interface subcommand.

   c. Encapsulation type *cisco* can be configured using the **encapsulation frame-relay cisco** subinterface subcommand.

   d. Encapsulation types must be the same on all VCs on the same physical access link.

   e. Different encapsulations can be configured for each VC on the same physical interface using the **frame-relay interface-dlci** *dlci encapsulation-type* command.

   f. Different encapsulations can be configured for each VC using the **encapsulation frame-relay encapsulation-type** subcommand under the **frame-relay interface-dlci** command.

4. Which of the following commands disables Frame Relay LMI?

   a. The **no frame-relay lmi** command under the physical interface.

   b. The **no keepalive** command under the physical interface.

   c. The **frame-relay lmi-interval 0** command under the physical interface.

   d. The **keepalive 0** command under the physical interface.

   e. It cannot be disabled, as it is required for a working Frame Relay access link.

5. Which of the following answers are true regarding the three options for Frame Relay payload compression?

   a. FRF.9 and packet-by-packet use a per-packet compression dictionary.

   b. Data-stream and FRF.9 compression use the LZS compression algorithm.

   c. The only method of enabling data-steam compression is through the **frame-relay payload-compress** subinterface subcommand.

   d. The data-stream compression type is Cisco proprietary.

6. R1 has a Frame Relay access link on s0/0. The attached Frame Relay switch has ten PVCs configured on the link, with DLCIs 80–89. Which of the following is true regarding definition of DLCIs and encapsulation on the link?

   a. The **frame-relay interface-dlci** command associates a DLCI with the subinterface under which it is configured.

   b. The LMI Status message from the switch can be used by the router to associate the DLCIs with the correct subinterface.

   c. PVCs using IETF encapsulation require a **frame-relay map** command on the related subinterface.

   d. The LMI Status message from the switch tells the router which encapsulation to use for each PVC.

   e. Different encapsulation types can be mixed over this same access link.

7. R1 has a Frame Relay access link on s0/0. The attached Frame Relay switch has ten PVCs configured on the link, with DLCIs 80–89. R1's configuration includes ten point-to-point subinterfaces, also numbered 80 through 89, but only four of those subinterfaces list a DLCI using the **frame-relay interface-dlci** command. All ten subinterfaces have IP addresses configured, but no other **frame-relay** commands are configured on the subinterfaces. Which of the following could be true regarding R1's use of Frame Relay?

   a. Six subinterfaces will not be able to send traffic.

   b. Six subinterfaces will learn their associated DLCIs as a result of received Inverse ARP messages.

   c. Six subinterfaces will learn their associated DLCIs as a result of sent Inverse ARP messages.

   d. Four subinterfaces need a **frame-relay map** command before they can successfully pass traffic.

   e. LMI will learn the missing DLCIs and assign them to the subinterface bearing the same value as the DLCI.

Foundation Topics

Frame Relay Concepts

Frame Relay remains the most commonly deployed WAN technology used by routers. A slow migration away from Frame Relay has already begun with the advent and rapid growth of IP-based VPNs and MPLS. However, Frame Relay will likely be a mainstay of enterprise networks for the fore-seeable future.

Frame Relay standards have been developed by many groups. Early on, Cisco and some other companies (called the *gang of four*) developed vendor standards to aid Frame Relay adoption and product development. Later, a vendor consortium called the *Frame Relay Forum (FRF)* formed for the purpose of furthering Frame Relay standards; the IETF concurrently defined several RFCs related to using Frame Relay as a Layer 2 protocol in IP networks. (Cisco IOS documentation frequently refers to FR standards via FRF Implementation Agreements [IAs]—for instance, the FRF.12 fragmentation specification.) Finally, ANSI and ITU built on those standards to finalize U.S. national and international standards for Frame Relay.

This section briefly covers some of the more commonly known features of Frame Relay, as well as specific examples of some of the less commonly known features. This section does not attempt to cover all of Frame Relay's core concepts or terms, mainly because most engineers already understand Frame Relay well. So, make sure to review the definitions listed at the end of this chapter to fill in any gaps in your Frame Relay knowledge.

Frame Relay Data Link Connection Identifiers

To connect two DTEs, an FR service uses a *virtual circuit (VC)* between pairs of routers. A router can then send an FR frame with the appropriate (typically) 10-bit *Data Link Connection Identifier (DLCI)* header field that identifies each VC. The intermediary FR switches forward the frame based on its DLCI, until the frame eventually exits the FR service out the access link to the router on the other end of the VC.

FR DLCIs are locally significant, meaning that a particular DLCI value only matters on a single link. As a result, the DLCI value for a frame may change as the frame passes through the network. The following five-step process shows the locally significant DLCI values for a VC in Figure 15-1:

1. Router A sends a frame with DLCI 41.

2. The FR service identifies the frame as part of the VC connecting Router A to Router B.

3. The FR service replaces the frame's DLCI field with a value of 40.

4. The FR service forwards the frame to Router B.

5. Router B sees the incoming DLCI as 40, identifying it as being from Router A.

Figure 15-1 *Comparing Local and Global Frame Relay DLCIs*

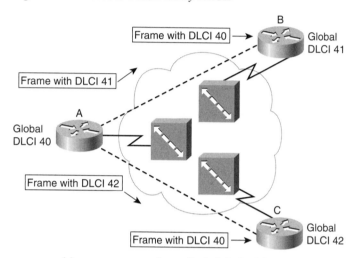

In practice, some providers use a convention called *global addressing*. The global DLCI convention simply allows humans to think of routers as having a single address, more akin to how MAC addresses are used. However, the addresses are still local, and a VC's DLCI may well change values as it passes through the network. For instance, the same VC from Router A to Router B in Figure 15-1 could use global addressing, listing Router A's DLCI as 40, and Router B's as 41. The logic based on the global addresses works like LANs. For example, for Router A to send a frame to Router B, Router A would send the frame to Router B's global address (41). Similarly, Router B would send frames to Router A's global address of 40 to send packets to Router A.

Local Management Interface

Local Management Interface (LMI) messages manage the local access link between the router and the Frame Relay switch. A Frame Relay DTE can send an LMI *Status Enquiry* message to the switch; the switch then replies with an LMI *Status* message to inform the router about the DLCIs of the defined VCs, as well as the status of each VC. By default, the LMI messages flow every 10 seconds. Every sixth message carries a full Status message, which includes more complete status information about each VC.

The LMI Status Enquiry (router) and Status (switch) messages function as a keepalive as well. A router considers its interface to have failed if the router ceases to receive LMI messages from the switch for a number (default 3) of keepalive intervals (default 10 seconds). As a result, FR LMI is actually enabled/disabled by using the **keepalive/no keepalive** interface subcommands on a Frame Relay interface.

Three LMI types exist, mainly because various vendors and standards organizations worked independently to develop Frame Relay standards. The earliest-defined type, called the Cisco LMI type, differs slightly from the later-defined ANSI and ITU types, as follows:

■ The allowed DLCI values

■ The DLCI used for sending LMI messages

Practically speaking, these issues seldom matter; by default, routers autosense the LMI type. If needed, the **frame-relay lmi-type type** interface subcommand can be used to set the LMI type on the access link. Table 15-2 lists the three LMI types, the **type** keyword values, along with some comparison points regarding LMI and permitted DLCIs.

Table 15-2 *Frame Relay LMI Types*

LMI Type	Source Document	Cisco IOS lmi-type Parameter	Allowed DLCI Range (Number)	LMI DLCI
Cisco	Proprietary	**Cisco**	16–1007 (992)	1023
ANSI	T1.617 Annex D	**Ansi**	16–991 (976)	0
ITU	Q.933 Annex A	**q933a**	16–991 (976)	0

Frame Relay Headers and Encapsulation

Routers create Frame Relay frames by using different consecutive headers. The first header is the ITU *Link Access Procedure for Frame-Mode Bearer Services (LAPF)* header. The LAPF header includes all the fields used by Frame Relay switches to deliver frames across the FR cloud, including the DLCI, DE, BECN, and FECN fields.

The Frame Relay encapsulation header follows the LAPF header, holding fields that are important only to the DTEs on the ends of a VC. For the encapsulation header, two options exist:

■ The earlier-defined Cisco-proprietary header

■ The IETF-defined RFC 2427 (formerly RFC 1490) encapsulation header

The **cisco** option works well with Cisco routers on each end of the VC, with the **ietf** option being required for multivendor interoperability. Both headers include a Protocol Type field to support multiple Layer 3 protocols over a VC; the most commonly used is the RFC 2427 *Network Layer Protocol ID (NLPID)* field. Figure 15-2 shows the general structure of the headers and trailers.

Figure 15-2 *Frame Relay Encapsulation Options*

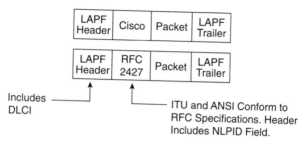

Each VC uses the Cisco encapsulation header unless configured explicitly to use the IETF header. Three methods can be used to configure a VC to use the IETF-style header:

- Use the **encapsulation frame-relay ietf** interface subcommand, which changes that interface's default for each VC to IETF instead of cisco

- Use the **frame-relay interface-dlci** *number* **ietf** interface subcommand, overriding the default for this VC

- Use the **frame-relay map dlci . . . ietf** command, which also over-rides the default for this VC

For example, on an interface with ten VCs, seven of which need to use IETF encapsulation, the interface default could be changed to IETF using the **encapsulation frame-relay ietf** interface subcommand. Then, the **frame-relay interface-dlci** *number* **cisco** command could be used for each of the three VCs that require Cisco encapsulation.

Frame Relay Congestion: DE, BECN, and FECN

FR networks, like any other multiaccess network, create the possibility for congestion caused by speed mismatches. For instance, imagine an FR network with 20 remote sites with 256-kbps links, and one main site with a T1 link. If all 20 remote sites were to send continuous frames to the main site at the same time, about 5 Mbps of data would need to exit the FR switch over the 1.5-Mbps T1 connected to the main router, causing the output queue on the FR switch to grow. Similarly, when the main site sends data to any one remote site, it sends at T1 speed, potentially causing the egress queue connected to the remote 256-kbps access link to back up as well. Beyond those two cases, which are typically called *egress blocking*, queues can grow inside the core of the FR network as well.

Frame Relay provides two methods of reacting to the inevitable congestion, as covered in the next two sections.

Adaptive Shaping, FECN, and BECN

Chapter 14, "Shaping and Policing," briefly covers the concept of adaptive traffic shaping, in which the shaper varies the shaping rate depending on whether the network is congested or not. To react to congestion that occurs somewhere inside the FR cloud, the router must receive some form of notice that the congestion is occurring. So, the FR LAPF header includes the *Forward Explicit Congestion Notification (FECN)* and *Backward Explicit Congestion Notification (BECN)* bits for signaling congestion on a particular VC.

FR switches use FECN and BECN to inform a router that a particular VC has experienced congestion. To do so, when a switch notices congestion caused by a VC, the switch sets the FECN bit in a frame that is part of that VC. The switch also tracks the VC that was congested so that it can look for the next frame sent over that VC, but going the opposite direction, as shown in step 4 of Figure 15-3. The switch then marks the BECN bit in that frame. The router receiving the frame with BECN set knows that a frame it sent experienced congestion, so the router can reduce its shaping rate. Figure 15-3 shows an example of the process.

Figure 15-3 *Basic Operation of FECN and BECN*

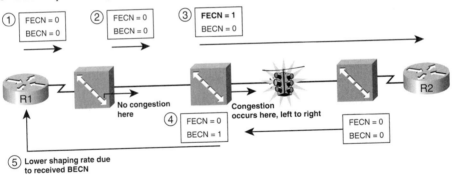

FECN can be set by the FR switches, but not by any of the routers, because the routers do not need to signal forward congestion. For example, if R1 thought congestion was occurring left to right in Figure 15-3, R1 could simply slow down its shaping rate. At the other end of the link, R2 is the destination of the frame, so it would never notice congestion for frames going left to right. So, only the switches need to set FECN.

BECN can be set by switches and by a router. Figure 15-3 shows a switch setting BECN on the next user frame. It can also send a Q.922 test frame, removing the need to wait on traffic sent over the VC, setting BECN in that frame. Finally, routers can be configured to watch for received frames with FECN set, reacting by returning a Q.922 test frame over that VC with the BECN bit set. This feature, sometimes called FECN reflection, is configured with the **shape fecn-adapt** (CB Shaping) or **traffic-shape fecn-adapt** (FRTS) command.

The Discard Eligibility Bit

When congestion occurs, queues begin to fill, and in some cases, frames must be tail-dropped from the queues. Switches can (but are not required to) examine the FR Discard Eligibility (DE) bit when frames need to be discarded, and purposefully discard frames with DE set instead of frames without DE set.

Both routers and switches can set the DE bit. Typically, a router makes the decision about setting the DE bit for certain frames, because the network engineer that controls the router is much more likely to know (and care) about which traffic is more important than other traffic. Marking DE can be performed with CB Marking, as covered in Chapter 12, "Classification and Marking," using the MQC **set fr-de** command.

Although routers typically mark DE, FR switches may also mark DE. For switches, the marking is typically done when the switch polices, but instead of discarding out-of-profile traffic, the switch marks DE. By doing so, downstream switches will be more likely to discard the marked frames that had already caused congestion.

Table 15-3 summarizes some of the key points regarding Frame Relay's FECN, BECN, and DE bits.

Table 15-3 *Frame Relay FECN, BECN, and DE Summary*

Bit	Meaning When Set	Where Set
FECN	Congestion in the same direction as this frame	By FR switches in user frames
BECN	Congestion in the opposite direction of this frame	By FR switches or routers in user or Q.922 test frames
DE	This frame should be discarded before non-DE frames	By routers or switches in user frames

Frame Relay Configuration

This section completes the FR configuration coverage for this book. Earlier, Chapter 6, "IP Forwarding (Routing)," covered issues with mapping Layer 3 addresses to FR DLCIs, and Chapter 9, "OSPF," covered issues with using OSPF over FR. This section covers the basic configuration and operational commands, along with FR payload compression and FR LFI options.

Frame Relay Configuration Basics

Two of the most important details regarding Frame Relay configuration are the association of DLCIs with the correct interface or subinterface, and the mapping of L3 addresses to those DLCIs. Interesting, both features can be configured using the same two commands—the **frame-relay map** and **frame-relay interface-dlci** commands. Chapter 6 already covered the details of mapping L3 addresses to DLCIs using InARP and static mapping. (If you have not reviewed those details since starting this chapter, it is probably a good time to do so.) This section focuses more on the association of DLCIs with a particular subinterface.

Although a router can learn each DLCI on the access link via LMI Status messages, these messages do not imply with which subinterface each DLCI should be used. To configure Frame Relay using subinterfaces, the DLCIs must be associated with the subinterface. Any DLCIs learned with LMI that are not associated with a subinterface are assumed to be used by the physical interface.

The more common method to make this association is to use the **frame-relay interface-dlci** subinterface subcommand. On point-to-point subinterfaces, only a single **frame-relay interface-dlci** command is allowed, whereas multipoint interfaces support multiple commands. The alternative method is to use the **frame-relay map** command. This command still maps Layer 3 addresses to DLCIs, but also implies an association of the configured DLCI with the subinterface under which the command is issued. And similar to **frame-relay interface-dlci** commands, only one **frame-relay map** command is allowed per point-to-point subinterface, per Layer 3 protocol. On multipoint subinterfaces, multiple commands are allowed per Layer 3 protocol.

Example 15-1 depicts a wide variety of Frame Relay configuration options, using **frame-relay interface-dlci** commands, and the related **show** commands. Based on Figure 15-4, this example implements the following requirements:

■ R1 uses a multipoint subinterface to connect to R2 and R3.

■ R1 uses a point-to-point subinterface to connect to R4.

■ The VC between R1 and R4 uses IETF encapsulation.

Figure 15-4 *Sample FR Network for Configuration Examples*

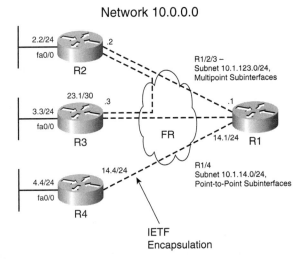

Example 15-1 *Basic Frame Relay Configuration Example*

```
! R1 configuration begins the example. Subint .14 shows the IETF option used on
! the frame-relay interface-dlci command. Subint .123 has two DLCIs associated
! with it, for the VCs to R2 and R3.
interface Serial0/0/0
 encapsulation frame-relay
!
interface Serial0/0/0.14 point-to-point
 ip address 10.1.14.1 255.255.255.0
 frame-relay interface-dlci 104 IETF
!
interface Serial0/0/0.123 multipoint
 ip address 10.1.123.1 255.255.255.0
 frame-relay interface-dlci 102
 frame-relay interface-dlci 103
! R2 configuration comes next. R2 assigns the DLCI for the VC to R1 and R3 to the
! .123 subinterface. Note the routers' subint numbers do not have to match.
interface Serial0/0/0
 encapsulation frame-relay
!
interface Serial0/0/0.123 multipoint
 ip address 10.1.123.2 255.255.255.0
 frame-relay interface-dlci 101
 frame-relay interface-dlci 103
! R3 configuration follows the same conventions as does R2's and is not shown.
! R4's configuration follows next, with the encapsulation frame-relay ietf command
! setting the encapsulation for all the VCs on interface s0/0/0. Also note that
! the frequency of LMI enquiries was changed from the default (10) to 8 with the
! keepalive 8 command.
interface Serial0/0/0
 encapsulation frame-relay IETF
 keepalive 8
!
interface Serial0/0/0.1 point-to-point
 ip address 10.1.14.4 255.255.255.0
 frame-relay interface-dlci 101
! The show frame-relay pvc command shows statistics and status per VC. The next
! command (on R1) filters the output to just include the lines with PVC status.
R1# show frame-relay pvc | incl PVC STATUS
DLCI = 100, DLCI USAGE = UNUSED, PVC STATUS = INACTIVE, INTERFACE = Serial0/0/0
DLCI = 102, DLCI USAGE = LOCAL, PVC STATUS = ACTIVE, INTERFACE = Serial0/0/0.123
DLCI = 103, DLCI USAGE = LOCAL, PVC STATUS = ACTIVE, INTERFACE = Serial0/0/0.123
DLCI = 104, DLCI USAGE = LOCAL, PVC STATUS = ACTIVE, INTERFACE = Serial0/0/0.14
DLCI = 105, DLCI USAGE = UNUSED, PVC STATUS = ACTIVE, INTERFACE = Serial0/0/0
DLCI = 106, DLCI USAGE = UNUSED, PVC STATUS = INACTIVE, INTERFACE = Serial0/0/0
DLCI = 107, DLCI USAGE = UNUSED, PVC STATUS = ACTIVE, INTERFACE = Serial0/0/0
DLCI = 108, DLCI USAGE = UNUSED, PVC STATUS = ACTIVE, INTERFACE = Serial0/0/0
DLCI = 109, DLCI USAGE = UNUSED, PVC STATUS = INACTIVE, INTERFACE = Serial0/0/0
```

continues

Example 15-1 *Basic Frame Relay Configuration Example (Continued)*

```
DLCI = 110, DLCI USAGE = UNUSED, PVC STATUS = INACTIVE, INTERFACE = Serial0/0/0
! The next command lists stats for a single VC on R1, with DLCI 102, which is the
! VC to R2. Note the counters for FECN, BECN, and DE, as well as the in and out
! bit rates just for this VC.
R1# show frame-relay pvc 102
PVC Statistics for interface Serial0/0/0 (Frame Relay DTE)
DLCI = 102, DLCI USAGE = LOCAL, PVC STATUS = ACTIVE, INTERFACE = Serial0/0/0.123

  input pkts 41          output pkts 54         in bytes 4615
  out bytes 5491         dropped pkts 0         in pkts dropped 0
  out pkts dropped 0     out bytes dropped 0
  in FECN pkts 0         in BECN pkts 0         out FECN pkts 0
  out BECN pkts 0        in DE pkts 0           out DE pkts 0
  out bcast pkts 27      out bcast bytes 1587
  5 minute input rate 0 bits/sec, 0 packets/sec
  5 minute output rate 0 bits/sec, 0 packets/sec
  pvc create time 00:29:37, last time pvc status changed 00:13:47
! The following output confirms that R1's link is using the Cisco LMI standard. Full
! LMI Status messages occur about every minute, with the Last Full Status message
! listed last. Note that the router sends Status Enquiries to the switch, with the
! switch sending Status messages; those counters should increment together.
R1# show frame-relay lmi
LMI Statistics for interface Serial0/0/0 (Frame Relay DTE) LMI TYPE = CISCO
  Invalid Unnumbered info 0      Invalid Prot Disc 0
  Invalid dummy Call Ref 0       Invalid Msg Type 0
  Invalid Status Message 0       Invalid Lock Shift 0
  Invalid Information ID 0        Invalid Report IE Len 0
  Invalid Report Request 0       Invalid Keep IE Len 0
  Num Status Enq. Sent 183       Num Status msgs Rcvd 183
  Num Update Status Rcvd 0       Num Status Timeouts 0
  Last Full Status Req 00:00:35  Last Full Status Rcvd 00:00:35
! The show interface command lists several details as well, including the interval
! for LMI messages (keepalive), LMI stats, LMI DLCI (1023), and stats for the FR
! broadcast queue. The broadcast queue holds FR broadcasts that must be replicated
! and sent over this VC, for example, OSPF LSAs.
R1# show int s 0/0/0
Serial0/0/0 is up, line protocol is up
! lines omitted for brevity
  Encapsulation FRAME-RELAY, loopback not set
  Keepalive set (10 sec)
  LMI enq sent  185, LMI stat recvd 185, LMI upd recvd 0, DTE LMI up
  LMI enq recvd 0, LMI stat sent  0, LMI upd sent  0
  LMI DLCI 1023  LMI type is CISCO  frame relay DTE
  FR SVC disabled, LAPF state down
  Broadcast queue 0/64, broadcasts sent/dropped 274/0, interface broadcasts 228
! Lines omitted for brevity
! R3 is using ANSI LMI, which uses DLCI 0, as confirmed next.
```

Example 15-1 *Basic Frame Relay Configuration Example (Continued)*

```
R3# sh frame lmi | include LMI TYPE
LMI Statistics for interface Serial0/0/0 (Frame Relay DTE) LMI TYPE = ANSI
R3# sh int s 0/0/0 | include LMI DLCI
LMI DLCI 0  LMI type is ANSI Annex D  frame relay DTE
```

At the end of Example 15-1, note that R3 is using the ANSI LMI type. R3 could have configured the LMI type statically using the **frame-relay lmi-type** {**ansi** | **cisco** | **q933a**} command, under the physical interface. However, R3 omitted the command, causing R3 to take the default action of autosensing the LMI type.

Frame Relay Payload Compression

Cisco IOS software supports three options for payload compression on Frame Relay VCs: *packet-by-packet*, *data-stream*, and *Frame Relay Forum Implementation Agreement 9 (FRF.9)*. FRF.9 is the only standardized protocol of the three options. FRF.9 compression and data-stream compression function basically the same way; the only real difference is that FRF.9 implies compatibility with non-Cisco devices.

All three FR compression options use LZS as the compression algorithm, but one key difference relates to their use of compression dictionaries. LZS defines dynamic dictionary entries that list a binary string from the compressed data, and an associated smaller string that represents it during transmission—thereby reducing the number of bits used to send data. The table of short binary codes, and their longer associated string of bytes, is called a *dictionary*. The packet-by-packet compression method also uses LZS, but the compression dictionary is built for each packet, then discarded—hence the name packet-by-packet. The other two methods do not clear the dictionary after each packet. Table 15-4 lists the three FR compression options and their most important distinguishing features.

Table 15-4 *FR Payload Compression Feature Comparison*

Feature	Packet-by-Packet	FRF.9	Data-Stream
Uses LZS algorithm?	Yes	Yes	Yes
Same dictionary for all packets?	No	Yes	Yes
Cisco-proprietary?	Yes	No	Yes

FR payload compression configuration is configured per VC. The configuration varies depending on whether point-to-point subinterfaces are used. On point-to-point subinterfaces, the **frame-relay payload-compress** *type* subinterface command is used; otherwise, the **frame-relay map** command must be configured along with the **payload-compress** *type* option. Example 15-2 shows Frame

Relay compression configured in the same network as shown in Figure 15-4 and Example 15-1. The VC from R1 to R3 (multipoint subinterface) uses data-stream compression, and the VC from R1 to R4 uses FRF.9.

Example 15-1 *Frame Relay Data-Stream Compression*

```
! Below, the configuration added to R1's Example 15-1 configuration is shown.
! R3 uses a frame-relay map command as well, and R4 uses the same
! frame-relay payload-compress command.
interface Serial0/0/0.14 point-to-point
 frame-relay payload-compress frf9 stac
!
interface Serial0/0/0.123 multipoint
 frame-relay map ip 10.1.123.3 103 broadcast payload-compress data-stream stac
! Next, R1 sends 5000 200-byte pings to R4 to create traffic. R4 shows the pre- and
! post-compression stats in the show compress command.
R4# show compress
 Serial0/0/0 - DLCI: 101
         Software compression enabled
         uncompressed bytes xmt/rcv 1021536/1021536
         compressed bytes   xmt/rcv 178090/177820
         Compressed bytes sent:    178090 bytes   12 Kbits/sec  ratio: 5.736
         Compressed bytes recv:    177820 bytes   12 Kbits/sec  ratio: 5.744
         1  min avg ratio xmt/rcv 3.506/3.301
         5  min avg ratio xmt/rcv 3.506/3.301
         10 min avg ratio xmt/rcv 3.506/3.301
         no bufs xmt 0 no bufs rcv 0
         resyncs 0
         Additional Stac Stats:
         Transmit bytes:  Uncompressed =      0 Compressed =    142922
         Received bytes:  Compressed =   142652 Uncompressed =       0
```

Frame Relay Fragmentation

Frame Relay Forum IA 12, or FRF.12, defines a standard method of performing LFI over a Frame Relay PVC. Cisco IOS supports two methods for configuring FRF.12. The legacy FRF.12 configuration requires FRTS to be configured, and requires a queuing tool to be applied to the shaped packets. (Example 14-7 in Chapter 14 shows an FRTS **map-class shape-with-LLQ** command that shapes and applies LLQ.)

Figure 15-5 shows the overall logic of how FRF.12 interleaves packets using LFI, when configured using legacy FRF.12 configuration. IOS creates a 2-queue software queuing system on the physical interface. Any packets leaving the FRTS LLQ go into the "high" Dual FIFO queue, with the packets and fragments from other queuing going into the Dual FIFO "normal" queue. On the interface, IOS treats the Dual FIFO queue as a priority queue, which causes interleaving.

Figure 15-5   *Interface Dual FIFO Queues with FRTS Plus FRF.12*

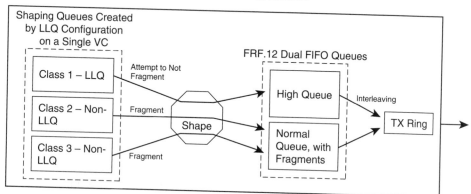

> **NOTE**   All packets can be fragmented, but Cisco rightfully suggests choosing a fragment size so that the packets typically placed into the LLQ PQ will not be fragmented. Only packets from the shaping LLQ are placed into the Dual FIFO interface high queue, and only those packets are interleaved.

To configure legacy FRF.12, the **frame-relay fragment size** command is added to the FRTS map class on both ends of the VC. For example, in Example 14-7, the **frame-relay fragment 120** command could be added to the shape-with-LLQ map class, with the same configuration on the router on the other end of the VC, to enable FRF.12. Note that because fragmentation of any kind implies that an additional fragmentation header is used, fragmentation must be added on both ends of the link or VC.

The second method of configuring FRF.12 is called *Frame Relay Fragmentation at the Interface*, and was added to Cisco IOS Software Release 12.2(13)T. This method does not require FRTS; the **frame-relay fragment** command simply sits directly on the physical interface. If no queuing tool is configured on the interface, the router creates Dual FIFO queuing on the interface, interleaving all non-fragmented packets between fragments of other packets. Optionally, configuration of a queuing tool that has a PQ feature (for example, LLQ) can be used instead, causing packets in the PQ to be immediately interleaved. Example 15-3 shows a sample configuration using the same router, R1, from the first two examples in this chapter. In this case, FRF.12 has been enabled on s0/0/0, with a fragment size of 120.

Example 15-2   *FRF.12 on the Interface—Configuration*

```
! No FRTS configuration exists—simply the frame-relay fragment 120 end-to-end
! command. Note that LLQ is not enabled in this case, so nonfragmented packets
! will be interleaved using Dual FIFO.
R1# show run int s 0/0/0
interface Serial0/0/0
 encapsulation frame-relay
 frame-relay fragment 120 end-to-end
! Next, fragmentation stats are listed.
```

continues

Example 15-2 *FRF.12 on the Interface—Configuration (Continued)*

```
R1# show frame-relay fragment 104
interface              dlci frag-type  size in-frag    out-frag   dropped-frag
Se0/0/0.14              104  end-to-end 120  2759       2762       0
! The show queueing command (yes, IOS misspells it) lists statistics for the Dual
! FIFO queuing system added to the interface when FRF.12 is configured.
R1# show queueing int s0/0/0
Interface Serial0/0/0 queueing strategy: priority

Output queue utilization (queue/count)
    high/354 medium/0 normal/1422 low/0
```

Table 15-5 summarizes the key points regarding both styles of FRF.12 configuration.

Table 15-5 *Comparing Legacy and Interface FRF.12*

Feature	Legacy FRF.12	FRF.12 on the Interface
Requires FRTS?	Yes	No
Interleaves by feeding Dual FIFO interface high queue from a shaping PQ?	Yes	No
Interleaves by using either Dual FIFO or a configured LLQ policy-map on the physical interface.	No	Yes
Config mode for the **frame-relay fragment** command.	**map-class**	Physical interface

In addition to FRF.12, Cisco IOS supports two other methods of LFI over Frame Relay, including FRF.11-c. This fragmentation method works only on Voice over Frame Relay (VoFR) VCs. With this tool, voice frames are never fragmented, and voice frames are always interleaved, without requiring any particular queuing tool. Once a VoFR VC has been configured, the LFI configuration is identical to the legacy style of FRF.12 configuration.

The last type of FR LFI uses MLP over Frame Relay; it also happens to be the only option for Frame Relay-to-ATM Service Interworking. MLP over FR uses PPP headers instead of the Cisco or RFC 2427 header shown in Figure 15-2, thereby enabling many PPP features supported by the PPP headers. MLP and LFI configuration would simply need to be added to that configuration to achieve LFI.

Foundation Summary

This section lists additional details and facts to round out the coverage of the topics in this chapter. Unlike most of the Cisco Press *Exam Certification Guides*, this "Foundation Summary" does not repeat information presented in the "Foundation Topics" section of the chapter. Please take the time to read and study the details in the "Foundation Topics" section of the chapter, as well as review items noted with a Key Topic icon.

Table 15-6 summarizes the key standards mentioned in the chapter.

Table 15-6   *Protocols and Standards for Chapter 18*

Topic	Standard
Frame Relay Encapsulation	RFC 2427
Frame Relay Compression	FRF.9
Frame Relay LFI	FRF.12, FRF.11-c
Frame Relay Service Interworking	FRF.8

Table 15-7 lists the Cisco IOS commands covered in this chapter.

Table 15-7   *Command Reference for Chapter 15*

Command	Mode and Function
frame-relay payload-compression {packet-by-packet | frf9 stac | data-stream stac}	Subinterface mode; defines the type of FR compression
encapsulation frame-relay [cisco | ietf]	Interface mode; enables FR, and chooses one of two encapsulation types
frame-relay broadcast-queue *size byte-rate packet-rate*	Interface mode; sets the FR broadcast queue size and rates
frame-relay fragment *fragment_size* **[switched]**	Map-class mode; enables fragmentation with fragments of the defined size
frame-relay fragment *fragment-size* **end-to-end**	Interface mode; enables interface FR fragmentation, based on size
frame-relay interface-dlci *dlci* **[ietf | cisco] [ppp** *virtual-template-name*]	Subinterface mode; associates a DLCI with the subinterface, and sets the encapsulation
frame-relay inverse-arp [*protocol*] [*dlci*]	Interface mode; enables InARP, per Layer 3 protocol and/or DLCI

continues

Table 15-7 *Command Reference for Chapter 15 (Continued)*

Command	Mode and Function
frame-relay lmi-type {**ansi** | **cisco** | **q933a**}	Interface mode; statically configures the LMI type
frame-relay map *protocol protocol-address* {*dlci* | **vc-bundle** *vc-bundle-name*}[**broadcast**] [**ietf** | **cisco**] [**payload-compression** {**packet-by-packet** | **frf9 stac** | **data-stream stac**]	Subinterface mode; maps Layer 3 protocol addresses of neighboring routers to DLCIs along with other settings associated with the PVC
keepalive *time-interval*	Interface mode; for FR, enables LMI messages every time interval
protocol *protocol* {*protocol-address* | **inarp**} [[**no**] **broadcast**]	PVC mode; maps a Layer 3 address to the PVC under which the command is issued
show compress	Displays compression statistics
show frame-relay fragment [**interface** *interface* [*dlci*]]	Displays fragmentation statistics
show frame-relay map	Displays mapping for physical and multipoint subinterfaces

Table 15-8 lists some of the ANSI and ITU standards for Frame Relay.

Table 15-8 *Frame Relay Protocol Specifications*

What the Specification Defines	ITU Document	ANSI Document
Data-link specifications, including LAPF header/trailer	Q.922 Annex A (Q.922-A)	T1.618
PVC management, LMI	Q.933 Annex A (Q.933-A)	T1.617 Annex D (T1.617-D)
SVC signaling	Q.933	T1.617
Multiprotocol encapsulation (originated in RFC 1490/2427)	Q.933 Annex E (Q.933-E)	T1.617 Annex F (T1.617-F)

Memory Builders

The CCIE Routing and Switching written exam, like all Cisco CCIE written exams, covers a fairly broad set of topics. This section provides some basic tools to help you exercise your memory about some of the broader topics covered in this chapter.

Fill in Key Tables from Memory

Appendix E, "Key Tables for CCIE Study," on the CD in the back of this book contains empty sets of some of the key summary tables in each chapter. Print Appendix E, refer to this chapter's tables in it, and fill in the tables from memory. Refer to Appendix F, "Solutions for Key Tables for CCIE Study," on the CD to check your answers.

Definitions

Next, take a few moments to write down the definitions for the following terms:

FRF, VC, PVC, SVC, DTE, DCE, LMI, access rate, access link, FRF.9, FRF.5, FRF.8, Service Interworking, FRF.12, FRF.11-c, VoFR, LAPF, NLPID, DE, FECN, BECN, Dual FIFO, LZS, DLCI

Refer to the glossary to check your answers.

Further Reading

- *Troubleshooting Remote Access Networks*, by Dr. Plamen Nedeltchev

- *ISDN and Broadband ISDN with Frame Relay and ATM*, by Dr. William Stallings

Part VI: IP Multicast

Blueprint topics covered in this chapter:

This chapter covers the following subtopics from the Cisco CCIE Routing and Switching written exam blueprint. Refer to the full blueprint in Table I-1 in the Introduction for more details on the topics covered in each chapter and their context within the blueprint.

- Internet Group Management Protocol (IGMP) v2

- Group Addresses

CHAPTER 16

Introduction to IP Multicasting

IP multicast concepts and protocols are an important part of the CCIE Routing and Switching written exam. Demand for IP multicast applications has increased dramatically over the last several years. Almost all major campus networks today use some form of multicasting. This chapter covers why multicasting is needed, the fundamentals of multicast addressing, and how multicast traffic is distributed and controlled over a LAN.

"Do I Know This Already?" Quiz

Table 16-1 outlines the major headings in this chapter and the corresponding "Do I Know This Already?" quiz questions.

Table 16-1   *"Do I Know This Already?" Foundation Topics Section-to-Question Mapping*

Foundation Topics Section	Questions Covered in This Section	Score
Why Do You Need Multicasting?	1	
Multicast IP Addresses	2–4	
Managing Distribution of Multicast Traffic	5–6	
LAN Multicast Optimizations	7	
Total Score		

In order to best use this pre-chapter assessment, remember to score yourself strictly. You can find the answers in Appendix A, "Answers to the 'Do I Know This Already?' Quizzes."

1. Which of the following reasons for using IP multicasting are valid for one-to-many applications?

    a. Multicast applications use connection-oriented service.

    b. Multicast uses less bandwidth than unicast.

    c. A multicast packet can be sent from one source to many destinations.

    d. Multicast eliminates traffic redundancy.

2. Which of the following statements is true of a multicast address?

    a. Uses a Class D address that can range from 223.0.0.0 to 239.255.255.255

    b. Uses a subnet mask ranging from 8 bits to 24 bits

    c. Can be permanent or transient

    d. Can be entered as an IP address on an interface of a router only if the router is configured for multicasting

3. Which of the following multicast addresses are reserved and not forwarded by multicast routers?

    a. 224.0.0.1 and 224.0.0.13

    b. 224.0.0.9 and 224.0.1.39

    c. 224.0.0.10 and 224.0.1.40

    d. 224.0.0.5 and 224.0.0.6

4. From the following pairs of Layer 3 multicast addresses, select a pair that will use the same Ethernet multicast MAC address of 0x0100.5e4d.2643.

    a. 224.67.26.43 and 234.67.26.43

    b. 225.77.67.38 and 235.77.67.38

    c. 229.87.26.43 and 239.87.26.43

    d. 227.77.38.67 and 238.205.38.67

5. From the following statements, select the true statement(s) regarding IGMP Query messages and IGMP Report messages.

    a. Hosts, switches, and routers originate IGMP Membership Report messages.

    b. Hosts, switches, and routers originate IGMP Query messages.

    c. Hosts originate IGMP Query messages and routers originate IGMP Membership messages.

    d. Hosts originate IGMP Membership messages and routers originate IGMP Query messages.

    e. Hosts and switches originate IGMP Membership messages and routers originate IGMP Query messages.

6. Seven hosts and a router on a multicast LAN network are using IGMPv2. Hosts 5, 6, and 7 are members of group 226.5.6.7, and the other four hosts are not. Which of the following answers is/are true about how the router will respond when Host 7 sends an IGMPv2 Leave message for the group 226.5.6.7?

- **a.** Sends an IGMPv2 General Query to multicast destination address 224.0.0.1
- **b.** Sends an IGMPv2 Group-Specific Query to multicast destination address 224.0.0.1
- **c.** Sends an IGMPv2 General Query to multicast destination address 226.5.6.7
- **d.** Sends an IGMPv2 Group-Specific Query to multicast destination address 226.5.6.7
- **e.** First sends an IGMPv2 Group-Specific Query to multicast destination address 226.5.6.7, and then sends an IGMPv2 General Query to multicast destination address 224.0.0.1

7. Which of the following statements is/are true regarding CGMP and IGMP snooping?

- **a.** CGMP and IGMP snooping are used to constrain the flooding of multicast traffic in LAN switches.
- **b.** CGMP is a Cisco-proprietary protocol and uses the well-known Layer 2 multicast MAC address 0x0100.0cdd.dddd.
- **c.** IGMP snooping is preferable in a mixed-vendor environment; however, if implemented using Layer 2–only LAN switches, it can cause a dramatic reduction in switch performance.
- **d.** CGMP is simple to implement, and in CGMP only routers send CGMP messages, while switches only listen for CGMP messages.
- **e.** All of these answers are correct.

Foundation Topics

Why Do You Need Multicasting?

"Necessity is the mother of all invention," a saying derived from Plato's *Republic*, holds very true in the world of technology. In the late 1980s, Dr. Steve Deering was working on a project that required him to send a message from one computer to a group of computers across a Layer 3 network. After studying several routing protocols, Dr. Deering concluded that the functionality of the routing protocols could be extended to support "Layer 3 multicasting." This concept led to more research, and in 1991, Dr. Deering published his doctoral thesis, "Multicast Routing in a Datagram Network," in which he defined the components required for IP multicasting, their functions, and their relationships with each other.

The most basic definition of IP multicasting is as follows:

> Sending a message from a single source to selected multiple destinations across a Layer 3 network in one data stream.

If you want to send a message from one source to one destination, you could send a unicast message. If you want to send a message from one source to all the destinations on a local network, you could send a broadcast message. However, if you want to send a message from one source to selected multiple destinations spread across a routed network in one data stream, the most efficient method is IP multicasting.

Demand for multicast applications is increasing with the advent of such applications as audio and video web content; broadcasting TV programs, radio programs, and concerts over the Internet; communicating stock quotes to brokers; transmitting a corporate message to employees; and transmitting data from a centralized warehouse to a chain of retail stores. Success of one-to-many multicast applications has created a demand for the second generation of multicast applications that are referred to as "many-to-many" and "many-to-few," in which there are many sources of multicast traffic. Examples of these types of applications include playing games on an intranet or the Internet and conducting interactive audio and video meetings. The primary focus of this chapter and the next chapter is to help you understand concepts and technologies required for implementing one-to-many multicast applications.

Problems with Unicast and Broadcast Methods

Why not use unicast or broadcast methods to send a message from one source to many destinations? Figure 16-1 shows a video server as a source of a video application and the video data that needs to be delivered to a group of receivers—H2, H3, and H4—two hops away across a WAN link.

Figure 16-1   *Unicast*

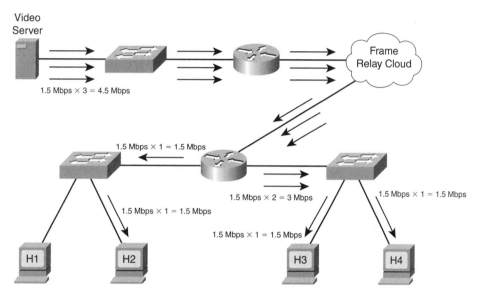

The unicast method requires that the video application send one copy of each packet to every group member's unicast address. To support full-motion, full-screen viewing, the video stream requires approximately 1.5 Mbps of bandwidth for each receiver. If only a few receivers exist, as shown in Figure 16-1, this method works fine but still requires $n \times 1.5$ Mbps of bandwidth, where n is the number of receiving hosts.

Figure 16-2 shows that as the number of receivers grows into the hundreds or thousands, the load on the server to create and send copies of the same data also increases, and replicated unicast transmissions consume a lot of bandwidth within the network. For 100 users, as indicated in the upper-left corner of Figure 16-2, the bandwidth required to send the unicast transmission increases to 150 Mbps. For 1000 users, the bandwidth required would increase to 1.5 Gbps.

Figure 16-2 *Unicast Does Not Scale to Large Numbers of Receivers*

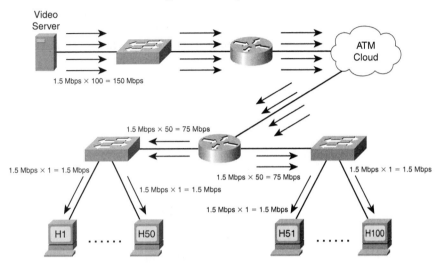

You can see from Figure 16-2 that the unicast method is not scalable. Figure 16-3 shows that the broadcast method requires transmission of data only once, but it has some serious issues. First, as shown in Figure 16-3, if the receivers are in a different broadcast domain from the sender, routers need to forward broadcasts. However, forwarding broadcasts might be the worst possible solution, because broadcasting a packet to all hosts in a network can waste bandwidth and increase processing load on all the network devices if only a small group of hosts in the network actually needs to receive the packet.

Figure 16-3 *Broadcast Wastes Bandwidth and Increases Processing Load on CPU*

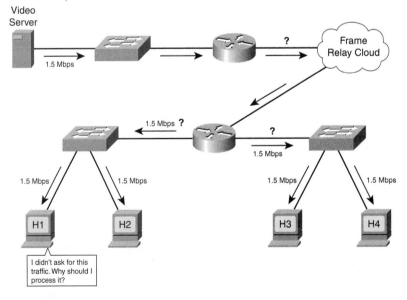

How Multicasting Provides a Scalable and Manageable Solution

The six basic requirements for supporting multicast across a routed network are as follows:

- A designated range of Layer 3 addresses that can only be used by multicast applications must exist. A network administrator needs to install a multicast application on a multicast server using a Layer 3 multicast address from the designated range.

- A multicast address must be used only as a destination IP address and specifically not as a source IP address. Unlike a unicast IP packet, a destination IP address in a multicast packet does not specify a recipient's address but rather signifies that the packet is carrying multicast traffic for a specific multicast application.

- The multicast application must be installed on all the hosts in the network that need to receive the multicast traffic for the application. The application must be installed using the same Layer 3 multicast address that was used on the multicast server. This is referred to as *launching an application* or *joining a group*.

- All hosts that are connected to a LAN must use a standard method to calculate a Layer 2 multicast address from the Layer 3 multicast address and assign it to their network interface cards (NICs). For example, if multiple routers are connected to an Ethernet segment and all of them are using the OSPF routing protocol, all the routers on their Ethernet interfaces will also be listening to the Layer 2 multicast address 0x0100.5e00.0005 in addition to their Burned-In Addresses (BIA). This Layer 2 multicast address 0x0100.5e00.0005 is calculated from the multicast Layer 3 address 224.0.0.5, which is reserved for the OSPF routing protocol.

- There must be a mechanism by which a host can dynamically indicate to the connected router whether it would like to receive the traffic for the installed multicast application. The Internet Group Management Protocol (IGMP) provides communication between hosts and a router connected to the same subnet. The Cisco Group Management Protocol (CGMP) or IGMP snooping helps switches learn which hosts have requested to receive the traffic for a specific multicast application and to which switch ports these hosts are connected.

- There must be a multicast routing protocol that allows routers to forward multicast traffic from multicast servers to hosts without overtaxing network resources. Some of the multicast routing protocols are Distance Vector Multicast Routing Protocol (DVMRP), Multicast Open Shortest Path First (MOSPF), and Protocol Independent Multicast dense mode (PIM-DM) and sparse mode (PIM-SM).

This chapter discusses the first five bulleted items, and Chapter 17, "IP Multicast Routing," covers the multicast routing protocols.

Figure 16-4 shows how multicast traffic is forwarded in a Layer 3 network. The purpose of this illustration is to give you an overview of how multicast traffic is forwarded and received by selected hosts.

Figure 16-4 *How Multicast Delivers Traffic to Selected Users*

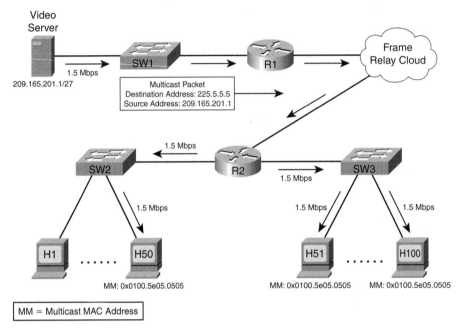

Assume that a video multicast application was installed on the video server using the special Layer 3 multicast address 225.5.5.5. Hosts 1 to 49, located across a WAN link, are not interested at this time in receiving traffic for this application. Hosts 50 to 100 are interested in receiving traffic for this application and launch this application on their PCs. When the host launches the application, the host *joins the group*, which means that the host now wants to receive multicast packets sent to 225.5.5.5. Hosts 50 to 100 join group 225.5.5.5 and indicate to R2 their desire to receive traffic for this multicast application by using IGMP. The multicast application calculates the Layer 2 multicast address 0x0100.5e05.0505 from the Layer 3 multicast address 225.5.5.5, and NICs of hosts 50 to 100 are listening to this address in addition to their BIAs.

A multicast routing protocol is configured on R1 and R2 so that they can forward the multicast traffic. R2 has one WAN link connected to the Frame Relay cloud and two Ethernet links connected to two switches, SW2 and SW3. R2 knows that it has on both Ethernet links hosts that would like to receive multicast traffic for the group 225.5.5.5 because these hosts have indicated their desire to receive traffic for the group using IGMP. Both switches have also learned on which ports they have hosts that would like to receive the multicast traffic for this application by using either CGMP or IGMP snooping.

A multicast packet travels from the video server over the Ethernet link to R1, and R1 forwards a single copy of the multicast packet over the WAN link to R2. When R2 receives a multicast packet on the WAN link with the destination address 225.5.5.5, it makes a copy of the packet and forwards a copy on each Ethernet link. Because it is a multicast packet for the group (application) 225.5.5.5, R2 calculates the Layer 2 destination multicast address of 0x0100.5e05.0505 and uses it as the destination MAC address on each packet it forwards to both switches. When the switches receive these packets, they forward them on appropriate ports to hosts. When the hosts receive the packets, their NICs compare the destination MAC address with the multicast MAC address they are listening to, and, because they match, inform the higher layers to process the packet.

You can see from Figure 16-4 that the multicast traffic is sent once over the WAN links and is received by the hosts that have requested it. Should additional hosts request to receive the same multicast traffic, neither the multicast server nor the network resources would incur any additional burden, as shown in Figure 16-5.

Figure 16-5   *Multicasting Is Scalable*

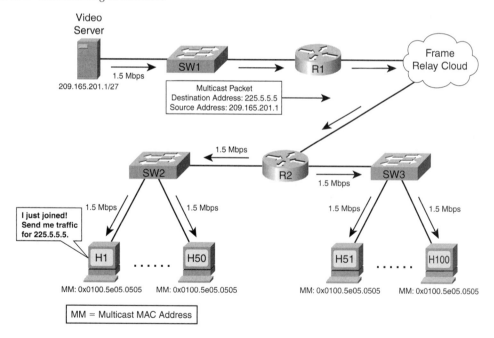

Assume that hosts 1 to 49 have also indicated their desire to receive traffic for the multicast group 225.5.5.5 using IGMP. R2 is already forwarding the traffic to both switches. Either CGMP or

IGMP snooping can help SW2 (shown in Figure 16-5) learn that hosts 1 to 49 have also requested the multicast traffic for the group so that it can start forwarding the multicast traffic on ports connected to hosts 1 to 49. The additional 49 users are now receiving multicast traffic, and the load on the multicast server, load on other network devices, and demand for bandwidth on the WAN links remain the same. The load on SW2 shown in Figure 16-5 increases because it has to make 49 more copies of the multicast traffic and forward it on 49 more ports; however, it is now operating at the same level as the other switch. You can see that IP multicast is scalable.

Although multicast offers many advantages, it also has some disadvantages. Multicast is UDP-based and hence unreliable. Lack of TCP windowing and "slow start" mechanisms can result in network congestion. Some multicast protocol mechanisms occasionally generate duplicate packets and deliver packets out of order.

Multicast IP Addresses

Multicast applications always use a multicast IP address. This multicast address represents the multicast application and is referred to as a multicast *group*. Unlike a unicast IP address, which uniquely identifies a single IP host, a multicast address used as a destination address on an IP packet signifies that the packet is carrying traffic for a specific multicast application. For example, if a multicast packet is traveling over a network with a destination address 225.5.5.5, it is proclaiming to the network devices that, "I am carrying traffic for the multicast application that uses multicast group address 225.5.5.5; do you want it?" A multicast address is never assigned to a network device, so it is never used as a source address. A source address on a multicast packet, or any IP packet, is always a unicast address.

Multicast Address Range and Structure

The Internet Assigned Numbers Authority (IANA) has assigned class D IP addresses to multicast applications. The first 4 bits of the first octet for a class D address are always 1110. IP multicast addresses range from 224.0.0.0 through 239.255.255.255. As these addresses are used to represent multicast groups (applications) and not hosts, there is no need for a subnet mask for multicast addresses because they are not hierarchical. In other words, there is only one requirement for a multicast address: The first 4 bits of the first octet must be 1110. The last 28 bits are unstructured.

Well-Known Multicast Addresses

IANA controls the assignment of IP multicast addresses. To preserve multicast addresses, IANA is reluctant to assign individual IP multicast addresses to new applications without a good technical justification. However, IANA has assigned individual IP multicast addresses to popular network protocols.

IANA has assigned several ranges of multicast IP addresses for specific types of reasons. Those types are as follows:

- Permanent multicast groups, in the range 224.0.0.0–224.0.1.255

- Addresses used with Source-Specific Multicast (SSM), in the range 232.0.0.0–232.255.255.255

- GLOP addressing, in the range 233.0.0.0–233.255.255.255

- Private multicast addresses, in the range 239.0.0.0–239.255.255.255

This section provides some insights into each of these four types of reserved IP multicast addresses. The rest of the multicast addresses are referred to as *transient* groups, which are covered later in this chapter in the section "Multicast Addresses for Transient Groups."

Multicast Addresses for Permanent Groups

IANA has reserved two ranges of permanent multicast IP addresses. The main distinction between these two ranges of addresses is that the first range is used for packets that should not be forwarded by routers, and the second group is used when packets should be forwarded by routers.

The range of addresses used for local (not routed) purposes is 224.0.0.0 through 224.0.0.255. These addresses should be somewhat familiar from the routing protocol discussions earlier in the book; for example, the 224.0.0.5 and 224.0.0.6 IP addresses used by OSPF fit into this first range of permanent addresses. Other examples include the IP multicast destination address of 224.0.0.1, which specifies that all multicast-capable hosts on a local network segment should examine this packet. Similarly, the IP multicast destination address of 224.0.0.2 on a packet specifies that all multicast-capable routers on a local network segment should examine this packet.

The range of permanent group addresses used when the packets should be routed is 224.0.1.0 through 224.0.1.255. This range includes 224.0.1.39 and 224.0.1.40, which are used by Cisco-proprietary Auto-Rendezvous Point (Auto-RP) protocols (covered in Chapter 17). Table 16-2 shows some of the well-known addresses from the permanent address range.

Table 16-2 *Some Well-Known Reserved Multicast Addresses*

Address	Usage
224.0.0.1	All multicast hosts
224.0.0.2	All multicast routers
224.0.0.4	DVMRP routers
224.0.0.5	All OSPF routers
224.0.0.6	OSPF designated routers

Table 16-2 *Some Well-Known Reserved Multicast Addresses (Continued)*

Address	Usage
224.0.0.9	RIPv2 routers
224.0.0.10	EIGRP routers
224.0.0.13	PIM routers
224.0.0.22	IGMPv3
224.0.0.25	RGMP
224.0.1.39	Cisco-RP-Announce
224.0.1.40	Cisco-RP-Discovery

Multicast Addresses for Source-Specific Multicast Applications and Protocols

IANA has allocated the range 232.0.0.0 through 232.255.255.255 for SSM applications and protocols. The purpose of these applications is to allow a host to select a source for the multicast group. SSM makes multicast routing efficient, allows a host to select a better-quality source, and helps network administrators minimize multicast denial-of-service (DoS) attacks.

> **NOTE** Only IGMPv3-capable hosts can use the SSM feature. IGMPv3 is a new protocol. At the time of this writing, a very limited number of IGMPv3 applications were available. Hence, use of these addresses is minimal.

Multicast Addresses for GLOP Addressing

IANA has reserved the range 233.0.0.0 through 233.255.255.255 (RFC 2770), called GLOP addressing, on an experimental basis. It can be used by anyone who owns a registered autonomous system number (ASN) to create 256 global multicast addresses that can be owned and used by the entity. IANA reserves addresses to ensure global uniqueness of addresses; for similar reasons, each autonomous system should be using an assigned unique ASN.

By using a value of 233 for the first octet, and by using the ASN for the second and third octets, a single autonomous system can create globally unique multicast addresses as defined in the GLOP addressing RFC. For example, the autonomous system using registered ASN 5663 could covert ASN 5663 to binary (0001011000011111). The first 8 bits, 00010110, equals 22 in decimal notation, and the last 8 bits, 00011111, equals 31 in decimal notation. Mapping the first 8 bits to the second octet and the last 8 bits to the third octet in the 233 range addresses, the entity who owns the ASN 5663 is automatically allocated the address range 233.22.31.0 through 233.22.31.255.

> **NOTE** GLOP is not an acronym and does not stand for anything. One of the authors of RFC 2770, David Meyer, started referring to this range of addresses as "GLOP" addressing, and since then the range has been identified by the name GLOP addressing.

Multicast Addresses for Private Multicast Domains

The last of the reserved multicast address ranges mentioned here is the range of *administratively scoped* addresses. IANA has assigned the range 239.0.0.0 through 239.255.255.255 (RFC 2365) for use in private multicast domains, much like the IP unicast ranges defined in RFC 1918, namely 10.0.0.0/8, 172.16.0.0/12, and 192.168.0.0/16. IANA will not assign these administratively scoped multicast addresses to any other protocol or application. Network administrators are free to use multicast addresses in this range; however, they must configure their multicast routers to ensure that multicast traffic in this address range does not leave their multicast domain boundaries.

Multicast Addresses for Transient Groups

When an enterprise wants to use globally unique unicast addresses, it needs to get a block of addresses from its ISP or from IANA. However, when an enterprise wants to use a multicast address for a global multicast application, it can use any multicast address that is not part of the well-known permanent multicast address space covered in the previous sections. These remaining multicast addresses are called *transient groups* or *transient multicast addresses*. This means that the entire Internet must share the transient multicast addresses; they must be dynamically allocated when needed and must be released when no longer in use.

Because these addresses are not permanently assigned to any application, they are called transient. Any enterprise can use these multicast addresses without requiring any registration or permission from IANA, but the enterprise is expected to release these multicast addresses after their use. At the time of this writing, there is no standard method available for using the transient multicast addresses. However, a great deal of work is being done by IETF to define and implement a standard method for dynamically allocating multicast addresses.

Summary of Multicast Address Ranges

Table 16-3 summarizes various multicast address ranges and their use.

Table 16-3 *Multicast Address Ranges and Their Use*

Key
Topic

Multicast Address Range	Usage
224.0.0.0 to 239.255.255.255	This range represents the entire IPv4 multicast address space. It is reserved for multicast applications.
224.0.0.0 to 224.0.0.255	This range is part of the permanent groups. Addresses from this range are assigned by IANA for network protocols on a local segment. Routers do not forward packets with destination addresses used from this range.
224.0.1.0 to 224.0.1.255	This range is also part of the permanent groups. Addresses from this range are assigned by IANA for the network protocols that are forwarded in the entire network. Routers forward packets with destination addresses used from this range.
232.0.0.0 to 232.255.255.255	This range is used for SSM applications.
233.0.0.0 to 233.255.255.255	This range is called the GLOP addressing. It is used for automatically allocating 256 multicast addresses to any enterprise that owns a registered ASN.
239.0.0.0 to 239.255.255.255	This range is used for private multicast domains. These addresses are called administratively scoped addresses.
Remaining ranges of addresses in the multicast address space	Addresses from these ranges are called transient groups. Any enterprise can allocate a multicast address from the transient groups for a global multicast application and should release it when the application is no longer in use.

Mapping IP Multicast Addresses to MAC Addresses

Assigning a Layer 3 multicast address to a multicast group (application) automatically generates a Layer 2 multicast address. Figure 16-6 shows how a multicast MAC address is calculated from a Layer 3 multicast address. The MAC address is formed using an IEEE-registered OUI of 01005E, then a binary 0, and then the last 23 bits of the multicast IP address. The method is identical for Ethernet and Fiber Distributed Data Interface (FDDI).

Figure 16-6 *Calculating a Multicast Destination MAC Address from a Multicast Destination IP Address*

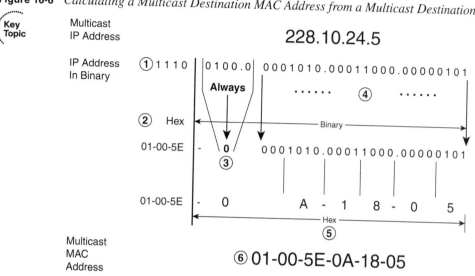

To understand the mechanics of this process, use the following six steps, which are referenced by number in Figure 16-6:

Step 1   Convert the IP address to binary. Notice the first 4 bits; they are always 1110 for any multicast IP address.

Step 2   Replace the first 4 bits 1110 of the IP address with the 6 hexadecimal digits (or 24 bits) 01-00-5E as multicast OUI, in the total space of 12 hexadecimal digits (or 48 bits) for a multicast MAC address.

Step 3   Replace the next 5 bits of the binary IP address with one binary 0 in the multicast MAC address space.

Step 4   Copy the last 23 bits of the binary IP address in the last 23-bit space of the multicast MAC address.

Step 5   Convert the last 24 bits of the multicast MAC address from binary to 6 hexadecimal digits.

Step 6   Combine the first 6 hexadecimal digits 01-00-5E with the last 6 hexadecimal digits, calculated in Step 5, to form a complete multicast MAC address of 12 hexadecimal digits.

Unfortunately, this method does not provide a unique multicast MAC address for each multicast IP address, because only the last 23 bits of the IP address are mapped to the MAC address. For example, the IP address 238.10.24.5 produces exactly the same MAC address, 0x01-00-5E-0A-18-05, as 228.10.24.5. In fact, because 5 bits from the IP address are always mapped to 0, 2^5 (32)

different class D IP addresses produce exactly the same MAC address. IETF points out that the chances of two multicast applications on the same LAN producing the same MAC address are very low. If it happens accidentally, a packet from a different IP multicast application can be identified at Layer 3 and discarded; however, network administrators should be careful when they implement multicast applications so that they can avoid using IP addresses that produce identical MAC addresses.

Managing Distribution of Multicast Traffic with IGMP

NOTE   The current CCIE Routing and Switching blueprint (v3) specifically includes IGMPv2 but not IGMPv1. For perspective, however, this section of the chapter touches on IGMPv1.

Refer to Figure 16-4. Assume that R2 has started receiving multicast traffic from the server. R2 has to make a decision about forwarding this traffic on the Ethernet links. R2 needs to know the answers to the following questions:

■   Is there any host connected to any of my Ethernet links that has shown interest in receiving this traffic?

■   If none of the hosts has shown any interest in receiving this traffic, why should I forward it on the Ethernet links and waste bandwidth?

■   If any host has shown interest in receiving this traffic, where is it located? Is it connected to one of my Ethernet links or to both?

As you can see, a mechanism is required for hosts and a local router to communicate with each other. The IGMP was designed to enable communication between a router and connected hosts.

Not only do routers need to know out which LAN interface to forward multicast packets, but switches also need to know on which ports they should forward the traffic. By default, if a switch receives a multicast frame on a port, it will flood the frame throughout the VLAN, just like it would do for a broadcast or unknown unicast frame. The reason is that switches will never find a multicast MAC address in their Content Addressable Memory (CAM) table, because a multicast MAC address is never used as a source address.

A switch's decision to flood multicast frames means that if any host or hosts in a VLAN request to receive the traffic for a multicast group, all the remaining hosts in the same VLAN, whether they have requested to receive the traffic for the multicast group, will receive the multicast traffic. This behavior is contrary to one of the major goals of multicast design, which is to deliver multicast traffic to only those hosts that have requested it, while maximizing bandwidth efficiency. To forward traffic more efficiently in Figure 16-4, SW2 and SW3 need to know the answers to the following questions:

- Should I forward this multicast traffic on all the ports in this VLAN or only on specific ports?

- If I should forward this multicast traffic on specific ports of a VLAN, how will I find those port numbers?

Three different tools, namely CGMP, IGMP snooping, and RGMP, allow switches to optimize their multicast forwarding logic by answering these kinds of questions. These topics are covered in more depth later in the chapter. For now, this section focuses on how routers and hosts use IGMP to make sure the router knows whether it should forward multicasts out the router's LAN interfaces.

Joining a Group

Before a host can receive any multicast traffic, a multicast application must be installed and running on that host. The process of installing and running a multicast application is referred to as *launching an application* or *joining a multicast group*. After a host joins a group, the host software calculates the multicast MAC address, and its NIC then starts listening to the multicast MAC address, in addition to its BIA.

Before a host (or a user) can join a group, the user needs to know what groups are available and how to join them. For enterprise-scale multicast applications, the user may simply find a link on a web page and click it, prompting the user's multicast client application to start working with the correct multicast address—totally hiding the multicast address details. Alternately, for an internally developed multicast application, the multicast address can be preconfigured on the client application. For example, a user might be required to log on to a server and authenticate with a name and a password; if the user is authenticated, the multicast application automatically installs on the user's PC, which means the user has joined the multicast group. When the user no longer wants to use the multicast application, the user must leave the group. For example, the user may simply close the multicast application to leave the group.

The process by which a human discovers which multicast IP address to listen for and join can be a challenge, particularly for multicast traffic on the Internet. The problem is similar to when you have a satellite or digital cable TV system at home—you might have literally thousands of channels, but finding the channel that has the show you want to watch might require a lot of surfing through the list of channels and time slots. For IP multicast, a user needs to discover what applications they may want to use, and the multicast IP addresses used by the applications. A lot of work remains to be done in this area, but some options are available. For example, online TV program guides and web-based schedules advertise events that will use multicast groups and specify who to contact if you want to see the event, lecture, or concert. Tools like Session Description Protocol (SDP) and Service Advertising Protocol (SAP) also describe multicast events and advertise them. However, a detailed discussion of the different methods, their limitations, and procedures for using them is beyond the scope of this book. The rest of the discussion in this section assumes that hosts have somehow learned about a multicast group.

Internet Group Management Protocol

IGMP has evolved from the Host Membership Protocol, described in Dr. Steve Deering's doctoral thesis, to IGMPv1 (RFC 1112), to IGMPv2 (RFC 2236), to the latest, IGMPv3 (RFC 3376). IGMP messages are sent in IP datagrams with IP protocol number 2, with the IP Time-to-Live (TTL) field set to 1. IGMP packets pass only over a LAN and are not forwarded by routers, due to their TTL field values.

The two most important goals of IGMP are as follows:

Key Topic

■ To inform a local multicast router that a host wants to receive multicast traffic for a specific group

■ To inform local multicast routers that a host wants to leave a multicast group (in other words, the host is no longer interested in receiving the multicast group traffic)

Multicast routers use IGMP to maintain information for each router interface about which multicast group traffic they should forward and which hosts want to receive it.

The following section examines IGMPv2 in detail and introduces important features of IGMPv3. IGMPv1 is no longer on the CCIE Routing Switching exam blueprint, so the focus begins with IGMPv2. In the figures that show the operation of IGMP, Layer 2 switches are not shown because IGMP is used for communication between hosts and routers. Later in the chapter, the sections "Cisco Group Management Protocol," "IGMP Snooping," and "Router-Port Group Management Protocol" discuss the operation of multicasting at Layer 2.

IGMP Version 2

Figure 16-7 shows the 8-octet format of an IGMPv2 message.

Figure 16-7 *IGMPv2 Message Format*

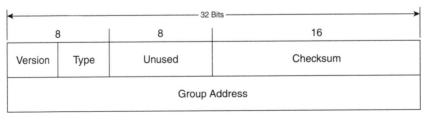

IGMPv2 has four fields, which are defined as follows:

- **Type**—8-bit field that is one of four message types defined by IGMPv2:

    — **Membership Query (Type code = 0x11)**—Used by multicast routers to discover the presence of group members on a subnet. A General Membership Query message sets the Group Address field to 0.0.0.0. A Group-Specific Query sets the Group Address field to the address of the group being queried. It is sent by a router after it receives the IGMPv2 Leave Group message from a host. It is used to determine whether a specific multicast group has any remaining members on a subnet.

    — **Version 1 Membership Report (Type code = 0x12)**—Used by IGMPv2 hosts for backward compatibility with IGMPv1.

    — **Version 2 Membership Report (Type Code = 0x16)**—Sent by a group member to inform the router that at least one group member is present on the subnet.

    — **Leave Group (Type code = 0x17)**—Sent by a group member if it was the last member to send a Membership Report to inform the router that it is leaving the group.

- **Maximum Response Time**—8-bit field included only in Query messages. The units are 1/10 of a second, with 100 (10 seconds) being the default. The values range from 1 to 255 (0.1 to 25.5 seconds).

- **Checksum**—Carries the 16-bit checksum computed by the source. The IGMP checksum is computed over the whole IP payload, not just over the first 8 octets, even though IGMPv2 messages are only 8 bytes in length.

- **Group Address**—Set to 0.0.0.0 in General Query messages and to the group address in Group-Specific messages. Membership Report messages carry the address of the group being reported in this field; Leave Group messages carry the address of the group being left in this field.

IGMPv2 supports complete backward compatibility with IGMPv1. The IGMPv2 Type codes 0x11 and 0x12 match the type codes for IGMPv1 for the Membership Query and Membership Report messages. This enables IGMPv2 hosts and routers to recognize IGMPv1 messages when IGMPv1 hosts or routers are on the network.

One of the primary reasons for developing IGMPv2 was to provide a better Leave mechanism to shorten the leave latency compared to IGMPv1. IGMPv2 has the following features:

- **Leave Group messages**—Provide hosts with a method for notifying routers that they want to leave the group.

- **Group-Specific Query messages**—Permit the router to send a query for a specific group instead of all groups.

- **Maximum Response Time field**—A field in Query messages that permits the router to specify the MRT. This field allows for tuning the response time for the Host Membership Report. This feature can be useful when a large number of groups are active on a subnet and you want to decrease the burstiness of the responses by spreading the responses over a longer period of time.

- **Querier election process**—Provides the method for selecting the preferred router for sending Query messages when multiple routers are connected to the same subnet.

IGMPv2 helps reduce surges in IGMPv2 Solicited Report messages sent by hosts in response to IGMPv2 Query messages by allowing the network administrator to change the Query Response Interval. The IGMPv2 Query message includes an MRT field, stating an MRT to be used by all IGMPv2 hosts on the LAN. Setting MRT, which ranges from 0.1 to 25.5 seconds, to a value slightly longer than IGMPv1's default of 10 seconds spreads the hosts' collective IGMPv2 Solicited Report messages over a longer time period, resulting in more uniform consumption of subnet bandwidth and router resources.

A multicast host can send an IGMP Report in response to a Query or simply send a Report when the host's application first comes up. The IGMPv2 router acting as the IGMPv2 querier sends general IGMP Query messages every 125 seconds. The operations of IGMPv2 General Query messages and Report messages are covered next.

IGMPv2 Host Membership Query Functions

A multicast router uses the IGMPv2 Host Membership Query message to determine whether it has any host on any of its LAN interfaces that wants multicast traffic for any group. The IGMPv2 Host Membership Query message is sent only by multicast routers on LAN interfaces. For example, Figure 16-8 shows the IGMPv2 Host Membership Query process. It lists two steps, with the second step being the router sending the Query.

Figure 16-8 *IGMPv2 Host Membership Query Process*

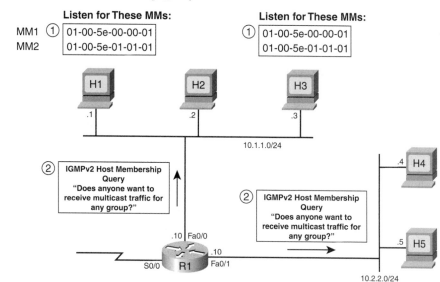

The details of the two steps are as follows:

1. Hosts H1 and H3 join multicast group 226.1.1.1. The Join causes these hosts to prepare to receive messages sent to both 226.1.1.1 (the joined group) and 224.0.0.1 (the address to which IGMPv2 Queries will be sent). Multicast hosts must listen to the well-known 224.0.0.1 multicast group address to participate in IGMP and, as a result, to receive multicast queries sent by the router. The Join causes these hosts to calculate the two multicast MAC (MM) addresses, 01-00-5e-01-01-01 (from 226.1.1.1) and 01-00-5e-00-00-01 (from 224.0.0.1), and then listen for frames sent to these two MMs.

2. R1 sends an IGMPv2 Host Membership Query out each LAN interface, looking for any host interested in receiving packets for any multicast group. R1 periodically sends IGMPv2 Queries on each LAN interface, by default, every 60 seconds. This time period is called the Query Interval. R1's Queries use a destination IP address and MAC address of 224.0.0.1 and 01-00-5e-00-00-01, with the source IP address and MAC address of R1's interface IP address and BIA, respectively. After sending IGMPv2 Queries, R1 expects any host that has joined group 226.1.1.1, or any other group, to reply with an IGMPv2 Report. The IGMPv2 Queries also use a TTL of 1, preventing the packet from being routed.

   The IGMPv2 Query message's Group Address field (see Figure 16-7) is always 0.0.0.0. By sending the IGMPv2 Query message with the Group Address 0.0.0.0, the router is asking the hosts on each LAN, "Does anyone want to receive multicast traffic for any group?"

At this point, router R1 still does not know whether any hosts need to receive any multicast traffic. The next section covers how the hosts respond with IGMP Report messages to inform R1 of their interest in receiving multicast packets.

IGMPv2 Host Membership Report Functions

Hosts use IGMPv2 Host Membership Report messages to reply to IGMP Queries and inform the routers of their desire to receive multicasts. Multicast hosts use IGMPv2 Host Membership Report messages to communicate to a local router for which multicast groups they want to receive traffic.

In IGMPv2, a host sends a Host Membership Report under the following two conditions:

- When a host receives an IGMPv2 Query from a local router, it is supposed to send an IGMPv2 Host Membership Report for all the multicast groups for which it wants to receive multicast traffic. This Report is called an IGMPv2 Solicited Host Membership Report.

- When a host joins a new group, the host immediately sends an IGMPv2 Host Membership Report to inform a local router that it wants to receive multicast traffic for the group it has just joined without waiting to receive an IGMPv2 Query. This Report is called an IGMPv2 Unsolicited Host Membership Report.

The operations of Solicited Host Membership Report and Unsolicited Host Membership Report are explained in the following sections.

> **NOTE**   The term *Solicited Host Membership Report* is not defined in RFC 2236. It is used in this book to specify whether the IGMPv2 Report was sent in response to a Query (solicited).

IGMPv2 Solicited Host Membership Report

Figure 16-9 shows operation of the IGMPv2 Solicited Host Membership Report process and the Report Suppression mechanism. Figure 16-9 picks up the example from Figure 16-8, in which router R1 had sent an IGMPv2 Query.

Figure 16-9 *IGMPv2 Solicited Host Membership Report and Report Suppression Processes*

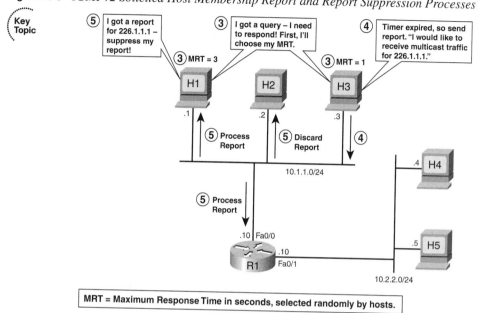

MRT = Maximum Response Time in seconds, selected randomly by hosts.

If many hosts have launched multicast applications and if all of them respond to the Host Membership Query with the Host Membership Report, many redundant reports could be sent to the router. This wastes bandwidth and unnecessarily increases the processing load on the router. A multicast router needs to receive only one report for each application on each of its LAN interfaces. A multicast router begins forwarding multicast traffic on a LAN interface whether 1 user or 200 users request to receive the traffic for a given multicast group.

The Report Suppression mechanism helps to solve these problems. It uses the IGMPv2 Maximum Response Time (MRT) timer to suppress many of the unnecessary IGMP Reports. This timer is called the *Query Response Interval*. In other words, when any host receives an IGMPv2 Query, it has a maximum of the configured MRT to send the IGMP Report if it wants to receive multicast traffic for that application. Each host that wants to send the Solicited Host Membership Report picks randomly a time between 0 and the MRT and starts a timer. When this timer expires, the host will send a report. However, if a host receives a report sent by another host for the same multicast group for which it was planning to send the report, it does not send the report. This is called *Report Suppression* and is designed to reduce redundant reports. The unit of measurement for the MRT is 0.1 second. For example, a 3-second MRT is expressed as 30.

The following three steps, referenced in Figure 16-9 and a continuation of the steps referenced in Figure 16-8, describe the sequence of events for the IGMPv2 Solicited Host Membership Report and Report Suppression mechanism:

1. Hosts H1 and H3 would like to send IGMPv2 Solicited Host Membership Reports. Assume that H1 and H3 have received an IGMPv2 Query (as shown in step 2 of Figure 16-8). Because both H1 and H3 have joined the group 226.1.1.1, they need to send an IGMPv2 Solicited Host Membership Report. Further assume that H1 and H3 have randomly picked an MRT of 3 seconds and 1 second, respectively.

2. H3's timer expires in 1 second; it prepares and sends the IGMPv2 Solicited Host Membership Report with the TTL value of 1. H3 uses the destination IP address 226.1.1.1 and the source IP address 10.1.1.3, the destination MAC address 01-00-5e-01-01-01 calculated from the Layer 3 address 226.1.1.1, and its BIA address as the source address.

3. Hosts H1, H2, and R1 receive the IGMPv2 Solicited Host Membership Report, but only H1 and R1 process the Report. The NIC of H2 discards the frame sent by H3 because it is not listening to the address 01-00-5e-01-01-01. H1 realizes that H3 has already made a request to the router to forward the traffic for the same multicast group 226.1.1.1. Therefore, H1 suppresses its own Report and does not send it. By using the Group Address of 226.1.1.1, H3 is telling the multicast router, "I would like to receive multicast traffic for group 226.1.1.1."

R1 has now received the IGMPv2 Solicited Host Membership Report on its fa0/0 interface requesting traffic for multicast group 226.1.1.1, but it has not received a Host Membership Report on its fa0/1 interface. Figure 16-10 shows that R1 has started forwarding multicast traffic for group 226.1.1.1 on its fa0/0 interface.

Figure 16-10   *R1 Forwarding Traffic for Group 226.1.1.1 on Its Fa0/0 Interface*

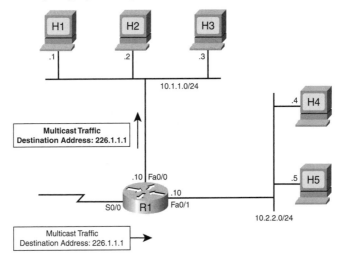

IGMPv2 Unsolicited Host Membership Report

In IGMPv2, a multicast router sends IGMP Host Membership Query messages by default every 125 seconds (Query Interval) on each of its LAN interfaces to determine whether any host wants to receive multicast traffic for any group. However, a host does not have to receive the Host Membership Query message from the router to send a Host Membership Report. A host can send an IGMPv2 Unsolicited Host Membership Report anytime a user launches a multicast application. This feature reduces the waiting time for a host to receive traffic for a multicast group. For example, Figure 16-11 shows that a user has launched a multicast application that uses 226.1.1.1 on H4, which sends an IGMPv2 Unsolicited Host Membership Report that will be received by R1 on its fa0/1 interface, and R1 will then start forwarding traffic for 226.1.1.1 on its fa0/1 interface.

Figure 16-11 *H4 Sends IGMPv2 Unsolicited Host Membership Report*

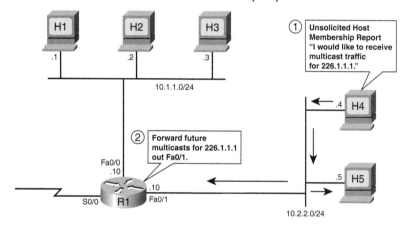

IGMPv2 improves the Query/Report process by using the IGMPv2 Group-Specific Query. In IGMPv2, when a host leaves a group, it sends an IGMPv2 Leave message. When an IGMPv2 router receives a Leave message, instead of waiting for the normal Query Interval timer (125 seconds by default) to expire, the IGMPv2 router immediately sends a Group-Specific Query for that group. The Group-Specific Query asks only whether any remaining hosts still want to receive packets for that single multicast group. As a result, the router quickly knows whether to continue to forward that multicast group on that LAN.

The main advantage of IGMPv2 over IGMPv1 is IGMPv2's shorter leave latency. An IGMPv1 router takes, by default, 3 minutes to conclude that the last host on the subnet has left a group and no host on the subnet wants to receive traffic for the group. Meanwhile, the IGMPv1 router continues forwarding the group traffic on the subnet and wastes bandwidth. On the other hand, an IGMPv2 router concludes in 3 seconds that no host on the subnet wants to receive traffic for a group and stops forwarding it on the subnet.

The functions of the IGMPv2 Leave message and IGMPv2 Group-Specific Query message are explained in detail in the next section.

IGMPv2 Leave Group and Group-Specific Query Messages

The IGMPv2 Leave Group message is used to significantly reduce the leave latency, while the IGMPv2 Group-Specific Query message prevents a router from incorrectly stopping the forwarding of packets on a LAN when a host leaves a group. As a result, both of these IGMPv2 functions work together.

> **NOTE** IGMPv2 RFC 2236 recommends that a host sends a Leave Group message only if the leaving member was the last host to send a Membership Report in response to a Query. However, most IGMPv2 vendor operating systems have implemented the Leave Group processing by always sending a Leave Group message when any host leaves the group.

Figure 16-12 shows the operation of the IGMPv2 Leave process and the IGMP Group-Specific Query. In Figure 16-12, hosts H1 and H3 are currently members of group 226.1.1.1; H1 wants to leave the group.

Figure 16-12 *How Group-Specific Queries Work with the IGMPv2 Leave Process*

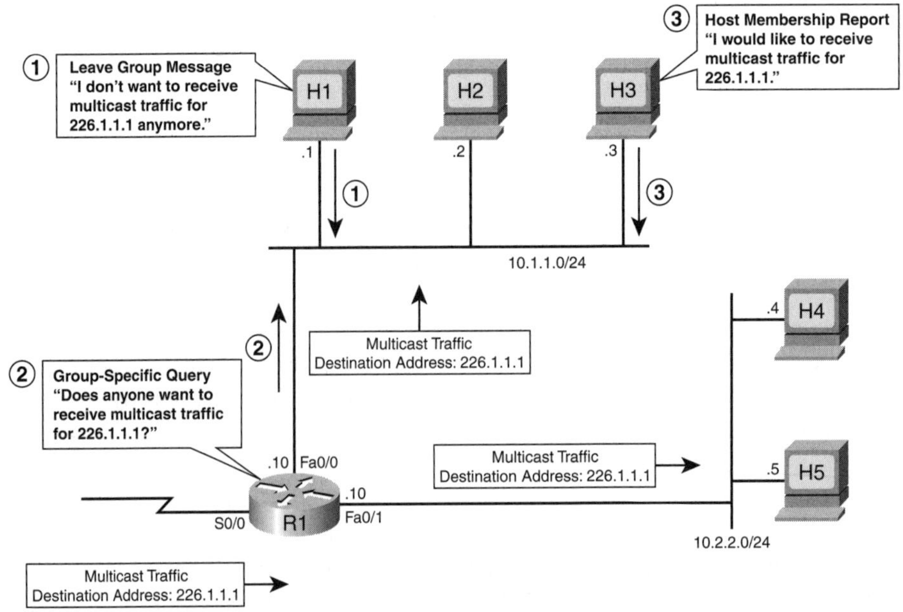

The following three steps, referenced in Figure 16-12, describe the sequence of events for the IGMPv2 Leave mechanism when H1 leaves:

1. H1 sends an IGMPv2 Leave Group message. The destination address on the packet is 224.0.0.2, which is a well-known multicast address for All Multicast Routers to inform all routers on the subnet that, "I don't want to receive multicast traffic for 226.1.1.1 anymore."

2. R1 sends a Group-Specific Query. Routers do not keep track of hosts that are members of the group, only the group memberships that are active. Because H1 has decided to leave 226.1.1.1, R1 can stop forwarding traffic for 226.1.1.1 on its fa0/0 interface if H1 is the last member of 226.1.1.1 on the interface. However, R1 needs to make sure that no other hosts of this interface still need to receive packets from group 226.1.1.1. Therefore, R1 sends a Group-Specific Query to determine whether any hosts are still members of 226.1.1.1. R1 uses 226.1.1.1 as the destination address on the packet so that only hosts that are members of this group will receive the message and respond. Through this message, R1 is asking any remaining hosts on the subnet, "Does anyone want to receive multicast traffic for 226.1.1.1?"

3. H3 sends a Membership Report. H3 is still a member of group 226.1.1.1. It hears the Group-Specific Query and responds with an IGMPv2 Membership Report to inform the routers on the subnet that it is still a member of group 226.1.1.1 and would like to keep receiving traffic for group 226.1.1.1.

NOTE The Report Suppression mechanism explained earlier for the General Group Query is also used for the Group-Specific Query.

IGMPv2 routers repeat the process of Step 2 in this example each time they receive a Leave message as shown in Step 1. In the previous example, the router (R1) did not stop sending traffic as a result of the process. In the next example, H3 is the only remaining member of group 226.1.1.1 on the subnet. Assume that now H3 also wants to leave the group, as shown in Figure 16-13.

Figure 16-13 *IGMPv2 Leave Process—No Response to the Group-Specific Query*

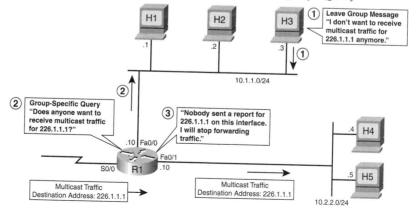

The following three steps, referenced in Figure 16-13, describe the sequence of events for the IGMPv2 Leave mechanism when H3 leaves:

1. H3 sends an IGMPv2 Leave Group message. The destination address on the packet is 224.0.0.2 to inform all routers on the subnet that, "I don't want to receive multicast traffic for 226.1.1.1 anymore."

2. R1 sends a Group-Specific Query. R1 receives the Leave Group message from H3. R1 sends a Group-Specific Query to determine whether any hosts are still members of group 226.1.1.1. R1 uses 226.1.1.1 as the destination address on the packet so that only hosts that are members of this group will receive the message and respond.

3. No reports are received, so R1 stops forwarding group traffic. Because there are now no remaining members of 226.1.1.1 on the subnet, R1 does not receive a response to the Group-Specific Query from any host. As a result, R1 stops forwarding multicasts for 226.1.1.1 out its fa0/1 interface.

Step 3 of this example provides a nice backdrop from which to describe the concepts of a *Last Member Query Interval* and a *Last Member Query Count*. These values determine how long it takes a router to believe that all hosts on a LAN have left a particular group. By default, routers use an MRT of 10 (1 second) for Group-Specific Queries; because a router should receive a response to a Group-Specific Query in that amount of time, the router uses the MRT value as the value of the Last Member Query Interval. So, the router uses the following process:

1. Send a Group-Specific Query in response to an IGMP Leave.

2. If no Report is received within the Last Member Query Interval, repeat Step 1.

3. Repeat Step 1 the number of times defined by the value of the Last Member Query Count.

The Last Member Query Count is the number of consecutive Group-Specific Queries sent for the same group before the router concludes that there are no active members of the group on a subnet. The default value for the Last Member Query Count is 2. So the leave latency is typically less than 3 seconds, compared to up to 3 minutes with IGMPv1.

IGMPv2 Querier

IGMPv2 defines a querier election process that is used when multiple routers are connected to a subnet. When IGMPv2 routers start, they each send an IGMPv2 General Query message to the well-known All Hosts group 224.0.0.1 using their interface address as the source address. When an IGMPv2 router receives a General Query message, it compares the source IP address of the General Query message with its own interface address. The router with the lowest IP address on the subnet is elected as the IGMP querier. The nonquerier routers stop sending their queries but monitor how frequently the querier is sending general IGMPv2 Queries. When the elected querier does not send a query for two consecutive Query Intervals plus one half of one Query Response

Interval, it is considered to be dead, and a new querier is elected. RFC 2236 refers to this time interval as the *Other Querier Present Interval*. The default value for the Other Querier Present Interval is 255 seconds, because the default General IGMPv2 Query Interval is 125 seconds and the default Query Response Interval is 10 seconds.

IGMPv1 and IGMPv2 Interoperability

IGMPv2 is designed to be backward compatible with IGMPv1. RFC 2236 defines some special interoperability rules. The next few sections explore the following interoperability scenarios:

- **IGMPv2 Host and IGMPv1 Routers**—Defines how an IGMPv2 host should behave in the presence of an IGMPv1 router on the same subnet.

- **IGMPv1 Host and IGMPv2 Routers**—Defines how an IGMPv2 router should behave in the presence of an IGMPv1 host on the same subnet.

IGMPv2 Host and IGMPv1 Routers

When a host sends the IGMPv2 Report with the message type 0x16, which is not defined in IGMPv1, a version 1 router would consider 0x16 an invalid message type and ignore it. Therefore, a version 2 host must send IGMPv1 Reports when a version 1 router is active. But how does an IGMPv2 host detect the presence of an IGMPv1 router on the subnet?

IGMPv2 hosts determine whether the querying router is an IGMPv1 or IGMPv2 host based on the value of the MRT field of the periodic general IGMP Query. In IGMPv1 Queries, this field is zero, whereas in IGMPv2 it is nonzero and represents the MRT value. When an IGMPv2 host receives an IGMPv1 Query, it knows that the IGMPv1 router is present on the subnet and marks the interface as an IGMPv1 interface. The IGMPv2 host then stops sending IGMPv2 messages.

Whenever an IGMPv2 host receives an IGMPv1 Query, it starts a 400-second *Version 1 Router Present Timeout* timer. This timer is reset whenever it receives an IGMPv1 Query. If the timer expires, which indicates that there are no IGMPv1 routers present on the subnet, the IGMPv2 host starts sending IGMPv2 messages.

IGMPv1 Host and IGMPv2 Routers

IGMPv2 routers can easily determine if any IGMPv1 hosts are present on a LAN based on whether any hosts send an IGMPv1 Report message (type 0x12) or IGMPv2 Report message (type 0x16). Like IGMPv1 routers, IGMPv2 routers send periodic IGMPv2 General Queries. An IGMPv1 host responds normally because IGMPv2 General Queries are very similar in format to IGMPv1

Queries—except for the second octet, which is ignored by IGMPv1 hosts. So, an IGMPv2 router will examine all Reports to find out if any IGMPv1 hosts exist on a LAN.

> **NOTE** If IGMPv2 hosts are also present on the same subnet, they would send IGMPv2 Membership Reports. However, IGMPv1 hosts do not understand IGMPv2 Reports and ignore them; they do not trigger Report Suppression in IGMPv1 hosts. Therefore, sometimes an IGMPv2 router receives both an IGMPv1 Report and an IGMPv2 Report in response to a General Query.

While an IGMPv2 router knows that an IGMPv1 host is present on a LAN, the router ignores Leave messages and the Group-Specific Queries triggered by receipt of the Leave messages. This is necessary because if an IGMPv2 router responds to a Leave Group message with a Group-Specific Query, IGMPv1 hosts will not understand it and thus ignore the message. When an IGMPv2 router does not receive a response to its Group-Specific Query, it may erroneously conclude that nobody wants to receive traffic for the group and thus stop forwarding it on the subnet. So with one or more IGMPv1 hosts listening for a particular group, the router essentially suspends the optimizations that reduce leave latency.

IGMPv2 routers continue to ignore Leave messages until the *IGMPv1-host-present countdown timer* expires. RFC 2236 defines that when IGMPv2 routers receive an IGMPv1 Report, they must set an IGMPv1-host-present countdown timer. The timer value should be equal to the Group Membership Interval, which defaults to 180 seconds in IGMPv1 and 260 seconds in IGMPv2. (Group Membership Interval is a time period during which, if a router does not receive an IGMP Report, the router concludes that there are no more members of the group on a subnet.)

IGMPv2 Timers

Table 16-4 summarizes important timers used in IGMPv2, their usage, and default values.

Table 16-4 *Important IGMPv2 Timers*

Timer	Usage	Default Value
Query Interval	A time period between General Queries sent by a router.	125 seconds
Query Response Interval	The maximum response time for hosts to respond to the periodic general Queries.	10 seconds; can be between .1 and 25.5 seconds
Group Membership Interval	A time period during which, if a router does not receive an IGMP Report, the router concludes that there are no more members of the group on the subnet.	260 seconds

Table 16-4 *Important IGMPv2 Timers (Continued)*

Timer	Usage	Default Value
Other Querier Present Interval	A time period during which, if the IGMPv2 non-querier routers do not receive an IGMP Query from the querier router, the nonquerier routers conclude that the querier is dead.	255 seconds
Last Member Query Interval	The maximum response time inserted by IGMPv2 routers into the Group-Specific Queries and the time period between two consecutive Group-Specific Queries sent for the same group.	1 second
Version 1 Router Present Timeout	A time period during which, if an IGMPv2 host does not receive an IGMPv1 Query, the IGMPv2 host concludes that there are no IGMPv1 routers present and starts sending IGMPv2 messages.	400 seconds

IGMP Version 3

In October 2002, RFC 3376 defined specifications for IGMPv3, which is a major revision of the protocol and is very complex. To use the new features of IGMPv3, last-hop routers have to be updated, host operating systems have to be modified, and applications have to be specially designed and written. At the time of this writing (mid-2007), a limited number of IGMPv3 applications are available. Therefore, this section does not examine IGMPv3 in detail; instead, it summarizes IGMPv3's major features.

In IGMPv1 and IGMPv2, when a host makes a request to join a group, a multicast router forwards the traffic for the group to the subnet regardless of the source IP address of the packets. For example, assume that a multimedia conference is in session. A group member decides to maliciously disturb the session by sending "bogus data or noise" by either talking or sending music to the same group. Although multimedia applications allow a user to mute any of the other members, it does not stop the unwanted traffic from being delivered to the host. If a group of hackers decides to flood a company's network with bogus high-bandwidth data using the same multicast group address that the company's employees have joined, it can create a DoS attack for the company by overwhelming low-speed links. Neither IGMPv1 nor IGMPv2 has a mechanism to prevent such an attack.

IGMPv3 allows a host to filter incoming traffic based on the source IP addresses from which it is willing to receive packets, through a feature called *Source-Specific Multicast (SSM)*. IGMPv3 is designed to support source filtering. It allows a host to indicate interest in receiving packets only from specific source addresses, or from all but specific source addresses, sent to a particular multicast address. Figure 16-14 shows basic operation of the IGMPv3 Membership Report process.

Figure 16-14 *IGMPv3 Membership Report*

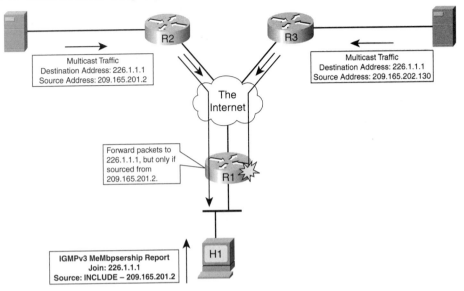

In Figure 16-14, the multicast traffic for the group 226.1.1.1 is available from two sources. R1 receives traffic from both the sources. H1 prepares an IGMPv3 Membership Report using the destination address 224.0.0.22, specially assigned by IANA for the IGMPv3 Membership Report. The message type is 0x22 (defined in RFC 3376), with a note "Source–INCLUDE— 209.165.201.2," which means, "I would like to join multicast group 226.1.1.1, but only if the group traffic is coming from the source 209.165.201.2."

How does a host learn group source addresses? A lot of work remains to be done by application designers to develop SSM applications. Cisco has designed URL Rendezvous Directory (URD) and IGMP v3lite to use the new features of IGMPv3 until IGMPv3 applications are available and operating systems are updated. A detailed discussion of URD and IGMP v3lite is beyond the scope of this book. IGMPv3 is compatible with IGMPv1 and IGMPv2.

> **NOTE**   The following URL provides more information on URD and IGMP v3lite:
> http://www.cisco.com/univercd/cc/td/doc/product/software/ios121/121newft/121t/121t5/ dtigmpv3.htm

Comparison of IGMPv1, IGMPv2, and IGMPv3

Table 16-5 compares the important features of IGMPv1, IGMPv2, and IGMPv3.

Table 16-5   *Comparison of IGMPv1, IGMPv2, and IGMPv3*

Feature	IGMPv1	IGMPv2	IGMPv3
First Octet Value for the Query Message	0x11	0x11	0x11
Group Address for the General Query	0.0.0.0	0.0.0.0	0.0.0.0
Destination Address for the General Query	224.0.0.1	224.0.0.1	224.0.0.1
Default Query Interval	60 seconds	125 seconds	125 seconds
First Octet Value for the Report	0x12	0x16	0x22
Group Address for the Report	Joining multicast group address	Joining multicast group address	Joining multicast group address and source address
Destination Address for the Report	Joining multicast group address	Joining multicast group address	224.0.0.22
Is Report Suppression Mechanism Available?	Yes	Yes	No
Can Maximum Response Time Be Configured?	No, fixed at 10 seconds	Yes, 0 to 25.5 seconds	Yes, 0 to 53 minutes
Can a Host Send a Leave Group Message?	No	Yes	Yes
Destination Address for the Leave Group Message		224.0.0.2	224.0.0.22
Can a Router Send a Group-Specific Query?	No	Yes	Yes
Can a Host Send Source- and Group-Specific Reports?	No	No	Yes
Can a Router Send Source- and Group-Specific Queries?	No	No	Yes
Rule for Electing a Querier	None—depends on multicast routing protocol	Router with the lowest IP address on the subnet	Router with the lowest IP address on the subnet
Compatible with Other Versions of IGMP?	No	Yes, only with IGMPv1	Yes, with both IGMPv1 and IGMPv2

LAN Multicast Optimizations

This final major section of this chapter introduces the basics of three tools that optimize the flow of multicast over a LAN. Specifically, this section covers the following topics:

- Cisco Group Management Protocol (CGMP)

- IGMP snooping

- Router-Port Group Management Protocol (RGMP)

Cisco Group Management Protocol

IGMP helps routers to determine how to distribute multicast traffic. However, IGMP works at Layer 3, and switches do not understand IGMP messages. Switches, by default, flood multicast traffic to all the hosts in a broadcast domain, which wastes bandwidth. Figure 16-15 illustrates the problem.

Figure 16-15 *Switches Flood Multicast Traffic*

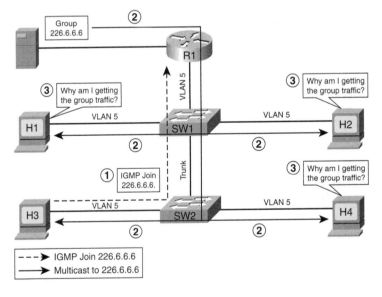

Hosts H1, H2, H3, H4, and R1 are all in the same broadcast domain of VLAN 5. The following three steps, referenced in Figure 16-15, describe the sequence of events when H3 sends an IGMP Join message:

1. H3 sends an IGMP Join message for group 226.6.6.6.

2. R1 forwards the group traffic to SW1. The destination MAC address on the frame is 0x0100.5e06.0606. SW1 cannot find this address in its CAM table because it is never used by any device as a source address. Therefore, SW1 starts forwarding the group traffic to H1, H2, and SW2 because the group traffic is for VLAN 5. Similarly, SW2 starts forwarding the group traffic to H3 and H4.

3. All the hosts, H1 to H4, receive the group traffic, but only H3 requested it. H3 requested the group traffic and has started receiving it. However, H1, H2, and H4 did not ask for the group traffic, and they are flooded by switches with the group traffic.

In this illustration, only four hosts are shown in the broadcast domain of VLAN 5. What happens if a broadcast domain is flat and has hundreds of users? If a single host joins a multicast group, all the hosts would be flooded with the group traffic whether they have requested the group traffic. The goal of multicasting is to deliver the group traffic to only those hosts that have requested it and maximize the use of bandwidth.

There are two popular methods for helping Layer 2 switches determine how to distribute the multicast traffic to hosts:

- CGMP, which is Cisco proprietary and discussed throughout the rest of this section.

- IGMP snooping, discussed in the next section.

CGMP, a Layer 2 protocol, is configured on both a Cisco router and switches and permits the router to communicate Layer 2 information it has learned from IGMP to switches. A multicast router knows the MAC addresses of the multicast hosts, and the groups to which they listen, based on IGMP communication with hosts. The goal of CGMP is to enable the router to communicate this information through CGMP messages to switches so that switches can dynamically modify their CAM table entries. Only the routers produce CGMP messages, while switches only listen to the CGMP messages. To do this, CGMP must be enabled at both ends of the router-switch connection over which CGMP is operating, because both devices must know to use CGMP.

The destination address on the CGMP messages is always the well-known CGMP multicast MAC address 0x0100.0cdd.dddd. The use of the multicast destination MAC address on the CGMP messages forces switches to flood the message through all the ports so that all the switches in a network receive the CGMP messages. The important information in the CGMP messages is one or more pairs of MAC addresses:

- Group Destination Address (GDA)

- Unicast Source Address (USA)

The following five steps describe the general process of CGMP. Later, these steps are explained using a detailed example.

1. When a CGMP-capable router gets connected to the switch, it sends a CGMP Join message with the GDA set to zero and the USA set to its own MAC address. The CGMP-capable switch now knows that a multicast router is connected to the port on which it received the router's CGMP message. The router repeats the message every 60 seconds. A router can also tell the switch that it no longer participates in CGMP by sending a CGMP Leave message with the GDA set to zero and the USA set to its own MAC address.

2. When a host joins a group, it sends an IGMP Join message. Normally, a multicast router examines only Layer 3 information in the IGMP Join message, and the router does not have to process any Layer 2 information. However, when CGMP is configured on a router, the router also examines the Layer 2 destination and source MAC addresses of the IGMP Join message. The source address is the unicast MAC address of the host that sent the IGMP Join message. The router then generates a CGMP Join message that includes the multicast MAC address associated with the multicast IP address (to the GDA field of the CGMP join) and the unicast MAC address of the host (to the USA field of the CGMP message). The router sends the CGMP Join message using the well-known CGMP multicast MAC address 0x0100.0cdd.dddd as the destination address.

3. When switches receive a CGMP Join message, they search in their CAM tables for the port number associated with the host MAC address listed in the USA field. Switches create a new CAM table entry (or use an existing entry if it was already created before) for the multicast MAC address listed in the GDA field of the CGMP Join message, add the port number associated with the host MAC address listed in the USA field to the entry, and forward the group traffic on the port.

4. When a host leaves a group, it sends an IGMP Leave message. The router learns the host's unicast MAC address (USA) and the IP multicast group it has just left. Because the Leave messages are sent to the All Multicast Routers MAC address 0x0100.5e00.0002 and not to the multicast group address the host has just left, the router calculates the multicast MAC address (GDA) from the IP multicast group the host has just left. The router then generates a CGMP Leave message, copies the multicast MAC address it has just calculated in the GDA field and unicast MAC address in the USA field of the CGMP Leave message, and sends it to the well-known CGMP multicast MAC address.

5. When switches receive a CGMP Leave message, they again search for the port number associated with the host MAC address listed in the USA field. Switches remove this port from the CAM table entry for the multicast MAC address listed in the GDA field of the CGMP Leave message and stop forwarding the group traffic on the port.

Thus, CGMP helps switches send group traffic to only those hosts that want it, which helps to avoid wasted bandwidth.

Figure 16-16, 16-17, and 16-18 show a complete example of how routers and switches use CGMP in response to a host joining and then leaving a group. Figure 16-16 begins the example by showing a router's reaction to an IGMP Report, which is to send a CGMP Join to the switches on a LAN. The following two steps, referenced in Figure 16-16, describe the sequence of events when H3 sends an IGMP Join message:

1. H3 sends an IGMP Join message for 226.6.6.6. At Layer 2, H3 uses 0x0100.5e06.0606 (the multicast MAC address associated with 226.6.6.6) as the destination address of a frame and its own BIA 0x0006.7c11.1103 as the source MAC address.

2. R1 generates a CGMP Join message. When a CGMP-capable router receives an IGMP Join message, it generates a Layer 2 CGMP Join message. The destination address on the frame is the well-known multicast MAC address 0x0100.0cdd.dddd, which is understood only by Cisco switches but is forwarded by all switches. R1 sets the GDA to the group MAC address 0x0100.5e06.0606 and sets the USA to H3's MAC address 0x0006.7c11.1103, which communicates to switches that, "A host with the USA 0x0006.7c11.1103 has requested multicast traffic for the GDA 0x0100.5e06.0606, so map your CAM tables accordingly." This message is received by both switches.

Figure 16-16 *CGMP Join Message Process*

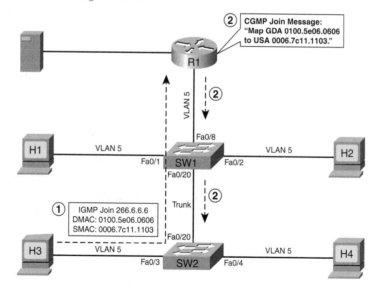

SW1 and SW2 search their CAM table entries and find that a host with the USA 0x0006.7c11.1103 is located on their port number fa0/20 and fa0/3, respectively. Figure 16-17 shows that SW1 and SW2 have mapped the GDA 0x0100.5e06.0606 to their port numbers fa0/20 and fa0/3, respectively.

Figure 16-17 *Switches Map GDA to Port Numbers and Don't Flood All the Hosts in a Broadcast Domain*

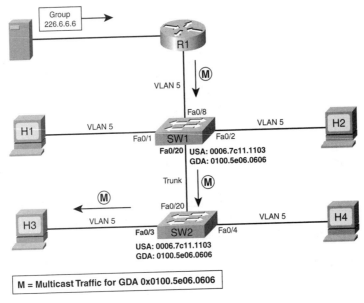

When R1 forwards multicast traffic with GDA 0x0100.5e06.0606 to SW1, as shown in Figure 16-17, SW1 searches its CAM table and notices that this traffic should be forwarded only on port fa0/20. Therefore, only SW2 receives the group traffic. Similarly, SW2 searches its CAM table and forwards the group traffic only on its port fa0/3, and only H3 receives the group traffic.

CGMP optimizes the forwarding of IGMP traffic as well. Although not shown in the figures, assume that H1 sends an IGMP Join message for 226.6.6.6. R1 will send another CGMP Join message, and SW1 will add the GDA 0x0100.5e06.0606 to its port fa0/1 also. When a router sends IGMP General Queries, switches forward them to host members who have joined any group, for example, H1 and H3. When hosts send IGMP Reports, switches forward them to the members of the group and the router.

The final step of the example, shown in Figure 16-18, demonstrates what happens when H3 leaves the group. Note that for this example, H1 has also joined the same multicast group.

Figure 16-18 *CGMP Leave Message Process*

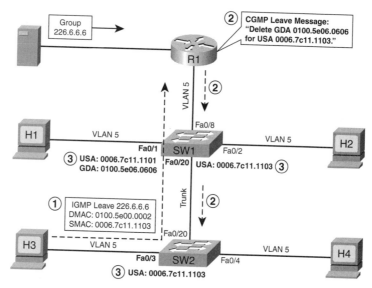

The following three steps, referenced in Figure 16-18, describe the sequence of events when H3 sends an IGMP Leave message:

1. H3 sends an IGMP Leave message for 226.6.6.6. At Layer 2, H3 uses the All Multicast Routers MAC address 0x0100.5e00.0002 as the destination address and its own BIA 0x0006.7c11.1103 as the source address.

2. R1 generates a CGMP Leave message. When a CGMP-capable router receives an IGMP Leave message, it generates a Layer 2 CGMP Leave message. The destination address on the frame is the well-known multicast MAC address 0x0100.0cdd.dddd. R1 calculates the group MAC address 0x0100.5e06.0606 from the Layer 3 address 226.6.6.6 and sets the GDA to that value. It sets the USA to H3's MAC unicast MAC address of 0x0006.7c11.1103. This Leave message communicates to switches that, "A host with the USA 0x0006.7c11.1103 does not want to receive multicast traffic for GDA 0x0100.5e06.0606, so update your CAM tables accordingly." This message is received by both switches.

3. Switches update their CAM table entries. SW1 and SW2 search their CAM table entries and find that a host with the USA 0x0006.7c11.1103 is located on their port numbers fa0/20 and fa0/3, respectively. Figure 16-19 shows that SW1 and SW2 have removed the GDA 0x0100.5e06.0606 from their port numbers fa0/20 and fa0/3, respectively.

H1 is still a member of the group 266.6.6.6, so R1 keeps forwarding the traffic with GDA 0x0100.5e06.0606 to SW1, as shown in Figure 16-18. SW1 searches its CAM table and finds that this traffic should be forwarded only on port fa0/1. Therefore, only H1 receives the group traffic.

Continuing the example further, now assume that H1 sends an IGMP Leave message for 226.6.6.6. R1 will send a Group-Specific Query for 226.6.6.6. Because no host is currently a member of this group, R1 does not receive any IGMP Membership Reports for the group. R1 sends the CGMP Leave message with the GDA set to the group MAC address and the USA set to 0. This message communicates to switches that, "No hosts are interested in receiving the multicast group traffic for the MAC address 0x0100.5e06.0606, so remove all the CAM table entries for this group."

Table 16-6 summarizes the possible combinations of the GDA and the USA in CGMP messages and the meanings of each. The first five messages have been discussed.

Table 16-6 *CGMP Messages*

Type	Group Destination Address	Unicast Source Address	Meaning
Join	Group MAC	Host MAC	Add USA port to group
Leave	Group MAC	Host MAC	Delete USA port from group
Join	Zero	Router MAC	Learn which port connects to the CGMP router
Leave	Zero	Router MAC	Release CGMP router port
Leave	Group MAC	Zero	Delete the group from the CAM
Leave	Zero	Zero	Delete all groups from the CAM

The last Leave message in Table 16-6, Delete All Groups, is used by the router for special maintenance functions. For example, when the **clear ip cgmp** command is entered at the router for clearing all the CGMP entries on the switches, the router sends the CGMP Leave message with GDA set to zero and USA set to zero. When switches receive this message, they delete all group entries from the CAM tables.

IGMP Snooping

What happens if your network has non-Cisco switches? You cannot use CGMP because it is Cisco proprietary. IGMP snooping can be used for a multivendor switched network to control distribution of multicast traffic at Layer 2. IGMP snooping requires the switch software to eavesdrop on the IGMP conversation between multicast hosts and the router. The switch examines IGMP messages and learns the location of multicast routers and group members.

> **NOTE** Many Cisco switches support IGMP snooping, including the 3550 and 3560 switches used in the CCIE Routing and Switching lab exam.

The following three steps describe the general process of IGMP snooping. Later, these steps are explained in detail.

1. To detect whether multiple routers are connected to the same subnet, Cisco switches listen to the following routing protocol messages to determine on which ports routers are connected:

    — IGMP General Query message with GDA 01-00-5e-00-00-01

    — OSPF messages with GDA 01-00-5e-00-00-05 or 01-00-5e-00-00-06

    — Protocol Independent Multicast (PIM) version 1 and Hot Standby Routing Protocol (HSRP) Hello messages with GDA 01-00-5e-00-00-02

    — PIMv2 Hello messages with GDA 01-00-5e-00-00-0d

    — Distance Vector Multicast Routing Protocol (DVMRP) Probe messages with GDA 01-00-5e-00-00-04

    As soon as the switch detects router ports in a VLAN, they are added to the port list of all GDAs in that VLAN.

2. When the switch receives an IGMP Report on a port, its CPU looks at the GDA, creates an entry in the CAM table for the GDA, and adds the port to the entry. The router port is also added to the entry. The group traffic is now forwarded on this port and the router port. If other hosts send their IGMP Reports, the switch adds their ports to the group entry in the CAM table and forwards the group traffic on these ports.

3. Similarly, when the switch receives an IGMP Leave message on a port, its CPU looks at the GDA, removes the port from the group entry in the CAM table, and does not forward the group traffic on the port. The switch checks whether this is the last nonrouter port for the GDA. If it is not the last nonrouter port for the GDA, which means there is at least one host in the VLAN that wants the group traffic, the switch discards the Leave message; otherwise, it sends the Leave message to the router.

Thus, IGMP snooping helps switches send group traffic to only those hosts that want it and helps to avoid wasted bandwidth.

For efficient operations, IGMP snooping requires hardware filtering support in a switch so that it can differentiate between IGMP Reports and actual multicast traffic. The switch CPU needs to see IGMP Report messages (and Multicast Routing Protocol messages) because the IGMP snooping process requires the CPU. However, the forwarding of multicast frames does not require the CPU, instead requiring only a switch's forwarding ASICs. Older switches, particularly those that have no Layer 3 awareness, could not identify a packet as IGMP; these switches would have overburdened their CPUs by having to send all multicasts to the CPU. Most of today's more modern switches support enough Layer 3 awareness to recognize IGMP so that IGMP snooping does not overburden the CPU.

> **NOTE** CGMP was a popular Cisco switch feature in years past because IGMP implementations on some switches would have required too much work. Today, many of the Cisco current switch product offerings do not even support CGMP, in deference to IGMP snooping.

Figure 16-19 shows an example of the IGMP snooping process.

Figure 16-19 *Joining a Group Using IGMP Snooping and CAM Table Entries*

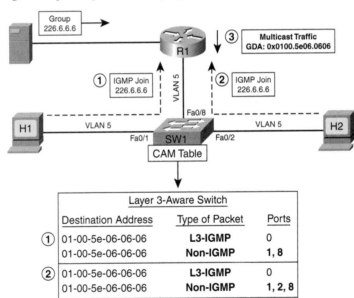

The following three steps, referenced in Figure 16-19, describe the sequence of events when H1 and H2 send IGMP Join messages:

1. H1 sends an IGMP Join message for 226.6.6.6. At Layer 2, H1 uses the multicast MAC address 0x0100.5e06.0606 (the MAC for group 226.6.6.6) as the destination address and uses its own BIA 0x0006.7c11.1101 as the source address. SW1 receives the packet on its fa0/1 port and, noticing that it is an IGMP packet, forwards the packet to the switch CPU. The CPU

uses the information to set up a multicast forwarding table entry, as shown in the CAM table that includes the port numbers 0 for CPU, 1 for H1, and 8 for R1. Notice that the CAM table lists two entries for the same destination MAC address 0x0100.5e06.0606—one for the IGMP frames for port 0 and the other for the non-IGMP frames for ports 1 and 8. The CPU of the switch instructs the switching engine to not forward any non-IGMP frames to port 0, which is connected to the CPU.

2. H2 sends an IGMP Join message for 226.6.6.6. At Layer 2, H2 uses the multicast MAC address 0x0100.5e06.0606 as the destination address and uses its own BIA 0x0006.7c11.1102 as the source address. SW1 receives the packet on its fa0/2 port, and its switching engine examines the packet. The process of analyzing the packet, as described in Step 1, is repeated and the CAM table entries are updated as shown.

3. Router R1 forwards the group traffic. R1 is receiving multicast traffic for group 226.6.6.6 and starts forwarding the traffic to SW1. SW1 starts receiving the multicast traffic on its port fa0/8. The switching engine would examine the packet and determine that this is a non-IGMP packet, search its CAM table, and determine that it should forward the packet on ports fa0/1 and fa0/2.

Compared to CGMP, IGMP snooping is less efficient in maintaining group information. In Figure 16-20, when R1 periodically sends IGMP General Queries to the All Hosts group, 224.0.0.1 (GDA 0x0100.5e00.0001), SW1 intercepts the General Queries and forwards them through all ports in VLAN 5. In CGMP, due to communication from the router through CGMP messages, the switch knows exactly on which ports multicast hosts are connected and, therefore, forwards IGMP General Queries only on those ports. Also, in IGMP snooping, when hosts send IGMP Reports, the switch must intercept them to maintain GDA information in the CAM table. As a result, the hosts do not receive each other's IGMP Report, which breaks the Report Suppression mechanism and forces each host to send an IGMP Report. However, the switch sends only one IGMP Report per group to the router. In CGMP, the switch does not have to intercept IGMP Reports, because maintaining group information in the switch is not dependent on examining IGMP packets from hosts; instead, the switch uses CGMP messages from the router.

Figure 16-20 shows the Leave process for IGMP snooping.

Figure 16-20 *Leaving a Group Using IGMP Snooping and CAM Table Entries*

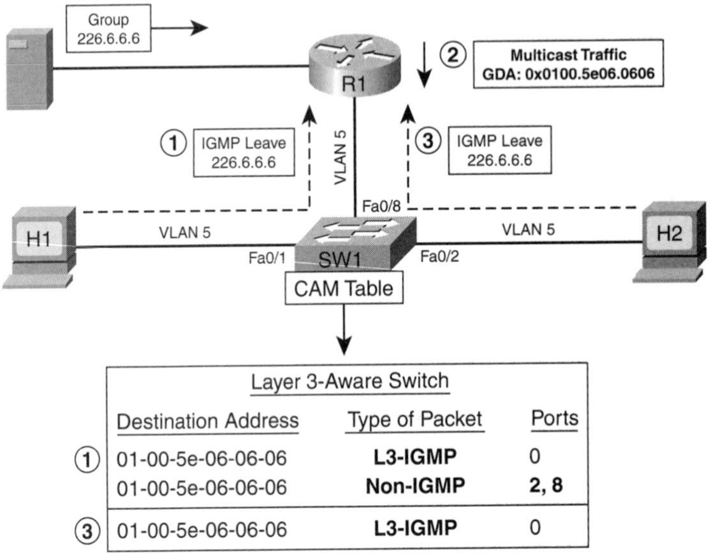

The following three steps, referenced in Figure 16-20, describe the sequence of events when H1 and H2 send IGMP Leave messages:

1. H1 sends an IGMP Leave message for 226.6.6.6, but SW1 does not forward it to router R1 in this case. At Layer 2, H1 uses the All Multicast Routers MAC address 0x0100.5e00.0002 as the destination address and uses its own BIA 0x0006.7c11.1101 as the source address. SW1 captures the IGMP Leave message on its fa0/1 port, and its switching engine examines the packet. The switch sends an IGMP General Query on port fa0/1 to determine whether there are any other hosts that are members of this group on the port. (This feature was designed to protect other hosts if they are connected to the same switch port using a hub.) If an IGMP Report is received on port fa0/1, the switch discards the Leave message received from H1. Because, in this example, there is only one host connected to port fa0/1, the switch does not receive any IGMP Report and deletes the port fa0/1 from the CAM table entry, as shown in Figure 16-20. H2 connected with port fa0/2 is still a member of the group, and its port number is in the CAM table entry. Hence, SW1 does not forward the IGMP Leave message to the router.

2. Router R1 continues forwarding the group traffic. R1 continues forwarding multicast traffic for group 226.6.6.6 to SW1 because R1 did not even know that H1 left the group. Based on the updated CAM table entry for the group shown in Figure 16-20, SW1 now forwards this traffic only on port fa0/2.

3. H2 sends an IGMP Leave message for 226.6.6.6, and SW1 does forward it to router R1 in this case. At Layer 2, H2 uses the All Multicast Routers MAC address 0x0100.5e00.0002 as the destination address and uses its own BIA 0x0006.7c11.1102 as the source address. Again, SW1 captures the IGMP Leave message on its fa0/2 port and its switching engine examines the packet. The switch sends an IGMP General Query on port fa0/2 to determine whether there are any other hosts that are members of this group on the port. Because, in this example, there is only one host connected to port fa0/2, the switch does not receive any IGMP Report and deletes the port fa0/2 from the CAM table entry. After SW1 deletes the port, it realizes that this was the last nonrouter port for the CAM table entry for 0x0100.5e06.0606. Therefore, SW1 deletes the CAM table entry for this group, as shown in Figure 16-20, and forwards the IGMP Leave message to R1, which sends an IGMP Group-Specific Query and, when no hosts respond, stops forwarding traffic for 226.6.6.6 toward SW1.

IGMP snooping becomes more complicated when multiple multicast routers are used and many LAN switches are interconnected via high-speed trunks. Also, CGMP and IGMP snooping control distribution of multicast traffic only on ports where hosts are connected. They do not provide any control mechanism for ports where routers are connected. The next section briefly examines how Router-Port Group Management Protocol (RGMP) helps switches control distribution of multicast traffic on ports where routers are connected.

Router-Port Group Management Protocol

RGMP is a Layer 2 protocol that enables a router to communicate to a switch which multicast group traffic the router does and does not want to receive from the switch. By being able to restrict the multicast destinations that a switch forwards to a router, a router can reduce its overhead. In fact, RGMP was designed to help routers reduce overhead when they are attached to high-speed LAN backbones.

Although RGMP is Cisco proprietary, oddly enough it cannot work concurrently with Cisco-proprietary CGMP. When RGMP is enabled on a router or a switch, CGMP is silently disabled; if CGMP is enabled on a router or a switch, RGMP is silently disabled. Note also that while it is proprietary, RGMP is published as informational RFC 3488.

RGMP works well in conjunction with IGMP snooping. In fact, IGMP snooping would typically learn the ports of all multicast routers by listening for IGMP and multicast routing protocol traffic. In some cases, some routers may not want all multicast traffic, so RGMP provides a means to reduce the unwanted traffic. The subtle key to the need for RGMP when using IGMP snooping is to realize this important fact about IGMP snooping:

> IGMP snooping helps switches control distribution of multicast traffic on ports where multicast hosts are connected, but it does not help switches control distribution of multicast traffic on ports where multicast routers are connected.

For example, consider the simple network shown in Figure 16-21. SW2 has learned of routers R3 and R4 with IGMP snooping, so it forwards multicasts sent to all multicast groups out to both R3 and R4.

Figure 16-21 *IGMP Snooping Without RGMP*

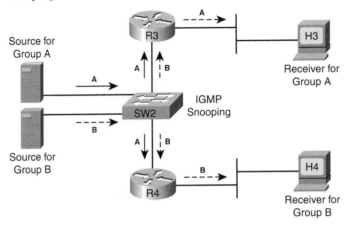

As you can see from Figure 16-21, R3 needs to receive traffic only for group A, and R4 needs to receive traffic only for group B. However, IGMP snooping causes the switch to forward all multicast packets to each router. To combat that problem, RGMP can be used by a router to tell the switch to only forward packets for particular multicast groups. For example, Figure 16-22 shows the same network as Figure 16-21, but with RGMP snooping. In this case, RGMP Join messages are enabled in both the routers and the switch, with the results shown in Figure 16-22.

Figure 16-22 *More Efficient Forwarding with RGMP Added to IGMP Snooping*

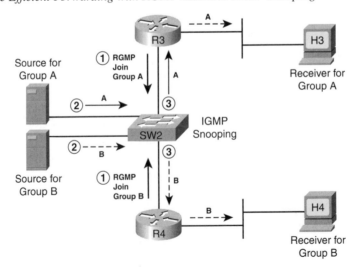

Figure 16-22 shows the following three main steps, with the first step showing the RGMP function with the RGMP Join message. The Join message allows a router to identify the groups for which the router wants to receive traffic:

1. R3 sends an RGMP Join for group A, and R4 sends an RGMP Join for group B. As a result, SW2 knows to forward multicasts for group A only to R3, and for group B only to R4.

2. The sources send a packet to groups A and B, respectively.

3. SW2 forwards the traffic for group A only to R3 and the packets for group B only to R4.

While Figure 16-22 shows just one example and one type of RGMP message, RGMP includes four different messages. All the RGMP messages are generated by a router and are sent to the multicast IP address 224.0.0.25. The following list describes the four RGMP messages:

■ When RGMP is enabled on a router, the router sends RGMP Hello messages by default every 30 seconds. When the switch receives an RGMP Hello message, it stops forwarding all multicast traffic on the port on which it received the Hello message.

■ When the router wants to receive traffic for a specific multicast group, the router sends an RGMP Join *G* message, where *G* is the multicast group address, to the switch. When the switch receives an RGMP Join message, it starts forwarding the requested group traffic on the port on which it received the Hello message.

■ When the router does not want to receive traffic for a formerly RGMP-joined specific multicast group, the router sends an RGMP Leave *G* message, where *G* is the multicast group address, to the switch. When the switch receives an RGMP Leave message, it stops forwarding the group traffic on the port on which it received the Hello message.

■ When RGMP is disabled on the router, the router sends an RGMP Bye message to the switch. When the switch receives an RGMP Bye message, it starts forwarding all IP multicast traffic on the port on which it received the Hello message.

NOTE   The following URL provides more information on RGMP: http://www.cisco.com/en/US/products/hw/switches/ps700/ products_tech_note09186a008011c11b.shtml

Foundation Summary

This section lists additional details and facts to round out the coverage of the topics in this chapter. Unlike most of the Cisco Press *Exam Certification Guides*, this "Foundation Summary" does not repeat information presented in the "Foundation Topics" section of the chapter. Please take the time to read and study the details in the "Foundation Topics" section of the chapter, as well as review items noted with a Key Topic icon.

Table 16-7 lists some of the key protocols and facts regarding IGMP.

Table 16-7 *Protocols and Standards for Chapter 16*

Name	Standard
GLOP Addressing in 233/8	RFC 2770
Administratively Scoped IP Multicast	RFC 2365
IGMP version 0	RFC 988
Host Extensions for IP Multicasting [IGMPv1]	RFC 1112
Internet Group Management Protocol, Version 2	RFC 2236
Internet Group Management Protocol, Version 3	RFC 3376
Multicast Listener Discovery (MLD) for IPv6	RFC 2710
Cisco Systems Router-Port Group Management Protocol (RGMP)	RFC 3488

Configuring multicasting on a Cisco router is relatively easy. You must first configure a multicast routing protocol on a Cisco router. The multicast routing protocols are covered in the next chapter, which also presents all the important configuration commands in the "Foundation Summary" section.

Memory Builders

The CCIE Routing and Switching written exam, like all Cisco CCIE written exams, covers a fairly broad set of topics. This section provides some basic tools to help you exercise your memory about some of the broader topics covered in this chapter.

Fill in Key Tables from Memory

Appendix E, "Key Tables for CCIE Study," on the CD in the back of this book contains empty sets of some of the key summary tables in each chapter. Print Appendix E, refer to this chapter's tables in it, and fill in the tables from memory. Refer to Appendix F, "Solutions for Key Tables for CCIE Study," on the CD to check your answers.

Definitions

Next, take a few moments to write down the definitions for the following terms:

multicasting, multicast address range, multicast address structure, permanent multicast group, source-specific addresses, GLOP addressing, administratively scoped addresses, transient multicast group, multicast MAC address, joining a group, IGMP, MRT, Report Suppression mechanism, IGMPv2 Host Membership Query, IGMPv2 Leave, IGMPv2 Group-Specific Query, IGMPv2 Host Membership Report, SSM, IGMPv3 Host Membership Query, IGMPv3 Host Membership Report, querier election, CGMP, IGMP snooping, RGMP

Refer to the glossary to check your answers.

Further Reading

Beau Williamson, *Developing IP Multicast Networks*, Volume I, Cisco Press, 2000.

References in This Chapter

- Beau Williamson, *Developing IP Multicast Networks,* Volume I, Cisco Press, 2000 (Chapter 3):

  — IGMP Version 2, page 64

  — IGMPv1–IGMPv2 Interoperability, pages 73–76

- Cisco Systems, Inc.:

  — "Multicast in a Campus Network: CGMP and IGMP Snooping (Document ID 10559)," http://www.cisco.com/warp/public/473/22.html.

  — Router-Port Group Management Protocol, http://www.cisco.com/univercd/cc/td/doc/product/software/ios120/120newft/120limit/120s/120s10/dtrgmp.htm.

Blueprint topics covered in this chapter:

This chapter covers the following subtopics from the Cisco CCIE Routing and Switching written exam blueprint. Refer to the full blueprint in Table I-1 in the Introduction for more details on the topics covered in each chapter and their context within the blueprint.

- IGMPv2

- Group Addresses

- Shared Trees

- Source Trees

- Protocol Independent Multicast (PIM) Mechanics

- PIM Sparse Mode

- Auto-RP

- Anycast RP

CHAPTER 17

IP Multicast Routing

In Chapter 16, "Introduction to IP Multicasting," you learned how a multicast router communicates with hosts and then decides whether to forward or stop the multicast traffic on a subnet. But how does a multicast router receive the group traffic? How is the multicast traffic forwarded from a source so that all the group users receive it? This chapter provides answers to those questions.

This chapter first defines the multicast routing problem by identifying the difference between unicast and multicast routing. It then provides an overview of the basic design concepts of multicast routing protocols, and shows how they solve multicast routing problems. Next, the chapter covers the operations of the Protocol Independent Multicast routing protocol in dense mode (PIM-DM) and sparse mode (PIM-SM). The chapter also covers the basic functions of Distance Vector Multicast Routing Protocol (DVMRP) and Multicast OSPF (MOSPF).

"Do I Know This Already?" Quiz

Table 17-1 outlines the major headings in this chapter and the corresponding "Do I Know This Already?" quiz questions.

Table 17-1 *"Do I Know This Already?" Foundation Topics Section-to-Question Mapping*

Foundation Topics Section	Questions Covered in This Section	Score
Multicast Routing Basics	1	
Dense-Mode Routing Protocols	2–4	
Sparse-Mode Routing Protocols	5–8	
Total Score		

In order to best use this pre-chapter assessment, remember to score yourself strictly. You can find the answers in Appendix A, "Answers to the 'Do I Know This Already?' Quizzes."

1. When a multicast router receives a multicast packet, which one of the following tasks will it perform first?

   a. Examine the IP multicast destination address on the packet, consult the multicast routing table to determine the next-hop address, and forward the packet through appropriate interface(s).

   b. Depending on the multicast routing protocol configured, either forward the packet on all the interfaces or forward the packet on selected interfaces except the one on which the packet was received.

   c. Determine the interface this router would use to send packets to the source of the packet, and decide whether the packet arrived in that interface or not.

   d. Send a Prune message to its upstream neighbor if it does not have any directly connected group members or active downstream routers.

2. A PIM router receives a PIM Assert message on a LAN interface. Which of the following statements is (are) true about the response of the router?

   a. The router does not have to take any action.

   b. If the router is configured with the PIM-DM routing protocol, it will process the Assert message; otherwise, it will ignore it.

   c. If the router is configured with the PIM-SM routing protocol, it will process the Assert message; otherwise, it will ignore it.

   d. The router will send a PIM Assert message.

3. When a PIM-DM router receives a Graft message from a downstream router after it has sent a Prune message to its upstream router for the same group, which of the following statements is (are) true about its response?

   a. It will send a Graft message to the downstream router and a Prune message to the upstream router.

   b. It will send a Prune message to the downstream router and a Graft message to the upstream router.

   c. It will re-establish adjacency with the upstream router.

   d. It will send a Graft message to the upstream router.

4. On router R1, the **show ip mroute 239.5.130.24** command displays **Serial2, Prune/Dense, 00:01:34/00:01:26** for the (S, G) entry under the outgoing interface list. Which of the following statements provide correct interpretation of this information?

   a. Router R1 has sent a Prune message on its Serial2 interface to its upstream router 1 minute and 34 seconds ago.

   b. Router R1 will send a Graft message on its Serial2 interface to its upstream router after 1 minute and 26 seconds.

   c. Router R1 received a Prune message on its Serial2 interface from its downstream router 1 minute and 34 seconds ago.

   d. Router R1 will send a Prune message on its Serial2 interface to its upstream router after 1 minute and 26 seconds.

   e. Router R1 will forward the traffic for the group on its Serial2 interface after 1 minute and 26 seconds.

5. From the following statements, select the true statement(s) regarding when a PIM-SM RP router will send the unicast PIM Register-Stop messages to the first-hop DR.

   a. If the RP has no need for the traffic

   b. If the RP is already receiving traffic on the shared tree

   c. When the RP begins receiving multicast traffic via SPT from the source

   d. When the RP sends multicast traffic via SPT to the downstream router

6. R1, a PIM-SM router, sends an (S,G) RP-bit Prune to its upstream neighbor. Assume that all the PIM-SM routers in the network are using the Cisco default **spt-threshold** value. Which of the following statements is (are) true about the status of different routers in the PIM-SM network at this time?

   a. At R1, the root-path tree and shortest-path tree diverge.

   b. R1 is switching over from shortest-path tree to root-path tree.

   c. R1 is switching over from root-path tree to shortest-path tree.

   d. At R1, the RPF neighbor for the (S,G) entry is different from the RPF neighbor of the (*, G) entry.

7. In a PIM-SM LAN network using Auto-RP, one of the routers is configured to send Cisco-RP-Announce and Cisco-RP-Discovery messages. All the routers show all the interfaces with correct PIM neighbors in sparse mode. However, the network administrator is puzzled by inconsistent RP mapping information shown on many routers. Some routers show correct RP mappings, but many leaf routers do not show any RP mappings. Which of the following statements represent(s) the most likely cause(s) for the above problem?

   a. The links between the leaf routers and the mapping agent are congested.

   b. All the interfaces of all the routers are configured with the command **ip pim sparse-mode**.

   c. The leaf routers are configured with a static RP address using an **override** option.

   d. The RPF check on the leaf routers is failing.

8. PIM-SM router R1 has two interfaces listed, s0/0 and fa0/0, in its (*,G) entry for group 227.7.7.7 in its multicast routing table. Assuming nothing changes in that (*,G) entry in the next 10 minutes, which of the following could be true?

   a. R1 is sending PIM Join messages toward the RP.

   b. R1 does not need to send Join messages toward the RP as long as the RP is continuing to forward multicasts for group 227.7.7.7 to R1.

   c. R1 is receiving PIM Join messages periodically on one or both of interfaces s0/0 and fa0/0.

   d. R1 is receiving IGMP Report messages periodically on interface fa0/0.

   e. The RP has been sending PIM Prune messages to R1 periodically, but R1 has been replying with PIM Reject messages because it still needs to receive the packets.

Foundation Topics

Multicast Routing Basics

The main function of any routing protocol is to help routers forward a packet in the right direction, causing the packet to keep moving closer to its desired destination, ultimately reaching its destination. To forward a unicast packet, a router examines the packet's destination address, finds the next-hop address from the unicast routing table, and forwards the packet through the appropriate interface. A unicast packet is forwarded along a single path from the source to the destination.

The top part of Figure 17-1 shows how a router can easily make a decision about forwarding a unicast packet by consulting its unicast routing table. However, when a router receives a multicast packet, as shown at the bottom of Figure 17-1, it cannot forward the packet because multicast IP addresses are not listed in the unicast routing table. Also, routers often have to forward multicast packets out multiple interfaces to reach all receivers. These requirements make the multicast forwarding process more complex than unicast forwarding.

Figure 17-1 *Multicast Routing Problem*

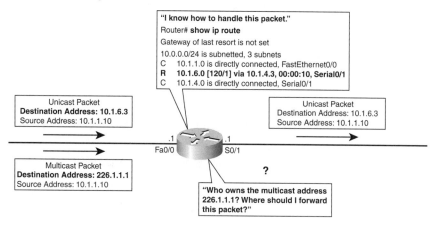

Figure 17-1 shows that the router has received a multicast packet with the destination address 226.1.1.1. The destination address represents a dynamically changing group of recipients, not any one recipient's address. How can the router find out where these users are? Where should the router forward this packet?

An analogy may help you to understand better the difficulty of multicast routing. Assume that you want to send party invitations through the mail, but instead of creating dozens of invitations, you create only one. Before mailing the invitation, you put a destination address on it, "This envelope contains my party invitation," and then drop it in a mailbox. When the postal system examines the destination address on your envelope, where should it deliver your envelope? And because it is only one invitation, does the postal system need to make copies? Also, how can the postal system figure out to which addresses to deliver the copies? By contrast, if IP multicast were the post office, it would know who you want to invite to the party, know where they are located, and make copies of the invitation and deliver them all to the correct addresses.

The next few sections discuss solutions for forwarding multicast traffic and controlling the distribution of multicast traffic in a routed network.

Overview of Multicast Routing Protocols

Routers can forward a multicast packet by using either a *dense-mode multicast routing protocol* or a *sparse-mode multicast routing protocol*. This section examines the basic concepts of multicast forwarding using dense mode, the Reverse Path Forwarding (RPF) check, and multicast forwarding using sparse mode, all of which help to solve the multicast routing problem.

Multicast Forwarding Using Dense Mode

Dense-mode routing protocols assume that the multicast group application is so popular that every subnet in the network has at least one receiver wanting to receive the group traffic. Therefore, the design of a dense-mode routing protocol instructs the router to forward the multicast traffic on all the configured interfaces, with some exceptions to prevent looping. For example, a multicast packet is never forwarded out the interface on which it was received. Figure 17-2 shows how a dense-mode routing protocol receives a multicast on one interface, and then forwards copies out all other interfaces.

Figure 17-2 *R1 Forwarding a Multicast Packet Using a Dense-Mode Routing Protocol*

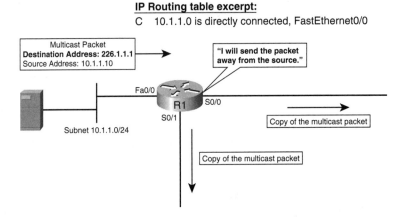

Figure 17-2 shows the dense-mode logic on R1, with R1 *flooding* copies of the packet out all interfaces except the one on which the packet was received. Although Figure 17-2 shows only one router, other routers can receive these multicasts and repeat the same process. All subnets will receive a copy of the original multicast packet.

Dense-mode protocols assume that all subnets need to receive a copy of the packets; however, dense-mode protocols do allow routers to ask to not receive traffic sent to a particular multicast group. Dense-mode routers typically do not want to receive multicast packets for a particular group if both of the following are true:

- The router does not have any active downstream routers that need packets for that group.

- The router does not know of any hosts on directly connected subnets that have joined that group.

When both of these conditions are true, the router needs to inform its upstream router not to send traffic for the group, which it does by using a special message called a Prune message. The mechanics of how dense-mode routers communicate with each other is discussed in detail under the PIM-DM section later in this chapter.

DVMRP, PIM-DM, and MOSPF are the dense-mode routing protocols discussed in this chapter, with most of the attention being paid to PIM-DM.

Reverse Path Forwarding Check

Routers cannot simply use logic by which they receive a multicast packet and then forward a copy of it out all other interfaces, without causing multicast packets to loop around the internetwork. To prevent such loops, routers do not forward multicasts out the same interface on which they were received. Multicast routers use a *Reverse Path Forwarding (RPF) check* to prevent loops. The RPF check adds this additional step to a dense-mode router's forwarding logic:

Look at the source IP address of the multicast packet. If my route that matches the source lists an outgoing interface that is the actual interface on which the packet was received, the packet passes the RPF check. If not, do not replicate and forward the packet.

Figure 17-3 shows an example in which R3 uses the RPF check on two separate copies of the same original multicast packet. Host S1 sends a multicast packet, with R1 flooding it to R2 and R3. R2 receives its copy, and floods it as well. As a result, R3 receives the same packet from two routers: on its s0/0 interface from R2 and on its s0/1 interface from R1. Without the RPF check, R3 would forward the packet it got from R1 to R2, and vice versa, and begin the process of looping packets. With this same logic, R1 and R2 also keep repeating the process. This duplication creates multicast routing loops and generates multicast storms that waste bandwidth and router resources.

Figure 17-3 *R3 Performs the RPF Check*

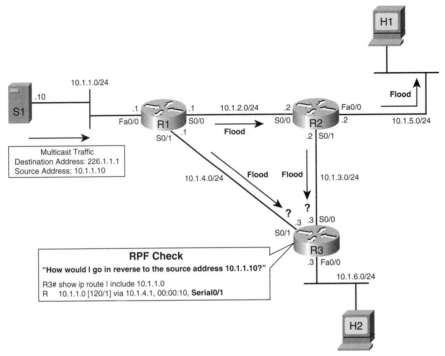

A multicast router does not forward any multicast packet unless the packet passes the RPF check. In Figure 17-3, R3 has to decide whether it should accept the multicast packets coming from R1 and R2. R3 makes this decision by performing the RPF check, described in detail as follows:

1. R3 examines the source address of each incoming multicast packet, which is 10.1.1.10. The source address is used in the RPF check of Step 2.

2. R3 determines the reverse path interface based on its route used to forward packets to 10.1.1.10. In this case, R3's route to 10.1.1.0/24 is matched, and it lists an outgoing interface of s0/1, making s0/1 R3's RPF interface for IP address 10.1.1.10.

3. R3 compares the reverse path interface determined in Step 2 with the interface on which the multicast packet arrived. If they match, it accepts the packet and forwards it; otherwise, it drops the packet. In this case, R3 floods the packet received on s0/1 from R1, but it ignores the packet received on s0/0 from R2.

The RPF check implements a strategy by which routers accept packets that arrive over the shortest path, and discard those that arrive over longer routes. Multicast routing protocols cannot use the destination address to help routers forward a packet, because that address represents the group traffic. So, multicast routing protocols use the RPF check to determine whether the packet arrived at the router using the shortest-path route from the source to the router. If it did, multicast routing protocols accept the packet and forward it; otherwise, they drop the packet and thereby avoid routing loops and duplication.

Different multicast routing protocols determine their RPF interfaces in different ways, as follows:

■ Distance Vector Multicast Routing Protocol (DVMRP) maintains a separate multicast routing table and uses it for the RPF check.

■ Protocol Independent Multicast (PIM) and Core-Based Tree (CBT) generally use the unicast routing table for the RPF check, as shown in Figure 17-3.

■ PIM and CBT can also use the DVMRP route table, the Multiprotocol Border Gateway Protocol (MBGP) route table, or statically configured multicast route(s) for the RPF check.

■ Multicast OSPF does not use the RPF check, because it computes both forward and reverse shortest-path source-rooted trees by using the Dijkstra algorithm.

Multicast Forwarding Using Sparse Mode

A dense-mode routing protocol is useful when a multicast application is so popular that you need to deliver the group traffic to almost all the subnets of a network. However, if the group users are located on a few subnets, a dense-mode routing protocol will still flood the traffic in the entire internetwork, wasting bandwidth and resources of routers. In those cases, a sparse-mode routing protocol, such as PIM-SM, could be used to help reduce waste of network resources.

The fundamental difference between dense-mode and sparse-mode routing protocols relates to their default behavior. By default, dense-mode protocols keep forwarding the group traffic unless a downstream router sends a message stating that it does not want that traffic. Sparse-mode protocols do not forward the group traffic to any other router unless it receives a message from that router requesting copies of packets sent to a particular multicast group. A downstream router requests to receive the packets only for one of two reasons:

■ The router has received a request to receive the packets from some downstream router.

■ A host on a directly connected host has sent an IGMP Join message for that group.

Figure 17-4 shows an example of what must happen with PIM-SM before a host (H2 in this case) can receive packets sent by host S1 to multicast group address 226.1.1.1. The PIM sparse-mode operation begins with the packet being forwarded to a special router called the *rendezvous point (RP)*. Once the group traffic arrives at an RP, unlike the dense-mode design, the RP does not automatically forward the group traffic to any router; the group traffic must be specifically requested by a router.

Figure 17-4 *R1 Forwarding a Multicast Packet Using a Sparse-Mode Routing Protocol*

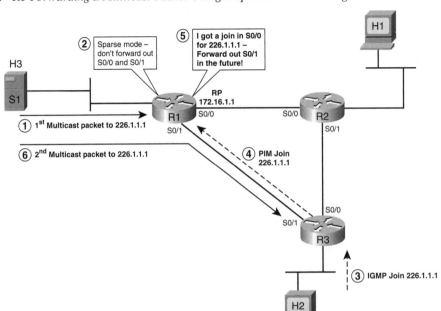

> **NOTE** Throughout this chapter, the solid arrowed lines in the figures represent multicast packets, with dashed arrowed lines representing PIM and IGMP messages.

Before you look at the numbered steps in Figure 17-4, consider the state of this internetwork. PIM-SM is configured on all the routers, R1 is selected as an RP, and in all three routers, the IP address 172.16.1.1 of R1 is configured statically as the RP address. Usually, a loopback interface address is used as an RP address and the loopback network is advertised in the unicast routing protocol so that all the routers learn how to locate an RP. At this point, R1, as the RP, may receive multicast packets sent to 226.1.1.1, but it will not forward them.

The following list describes the steps shown in Figure 17-4:

1. Host S1 sends a multicast to the RP, with destination address 226.1.1.1.

2. R1 chooses to ignore the packet, because no routers or local hosts have told the RP (R1) that they want to receive copies of multicast packets.

3. Host H2 sends an IGMP Join message for group 226.1.1.1.

4. R3 sends a PIM Join message to the RP (R1) for address 26.1.1.1.

5. R1's logic now changes, so future packets sent to 226.1.1.1 will be forwarded by R1 out s0/1 to R3.

6. Host S1 sends a multicast packet to 226.1.1.1, and R1 forwards it out s0/1 to R3.

In a PIM-SM network, it is critical for all the routers to somehow learn the IP address of an RP. One option in a small network is to statically configure the IP address of an RP in every router. Later in the chapter, the section "Dynamically Finding RPs and Using Redundant RPs" covers how routers can dynamically discover the IP address of the RP.

The example in Figure 17-4 shows some of the savings in using a sparse-mode protocol like PIM-SM. R2 has not received any IGMP Join messages on its LAN interface, so it does not send any request to the RP to forward the group traffic. As a result, R1 does not waste link bandwidth on the link from R1 to R2. R3 will not forward multicasts to R2 either in this case.

> **NOTE**   In Figure 17-4, R3 first performs its RPF check by using the IP address of the RP rather than the IP address of the source of the packet, because it is receiving the group traffic from the RP. If the RPF check succeeds, R3 forwards the traffic on its LAN.

Multicast Scoping

Multicast scoping confines the forwarding of multicast traffic to a group of routers, for administrative, security, or policy reasons. In other words, multicast scoping is the practice of defining boundaries that determine how far multicast traffic will travel in your network. The following sections discuss two methods of multicast scoping:

- TTL scoping

- Administrative scoping

TTL Scoping

With TTL scoping, routers compare the TTL value on a multicast packet with a configured TTL value on each outgoing interface. A router forwards the multicast packet only on those interfaces whose configured TTL value is less than or equal to the TTL value of the multicast packet. In effect, TTL scoping resets the TTL value at which the router discards multicasts from the usual value of 0 to some higher number. Figure 17-5 shows an example of a multicast router with various TTL threshold values configured on its interfaces.

In Figure 17-5, a multicast packet arrives on the s1 interface with a TTL of 18. The router decreases the packet's TTL by 1 to 17. Assume that the router is configured with a dense-mode routing protocol on all four interfaces and the RPF check succeeds—in other words, the router will want to forward a copy of the packet on each interface. The router compares the remaining TTL of the packet, which is now 17, with the TTL threshold of each outgoing interface. If the packet's TTL is higher than or equal to the interface TTL, it forwards a copy of the packet on that interface; otherwise, it does not forward it. On a Cisco router, the default TTL value on all the interfaces is 0.

Figure 17-5 *Multicast Scoping Using TTL Thresholds*

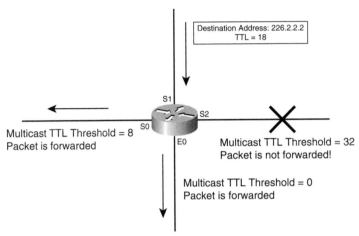

On the s0 and s2 interfaces in Figure 17-5, the network administrator has configured the TTL as 8 and 32, respectively. A copy of the packet is forwarded on the s0 and e0 interfaces because their TTL thresholds are less than 17. However, the packet is not forwarded on the s2 interface because its TTL threshold is 32, which is higher than 17.

TTL scoping has some weaknesses. First, it is difficult to implement in a large and complex network, because estimating correct TTL thresholds on many routers and many interfaces so that the network correctly confines only the intended sessions becomes an extremely demanding task. Another problem with TTL scoping is that a configured TTL threshold value on an interface applies to all multicast packets. If you want flexibility for some multicast sessions, you have to manipulate the applications to alter the TTL values when packets leave the servers.

Administrative Scoping

Recall from Chapter 16 that administratively scoped multicast addresses are private addresses in the range 239.0.0.0 to 239.255.255.255. They can be used to set administrative boundaries to limit the forwarding of multicast traffic outside of a domain. It requires manual configuration. You can configure and apply a filter on a router's interface so that multicast traffic with group addresses in the private address range is not allowed to enter or exit the interface.

> **NOTE** This chapter assumes that you have read Chapter 16 or are thoroughly familiar with the operation of IGMP; if neither is true, read Chapter 16 before continuing with this chapter.

Dense-Mode Routing Protocols

There are three dense-mode routing protocols:

■ Protocol Independent Multicast Dense Mode (PIM-DM)

- Distance Vector Multicast Routing Protocol (DVMRP)

- Multicast Open Shortest Path First (MOSPF)

This section covers the operation of PIM-DM in detail and provides an overview of DVMRP and MOSPF.

Operation of Protocol Independent Multicast Dense Mode

Protocol Independent Multicast (PIM) defines a series of protocol messages and rules by which routers can provide efficient forwarding of multicast IP packets. PIM previously existed as a Cisco-proprietary protocol, although it has been offered as an experimental protocol via RFCs 2362, 3446, and 3973. The PIM specifications spell out the rules mentioned in the earlier examples in this chapter—things like the RPF check, the PIM dense-mode logic of flooding multicasts until routers send Prune messages, and the PIM Sparse-mode logic of not forwarding multicasts anywhere until a router sends a Join message. This section describes the PIM-DM protocols in more detail.

PIM gets its name from its ability to use the unicast IP routing table for its RPF check—independent of whatever unicast IP routing protocol(s) was used to build the unicast routing table entries. In fact, the name "PIM" really says as much about the two other dense-mode protocols—DVMRP and MOSPF—as it does about PIM. These other two protocols do not use the unicast IP routing table for their RPF checks, instead building their own independent tables. PIM simply relies on the unicast IP routing table, independent of which unicast IP routing protocol built a particular entry in the routing table.

Forming PIM Adjacencies Using PIM Hello Messages

PIM routers form adjacencies with neighboring PIM routers for the same general reasons, and with the same general mechanisms, as many other routing protocols. PIMv2, the current version of PIM, sends Hello messages every 30 seconds (default) on every interface on which PIM is configured. By receiving Hellos on the same interface, routers discover neighbors, establish adjacency, and maintain adjacency. PIMv2 Hellos use IP protocol number 103 and reserved multicast destination address 224.0.0.13, called the All-PIM-Routers multicast address. The Hello messages contain a Holdtime value, typically three times the sender's PIM hello interval. If the receiver does not receive a Hello message from the sender during the Holdtime period, it considers the sending neighbor to be dead.

NOTE The older version, PIMv1, does not use Hellos, instead using a PIM Query message. PIMv1 messages are encapsulated in IP packets with protocol number 2 and use the multicast destination address 224.0.0.2.

As you will see in the following sections, establishing and maintaining adjacencies with directly connected neighbors is very important for the operation of PIM. A PIM router sends other PIM messages only on interfaces on which it has known active PIM neighbors.

Source-Based Distribution Trees

Dense-mode routing protocols are suitable for dense topology in which there are many multicast group members relative to the total number of hosts in a network. When a PIM-DM router receives a multicast packet, it first performs the RPF check. If the RPF check succeeds, the router forwards a copy of the packet to all the PIM neighbors except the one on which it received the packet. Each PIM-DM router repeats the process and floods the entire network with the group traffic. Ultimately, the packets are flooded to all leaf routers that have no downstream PIM neighbors.

The logic described in the previous paragraph actually describes the concepts behind what PIM calls a *source-based distribution tree*. It is also sometimes called a *shortest-path tree (SPT)*, or simply a *source tree*. The tree defines a path between the source host that originates the multicast packets and all subnets that need to receive a copy of the multicasts sent by that host. The tree uses the source as the root, the routers as the nodes in the tree, and the subnets connected to the routers as the branches and leaves of the tree. Figure 17-3, earlier in the chapter, shows the concept behind an SPT.

The configuration required on the three routers in Figure 17-3 is easy—just add the global command **ip multicast-routing** on each router and the interface command **ip pim dense-mode** on all the interfaces of all the routers.

PIM-DM might have a different source-based distribution tree for each combination of source and multicast group, because the SPT will differ based on the location of the source and the locations of the hosts listening for each multicast group address. The notation (S,G) refers to a particular SPT, or to an individual router's part of a particular SPT, where S is the source's IP address and G is the multicast group address. For example, the (S,G) notation for the example in Figure 17-3 would be written as (10.1.1.10, 226.1.1.1).

Example 17-1 shows part of the (S,G) SPT entry on R3, from Figure 17-3, for the (10.1.1.0, 226.1.1.1) SPT. Host S1 is sending packets to 226.1.1.1, and host H2 sends an IGMP Join message for the group 226.1.1.1. Example 17-1 shows a part of R3's multicast routing table, as displayed using the **show ip mroute** command.

Example 17-1 *Multicast Route Table Entry for the Group 226.1.1.1 for R3*

```
(10.1.1.10/32, 226.1.1.1), 00:00:12/00:02:48, flags: CT
  Incoming interface: Serial0/1, RPF nbr 10.1.4.1
  Outgoing interface list:
    FastEthernet0/0, Forward/Dense, 00:00:12/00:00:00
```

The interpretation of the information shown in Example 17-1 is as follows:

- The first line shows that the (S, G) entry for (10.1.1.10/32, 226.1.1.1) has been up for 12 seconds, and that if R3 does not forward an (S, G) packet in 2 minutes and 48 seconds, it will expire. Every time R3 forwards a packet using this entry, the timer is reset to 3 minutes.

- The C flag indicates that R3 has a directly connected group member for 226.1.1.1. The T flag indicates that the (S,G) traffic is forwarded on the shortest-path tree.

- The incoming interface for the group 226.1.1.1 is s0/1 and the RPF neighbor (the next-hop IP address to go in the reverse direction toward the source address 10.1.1.10) is 10.1.4.1.

- The group traffic is forwarded out on the fa0/0 interface. This interface has been in the forwarding state for 12 seconds. The second timer is listed as 00:00:00, because it cannot expire with PIM-DM, as this interface will continue to forward traffic until pruned.

> **NOTE**   The multicast routing table flags mentioned in this list, as well as others, are summarized in Table 17-6 in the "Foundation Summary" section of this chapter.

The next two sections show how PIM-DM routers use information learned from IGMP to dynamically expand and contract the source-based distribution trees to satisfy the needs of the group users.

> **NOTE**   According to PIM-DM specifications, multicast route tables only need (S,G) entries. However, for each (S,G) entry, a Cisco router creates a (*,G) entry as a parent entry, for design efficiency. The (*,G) entry is not used for forwarding the multicast traffic for a group that uses PIM-DM. Therefore, for simplicity and clarity, the (*,G) entries are not shown in the examples that use PIM-DM. Had you built the same network as illustrated in Figure 17-3, and configured PIM-DM, the (*,G) entries would also be listed in the **show ip mroute** command output.

Prune Message

PIM-DM creates a new SPT when a source first sends multicast packets to a new multicast group address. The SPT includes all interfaces except RPF interfaces, because PIM-DM assumes that all hosts need to receive a copy of each multicast packet. However, some subnets may not need a copy of the multicasts, so PIM-DM defines a process by which routers can remove interfaces from an SPT by using PIM Prune messages.

For example, in Figure 17-3, hosts H1 and H2 need a copy of the multicast packets sent to 226.1.1.1. However, as shown, when R2 gets the multicast from R1, R2 then forwards the multicasts to R3. As it turns out, R3 is dropping the packets for the group traffic from 10.1.1.1, sent to 226.1.1.1, because those packets fail R3's RPF check. In this case, R3 can cause R2 to remove its s0/1 interface from its outgoing interface list for (10.1.1.10, 226.1.1.1) by sending a

Prune message to R2. As a result, R2 will not forward the multicasts to R3, thereby reducing the amount of wasted bandwidth.

NOTE The term *outgoing interface list* refers to the list of interfaces in a forwarding state, listed for an entry in a router's multicast routing table.

The following is a more formal definition of a PIM Prune message:

The PIM Prune message is sent by one router to a second router to cause the second router to remove the link on which the Prune is received from a particular (S,G) SPT.

Figure 17-6 shows the same internetwork and example as Figure 17-3, but with R3's Prune messages sent to R2.

Figure 17-6 *R3 Sends a Prune Message to R2*

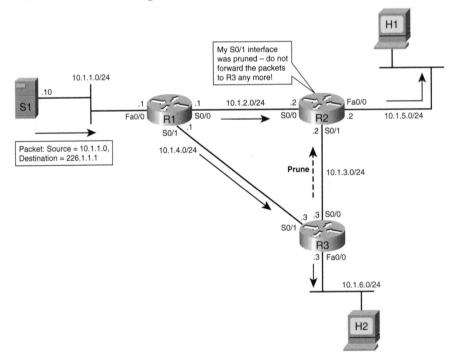

As a result of the Prune message from R3 to R2, R2 will prune its s0/1 interface from the SPT for (10.1.1.10,226.1.1.1). Example 17-2 shows the multicast route table entry for R2 in Figure 17-6, with the line that shows the pruned state highlighted.

Example 17-2 *Multicast Route Table Entry for the Group 226.1.1.1 for R2*

```
(10.1.1.10/32, 226.1.1.1), 00:00:14/00:02:46, flags: CT
  Incoming interface: Serial0/0, RPF nbr 10.1.2.1
  Outgoing interface list:
    FastEthernet0/0, Forward/Dense, 00:00:14/00:00:00
    Serial0/1, Prune/Dense, 00:00:08/00:02:52
```

Most of the information shown in Example 17-2 is similar to the information shown in Example 17-1. Notice the Serial0/1 information shown under the outgoing interface list. It shows that this interface was pruned 8 seconds ago because R3 sent a Prune message to R2. This means that, at this time, R2 is not forwarding traffic for 226.1.1.1 on its s0/1 interface.

Because PIM-DM's inherent tendency is to flood traffic through an internetwork, the pruned s0/1 interface listed in Example 17-2 will be changed back to a forwarding state after 2 minutes and 52 seconds. In PIM-DM, when a router receives a Prune message on an interface, it starts a (default) 3-minute Prune timer, counting down to 0. When the Prune timer expires, the router changes the interface to a forwarding state again. If the downstream router does not want the traffic, it can again send a Prune message. This feature keeps a downstream router aware that the group traffic is available on a particular interface from the upstream neighbor.

> **NOTE**   PIMv2 offers a better solution to maintaining the pruned state of an interface, using State Refresh messages. These messages are covered later in the chapter, in the section "Steady-State Operation and the State Refresh Message."

Note that a multicast router can have more than one interface in the outgoing interface list, but it can have only one interface in the incoming interface list. The only interface in which a router will receive and process multicasts from a particular source is the RPF interface. Routers still perform an RPF check, with the incoming interface information in the beginning of the **show ip mroute** output stating the RPF interface and neighbor.

PIM-DM: Reacting to a Failed Link

When links fail, or any other changes affect the unicast IP routing table, PIM-DM needs to update the RPF interfaces based on the new unicast IP routing table. Because the RPF interface may change, (S,G) entries may also need to list different interfaces in the outgoing interface list. This section describes an example of how PIM-DM reacts.

Figure 17-7 shows an example in which the link between R1 and R3, originally illustrated in Figure 17-6, has failed. After the unicast routing protocol converges, R3 needs to update its RPF neighbor IP address from 10.1.4.1 (R1) to 10.1.3.2 (R2). Also in this case, H1 has issued an IGMP Leave message.

Figure 17-7 *Direct Link Between R1 and R3 Is Down and Host H1 Sends an IGMP Leave Message*

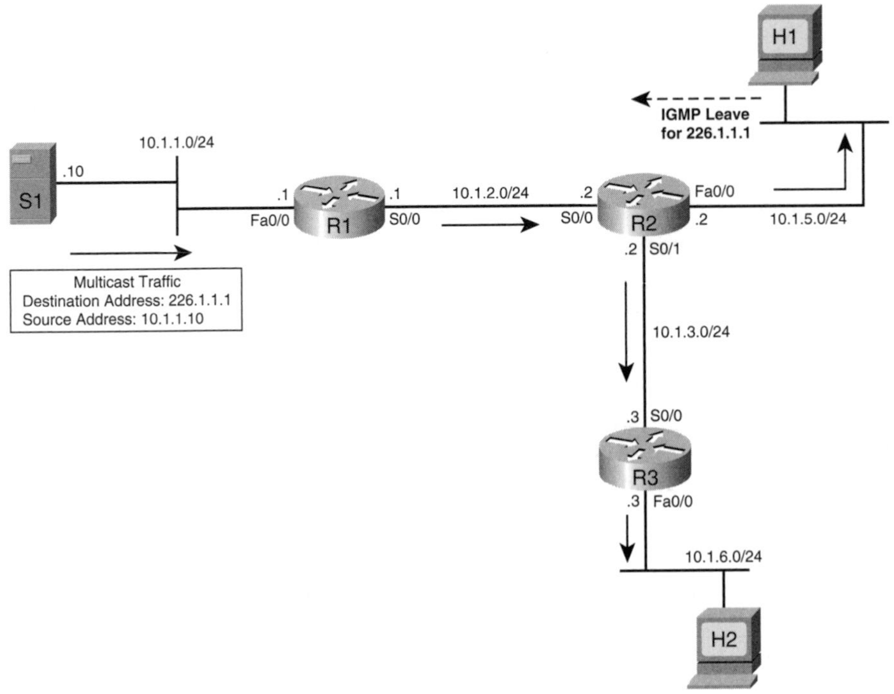

Example 17-3 shows the resulting multicast route table entry for R3 in Figure 17-7. Note that the RPF interface and neighbor IP address has changed to point to R2.

Example 17-3 *Multicast Route Table Entry for the Group 226.1.1.1 for R3*

```
(10.1.1.10/32, 226.1.1.1), 00:02:16/00:01:36, flags: CT
  Incoming interface: Serial0/0, RPF nbr 10.1.3.2
  Outgoing interface list:
    FastEthernet0/0, Forward/Dense, 00:02:16/00:00:00
```

Example 17-3 shows how R3's view of the (10.1.1.10,226.1.1.1) SPT has changed. However, R2 had pruned its s0/1 interface from that SPT, as shown in Figure 17-6. So, R2 needs to change its s0/1 interface back to a forwarding state for SPT (10.1.1.10, 226.1.1.1). Example 17-4 shows the resulting multicast route table entry for (10.1.1.10, 226.1.1.1) in R2.

Example 17-4 *Multicast Route Table Entry for the Group 226.1.1.1 for R2*

```
(10.1.1.10/32, 226.1.1.1), 00:03:14/00:02:38, flags: T
  Incoming interface: Serial0/0, RPF nbr 10.1.2.1
  Outgoing interface list:
  Serial0/1, Forward/Dense, 00:02:28/00:00:00
```

> **NOTE**   R2 changed its s0/1 to a forwarding state because of a PIM Graft message sent by R3. The upcoming section "Graft Message" explains the details.

In Example 17-4, notice the outgoing interface list for R2. R2 has now removed interface fa0/0 from the outgoing interface list and stopped forwarding traffic on the interface because it received no response to the IGMP Group-Specific query for group 226.1.1.1. As a result, R2 has also removed the C flag (C meaning "connected") from its multicast routing table entry for (10.1.1.10, 226.1.1.1). Additionally, R2 forwards the traffic on its s0/1 interface toward R3 because R3 is still forwarding traffic on its fa0/0 interface and has not yet sent a Prune message to R2.

Rules for Pruning

This section explains two key rules that a PIM-DM router must follow to decide when it can request a prune. Before explaining another example of how PIM-DM reacts to changes in an internetwork, a couple of new multicast terms must be defined. To simplify the wording, the following statements define *upstream router* and *downstream router* from the perspective of a router named R1.

- R1's upstream router is the router from which R1 receives multicast packets for a particular SPT.

- R1's downstream router is a router to which R1 forwards some multicast packets for a particular SPT.

For example, R1 is R2's upstream router for the packets that S1 is sending to 226.1.1.1 in Figure 17-7. R3 is R2's downstream router for those same packets, because R2 sends those packets to R3.

PIM-DM routers can choose to send a Prune message for many reasons, one of which was covered earlier with regard to Figure 17-6. The main reasons are summarized here:

- When receiving packets on a non-RPF interface.

- When a router realizes that both of the following are true:

  — No locally connected hosts in a particular group are listening for packets.

  — No downstream routers are listening for the group.

This section shows the logic behind the second reason for sending prunes. At this point in the explanation of Figures 17-6 and 17-7, the only host that needs to receive packets sent to 226.1.1.1 is H2. What would the PIM-DM routers in this network do if H2 leaves group 226.1.1.1? Figure 17-8 shows just such an example, with H2 sending an IGMP Leave message for group 226.1.1.1. Figure 17-8 shows how PIM-DM uses this information to dynamically update the SPT.

Figure 17-8 *R3 and R2 Sending Prune Messages*

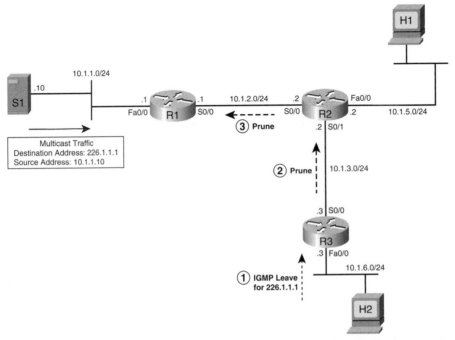

Figure 17-8 shows three steps, with the logic in Steps 2 and 3 being similar but very important:

1. H2 leaves the multicast group by using an IGMP Leave message.

2. R3 uses an IGMP Query to confirm that no other hosts on the LAN want to receive traffic for group 226.1.1.1. So, R3 sends a Prune, referencing the (10.1.1.20, 226.1.1.1) SPT, out its RPF interface R2.

3. R2 does not have any locally connected hosts listening for group 226.1.1.1. Now, its only downstream router has sent a Prune for the SPT with source 10.1.1.10, group 226.1.1.1. Therefore, R2 has no reason to need packets sent to 226.1.1.1 any more. So, R2 sends a Prune, referencing the (10.1.1.20, 226.1.1.1) SPT, out its RPF interface R1.

After the pruning is complete, both R3 and R2 will not be forwarding traffic sent to 226.1.1.1 from source 10.1.1.10. In the routers, the **show ip mroute** command shows that fact using the P (prune) flag, which means that the router has completely pruned itself from that particular (S,G) SPT.

Example 17-5 shows R3's command output with a null outgoing interface list.

Example 17-5 *Multicast Route Table Entry for the Group 226.1.1.1 for R3*

```
(10.1.1.10/32, 226.1.1.1), 00:03:16/00:01:36, flags: PT
  Incoming interface: Serial0/0, RPF nbr 10.1.3.2
    Outgoing interface list: Null
```

After all the steps in Figure 17-8 have been completed, R1 also does not need to send packets sent by 10.1.1.10 to 226.1.1.1 out any interfaces. After receiving a Prune message from R2, R1 has also updated its outgoing interface list, which shows that there is only one outgoing interface and that it is in the pruned state at this time. Example 17-6 shows the details.

Example 17-6 *Multicast Route Table Entry for the Group 226.1.1.1 for R1*

```
(10.1.1.10/32, 226.1.1.1), 00:08:35/00:02:42, flags: CT
  Incoming interface: FastEthernet0/0, RPF nbr 0.0.0.0
  Outgoing interface list:
    Serial0/0, Prune/Dense, 00:00:12/00:02:48
```

Of particular interest in the output, R1 has also set the C flag, but for R1 the C flag does not indicate that it has directly connected group members. In this case, the combination of a C flag and an RPF neighbor of 0.0.0.0 indicates that the connected device is the source for the group.

In reality, there is no separate Prune message and Join message; instead, PIM-DM and PIM-SM use a single message called a Join/Prune message. A Prune message is actually a Join/Prune message with a group address listed in the Prune field, and a Join message is a Join/Prune message with a group address listed in the Join field.

Steady-State Operation and the State Refresh Message

As mentioned briefly earlier in the chapter, with PIM-DM, an interface stays pruned only for 3 minutes by default. Prune messages list a particular source and group (in other words, a particular (S,G) SPT). Whenever a router receives a Prune message, it finds the matching (S,G) SPT entry and marks the interface on which the Prune message was received as "pruned." However, it also sets a Prune timer, default 3 minutes, so that after 3 minutes, the interface is placed into a forwarding state again.

So, what happens with PIM-DM and pruned links? Well, the necessary links are pruned, and 3 minutes later they are added back. More multicasts flow, and the links are pruned. Then they are added back. And so on. So, when Cisco created PIM V2 (published as experimental RFC 3973), it included a feature called *state refresh*. State Refresh messages can prevent this rather inefficient behavior in PIM-DM version 1 of pruning and automatically unpruning interfaces.

Figure 17-9 shows an example that begins with the same state as the network described at the end of the preceding section, "Rules for Pruning," where the link between R1 and R2 and the link between R2 and R3 have been pruned. Almost 3 minutes have passed, and the links are about to be added to the SPT again due to the expiration of the Prune timers.

Figure 17-9   *How PIM-DM Version 2 Uses State Refresh Messages*

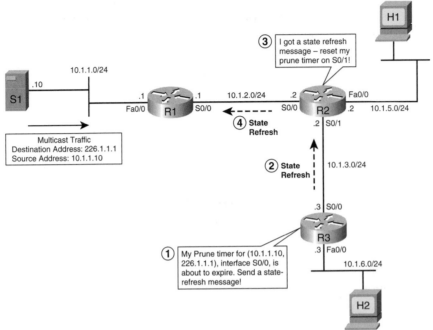

The PM State Refresh message can be sent, just before a neighbor's Prune timer expires, to keep the interface in a pruned state. In Figure 17-9, the following steps do just that:

1. R3 monitors the time since it sent the last Prune to R2. Just before the Prune timer expires, R3 decides to send a State Refresh message to R2.

2. R3 sends the State Refresh message to R2, referencing SPT (10.1.1.10, 226.1.1.1).

3. R2 reacts by resetting its Prune timer for the interface on which it received the State Refresh message.

4. Because R2 had also pruned itself by sending a Prune message to R1, R2 also uses State Refresh messages to tell R1 to leave its s0/0 interface in a pruned state.

As long as R3 keeps sending a State Refresh message before the Prune timer on the upstream router (R2) expires, the SPT will remain stable, and there will not be the periodic times of flooding of more multicasts for that (S,G) tree.

Graft Message

When new hosts join a group, routers may need to change the current SPT for a particular (S,G) entry. With PIM-DM, one option could be to wait on the pruned links to expire. For example, in Figure 17-9, R3 could simply quit sending State Refresh messages, and within 3 minutes at most,

R3 would be receiving the multicast packets for some (S,G) SPT again. However, waiting on the (default) 3-minute Prune timer to expire is not very efficient. To allow routers to "unprune" a previously pruned interface from an SPT, PIM-DM includes the *Graft* message, which is defined as follows:

A router sends a Graft message to an upstream neighbor—a neighbor to which it had formerly sent a Prune message—causing the upstream router to put the link back into a forwarding state (for a particular (S,G) SPT).

Figure 17-10 shows an example that uses the same ongoing example network. The process shown in Figure 17-10 begins in the same state as described at the end of the preceding section, "Steady-State Operation and the State Refresh Message." Neither host H1 nor H2 has joined group 226.1.1.1, and R2 and R3 have been totally pruned from the (10.1.1.10, 226.1.1.1) SPT. Referring to Figure 17-10, R1's s0/0 interface has been pruned from the (S,G) SPT, so R2 and R3 are not receiving the multicasts sent by server S1 to 226.1.1.1. The example then begins with host H2 joining group 226.1.1.1 again.

Figure 17-10 *R3 and R2 Send Graft Messages*

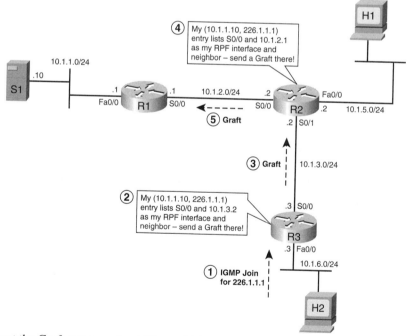

Without the Graft message, host H2 would have to wait for as much as 3 minutes before it would receive the group traffic. However, with the following steps, as listed in Figure 17-10, H2 will receive the packets in just a few seconds:

1. Host H2 sends an IGMP Join message.

2. R3 looks for the RPF interface for its (S, G) state information for the group 226.1.1.1 (see earlier Example 17-5), which shows the incoming interface as s0/0 and RPF neighbor as 10.1.3.2 for the group.

3. R3 sends the Graft message out s0/0 to R2.

4. R2 now knows it needs to be receiving messages from 10.1.1.10, sent to 226.1.1.1. However, R2's (S,G) entry also shows a P flag, meaning R2 has pruned itself from the SPT. So, R2 finds its RPF interface and RPF neighbor IP address in its (S,G) entry, which references interface s0/0 and router R1.

5. R2 sends a graft to R1.

At this point, R1 immediately puts its s0/0 back into the outgoing interface list, as does R2, and now H2 receives the multicast packets. Note that R1 also sends a Graft Ack message to R2 in response to the Graft message, and R2 sends a Graft Ack in response to R3's Graft message as well.

LAN-Specific Issues with PIM-DM and PIM-SM

This section covers three small topics related to operations that only matter when PIM is used on LANs:

■ Prune Override

■ Assert messages

■ Designated routers

Both PIM-DM and PIM-SM use these features in the same way.

Prune Override

In both PIM-DM and PIM-SM, the Prune process on multiaccess networks operates differently from how it operates on point-to-point links. The reason for this difference is that when one router sends a Prune message on a multiaccess network, other routers might not want the link pruned by the upstream router. Figure 17-11 shows an example of this problem, along with the solution through a PIM Join message that is called a *Prune Override*. In this figure, R1 is forwarding the group traffic for 239.9.9.9 on its fa0/0 interface, with R2 and R3 receiving the group traffic on their e0 interfaces. R2 does not have any connected group members, and its outgoing interface list would show null. The following list outlines the steps in logic shown in Figure 17-11, in which R3 needs to send a Prune Override:

1. R2 sends a Prune for group 239.9.9.9 because R2 has a null outgoing interface list for the group.

2. R1, realizing that it received the Prune on a multiaccess network, knows that other routers might still want to get the messages. So, instead of immediately pruning the interface, R1 sets a 3-second timer that must expire before R1 will prune the interface.

3. R3 also receives the Prune message sent by R2, because Prune messages are multicast to All-PIM-Routers group address 224.0.0.13. R3 still needs to get traffic for 239.9.9.9, so R3 sends a Join message on its e0 interface.

4. (Not shown in Figure 17-11) R1 receives the Join message from R3 before removing its LAN interface from the outgoing interface list. As a result, R1 does not prune its Fa0/0 interface.

Figure 17-11 *Prune Override*

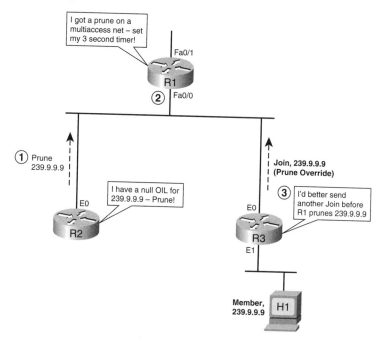

This process is called *Prune Override* because R3 overrides the Prune sent by R2. The Prune Override is actually a Join message, sent by R3 in this case. The message itself is no different from a normal Join. As long as R1 receives a Join message from R3 before its 3-second timer expires, R3 continues to receive traffic without interruption.

Assert Message

The final PIM-DM message covered in this chapter is the PIM Assert message. The Assert message is used to prevent wasted effort when more than one router attaches to the same LAN. Rather than sending multiple copies of each multicast packet onto the LAN, the PIM Assert message allows the routers to negotiate. The winner gets the right to be responsible for forwarding multicasts onto the LAN.

Figure 17-12 shows an example of the need for the Assert message. R2 and R3 both attach to the same LAN, with H1 being an active member of the group 227.7.7.7. Both R2 and R3 are receiving the group traffic for 227.7.7.7 from the source 10.1.1.10.

Figure 17-12 *R2 and R3 Sending Assert Messages*

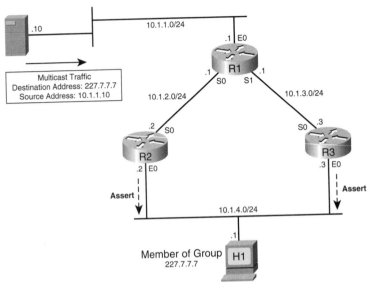

The goal of the Assert message is to assign the responsibility of forwarding group traffic on the LAN to the router that is closest to the source. When R2 and R3 receive group traffic from the source on their s0 interfaces, they forward it on their e0 interfaces. Both of them have their s0 interfaces in the incoming interface list and e0 interfaces in the outgoing interface list. Now, R2 and R3 receive a multicast packet for the group on their e0 interfaces, which will cause them to send an Assert message to resolve who should be the forwarder.

The Assert process picks a winner based on the routing protocol and metric used to find the route to reach the unicast address of the source. In this example, that means that R2 or R3 will win based on the routes they each use to reach 10.1.1.10. R2 and R3 send and receive Assert messages that include their respective administrative distances of the routing protocols used to learn the route that matches 10.1.1.10, as well as the metric for those routes. The routers on the LAN compare their own routing protocol administrative distance and metrics to those learned in the Assert messages. The winner of the Assert process is determined as follows:

1. The router advertising the lowest administrative distance of the routing protocol used to learn the route wins.

2. If a tie, the router with the lowest advertised routing protocol metric for that route wins.

3. If a tie, the router with the highest IP address on that LAN wins.

Designated Router

PIM Hello messages are also used to elect a designated router (DR) on a multiaccess network. A PIM-DM or PIM-SM router with the highest IP address becomes a DR.

The PIM DR concept applies mainly when IGMPv1 is used. IGMPv1 does not have a mechanism to elect a Querier—that is to say that IGMPv1 has no way to decide which of the many routers on a LAN should send IGMP Queries. When IGMPv1 is used, the PIM DR is used as the IGMP Querier. IGMPv2 can directly elect a Querier (the router with the lowest IP address), so the PIM DR is not used as the IGMP Querier when IGMPv2 is used.

Note that on a LAN, one router might win the Assert process for a particular (S,G) SPT, while another might become the IGMP Querier (PIM DR for IGMPv1, IGMP Querier for IGMPv2). The winner of the Assert process is responsible for forwarding multicasts onto the LAN, whereas the IGMP Querier is responsible for managing the IGMP process by being responsible for sending IGMP Query messages on the LAN. Note also that the IGMPv2 Querier election chooses the lowest IP address, and the Assert process uses the highest IP address as a tiebreaker, making it slightly more likely that different routers are chosen for each function.

Summary of PIM-DM Messages

This section concludes the coverage of PIM-DM. Table 17-2 lists the key PIM-DM messages covered in this chapter, along with a brief definition of their use.

Table 17-2 *Summary of PIM-DM Messages*

PIM Message	Definition
Hello	Used to form neighbor adjacencies with other PIM routers, and to maintain adjacencies by monitoring for received Hellos from each neighbor. Also used to elect a PIM DR on multiaccess networks.
Prune	Used to ask a neighboring router to remove the link over which the Prune flows from that neighboring router's outgoing interface list for a particular (S,G) SPT.
State Refresh	Used by a downstream router, sent to an upstream router on an RPF interface, to cause the upstream router to reset its Prune timer. This allows the downstream router to maintain the pruned state of a link, for a particular (S,G) SPT.
Assert	Used on multiaccess networks to determine which router wins the right to forward multicasts onto the LAN, for a particular (S,G) SPT.
Prune Override (Join)	On a LAN, a router may multicast a Prune message to its upstream routers. Other routers on the same LAN, wanting to prevent the upstream router from pruning the LAN, immediately send another Join message for the (S,G) SPT. (The Prune Override is not actually a Prune Override message—it is a Join. This is the only purpose of a Join message in PIM-DM, per RFC 3973.)
Graft/Graft-Ack	When a pruned link needs to be added back to an (S,G) SPT, a router sends a Graft message to its RPF neighbor. The RPF neighbor acknowledges with a Graft-Ack.

The next two short sections introduce two other dense-mode protocols, DVMRP and MOSPF.

Distance Vector Multicast Routing Protocol

RFC 1075 describes Version 1 of DVMRP. DVMRP has many versions. The operation of DVMRP is similar to PIM-DM. The major differences between PIM-DM and DVMRP are defined as follows:

- Cisco IOS does not support a full implementation of DVMRP; however, it does support connectivity to a DVMRP network.

- DVMRP uses its own distance vector routing protocol that is similar to RIPv2. It sends route updates every 60 seconds and considers 32 hops as infinity. Use of its own routing protocol adds more overhead to DVMRP operation compared to PIM-DM.

- DVMRP uses Probe messages to find neighbors using the All DVMRP Routers group address 224.0.0.4.

- DVMRP uses a truncated broadcast tree, which is similar to an SPT with some links pruned.

Multicast Open Shortest Path First

MOSPF is defined in RFC 1584, "Multicast Extensions to OSPF," which is an extension to the OSPFv2 unicast routing protocol. The basic operation of MOSPF is described here:

- MOSPF uses the group membership LSA, Type 6, which it floods throughout the originating router's area. As with unicast OSPF, all MOSPF routers in an area must have identical link-state databases so that every MOSPF router in an area can calculate the same SPT.

- The SPT is calculated "on-demand," when the first multicast packet for the group arrives.

- Through the SPF calculation, all the routers know where the attached group members are, based on the group membership LSAs.

- After the SPF calculation is completed, entries are made into each router's multicast forwarding table.

- Just like unicast OSPF, the SPT is loop free, and every router knows the upstream interface and downstream interfaces. As a result, an RPF check is not required.

- Obviously, MOSPF can only work with the OSPF unicast routing protocol. MOSPF is suitable for small networks. As more hosts begin to source multicast traffic, routers have to perform a higher number of Dijkstra algorithm computations, which demands an increasing level of router CPU resources. Cisco IOS does not support MOSPF.

Sparse-Mode Routing Protocols

There are two sparse-mode routing protocols:

- Protocol Independent Multicast Sparse Mode (PIM-SM)

- Core-Based Tree (CBT)

This section covers the operation of PIM-SM.

Operation of Protocol Independent Multicast Sparse Mode

PIM-SM works with a completely opposite strategy from that of PIM-DM, although the mechanics of the protocol are not exactly opposite. PIM-SM assumes that no hosts want to receive multicast packets until they specifically ask to receive them. As a result, until a host in a subnet asks to receive multicasts for a particular group, multicasts are never delivered to that subnet. With PIM-SM, downstream routers must request to receive multicasts using PIM Join messages. Also, once they are receiving those messages, the downstream router must continually send Join messages to the upstream router—otherwise, the upstream router stops forwarding, putting the link in a pruned state. This process is opposite to that used by PIM-DM, in which the default is to flood multicasts, with downstream routers needing to continually send Prunes or State Refresh messages to keep a link in a pruned state.

PM-SM makes the most sense with a small percentage of subnets that need to receive packets sent to any multicast group.

Similarities Between PIM-DM and PIM-SM

PIM-SM has many similarities to PIM-DM. Like PIM-DM, PIM-SM uses the unicast routing table to perform RPF checks—regardless of what unicast routing protocol populated the table. (Like PIM-DM, the "protocol independent" part of the PIM acronym comes from the fact that PIM-SM is not dependent on any particular unicast IP routing protocol.) In addition, PIM-SM also uses the following mechanisms that are used by PIM-DM:

- PIM Neighbor discovery through exchange of Hello messages.

- Recalculation of the RPF interface when the unicast routing table changes.

- Election of a DR on a multiaccess network. The DR performs all IGMP processes when IGMPv1 is in use on the network.

- The use of Prune Overrides on multiaccess networks.

- Use of Assert messages to elect a designated forwarder on a multiaccess network. The winner of the Assert process is responsible for forwarding unicasts onto that subnet.

> **NOTE** The preceding list was derived, with permission, from *Routing TCP/IP*, Volume II, by Jeff Doyle and Jennifer DeHaven Carroll.

These mechanisms are described in the "Operation of Protocol Independent Multicast Dense Mode" section and thus are not repeated in this section.

Sources Sending Packets to the Rendezvous Point

PIM-SM uses a two-step process to initially deliver multicast packets from a particular source to the hosts wanting to receive packets. Later, the process is improved beyond these initial steps. The steps for the initial forwarding of multicasts with PIM-SM are as follows:

1. Sources send the packets to a router called the rendezvous point (RP).

2. The RP sends the multicast packets to all routers/hosts that have registered to receive packets for that group. This process uses a shared tree.

> **NOTE** In addition to these two initial steps, routers with local hosts that have sent an IGMP Join for a group can go a step further, joining the source-specific tree for a particular (S,G) SPT.

This section describes the first of these two steps, in which the source sends packets to the RP. To make that happen, the router connected to the same subnet as the source host must register with the RP. The RP accepts the registration only if the RP knows of any routers or hosts that need to receive a copy of those multicasts.

Figure 17-13 shows an example of the registration process in which the RP knows that no hosts currently want the IP multicasts sent to group 228.8.8.8—no matter which source is sending them. The configuration for this example is simple, with all the routers configured with the global command **ip multicast-routing** and the interface command **ip pim sparse-mode** on all the interfaces. Also, all routers have statically configured R3 as the RP by using the global command **ip pim rp-address 10.1.10.3**. Usually, a loopback interface address is used as an RP address. The loopback network 10.1.10.3/32 of R3 is advertised in the unicast routing protocol so that all the routers know how to reach the RP.

Figure 17-13   *Source Registration Process when RP Has Not Received a Request for the Group from Any PIM-SM Router*

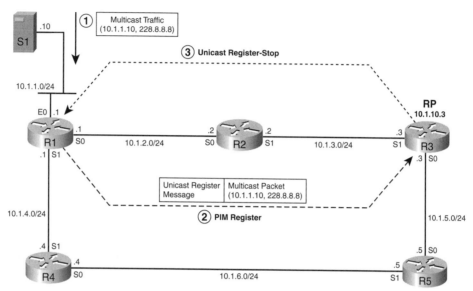

The following three steps, referenced in Figure 17-13, describe the sequence of events for the Source Registration process when the RP has not received a request for the group from any PIM-SM router because no host has yet joined the group.

1.   Host S1 begins sending multicasts to 228.8.8.8, and R1 receives those multicasts because it connects to the same LAN.

2.   R1 reacts by sending unicast PIM Register messages to the RP. The Register messages are unicasts sent to the RP IP address, 10.1.10.3 in this case.

3.   R3 sends unicast Register-Stop messages back to R1 because R3 knows that it does not have any need to forward packets sent to 228.8.8.8.

In this example, the router near the source (R1) is attempting to register with the RP, but the RP tells R1 not to bother any more, because no one wants those multicast messages. R1 has not forwarded any of the native multicast messages at this point, in keeping with the PIM-SM strategy of not forwarding multicasts until a host has asked for them. However, the PIM Register message shown in Figure 17-13 encapsulates the first multicast packet. As will be seen in Figure 17-14, the encapsulated packet would be forwarded by the RP had any senders been interested in receiving the packets sent to that multicast group.

The source host may keep sending multicasts, so R1 needs to keep trying to register with the RP in case some host finally asks to receive the packets. So, when R1 receives the Register-Stop messages, it starts a 1-minute Register-Suppression timer. 5 seconds before the timer expires,

R1 sends another Register message with a flag set, called the Null-Register bit, without any encapsulated multicast packets. As a result of this additional Register message, one of two things will happen:

- If the RP still knows of no hosts that want to receive these multicast packets, it sends another Register-Stop message to R1, and R1 resets its Register-Suppression timer.

- If the RP now knows of at least one router/host that needs to receive these multicast packets, it does not reply to this briefer Register message. As a result, R1, when its timer expires, again sends its multicast packets to R3 (RP) encapsulated in PIM Register messages.

Joining the Shared Tree

So far, this section on PIM-SM has explained the beginnings of the registration process, by which a router near the source of multicast packets registers with the RP. Before completing that discussion, however, the concept of the shared tree for a multicast group, also called the *root-path tree (RPT)*, must be explained. As mentioned earlier, PIM-SM initially causes multicasts to be delivered in a two-step process: first, packets are sent from the source to the RP, and then the RP forwards the packets to the subnets that have hosts that need a copy of those multicasts. PIM-SM uses this shared tree in the second part of the process.

The RPT is a tree, with the RP at the root, that defines over which links multicasts should be forwarded to reach all required routers. One such tree exists for each multicast group that is currently active in the internetwork. So, once the multicast packets sent by each source are forwarded to the RP, the RP uses the RPT for that multicast group to determine where to forward these packets.

PIM-SM routers collectively create the RPT by sending PIM Join messages toward the RP. In PIM-SM, multicast traffic is sent only to routers that specifically request it. PIM-SM routers request the traffic by joining the RPT by sending a Join toward the RP.

PIM-SM routers choose to send a Join under two conditions:

- When a PIM-SM router receives a PIM Join message on any interface other than the interface used to route packets toward the RP

- When a PIM-SM router receives an IGMP Membership Report message from a host on a directly connected subnet

Figure 17-14 shows an example of the PIM-SM join process, using the same network as Figure 17-12 but with H1 joining group 228.8.8.8. The routers react to the IGMP Join by sending a Join toward the RP, to become part of the shared SPT (*,228.8.8.8).

Figure 17-14 *Creating a Shared Tree for (*,228.8.8.8)*

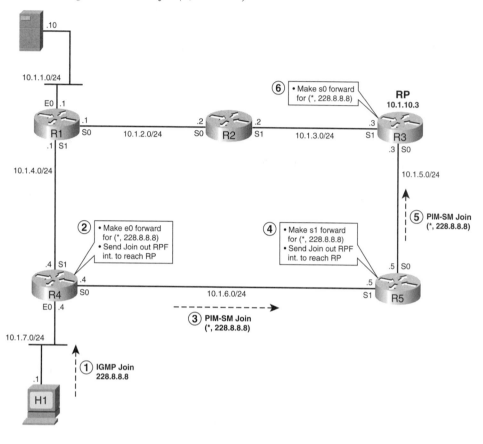

Figure 17-14 shows how H1 causes a shared tree (*,228.8.8.8) to be created, as described in the following steps:

1. H1 sends an IGMP Join message for the group 228.8.8.8.

2. R4 realizes it now needs to ask the RP to send it packets sent to 228.8.8.8, so R4 sends a PIM Join for the shared tree for group 228.8.8.8 toward the RP. R4 also puts its e0 interface into a forwarding state for the RPT for group 228.8.8.8.

3. R4 sends the Join to the RP.

4. R5 receives the Join on its s1 interface, so R5 puts its s1 interface in a forwarding state for the shared tree (represented by (*,228.8.8.8)). R5 also knows it needs to forward the Join toward the RP.

5. R5 sends the Join toward the RP.

6. R3, the RP, puts its s0 interface in a forwarding state for the (*,288.8.8.8) shared tree.

By the end of this process, the RP knows that at least one host wants packets sent to 228.8.8.8. The RPT for group 228.8.8.8 is formed with R3's s0 interface, R5's s1 interface, and R4's e0 interface.

NOTE The notation (*,G) represents a single RPT. The * represents a wildcard, meaning "any source," because the PIM-SM routers use this shared tree regardless of the source of the packets. For example, a packet sent from any source IP address, arriving at the RP, and destined to group 228.8.8.8, would cause the RP to use its (*,228.8.8.8) multicast routing table entries, because these entries are part of the RPT for group 228.8.8.8.

Completion of the Source Registration Process

So far in this description of PIM-SM, a source (10.1.1.10) sent packets to 228.8.8.8, as shown in Figure 17-13—but no one cared at the time, so the RP did not forward the packets. Next, you learned what happens when a host does want to receive packets, with the routers reacting to create the RPT for that group. This section completes the story by showing how an RP reacts to a PIM Register message when the RP knows that some hosts want to receive those multicasts.

When the RP receives a Register message for an active multicast group—in other words, the RP believes that it should forward packets sent to the group—the RP does not send a Register-Stop message, as was shown back in Figure 17-13. Instead, it reacts to the Register message by de-encapsulating the multicast packet, and forwarding it.

The behavior of the RP in reaction to the Register message points out the second major function of the Register message. Its main two functions are as follows:

- To allow a router to inform the RP that it has a local source for a particular multicast group

- To allow a router to forward multicasts to the RP, encapsulated inside a unicast packet, until the registration process is completed

To show the complete process, Figure 17-15 shows an example. In the example, host H1 has already joined group 228.8.8.8, as shown in Figure 17-14. The following steps match those identified in Figure 17-15. Note that Step 3 represents the forwarding of the multicasts that were encapsulated inside Register messages at Step 2.

1. Host S1 sends multicasts to 228.8.8.8.

2. Router R1 encapsulates the multicasts, sending them inside Register messages to the RP, R3.

3. R3, knowing that it needs to forward the multicast packets, de-encapsulates the packets and sends them toward H1. (This action allows R1 and R3 to distribute the multicasts while the registration process completes.) R5 forwards the group traffic to R4 and R4 forwards it on its LAN.

4. R3 joins the SPT for source 10.1.1.10, group 228.8.8.8, by sending a PIM-SM Join message for group (10.1.1.10,228.8.8.8) toward the source 10.1.1.10.

5. When R1 and R2 receive the PIM-SM Join message from R2 requesting the group traffic from the source, they start forwarding group traffic toward the RP. At this point, R3 (the RP) now receives this traffic on the SPT from the source. However, R1 is also still sending the Register messages with encapsulated multicast packets to R3.

6. R3 sends unicast Register-Stop messages to R1. When R1 receives the Register-Stop messages from R3, it stops sending the encapsulated unicast Register messages to R3.

Figure 17-15 *Source Registration when the RP Needs to Receive Packets Sent to that Group*

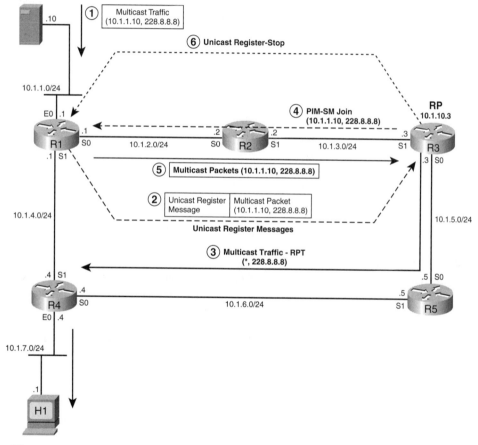

The process may seem like a lot of trouble, but at the end of the process, multicasts are delivered to the correct locations. The process uses the efficient SPT from the source to the RP, and the shared tree (*,228.8.8.8) from the RP to the subnets that need to receive the traffic.

Note that the PIM protocols could have just let a router near the source, such as R1 in this example, continue to encapsulate multicasts inside the unicast Register messages. However, it is inefficient to make R1 encapsulate every multicast packet, make R3 de-encapsulate every packet, and then make R3 forward the traffic. So, PIM-SM has the RP, R3 in this case, join the group-specific tree for that (S,G) combination.

Shared Distribution Tree

In Figure 17-15, the group traffic that flows over the path from the RP (R3) to R5 to R4 is called a *shared distribution tree*. It is also called a *root-path tree (RPT)* because it is rooted at the RP. If the network has multiple sources for the same group, traffic from all the sources would first travel to the RP (as shown with the traffic from host S1 in Figure 17-14), and then travel down this shared RPT to all the receivers. Because all sources in the multicast group use a common shared tree, a wildcard notation of (*,G) is used to identify an RPT, where * represents all sources and G represents the multicast group address. The RPT for the group 228.8.8.8 shown in Figure 17-14 would be written as (*,228.8.8.8).

Example 17-7 shows the multicast route table entry for R4 in Figure 17-15. On a Cisco router, the **show ip mroute** command displays the multicast route table entries.

Example 20-7 *Multicast Route Table Entry for the Group 228.8.8.8 for R4*

```
(*, 228.8.8.8), 00:00:08/00:02:58, RP 10.1.10.3, flags: SC
  Incoming interface: Serial0, RPF nbr 10.1.6.5
  Outgoing interface list:
    Ethernet0, Forward/Sparse, 00:00:08/00:02:52
```

The interpretation of the information shown in Example 17-7 is as follows:

■ The first line shows that the (*,G) entry for the group 228.8.8.8 was created 8 seconds ago, and if R4 does not forward group packets using this entry in 2 minutes and 58 seconds, it will expire. Every time R4 forwards a packet, the timer is reset to 3 minutes. This entry was created because R4 received an IGMP Join message from H1.

■ The RP for this group is 10.1.10.3 (R3). The S flag indicates that this group is using the sparse-mode (PIM-SM) routing protocol. The C flag indicates that R4 has a directly connected group member for 228.8.8.8.

■ The incoming interface for this (*,228.8.8.8) entry is s0 and the RPF neighbor is 10.1.6.5. Note that for the SPT, the RPF interface is chosen based on the route to reach the RP, not the route used to reach a particular source.

■ Group traffic is forwarded out on the Ethernet0 interface. In this example, Ethernet0 was added to the outgoing interface list because an IGMP Report message was received on this interface from H1. This interface has been in the forwarding state for 8 seconds. The Prune timer indicates that if an IGMP Join is not received again on this interface within the next 2 minutes and 52 seconds, it will be removed from the outgoing interface list.

Steady-State Operation by Continuing to Send Joins

To maintain the forwarding state of interfaces, PIM-SM routers must send PIM Join messages periodically. If a router fails to send Joins periodically, PIM-SM moves interfaces back to a pruned state.

PIM-SM routers choose to maintain the forwarding state on links based on two general criteria:

■ A downstream router continues to send PIM joins for the group.

■ A locally connected host still responds to IGMP Query messages with IGMP Report messages for the group.

Figure 17-16 shows an example in which R5 maintains the forwarding state of its link to R3 based on both of these reasons. H2 has also joined the shared tree for 228.8.8.8. H1 had joined earlier, as shown in Figures 17-14 and 17-15.

Figure 17-16 *Host H2 Sends an IGMP Join Message*

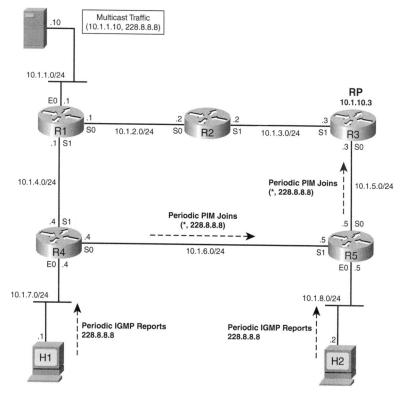

Example 17-8 shows the multicast route table entry for R5 in Figure 17-16, with these two interfaces in a forwarding state.

Example 17-8 *Multicast Route Table Entry for the Group 228.8.8.8 for R5*

```
(*,228.8.8.8), 00:00:05/00:02:59, RP 10.1.10.3, flags: SC
  Incoming interface: Serial0, RPF nbr 10.1.5.3
  Outgoing interface list:
    Serial1, Forward/Sparse, 00:01:15/00:02:20
    Ethernet0, Forward/Sparse, 00:00:05/00:02:55
```

In Example 17-8, two interfaces are listed in the outgoing interface list. The s1 interface is listed because R5 has received a PIM-SM Join message from R4. In PIM-SM, the downstream routers need to keep sending PIM-SM Join messages every 60 seconds to the upstream router. When R5 receives another PIM-SM Join from R4 on its s1 interface, it resets the Prune timer to the default value of 3 minutes. If R5 does not receive a PIM-SM Join from R4 before R5's Prune timer on that interface expires, R5 places its s1 interface in a pruned state and stops forwarding the traffic on the interface.

By contrast, R5's e0 interface is listed as forwarding in R5's outgoing interface list because R5 has received an IGMP Join message from H2. Recall from Chapter 16 that a multicast router sends an IGMP general query every 60 or 125 seconds (depending on the IGMP version) on its LAN interfaces. It must receive at least one IGMP Report/Join message as a response for a group; otherwise, it stops forwarding the group traffic on the interface. When R5 receives another IGMP Report message on its e0 interface, it resets the Prune timer for the entry to the default value of 3 minutes.

Note also that on R5, the receipt of the PIM Join from R4, or the IGMP Report on e0, triggers R5's need to send the PIM Join toward the RP.

Examining the RP's Multicast Routing Table

In the current state of the ongoing example, as last shown in Figure 17-16, the RP (R3) has joined the SPT for source 10.1.1.10, group 228.8.8.8. The RP also is the root of the shared tree for group 228.8.8.8. Example 17-9 shows both entries in R3's multicast route table.

Example 17-9 *Multicast Route Table Entry for the Group 228.8.8.8 for R3*

```
(*,228.8.8.8), 00:02:27/00:02:59, RP 10.1.10.3, flags: S
  Incoming interface: Null, RPF nbr 0.0.0.0
  Outgoing interface list:
    Serial0, Forward/Sparse, 00:02:27/00:02:33
(10.1.1.10/32, 228.8.8.8), 00:02:27/00:02:33, flags: T
  Incoming interface: Serial1, RPF nbr 10.1.3.2,
  Outgoing interface list:
  Outgoing interface list: Null
```

The first entry shows the shared tree, as indicated by the S flag. Notice the incoming interface is Null because R3, as RP, is the root of the tree. Also, the RPF neighbor is listed as 0.0.0.0 for the same reason. In other words, it shows that the shared-tree traffic for the group 228.8.8.8 has originated at this router and it does not depend on any other router for the shared-tree traffic.

The second entry shows the SPT entry on R3 for multicast group 228.8.8.8, source 10.1.1.10. The T flag indicates that this entry is for an SPT, and the source is listed at the beginning of that same line (10.1.1.10). The incoming interface is s1 and the RPF neighbor for the source address 10.1.1.10 is 10.1.3.2.

As you can see, an RP uses the SPT to pull the traffic from the source to itself and uses the shared tree to push the traffic down to the PIM-SM routers that have requested it.

Shortest-Path Tree Switchover

PIM-SM routers could continue forwarding packets via the PIM-SM two-step process, whereby sources send packets to the RP, and the RP sends them to all other routers using the RPT. However, one of the most fascinating aspects of PIM-SM operations is that each PIM-SM router can build the SPT between itself and the source of a multicast group and take advantage of the most efficient path available from the source to the router. In Figure 17-16, R4 is receiving the group traffic from the source via the path R1-R2-R3-R5-R4. However, it is obvious that it would be more efficient for R4 to receive the group traffic directly from R1 on R4's s1 interface.

In the section "Completion of the Source Registration Process," earlier in this chapter, you saw that the PIM-SM design allows an RP to build an SPT between itself and the router that is directly connected with the source (also called the source DR) to pull the group traffic. Similarly, the PIM-SM design also allows any other PIM-SM router to build an SPT between the router and the source DR. This feature allows a PIM-SM router to avoid using the inefficient path, such as the one used by R4 in Figure 17-16. Also, once the router starts receiving the group traffic over the SPT, it can send a Prune message to the upstream router of the shared tree to stop forwarding the traffic for the group.

The question is, when should a router switch over from RPT to SPT? RFC 2362 for PIM-SM specifies that, "The recommended policy is to initiate the switch to the SP-tree after receiving a significant number of data packets during a specified time interval from a particular source." What number should be considered as a significant number? The RFC does not specify that. Cisco routers, by default, switch over from the RPT to the source-specific SPT after they receive the first packet from the shared tree.

> **NOTE**   You can change this behavior by configuring the global command **ip pim spt-threshold** *rate* on any router for any group. Once the traffic rate exceeds the stated rate (in kbps), the router joins the SPT. The command impacts the behavior only on the router(s) on which it is configured.

If a router is going to switch to SPT, why join the RPT first? In PIM-SM, a router does not know the IP address of a source until it receives at least one packet for the group from the source. After it receives one packet on the RPT, it can learn the IP address of a source, and initialize a switchover to the SPT for that (source,group) combination.

With the default Cisco PIM-SM operation, when multicast packets begin arriving on R4's s0 interface via the shared tree, R4 attempts to switch to the SPT for source 10.1.1.10. Figure 17-17 shows the general steps.

Figure 17-17 *R4 Initializing Switchover from RPT to SPT by Sending a PIM-SM Join to R1*

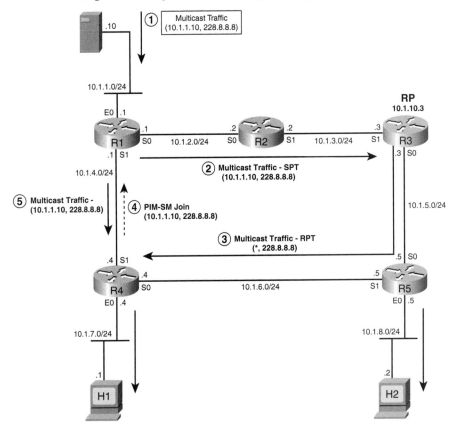

The first three steps Figure 17-17 are as follows:

1. The source (S1,10.1.1.10) sends a multicast packet to the first-hop router R1.

2. R1 forwards the packet to the RP (R3).

3. The RP forwards the packet to R4 via the shared tree.

At Step 3, R4 learned that the source address of the multicast group 228.8.8.8 is 10.1.1.10. So, besides forwarding the packet at Step 3, R4 can use that information to join the SPT for group 228.8.8.8, from source 10.1.1.10, using the following steps from Figure 17-17.

4. R4 consults its unicast routing table, finds the next-hop address and outgoing interface it would use to reach source 10.1.1.10, and sends the PIM-SM Join message out that interface (s1) to R1. This PIM-SM Join message is specifically for the SPT of (10.1.1.10,228.8.8.8). The Join travels hop by hop until it reaches the source DR.

5. As a result of the Join, R1 places its s1 interface in a forwarding state for SPT (10.1.1.10,228.8.8.8). So, R1 starts forwarding multicasts from 10.1.1.10 to 228.8.8.8 out its s1 interface as well.

R4 now has a multicast routing table entry for the SPT, as shown in Example 17-10.

Example 17-10 *Multicast Route Table Entry for the Group 228.8.8.8 for R4*

```
(*,228.8.8.8), 00:02:36/00:02:57, RP 10.1.10.3, flags: SCJ
  Incoming interface: Serial0, RPF nbr 10.1.6.5
  Outgoing interface list:
    Ethernet0, Forward/Sparse, 00:02:36/00:02:13
(10.1.1.10/32, 228.8.8.8), 00:00:23/00:02:33, flags: CJT
  Incoming interface: Serial1, RPF nbr 10.1.4.1,
  Outgoing interface list:
  Ethernet0, Forward/Sparse, 00:00:23/00:02:37
```

In Example 17-10, you see two entries for the group. The J flag (for join) on both the entries indicates that the traffic was switched from RPT to SPT, and now the (S,G) entry will be used for forwarding multicast packets for the group. Notice that the incoming interfaces for the (*,G) entry and (S,G) entry are different.

Pruning from the Shared Tree

When a PIM-SM router has joined a more efficient SPT, it may not need to receive multicast packets over the RPT any more. For example, when R4 in Figure 17-17 notices that it is receiving the group traffic over RPT and SPT, it can and should ask the RP to stop sending the traffic.

To stop the RP from forwarding traffic to a downstream router on the shared tree, the downstream router sends a PIM-SM Prune message to the RP. The Prune message references the (S,G) SPT, which identifies the IP address of the source. Essentially, this prune means the following to the RP:

> Stop forwarding packets from the listed source IP address, to the listed group address, down the RPT.

For example, in Figure 17-18, which continues the example shown in Figure 17-17, R4 sends a Prune out its s0 interface toward R5. The Prune lists (S,G) entry (10.1.1.10,228.8.8.8), and it sets a bit called the RP-tree bit (RPT-bit). By setting the RPT-bit in the Prune message, R4 informs

R5 (the upstream router) that it has switched to SPT and the Prune message is for the redundant traffic for the group 228.8.8.8, from 10.1.1.10, that R4 is receiving on the shared tree.

Figure 17-18 *R4 Sends PIM-SM Prune with RP Bit Set to R5*

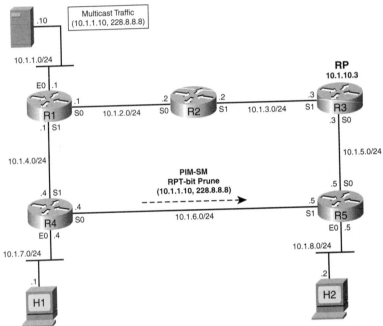

To stop the packets from being sent over the RPT to R4, R5 must prune its interface s1 in the RPT (*, 228.8.8.8). R5 may go on to join the SPT for (10.1.1.10,228.8.8.8.8) as well.

This concludes the coverage of the operations of PIM-SM. The next section covers some details about how routers can learn the IP address of the PIM RP.

Dynamically Finding RPs and Using Redundant RPs

In a PIM-SM network, every router must somehow learn the IP address of an RP. A PIM-SM router can use one of the following three methods to learn the IP address of an RP:

- The RP address can be statically configured on all the PIM-SM routers with the Cisco IOS global command **ip pim rp-address** *address*. This is the method used for the five-router topology shown in Figure 17-19.

- The Cisco-proprietary Auto-RP protocol can be used to designate the RP and advertise its IP address so that all PIM-SM routers can learn its IP address automatically.

- A standard BootStrap Router (BSR) protocol can be used to designate the RP and advertise its IP address so that all the PIM-SM routers can learn its IP address automatically.

Additionally, because PIM-SM relies so heavily on the RP, it makes sense to have redundant RPs. Cisco IOS offers two methods of providing redundant RPs, which are also covered in this section:

- Anycast RP using the Multicast Source Discovery Protocol (MSDP)

- BootStrap Router (BSR)

Dynamically Finding the RP Using Auto-RP

Static RP configuration is suboptimal under the following conditions:

- When an enterprise has a large number of PIM-SM routers and the enterprise wants to use many different RPs for different groups, it becomes time consuming and cumbersome to statically configure the IP addresses of many RPs for different groups on all the routers.

- When an RP fails or needs to be changed because a new RP is being installed, it becomes extremely difficult in a statically configured PIM-SM domain to switch over to an alternative RP without considerable downtime.

Auto-RP provides an alternative in which routers dynamically learn the unicast IP address used by each RP. Auto-RP uses a two-step process, which is shown in Figure 17-19 and Figure 17-20. In the first step, the RP sends RP-Announce messages to the reserved multicast address 224.0.1.39, stating that the router is an RP. The RP-Announce message also allows the router to advertise the multicast groups for which it is the RP, thereby allowing some load-balancing of the RP workload among different routers. The RP continues to send these RP-Announce messages every minute.

Figure 17-19 *R3 Sends RP-Announce Messages*

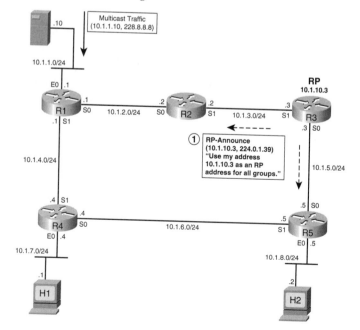

For example, Figure 17-19 shows R3 as an RP that uses Auto-RP. R3 supports all multicast groups in this case. The RP-Announce message is shown as Step 1, to link it with Step 2 in Figure 17-20.

Key Topic

The second step for Auto-RP requires that one router be configured as a mapping agent. The mapping agent is usually the same router that was selected as an RP, but can be a different PIM-SM router. The mapping agent learns all the RPs and the multicast groups they each support. Then, the mapping agent multicasts another message, called RP-Discovery, that identifies the RP for each range of multicast group addresses. This message goes to reserved multicast address 224.0.1.40. It is this RP-Discovery message that actually informs the general router population as to which routers they should use as RPs.

For example, in Figure 17-20, R2 is configured as a mapping agent. To receive all RP-Announce messages, R2 locally joins the well-known Cisco-RP-Announce multicast group 224.0.1.39. In other words, the mapping agent has become a group member for 224.0.1.39 and is listening for the group traffic. When R2 receives the RP-Announce packets shown in Figure 17-19, it examines the packet, creates group-to-RP mappings, and maintains this information in its cache, as shown in Figure 17-20.

Figure 17-20 *R2 Creates Group-to-RP Mappings and Sends Them in RP-Discovery Messages*

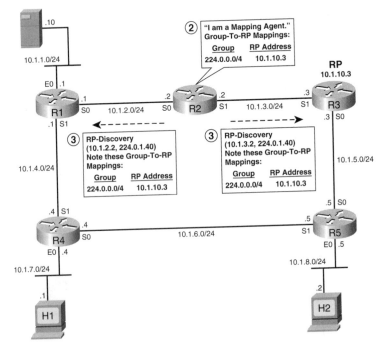

At first glance, the need for the mapping agent may not be obvious. Why not just let the RPs announce themselves to all the other routers? Well, if Auto-RP supported only one RP, or even only one RP to support each multicast group, the mapping agent would be a waste of effort. However, to support RP redundancy—in other words, to support multiple RPs that can act as RP for the same multicast group—the Auto-RP mapping agent decides which RP should be used to support each group at the moment. To do so, the mapping agent selects the router with the highest IP address as an RP for the group. (Note that you can also configure multiple mapping agents, for redundancy.)

As soon as Cisco routers are configured with PIM-SM and Auto-RP, they automatically join the well-known Cisco-RP-Discovery multicast group 224.0.1.40. That means they are listening to the group address 224.0.1.40, and when they receive a 224.0.1.40 packet, they learn group-to-RP mapping information and maintain it in their cache. When a PIM-SM router receives an IGMP Join message for a group or PIM-SM Join message from a downstream router, it checks the group-to-RP mapping information in its cache. Then it can proceed as described throughout the PIM-SM explanations in this chapter, using that RP as the RP for that multicast group.

The following list summarizes the steps used by Auto-RP:

1. Each RP is configured to use Auto-RP and to announce itself and its supported multicast groups via RP-Announce messages (224.0.1.39).

2. The Auto-RP mapping agent, which may or may not also be an RP router, gathers information about all RPs by listening to the RP-Announce messages.

3. The mapping agent builds a mapping table that lists the currently best RP for each range of multicast groups, with the mapping agent picking the RP with the highest IP address if multiple RPs support the same multicast groups.

4. The mapping agent sends RP-Discover messages to 224.0.1.40 advertising the mappings.

5. All routers listen for packets sent to 224.0.1.40 to learn the mapping information and find the correct RP to use for each multicast group.

Finally, one last small but important point deserves some attention before moving on to BSR. Auto-RP creates a small chicken-and-egg problem in that the purpose of Auto-RP is to find the RPs, but to get the RP-Announce and RP-Discovery messages, PIM-SM routers would need to send a Join toward the RP, which they do not know yet. To overcome this problem, Cisco added a variation of PIM called *sparse-dense mode*. In PIM sparse-dense mode, a router uses PIM-DM rules when it does not know the location of the RP, and PIM-SM rules when it does know the location of the RP. So, under normal conditions with Auto-RP, the routers would use dense mode long enough to learn the group-to-RP mappings from the mapping agent, and then switch over to sparse mode. Also, if any other multicast traffic occurred before the routers learned of the RPs using Auto-RP, the multicast packets would still be forwarded using dense-mode rules. (PIM sparse-dense mode is configured per interface using the **ip pim sparse-dense-mode** interface subcommand.)

Dynamically Finding the RP Using BSR

Cisco provided the proprietary Auto-RP feature to solve a couple of specific problems. PIM Version 2, which came later, provided a different solution to the same problem, namely the BootStrap Router (BSR) feature. From a very general perspective, BSR works similarly to Auto-RP. Each RP sends a message to another router, which collects the group-to-RP mapping information. That router then distributes the mapping information to the PIM routers. However, any examination of BSR beyond that level of detail shows that these two tools do differ in many ways.

It is helpful to first understand the concept of the bootstrap router, or BSR router, before thinking about the RPs. One router acts as BSR, which is similar to the mapping agent in Auto-RP. The BSR receives mapping information from the RPs, and then it advertises the information to other routers. However, there are some specific differences between the actions of the BSR, and their implications, and the actions of the Auto-RP mapping agent:

■ The BSR router does not pick the best RP for each multicast group; instead, the BSR router sends all group-to-RP mapping information to the other PIM routers inside bootstrap messages.

■ PIM routers each independently pick the currently best RP for each multicast group by running the same hash algorithm on the information in the bootstrap message.

■ The BSR floods the mapping information in a bootstrap message sent to the all-PIM-routers multicast address (224.0.0.13).

■ The flooding of the bootstrap message does not require the routers to have a known RP or to support dense mode. (This will be described in more detail in the next few pages.)

Figure 17-21 shows an example, described next, of how the BSR floods the bootstrap message. PIMv2 creates specific rules for BSR bootstrap messages, stating that PIM routers should flood these messages. PIM-SM routers flood bootstrap messages out all non-RPF interfaces, which in effect guarantees that at least one copy of the message makes it to every router. Note that this logic is not dependent on a working dense- or spare-mode implementation. As a result, BSR overcomes the chicken-and-egg problem of Auto-RP.

For example, in Figure 17-21, imagine that R4's s1 interface is its RPF interface to reach R2, and R5's RPF interface to reach R2 is its s0 interface. So, they each forward the bootstrap messages at Step 3 of Figure 17-21. However, because R4 receives the bootstrap message from R5 on one of R4's non-RPF interfaces, R4 discards the packet, thereby preventing loops. R5 also does not forward the bootstrap message any further for the same basic reasons.

Figure 17-21 *BSR Flooding Bootstrap Messages*

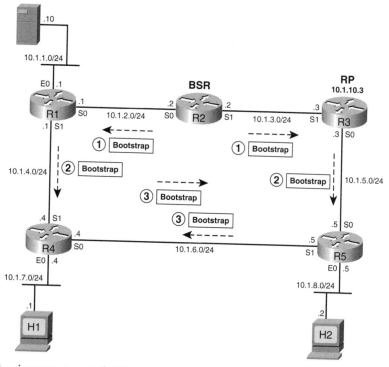

The other important part of BSR operation is for each candidate RP (c-RP) to inform the BSR router that it is an RP and to identify the multicast groups it supports. This part of the process with BSR is simple if you keep in mind the following point:

> All PIM routers already know the unicast IP address of the BSR based on the earlier receipt of bootstrap messages.

So, the c-RPs simply send unicast messages, called c-RP Advertisements, to the BSR. These c-RP advertisements include the IP address used by the c-RP, and the groups it supports.

The BSR feature supports redundant RPs and redundant BSRs. As mentioned earlier, the bootstrap message sent by the BSR router includes all candidate RPs, with each router using the same hash algorithm to pick the currently best RP for each multicast group. The mapping information can list multiple RPs that support the same group addresses.

Additionally, multiple BSR routers can be configured. In that case, each candidate BSR (c-BSR) router sends bootstrap messages that include the priority of the BSR router and its IP address. The highest-priority BSR wins, or if a tie occurs, the highest BSR IP address wins. Then, the winning BSR, called the preferred BSR, continues to send bootstrap messages, while the other BSRs monitor those messages. If the preferred BSR's bootstrap messages cease, the redundant BSRs can attempt to take over.

Anycast RP with MSDP

The final tool covered here for finding a router's RP is called Anycast RP with Multicast Source Discovery Protocol (MSDP). Anycast RP is actually an implementation feature more than a new feature with new configuration commands. As will be explained in the upcoming pages, Anycast RP can actually use static RP configuration, Auto-RP, and BSR.

The key differences between using Anycast RP and using either Auto-RP or BSR relate to how the redundant RPs are used. The differences are as follows:

■ **Without Anycast RP**—RP redundancy allows only one router to be the active RP for each multicast group. Load sharing of the collective work of the RPs is accomplished by using one RP for some groups and another RP for other groups.

■ **With Anycast RP**—RP redundancy and load sharing can be achieved with multiple RPs concurrently acting as the RP for the same group

The way Anycast RP works is to have each RP use the same IP address. The RPs must advertise this address, typically as a /32 prefix, with its IGP. Then, the other methods of learning an RP—static configuration, Auto-RP, and BSR—all view the multiple RPs as a single RP. At the end of the process, any packets sent to "the" RP are routed per IGP routes to the closest RP. Figure 17-22 shows an example of the process.

Figure 17-22 *Learning the RP Address with Anycast RP*

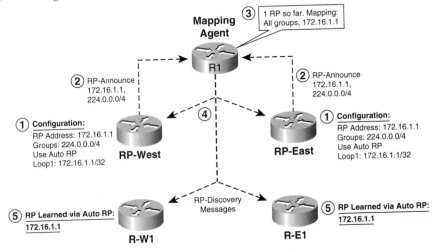

Figure 17-22 shows a design using two RPs (RP-East and RP-West) along with Auto-RP. The steps shown in the figure are as follows:

1. Both RPs are configured with 172.16.1.1/32, and configured to use that IP address for RP functions. In this case, both are configured to be the RP for all multicast groups.

2. Both RPs act as normal for Auto-RP by sending RP-Announce messages to 224.0.1.39.

3. The Auto-RP mapping agent builds its mapping table with a single entry, because it cannot tell the difference between the two RPs, because both use IP address 172.16.1.1.

4. The Auto-RP mapping agent acts as normal, sending an RP-Discovery message to 224.0.1.40. It includes (in this case) a single mapping entry: all groups map to 172.16.1.1.

5. All the routers, including routers R-W1 and R-E1, learn via Auto-RP that the single RP for all groups is 172.16.1.1.

The last step described in the list brings the discussion to the main benefit of Anycast RP. At this point, the core Auto-RP function of advertising the IP address of the RP is complete. Of course, the IP address exists on two routers in Figure 17-22, but it could be more than that in other designs. Because of the IGP routes, when routers in the western part of the network (like R-W1) send packets to the RP at 172.16.1.1, they are actually sending the packets to RP-West. Likewise, when routers in the eastern part of the network (like R-E1) send packets to the RP (172.16.1.1), they are actually sending the packets to RP-East. This behavior is only achieved by using the Anycast RP implementation option beyond simply using Auto-RP.

The two biggest benefits of this design with Anycast RP are as follows:

■ Multiple RPs share the load for a single multicast group.

■ Recovery after a failed RP happens quickly. If an RP fails, multicast traffic is only interrupted for the amount of time it takes the IGP to converge to point to the other RP sharing the same IP address.

The design of Anycast RP creates a problem that must be overcome using MSDP. The problem relates to the fact that each individual RP builds its own shared tree, but any multicast source sends packets to one of the RPs. For example, Figure 17-23 shows the same network as Figure 17-22, but now with a multicast source in the western part of the network. The routers in the west side of the figure receive the packets as distributed by RP-West via its shared tree. However, the routers in RP-East's shared tree do not get the packets because RP-East never gets the packet sent by the server in the west side.

The solution to this problem is for the RPs to tell each other about all known sources by using MSDP. MSDP allows RPs to send messages to each other, revealing the IP addresses of each source for each multicast group. In Figure 17-23, RP-West could tell RP-East about the multicast source for 226.1.1.1 at unicast IP address 172.16.5.5. Then, RP-East can join the SPT of source 172.16.5.5, group 226.1.1.1, just as it would have done if it had received the multicast traffic directly from 172.16.5.5.

Figure 17-23 *The Anycast RP Problem (Later Solved with MSDP)*

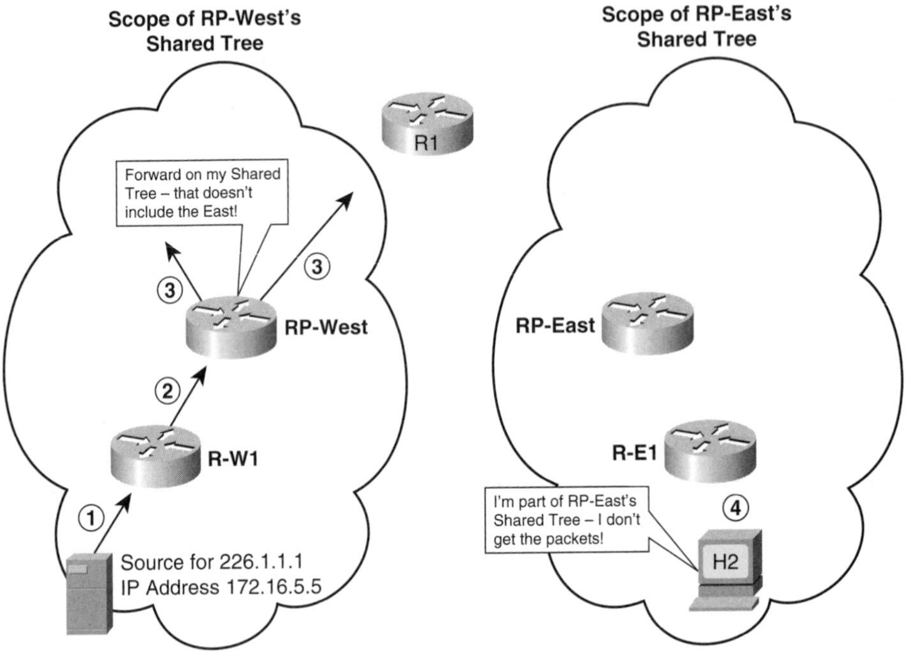

Summary: Finding the RP

This section covers the concepts behind four separate methods for finding the RP. Three are specific configuration features, namely static configuration, Auto-RP, and BSR. The fourth, Anycast RP, actually uses any of the first three methods, but with the design that includes having the RPs use the same unicast IP address to achieve better redundancy features. Table 17-3 summarizes the methods of finding the RP with PIM-SM.

Table 17-3 *Comparison of Methods of Finding the RP*

Method	RP Details	Mapping Info	Redundant RP Support?	Load Sharing of One Group?
Static	Simple reference to unicast IP address.	—	No	No
Auto-RP	Sends RP-Announce to 224.0.1.39; relies on sparse-dense mode.	Mapping agent sends via RP-Discovery to 224.0.1.40	Yes	No

Table 17-3 *Comparison of Methods of Finding the RP (Continued)*

Method	RP Details	Mapping Info	Redundant RP Support?	Load Sharing of One Group?
BSR	Sends c-RP advertisements as unicasts to BSR IP address; does not need sparse-dense mode.	Sends bootstrap messages flooded over non-RPF path	Yes	No
Anycast RP	Each RP uses identical IP addresses.	Can use Auto-RP or BSR normal processes	Yes	Yes

Bidirectional PIM

PIM-SM works efficiently with a relatively small number of multicast senders. However, in cases with a large number of senders and receivers, PIM-SM becomes less efficient. Bidirectional PIM addresses this relative inefficiency by slightly changing the rules used by PIM-SM.

To appreciate bidirectional PIM, a brief review of PIM-SM's normal operations is useful. While many variations can occur, the following general steps can be used by PIM-SM:

1. The RP builds a shared tree, with itself as the root, for forwarding multicast packets.

2. When a source first sends multicasts, the router nearest the source forwards the multicasts to the RP, encapsulated inside a PIM Register message.

3. The RP joins the source-specific tree for that source by sending a PIM Join toward that source.

4. Later, the routers attached to the same LANs as the receivers can send a PIM Join toward the source to join the SPT for that source.

With bidirectional PIM, the last three steps in this list are not performed. Bidirectional PIM instead follows these steps:

1. As with normal PIM-SM, the RP builds a shared tree, with itself as the root, for forwarding multicast packets.

2. When a source sends multicasts, the router receiving those multicasts does not use a PIM Register message. Instead, it forwards the packets in the opposite direction of the shared tree, back up the tree toward the RP. This process continues for all multicast packets from the source.

3. The RP forwards the multicasts via the shared tree.

4. All packets are forwarded per Steps 2 and 3. The RP does not join the source tree for the source, and the leaf routers do not join the SPT, either.

The name "bidirectional" comes from Step 2, in which the router near the source forwards packets back up the tree toward the RP. The other direction in the tree is used at Step 3, with the RP forwarding multicasts using the shared tree.

Comparison of PIM-DM and PIM-SM

One of the most confusing parts of the PIM-DM and PIM-SM designs is that it appears that if sources keep sending, and receivers keep listening, there is no difference between the end results of the end-user multicast packet flow using these two options. Once PIM-SM completes its more complicated processes, the routers near the receivers have all joined the SPT to the source, and the most efficient forwarding paths are used for each (S,G) tree.

Although its underlying operation is a bit more complicated, PIM-SM tends to be the more popular option today. PIM-SM's inherent strategy of not forwarding multicasts until hosts request them makes it more efficient during times of low usage. When the numbers of senders and receivers increases, PIM-SM quickly moves to use the SPT—the same SPT that would have been derived using PIM-DM. As such, PIM-SM has become a more popular option for most enterprise implementations today. It has also become a popular option for interdomain multicast as well.

Table 17-4 summarizes the important features of PIM-DM and PIM-SM.

Table 17-4 *Comparison of PIM-DM and PIM-SM*

Feature	PIM-DM	PIM-SM
Destination address for Version 1 Query messages, and IP protocol number	224.0.0.2 and 2	224.0.0.2 and 2
Destination address for Version 2 Hello messages, and IP protocol number	224.0.0.13 and 103	224.0.0.13 and 103
Default interval for Query and Hello messages	30 seconds	30 seconds
Default Holdtime for Versions 1 and 2	90 seconds	90 seconds
Rule for electing a designated router on a multiaccess network	Router with the highest IP address on the subnet	Router with the highest IP address on the subnet
Main design principle	A router automatically receives the traffic. If it does not want the traffic, it has to say no (send a Prune message) to its sender.	Unless a router specifically makes a request to an RP, it does not receive multicast traffic.

Table 17-4 *Comparison of PIM-DM and PIM-SM (Continued)*

Feature	PIM-DM	PIM-SM
SPT or RPT?	Uses only SPT	First uses RPT and then switches to SPT
Uses Join/Prune messages?	Yes	Yes
Uses Graft and Graft-Ack messages?	Yes	No
Uses Prune Override mechanism?	Yes	Yes
Uses Assert message?	Yes	Yes
Uses RP?	No	Yes
Uses source registration process?	No	Yes

Foundation Summary

This section lists additional details and facts to round out the coverage of the topics in this chapter. Unlike most of the Cisco Press *Exam Certification Guides*, this "Foundation Summary" does not repeat information presented in the "Foundation Topics" section of the chapter. Please take the time to read and study the details in the "Foundation Topics" section of the chapter, as well as review items noted with a Key Topic icon.

Table 17-5 lists the protocol standards referenced in this chapter.

Table 17-5 *RFC Reference for Chapter 20*

RFC	What It Defines
3973	PIM-DM
3618	MSDP
3446	Anycast RP
2362	PIM-SM
1584	Multicast Extensions to OSPF

Table 17-6 lists some of the most common Cisco IOS commands related to the topics in this chapter and Chapter 16.

Table 17-6 *Command Reference for Chapters 16 and 17*

Command	Command Mode and Description
ip multicast-routing	Global mode; required first command on Cisco routers to use multicasting.
ip pim dense-mode[1]	Interface config mode; configures the interface to use PIM-DM routing protocol.
ip pim sparse-mode[1]	Interface config mode; configures the interface to use PIM-SM routing protocol.
ip pim sparse-dense-mode	Interface config mode; configures the interface to use PIM-SM routing protocol for a group if the RP address is known; otherwise, uses PIM-DM routing protocol.

Table 17-6 *Command Reference for Chapters 16 and 17 (Continued)*

Command	Command Mode and Description
ip igmp version {**1**	**2**}	Interface config mode; sets the IGMP version on an interface. The default is 2.
ip igmp query-interval *seconds*	Interface config mode; changes the interval for IGMP queries sent by the router from the default 60 seconds.
ip igmp query-max-response-time *seconds*	Interface config mode; changes the Max Response Time advertised in IGMP Queries from the default of 10 seconds for IGMPv2 and IGMPv3.
ip igmp join-group *group-address*	Interface config mode; configures a router to join a multicast group. The group-address is a multicast IP address in four-part dotted-decimal notation.
ip multicast boundary *access-list* [**filter-autorp**]	Interface config mode; configures an interface as a multicast boundary for administrative scoping. A numbered or named access list controls the range of group addresses affected by the boundary. (Optional) **filter-autorp** filters Auto-RP messages denied by the boundary ACL.
ip multicast ttl-threshold *ttl-value*	Interface config mode; configures an interface as a multicast boundary for TTL scoping. Time-to-Live value represents number of hops, ranging from 0 to 255. The default value is 0, which means that all multicast packets are forwarded out the interface.
ip cgmp	Interface config mode; enables support for CGMP on an interface.
ip pim version {**1**	**2**}	Interface config mode; sets the PIM version on an interface. The default is 2.
ip pim query-interval *seconds*	Interface config mode; changes the interval for PIMv2 Hello or PIMv1 Router Query messages from the default 60 seconds.
ip pim message-interval *seconds*	Interface config mode; changes the interval for sparse-mode Join/Prune messages from the default 60 seconds.
ip pim spt-threshold {**kbps**	**infinity**} [**group-list** *access-list-number*]	Global mode; specifies the incoming rate for the multicast traffic for a PIM-SM router to switch from RPT to SPT. The default is to switch after the first multicast packet is received. If the **group-list** option is used, the command parameters are applied only to the groups permitted by the access list; otherwise, they are applied to all groups.

continues

Table 17-6 *Command Reference for Chapters 16 and 17 (Continued)*

Command	Command Mode and Description
ip pim rp-address *rp-address* [*access-list*] [**override**]	Global mode; statically configures the IP address of an RP where *rp-address* is a unicast IP address in four-part, dotted notation. (Optional) *access-list* represents a number or name of an access list that defines for which multicast groups the RP should be used. (Optional) **override** indicates that if there is a conflict, the RP configured with this command prevails over the RP learned dynamically by Auto-RP or any other method.
ip pim send-rp-announce *interface-type interface-number* **scope** *ttl-value* [**group-list** *access-list*] [**interval** *seconds*]	Global mode; configures the router to be an RP, and the router sends RP-Announce messages using the Auto-RP method for the interface address selected. Scope represents the TTL. (Optional) **group-list** defines the multicast groups for which this router is RP. (Optional) **interval** changes the announcement frequency from the default 60 seconds.
ip pim send-rp-discovery [*interface-type interface-number*] **scope** *ttl-value*	Global mode; configures the router to be a mapping agent, and the router sends RP-Discovery messages using the Auto-RP method. **scope** represents the TTL. (Optional) The IP address of the interface specified is used as the source address for the messages. The default is to use the IP address of the interface on which the message is sent as the source address.
ip pim rp-announce-filter rp-list *access-list* **group-list** *access-list*	Global mode; configures a mapping agent to filter RP-Announce messages coming from specific RPs. **rp-list** *access-list* specifies a number or name of a standard access list that specifies that this filter is only for the RP addresses permitted in this ACL. **group-list** *access-list* specifies a number or name of a standard access list that describes permitted group addresses. The filter defines that only the group range permitted in the **group-list** *access-list* should be accepted from the RP-Announcements received from the RP addresses permitted by the **rp-list** *access-list*.
show ip igmp groups [*group-name* | *group-address* | *interface-type interface-number*] [**detail**]	User mode; displays the list of multicast groups for which the router has directly connected group members, learned via IGMP.
show ip mroute [*group-address* | *group-name*] [*source-address* | *source-name*] [*interface-type interface-number*] [**summary**] [**count**] [**active** *kbps*]	User mode; displays the contents of the IP multicast routing table.

Table 17-6 *Command Reference for Chapters 16 and 17 (Continued)*

Command	Command Mode and Description
show ip pim neighbor [*interface-type interface-number*]	User mode; displays the list of neighbors discovered by PIM.
show ip pim rp [**mapping** [**elected** | **in-use**] | **metric**] [*rp-address*]	User mode; displays the active RPs associated with multicast groups.
show ip rpf {*source-address* | *source-name*} [**metric**]	User mode; displays the information IP multicasting routing uses to perform the RPF check.
clear ip cgmp [*interface-type interface-number*]	Enable mode; the router sends a CGMP Leave message and instructs the switches to clear all group entries they have cached.
debug ip igmp	Enable mode; displays IGMP messages received and sent, and IGMP-host-related events.
debug ip pim	Enable mode; displays PIM messages received and sent, and PIM-related events.

[1]When you configure any one of these commands on a LAN interface, IGMPv2 is automatically enabled on the interface.

Table 17-7 summarizes important flags displayed in an mroute entry when you use the command **show ip mroute**.

Table 17-7 *mroute Flags*

Flag	Description
D (dense)	Entry is operating in dense mode.
S (sparse)	Entry is operating in sparse mode.
C (connected)	A member of the multicast group is present on the directly connected interface.
L (local)	The router itself is a member of the multicast group.
P (pruned)	Route has been pruned.
R (RP-bit set)	Indicates that the (S,G) entry is pointing toward the RP. The RP is typically in a pruned state along the shared tree after a downstream router has switched to SPT for a particular source.
F (register flag)	Indicates that the software is registering for a multicast source.

continues

Table 17-7 *mroute Flags*

Flag	Description
T (SPT-bit set)	Indicates that packets have been received on the shortest-path source tree.
J (join SPT)	This flag has meaning only for sparse-mode groups. For (*,G) entries, the J flag indicates that the rate of traffic flowing down the shared tree has exceeded the SPT-Threshold set for the group. This calculation is done once a second. On Cisco routers, the default SPT-Threshold value is 0 kbps. When the J flag is set on the (*,G) entry and the router has a directly connected group member denoted by the C flag, the next (S,G) packet received down the shared tree will trigger a switch over from RPT to SPT for source S and group G. For (S,G) entries, the J flag indicates that the entry was created because the router has switched over from RPT to SPT for the group. When the J flag is set for the (S,G) entries, the router monitors the traffic rate on SPT and switches back to RPT for this source if the traffic rate on the source tree falls below the group's SPT-Threshold for more than 1 minute.

Memory Builders

The CCIE Routing and Switching written exam, like all Cisco CCIE written exams, covers a fairly broad set of topics. This section provides some basic tools to help you exercise your memory about some of the broader topics covered in this chapter.

Fill in Key Tables from Memory

Appendix E, "Key Tables for CCIE Study," on the CD in the back of this book contains empty sets of some of the key summary tables in each chapter. Print Appendix E, refer to this chapter's tables in it, and fill in the tables from memory. Refer to Appendix F, "Solutions for Key Tables for CCIE Study," on the CD to check your answers.

Definitions

Next, take a few moments to write down the definitions for the following terms:

dense-mode protocol, RPF check, sparse-mode protocol, RP, multicast scoping, TTL scoping, administrative scoping, PIM-DM, PIM Hello message, designated router, source-based distribution tree, multicast state information, Join/Prune message, upstream router, downstream router, Graft message, Graft Ack message, Prune Override, Assert message, DVMRP, MOSPF, PIM-SM, source DR, source registration, shared distribution tree, shortest-path tree switchover, PIM-SM (S, G) RP-bit Prune, Auto-RP

Refer to the glossary to check your answers.

Further Reading

Developing IP Multicast Networks, Volume I, by Beau Williamson (Cisco Press, 2000).

Part VII: Security

Chapter 18: Security

Blueprint topics covered in this chapter:

This chapter covers the following subtopics from the Cisco CCIE Routing and Switching written exam blueprint. Refer to the full blueprint in Table I-1 in the Introduction for more details on the topics covered in each chapter and their context within the blueprint.

- Storm Control

- Dynamic Multiport VPN (DMVPN)

- Extended IP Access Lists

- Unicast Reverse Path Forwarding (uRPF)

- IP Source Guard

- Context-Based Access Control (CBAC)

Security

Over the years, the CCIE program has expanded to add several CCIE certifications besides the Routing and Switching track. As a result, some topics previously covered in the Routing and Switching exam have been removed, or shortened, because they are more appropriate for another CCIE track. For example, the CCIE Routing and Switching track formerly covered voice to some degree, but the CCIE Voice track now covers voice to a much deeper level.

The topics in this chapter are certainly covered in more detail in the CCIE Security written and lab exams. However, because security has such an important role in networks, and because many security features relate specifically to router and switch operations, some security details remain within the CCIE Routing and Switching track. This chapter covers many of the core security features related to routers and switches.

"Do I Know This Already?" Quiz

Table 18-1 outlines the major headings in this chapter and the corresponding "Do I Know This Already?" quiz questions.

Table 18-1 *"Do I Know This Already?" Foundation Topics Section-to-Question Mapping*

Foundation Topics Section	Questions Covered in This Section	Score
Router and Switch Device Security	1–3	
Layer 2 Security	4–7	
Layer 3 Security	8–10	
Total Score		

To best use this prechapter assessment, remember to score yourself strictly. You can find the answers in Appendix A, "Answers to the 'Do I Know This Already?' Quizzes."

1. Consider the following configuration commands, which will be pasted into a router's configuration. Assuming no other AAA configuration or other security-related configuration exists before pasting in this configuration, which of the following is true regarding the process and sequences for authentication of a user attempting to enter privileged mode?

```
enable secret fred
enable authentication wilma
username barney password betty
aaa new-model
aaa authentication enable default group radius local
aaa authentication enable wilma group fred local
aaa authentication login default group radius local
aaa authentication login fred line group radius none
radius-server host 10.1.1.1 auth-port 1812 acct-port 1646
radius-server host 10.1.1.2 auth-port 1645 acct-port 1646
radius-server key cisco
radius-server host 10.1.1.3 auth-port 1812 acct-port 1646
radius-server host 10.1.1.4 auth-port 1645 acct-port 1646
radius-server key cisco
aaa group server radius fred
server 10.1.1.3 auth-port 1645 acct-port 1646
server 10.1.1.4 auth-port 1645 acct-port 1646
line con 0
 password cisco
 login authentication fred
line vty 0 4
 password cisco
```

   a. The user will only need to supply a password of fred without a username.

   b. The RADIUS server at either 10.1.1.1 or 10.1.1.2 must approve the username/password supplied by the user.

   c. The RADIUS server at 10.1.1.3 is checked first; if no response, then the server at 10.1.1.4 is checked.

   d. None of these answers is correct.

2. Using the same exhibit and conditions as question 1, which of the following is true regarding the process and sequences for authentication of a user attempting to log in through the console?

   a. A simple password of cisco will be required.

   b. The user will supply a username/password, which will be authenticated if either server 10.1.1.1 or 10.1.1.2 returns a RADIUS message approving the user.

   c. The username/password is presented to the RADIUS server at 10.1.1.3 first; if no response, then the server at 10.1.1.4 is checked next.

   d. None of these answers is correct.

3. Using the same exhibit and conditions as question 1, which of the following is true regarding the process and sequences for authentication of a user attempting to log in via Telnet?

   a. A simple password of cisco will be required.

   b. The router will attempt authentication with RADIUS server 10.1.1.1 first; if no response, then 10.1.1.2; if no response, then it will require password cisco.

   c. The router will attempt authentication with RADIUS server 10.1.1.1 first; if no response, then 10.1.1.2; if no response, then it will require a username/password of betty/barney.

   d. The username/password is presented to the RADIUS server at 10.1.1.3 first; if no response, then the server at 10.1.1.4 is checked next.

   e. If neither 10.1.1.1 nor 10.1.1.2 respond, the user cannot be authenticated and is rejected.

   f. None of the other answers is correct.

4. Which of the following are considered best practices for Layer 2 security?

   a. Inspect ARP messages to prevent hackers from causing hosts to create incorrect ARP table entries.

   b. Enable port security.

   c. Put all management traffic in VLAN 1, but no user traffic.

   d. Configure DTP to use the auto setting.

   e. Shut down unused ports.

5. Assuming a Cisco 3550 switch, which of the following is true regarding the port security feature?

   a. The default maximum number of MACs allowed to be reached on an interface is three.

   b. Sticky-learned MAC addresses are automatically added to the startup configuration once they are learned the first time.

   c. Dynamic (non-sticky) learned MAC addresses are added to the running configuration, but they can be saved using the **copy run start** command.

   d. A port must be set to be a static access or trunking port for port security to be allowed on the interface.

   e. None of the other answers is correct.

6. Which of the following is true regarding the use of IEEE 802.1X for LAN user authentication?

    a. The EAPoL protocol is used between the authenticator and authentication server.

    b. The supplicant is client software on the user's device.

    c. A switch acts in the role of 802.1X authentication server.

    d. The only traffic allowed to exit a currently unauthenticated 802.1X port are 802.1X-related messages.

7. The following ACE is typed into configuration mode on a router: **access-list 1 permit 10.44.38.0 0.0.3.255**. If this statement had instead used a different mask, with nothing else changed, which of the following choices for mask would result in a match for source IP address 10.44.40.18?

    a. 0.0.1.255

    b. 0.0.5.255

    c. 0.0.7.255

    d. 0.0.15.255

8. An enterprise uses a registered class A network. A smurf attack occurs from the Internet, with the enterprise receiving lots of ICMP Echoes, destined to subnet broadcast address 9.1.1.255, which is the broadcast address of an actual deployed subnet (9.1.1.0/24) in the enterprise. The packets all have a source address of 9.1.1.1. Which of the following tools might help mitigate the effects of the attack?

    a. Ensure that the **no ip directed-broadcast** command is configured on the router interfaces connected to the 9.1.1.0/24 subnet.

    b. Configure an RPF check so that the packets would be rejected based on the invalid source IP address.

    c. Routers will not forward packets to subnet broadcast addresses, so there is no need for concern in this case.

    d. Filter all packets sent to addresses in subnet 9.1.1.0/24.

9. Which of the following statements is true regarding the router Cisco IOS Software TCP intercept feature?

    a. Always acts as a proxy for incoming TCP connections, completing the client-side connection, and only then creating a server-side TCP connection.

    b. Can monitor TCP connections for volume and for incomplete connections, as well as serve as a TCP proxy.

    c. If enabled, must operate on all TCP connection requests entering a particular interface.

    d. None of the other answers is correct.

Foundation Topics

Router and Switch Device Security

Securing access to a router or switch CLI is one of the first steps in securing a routed/switched network. Cisco includes several basic mechanisms appropriate for protecting devices in a lab, as well as more robust security features appropriate for devices deployed in production environments. Additionally, these same base authentication features can be used to authenticate dial PPP users. The first section of this chapter examines each of these topics.

Simple Password Protection for the CLI

Figure 18-1 provides a visual reminder of some hopefully familiar details about how users can reach a router's CLI user mode, and move into enable (privileged) mode using the **enable** command.

Figure 18-1 *Router User and Enable Modes*

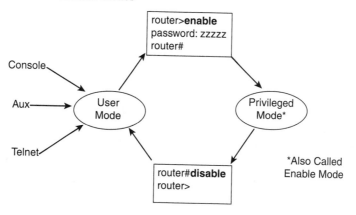

Figure 18-1 shows three methods to reach user mode on a router. The figure also applies to Cisco IOS–based switches, except that Cisco switches do not have auxiliary ports.

Cisco IOS can be configured to require simple password protection for each of the three methods to access user mode. To do so, the **login** line subcommand is used to tell Cisco IOS to prompt the user for a password, and the **password** command defines the password. The configuration mode implies for which of the three access methods the password should be required. Example 18-1 shows a simple example.

Example 18-1   *Simple User Mode CLI Password Protection*

```
! The login and password commands under line con 0 tell the router to supply a password
! prompt, and define the password required at the console port, respectively.
line con 0
 login
 password fred
!
line vty 0 15
 login
 password barney
```

These passwords are stored as clear text in the configuration, but they can be encrypted by including the **service password-encryption** global command. Example 18-2 shows the results of adding this command.

Example 18-2   *Using the* **service password-encryption** *Command*

```
! The service password-encryption global command causes all existing clear-text
! passwords in the running config to be encrypted.
service password-encryption
! The "7" in the password commands means that the following value is the
! encrypted password per the service password-encryption command.
line con 0
 password 7 05080F1C2243
 login
line vty 0 4
 password 7 00071A150754
 login
```

Note that when the **service password-encryption** command is added to the configuration, all clear-text passwords in the running configuration are changed to an encrypted value. The passwords in the startup configuration are not changed until the **copy running-config startup-config** (or **write memory** for all you fellow old-timers out there) command has been used to save the configuration. Also, after disabling password encryption (**no service password-encryption**), passwords are not automatically decrypted—instead, Cisco IOS waits for a password to be changed before listing the password in its unencrypted form.

Note that the encryption used by the **service password-encryption** command is weak. Publicly available tools can decrypt the password. The encryption is useful to prevent the curious from logging into a router or switch, but it provides no real protection against even a hacker with modest ability.

Better Protection of Enable and Username Passwords

The password required by the **enable** command can be defined by either the **enable password** *pw* command or the **enable secret** *pw* command. If both are configured, the **enable exec** command only accepts the password defined in the **enable secret** command.

The password in the **enable password** command follows the same encryption rules as login passwords, only being encrypted if the **service password-encryption** command is configured. However, the **enable secret** password is not affected by **service password-encryption**. Instead, it is always stored as an MD5-hashed value, instead of being encrypted, resulting in a much harder to break password. Example 18-3 shows how Cisco IOS represents this subtle difference in how the password values are stored.

Example 18-3 *Differences in Hashed/Encrypted Enable Passwords*

```
! The enable password lists a 7 in the output to signify an encrypted value
! per the service password-encryption command; the
! enable secret command lists a 5, signifying an MD5-hashed value.
service password-encryption
!
enable secret 5 $1$GvDM$ux/PhTwSscDNOyNIyr5Be/
enable password 7 070C285F4D064B
```

The **username** *name* **password** *password* command has a feature similar to the **enable secret** command. The **service password-encryption** command encrypts the password listed in the **username** *name* **password** *password* command; however, the **username** *name* **secret** *password* command uses the same MD5 hash as the **enable secret** command to better protect the password. And, as with **enable secret**, a 5 is listed in the command as stored in the configuration—for example, **username barney secret 5 1oMnb$EGf1zE5QPip4UW7TTqQTR**.

User Mode and Privileged Mode AAA Authentication

The term *authentication, authorization, and accounting (AAA)* refers to a variety of common security features. This section focuses on the first "A" in AAA—authentication—and how it is used to manage access to a router or IOS switch's user mode and privileged mode.

The strongest authentication method to protect the CLI is to use a TACACS+ or RADIUS server. The *Cisco Secure Access Control Server (ACS)* is a Cisco Systems software product that can be installed on Unix, Linux, and several Windows platforms, holding the set of usernames and passwords used for authentication. The routers and switches then need to receive the username and password from the user, send it as encrypted traffic to the server, and receive a reply—either accepting or rejecting the user. Table 18-2 summarizes some of the key facts about RADIUS and TACACS+.

Table 18-2 *Comparing RADIUS and TACACS+ for Authentication*

	RADIUS	**TACACS+**
Scope of Encryption: packet payload or just the password	Password only	Entire payload
Layer 4 Protocol	UDP	TCP
Well-Known Port/IOS Default Port Used for authentication	1812/1645[1]	49/49
Standard or Cisco-Proprietary	RFC 2865	Proprietary

[1]Radius originally defined port 1645 as the well-known port, which was later changed to port 1812.

Using a Default Set of Authentication Methods

AAA authentication configuration includes commands by which a set of authentication methods is defined. A single *authentication method* is exactly what it sounds like—a way to authenticate a user. For example, one method is to ask a RADIUS server to authenticate a login user; another is to let a router look at a set of locally defined **username** commands. A set of configuration methods represents an ordered list of authentication methods, each of which is tried in order until one of the methods returns an authentication response, either accepting or rejecting the user.

The simplest AAA configuration defines a default set of authentication methods used for all router or switch logins, plus a second set of default authentication methods used by the **enable** command. The defined default login authentication methods apply to all login access—console, Telnet, and aux (routers only). The default authentication methods used by the **enable** command simply dictate what Cisco IOS does when a user types the **enable** command. The overall configuration uses the following general steps:

Step 1   Enable AAA authentication with the **aaa new-model** global command.

Step 2   If using RADIUS or TACACS+, define the IP address(es) and encryption keys used by the server(s) by using the **radius-server host**, **radius-server key**, **tacacs-server host**, and **tacacs-server key** commands.

Step 3   Define the default set of authentication methods used for all CLI access by using the **aaa authentication login default** command.

Step 4   Define the default set of authentication methods used for enable-mode access by using the **aaa authentication enable default** command.

Example 18-4 shows a sample router configuration using these commands. In this case, two RADIUS servers are configured. One of the servers uses the Cisco IOS default port of 1645, and the other uses the reserved well-known port 1812. Per the following configuration, this router attempts the following authentication:

■ When a login attempt is made, Cisco IOS attempts authentication using the first RADIUS server; if there's no response, IOS tries the second RADIUS server; if there's no response, the user is allowed in (authentication mode **none**).

■ When any user issues the **enable** command, the router tries the RADIUS servers, in order; if none of the RADIUS servers replies, the router will accept the single username/password configured on the router of **cisco/cisco**.

Example 18-4   *Differences in Hashed/Encrypted Enable Passwords*

```
! The next command shows that the enable secret password is still configured,
! but it will not be used. The username command defines a user/password that
! will be used for enable authentication if the RADIUS servers are not reachable.
! Note that the 0 in the username command means the password is not encrypted.
```

Example 18-4 *Differences in Hashed/Encrypted Enable Passwords (Continued)*

```
R1# show running-config
! lines omitted for brevity
enable secret 5 $1$GvDM$ux/PhTwSscDNOyNIyr5Be/
username cisco password 0 cisco
! Next, AAA is enabled, and the default enable and login authentication is
! defined.
aaa new-model
aaa authentication enable default group radius local
aaa authentication login default group radius none
! Next, the two RADIUS servers are configured. The port numbers were omitted when
! the radius-server host 10.1.1.2 command was issued, and IOS filled in its
! default. Similarly, radius-server host 10.1.1.1 auth-port 1812 was issued,
! with IOS adding the accounting port number default into the command.
radius-server host 10.1.1.1 auth-port 1812 acct-port 1646
radius-server host 10.1.1.2 auth-port 1645 acct-port 1646
radius-server key cisco
! Before adding AAA configuration, both the console and vtys had both the login
! and password commands as listed in Example 18-1. The act of enabling AAA
! deleted the login command, which now by default uses the settings on global
! command aaa authentication login default. The passwords remaining below would
! be used only if the aaa authentication login command listed a method of "line."
line con 0
 password cisco
line vty 0 4
 password cisco
```

Using Multiple Authentication Methods

AAA authentication allows reference to multiple servers and to multiple authentication methods so that a user can be authenticated even if one authentication method is not working. The **aaa authentication** command supports up to four methods on a single command. Additionally, there is no practical limit to the number of RADIUS or TACACS+ servers that can be referenced in a RADIUS or TACACS+ server group. The logic used by Cisco IOS when using these methods is as follows:

Key
Topic

■ Use the first listed method first; if that method does not respond, move on to the next, and then the next, and so on until a method responds. Use the first-responding-method's decision (allow or reject).

■ If a method refers to a set of more than one server, try the first server, with "first" being based on the order of the commands in the configuration file. If no response, move on to the next sequential server, and so on, until a server responds. Use the first-responding-server's decision (allow or reject).

■ If no response occurs for any method, reject the request.

For example, Example 18-4 listed RADIUS servers 10.1.1.1 and 10.1.1.2, in that order, so those servers would be checked in that same order. If neither replies, then the next method would be used—**none** for login sessions (meaning automatically allow the user in), and **local** (meaning authenticate based on configured **username** commands).

Table 18-3 lists the authentication methods allowed for login and enable (privileged exec) mode, along with a brief description.

Table 18-3 *Authentication Methods for Login and Enable*

Method	Meaning
group radius	Use the configured RADIUS servers
group tacacs+	Use the configured TACACS+ servers
group *name*	Use a defined group of either RADIUS or TACACS+ servers
enable	Use the enable password, based on **enable secret** or **enable password** commands
line[1]	Use the password defined by the **password** command in **line** configuration mode
local	Use **username** commands in the local configuration; treats the username as case insensitive, but the password as case sensitive
local-case	Use **username** commands in the local configuration; treats both the username and password as case sensitive
none	No authentication required; user is automatically authenticated

[1]Cannot be used for enable authentication.

Groups of AAA Servers

By default, Cisco IOS automatically groups RADIUS and TACACS+ servers configured with the **radius-server host** and **tacacs-server host** commands into groups, aptly named *radius* and *tacacs+*. The **aaa authentication** command includes the keywords **group radius** or **group tacacs+** to refer to these default groups. By default, all defined RADIUS servers end up in the radius group, and all defined TACACS+ servers end up in the tacacs+ group.

In some cases, particularly with larger-scale dial implementations, a design may call for the separation of different sets of RADIUS or TACACS+ servers. To do so, servers can be grouped by name. Example 18-5 shows an example configuration with two servers in a RADIUS group named fred, and shows how the **aaa authentication** command can refer to the group.

Example 18-5 *Configuring a RADIUS Server Group*

```
! The next three commands create RADIUS group fred. Note that the servers are
! configured inside AAA group config mode, using the server subcommand. Note that
! IOS added the auth-port and acct-port parameters automatically.
```

Example 18-5 *Configuring a RADIUS Server Group (Continued)*

```
R1(config)# aaa group server radius fred
R1(config-group)# server 10.1.1.3 auth-port 1645 acct-port 1646
R1(config-group)# server 10.1.1.4 auth-port 1645 acct-port 1646
! To use group fred instead of the default group, the aaa authentication
! commands need to refer to group fred, as shown next.
aaa new-model
aaa authentication enable default group fred local
aaa authentication login default group fred none
```

Overriding the Defaults for Login Security

The console, vty, and aux (routers only) lines can override the use of the default login authentication methods. To do so, in line configuration mode, the **login authentication** *name* command is used to point to a named set of configuration methods. Example 18-6 shows a named group of configuration methods called **for-console**, **for-vty**, and **for-aux**, with each applied to the related login method. Each of the named groups defines a different set of authentication methods. Example 18-6 shows an example that implements the following requirements:

- **console**—Try the RADIUS servers, and use the line password if no response

- **vty**—Try the RADIUS servers, and use local usernames/passwords if no response

- **aux**—Try the RADIUS servers, and do not authenticate if no response

Example 18-6 *Overriding the Default Login Authentication Method*

```
! The configuration shown here has been added to the configuration from earlier
! examples.
aaa authentication login for-console group radius line
aaa authentication login for-vty group radius local
aaa authentication login for-aux group radius
! The methods are enabled below with the login authentication commands. Note that
! the local passwords still exist on the console and vtys; for the console,
! that password would be used (based on the line keyword in the aaa
! authentication command above) if the RADIUS servers are all nonresponsive.
! However, the vty password command would not be used by this configuration.
line con 0
 password 7 14141B180F0B
 login authentication for-console
line aux 0
 login authentication for-aux
line vty 0 4
 password 7 104D000A0618
 login authentication for-vty
```

PPP Security

PPP provides the capability to use PAP and CHAP for authentication, which is particularly useful for dial applications. The default authentication method for CHAP/PAP is the reliance on a locally configured set of **username** *name* **password** *password* commands.

Cisco IOS supports the use of AAA authentication for PPP using the same general set of commands as used for login authentication. The configuration steps are as follows:

Step 1 Just as with login authentication, enable AAA authentication with the **aaa new-model** global command.

Step 2 Just as with login authentication, if used, configure RADIUS and/or TACACS+ servers, using the same commands and syntax as used for login and enable authentication.

Step 3 Similar to login authentication, define PPP to use a default set of authentication methods with the **aaa authentication ppp default** command. (The only difference is that the **ppp** keyword is used instead of **login**.)

Step 4 Similar to login authentication, use the **aaa authentication ppp** *list-name method1* [*method2*...] command to create a named group of methods that can be used instead of the default set.

Step 5 To use a named group of authentication methods instead of the default set, use the **ppp authentication** {*protocol1* [*protocol2*...]} *list-name* command. For example, the command **ppp authentication chap fred** references the authentication methods defined by the **aaa authentication ppp fred** command.

Layer 2 Security

The Cisco SAFE Blueprint document (available at http://www.cisco.com/go/safe) suggests a wide variety of best practices for switch security. In most cases, the recommendations depend on one of three general characterizations of the switch ports, as follows:

- **Unused ports**—Switch ports that are not yet connected to any device—for example, switch ports that are pre-cabled to a faceplate in an empty cubicle

- **User ports**—Ports cabled to end-user devices, or any cabling drop that sits in some physically unprotected area

- **Trusted ports or trunk ports**—Ports connected to fully trusted devices, like other switches known to be located in an area with good physical security

The following list summarizes the best practices that apply to both unused and user ports. The common element between these types of ports is that a malicious person can gain access once they get inside the building, without having to gain further access behind the locked door to a wiring closet or data center.

- Disable unneeded dynamic protocols like CDP and DTP.

- Disable trunking by configuring these ports as access ports.

- Enable BPDU Guard and Root Guard to prevent STP attacks and keep a stable STP topology.

- Use either Dynamic ARP Inspection (DAI) or private VLANs to prevent frame sniffing.

- Enable port security to at least limit the number of allowed MAC addresses, and possibly restrict the port to use only specific MAC addresses.

- Use 802.1X user authentication.

- Use DHCP snooping and IP Source Guard to prevent DHCP DoS and man-in-the-middle attacks.

Besides the preceding recommendations specifically for unused ports and user ports, the Cisco SAFE Blueprint makes the following additional recommendations:

- For any port (including trusted ports), consider the general use of private VLANs to further protect the network from sniffing, including preventing routers or L3 switches from routing packets between devices in the private VLAN.

- Configure VTP authentication globally on each switch to prevent DoS attacks.

- Disable unused switch ports and place them in an unused VLAN.

- Avoid using VLAN 1.

- For trunks, do not use the native VLAN.

The rest of this section's coverage of switch security addresses the points in these two lists of best practices, with the next subsection focusing on best practices for unused and user ports (based on the first list), and the following subsection focusing on the general best practices (based on the second list).

Switch Security Best Practices for Unused and User Ports

The first three items in the list of best practices for unused and user ports are mostly covered in earlier chapters. For a brief review, Example 18-7 shows an example configuration on a Cisco 3550 switch, with each of these items configured and noted. In this example, fa0/1 is a currently unused port. CDP has been disabled on the interface, but it remains enabled globally, on the presumption that some ports still need CDP enabled. DTP has been disabled as well, and STP Root Guard and BPDU Guard are enabled.

Example 18-7 *Disabling CDP and DTP and Enabling Root Guard and BPDU Guard*

```
! The cdp run command keeps CDP enabled globally, but it has been disabled on
! fa0/1, the unused port.
cdp run
int fa0/0
 no cdp enable
! The switchport mode access interface subcommand prevents the port from trunking,
! and the switchport nonegotiate command prevents any DTP messages
! from being sent or processed.
 switchport mode access
 switchport nonegotiate
! The last two interface commands enable Root Guard and BPDU Guard, per interface,
! respectively. BPDU Guard can also be enabled for all ports with PortFast
! enabled by configuring the spanning-tree portfast bpduguard enable global
! command.
 spanning-tree guard root
 spanning-tree bpduguard enable
```

Port Security

Switch port security monitors a port to restrict the number of MAC addresses associated with that port in the Layer 2 switching table. It can also enforce a restriction for only certain MAC addresses to be reachable out the port.

To implement port security, the switch adds more logic to its normal process of examining incoming frames. Instead of automatically adding a Layer 2 switching table entry for the source MAC and port number, the switch considers the port security configuration and whether it allows that entry. By preventing MACs from being added to the switch table, port security can prevent the switch from forwarding frames to those MACs on a port.

Port security supports the following key features:

- Limiting the number of MACs that can be associated with the port

- Limiting the actual MAC addresses associated with the port, based on three methods:

  — Static configuration of the allowed MAC addresses

  — Dynamic learning of MAC addresses, up to the defined maximum, where dynamic entries are lost upon reload

  — Dynamically learning but with the switch saving those entries in the configuration (called *sticky learning*)

Port security protects against a couple of types of attacks. Once a switch's forwarding table fills, the switch times out older entries. When the switch receives frames destined for those MACs that are no longer in the table, the switch floods the frames out all ports. An attacker could cause the switch to fill its switching table by sending lots of frames, each with a different source MAC, forcing the switch to time out the entries for most or all of the legitimate hosts. As a result, the switch floods legitimate frames because the destination MACs are no longer in the CAM, allowing the attacker to see all the frames.

An attacker could also claim to be the same MAC address as a legitimate user by simply sending a frame with that same MAC address. As a result, the switch would update its switching table, and send frames to the attacker, as shown in Figure 18-2.

Figure 18-2 *Claiming to Use Another Host's MAC Address*

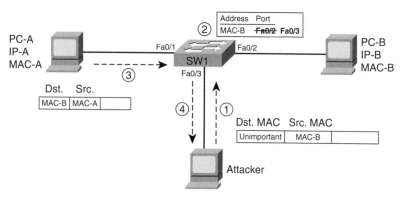

1. Attacker sources frame using PC-B's actual MAC.
2. SW1 updates its MAC address table.
3. Another frame is sent to destination MAC-B.
4. SW1 forwards frame to attacker.

Port security prevents both styles of these attacks by limiting the number of MAC addresses and by limiting MACs to particular ports. Port security configuration requires just a few configuration steps, all in interface mode. The commands are summarized in Table 18-4.

Table 18-4 *Port Security Configuration Commands*

Command	Purpose
switchport mode {**access** I **trunk**}	Port security requires that the port be statically set as either access or trunking
switchport port-security [**maximum** *value*]	Enables port security on an interface, and optionally defines the number of allowed MAC addresses on the port (default 1)
switchport port-security mac-address *mac-address* [**vlan** {*vlan-id* I {**access** I **voice**}}	Statically defines an allowed MAC address, for a particular VLAN (if trunking), and for either the access or voice VLAN

continues

Table 18-4   *Port Security Configuration Commands (Continued)*

Command	Purpose
switchport port-security mac-address sticky	Tells the switch to remember the dynamically learned MAC addresses
**switchport port-security [aging] [violation {protect	restrict	shutdown}]**	Defines the Aging timer and actions taken when a violation occurs

Of the commands in Table 18-4, only the first two are required for port security. With just those two commands, a port allows the first-learned MAC address to be used, but no others. If that MAC address times out of the CAM, another MAC address may be learned on that port, but only one is allowed at a time.

The next two commands in the table allow for the definition of MAC addresses. The third command statically defines the permitted MAC addresses, and the fourth command allows for sticky learning. Sticky learning tells the switch to learn the MACs dynamically, but then add the MACs to the running configuration. This allows port security to be enabled and existing MAC addresses to be learned, but then have them locked into the configuration as static entries simply by saving the running configuration. (Note that the **switchport port-security maximum** *x* command would be required to allow more than one MAC address, with x being the maximum number.)

The last command in the table tells the switch what to do when violations occur. The **protect** option simply tells the switch to perform port security. The **restrict** option tells it to also send SNMP traps and issue log messages regarding the violation. Finally, the **shutdown** option puts the port in a err-disabled state, and requires a **shutdown/no shutdown** combination on the port to recover the port's forwarding state.

Example 18-8 shows a sample configuration, based on Figure 18-3. In the figure, Server 1 and Server 2 are the only devices that should ever be connected to interfaces Fast Ethernet 0/1 and 0/2, respectively. In this case, a rogue device has attempted to connect to fa0/1.

Figure 18-3   *Port Security Configuration Example*

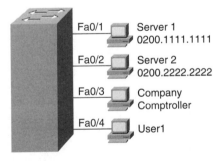

Fa0/1 — Server 1 0200.1111.1111
Fa0/2 — Server 2 0200.2222.2222
Fa0/3 — Company Comptroller
Fa0/4 — User1

Example 18-8 *Using Port Security to Define Correct MAC Addresses Connected to Particular Interfaces*

```
! FA0/1 has been configured to use a static MAC address, defaulting to allow
! only one MAC address.
interface FastEthernet0/1
 switchport mode access
 switchport port-security
 switchport port-security mac-address 0200.1111.1111
! FA0/2 has been configured to use a sticky-learned MAC address, defaulting to
! allow only one MAC address.
interface FastEthernet0/2
 switchport mode access
 switchport port-security
 switchport port-security mac-address sticky
! FA0/1 shows as err-disabled, as a device that was not 0200.1111.1111 tried to
! connect. The default violation mode is shutdown, as shown. It also lists the
! fact that a single MAC address is configured, that the maximum number of MAC
! addresses is 1, and that there are 0 sticky-learned MACs.
fred# show port-security interface fastEthernet 0/1
Port Security : Enabled
Port status : Err-Disabled
Violation mode : Shutdown
Maximum MAC Addresses : 1
Total MAC Addresses : 1
Configured MAC Addresses : 1
Sticky MAC Addresses : 0
Aging time : 0 mins
Aging type : Absolute
SecureStatic address aging : Disabled
Security Violation count : 1
! FA0/2 shows as SecureUp, meaning that port security has not seen any violations
! on this port. Note also at the end of the stanza that the security violations
! count is 0. It lists the fact that one sticky MAC address has been learned.
fred# show port-security interface fastEthernet 0/2
Port Security : Enabled
Port status : SecureUp
Violation mode : Shutdown
Maximum MAC Addresses : 1
Total MAC Addresses : 1
Configured MAC Addresses : 0
Sticky MAC Addresses : 1
Aging time : 0 mins
Aging type : Absolute
SecureStatic address aging : Disabled
Security Violation count : 0
! Note the updated configuration in the switch. Due to the sticky option, the
! switch added the last shown configuration command.
```

Key Topic

continues

Example 18-8 *Using Port Security to Define Correct MAC Addresses Connected to Particular Interfaces (Continued)*

```
Fred# show running-config
(Lines omitted for brevity)
interface FastEthernet0/2
 switchport mode access
 switchport port-security
 switchport port-security mac-address sticky
 switchport port-security mac-address sticky 0200.2222.2222
```

The final part of the example shows that sticky learning updated the running configuration. The MAC address is stored in the running configuration, but it is stored in a command that also uses the **sticky** keyword, differentiating it from a truly statically configured MAC. Note that the switch does not automatically save the configuration in the startup-config file.

Dynamic ARP Inspection

A switch can use DAI to prevent certain types of attacks that leverage the use of IP ARP messages. To appreciate just how those attacks work, you need to keep in mind several detailed points about the contents of ARP messages. Figure 18-4 shows a simple example with the appropriate usage of ARP messages, with PC-A finding PC-B's MAC address.

Figure 18-4 *Normal Use of ARP, Including Ethernet Addresses and ARP Fields*

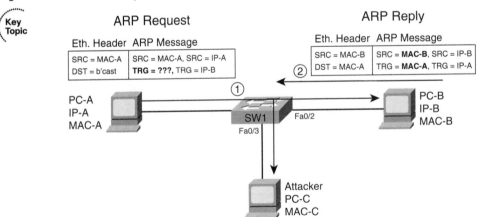

1. PC-A Sends ARP Broadcast Looking for IP-B's MAC Address (Target MAC)
2. PC-B Sends LAN Unicast ARP Reply

The ARP message itself does not include an IP header. However, it does include four important addressing fields: the source MAC and IP address of the sender of the message, and the target MAC and IP address. For an ARP request, the target IP lists the IP address whose MAC needs to be found, and the target MAC Address field is empty, as that is the missing information. Note that the ARP reply (a LAN unicast) uses the source MAC field to imply the MAC address value—for example, PC-B sets the source MAC inside the ARP message to its own MAC address, and the source IP to its own IP address.

An attacker can form a man-in-the-middle attack in a LAN by creative use of *gratuitous ARPs*. A gratuitous ARP occurs when a host sends an ARP reply, without even seeing an ARP request, and with a broadcast destination Ethernet address. The more typical ARP reply in Figure 18-4 shows the ARP reply as a unicast, meaning that only the host that sent the request will learn an ARP entry; by broadcasting the gratuitous ARP, all hosts on the LAN will learn an ARP entry.

While gratuitous ARPs can be used to good effect, they can also be used by an attacker. The attacker can send a gratuitous ARP, claiming to be an IP address of a legitimate host. All the hosts in the subnet (including routers and switches) update their ARP tables, pointing to the attacker's MAC address—and then later sending frames to the attacker instead of to the true host. Figure 18-5 depicts the process.

Figure 18-5 *Man-in-the-Middle Attack Using Gratuitous ARPs*

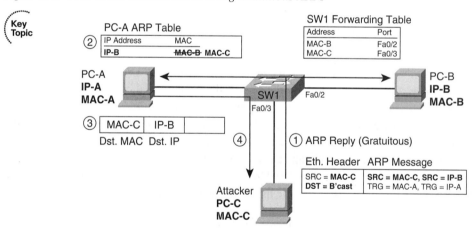

The steps shown in Figure 18-5 can be explained as follows:

1.   The attacker broadcasts gratuitous ARP listing IP-B, but with MAC-C as the source IP and MAC.

2.   PC-A updates its ARP table to list IP-B's associated address as MAC-C.

3.   PC-A sends a frame to IP-B, but with destination MAC MAC-C.

4.   SW1 forwards the frame to MAC-C, which is the attacker.

The attack results in other hosts, like PC-A, sending frames meant for IP-B to MAC address MAC-C—the attacker's PC. The attacker then simply forwards another copy of each frame to

PC-B, becoming a man in the middle. As a result, the user can continue to work, and the attacker can gain a much larger amount of data.

Switches use DAI to defeat ARP attacks by examining the ARP messages and then filtering inappropriate messages. DAI considers each switch port to be either untrusted (the default) or trusted, performing DAI messages only on untrusted ports. DAI examines each ARP request or reply (on untrusted ports) to decide if it is inappropriate; if inappropriate, the switch filters the ARP message. DAI determines if an ARP message is inappropriate by using the following logic:

1. If an ARP reply lists a source IP address that was not DHCP-assigned to a device off that port, DAI filters the ARP reply.

2. DAI uses additional logic like Step 1, but uses a list of statically defined IP/MAC address combinations for comparison.

3. For a received ARP reply, DAI compares the source MAC address in the Ethernet header to the source MAC address in the ARP message. These MACs should be equal in normal ARP replies; if they are not, DAI filters the ARP message.

4. Like Step 3, but DAI compares the destination Ethernet MAC and the target MAC listed in the ARP body.

5. DAI checks for unexpected IP addresses listed in the ARP message, such as 0.0.0.0, 255.255.255.255, multicasts, and so on.

Table 18-5 lists the key Cisco 3550 switch commands used to enable DAI. DAI must first be enabled globally. At that point, all ports are considered to be untrusted by DAI. Some ports, particularly ports connected to devices in secure areas (ports connecting servers, other switches, and so on), need to be explicitly configured as trusted. Then, additional configuration is required to enable the different logic options. For example, DHCP snooping needs to be enabled before DAI can use the DHCP snooping binding database to perform the logic in Step 1 in the preceding list. Optionally, you can configure static IP addresses, or perform additional validation (per the last three points in the preceding list) using the **ip arp inspection validate** command.

Table 18-5 *Cisco IOS Switch Dynamic ARP Inspection Commands*

Command	Purpose
ip arp inspection vlan *vlan-range*	Global command to enable DAI on this switch for the specified VLANs.
[**no**] **ip arp inspection trust**	Interface subcommand that enables (with **no** option) or disables DAI on the interface. Defaults to enabled once the **ip arp inspection** global command has been configured.
ip arp inspection filter *arp-acl-name* **vlan** *vlan-range* [**static**]	Global command to refer to an ARP ACL that defines static IP/MAC addresses to be checked by DAI for that VLAN (Step 2 in the preceding list).

Table 18-5 *Cisco IOS Switch Dynamic ARP Inspection Commands (Continued)*

Command	Purpose
ip arp inspection validate {[src-mac] [dst-mac] [ip]}	Enables additional optional checking of ARP messages (per Steps 3–5 in the preceding list).
ip arp inspection limit {**rate** *pps* [**burst interval** *seconds*] | **none**}	Limits the ARP message rate to prevent DoS attacks carried out by sending a large number or ARPs.

Because DAI causes the switch to perform more work, an attacker could attempt a DoS attack on a switch by sending large numbers of ARP messages. DAI automatically sets a limit of 15 ARP messages per port per second to mitigate that risk; the settings can be changed using the **ip arp inspection limit** interface subcommand.

DHCP Snooping

DHCP snooping prevents the damage inflicted by several attacks that use DHCP. DHCP snooping causes a switch to examine DHCP messages and filter those considered to be inappropriate. DHCP snooping also builds a table of IP address and port mappings, based on legitimate DHCP messages, called the *DHCP snooping binding table*. The DHCP snooping binding table can then be used by DAI and by the IP Source Guard feature.

Figure 18-6 shows a man-in-the-middle attack that leverages DHCP. The legitimate DHCP server sits at the main site, whereas the attacker sits on the local LAN, acting as a DHCP server.

Figure 18-6 *Man-in-the-Middle Attack Using DHCP*

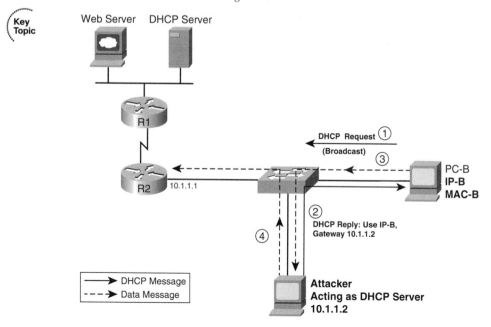

The following steps explain how the attacker's PC can become a man in the middle in Figure 18-6:

1. PC-B requests an IP address using DHCP.

2. The attacker PC replies, and assigns a good IP/mask, but using its own IP address as the default gateway.

3. PC-B sends data frames to the attacker, thinking that the attacker is the default gateway.

4. The attacker forwards copies of the packets, becoming a man in the middle.

NOTE   PC-B will use the first DHCP reply, so with the legitimate DHCP server only reachable over the WAN, the attacker's DHCP response should be the first response received by PC-B.

DHCP snooping defeats such attacks for ports it considers to be untrusted. DHCP snooping allows all DHCP messages on trusted ports, but it filters DHCP messages on untrusted ports. It operates based on the premise that only DHCP clients should exist on untrusted ports; as a result, the switch filters incoming DHCP messages that are only sent by servers. So, from a design perspective, unused and unsecured user ports would be configured as untrusted to DHCP snooping.

DHCP snooping also needs to examine the DHCP client messages on untrusted ports, because other attacks can be made using DHCP client messages. DHCP servers identify clients based on their stated *client hardware address* as listed in the DHCP request. A single device could pose as multiple devices by sending repeated DHCP requests, each with a different DHCP client hardware address. The legitimate DHCP server, thinking the requests are from different hosts, assigns an IP address for each request. The DHCP server will soon assign all IP addresses available for the subnet, preventing legitimate users from being assigned an address.

For untrusted ports, DHCP snooping uses the following general logic for filtering the packets:

1. It filters all messages sent exclusively by DHCP servers.

2. The switch checks DHCP *release* and *decline* messages against the DHCP snooping binding table; if the IP address in those messages is not listed with the port in the DHCP snooping binding table, the messages are filtered.

3. Optionally, it compares a DHCP request's client hardware address value with the source MAC address inside the Ethernet frame.

Of the three entries in this list, the first takes care of the fake DHCP server man-in-the-middle attack shown in Figure 18-6. The second item prevents an attacking host from releasing a legitimate host's DHCP lease, then attempting to request an address and be assigned the same IP address—thereby taking over any existing connections from the original host. Finally, the last item in the list prevents the DoS attack whereby a host attempts to allocate all the IP addresses that the DHCP server can assign in the subnet.

Table 18-6 lists the key configuration commands for configuring DHCP snooping on a Cisco 3550 switch.

Table 18-6 *Cisco IOS Switch Dynamic ARP Inspection Commands*

Command	Purpose
ip dhcp snooping vlan *vlan-range*	Global command to enable DHCP snooping for one or more VLANs
[**no**] **ip dhcp snooping trust**	Interface command to enable or disable a trust level on an interface; **no** version (enabled) is the default
ip dhcp snooping binding *mac-address* **vlan** *vlan-id* *ip-address* **interface** *interface-id* **expiry** *seconds*	Global command to add static entries to the DHCP snooping binding database
ip dhcp snooping verify mac-address	Interface subcommand to add the optional check of the Ethernet source MAC address to be equal to a DHCP request's client ID
ip dhcp snooping limit rate *rate*	Sets the maximum number of DHCP messages per second to mitigate DoS attacks

IP Source Guard

The Cisco IOS switch IP Source Guard feature adds one more check to the DHCP snooping logic. When enabled along with DHCP snooping, IP Source Guard checks the source IP address of received packets against the DHCP snooping binding database. Alternatively, it checks both the source IP and source MAC addresses against that same database. If the entries do not match, the frame is filtered.

To better appreciate this feature, consider the example DHCP snooping binding database shown in Example 18-9. Note that each of the entries lists the MAC address and IP address, VLAN, and interface. These entries were gleaned from ports untrusted by DHCP snooping, with the DHCP snooping feature building these entries based on the source MAC address and source IP address of the DHCP requests.

Example 18-9 *Sample DHCP Snooping Binding Database*

```
SW1# show ip dhcp snooping binding
Mac Address         Ip Address        Lease(sec)  Type           VLAN  Interface
------------------  ---------------   ----------  -------------  ----  ------------------
02:00:01:02:03:04   172.16.1.1        3412        dhcp-snooping  3     FastEthernet0/1
02:00:AA:BB:CC:DD   172.16.1.2        4916        dhcp-snooping  3     FastEthernet0/2
```

IP Source Guard is enabled using interface subcommands. To check just the source IP address, use the **ip verify source** interface subcommand; alternately, the **ip verify source port-security** interface subcommand enables checking of both the source IP and MAC addresses. Optionally, you can use the **ip source binding** *mac-address* **vlan** *vlan-id ip-address* **interface** *interface-id* global command to create static entries that will be used in addition to the DHCP snooping binding database. For example, with IP Source Guard enabled using the **ip verify source** command under interface fa0/1, the only packets allowed coming into interface fa0/1 would be those with source IP address 172.16.1.1.

802.1X Authentication Using EAP

Switches can use IEEE 802.1X to perform user authentication, rather than the types of device authentication performed by many of the other features described in this section. User authentication requires the user to supply a username and password, verified by a RADIUS server, before the switch will enable the switch port for normal user traffic. Requiring a username and password prevents the attacker from simply using someone else's PC to attack the network without first breaking the 802.1X authentication username and password.

IEEE 802.1X defines some of the details of LAN user authentication, but it also uses the Extensible Authentication Protocol (EAP), an Internet standard (RFC 3748), as the underlying protocol used for authentication. EAP includes the protocol messages by which the user can be challenged to provide a password, as well as flows that create one-time passwords (OTPs) per RFC 2289. Figure 18-7 shows the overall flow of LAN user authentication, without the details behind each message.

Figure 18-7 *802.1X for LAN User Authentication*

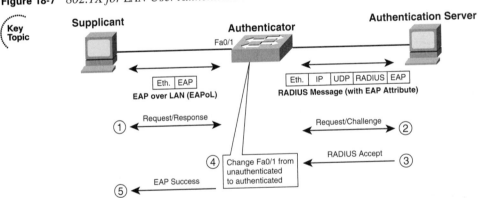

Figure 18-7 introduces a couple of general concepts plus several new terms. First, EAP messages are encapsulated directly inside an Ethernet frame when sent between the 802.1X *supplicant* (user device) and the 802.1X *authenticator* (switch). These frames are called *EAP over LAN (EAPoL)* frames. However, RADIUS expects the EAP message as a data structure called a *RADIUS attribute*, with these attributes sitting inside a normal RADIUS message. To support the two protocols, the switch translates between EAPoL and RADIUS for messages that need to flow between the supplicant and authentication server.

The rest of Figure 18-7 shows a simplistic view of the overall authentication flow. The switch and supplicant create an OTP using a temporary key, with the switch then forwarding the authentication request to the authentication server. The switch, as authenticator, must be aware of the results (Step 3), because the switch has a duty to enable the port once authenticated.

The 802.1X roles shown in Figure 18-7 are summarized as follows:

- **Supplicant**—The 802.1X driver that supplies a username/password prompt to the user and sends/receives the EAPoL messages

- **Authenticator**—Translates between EAPoL and RADIUS messages in both directions, and enables/disables ports based on the success/failure of authentication

- **Authentication server**—Stores usernames/passwords and verifies that the correct values were submitted before authenticating the user

802.1X switch configuration resembles the AAA configuration covered in the section titled "Using a Default Set of Authentication Methods" earlier in this chapter. The switch configuration treats 802.1X user authentication as another option for AAA authentication, using the following steps:

Step 1   As with other AAA authentication methods, enable AAA with the **aaa new-model** global command.

Step 2   As with other configurations using RADIUS servers, define the RADIUS server(s) IP address(es) and encryption key(s) using the **radius-server host** and **radius-server key** commands.

Step 3   Similar to login authentication configuration, define the 802.1X authentication method (RADIUS only today) using the **aaa authentication dot1x default** command or, for multiple groups, the **aaa authentication dot1x group** *name* global command.

Step 4   Enable 802.1X globally using the **dot1x system auth-control** global command.

Step 5   Set each interface to use one of three operational settings using the **dot1x port-control {auto | force-authorized | force-unauthorized}** interface subcommand:

- Using 802.1X (**auto**)

- Not using 802.1X, but the interface is automatically authorized (**force-authorized**) (default)

- Not using 802.1X, but the interface is automatically unauthorized (**force-unauthorized**)

Example 18-10 shows a simple 802.1X configuration on a Cisco 3550 switch. The example shows a reasonable configuration based on Figure 18-3 earlier in the chapter, with servers off ports fa0/1 and fa0/2, and two users off ports fa0/3 and fa0/4. Also, consider fa0/5 as an unused port. Note that at the time of this writing, RADIUS is the only available authentication method for 802.1X in the Cisco 3550 and 3560 switches.

Example 18-10 *Example Cisco 3550 802.1X Configuration*

```
! The first three commands enable AAA, define that 802.1x should use the RADIUS
! group comprised of all defined RADIUS servers, and enable 802.1X globally.
aaa new-model
aaa authentication dot1x default group radius
dot1x system auth-control
! Next, commands shown previously are used to define the default radius group.
! These commands are unchanged compared to earlier examples.
radius-server host 10.1.1.1 auth-port 1812 acct-port 1646
radius-server host 10.1.1.2 auth-port 1645 acct-port 1646
radius-server key cisco
! The server ports (fa0/1 and fa0/2), inside a secure datacenter, do not require
! 802.1x authentication.
int fa0/1
 dot1x port-control force-authorized
int fa0/2
 dot1x port-control force-authorized
! The client ports (fa0/3 and fa0/4) require 802.1x authentication.
int fa0/3
 dot1x port-control auto
int fa0/4
 dot1x port-control auto
! The unused port (fa0/5) is configured to be in a permanently unauthorized
! state until the dot1x port-control command is reconfigured for this port. As
! such, the port will only allow CDP, STP, and EAPoL frames.
int fa0/5
 dot1x port-control force-unauthorized
```

Storm Control

Cisco IOS for Catalyst switches supports rate-limiting traffic at Layer 2 using the **storm-control** commands. Storm control can be configured to set rising and falling thresholds for each of the three types of port traffic: unicast, multicast, and broadcast. Each rate limit can be configured on a per-port basis.

You can configure storm control to operate on each traffic type based on either packet rate or a percentage of the interface bandwidth. You can also specify rising and falling thresholds for each traffic type. If you don't specify a falling threshold, or if the falling threshold is the same as the rising threshold, the switch port will forward all traffic up to the configured limit and will not wait for that traffic to pass a specified falling threshold before forwarding it again.

When any of the configured thresholds is passed, the switch can take any of three additional actions, also on a per-port basis. The first, and the default, is that the switch can rate-limit by discarding excess traffic according to the configured command(s) and take no further action. The other two actions include performing the rate-limiting function and either shutting down the port or sending an SNMP trap.

Let's say we have the following goals for a storm-control configuration:

- Limit broadcast traffic to 100 packets per second. When broadcast traffic drops back to 50 packets per second, begin forwarding broadcast traffic again.

- Limit multicast traffic to 0.5 percent of the 100-Mbps interface rate, or 500 kbps. When multicast traffic drops back to 400 kbps, begin forwarding multicast traffic again.

- Limit unicast traffic to 80 percent of the 100-Mbps interface rate, or 80 Mbps. Forward all unicast traffic up to this limit.

- When any of these three conditions occurs and results in rate-limiting, send an SNMP trap.

The configuration that results is shown in Example 18-11.

Example 18-11 *Storm Control Configuration Example*

```
Cat3560(config)# interface FastEthernet0/10
Cat3560(config-if)# storm-control broadcast level pps 100 50
Cat3560(config-if)# storm-control multicast level 0.50 0.40
Cat3560(config-if)# storm-control unicast level 80.00
Cat3560(config-if)# storm-control action trap
Cat3560(config-if)# end
Cat3560# show storm-control fa0/10 unicast
Interface  Filter State   Upper        Lower         Current
---------  -------------  -----------  -----------   ----------
Fa0/10     Forwarding     80.00%       80.00%        0.00%
Cat3560# show storm-control fa0/10 broadcast
Interface  Filter State   Upper        Lower         Current
---------  -------------  -----------  -----------   ----------
Fa0/10     Forwarding     100 pps      50 pps        0 pps
Cat3560# show storm-control fa0/10 multicast
Interface  Filter State   Upper        Lower         Current
---------  -------------  -----------  -----------   ----------
Fa0/10     Forwarding     0.50%        0.40%         0.00%
Jun 10 14:24:47.595: %STORM_CONTROL-3-FILTERED: A Multicast storm detected on
    Fa0/19. A packet filter action has been applied on the interface.
! The preceding output indicates that the multicast storm threshold was
! exceeded and the switch took the action of sending
! an SNMP trap to indicate this condition.
```

One important caveat about storm control is that it supports only physical ports. The configuration commands are available on EtherChannel (port-channel) interfaces, but they have no effect.

General Layer 2 Security Recommendations

Recall that the beginning of the "Layer 2 Security" section outlined the Cisco SAFE Blueprint recommendations for user and unused ports and some general recommendations. The general recommendations include configuring VTP authentication globally on each switch, putting unused switch ports in an unused VLAN, and simply not using VLAN 1. The underlying configuration for each of these general recommendations is covered in Chapter 2.

Additionally, Cisco recommends not using the native VLANs on trunks. The reason is that in some cases, an attacker on an access port might be able to hop from its access port VLAN to a trunk's native VLAN by sending frames that begin with multiple 802.1Q headers. This attack has been proven to be ineffective against Cisco switches; however, the attack takes advantage of unfortunate sequencing of programming logic in how a switch processes frames, so best practices call for not using native VLANs on trunks anyway. Simply put, by following this best practice of not using the native VLAN, even if an attacker managed to hop VLANs, if there are no devices inside that native VLAN, no damage could be inflicted. In fact, Cisco goes on to suggest using a different native VLAN for each trunk, to further restrict this type of attack.

The last general Layer 2 security recommendation covered in this chapter is to consider the use of private VLANs to further restrict traffic. As covered in Chapter 2, private VLANs restrict hosts on some ports from sending frames directly to each other. Figure 18-8 shows the allowed flows as dashed lines. The absence of a line between two devices means that private VLANs would prevent them from communicating. For example, PC1 and PC2 are not allowed to send frames to one another.

Private VLANs are created with some number of promiscuous ports in the primary VLAN, with other isolated and community ports in one or more secondary VLANs. Isolated ports can send frames only to promiscuous ports, whereas community ports can send frames to promiscuous ports and other community ports in the same secondary VLAN.

Private VLANs could be applied generally for better security by making user ports isolated, only allowing them access to promiscuous ports like routers, servers, or other network services. However, other, more recent additions to Cisco switches, like DHCP snooping, DAI, and IP Source Guard, are typically better choices.

Figure 18-8 *Private VLAN Allowed Flows*

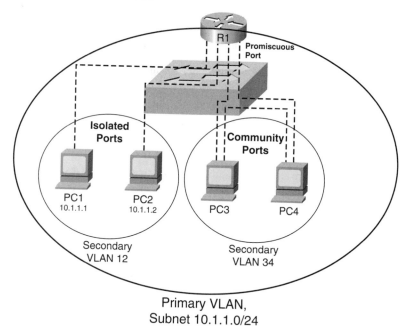

If private VLANs are used, Cisco also recommends additional protection against a trick by which an attacker can use the default gateway to overcome the protections provided by private VLANs. For example, in Figure 18-8, PC1 could send a frame with R1's destination MAC address, but with PC2's destination IP address (10.1.1.2). The switch forwards the frame to R1 because R1's port is promiscuous. R1 then routes the packet to PC2, effectively getting around the private VLAN intent. To solve such a problem, the router simply needs an inbound ACL on its LAN interface that denies traffic whose source and destination IP addresses are in the same local connected subnet. In this example, an **access-list 101 deny ip 10.1.1.0. 0.0.0.255 10.1.1.0 0.0.0.255** command would prevent this attack. (Of course, a few **permit** clauses would also be appropriate for the ACL.)

Layer 3 Security

The Cisco SAFE Blueprint also lists several best practices for Layer 3 security. The following list summarizes the key Layer 3 security recommendations from the SAFE Blueprint.

1. Enable secure Telnet access to a router user interface, and consider using Secure Shell (SSH) instead of Telnet.

2. Enable SNMP security, particularly adding SNMPv3 support.

3. Turn off all unnecessary services on the router platform.

4. Turn on logging to provide an audit trail.

5. Enable routing protocol authentication.

6. Enable the CEF forwarding path to avoid using flow-based paths like fast switching.

Additionally, RFCs 2827 and 3704 outline other recommended best practices for protecting routers, Layer 3 forwarding (IP routing), and the Layer 3 control plane (routing protocols). RFC 2827 addresses issues with the use of the IP Source and Destination fields in the IP header to form some kind of attack. RFC 3704 details some issues related to how the tools of 2827 may be best deployed over the Internet. Some of the details from those RFCs are as follows:

1. If a company has registered a particular IP prefix, packets with a source address inside that prefix should not be sent into that autonomous system from the Internet.

2. Packets should never have anything but a valid unicast source IP address, so packets with source IP addresses of loopback (127.0.0.1), 127.x.x.x, broadcast addresses, multicast addresses, and so on, should be filtered.

3. Directed (subnet) broadcasts should not be allowed unless a specific need exists.

4. Packets for which no return route exists to the source IP address of the packet should be discarded (reverse-path-forwarding [RPF] check).

This section does not attempt to cover every portion of Layer 3 security, given the overall purpose of this book. The remainder of this chapter first provides some reference information regarding IP ACLs, which of course are often used to filter packets. This section ends with coverage of some of the more common Layer 3 attacks, and how Layer 3 security can mitigate those attacks.

IP Access Control List Review

A relatively deep knowledge of IP ACL configuration and use is assumed to be pre-requisite knowledge for readers of this book. In fact, many of the examples in the earlier sections of the book did not take the space required to explain the detailed logic of ACLs used in the examples. However, some reference information, as well as statements regarding some of the rules and practices regarding IP ACLs, is useful for general CCIE Routing and Switching exam study. Those details are presented in this section.

First, Table 18-7 lists the majority of the Cisco IOS commands related to IP ACLs.

Table 18-7 *IP ACL Command Reference*

Command	Configuration Mode and Description
access-list *access-list-number* {**deny** I **permit**} *source* [*source-wildcard*] [**log**]	Global command for standard numbered access lists.
access-list *access-list-number* [**dynamic** *dynamic-name* [**timeout** *minutes*]] {**deny** I **permit**} *protocol source source-wildcard destination destination-wildcard* [**precedence** *precedence*] [**tos** *tos*] [**log** I **log-input**] [**time-range** *time-range-name*] [**fragments**]	Generic syntax used with a wide variety of protocols. The options beginning with **precedence** are also included for TCP, UDP, and ICMP.
access-list *access-list-number* [**dynamic** *dynamic-name* [**timeout** *minutes*]] {**deny** I **permit**} **tcp** *source source-wildcard* [*operator* [*port*]] *destination destination-wildcard* [*operator* [*port*]] [**established**]	Version of **access-list** command with TCP-specific parameters; identical options exist for UDP, except for the **established** keyword.
access-list *access-list-number* {**deny** I **permit**} **icmp** *source source-wildcard destination destination-wildcard* [*icmp-type* [*icmp-code*] I *icmp-message*]	Version of **access-list** command to match ICMP packets.
access-list *access-list-number* **remark** *text*	Defines a remark.
ip access-list {**standard** I **extended**} *access-list-name*	Global command to create a named ACL.
[*sequence-number*] **permit** I **deny** *protocol source source-wildcard destination destination-wildcard* [**precedence** *precedence*] [**tos** *tos*] [**log** I **log-input**] [**time-range** *time-range-name*] [**fragments**]	Named ACL subcommand used to define an individual entry in the list; similar options for TCP, UDP, ICMP, and others.
ip access-group {*number* I *name* [**in** I **out**]}	Interface subcommand to enable access lists.
access-class *number* I *name* [**in** I **out**]	Line subcommand for standard or extended access lists.
access-list compiled	Global command to compile ACLs on Cisco 7200s/7500s.
ip access-list resequence *access-list-name starting-sequence-number increment*	Global command to redefine sequence numbers for a crowded ACL.
show ip interface [*type number*]	Includes a reference to the access lists enabled on the interface.
show access-lists [*access-list-number* I *access-list-name*]	Shows details of configured access lists for all protocols.
show ip access-list [*access-list-number* I *access-list-name*]	Shows IP access lists.

ACL Rule Summary

Cisco IOS processes the *Access Control Entries (ACEs)* of an ACL sequentially, either permitting or denying a packet based on the first ACE matched by that packet in the ACL. For an individual ACE, all the configured values must match before the ACE is considered a match. Table 18-8 lists several examples of named IP ACL **permit** and **deny** commands that create an individual ACE, along with their meanings.

Table 18-8 *Examples of ACL ACE Logic and Syntax*

Access List Statement	What It Matches
deny ip any host 10.1.1.1	IP packets with any source IP and destination IP = 10.1.1.1 only.
deny tcp any gt 1023 host 10.1.1.1 eq 23	IP packets with a TCP header, with any source IP, a source TCP port greater than (**gt**) 1023, plus a destination IP of 10.1.1.1, and a destination TCP port of 23.
deny tcp any host 10.1.1.1 eq 23	Same as previous example except that any source port matches, as that parameter was omitted.
deny tcp any host 10.1.1.1 eq telnet	Same results as the previous example; the syntax uses the **telnet** keyword instead of port 23.
deny udp 1.0.0.0 0.255.255.255 lt 1023 any	A packet with a source address in network 1.0.0.0/8, using UDP with a source port less than 1023, with any destination IP address.

The Port Number field is only matchable when the protocol type in an extended IP ACL ACE is UDP or TCP. In these cases, the port number is positional in that the source port matching parameter occurs right after the source IP address, and the destination port parameter occurs right after the destination IP address. Several examples were included in Table 18-8. Table 18-9 summarizes the matching logic used to match UDP and TCP ports.

Table 18-9 *IP ACE Port Matching.*

Keyword	Meaning
gt	Greater than
lt	Less than
eq	Equals
ne	Not equal
range *x-y*	Range of port numbers, inclusive

ICMP does not use port numbers, but it does include different message types, and some of those even include a further message code. The IP ACL commands allow these to be matched using a rather long list of keywords, or with the numeric message type and message code. Note that these parameters are also positional, following the destination IP address. For example, the named ACL command **permit icmp any any echo-reply** is correct, but the command **permit icmp any echo-reply any** is syntactically incorrect and would be rejected.

Several other parameters can also be checked. For example, the IP precedence bits can be checked, as well as the entire ToS byte. The **established** parameter matches if the TCP header has the ACK flag set—indicative of any TCP segment except the first segment of a new connection setup. (The **established** keyword will be used in an example later in the chapter.) Also, the **log** and **log-input** keywords can be used to tell Cisco IOS to generate periodic log messages when the ACE is matched—one message on initial match, and one every 5 minutes afterwards. The **log-input** option includes more information than the **log** option, specifically information about the incoming interface of the packet that matched the ACE.

For ACL configuration, several facts need to be kept in mind. First, standard ACLs can only match the source IP address field. Numbered standard ACLs are identified with ACL numbers of either 1–99 or 1300–1999, inclusive. Extended numbered IP ACLs range from 100–199 and 2000–2699, again inclusive. Additionally, newly configured ACEs in numbered IP ACLs are always added at the end of the existing ACL, and ACEs in numbered IP ACLs cannot be deleted one at a time. As a result, to insert a line into the middle of a numbered ACL, the entire numbered ACL may need to be deleted (using the **no access-list** *number* global command) and then reconfigured. Named ACLs overcome that problem by using an implied or explicit sequence number, with Cisco IOS listing and processing the ACEs in an ACL in sequence number order.

Wildcard Masks

ACEs use *wildcard masks* (WC masks) to define the portion of the IP address that should be examined. WC masks represent a 32-bit number, with the mask's 0 bits telling Cisco IOS that those corresponding bits in the IP address must be compared when performing the matching logic. The binary 1s in the WC mask tell Cisco IOS that those bits do not need to be compared; as a result, these bits are often called "don't care" bits. Table 18-10 lists several example WC masks, and the implied meanings.

Table 18-10   *Sample Access List Wildcard Masks*

Wildcard Mask	Description
0.0.0.0	The entire IP address must match.
0.0.0.255	Just the first 24 bits must match.
0.0.255.255	Just the first 16 bits must match.
0.255.255.255	Just the first 8 bits must match.

continues

Table 18-10   *Sample Access List Wildcard Masks*

Wildcard Mask	Description
255.255.255.255	Automatically considered to match because all 32 bits are "don't care" bits.
0.0.15.255	Just the first 20 bits must match.
0.0.3.255	Just the first 22 bits must match.
17.44.97.33	A valid WC mask, it means match all bits except bits 4, 8, 11, 13, 14, 18, 19, 24, 27, and 32.

That last entry is unlikely to be useful in an actual production network, but unlike IP subnet masks, the WC mask does not have to list a single unbroken set of 0s and another unbroken string of 1s. A much more likely WC mask is one that matches a particular mask or prefix length. To find a WC mask to match hosts in a known prefix, use the following simple math: in decimal, subtract the subnet mask from 255.255.255.255. The result is the "right" WC mask to match that prefix length. For instance, a subnet mask of 255.255.255.0, subtracted from 255.255.255.255, gives you 0.0.0.255 as a WC mask. This mask only checks the first 24 bits—which in this case is the network and subnet part of the address. Similarly, if the subnet mask is 255.255.240.0, subtracting from 255.255.255.255 gives you 0.0.15.255.

General Layer 3 Security Considerations

This section explains a few of the more common ways to avoid Layer 3 attacks.

Smurf Attacks, Directed Broadcasts, and RPF Checks

A smurf attack occurs when a host sends a large number of ICMP Echo Requests with some atypical IP addresses in the packet. The destination address is a *subnet broadcast address*, also known as a *directed broadcast address*. Routers forward these packets based on normal matching of the IP routing table, until the packet reaches a router connected to the destination subnet. This final router then forwards the packet onto the LAN as a LAN broadcast, sending a copy to every device. Figure 18-9 shows how the attack develops.

The other feature of a smurf attack is that the source IP address of the packet sent by the attacker is the IP address of the attacked host. For example, in Figure 18-9, many hosts may receive the ICMP Echo Request at Step 2. All those hosts then reply with an Echo Reply, sending it to 10.1.1.2—the address that was the source IP address of the original ICMP Echo at Step 1. Host 10.1.1.2 receives a potentially large number of packets.

Figure 18-9   *Smurf Attack*

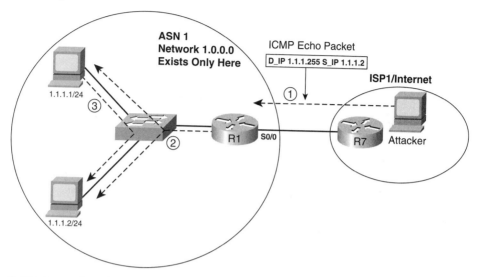

1. Attacker sends packet destined to subnet broadcast, source
   1.1.1.2 (for secondary attack).
2. R1 forwards packet as LAN broadcast.
3. R1 replies with ICMP echo reply packet sent to 1.1.1.2.

Several solutions to this problem exist. First, as of Cisco IOS Software version 12.0, IOS defaults each interface to use the **no ip directed-broadcast** command, which prevents the router from forwarding the broadcast onto the LAN (Step 2 in Figure 18-9). Also, a Reverse-Path-Forwarding (RPF) check could be enabled using the **ip verify unicast source reachable-via** {**rx** | **any**} [**allow-default**] [**allow-self-ping**] [*list*] interface subcommand. This command tells Cisco IOS to examine the source IP address of incoming packets on that interface. Two styles of check can be made with this command:

- **Strict RPF**—Using the **rx** keyword, the router checks to see if the matching route uses an outgoing interface that is the same interface on which the packet was received. If not, the packet is discarded. (An example scenario using Figure 18-9 will be explained shortly.)

- **Loose RPF**—Using the **any** keyword, the router checks for any route that can be used to reach the source IP address.

The command can also ignore default routes when it performs the check (default) or use default routes when performing the check by including the **allow-default** keyword. Also, although not recommended, the command can trigger a ping to the source to verify connectivity. Finally, the addresses for which the RPF check is made can be limited by a referenced ACL.

For example, in Figure 18-9, if R1 used strict RPF on s0/0, it would notice that its route to reach 1.1.1.2 (the source IP address of the packet at Step 1) did not refer to s0/0 as the outgoing interface—thereby discarding the packet. However, with loose RPF, R1 would have found a connected route that matched 1.1.1.2, so it would have allowed the packet through. Finally, given that AS1 should never receive packets with source addresses in network 1.0.0.0, as it owns that entire class A network, R1 could simply use an inbound ACL to discard any packets sourced from 1.0.0.0/8 as they enter s0/0 from the Internet.

Fraggle attacks use similar logic as smurf attacks, but instead of ICMP, fraggle attacks use the UDP Echo application. These attacks can be defeated using the same options as listed for smurf attacks.

Inappropriate IP Addresses

Besides smurf and fraggle attacks, other attacks involve the use of what can be generally termed inappropriate IP addresses, both for the source IP address and destination IP address. By using inappropriate IP addresses, the attacker can remain hidden and elicit cooperation of other hosts to create a distributed denial-of-service (DDoS) attack.

One of the Layer 3 security best practices is to use ACLs to filter packets whose IP addresses are not appropriate—for instance, the smurf attack listed a valid source IP address of 1.1.1.2, but packets with that source address should never enter AS1 from the Internet. The Internet Assigned Numbers Authority (IANA) manages the assignment of IP prefix ranges. It lists the assigned ranges in a document found at http://www.iana.org/assignments/ipv4-address-space. A router can then be configured with ACLs that prevent packets based on known assigned ranges and on known unassigned ranges. For example, in Figure 18-9, an enterprise router should never need to forward a packet onto the Internet if that packet has a source IP address from another company's registered IP prefix. In the smurf attack case, such an ACL used at the attacker's ISP would have prevented the first packet from getting to AS1.

Routers should also filter packets that use IP addresses that should be considered bogus or inappropriate. For example, a packet should never have a broadcast or multicast source IP address in normal use. Also, an enterprise router should never receive a packet from an ISP with that packet's source IP address being a private network per RFC 1918. Additionally, that same router should not receive packets sourced from IP addresses in ranges currently unallocated by IANA. These types of IP addresses are frequently called *bogons*, which is a derivation of the word bogus.

Creating an ACL to match these bogon IP addresses is not particularly difficult, but it does require a lot of administrative effort, particularly to update it based on changes to IANA's assigned prefixes. You can use freeware called the Router Audit Tool (RAT) that makes recommendations for router security, including bogon ACLs. You can also use the Cisco IOS *AutoSecure* feature, which automatically configures ACLs to prevent the use of such bogus IP addresses.

TCP SYN Flood, the Established Bit, and TCP Intercept

A TCP SYN flood is an attack directed at servers by initiating large numbers of TCP connections, but not completing the connections. Essentially, the attacker initiates many TCP connections, each with only the TCP SYN flag set, as usual. The server then sends a reply (with TCP SYN and ACK flags set)—but then the attacker simply does not reply with the expected third message in the three-way TCP connection setup flow. The server consumes memory and resources while waiting on its timeouts to occur before clearing up the partially initialized connections. The server might also reject additional TCP connections, and load balancers in front of a server farm might unbalance the load of actual working connections as well.

Stateful firewalls can prevent TCP SYN attacks. Both the Cisco PIX Firewall and the Cisco IOS Firewall feature set can be used to do this. The methods used are not part of the CCIE Routing and Switching written exam, but instead are covered in the CCIE Security exam; the impact of TCP SYN attacks can be reduced or eliminated by using a few other tools in Cisco IOS.

One way to prevent SYN attacks is to simply filter packets whose TCP header shows only the SYN flag set—in other words, filter all packets that are the first packet in a new TCP connection. In many cases, a router should not allow TCP connections to be established by a client on one side to a server on the other, as shown in Figure 18-10. In these cases, filtering the initial TCP segment prevents the SYN attack.

Figure 18-10 *Example Network: TCP Clients in the Internet*

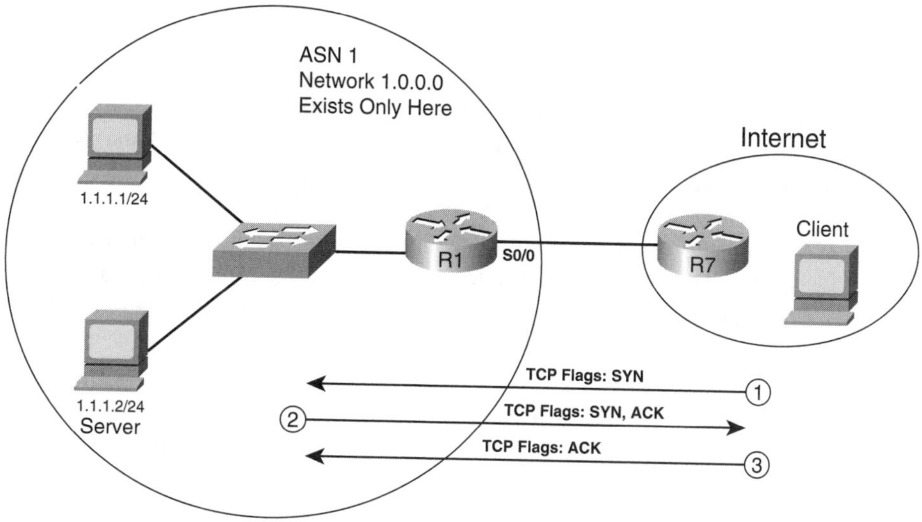

Cisco IOS ACLs cannot directly match the TCP SYN flag. However, an ACE can use the **established** keyword, which matches TCP segments that have the ACK flag set. The **established** keyword essentially matches all TCP segments except the very first TCP segment in a new connection. Example 18-12 shows the configuration that would be used on R1 to deny new connection requests from the Internet into the network on the left.

Example 18-12 *Using an ACL with the* **established** *Keyword*

```
! The first ACE matches TCP segments that are not the first segment, and permits
! them. The second ACE matches all TCP segment between the same set of IP
! addresses, but because all non-initial segments have already been matched, the
! second ACE only matches the initial segments.
ip access-list extended prevent-syn
 permit tcp any 1.0.0.0 0.255.255.255 established
 deny tcp any 1.0.0.0 0.255.255.255
 permit (whatever)
!
interface s0/0
 ip access-group prevent-syn in
```

The ACL works well when clients outside a network are not allowed to make TCP connections into the network. However, in cases where some inbound TCP connections are allowed, this ACL cannot be used. Another Cisco IOS feature, called *TCP intercept*, provides an alternative that allows TCP connections into the network, but monitors those TCP connections for TCP SYN attacks.

TCP intercept operates in one of two different modes. In *watch mode,* it keeps state information about TCP connections that match a defined ACL. If a TCP connection does not complete the three-way handshake within a particular time period, TCP intercept sends a TCP reset to the server, cleaning up the connection. It also counts the number of new connections attempted over time, and if a large number occurs in 1 second ("large" defaulting to 1100), the router temporarily filters new TCP requests to prevent a perceived SYN attack.

In *intercept mode*, the router replies to TCP connection requests instead of forwarding them to the actual server. Then, if the three-way handshake completes, the router creates a TCP connection between itself and the server. At that point, the router knits the two connections together. This takes more processing and effort, but it provides better protection for the servers.

Example 18-13 shows an example using TCP intercept configuration, in watch mode, plus a few changes to its default settings. The example allows connections from the Internet into AS1 in Figure 18-10.

Example 18-13 *Configuring TCP Intercept*

```
! The following command enables TCP intercept for packets matching ACL
! match-tcp-from-internet. Also, the mode is set to watch, rather than the
! default of intercept. Finally, the watch timeout has been reset from the
! default of 30 seconds; if the TCP connection remains incomplete as of the
! 20-second mark, TCP intercept resets the connection.
ip tcp intercept-list match-tcp-from-internet
ip tcp intercept mode watch
ip tcp intercept watch-timeout 20
! The ACL matches packets sent into 1.0.0.0/8 that are TCP. It is referenced by
! the ip tcp intercept-list command listed above.
ip access-list extended match-tcp-from-internet
 permit tcp any 1.0.0.0 0.255.255.255
! Note below that the ACL is not enabled on any interfaces.
interface s0/0
! Note: there is no ACL enabled on the interface!
```

Context-Based Access Control

In some cases, access-list filtering may be enough to control and secure a router interface. However, as attackers have become more sophisticated, Cisco has developed better tools to deal with threats. The challenge, as always, is to make security features relatively transparent to network users while thwarting attackers. CBAC is one of those features.

A function of the firewall feature set in Cisco IOS, CBAC takes access-list filtering a step or two farther by providing dynamic inspection of traffic that you specify as it traverses a firewall router. It does this based on actual protocol commands, such as the FTP **get** command—not simply on Layer 4 port numbers. Based on where the traffic originates, CBAC decides what traffic should be permitted to cross the firewall. When it sees a session initiate on the trusted network for a particular protocol, which would normally be blocked inbound based on other filtering methods, CBAC creates temporary openings in the firewall to permit the corresponding inbound traffic to enter from the untrusted network. It permits only the desired traffic, rather than opening the firewall to all traffic for a particular protocol.

CBAC works on TCP and UDP traffic, and it supports protocols such as FTP that require multiple, simultaneous sessions or connections. You would typically use CBAC to protect your internal network from external threats by configuring it to inspect inbound traffic from the outside world for those protocols. With CBAC, you configure the following:

- Protocols to inspect

- Interfaces on which to perform the inspection

- Direction of the traffic to inspect, per interface

TCP Versus UDP with CBAC

TCP has clear-cut connections, so CBAC (and other stateful inspection and filtering methods) can handle it rather easily. However, CBAC works at a deeper level than simply protocols and port numbers. For example, with FTP traffic, CBAC recognizes and inspects the specific FTP control-channel commands to decide when to open and close the temporary firewall openings.

By comparison to TCP, UDP traffic is connectionless and therefore more difficult to handle. CBAC manages UDP by approximating based on factors such as whether the source and destination addresses and ports of UDP frames are the same as those that came recently, and their relative timing. You can configure a global idle timeout that CBAC uses to determine whether a segment arrived "close enough" in time to be considered part of the same flow. You can also configure other timeouts, including protocol-specific timeouts for TCP and UDP traffic.

CBAC Protocol Support

CBAC can inspect any of the following protocols:

- Any generic TCP session, regardless of application layer protocol

- All UDP "sessions"

- FTP

- SMTP

- TFTP

- H.323 (NetMeeting, ProShare, etc.)

- Java

- CU-SeeMe

- Unix R commands (**rlogin**, **rexec**, **rsh**, etc.)

- RealAudio

- Sun RPC

- SQL*Net

- StreamWorks

- VDOLive

CBAC Caveats

As powerful as CBAC is for dynamic inspection and filtering, however, CBAC has some limitations. You should be aware of a few restrictions and caveats about how CBAC works:

- CBAC comes after access-list filters are applied to an interface. If an access list blocks a particular type of traffic on an interface where you are using CBAC to inspect inbound traffic, that traffic will be denied before CBAC sees it.

- CBAC cannot protect against attacks that originate inside your network, where most attacks originate.

- CBAC works only on protocols that you specify it should inspect, leaving all other filtering to access lists and other filtering methods.

- CBAC inspects only TCP- and UDP-transported traffic. It does not inspect any other protocol, including ICMP.

- CBAC does not inspect traffic destined to or originated from the firewall router itself, only traffic that traverses the firewall router.

- CBAC has restrictions on handling encrypted traffic. See the link in the "Further Reading" section for more details.

CBAC Configuration Steps

Although configuring CBAC is not difficult, it does involve several steps, which are as follows:

Step 1   Choose an interface ("inside" or "outside").

Step 2   Configure an IP access list for that interface.

Step 3   Configure global timeouts and thresholds using the **ip inspect** commands.

Step 4   Define an inspection rule and an optional rule-specific timeout value using the **ip inspect name** *protocol* commands. For example, **ip inspect name actionjackson ftp timeout 3600**.

Step 5   Apply the inspection rule to an interface. For example, in interface configuration mode, **ip inspect actionjackson in**.

CBAC is a powerful IOS firewall feature set option that you should understand at the functional level before attempting the CCIE Routing and Switching qualifying exam. See the "Further Reading" section for a link to more information and configuration details on CBAC.

Dynamic Multipoint VPN

IPsec is a commonly implemented method of forming secure tunnels from site to site or from remote users to a central site. However, it has limitations. In a site-to-site, hub-and-spoke environment, for example, all VPN traffic from spoke to spoke must traverse the hub site, where it must be unencrypted, routed, and then encrypted again. This is a lot of work for a VPN Concentrator, especially in a large environment with many spoke sites where a lot of traffic must flow between spokes. One result is additional network overhead and memory and CPU requirements at the central site. Another is significant configuration complexity at the hub router.

Dynamic Multipoint VPN (DMVPN) takes advantage of IPsec, GRE tunnels, and Next Hop Resolution Protocol (NHRP) to make IPsec scale better in a hub-and-spoke environment. DMVPN also supports traffic segmentation across VPNs and is VRF-aware.

In a typical hub-and-spoke IPsec VPN environment, the hub router must have separate, statically configured crypto maps, crypto access lists, GRE tunnels, and **isakmp peer** statements for each spoke router. This is one of the limits of traditional hub-and-spoke VPN scalability that DMVPN eliminates. In a DMVPN environment, the spoke router connection information is not explicitly configured on the hub router. Instead, the hub router is configured for a single multipoint GRE (mGRE) tunnel interface and a set of profiles that apply to the spoke routers. Each spoke router points to one or more hubs, facilitating redundancy and load sharing. DMVPN additionally supports multicast traffic from hub to spoke routers.

The benefits of DMVPN compared to a traditional IPsec hub-and-spoke VPN environment include these:

Key Topic

- Simpler hub router configuration. A DMVPN hub router requires only one multipoint GRE tunnel interface, one IPsec profile, and no crpyto access lists.

- Zero-touch at the hub router for provisioning spoke routers. The hub router does not require configuration when new spoke routers are brought online.

- Automatically initiated IPsec encryption, facilitated by NHRP.

- Dynamic addressing support for spoke routers. Instead of static configuration, the hub learns spoke router addresses when they register to the network.

- Dynamically created spoke-to-spoke tunnels. Spoke routers learn about each other using NHRP so that they can form tunnels between each other automatically instead of requiring spoke-to-spoke traffic to be encrypted, unencrypted, and routed at the hub router.

- VRF integration for MPLS environments.

A dynamic routing protocol (EIGRP, OSPF, BGP, RIP, or even ODR for small deployments) is required between the hub and the spokes. (Cisco recommends a distance vector protocol, and therefore prefers EIGRP for large-scale deployments.) This is how spoke routers learn about the networks at other spoke routers. In a DMVPN environment, the next-hop IP address for a spoke network is the tunnel interface for that spoke.

Figure 18-11 shows a DMVPN network with one hub and three spoke routers. In this network, each spoke router has a permanent IPsec tunnel to the hub router. Each of the spokes, which are NHRP clients, registers with the NHRP server (the hub router). When a spoke router needs to send traffic to a private network on another spoke router, which it has learned about by using the dynamic routing protocol running between the hub and the spokes, that spoke router queries the NHRP server in the hub router for the outside IP address of the destination spoke router. When the NHRP server returns that information, the originating spoke router initiates a dynamic IPsec tunnel to the other spoke router over the mGRE tunnel. After the required traffic has passed and the connection has been idle for a preconfigured time, the dynamic IPsec tunnel is torn down to save router resources (IPsec security associations, or SAs).

Figure 18-11   *Basic DMVPN Network*

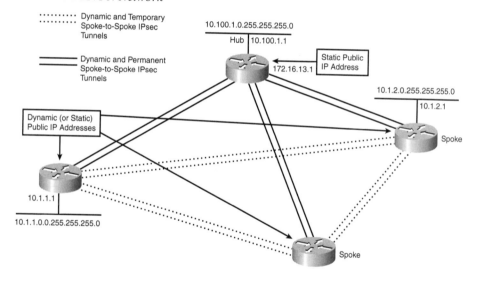

NOTE   Figure 18-11 is redrawn from Figure 1 in "Dynamic Multipoint VPN (DMVPN)" at http://www.cisco.com/en/US/products/sw/iosswrel/ps1839/products_feature_guide09186a0080110ba1.html.

For more details on DMVPN, see the link in the "Further Reading" section at the end of the chapter. You should be familiar with the concepts of DMVPN, but not the configuration details, for the CCIE Routing and Switching qualification exam.

Foundation Summary

This section lists additional details and facts to round out the coverage of the topics in this chapter. Unlike most of the Cisco Press Exam Certification Guides, this "Foundation Summary" does not repeat information presented in the "Foundation Topics" section of the chapter. Please take the time to read and study the details in the "Foundation Topics" section of the chapter, as well as review items noted with a Key Topic icon.

Table 18-11 lists some of the key protocols covered in this chapter.

Table 18-11   *Protocols and Standards for Chapter 18*

Name	Standard
RADIUS	RFC 2865
Port-Based Network Access Control	IEEE 802.1X
EAP	RFC 3748
A One-Time Password System	RFC 2289
Router Security	RFCs 2827 and 3704
Next Hop Resolution Protocol (NHRP)	RFC 2332

Table 18-12 lists some of the most popular router IOS commands related to the topics in this chapter.

Table 18-12   *Router IOS Commands Related to Chapter 18*

Command	Description
service password-encryption	Global command to enable simple encryption of passwords
server *ip-address* [**auth-port** *port-number*] [**acct-port** *port-number*]	Global command to define a RADIUS server and ports used
aaa group server radius | tacacs+ *group-name*	Global command to create the name of a group of AAA servers
server *ip-address*	AAA group mode; defines a TACACS+ server
server *ip-address* [**auth-port** *port-number*] [**acct-port** *port-number*]	AAA group mode; defines a RADIUS server and ports used
radius-server host {*hostname* | *ip-address*} [**auth-port** *port-number*] [**acct-port** *port-number*] [**timeout** *seconds*] [**retransmit** *retries*] [**key** *string*] [**alias**{*hostname* | *ip-address*}]	Global mode; defines details regarding a single RADIUS server

Table 18-12   *Router IOS Commands Related to Chapter 18 (Continued)*

Command	Description
radius-server key {**0** *string* | **7** *string* | *string*}	Global mode; defines the key used to encrypt RADIUS passwords
tacacs-server host {*host-name* | *host-ip-address}* [**key** *string*] [**nat**] [**port** [*integer*]] [**single-connection**] [**timeout** [*integer*]]	Global mode; defines details regarding a single TACACS+ server
tacacs-server key *key*	Global mode; defines the key used to encrypt the TACACS+ payload
aaa authentication enable default *method1* [*method2...*]	Global mode; defines the default authentication methods used by the **enable** command
aaa authentication login {**default** | *list-name*} *method1* [*method2...*]	Global mode; defines the default authentication methods used by console, vty, and aux logins
aaa authentication ppp {**default** | *list-name*} *method1* [*method2...*]	Global mode; defines the default authentication methods used by PPP
aaa new-model	Global mode; enables AAA globally in a router/switch
login authentication {**default** | *list-name*}	Line mode; defines the AAA group to use for authentication
ppp authentication {*protocol1* [*protocol2...*]} [**if-needed**] [*list-name* | **default**] [**callin**] [**one-time**] [**optional**]	Interface mode; defines the type of AAA authentication used by PPP
auto secure [**management** | **forwarding**] [**no-interact**]	Global mode; automatically configures IOS with Cisco's recommended device security configuration
enable password [**level** *level*] {*password* | [*encryption-type*] *encrypted-password*}	Global mode; defines the enable password
enable secret [**level** *level*] {*password* | [*encryption-type*] *encrypted-password*}	Global mode; defines the enable password that is MD5 hashed
ip verify unicast reverse-path [*list*]	Interface subcommand; enables strict RPF
ip verify unicast source reachable-via {**rx** | **any**} [**allow-default**] [**allow-self-ping**] [*list*]	Interface subcommand; enables strict or loose RPF
username *name* {**nopassword** | **password** *password*}	Global mode; defines local usernames and passwords
username *name* **secret** {[**0**] *password* | **5** *encrypted-secret*}	Global mode; defines local usernames and MD5-hashed passwords

continues

Table 18-12 *Router IOS Commands Related to Chapter 18 (Continued)*

Command	Description
ip tcp intercept list *access-list-number*	Global mode; identifies an ACL to be used by TCP intercept
ip tcp intercept mode {**intercept** | **watch**}	Global mode; defines the mode used by TCP intercept
ip tcp intercept watch-timeout *seconds*	Global mode; defines the timeout used before acting to clean up an incomplete TCP connection
ip inspect name *inspection-name protocol* [timeout *seconds*]	Configures inspection rules for CBAC
ip inspect *inspection-name* {**in** | **out**}	Applies a CBAC inspection rule to an interface

Table 18-13 lists some of the Cisco 3550 switch commands used in this chapter. Also, refer to Tables 18-4 through 18-7. Note that all commands in Table 18-13 were copied from the version 12.2(25)SEB 3550 Command Reference at Cisco.com; the syntax may vary on different Cisco IOS–based switches.

Table 18-13 *Catalyst IOS Commands Related to Chapter 21*

Command	Description
spanning-tree guard root	Interface mode; enables Root Guard.
aaa authentication dot1x {**default**} *method1*	Global mode; defines the default authentication method for 802.1X. Only one method is available, because only RADIUS is supported.
arp access-list *acl-name*	Global command; creates an ARP ACL with the stated name.
dot1x system-auth-control	Global command that enables 802.1X.
dot1x port-control {**auto** | **force-authorized** | **force-unauthorized**}	Interface subcommand to define 802.1X actions on the interface.
dot1x timeout {**quiet-period** *seconds* | **reauth-period** *seconds* | **server-timeout** *seconds* | **supp-timeout** *seconds* | **tx-period** *seconds*}	Global command to set 802.1X timers.

Memory Builders

The CCIE Routing and Switching written exam, like all Cisco CCIE written exams, covers a fairly broad set of topics. This section provides some basic tools to help you exercise your memory about some of the broader topics covered in this chapter.

Fill in Key Tables from Memory

Appendix E, "Key Tables for CCIE Study," on the CD in the back of this book contains empty sets of some of the key summary tables in each chapter. Print Appendix E, refer to this chapter's tables in it, and fill in the tables from memory. Refer to Appendix F, "Solutions for Key Tables for CCIE Study," on the CD to check your answers.

Definitions

Next, take a few moments to write down the definitions for the following terms:

AAA, authentication method, RADIUS, TACACS+, MD5 hash, enable password, enable secret, ACS, SAFE Blueprint, DAI, port security, IEEE 802.1X, DHCP snooping, IP Source Guard, man-in-the-middle attack, sticky learning, fraggle attack, DHCP snooping binding database, EAP, EAPoL, OTP, Supplicant, authenticator, authentication server, smurf attack, TCP SYN flood, TCP intercept, ACE, storm control, CBAC, inspection rule, DMVPN

Refer to the glossary to check your answers.

Further Reading

Appendix E, "Key Tables for CCIE Study," on the CD in the back of this book contains empty sets of some of the key summary tables in each chapter. Print Appendix E, refer to this chapter's tables in it, and fill in the tables from memory. Refer to Appendix F, "Solutions for Key Tables for CCIE Study," on the CD to check your answers.

Network Security Principles and Practices, by Saadat Malik

Network Security Architectures, by Sean Convery

Cisco SAFE Blueprint Introduction: http://www.cisco.com/go/safe

"Configuring Context-Based Access Control": http://www.cisco.com/en/US/docs/ios/12_0/security/configuration/guide/sccbac.html

"Dynamic Multipoint VPN (DMVPN)": http://www.cisco.com/en/US/products/sw/iosswrel/ps1839/products_feature_guide09186a0080110ba1.html

Part VIII: MPLS

Chapter 19: Multiprotocol Label Switching

Blueprint topics covered in this chapter:

This chapter covers the following subtopics from the Cisco CCIE Routing and Switching written exam blueprint. Refer to the full blueprint in Table I-1 in the Introduction for more details on the topics covered in each chapter and their context within the blueprint.

- Label Switching Router (LSR)

- Label Switched Path (LSP)

- Route Descriptor

- Label Format

- Label Imposition/Disposition

- Label Distribution

Multiprotocol Label Switching

Multiprotocol Label Switching (MPLS) remains a vitally important part of many service provider (SP) networks. MPLS is still growing in popularity in enterprise networks as well, particularly in larger enterprise internetworks. This chapter introduces the core concepts with MPLS, particularly its use for unicast IP forwarding and for MPLS VPNs.

"Do I Know This Already?" Quiz

Table 19-1 outlines the major headings in this chapter and the corresponding "Do I Know This Already?" quiz questions.

Table 19-1 *"Do I Know This Already?" Foundation Topics Section-to-Question Mapping*

Foundation Topics Section	Questions Covered in This Section	Score
MPLS Unicast IP Forwarding	1–4	
MPLS VPNs	5–8	
Other MPLS Applications	9	
Total Score		

In order to best use this pre-chapter assessment, remember to score yourself strictly. You can find the answers in Appendix A, "Answers to the 'Do I Know This Already?' Quizzes."

1. Imagine a frame-based MPLS network configured for simple unicast IP forwarding, with four routers, R1, R2, R3, and R4. The routers connect in a mesh of links so that they are all directly connected to the other routers. R1 uses LDP to advertise prefix 1.1.1.0/24, label 30, to the other three routers. What must be true in order for R2 to advertise a label for 1.1.1.0/24 to R1 using LDP?

   a. R2 must learn an IGP route to 1.1.1.0/24.

   b. R2 will not advertise a label to R1 due to split horizon rules.

   c. R2 can advertise a label back to R1 before learning an IGP route to 1.1.1.0/24.

   d. R2 must learn a route to 1.1.1.0/24 using MP-BGP before advertising a label.

   2. In a frame-based MPLS network configured for unicast IP forwarding, LSR R1 receives a labeled packet, with a label value of 55. Which of the following could be true?

   a. R1 makes its forwarding decision by comparing the packet to the IPv4 prefixes found in the FIB.

   b. R1 makes its forwarding decision by comparing the packet to the IPv4 prefixes found in the LFIB.

   c. R1 makes its forwarding decision by comparing the packet to the MPLS labels found in the FIB.

   d. R1 makes its forwarding decision by comparing the packet to the MPLS labels found in the LFIB.

   3. R1, R2, and R3 are all MPLS LSRs that use LDP and connect to the same LAN. None of the three LSRs advertise a transport IP address. Which of the following could be true regarding LDP operation?

   a. The LSRs discover the other two routers using LDP Hellos sent to IP address 224.0.0.20.

   b. Each pair of LSRs forms a TCP connection before advertising MPLS labels.

   c. The three LSRs must use their LAN interface IP addresses for any LDP TCP connections.

   d. The LDP Hellos use port 646, with the TCP connections using port 711.

   4. In a frame-based MPLS network configured for simple unicast IP forwarding, MPLS TTL propagation has been enabled for all traffic. Which of the following could be true?

   a. A **traceroute** command issued from outside the MPLS network will list IP addresses of the LSRs inside the MPLS network.

   b. A **traceroute** command issued from outside the MPLS network will not list IP addresses of the LSRs inside the MPLS network.

   c. Any IP packet with a TCP header, entering the MPLS network from outside the MPLS network, would not have its IP TTL field copied into the MPLS TTL field.

   d. An ICMP echo sent into the MPLS network from outside the MPLS network would have its IP TTL field copied into the MPLS TTL field.

   5. Which of the following is an extension to the BGP NLRI field?

   a. VRF

   b. Route Distinguisher

   c. Route Target

   d. BGP Extended Community

6. Which of the following controls into which VRFs a PE adds routes when receiving an IBGP update from another PE?

   a. Route Distinguisher

   b. Route Target

   c. IGP metric

   d. AS Path length

7. An ingress PE router in an internetwork configured for MPLS VPN receives an unlabeled packet. Which of the following is true?

   a. It injects a single MPLS header.

   b. It injects at least two MPLS headers.

   c. It injects (at least) a VPN label, which is used by any intermediate P routers.

   d. It uses both the FIB and LFIB to find all the required labels to inject before the IP header.

8. An internetwork configured to support MPLS VPNs uses PHP. An ingress PE receives an unlabeled packet and then injects the appropriate label(s) to the packet before sending the packet into the MPLS network. Which of the following is/are true about this packet?

   a. The number of MPLS labels in the packet will only change when the packet reaches the egress PE router, which extracts the entire MPLS header.

   b. The number of MPLS labels in the packet will change before the packet reaches the egress PE.

   c. The PHP feature will cause the egress PE to act differently than it would without PHP enabled.

   d. None of the other answers is correct.

9. Which of the following answers help define which packets are in the same MPLS FEC when using MPLS VPNs?

   a. IPv4 prefix

   b. ToS byte

   c. The MPLS VRF

   d. The TE tunnel

Foundation Topics

MPLS defines protocols that create a different paradigm for how routers forward packets. Instead of forwarding packets based on the packets' destination IP address, MPLS defines how routers can forward packets based on an MPLS label. By disassociating the forwarding decision from the destination IP address, MPLS allows forwarding decisions based on other factors, such as traffic engineering, QoS requirements, and the privacy requirements for multiple customers connected to the same MPLS network, while still considering the traditional information learned using routing protocols.

MPLS includes a wide variety of applications, with each application considering one or more of the possible factors that influence the MPLS forwarding decisions. For the purposes of the CCIE Routing and Switching written exam, this book covers two such applications in the first two major sections of this chapter:

■ MPLS unicast IP

■ MPLS VPNs

This chapter ends with a brief introduction to many of the other MPLS applications. Also, as usual, please take the time to check http://www.ciscopress.com/title/9781587201967 for the latest version of Appendix C, "CCIE Routing and Switching Exam Updates," to find out if you should read further about any of the MPLS topics.

> **NOTE** MPLS includes frame-mode MPLS and cell-mode MPLS, while this chapter only covers frame-mode MPLS. The generalized comments in this chapter may not apply to cell-mode MPLS.

MPLS Unicast IP Forwarding

MPLS can be used for simple unicast IP forwarding. With MPLS unicast IP forwarding, the MPLS forwarding logic forwards packets based on labels. However, when choosing the interfaces out which to forward the packets, MPLS considers only the routes in the unicast IP routing table, so the end result of using MPLS is that the packet flows over the same path as it would have if MPLS were not used, but all other factors were unchanged.

MPLS unicast IP forwarding does not provide any significant advantages by itself; however, many of the more helpful MPLS applications, such as MPLS VPNs and MPLS traffic engineering (TE), use MPLS unicast IP forwarding as one part of the MPLS network. So to understand MPLS as you would typically implement it, you need a solid understanding of MPLS in its most basic form: MPLS unicast IP forwarding.

MPLS requires the use of control plane protocols (for example, OSPF and LDP) to learn labels, correlate those labels to particular destination prefixes, and build the correct forwarding tables. MPLS also requires a fundamental change to the data plane's core forwarding logic. This section begins by examining the data plane, which defines the packet-forwarding logic. Following that, this section examines the control plane protocols, particularly the Label Distribution Protocol (LDP), which MPLS routers use to exchange labels for unicast IP prefixes.

MPLS IP Forwarding: Data Plane

MPLS defines a completely different packet-forwarding paradigm. However, hosts do not and should not send and receive labeled packets, so at some point, some router will need to add a label to the packet and, later, another router will remove the label. The MPLS routers—the routers that inject (push), remove (pop), or forward packets based on their labels—use MPLS forwarding logic.

MPLS relies on the underlying structure and logic of Cisco Express Forwarding (CEF) while expanding the logic and data structures as well. First, a review of CEF is in order, followed by details about a new data structure called the MPLS *Label Forwarding Information Base (LFIB)*.

CEF Review

A router's unicast IP forwarding control plane uses routing protocols, static routes, and connected routes to create a *Routing Information Base (RIB)*. With CEF enabled, a router's control plane processing goes a step further, creating the CEF *Forwarding Information Base (FIB)*, adding a FIB entry for each destination IP prefix in the routing table. The FIB entry details the information needed for forwarding: the next-hop router and the outgoing interface. Additionally, the CEF *adjacency table* lists the new data-link header that the router will then copy in front of the packet before forwarding.

For the data plane, a CEF router compares the packet's destination IP address to the CEF FIB, ignoring the IP routing table. CEF optimizes the organization of the FIB so that the router spends very little time to find the correct FIB entry, resulting in a smaller forwarding delay and a higher volume of packets per second through a router. For each packet, the router finds the matching FIB entry, then finds the adjacency table entry referenced by the matching FIB entry, and forwards the packet. Figure 19-1 shows the overall process.

Figure 19-1 *IP Routing Table and CEF FIB—No MPLS*

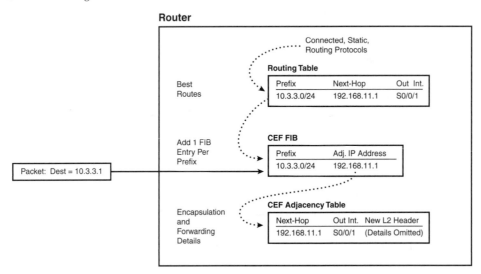

With this backdrop in mind, the text next looks at how MPLS changes the forwarding process using labels.

Overview of MPLS Unicast IP Forwarding

The MPLS forwarding paradigm assumes that hosts generate packets without an MPLS label; then, some router imposes an MPLS label, other routers forward the packet based on that label, and then other routers remove the label. The end result is that the host computers have no awareness of the existence of MPLS. To appreciate this overall forwarding process, Figure 19-2 shows an example, with steps showing how a packet is forwarded using MPLS.

Figure 19-2 *MPLS Packet Forwarding—End to End*

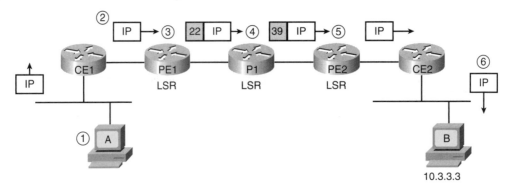

The steps from the figure are explained as follows:

1. Host A generates and sends an unlabeled packet destined to host 10.3.3.3.

2. Router CE1, with no MPLS features configured, forwards the unlabeled packet based on the destination IP address, as normal, without any labels. (Router CE1 may or may not use CEF.)

3. MPLS router PE1 receives the unlabeled packet and decides, as part of the MPLS forwarding process, to impose (push) a new label (value 22) into the packet and forwards the packet.

4. MPLS router P1 receives the labeled packet. P1 swaps the label for a new label value (39) and then forwards the packet.

5. MPLS router PE2 receives the labeled packet, removes (pops) the label, and forwards the packet toward CE2.

6. Non-MPLS router CE2 forwards the unlabeled packet based on the destination IP address, as normal. (CE2 may or may not use CEF.)

The steps in Figure 19-2 show a relatively simple process and provide a great backdrop from which to introduce a few terms. The term *Label Switch Router (LSR)* refers to any router that has awareness of MPLS labels, for example, routers PE1, P1, and PE2 in Figure 19-2. Table 19-2 lists the variations of the term LSR, and a few comments about the meaning of each term.

Table 19-2 *MPLS LSR Terminology Reference*

Key
Topic

LSR Type	Actions Performed by This LSR Type
Label Switch Router (LSR)	Any router that pushes labels onto packets, pops labels from packets, or simply forwards labeled packets.
Edge LSR (E-LSR)	An LSR at the edge of the MPLS network, meaning that this router processes both labeled and unlabeled packets.
Ingress E-LSR	For a particular packet, the router that receives an unlabeled packet and then inserts a label stack in front of the IP header.
Egress E-LSR	For a particular packet, the router that receives a labeled packet and then removes all MPLS labels, forwarding an unlabeled packet.
ATM-LSR	An LSR that runs MPLS protocols in the control plane to set up ATM virtual circuits. Forwards labeled packets as ATM cells.
ATM E-LSR	An E-edge LSR that also performs the ATM Segmentation and Reassembly (SAR) function.

MPLS Forwarding Using the FIB and LFIB

To forward packets as shown in Figure 19-2, LSRs use both the CEF FIB and the MPLS LFIB when forwarding packets. Both the FIB and LFIB hold any necessary label information, as well as the outgoing interface and next-hop information.

The FIB and LFIB differ in that routers use one table to forward incoming unlabeled packets, and the other to forward incoming labeled packets, as follows:

- **FIB**—Used for incoming unlabeled packets. Cisco IOS matches the packet's destination IP address to the best prefix in the FIB and forwards the packet based on that entry.

- **LFIB**—Used for incoming labeled packets. Cisco IOS compares the label in the incoming packet to the LFIB's list of labels and forwards the packet based on that LFIB entry.

Figure 19-3 shows how the three LSRs in Figure 19-2 use their respective FIBs and LFIB. Note that Figure 19-3 just shows the FIB on the LSR that forwards the packet using the FIB and the LFIB on the two LSRs that use the LFIB, although all LSRs have both a FIB and an LFIB.

Figure 19-3 *Usage of the CEF FIB and MPLS LFIB for Forwarding Packets*

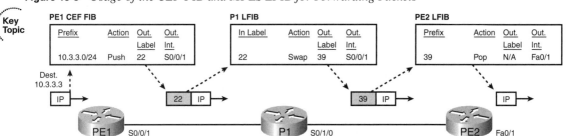

The figure shows the use of the FIB and LFIB, as follows:

- **PE1**—When the unlabeled packet arrives at PE1, PE1 uses the FIB. PE1 finds the FIB entry that matches the packet's destination address of 10.3.3.1—namely, the entry for 10.3.3.0/24 in this case. Among other things, the FIB entry includes the instructions to push the correct MPLS label in front of the packet.

- **P1**—Because P1 receives a labeled packet, P1 uses its LFIB, finding the label value of 22 in the LFIB, with that entry stating that P1 should swap the label value to 39.

- **PE2**—PE2 uses the LFIB as well, because PE2 receives a labeled packet; the matching LFIB entry lists a pop action, so PE2 removes the label, forwarding an unlabeled packet to CE2.

Note that P1 and PE2 in this example never examined the packet's destination IP address as part of the forwarding process. Because the forwarding process does not rely on the destination IP address, MPLS can then enable forwarding processes based on something other than the destination IP address, such as forwarding based on the VPN from which the packet originated, forwarding to balance traffic with traffic engineering, and forwarding over different links based on QoS goals.

The MPLS Header and Label

The MPLS header is a 4-byte header, located immediately before the IP header. Many people simply refer to the MPLS header as the MPLS label, but the label is actually a 20-bit field in the MPLS header. You may also see this header referenced as an MPLS *shim header*. Figure 19-4 shows the entire label, and Table 19-3 defines the fields.

Figure 19-4 *The MPLS Header*

20	3	1	8
Label	EXP	S	TTL

Table 19-3 *MPLS Header Fields*

Field	Length (Bits)	Purpose
Label	20	Identifies the portion of a label switched path (LSP).
Experimental (EXP)	3	Used for QoS marking; the field is no longer used for truly experimental purposes.
Bottom-of-Stack (S)	1	Flag, which when set to 1, means that this is the label immediately preceding the IP header.
Time-to-Live (TTL)	8	Used for the same purposes as the IP header's TTL field.

Of the four fields in the MPLS header, the first two, Label and EXP, should already be familiar. The 20-bit Label is usually listed as a decimal value in **show** commands. The MPLS EXP bits allow for QoS marking, which can be done using CB Marking, as covered in Chapter 12, "Classification and Marking." The S bit will make more sense once you examine how MPLS VPNs work, but in short, when packets hold multiple MPLS headers, this bit allows an LSR to recognize the last MPLS header before the IP header. Finally, the TTL field requires a little more examination, as covered in the next section.

The MPLS TTL Field and MPLS TTL Propagation

The IP header's TTL field supports two important features: a mechanism to identify looping packets, and a method for the **traceroute** command to find the IP address of each router in a particular end-to-end route. The MPLS header's TTL field supplies the same features—in fact, using all defaults, the presence or absence of MPLS LSRs in a network has no impact on the end results of either of the TTL-related processes.

MPLS needs a TTL field so that LSRs can completely ignore the encapsulated IP header when forwarding IP packets. Essentially, the LSRs will decrement the MPLS TTL field, and not the IP TTL field, as the packet passes through the MPLS network. To make the whole process work, using all default settings, ingress E-LSRs, LSRs, and egress E-LSRs work as follows:

- **Ingress E-LSRs**— After an ingress E-LSR decrements the IP TTL field, it pushes a label into an unlabeled packet and then copies the packet's IP TTL field into the new MPLS header's TTL field.

- **LSRs**—When an LSR swaps a label, the router decrements the MPLS header's TTL field, and always ignores the IP header's TTL field.

- **Egress E-LSRs**—After an egress E-LSR decrements the MPLS TTL field, it pops the final MPLS header and then copies the MPLS TTL field into the IP header TTL field.

Figure 19-5 shows an example in which a packet arrives at PE1, unlabeled, with IP TTL 4. The callouts in the figure list the main actions for the three roles of the LSRs as described in the previous list.

Figure 19-5 *Example of MPLS TTL Propagation*

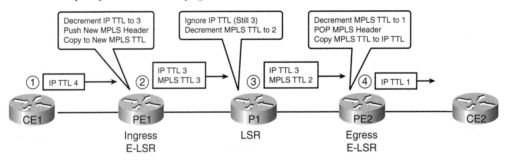

The term *MPLS TTL propagation* refers to the combined logic as shown in the figure. In effect, the MPLS routers propagate the same TTL value across the MPLS network—the same TTL values that would have occurred if MPLS was not used at all. As you might expect, a truly looping packet would eventually decrement to TTL 0 and be discarded. Additionally, a **traceroute** command would receive ICMP Time Exceeded messages from each of the routers in the figure, including the LSRs.

However, many engineers do not want hosts outside the MPLS network to have visibility into the MPLS network with the **traceroute** command. SPs typically implement MPLS networks to create Layer 3 WAN services, and the SP's customers sit outside the MPLS network. If the SP's customers can find the IP addresses of the MPLS LSRs, it may annoy the customer who wants to see only customer routers, and it may create a security exposure for the SP.

 Key Topic

Cisco routers can be configured to disable MPLS TTL propagation. When disabled, the ingress E-LSR sets the MPLS header's TTL field to 255, and the egress E-LSR leaves the original IP header's TTL field unchanged. As a result, the entire MPLS network appears to be a single router hop from a TTL perspective, and the routers inside the MPLS network are not seen from the customer's **traceroute** command. Figure 19-6 shows the same example as in Figure 19-5 but now with MPLS TTL propagation disabled.

Figure 19-6 *Example with MPLS TTL Propagation Disabled*

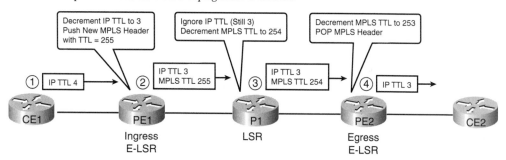

Cisco supports the ability to disable MPLS TTL propagation for two classes of packets. Most MPLS SPs may want to disable TTL propagation for packets forwarded by customers, but allow TTL propagation for packets created by the SP's routers. Using Figure 19-5 again for an example, an SP engineer may be logged in to router PE1 in order to issue a **traceroute** command. PE1 can be configured to use TTL propagation for locally created packets, which allows the **traceroute** command issued from PE1 to list all the routers in the MPLS cloud. At the same time, PE1 can be configured to disable TTL propagation for "forwarded" packets (packets received from customers), preventing the customer from learning router IP addresses inside the MPLS network. (The command is **no mpls ttl-propagation** [**local** | **forwarded**].)

> **NOTE**   Although the PE1 router has TTL-Propagation disabled, *all* routers in the MPLS domain should also have TTL disabled for consistent output of the TTL propagation.

MPLS IP Forwarding: Control Plane

For pure IP routing to work using the FIB, routers must use control plane protocols, like routing protocols, to first populate the IP routing table and then populate the CEF FIB. Similarly, for MPLS forwarding to work, MPLS relies on control plane protocols to learn which MPLS labels to use to reach each IP prefix, and then populate both the FIB and the LFIB with the correct labels.

MPLS supports many different control plane protocols. However, an engineer's choice of which control plane protocol to use is mainly related to the MPLS application used, rather than any detailed comparison of the features of each control plane protocol. For example, MPLS VPNs use two control plane protocols: LDP and multiprotocol BGP (MP-BGP).

While multiple control plane protocols may be used for some MPLS applications, MPLS unicast IP forwarding uses an IGP and one MPLS-specific control plane protocol: LDP. This section, still focused on unicast IP forwarding, examines the details of label distribution using LDP.

> **NOTE** The earliest pre-standard version of LDP was called *Tag Distribution Protocol (TDP)*. The term *tag switching* was also often used instead of label switching.

MPLS LDP Basics

For unicast IP routing, LDP simply advertises labels for each prefix listed in the IP routing table. To do so, LSRs use LDP to send messages to their neighbors, with the messages listing an IP prefix and corresponding label. By advertising an IP prefix and label, the LSR is essentially saying, "If you want to send packets to this IP prefix, send them to me with the MPLS label listed in the LDP update."

The LDP advertisement is triggered by a new IP route appearing in the unicast IP routing table. Upon learning a new route, the LSR allocates a label called a local label. The local label is the label that, on this one LSR, is used to represent the IP prefix just added to the routing table. An example makes the concept much clearer. Figure 19-7 shows a slightly expanded version of the MPLS network shown earlier in this chapter. The figure shows the basic process of what occurs when an LSR (PE2) learns about a new route (10.3.3.0/24), triggering the process of advertising a new local label (39) using LDP.

Figure 19-7 *LDP Process Triggered by New Unicast IP Route*

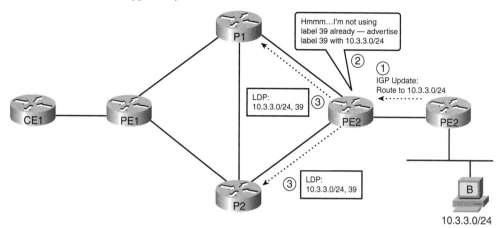

The figure shows the following simple three-step process on PE2:

1. PE2 learns a new unicast IP route, which appears in the IP routing table.

2. PE2 allocates a new *local label*, which is a label not currently advertised by that LSR.

3. PE2 uses LDP to advertise to neighbors the mapping between the IP prefix and label to all LDP neighbors.

Although the process itself is simple, it is important to note that PE2 must now be ready to process labeled packets that arrive with the new local label value in it. For example, in Figure 19-7, PE2 needs to be ready to forward packets received with label 39; PE2 will forward the packets with the same next-hop and outgoing interface information learned in the IGP Update at step 1 in the figure.

Although interesting, the process shown in Figure 19-7 shows only the advertisement of one segment of the full label switched path (LSP). An MPLS LSP is the combined set of labels that can be used to forward the packets correctly to the destination. For example, Figures 19-2 and 19-3 show a short LSP with label values 22 and 39, over which packets to subnet 10.3.3.0/24 were sent. Figure 19-7 shows the advertisement of one part, or segment, of the LSP.

NOTE LSPs are unidirectional.

The routers in the MPLS cloud must use some IP routing protocol to learn IP routes in order to trigger the LDP process of advertising labels. Typically, for MPLS unicast IP routing, you would use an IGP to learn all the IP routes, triggering the process of advertising the corresponding labels. For example, Figure 19-8 picks up the process where Figure 19-7 ended, with PE2 advertising a route for 10.3.3.0/24 using EIGRP, causing other routers to then use LDP to advertise labels.

Figure 19-8 *Completed Process of Advertising an Entire LSP*

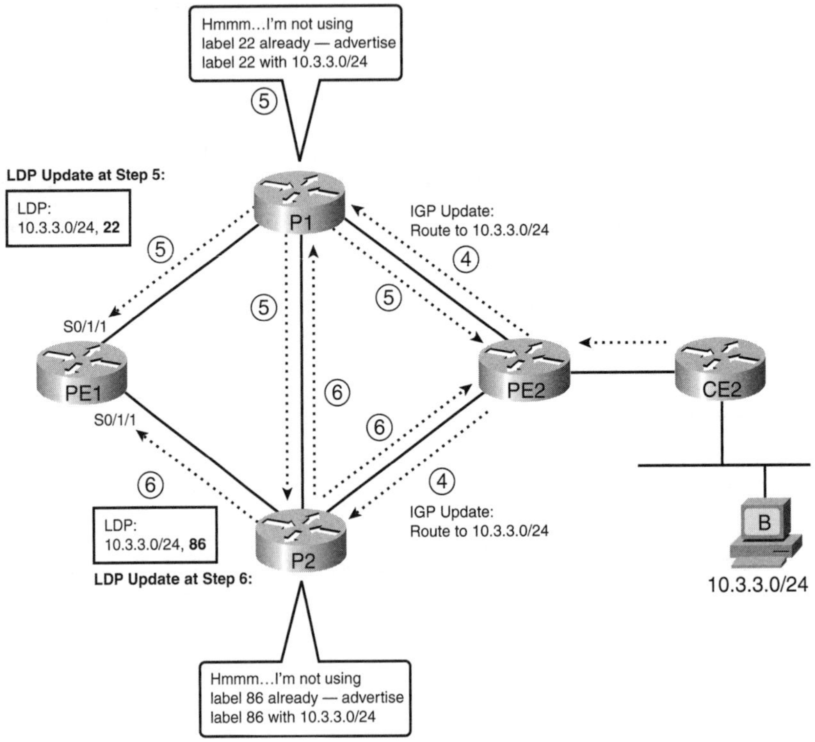

The steps in the figure are as follows, using numbering that continues the numbering from Figure 19-7:

4. PE2 uses EIGRP to advertise the route for 10.3.3.0/24 to both P1 and P2.

5. P1 reacts to the newly learned route by allocating a new local label (22) and using LDP to advertise the new prefix (10.3.3.0/24) to label (20) mapping. Note that P1 advertises this label to all its neighbors.

6. P2 also reacts to the newly learned route by allocating a new local label (86) and using LDP to advertise the new prefix (10.3.3.0/24) to label (86) mapping. P2 advertises this label to all its neighbors.

This same process occurs on each LSR, for each route in the LSR's routing table: each time an LSR learns a new route, the LSR allocates a new local label and then advertises the label and prefix mapping to all its neighbors—even when it is obvious that advertising the label may not be useful. For example, in Figure 19-8, P2 advertises a label for 10.3.3.0/24 back to router PE2—not terribly useful, but it is how frame-mode MPLS LSRs work.

Once the routers have all learned about a prefix using the IGP protocol, and LDP has advertised label/prefix mappings (bindings) to all other neighboring LSRs, each LSR has enough information with which to label switch packets from ingress E-LSR to egress E-LSR. For example, the same data plane process shown in Figures 19-2 and 19-3 could occur when PE1 receives an unlabeled packet destined to an address in 10.3.3.0/24. In fact, the labels advertised in Figures 19-7 and 19-8 purposefully match the earlier MPLS data plane figures (19-2 and 19-3). However, to complete the full process, you need to understand a bit more about what occurs inside an individual router, in particular, a data structure called the MPLS Label Information Base (LIB).

The MPLS Label Information Base Feeding the FIB and LFIB

LSRs store labels and related information inside a data structure called LIB. The LIB essentially holds all the labels and associated information that could possibly be used to forward packets. However, each LSR must choose the best label and outgoing interface to actually use and then populate that information into the FIB and the LFIB. As a result, the FIB and LFIB contain labels only for the currently used best LSP segment, while the LIB contains all labels known to the LSR, whether the label is currently used for forwarding or not.

To make a decision about the best label to use, LSRs rely on the routing protocol's decision about the best route. By relying on the routing protocol, the LSRs can take advantage of the routing protocol's loop-prevention features and react to the routing protocol's choice for new routes when convergence occurs. In short, an LSR makes the following decision:

> For each route in the routing table, find the corresponding label information in the LIB, based on the outgoing interface and next-hop router listed in the route. Add the corresponding label information to the FIB and LIB.

To better understand how an LSR adds information to the FIB and LFIB, this section continues the same example as used throughout the chapter so far. At this point, it is useful to examine the output of some **show** commands, but first, you need a little more detail about the example network and the configuration. Figure 19-9 repeats the same example network used in earlier figures in this chapter, with IP address and interface details included. The figure also notes on which interfaces MPLS has been enabled (dashed lines) and on which interfaces MPLS has not been enabled (solid lines).

Figure 19-9 *Example Network for Seeing the LIB, FIB, and LFIB*

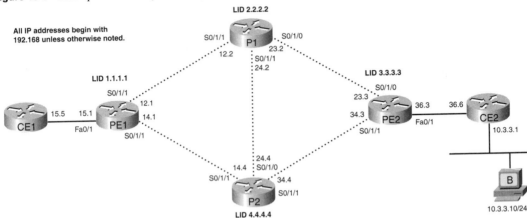

Legend:
MPLS-Enabled Links ....
Non-MPLS Enabled Links ─────────

The configuration of MPLS unicast IP routing is relatively simple. In this case, all six routers use EIGRP, advertising all subnets. The four LSRs enable MPLS globally and on the links noted with dashed lines in the figure. To enable MPLS for simple unicast IP forwarding, as has been described so far in this chapter, an LSR simply needs to enable CEF, globally enable MPLS, and enable MPLS on each desired interface. Also, because IOS uses TDP instead of LDP by default, this configuration overrides the default to use LDP. Example 19-1 shows a sample generic configuration.

Example 19-1 *MPLS Configuration on LSRs for Unicast IP Support*

```
! The first three commands enable CEF and MPLS globally, and
! use LDP instead of TDP
ip cef
mpls ip
mpls label protocol ldp
!
! Repeat the next two lines for each MPLS-enabled interface
interface type x/y/z
 mpls ip
! Normal EIGRP configuration next – would be configured for all interfaces
router eigrp 1
 network …
```

To see how LSRs populate the FIB and LFIB, consider subnet 10.3.3.0/24 again, and think about MPLS from router PE1's perspective. PE1 has learned a route for 10.3.3.0/24 with EIGRP. PE1 has also learned (using LDP) about two labels that PE1 can use when forwarding packets destined for 10.3.3.0/24—one label learned from neighboring LSR P1, and the other from neighboring LSR P2. Example 19-2 highlights these details. Note that the labels do match the figures and examples used earlier in this chapter.

Example 19-2 *PE1's LIB and IP Routing Table*

```
PE1# show ip route 10.0.0.0
Routing entry for 10.0.0.0/24, 1 known subnets
  Redistributing via eigrp 1
D       10.3.3.0 [90/2812416] via 192.168.12.2, 00:44:16, Serial0/0/1
PE1# show mpls ldp bindings 10.3.3.0 24
  tib entry: 10.3.3.0/24, rev 28
        local binding:  tag: 24
        remote binding: tsr: 2.2.2.2:0, tag: 22
        remote binding: tsr: 4.4.4.4:0, tag: 86
```

Example 19-2 shows some mundane information and a few particularly interesting points. First, the **show ip route** command does not list any new or different information for MPLS, but it is useful to note that PE1's best route to 10.3.3.0/24 is through P1. The **show ip mpls bindings 10.3.3.0 24** command lists the LIB entries from 10.3.3.0/24. Note that two remote bindings are listed—one from P1 (LDP ID 2.2.2.2) and one from P2 (LDP ID 4.4.4.4). This command also lists the local binding, which is the label that PE1 allocated and advertised to its neighbors.

> **NOTE**   The term *remote binding* refers to a label-prefix binding learned via LDP from some LDP neighbor.

From Example 19-2, you could anticipate that PE1 will use a label value of 22, and an outgoing interface of S0/0/1, when forwarding packets to 10.3.3.0/24. To see the details of how PE1 arrives at that conclusion, consider the linkages shown in Figure 19-10.

Figure 19-10 *PE1's Process to Determine the Outgoing Label*

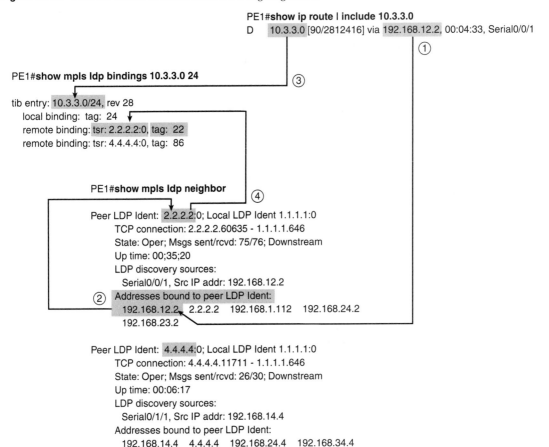

The figure shows the following steps:

1. The routing table entry to 10.3.3.0/24 lists a next-hop IP address of 192.168.12.2. PE1 compares that next-hop information to the list of interface IP addresses on each LDP peer and finds the LDP neighbor who has IP address 192.168.12.2.

2. That same stanza of the **show mpls ldp neighbor** command output identifies the LDP ID (LID) of this peer, namely 2.2.2.2.

3. PE1 notes that for that same prefix (10.3.3.0/24), the LIB contains one local label and two remote labels.

4. Among the known labels listed for prefix 10.3.3.0/24, one was learned from a neighbor whose LID is 2.2.2.2, with label (tag) value of 22.

NOTE Many IOS commands still use the older tag switching terminology—for example, the term Tag Switching Router (TSR) is listed instead of LSR in Figure 19-10.

As a result of these steps, PE1 knows it should use outgoing interface S0/1/0, with label 22, when forwarding packets to subnet 10.3.3.0/24.

Examples of FIB and LFIB Entries

As mentioned earlier in the chapter, the actual packet-forwarding process does not use the IP routing table (RIB) or the LIB—instead, the FIB is used to forward packets that arrived unlabeled, and the LFIB is used to forward packets that arrived already labeled. This section correlates the information in **show** commands to the conceptual view of the FIB and LFIB data structures shown back in Figure 19-3.

First, again focusing on PE1, PE1 simply adds information to the FIB stating that PE1 should impose an MPLS header, with label value 22. PE1 also populates the LFIB, with an entry for 10.3.3.0/24, using that same label value of 22 and an outgoing interface of S0/1/0. Example 19-3 shows the contents of the two tables.

Example 19-3 *FIB and LFIB Entries for 10.3.3.0/24 on PE1*

```
! This next command shows the FIB entry, which includes the local tag (24), the
! tags (label) imposed, and outgoing interface.
PE1# show ip cef 10.3.3.0
10.3.3.0/24, version 65, epoch 0, cached adjacency to Serial0/0/1
0 packets, 0 bytes
  tag information set
    local tag: 24
    fast tag rewrite with Se0/0/1, point2point, tags imposed: {22}
  via 192.168.12.2, Serial0/0/1, 0 dependencies
    next hop 192.168.12.2, Serial0/0/1
    valid cached adjacency
    tag rewrite with Se0/0/1, point2point, tags imposed: {22}
! The next command lists the LFIB entry for 10.3.3.0/24, listing the same basic
! information—the local tag, the outgoing tag (label), and outgoing interface.
PE1# show mpls forwarding-table 10.3.3.0 24
Local  Outgoing    Prefix       Bytes tag  Outgoing   Next Hop
tag    tag or VC   or Tunnel Id  switched   interface
24     22          10.3.3.0/24   0          Se0/0/1    point2point
```

In the data plane example of Figure 19-3, PE1 received an unlabeled packet and forwarded the packet to P1, with label 22. The information in the top part of Example 19-3, showing the FIB, matches that same logic, stating that a tag (label) value of 22 will be imposed by PE1.

Next, examine the LFIB at P1 as shown in Example 19-4. As shown in Figure 19-3, P1 swaps the incoming label of 22 with outgoing label 39. For perspective, the example also includes the LIB entries for 10.3.3.0/24.

Example 19-4 *FIB and LFIB Entries for 10.3.3.0/24 on P1*

```
P1# show mpls forwarding-table 10.3.3.0 24
Local   Outgoing    Prefix          Bytes tag  Outgoing    Next Hop
tag     tag or VC   or Tunnel Id    switched   interface
22      39                10.3.3.0/24       0         Se0/1/0     point2point
P1# show mpls ldp bindings 10.3.3.0 24
  tib entry: 10.3.3.0/24, rev 30
        local binding:  tag: 22
        remote binding: tsr: 1.1.1.1:0, tag: 24
        remote binding: tsr: 4.4.4.4:0, tag: 86
        remote binding: tsr: 3.3.3.3:0, tag: 39
```

The highlighted line in the output of the **show mpls forwarding-table** command lists the incoming label (22 in this case) and the outgoing label (39). Note that the incoming label is shown under the heading "local tag," meaning that label (tag) 22 was locally allocated by this router (P1) and advertised to other routers using LDP, as shown in Figure 19-8. P1 originally allocated and advertised label 22 to tell neighboring routers to forward packets destined to 10.3.3.0/24 to P1, with a label of 22. P1 knows that if it receives a packet with label 22, P1 should indeed swap the labels, forwarding the packet out S0/1/0 with a label of 39.

The LIB entries in Example 19-4 also reinforce the concept that (frame-mode) MPLS LSRs retain all learned labels in their LIBs, but only the currently used labels in the LFIB. The LIB lists P1's local label (22), and the three remote labels learned from P1's three LDP neighbors. To create the LFIB entry, P1 used the same kind of logic shown in Figure 19-10 to correlate the information in the routing table and LIB and choose a label value of 39 and outgoing interface S0/1/0 to forward packets to 10.3.3.0/24.

To see an example of the pop action, consider the LFIB for PE2, as shown in Example 19-5. When PE2 receives a labeled packet from P1 (label 39), PE2 will try to use its LFIB to forward the packet. When populating the LFIB, PE2 can easily realize that PE2 should pop the label and forward an unlabeled packet out its Fa0/1 interface. Those reasons include the fact that PE2 did not enable MPLS on Fa0/1 and that PE2 has not learned any labels from CE2. Example 19-5 shows the outgoing tag as "untagged."

Example 19-5 *FIB and LFIB Entries for 10.3.3.0/24 on PE2*

```
PE2# show mpls forwarding-table 10.3.3.0 24
Local   Outgoing    Prefix          Bytes tag   Outgoing    Next Hop
tag     tag or VC   or Tunnel Id    switched    interface
39      Untagged    10.3.3.0/24     0           Fa0/1       192.168.36.6
```

Note that while the text in Example 19-5 only showed LFIB entries, every LSR builds the appropriate FIB and LFIB entries for each prefix, in anticipation of receiving both unlabeled and labeled packets.

Label Distribution Protocol Reference

Before wrapping up the coverage of basic MPLS unicast IP forwarding, you should know a few more details about LDP itself. So far, this chapter has shown what LDP does, but it has not provided much information about how LDP accomplishes its tasks. This section hits the main concepts and summarizes the rest.

LDP uses a Hello feature to discover LDP neighbors and to determine to what IP address the ensuing TCP connection should be made. LDP multicasts the Hellos to IP address 224.0.0.2, using UDP port number 646 for LDP (TDP uses UDP port 711). The Hellos list each LSR's LDP ID (LID), which consists of a 32-bit dotted-decimal number and a 2-byte label space number. (For frame-based MPLS, the label space number is 0.) An LSR can optionally list a *transport address* in the Hello message, which is the IP address that the LSR wants to use for any LDP TCP connections. If a router does not advertise a transport address, other routers will use the IP address that is the first 4 bytes of the LDP ID for the TCP connections.

After discovering neighbors via an LDP Hello message, LDP neighbors form a TCP connection to each neighbor, again using port 646 (TDP 711). Because the TCP connection uses unicast addresses—either the neighbor's advertised transport address or the address in the LID—these addresses must be reachable according to the IP routing table. Once the TCP connection is up, each router advertises all of its bindings of local labels and prefixes.

Cisco routers choose the IP address in the LDP ID just like the OSPF router ID. LDP chooses the IP address to use as part of its LID based on the exact same logic as OSPF, as summarized in Table 19-4, along with other details.

Table 19-4 *LDP Reference*

LDP Feature	LDP Implementation
Transport protocols	UDP (Hellos), TCP (updates)
Port numbers	646 (LDP), 711 (TDP)
Hello destination address	224.0.0.2
Who initiates TCP connection	Highest LDP ID
TCP connection uses this address	Transport IP address (if configured), or LDP ID if no transport address is configured
LDP ID determined by these rules, in order or precedence	Configuration Highest IP address of an up/up loopback when LDP comes up Highest IP address of an up/up non-loopback when LDP comes up

This concludes the coverage of MPLS unicast IP forwarding for this chapter. Next, the chapter examines one of the more popular uses of MPLS, which happens to use unicast IP forwarding: MPLS VPNs.

MPLS VPNs

One of the most popular of the MPLS applications is called *MPLS virtual private networks (VPNs)*. MPLS VPNs allow a service provider, or even a large enterprise, to offer Layer 3 VPN services. In particular, SPs oftentimes replace older Layer 2 WAN services such as Frame Relay and ATM with an MPLS VPN service. MPLS VPN services enable the possibility for the SP to provide a wide variety of additional services to its customers because MPLS VPNs are aware of the Layer 3 addresses at the customer locations. Additionally, MPLS VPNS can still provide the privacy inherent in Layer 2 WAN services.

MPLS VPNs use MPLS unicast IP forwarding inside the SP's network, with additional MPLS-aware features at the edge between the provider and the customer. Additionally, MPLS VPNs use MP-BGP to overcome some of the challenges when connecting an IP network to a large number of customer IP internetworks—problems that include the issue of dealing with duplicate IP address spaces with many customers.

This section begins by examining some of the problems with providing Layer 3 services and then shows the core features of MPLS that solve those problems.

The Problem: Duplicate Customer Address Ranges

When an SP connects to a wide variety of customers using a Layer 2 WAN service such as Frame Relay or ATM, the SP does not care about the IP addressing and subnets used by those customers. However, in order to migrate those same customers to a Layer 3 WAN service, the SP must learn address ranges from the various customers and then advertise those routes into the SP's network. However, even if the SP wanted to know about all subnets from all its customers, many enterprises use the same address ranges—namely, the private IP network numbers, including the ever-popular network 10.0.0.0.

If you tried to support multiple customers using MPLS unicast IP routing alone, the routers would be confused by the overlapping prefixes, as shown in Figure 19-11. In this case, the network shows five of the SP's routers inside a cloud. Three customers (A, B, and C) are shown, with two customer routers connected to the SP's network. All three customers use network 10.0.0.0, with the three customer sites on the right all using subnet 10.3.3.0/24.

Figure 19-11 *The Main Challenge with Supporting Layer 3 VPNs*

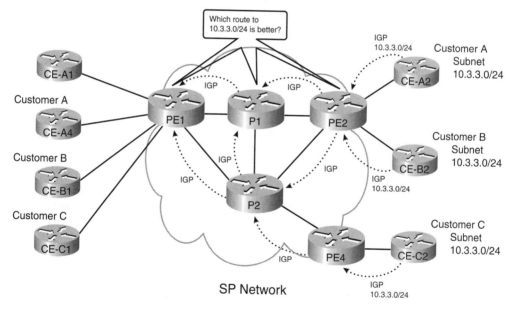

The first and most basic goal for a Layer 3 VPN service is to allow customer A sites to communicate with customer A sites—and only customer A sites. However, the network in Figure 19-11 fails to meet this goal for several reasons. Because of the overlapping address spaces, several routers would be faced with the dilemma of choosing one customer's route to 10.3.3.0/24 as the best route, and ignoring the route to 10.3.3.0/24 learned from another customer. For example, PE2 would learn about two different 10.3.3.0/24 prefixes. If PE2 chooses one of the two possible routes—for example, if PE2 picked the route to CE-A2 as best—then PE2 could not forward packets to customer B's 10.3.3.0/24 off router CE-B2. Also, a possibly worse effect is that hosts in one customer site may be able to send and receive packets with hosts in another customer's network. Following this same example, hosts in customer B and C sites could forward packets to subnet 10.3.3.0/24, and the routers might forward these packets to customer A's CE-A2 router.

The Solution: MPLS VPNs

The protocols and standards defined by MPLS VPNs solve the problems shown in Figure 19-11 and provide a much larger set of features. In particular, the MPLS VPN RFCs define the concept of using multiple routing tables, called *Virtual Routing and Forwarding (VRF) tables*, which separate customer routes to avoid the duplicate address range issue. This section defines some key terminology and introduces the basics of MPLS VPN mechanics.

MPLS uses three terms to describe the role of a router when building MPLS VPNs. Note that the names used for the routers in most of the figures in this chapter have followed the convention of identifying the type of router as CE, PE, or P, as listed here.

- **Customer edge (CE)**—A router that has no knowledge of MPLS protocols and does not send any labeled packets but is directly connected to an LSR (PE) in the MPLS VPN.

- **Provider edge (PE)**—An LSR that shares a link with at least one CE router, thereby providing function particular to the edge of the MPLS VPN, including IBGP and VRF tables

- **Provider (P)**—An LSR that does not have a direct link to a CE router, which allows the router to just forward labeled packets, and allows the LSR to ignore customer VPNs' routes

The key to understanding the general idea of how MPLS VPNs work is to focus on the control plane distinctions between PE routers and P routers. Both P and PE routers run LDP and an IGP to support unicast IP routing—just as was described in the first half of this chapter. However, the IGP advertises routes only for subnets inside the MPLS network, with no customer routes included. As a result, the P and PE routers can together label switch packets from the ingress PE to the egress PE.

PEs have several other duties as well, all geared toward the issue of learning customer routes and keeping track of which routes belong to which customers. PEs exchange routes with the connected CE routers from various customers, using either EBGP, RIP-2, OSPF, or EIGRP, noting which routes are learned from which customers. To keep track of the possibly overlapping prefixes, PE routers do not put the routes in the normal IP routing table—instead, PEs store those routes in separate per-customer routing tables, called VRFs. Then the PEs use IBGP to exchange these customer routes with other PEs—never advertising the routes to the P routers. Figure 19-12 shows the control plane concepts.

> **NOTE**   The term *global routing table* is used to refer to the IP routing table normally used for forwarding packets, as compared with the VRF routing tables.

Figure 19-12   *Overview of the MPLS VPN Control Plane*

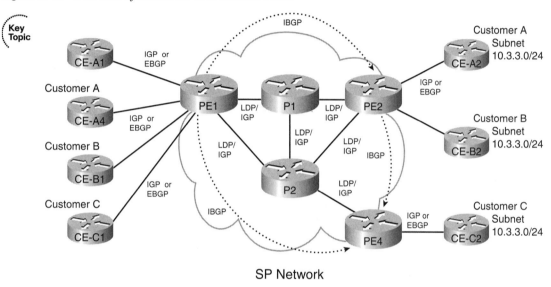

SP Network

The MPLS VPN data plane also requires more work and thought by the PE routers. The PE routers do not have any additional work to do, with one small exception, as compared with simple unicast IP routing. The extra work for the PE relates to the fact that the MPLS VPN data plane causes the ingress PE to place two labels on the packet, as follows:

- An outer MPLS header (S-bit = 0), with a label value that causes the packet to be label switched to the egress PE

- An inner MPLS header (S-bit = 1), with a label that identifies the egress VRF on which to base the forwarding decision

Figure 19-13 shows a general conceptual view of the two labels and the forwarding process. The figure shows a subset of Figure 19-12, with parts removed to reduce clutter. In this case, a host in customer A on the left side of the figure sends a packet to host 10.3.3.3, located on the right side of the figure.

Figure 19-13 *Overview of the MPLS VPN Data Plane*

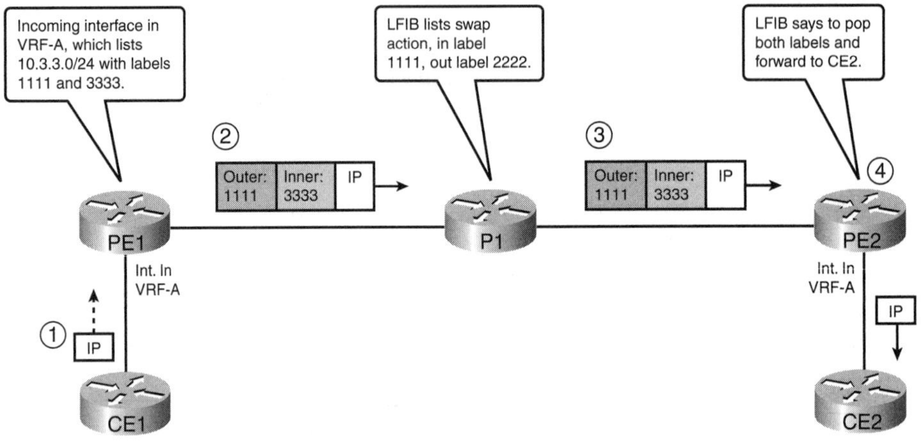

The figure shows the following steps:

1. CE1 forwards an unlabeled packet to PE1.

2. PE1, having received the packet in an interface assigned to VRF-A, compares the packet's destination (10.3.3.3) to the VRF-A CEF FIB, which is based on VRF-A's routing table. PE1 adds two labels based on the FIB and forwards the labeled packet.

3. P1, acting just the same as with unicast IP routing, processes the received labeled packet using its LFIB, which simply causes a label swap. P1 forwards the packet to PE2.

4. PE2's LFIB entry for label 2222 lists a pop action, causing PE2 to remove the outer label. PE2's LFIB entry for label 3333, populated based on the VRF for customer A's VPN, also lists a pop action and the outgoing interface. As a result, PE2 forwards the unlabeled packet to CE2.

NOTE In actual practice, Steps 3 and 4 differ slightly from the descriptions listed here, due to a feature called penultimate hop popping (PHP). This example is meant to show the core concepts. Figure 19-23, toward the end of this chapter, refines this logic when the router uses the PHP feature, which is on by default in MPLS VPNs.

The control plane and data plane processes described around Figures 19-12 and 19-13 outline the basics of how MPLS VPNs work. Next, the chapter takes the explanations a little deeper with a closer look at the new data structures and control plane processes that support MPLS VPNs.

The MPLS VPN Control Plane

The MPLS VPN control plane defines protocols and mechanisms to overcome the problems created by overlapping customer IP address spaces, while adding mechanisms to add more functionality to an MPLS VPN, particularly as compared to traditional Layer 2 WAN services. To understand the mechanics, you need a good understanding of BGP, IGPs, and several new concepts created by both MP-BGP RFCs and MPLS RFCs. In particular, this section introduces and explains the concepts behind three new concepts created for MPLS VPNs:

- VRFs

- Route Distinguishers (RDs)

- Route Targets (RTs)

The next several pages of text examine these topics in order. While reading the rest of the MPLS VPN coverage in this chapter, note that the text will keep expanding a single example. The example focuses on how the control plane learns about routes to the duplicate customer subnets 10.3.3.0/24 on the right side of Figure 19-12, puts the routes into the VRFs on PE2, and advertises the routes with RDs over to PE1 and then how RTs then dictate how PE1 adds the routes to its VRFs.

Virtual Routing and Forwarding Tables

To support multiple customers, MPLS VPN standards include the concept of a virtual router. This feature, called a VRF table, can be used to store routes separately for different customer VPNs. The use of separate tables solves part of the problems of preventing one customer's packets from leaking into another customer's network due to overlapping prefixes, while allowing all sites in the same customer VPN to communicate.

A VRF exists inside a single MPLS-aware router. Typically, routers need at least one VRF for each customer attached to that particular router. For example, in Figure 19-12, router PE2 connects to CE routers in customers A and B but not in customer C, so PE2 would not need a VRF for customer C. However, PE1 connects to CE routers for three customers, so PE1 will need three different VRFs.

For more complex designs, a PE might need multiple VRFs to support a single customer. Using Figure 19-12 again as an example, PE1 connects to two CEs of customer A (CE-A1 and CE-A4). If hosts near CE-A1 were allowed to access a centralized shared service (not shown in the figure) and hosts near CE-A4 were not allowed access, then PE1 would need two VRFs for customer A—one with routes for the shared service's subnets and one without those routes.

Each VRF has three main components, as follows:

■ An IP routing table (RIB)

■ A CEF FIB, populated based on that VRF's RIB

■ A separate instance or process of the routing protocol used to exchange routes with the CEs that need to be supported by the VRF

For example, Figure 19-14 shows more detail about router PE2 from Figure 19-12, now with MPLS VPNs implemented. In this case, PE2 will use RIP-2 as the IGP to both customer A (router CE-A2) and customer B (router CE-B2). (The choice of routing protocol used from PE-CE is unimportant to the depth of explanations shown here.)

Figure 19-14 *Adding Routes Learned from a CE to VRFs on Router PE2*

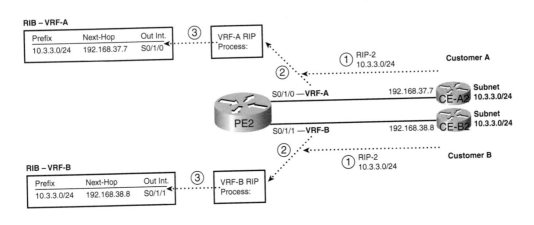

The figure shows three parallel steps that occur with each of the two customers. Note that step 1 for each customer does not occur at the same instant in time, nor does step 2, nor step 3; the figure lists these steps with the same numbers because the same function occurs at each step. The explanation of the steps is as follows:

1. The CE router, which has no knowledge of MPLS at all, advertises a route for 10.3.3.0/24 as normal—in this case with RIP-2.

2. In the top instance of step 2, the RIP-2 update arrives on PE3's S0/1/0, which has been assigned to customer A's VRF, VRF-A. PE2 uses a separate RIP process for each VRF, so PE2's VRF-A RIP process interprets the update. Similarly, the VRF-B RIP process analyzes the update received on S0/1/1 from CE-B2.

3. In the top instance of step 3, the VRF-A RIP process adds an entry for 10.3.3.0/24 to the RIB for VRF-A. Similarly, the bottom instance of step 3 shows the RIP process for VRF-B adding a route to prefix 10.3.3.0/24 to the VRF-B RIB.

> **NOTE** Each VRF also has a FIB, which was not included in the figure. IOS would add an appropriate FIB entry for each RIB entry.

MP-BGP and Route Distinguishers

Now that PE2 has learned routes from both CE-A2 and CE-B2, PE2 needs to advertise those routes to the other PEs, in order for the other PEs to know how to forward packets to the newly learned subnets. MPLS VPN protocols define the use of IBGP to advertise the routes—all the routes, from all the different VRFs. However, the original BGP specifications did not provide a way to deal with the fact that different customers may use overlapping prefixes.

MPLS deals with the overlapping prefix problem by adding another number in front of the original BGP NLRI (prefix). Each different number can represent a different customer, making the NLRI values unique. To do this, MPLS took advantage of a BGP RFC, called MP-BGP (RFC 4760), which allows for the re-definition of the NLRI field in BGP Updates. This re-definition allows for an additional variable-length number, called an *address family*, to be added in front of the prefix. MPLS RFC 4364, "BGP/MPLS IP Virtual Private Networks (VPNs)," defines a specific new address family to support IPv4 MPLS VPNs—namely, an MP-BGP address family called *Route Distinguishers (RDs)*.

RDs allow BGP to advertise and distinguish between duplicate IPv4 prefixes. The concept is simple: advertise each NLRI (prefix) as the traditional IPv4 prefix, but add another number (the RD) that uniquely identifies the route. In particular, the new NLRI format, called VPN-V4, has the following two parts:

■ A 64-bit RD

■ A 32-bit IPv4 prefix

For example, Figure 19-15 continues the story from Figure 19-14, with router PE2 using MP-BGP to advertise its two routes for IPv4 prefix 10.3.3.0/24 to PE1—one from VRF-A and one from VRF-B. The BGP Update shows the new VPN-V4 address family format for the NLRI information, using RD 1:111 to represent VPN-A, and 2:222 to represent VPN-B.

Figure 19-15 *Making Prefixes Unique Using an RD*

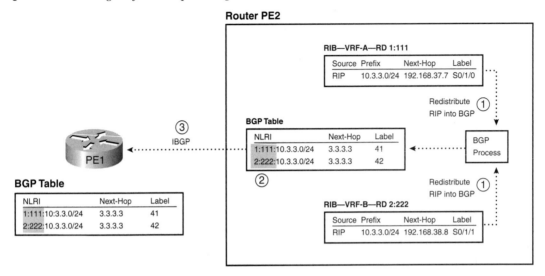

Without the RD as part of the VPN-V4 NLRI, PE1 would have learned about two identical BGP prefixes (10.3.3.0/24) and would have had to choose one of the two as the best route—giving PE1 reachability to only one of the two customer 10.3.3.0/24 subnets. With VPN-V4 NLRI, IBGP advertises two unique NLRI—a 1:111:10.3.3.0 (from VRF-A) and 2:222:10.3.3.0 (from VRF-B). As a result, PE1 keeps both NLRI in its BGP table. The specific steps shown in the figure are explained as follows:

1. PE2 redistributes from each of the respective per-VRF routing protocol instances (RIP-2 in this case) into BGP.

2. The redistribution process pulls the RD from each respective VRF and includes that RD with all routes redistributed from the VRF's routing table.

3. PE3 uses IBGP to advertise these routes to PE1, causing PE1 to know both routes for 10.3.3.0/24, each with the differing RD values.

NOTE Every VRF must be configured with an RD; the IOS **rd** VRF subcommand configures the value.

The RD itself is 8 bytes with some required formatting conventions. The first 2 bytes identify which of the three formats is followed. Incidentally, because IOS can tell which of the three formats is used based on the value, the IOS **rd** VRF subcommand only requires that you type the integer values for the last 6 bytes, with IOS inferring the first 2 bytes (the type) based on the value. The last 6 bytes, as typed in the **rd** command and seen in **show** commands, follow one of these formats:

- 2-byte-integer:4-byte-integer

- 4-byte-integer:2-byte-integer

- 4-byte-dotted-decimal:2-byte-integer

In all three cases, the first value (before the colon) should be either an ASN or an IPv4 address. The second value, after the colon, can be any value you wish. For example, you might choose an RD that lists an LSR's BGP ID using the third format, like 3.3.3.3:100, or you may use the BGP ASN, for example, 432:1.

At this point in the ongoing example, PE1 has learned about the two routes for 10.3.3.0/24—one for VPN-A and one for VPN-B—and the routes are in the BGP table. The next section describes how PE1 then chooses the VRFs into which to add these routes, based on the concept of a Route Target.

Route Targets

One of the most perplexing concepts for engineers, when first learning about MPLS VPNs, is the concept of Route Targets. Understanding the basic question of what RTs do is relatively easy, but understanding why MPLS needs RTs and how to best choose the actual values to use for RTs, can be a topic for long conversation when building an MPLS VPN. In fact, MPLS RTs enable MPLS to support all sorts of complex VPN topologies—for example, allowing some sites to be reachable from multiple VPNs, a concept called overlapping VPNs.

PEs advertise RTs in BGP Updates as BGP Extended Community path attributes (PAs). Generally speaking, BGP extended communities are 8 bytes in length, with the flexibility to be used for a wide variety of purposes. More specifically, MPLS defines the use of the BGP Extended Community PA to encode one or more RT values.

RT values follow the same basic format as the values of an RD. However, note that while a particular prefix can have only one RD, that same prefix can have one or more RTs assigned to it.

To best understand how MPLS uses RTs, first consider a more general definition of the purpose of RTs, followed by an example of the mechanics by which PEs use the RT:

> MPLS uses Route Targets to determine into which VRFs a PE places IBGP-learned routes.

Figure 19-16 shows a continuation of the same example in Figures 19-14 and 19-15, now focusing on how the PEs use the RTs to determine into which VRFs a route is added. In this case, the figure shows an *export RT*—a configuration setting in VRF configuration mode—with a different value configured for VRF-A and VRF-B, respectively. PE1 shows its import RT for each VRF—again a configuration setting in VRF configuration mode—which allows PE1 to choose which BGP table entries it pulls into each VRF's RIB.

Figure 19-16 *The Mechanics of the MPLS Route Target*

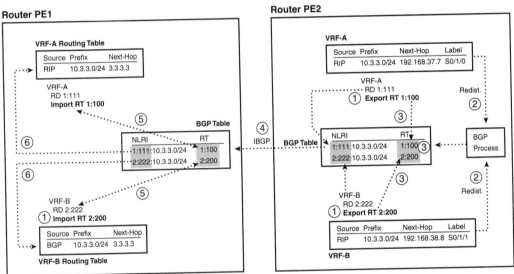

The figure has a lot of details, but the overall flow of concepts is not terribly difficult. Pay particular attention to the last two steps. Following the steps in the figure:

1. The two VRFs on PE2 are configured with an export RT value.

2. Redistribution out of the VRF into BGP occurs.

3. This step simply notes that the export process—the redistribution out of the VRF into BGP—sets the appropriate RT values in PE2's BGP table.

4. PE2 advertises the routes with IBGP.

5. PE1 examines the new BGP table entries and compares the RT values to the configured import RT values, which identifies which BGP table entries should go into which VRF.

6. PE1 redistributes routes into the respective VRFs, specifically the routes whose RTs match the import RT configured in the VRFs, respectively.

> **NOTE** It is sometimes helpful to think of the term *export* to mean "redistribute out of the VRF into BGP" and the term *import* to mean "redistribute into the VRF from BGP."

Each VRF needs to export and import at least one RT. The example in Figure 19-16 shows only one direction: exporting on the right (PE2) and importing on the left (PE1). However, PE2 needs to know the routes for the subnets connected to CE-A1 and CE-B1, so PE1 needs to learn those routes from the CEs, redistribute them into BGP with some exported RT value, and advertise them to PE2 using IBGP, with PE2 then importing the correct routes (based on PE2's import RTs) into PE2's VRFs.

In fact, for simple VPN implementations, in which each VPN consists of all sites for a single customer, most configurations simply use a single RT value, with each VRF for a customer both importing and exporting that RT value.

> **NOTE** The examples in this chapter show different numbers for the RD and RT values, so that it is clear what each number represents. In practice, you can set a VRF's RD and one of its RTs to the same value.

Overlapping VPNs

MPLS can support overlapping VPNs by virtue of the RT concept. An overlapping VPN occurs when at least one CE site needs to be reachable by CEs in different VPNs.

Many variations of overlapping VPNs exist. An SP may provide services to many customers, so the SP actually implements CE sites that need to be reached by a subset of customers. Some SP customers may want connectivity to one of their partners through the MPLS network—for example, customer A may want some of its sites to be able to send packets to some of customer B's sites.

Regardless of the business goals, the RT concept allows an MPLS network to leak routes from multiple VPNs into a particular VRF. BGP supports the addition of multiple Extended Community PAs to each BGP table entry. By doing so, a single prefix can be exported with one RT that essentially means "make sure all VRFs in VPN-A have this route," while assigning another RT value to that same prefix—an RT that means "leak this route into the VRFs of some overlapping VPN."

Figure 19-17 shows an example of the concepts behind overlapping MPLS VPNs, in particular, a design called a central services VPN. As usual, all customer A sites can send packets to all other customer A sites, and all customer B sites can send packets to all other customer B sites. Also, none of the customer A sites can communicate with the customer B sites. However, in addition to these usual conventions, CE-A1 and CE-B2 can communicate with CE-Serv, which connects to a set of centralized servers.

Figure 19-17 *Central Services VPN*

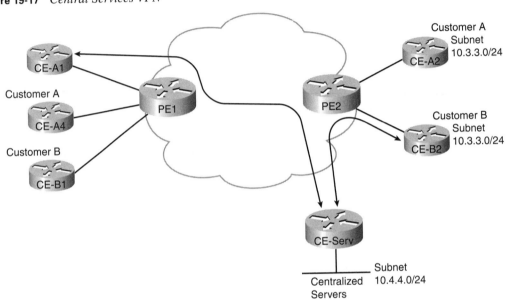

To accomplish these design goals, each PE needs several VRFs, with several VRFs exporting and importing multiple RTs. For example, PE1 needs two VRFs to support customer A—one VRF that just imports routes for customer A, and a second VRF that imports customer A routes as well as routes to reach the central services VPN. Similarly, PE2 needs a VRF for the central services VPN, which needs to import some of the routes in VPN-A and VPN-B.

The MPLS VPN Data Plane

The explanations of the VRF, RD, and RT features explain most of the details of the MPLS VPN control plane. VRFs allow PEs to store routes learned from various CEs, even if the prefixes overlap. The RD allows PEs to advertise routes as unique prefixes, even if the IPv4 prefixes happen to overlap. Finally, the RT tells the PEs which routes should be added to each VRF, which provides greater control and the ability to allow sites to be reachable from multiple VPNs.

At the end of the process, however, to support the forwarding of packets, ingress PEs need appropriate FIB entries, with Ps and PEs needing appropriate LFIB entries. This section focuses on explaining how LSRs fill the FIB and LFIB when using MPLS VPNs.

As usual for this chapter, this section focuses on how to forward packets to subnet 10.3.3.0/24 in the customer A VPN. To begin this examination of the MPLS VPN data plane, consider Figure 19-18. This figure repeats the same forwarding example in Figure 19-13 but now shows a few details about the FIB in the ingress PE and the LFIB entries in the P and egress PE routers.

Figure 19-18 *The Ingress PE FIB and Other Routers' LFIBs*

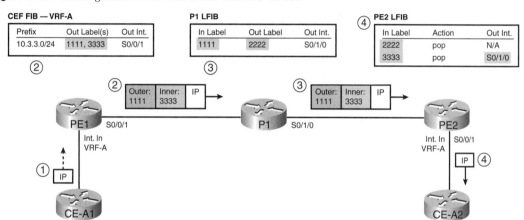

The numbered steps in the figure are as follows:

1. An unlabeled packet arrives on an interface assigned to VRF-A, which will cause ingress PE1 to use VRF-A's FIB to make a forwarding decision.

2. Ingress PE1's VRF-A FIB entry for 10.3.3.0/24 lists an outgoing interface of S0/0/1, and a label stack with two labels—an inner label of 3333 and an outer label of 1111. So PE1 forwards the packet with these two labels pushed in front of the IP header.

3. P1 uses the LFIB entry for incoming (local) label 1111, swapping this outer label value to 2222.

4. PE2 does two LFIB lookups. PE2 finds label 2222 in the table and pops that label, leaving the inner label. Then PE2 looks up the inner label 3333 in the LFIB, noting the pop action as well, along with the outgoing interface. So PE2 forwards the unlabeled packet out interface S0/1/0.

> **NOTE** As was the case with the example shown in Figure 19-13, the details at Steps 3 and 4 will differ slightly in practice, as a result of the PHP feature, which is explained around Figure 19-23 at the end of this chapter.

The example shows the mechanics of what happens in the data plane once the correct FIB and LFIB entries have been added. The rest of this topic about the MPLS VPN data plane examines how MPLS VPN LSRs build these correct entries. While reading this section, it is helpful to keep in mind a couple of details about the purpose of the inner and outer label used for MPLS VPNs:

- The outer label identifies the segments of the LSP between the ingress PE and the egress PE, but it does not identify how the egress PE should forward the packet.

- The inner label identifies the egress PE's forwarding details, in particular the outgoing interface for the unlabeled packet.

Building the (Inner) VPN Label

The inner label identifies the outgoing interface out which the egress PE should forward the unlabeled packet. This inner label, called the *VPN label*, must be allocated for each route added to each customer VRF. More specifically, a customer CE will advertise routes to the PE, with the PE storing those routes in that customer's VRF. In order to prepare to forward packets to those customer subnets, the PE needs to allocate a new local label, associate the label with the prefix (and the route's next-hop IP address and outgoing interface), and store that information in the LFIB.

Figure 19-19 shows PE2's routes for 10.3.3.0/24 in both VRF-A and VRF-B and the resulting LFIB entries. The figure shows the results of PE2's process of allocating a local label for each of the two routes and then also advertising those labels using BGP. (Note that the LFIB is not a per-VRF table; the LFIB is the one and only LFIB for PE2.)

Figure 19-19 *Creating the VPN Label LFIB Entry on the Egress PE*

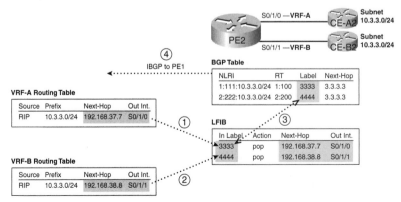

The steps shown in the figure are as follows:

1. After adding a route for 10.3.3.0/24 to VRF-A, PE2 allocates a local label (3333) to associate with the route. PE2 then stores the local label and corresponding next hop and outgoing interface from VRF-A's route for 10.3.3.0/24 into the LIB (not shown) and LFIB.

2. PE2 repeats the logic in Step 1 for each route in each VRF, including the route in VRF-B shown at Step 2. After learning a route for 10.3.3.0/24 in VRF-B, PE2 allocates a different label value (4444), associates that route's next-hop IP address and outgoing interface with the new label, and adds the information to a new LFIB entry.

3. PE2 adds the local labels to the BGP table entry for the routes, respectively, when redistributing routes into BGP.

4. PE2 uses IBGP to advertise the routes to PE1, with the BGP Update including the VPN label.

As a result of the first two steps in the figure, if PE3 receives a labeled packet and analyzes a label value of 3333, PE2 would be able to forward the packet correctly to CE-A2. Similarly, PE2 could correctly forward a received labeled packet with label 4444 to CE-B2.

> **NOTE**   Steps 3 and 4 in Figure 19-19 do nothing to aid PE2 to forward packets; these steps were included to be referenced at an upcoming step later in this section.

Creating LFIB Entries to Forward Packets to the Egress PE

The outer label defines the LSP from the ingress PE to the egress PE. More specifically, it defines an LSP used to forward packets to the BGP next-hop address as advertised in BGP Updates. In concept, the ingress PE adds the outer label to make a request of the core of the MPLS network to "deliver this packet to the egress PE—which advertised this particular BGP next-hop address."

MPLS VPNs use an IGP and LDP to learn routes and labels, specifically to learn the label values to use in the outer label. To link the concepts together, it can be helpful to think of the full control plane process related to the LSP used for the outer label, particularly Step 4 onward:

1. A PE, which will be an egress PE for this particular route, learns routes from some CE.

2. The egress PE uses IBGP to advertise the routes to an ingress PE.

3. The learned IBGP routes list some next-hop IP address.

4. For MPLS VPNs to work, the PE and P routers must have advertised a route to reach the BGP next-hop addresses.

5. Likewise, for MPLS VPNs to work, the PE and P routers must have advertised labels with LDP for the routes to reach the BGP next-hop addresses.

6.   Each P and PE router adds its part of the full end-to-end LSP into its LFIB, supporting the ingress PE's ability to send a packet to the egress PE.

For example, Figure 19-19 shows PE2 advertising two routes to PE1, both with BGP next-hop IP address 3.3.3.3. For MPLS to work, the collective PE and P routers need to advertise an IGP route to reach 3.3.3.3, with LDP advertising the labels, so that packets can be label switched toward the egress PE. Figure 19-20 shows the basic process; however, note that this part of the process works exactly like the simple IGP and LDP process shown for unicast IP forwarding in the first half of this chapter.

Figure 19-20   *Creating the LFIB Entries to Reach the Egress PE's BGP Next Hop*

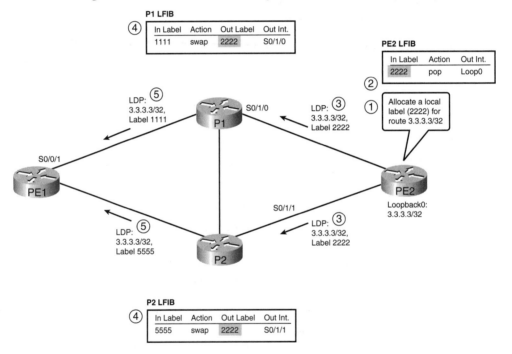

The steps in the figure focus on the LFIB entries for prefix 3.3.3.3/32, which matches PE2's BGP next-hop IP address, as follows. Note that the figure does not show all LDP advertisements but only those that are particularly interesting to the example.

1.   PE2, upon learning a route for prefix 3.3.3.3/32, allocates a local label of 2222.

2.   PE2 updates its LFIB for the local label, listing a pop action.

3.   As normal, PE2 advertises to its LDP neighbors the label binding of prefix 3.3.3.3/32 with label 2222.

4. P1 and P2 both independently learn about prefix 3.3.3.3/32 with the IGP, allocate a local label (1111 on P1 and 5555 on P2), and update their LFIBs.

5. P1 and P2 advertise the binding of 3.3.3.3/32, along with their respective local labels, to their peers.

Figure 19-18 showed the FIB and LFIB entries required for forwarding a packet from CE-A1 to CE-A2, specifically into subnet 10.3.3.0/24. Figures 19-19 and 19-20, and their associated text, explained how all the LFIB entries were created. Next, the focus turns to the FIB entry required on PE1.

Creating VRF FIB Entries for the Ingress PE

The last part of the data plane analysis focuses on the ingress PE. In particular, the ingress PE uses the following logic when processing an incoming unlabeled packet:

1. Process the incoming packet using the VRF associated with the incoming interface (statically configured).

2. Forward the packet using that VRF's FIB.

The FIB entry needs to have two labels to support MPLS VPNs: an outer label that identifies the LSP with which to reach the egress PE, and an inner label that identifies the egress PE's LFIB entry that includes the correct outgoing interface on the egress PE. Although it might be obvious by now, for completeness, the ingress PE learns the outer and inner label values as follows:

■ The outer label is based on the LIB entry, specifically for the LIB entry for the prefix that matches the BGP-learned next-hop IP address—not the packet's destination IP address.

■ The inner label is based on the BGP table entry for the route in the VRF that matches the packet's destination address.

Figure 19-21 completes the ongoing example by showing the process by which PE1 adds the correct FIB entry into VRF-A for the 10.3.3.0/24 prefix. The figure picks up the story at the point at which PE1 has learned all required BGP and LDP information, and it is ready to populate the VRF routing table and FIB.

Figure 19-21 *Creating the Ingress PE (PE1) FIB Entry for VRF-A*

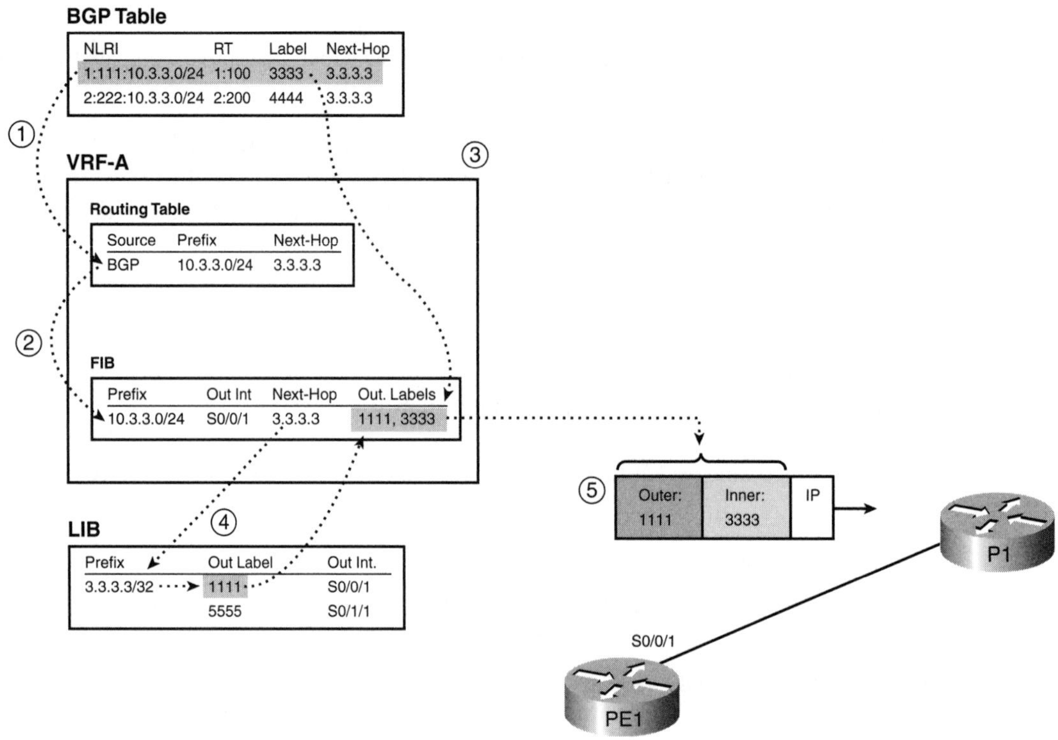

PE1's BGP table holds the VPN label (3333), while PE1's LIB holds the two labels learned from PE1's two LDP neighbors (P1 and P2, labels 2222 and 5555, respectively). In this case, PE1's best route that matches BGP next-hop 3.3.3.3 happens to point to P1 instead of P2, so this example uses label 1111, learned from P1.

The steps in the figure are explained as follows:

1. PE1 redistributes the route from BGP into the VRF-A routing table (based on the import RT).

2. PE1 builds a VRF-A FIB entry for the route just added to the VRF-A routing table.

3. This new FIB entry needs to include the VPN-label, which PE1 finds in the associated BGP table entry.

4. This new FIB entry also needs to include the outer label, the one used to reach the BGP next-hop IP address (3.3.3.3), so PE1 looks in the LIB for the best LIB entry that matches 3.3.3.3, and extracts the label (1111).

5. Ingress PE1 inserts the MPLS header including the two-label label stack.

At this point, when PE1 receives a packet in an interface assigned to VRF-A, PE1 will look in the VRF-A FIB. If the packet is destined for an address in prefix 10.3.3.0/24, PE1 will match the entry shown in the figure, and PE1 will forward the packet out S0/0/1, with labels 1111 and 3333.

Penultimate Hop Popping

The operation of the MPLS VPN data plane works well, but the process on the egress PE can be a bit inefficient. The inefficiency relates to the fact that the egress PE must do two lookups in the LFIB after receiving the packet with two labels in the label stack. For example, the data plane forwarding example used throughout this chapter has been repeated in Figure 19-22, with a summary description of the processing logic on each router. Note that the egress PE (PE2) must consider two entries in its LFIB.

Figure 19-22 *Two LFIB Lookups Required on the Egress PE*

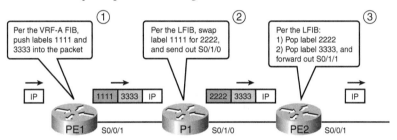

To avoid this extra work on the very last (ultimate) LSR, MPLS uses a feature called *penultimate hop popping (PHP)*. (*Penultimate* simply means "1 less than the ultimate.") So the penultimate hop is not the very last LSR to process a labeled packet, but the second-to-last LSR to process a labeled packet. PHP causes the penultimate-hop LSR to pop the outer label, so that the last LSR—the ultimate hop if you will—receives a packet that only has the VPN label in it. With only this single label, the egress PE needs to look up only one entry in the LFIB. Figure 19-23 shows the revised data plane flow with PHP enabled.

Figure 19-23 *Single LFIB Lookup on Egress PE Due to PHP*

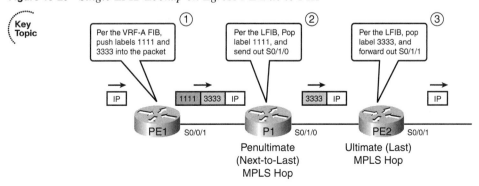

Other MPLS Applications

This last relatively short section of the chapter introduces the general idea about the protocols used by several other MPLS applications. To that end, this section introduces and explains the concept of a *Forwarding Equivalence Class (FEC)* and summarizes the concept of an FEC as used by various MPLS applications.

Frankly, this chapter has already covered all the concepts surrounding the term FEC. However, it is helpful to know the term and the FEC concept as an end to itself, because it helps when comparing various MPLS applications.

Generally speaking, an FEC is a set of packets that receives the same forwarding treatment by a single LSR. For simple MPLS unicast IP forwarding, each IPv4 prefix is an FEC. For MPLS VPNs, each prefix in each VRF is an FEC—making the prefix 10.3.3.0/24 in VRF-A a different FEC from the 10.3.3.0/24 prefix in VRF-B. Alternately, with QoS implemented, one FEC might be the set of packets in VRF-A, destined to 10.3.3.0/24, with DSCP EF in the packet, and another FEC might be packets in the same VPN, to the same subnet, but with a different DSCP value.

For each FEC, each LSR needs a label, or label stack, to use when forwarding packets in that FEC. By using a unique label or set of labels for each FEC, a router has the ability to assign different forwarding details (outgoing interface and next-hop router.)

Each of the MPLS applications can be compared by focusing on the information used to determine an FEC. For example, MPLS traffic engineering (TE) allows MPLS networks to choose to send some packets over one LSP and other packets over another LSP, based on traffic loading—even though the true end destination might be in the same location. By doing so, SPs can manage the flow of data over their high-speed core networks and prevent the problem of overloading the best route as determined by a routing protocol, while barely using alternate routes. To achieve this function, MPLS TE bases the FEC concept in part on the definition of an MPLS TE tunnel.

You can also compare different MPLS applications by listing the control plane protocols used to learn label information. For example, this chapter explained how MPLS VPN uses both LDP and MP-BGP to exchange label information, whereas other MPLS applications use LDP and something else—or do not even use LDP at all. Table 19-5 lists many of the common MPLS applications, the information that determines an FEC, and the control plane protocol that is used to advertise FEC-to-label bindings.

Table 19-5 *Control Protocols Used in Various MPLS Applications*

Key
Topic

Application	FEC	Control Protocol Used to Exchange FEC-to-Label Binding
Unicast IP routing	Unicast IP routes in the global IP routing table	Tag Distribution Protocol (TDP) or Label Distribution Protocol (LDP)
Multicast IP routing	Multicast routes in the global multicast IP routing table	PIM version 2 extensions
VPN	Unicast IP routes in the per-VRF routing table	MP-BGP
Traffic engineering	MPLS TE tunnels (configured)	RSVP or CR-LDP
MPLS QoS	IP routing table and the ToS byte	Extensions to TDP and LDP

Foundation Summary

Please take the time to read and study the details in the "Foundation Topics" section of the chapter, as well as review the items noted with a Key Topic icon.

Memory Builders

The CCIE Routing and Switching written exam, like all Cisco CCIE written exams, covers a fairly broad set of topics. This section provides some basic tools to help you exercise your memory about some of the broader topics covered in this chapter.

Fill in Key Tables from Memory

Appendix E, "Key Tables for CCIE Study," on the CD in the back of this book contains empty sets of some of the key summary tables in each chapter. Print Appendix E, refer to this chapter's tables in it, and fill in the tables from memory. Refer to Appendix F, "Solutions for Key Tables for CCIE Study," on the CD to check your answers.

Definitions

Next, take a few moments to write down the definitions for the following terms:

> FIB, LIB, LFIB, MPLS unicast IP routing, MPLS VPNs, LDP, TDP, LSP, LSP segment, MPLS TTL propagation, local label, remote label, label binding, VRF, RD, RT, overlapping VPN, inner label, outer label, VPN label, PHP, FEC, LSR, E-LSR, PE, CE, P, ingress PE, egress PE

Refer to the glossary to check your answers.

Further Reading

Cisco Press publishes a wide variety of MPLS books, which can be found at http://www.ciscopress.com. Additionally, you can see a variety of MPLS pages from http://www.cisco.com/go/mpls.

Part IX: IP Version 6

Chapter 20: IP Version 6

Blueprint topics covered in this chapter:

This chapter covers the following subtopics from the Cisco CCIE Routing and Switching written exam blueprint. Refer to the full blueprint in Table I-1 in the Introduction for more details on the topics covered in each chapter and their context within the blueprint.

- IPv6 Addressing and Types

- IPv6 Neighbor Discovery

- Basic IPv6 Functionality Protocols

- IPv6 Multicast and Related Multicast Protocols

- Tunneling Techniques

- OSPFv3

- EIGRP for IPv6

20

IP Version 6

This chapter begins with coverage of fundamental topics of IPv6, then progresses into IPv6 routing protocols and other key related technologies. As you will see, IPv6 has a great deal in common with IPv4. Once you understand the IPv6 addressing format and basic configuration commands, you should begin to feel comfortable with IPv6 as a Layer 3 protocol because it shares so many of IPv4's characteristics. IPv6 and IPv4 also have similar basic configuration options and **show** commands.

"Do I Know This Already?" Quiz

Table 20-1 outlines the major headings in this chapter and the corresponding "Do I Know This Already?" quiz questions.

Table 20-1 *"Do I Know This Already?" Foundation Topics Section-to-Question Mapping*

Foundation Topics Section	Questions Covered in This Section	Score
IPv6 Addressing and Address Types	1–3	
Basic IPv6 Functionality Protocols	4–5	
OSPFv3	6–8	
EIGRP for IPv6	9–10	
Tunneling Techniques	11–12	
IPv6 Multicast	13	
Total Score		

In order to best use this pre-chapter assessment, remember to score yourself strictly. You can find the answers in Appendix A, "Answers to the 'Do I Know This Already?' Quizzes."

1. Aggregatable global IPv6 addresses begin with what bit pattern in the first 16-bit group?

   a. 000/3

   b. 001/3

   c. 010/2

   d. 011/2

   e. None of these answers is correct.

2. Anycast addresses come from which address pool?

   a. Unicast

   b. Broadcast

   c. Multicast

   d. None of these answers is correct. Link-local and anycast addresses are drawn from reserved segments of the IPv6 address space.

3. How is the interface ID determined in modified EUI-64 addressing?

   a. From the MAC address of an Ethernet interface with zeros for padding

   b. From the MAC address of an Ethernet interface with hex FFFE inserted in the center

   c. By flipping the U/L bit in the Interface ID

   d. From a MAC address pool on a router that has no Ethernet interfaces

4. Neighbor discovery relies on which IPv6 protocol?

   a. ARPv6

   b. IGMPv4

   c. IPv6 multicast

   d. ICMPv6

5. Which protocol provides the same functions in IPv6 as IGMP does in IPv4 networks?

   a. ICMPv6

   b. ND

   c. MLD

   d. TLA

   e. No equivalent exists.

6. OSPFv3 provides which of the following authentication mechanisms?

   a. Null

   b. Simple password

   c. MD5

   d. None of these answers are correct.

7. OSPFv3 uses LSAs to advertise prefixes, as does OSPFv2. Which of these LSA types are exclusive to OSPFv3?

   a. Link LSA

   b. Intra-Area Prefix LSA

   c. Inter-Area Prefix LSA

   d. External LSA

   e. None of these answers are correct.

8. OSPFv3 requires only interface mode configuration to start on an IPv6-only router.

   a. True

   b. False

9. In EIGRP for IPv4, the default metric is based on k values for bandwidth and delay. Which of the following k values does IPv6 EIGRP use for its default metric calculation?

   a. Bandwidth

   b. Delay

   c. Reliability

   d. Load

   e. MTU

   f. All of these answers are correct.

10. IPv6 EIGRP shares a great deal in common with EIGRP for IPv4. Which of the following best characterizes IPv6 EIGRP behavior with respect to classful and classless networks?

   a. IPv6 EIGRP is classful by default, but can be configured for classless operation using the **no auto-summary** command under the routing process.

   b. IPv6 EIGRP is always classful.

   c. IPv6 EIGRP is always classless.

   d. IPv6 EIGRP defaults to classful operation but can be configured for classless operation on a per-interface basis.

11. Which of the following IPv6 tunnel types support only point-to-point communication?

   a. Manually configured

   b. Automatic 6to4

   c. ISATAP

   d. GRE

12. Which of the following IPv6 tunnel modes does Cisco recommend using instead of automatically configured IPv4-compatible tunnels?

   a. ISATAP

   b. 6to4

   c. GRE

   d. Manually configured

   e. None of these answers is correct.

13. Source-specific multicast is a variation on which PIM mode?

   a. PIM sparse mode

   b. PIM dense mode

   c. PIM sparse-dense mode

   d. Bidirectional PIM

   e. Anycast RP

   f. None of these answers are correct.

Foundation Topics

You must know IPv4 addressing intimately to even reach this point in your CCIE study efforts. This chapter takes advantage of that fact to help you better learn about IPv6 addressing by making comparisons between IPv4 and IPv6. But first, you need to briefly explore *why* we need IPv6 or, more precisely perhaps, why we will need it in the future.

IPv6 was created to meet the need for more host addresses than IPv4 can accommodate—a *lot* more. In the early 1990s, when the number of Internet-connected hosts began to show signs of massive growth, something of a crisis was brewing among the standards bodies about how to deal with that growth in a way that would scale not just to the short-term need, but long term as well.

It takes a lot of analysis and time to create a new addressing standard that meets those goals. Internet growth required faster solutions than a full-blown new addressing standard could support. Two methods were quickly implemented to meet the short-term need: RFC 1918 private IP addresses and NAT/PAT. In a way, these techniques have been so successful at reducing the growth of Internet routing tables that they have pushed out the need for IPv6 by at least a decade, but that need still exists. The day is coming when the world will simply have to move to IPv6 for reasons of application requirements, if not for near-term exhaustion of IPv4 addresses. One driver in this progression is peer-to-peer applications, which have grown greatly in popularity and are complex to support with NAT/PAT. Another is that the organic growth of the Internet around IPv4 has led to suboptimal and inadequate address allocation among the populated areas of the world, especially considering the surge in Internet growth in highly populated countries that were not part of the early Internet explosion.

IPv6 gives us a chance to allocate address ranges in a more sensible way, which will ultimately optimize Internet routing tables. At the same time, IPv6 provides an almost unimaginably vast pool of host IP addresses. At some point, NAT may become a distant memory of an archaic age.

Let's examine what makes IPv6 what it is and how it differs from IPv4. The key differences in IPv6 addressing compared to IPv4 follows:

- IPv6 addresses are 128 bits long, compared to 32 bits long for IPv4. In other words, IPv6 addresses are 2^{96} times more numerous than IPv4 addresses.

- IPv6 addresses are represented in hexadecimal rather than decimal and use colon-separated fields of 16 bits each, rather than decimal points between 8-bit fields, as in IPv4.

- In a Cisco IOS router, you can configure multiple IPv6 addresses on an interface (logical or physical), all of them with equal precedence in terms of the interface's behavior. By comparison, you can configure only one primary IPv4 address per interface with optional secondary addresses.

- Globally unique IPv6 addresses can be configured automatically by a router using the built-in autoconfiguration process without the assistance of protocols such as DHCP.

- IPv6 uses built-in neighbor discovery, by which an IPv6 node can discover its neighbors and any IPv6 routers on a segment, as well as whether any routers present are willing to serve as a default gateway for hosts.

- The concepts of private IPv4 addressing in RFC 1918 do not apply to IPv6; however, several different types of IPv6 addresses exist to provide similar functionality.

The preceding list provides several key differences between IPv4 and IPv6; the next section explores the details of these concepts and provides an introduction to IPv6 configuration in Cisco IOS.

IPv6 Addressing and Address Types

This section covers the basics of IPv6 addressing, starting with how IPv6 addresses are represented and then exploring the different types of IPv6 addresses. After laying that foundation, the "Basic IPv6 Functionality Protocols" section gets into the family of protocols that enables IPv6 to fully function as a network layer protocol.

IPv6 Address Notation

Because of the length of IPv6 addresses, it is impractical to represent them the same way as IPv4 addresses. At 128 bits, IPv6 addresses are four times the length of IPv4 addresses, so a more efficient way of representing them is called for. As a result, each of the eight groups of 16 bits in an IPv6 address is represented in hex, and these groups are separated by colons, as follows:

1234:5678:9ACB:DEF0:1234:5678:9ABC:DEF0

In IPv6, as in IPv4, unicast addresses have a two-level network:host hierarchy (known in IPv6 as the *prefix* and *interface ID*) that can be separated into these two parts on any bit boundary in the address. The prefix portion of the address includes a couple of components, including a *global routing prefix* and a *subnet*. However, the two-level hierarchy separates the prefix from the interface ID much like it divides the network and host portions of an IPv4 address. Instead of using a decimal or hex subnet mask, though, IPv6 subnets use slash notation to signify the network portion of the address, as follows:

1234:5678:9ABC:DEF0:1234:5678:9ABC:DEF0**/64**

An IPv6 address with a prefix length of 64 bits, commonly called a *164 address* in this context, sets aside the first half of the address space for the prefix and the last half for the interface ID. After more coverage of the ground rules for IPv6 addressing, this chapter covers the ways that prefixes and interface IDs are developed for unicast addresses, as well as the additional address types used in IPv6 networks.

Address Abbreviation Rules

Even in the relatively efficient format shown earlier, the previous IPv6 addresses can be cumbersome because of their sheer length. As a result, a couple of abbreviation methods are used to make it easier for us to work with them. These methods include the following:

■ Whenever one or more successive 16-bit groups in an IPv6 address consist of all 0s, that portion of the address can be omitted and represented by two colons (::). The two-colon abbreviation can be used only once in an address, to eliminate ambiguity.

■ When a 16-bit group in an IPv6 address begins with one or more 0s, the leading 0s can be omitted. This option applies regardless of whether the double-colon abbreviation method is used anywhere in the address.

Here are some examples of the preceding techniques, given an IPv6 address of 2001:0001:0000:0000:00A1:0CC0:01AB:397A. Valid ways of shortening this address using the preceding rules include these:

> 2001:1:0:0:A1:CC0:1AB:397A
> 2001:0001::00A1:0CC0:0174AB:397A
> 2001:1::A1:CC0:1AB:397A

All of these abbreviated examples unambiguously represent the given address and can be independently interpreted by any IPv6 host as the same address.

IPv6 Address Types

Like IPv4 addresses, several types of IPv6 addresses are required for the various applications of IPv6 as a Layer 3 protocol. In IPv4, the address types are unicast, multicast, and broadcast. IPv6 differs slightly in that broadcast addressing is not used; special multicast addresses take the place of IPv4 broadcast addresses. However, three address types remain in IPv6: unicast, multicast, and anycast. This section of the chapter discusses each one. Table 20-2 summarizes the IPv6 address types.

Table 20-2 *IPv6 Address Types*

Address Type	Range	Application
Aggregatable global unicast	2000::/3	Host-to-host communication; same as IPv4 unicast.
Multicast	FF00::/8	One-to-many and many-to-many communication; same as IPv4 multicast.
Anycast	Same as Unicast	Application-based, including load balancing, optimizing traffic for a particular service, and redundancy. Relies on routing metrics to determine the best destination for a particular host.
Link-local unicast	FE80::/10	Connected-link communications.
Solicited-node multicast	FF02::1:FF00:0/104	Neighbor solicitation.

Many of the terms in Table 20-2 are exclusive to IPv6. The following sections examine each of the address types listed in the table.

Unicast

Unicast IPv6 addresses have much the same functionality as unicast IPv4 addresses, but because IPv6's 128-bit address space provides so many more addresses to use, we have much more flexibility in assigning them globally. Because one of the intents for IPv6 addressing in public networks is to allow wide use of globally unique addresses, *aggregatable global* unicast IPv6 addresses are allocated in a way in which they can be easily summarized to reasonably contain the size of global IPv6 routing tables in service provider networks.

In addition to aggregatable global unicast addresses, several other aspects of IPv6 unicast addressing deserve mention here and follow in the next few sections.

Aggregatable Global Addresses

In current usage, aggregatable global addresses are assigned from the IPv6 addresses that begin with binary 001. This value can be written in prefix notation as 2000::/3, which means "all IPv6 addresses whose first 3 bits are equal to the first 3 bits of hex 2000." In practice, this includes IPv6 addresses that begin with hex 2 or 3. (Note that RFC 3587 later removed the restriction to only allocate aggregatable global unicast addresses from the 2000::/3, but in practice, these addresses are still allocated from this range.) To ensure that IPv6 addresses can be summarized efficiently when advertised toward Internet routers, several global organizations allocate these addresses to service providers and other users. See RFC 3587 and RFC 3177 for more details.

Aggregatable global address prefixes are structured so that they can be strictly summarized and aggregated through a hierarchy consisting of a private network and a series of service providers. Here is how that works, based on RFC 3177, starting after the first 3 bits in the prefix:

■ The next 45 bits represent the global routing prefix.

■ The last 16 bits in the prefix, immediately preceding the Interface ID portion of the address, are Site Level Aggregator (SLA), bits. These bits are used by an organization for its own internal addressing hierarchy. This field is also known as the Subnet ID.

■ The last 64 bits make up the interface ID.

Figure 20-1 shows the aggregatable global unicast IPv6 address format.

Figure 20-1 *IPv6 Address Format*

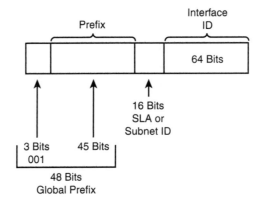

The interface ID portion of an aggregatable global IPv6 address can be explicitly assigned in Cisco IOS or derived using a number of methods explored later in this chapter in the "IPv6 Address Autoconfiguration" section. These addresses should use an Interface ID in the modified EUI-64 format, discussed later in this chapter. Depending on how these addresses are assigned, however, the Universal/Local bit, which is the 7th bit in the Interface ID field of an IPv6 address, can be set to 0 (locally administered) or 1 (globally unique) to indicate the nature of the Interface ID portion of the address.

Link-Local Addresses

As the term implies, link-local addresses are used on a data link or multiaccess network, such as a serial link or an Ethernet network. Because these addresses are link-local in scope, they are guaranteed to be unique only on that link or multiaccess network. Each interface type, regardless of whether it is serial, PPP, ATM, Frame Relay, Ethernet, or something else, gets a link-local address when IPv6 is enabled on that interface.

Link-local addresses always begin with FE80::/10. The Interface ID portion of the address is derived using the modified EUI-64 format, discussed later in this chapter. The remaining 54 bits of the prefix are always set to 0.

On Ethernet interfaces, the IEEE 802 MAC address is the basis for the Interface ID. For other interface types, routers draw from a pool of virtual MAC addresses to generate the Interface IDs. An example of a fully formed link-local address follows:

> FE80::207:85FF:FE80:71B8

As you might gather from the name, link-local addresses are used for communication between hosts that do not need to leave the local segment. By definition, routers do not forward link-local traffic to other segments. As you will see later in this chapter, link-local addresses are used for operations such as routing protocol neighbor communications, which are by their nature link-local.

IPv4-Compatible IPv6 Addresses

Many transition strategies have been developed for IPv4 networks to migrate to IPv6 service and for IPv6 networks to intercommunicate over IPv4 networks. Most of these strategies involve tunneling. Similarly, a mechanism exists for creating IPv6 addresses that are compatible with IPv4. These addresses use 0s in the first 96 bits of the address and one of the two formats for the remaining portion of the address. Take a look at an example, given the IPv4 address 10.10.100.16. The following are valid IPv4-compatible IPv6 addresses that correspond to this IPv4 address (all of these are in hexadecimal, as IPv6 addresses are universally represented):

> 0:0:0:0:0:10:10:100:16
> ::10:10:100:16
> ::A:A:64:10

IPv4-compatible IPv6 addresses are not widely used and do not represent a design best practice, but you should be familiar with their format. See the section "Tunneling," later in this chapter for more detail on IPv4-compatible address usage in the corresponding tunnel type and on the deprecation of this tunneling type in Cisco IOS.

Assigning an IPv6 Unicast Address to a Router Interface

To configure any IPv6 address or other IPv6 feature, you must first globally enable IPv6 on the router or switch:

```
Stengel(config)# ipv6 unicast-routing
```

Next, configure a global unicast address:

```
Stengel(config-if)# ipv6 address 2001:128:ab2e:1a::1/64
```

Routers automatically configure a link local IPv6 address on all IPv6-enabled interfaces. However, you can configure the link local address with the following command. (Note the the **link-local** keyword to designate the address type.)

```
Stengel(config-if)# ipv6 address fe80::1 link-local
```

Unlike IPv4, IPv6 allows you to assign many addresses to an interface. All IPv6 addresses configured on an interface get equal precedence in terms of IP routing behavior.

Multicast

Multicast for IPv6 functions much like IPv4 multicast. It allows multiple hosts to become members of (that is, receive traffic sent to) a multicast group without regard to their location or number. A multicast receiver is known as a group member, because it joins the multicast group to receive traffic. Multicast addresses in IPv6 have a specific format, which is covered in the next section.

Because IPv6 has no broadcast addressing concept, multicast takes the place of all functions that would use broadcast in an IPv4 network. For example, the IPv6 DHCP process uses multicast for sending traffic to an unknown host on a local network.

As in IPv4, IPv6 multicast addresses are always destinations; a multicast address cannot be used as a source of any IPv6 traffic.

IPv6 multicast is covered in more detail in the last section of this chapter.

IPv6 Multicast Address Format

Multicast addresses in IPv6 always begin with FF as the first octet in the address, or FF00::/8. The second octet specifies the lifetime and scope of the multicast group. Lifetime can be permanent or temporary. Scope can be local to any of the following:

- Node

- Link

- Site

- Organization

- Global

The multicast address format is shown in Figure 20-2.

Figure 20-2 *IPv6 Multicast Address Format*

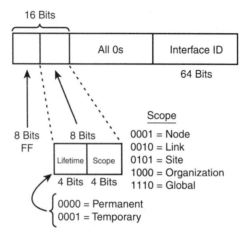

Table 20-3 shows several well-known IPv6 multicast group addresses and their functions.

Table 20-3 *IPv6 Multicast Well-Known Addresses*

Function	Multicast Group	IPv4 Equivalent
All hosts	FF02::1	Subnet broadcast address
All Routers	FF02::2	224.0.0.2
OSPFv3 routers	FF02::5	224.0.0.5
OSPFv3 designated routers	FF02::6	224.0.0.6
EIGRP routers	FF02::A	224.0.0.10
PIM routers	FF02::D	224.0.0.13

In an IPv6 network, as in IPv4, there is an all-nodes multicast group (FF02::1), of which all IPv6 hosts are members. All routers must join the all-routers multicast address (FF02::2). In addition, IPv6 multicast uses a *solicited-node group* that each router must join for all of its unicast and anycast addresses. The format for solicited-node multicast addresses is

FF02::1:FF00:0000/104

Note that all but the last 24 bits of the address are specified by the /104 prefix. Solicited-node addresses are built from this prefix concatenated with the low-order 24 bits (128 − 104 = 24) of the corresponding unicast or anycast address. For example, a unicast address of

      2001:1AB:2003:1::CBAC:DF01

has a corresponding solicited-node multicast address of

      FF02::1:FFAC:DF01

Solicited-node addresses are used in the Neighbor Discovery (ND) process, covered later in this chapter.

Multicast in IPv6 relies on a number of protocols with which you are already familiar, including PIM. Multicast Listener Discovery is another key part of IPv6 multicast. These topics and other related multicast subjects are covered later in this chapter in the "IPv6 Multicast" section.

Anycast

In some applications, particularly server farms or provider environments, it may be desirable to pool a number of servers to provide redundancy, load balancing, or both. Several protocols can provide this functionality in IPv4 networks.

IPv6 has built-in support for this application in the form of anycast addressing. Anycast addresses can be assigned to any number of hosts that provide the same service; when other hosts access this service, the specific server they hit is determined by the unicast routing metrics on the path to that particular group of servers. This provides geographic differentiation, enhanced availability, and load balancing for the service.

Anycast addresses are drawn from the IPv6 unicast address pool and, therefore, are not distinguishable from unicast addresses. RFC 2526 recommends a range of addresses for use by anycast applications. Once an address is assigned to more than one host, it becomes an anycast address by definition. Because anycast addresses cannot be used to source traffic, however, a router must know if one of its interface IPv6 addresses is an anycast address. Therefore, Cisco IOS Software requires the anycast keyword to be applied when an anycast address is configured, as in this example:

```
Mariano(config-if)# ipv6 address 3001:fffe::104/64 anycast
```

All IPv6 routers additionally must support the subnet router anycast address. This anycast address is a prefix followed by all 0s in the interface ID portion of the address. Hosts can use a subnet router anycast address to reach a particular router on the link identified by the prefix given in the subnet router anycast address.

The Unspecified Address

One additional type of IPv6 address deserves mention in this section, as it is used for a number of functions in IPv6 communications. This address, which is used for some types of requests covered later in this chapter, is represented simply by ::. The unspecified address is always a source address used by an interface that has not yet learned its unicast address. The unspecified address cannot be assigned to an interface, and it cannot be used as a destination address.

IPv6 Address Autoconfiguration

One of the goals of IPv6 is to make life easier for network administrators, especially in dealing with the almost unimaginably vast address space that IPv6 provides compared to IPv4. Automatic address configuration, or simply autoconfiguration, was created to meet that need.

An IPv6 host can automatically configure its complete address, or just the interface ID portion of its address, depending on which of the several methods for autoconfiguration it uses. Those methods include

- Stateful autoconfiguration

- Stateless autoconfiguration

- EUI-64

One method, *stateful autoconfiguration*, assigns a host or router its entire 128-bit IPv6 address using DHCP. Another method, *stateless autoconfiguration*, dynamically assigns the host or router interface a 64-bit prefix, and then the host or router derives the last 64 bits of its address using the EUI-64 process described in this section.

Because the EUI-64 format is seen so frequently, it is important to cover those details now. However, particularly for those who have not learned much about IPv6 before reading this chapter, it is better to defer the rest of the details about autoconfiguration until the section titled "IPv6 Address Autoconfiguration" later in this chapter.

EUI-64 Address Format

One key aspect of IPv6 addressing is automatic configuration, but how does an IPv6 host ensure that autoconfigured addresses are globally unique?

The answer to this question comes in two parts. The first part is to set aside a range and structure for aggregatable global addresses, as described earlier. Once a network administrator has set the prefix for a given network, the second part takes over. That second step is address autoconfiguration, but what format should a host use for these addresses to ensure that they are globally unique? That format is EUI-64.

With EUI-64, the interface ID is configured locally by the host to be globally unique. To do that, the host needs a globally unique piece of information that it already knows. That piece of information cannot be more than 64 bits long, because EUI-64 by definition requires a 64-bit prefix and a 64-bit interface ID. But it needs to be both long enough and from a source that is known to be globally unique.

To meet this need, Ethernet hosts and Cisco routers with Ethernet interfaces use their 48-bit MAC addresses as a seed for EUI-64 addressing. But because the MAC address is 48 bits long and the EUI-64 process makes up the last 64 bits of an IPv6 address, the host needs to derive the other 16 bits from another source. The IEEE EUI-64 standard places the hex value FFFE into the center of the MAC address for this purpose. Finally, EUI-64 sets the universal/local bit, which is the 7th bit in the Interface ID field of the address, to indicate global scope.

Here is an example. Given the IPv6 prefix 2001:128:1F:633 and a MAC address of 00:07:85:80:71:B8, the resulting EUI-64 address is

2001:128:1F:633:**<u>2</u>07:85<u>FF</u>:<u>FE</u>80:71B8**/64

The bold part of the address is the complete interface ID. Note how the underlined characters indicate the setting of the U/L bit and the insertion of FFFE after the OUI in the MAC address.

Configure this address on a router's Fast Ethernet interface, as shown in Example 20-1.

Example 20-1   *Configuring an EUI-64 IPv6 Address*

```
Matsui(config)# int fa0/0
Matsui(config-if)# ipv6 address 2001:128:1f:633::/64 eui-64
```

To view the result, use the relevant **show** commands. Example 20-2 shows a sample of the **show ipv6 interface brief** command. This shows both the global unicast addresses and link-local address assigned to this interface. The example shows interface Fa0/0 with the aggregatable global unicast address configured in Example 20-1, and the link-local unicast address automatically created by the router.

Example 20-2   *Checking an IPv6 Interface's Configured Addresses*

```
Matsui# show ipv6 interface brief
FastEthernet0/0              [up/up]
    FE80::207:85FF:FE80:71B8
    2001:128:1F:633:207:85FF:FE80:71B8
```

The shaded section of the unicast address in Example 20-2 shows the EUI-64-derived portion of the address. To see the full output, omit the **brief** keyword and specify the interface, as shown in

Example 20-3. In this example, the router explicitly informs you that the address was derived by EUI-64 by the "[EUI]" at the end of the global unicast address.

Example 20-3 *Detailed Interface Configuration Output*

```
Matsui# show ipv6 interface fa0/0
FastEthernet0/0 is up, line protocol is up
  IPv6 is enabled, link-local address is FE80::207:85FF:FE80:71B8
  No Virtual link-local address(es):
  Global unicast address(es):
    2001:128:1F:633:207:85FF:FE80:71B8, subnet is 2001:128:1F:633::/64 [EUI]
  Joined group address(es):
    FF02::1
    FF02::2
    FF02::A
    FF02::1:FF80:71B8
  MTU is 1500 bytes
  ICMP error messages limited to one every 100 milliseconds
  ICMP redirects are enabled
  ICMP unreachables are sent
  ND DAD is enabled, number of DAD attempts: 1
  ND reachable time is 30000 milliseconds
  ND advertised reachable time is 0 milliseconds
  ND advertised retransmit interval is 0 milliseconds
  ND router advertisements are sent every 200 seconds
  ND router advertisements live for 1800 seconds
  ND advertised default router preference is Medium
  Hosts use stateless autoconfig for addresses. IPv6 addressing:EUI-64;EUI-64 address
format
```

Basic IPv6 Functionality Protocols

IPv6 uses a number of protocols to support it. Because IPv6 is fundamentally similar to IPv4, some of these protocols will be familiar to you and are covered in other parts of this book—for example, ICMP, CDP, and DHCP. However, some aspects of IPv6 operation, and indeed some of its greatest strengths, require functional support from protocols not included in the IPv4 protocol suite. Key among them is Neighbor Discovery Protocol, which provides many functions critical in IPv6 networks. Other protocols, such as CDP, DNS, and ICMP, will be quite familiar.

Because neighbor discovery is such a critical function in IPv6 networks, this part of the chapter starts with that and then moves on to the more familiar protocols.

Neighbor Discovery

A major difference between IPv4 and IPv6 involves how IPv6 hosts learn their own addresses and learn about their neighbors, including other hosts and routers. Neighbor Discovery Protocol, also known as ND or NDP, facilitates this and other key functions. ND is defined in RFC 2461. The remainder of this section introduces ND functionality, lists its main features, and then lists the related ICMPv6 messages, which are beyond the scope of the exam but are useful for study and reference.

In IPv6 networks, ND Protocol uses ICMPv6 messages and solicited-node multicast addresses for its core functions, which center on discovering and tracking other IPv6 hosts on connected interfaces. ND is also used for address autoconfiguration.

Major roles of IPv6 ND include the following:

- Stateless address autoconfiguration (detailed in RFC 2462)

- Duplicate address detection (DAD)

- Router discovery

- Prefix discovery

- Parameter discovery (link MTU, hop limits)

- Neighbor discovery

- Neighbor address resolution (replaces ARP, both dynamic and static)

- Neighbor and router reachability verification

ND uses five types of ICMPv6 messages to do its work. Table 20-4 defines those functions and summarizes their goals.

Table 20-4 *ND Functions in IPv6*

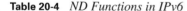

Message Type	Information Sought or Sent	Source Address	Destination Address	ICMP Type, Code
Router Advertisement (RA)	Routers advertise their presence and link prefixes, MTU, and hop limits.	Router's link-local address	FF02::1 for periodic broadcasts; address of querying host for responses to an RS	134, 0
Router Solicitation (RS)	Hosts query for the presence of routers on the link.	Address assigned to querying interface, if assigned, or :: if not assigned	FF02::2	133, 0

Table 20-4   *ND Functions in IPv6 (Continued)*

Message Type	Information Sought or Sent	Source Address	Destination Address	ICMP Type, Code
Neighbor Solicitation (NS)	Hosts query for other nodes' link-layer addresses. Used for duplicate address detection and to verify neighbor reachability.	Address assigned to querying interface, if assigned, or :: if not assigned	Solicited-node multicast address or the target node's address, if known	135, 0
Neighbor Advertise-ment (NA)	Sent in response to NS messages and periodically to provide information to neighbors.	Configured or automatically assigned address of originating interface	Address of node requesting the NA or FF02::1 for periodic advertisements	136, 0
Redirect	Sent by routers to inform nodes of better next-hop routers.	Link-local address of originating node	Source address of requesting node	137, 0

Neighbor Advertisements

IPv6 nodes send Neighbor Advertisement (NA) messages periodically to inform other hosts on the same network of their presence and link-layer addresses.

Neighbor Solicitation

IPv6 nodes send NS messages to find the link-layer address of a specific neighbor. This message is used in three operations:

■ Duplicate address detection

■ Neighbor reachability verification

■ Layer 3 to Layer 2 address resolution (as a replacement for ARP)

IPv6 does not include ARP as a protocol but rather integrates the same functionality into ICMP as part of neighbor discovery. The response to an NS message is an NA message.

Figure 20-3 shows how neighbor discovery enables communication between two IPv6 hosts.

Figure 20-3 *Neighbor Discovery Between Two Hosts*

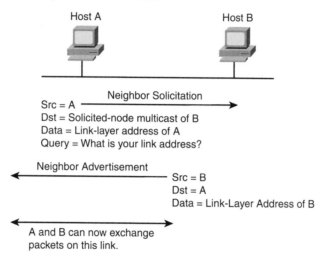

Host A   Host B

Neighbor Solicitation
Src = A ————————————————→
Dst = Solicited-node multicast of B
Data = Link-layer address of A
Query = What is your link address?

Neighbor Advertisement
←————————————————
Src = B
Dst = A
Data = Link-Layer Address of B

←————————————————→
A and B can now exchange
packets on this link.

> **NOTE**   Figures 20-3 and 20-4 were redrawn from Figures 12 and 13, respectively, in "Implementing IPv6 Addressing and Basic Connectivity" at http://www.cisco.com/en/US/products/sw/iosswrel/ps5187/products_configuration_guide_chapter09186a00806f3a6a.html.

Router Advertisement and Router Solicitation

A Cisco IPv6 router begins sending RA messages for each of its configured interface prefixes when the **ipv6 unicast-routing** command is configured. You can change the default RA interval (200 seconds) using the command **ipv6 nd ra-interval**. Router advertisements on a given interface include all of the 64-bit IPv6 prefixes configured on that interface. This allows for stateless address autoconfiguration using EUI-64 to work properly. RAs also include the link MTU, hop limits, and whether a router is a candidate default router.

IPv6 routers send periodic RA messages to inform hosts about the IPv6 prefixes used on the link and to inform hosts that the router is available to be used as a default gateway. By default, a Cisco router running IPv6 on an interface advertises itself as a candidate default router. If you do not want a router to advertise itself as a default candidate, use the command **ipv6 nd ra-lifetime 0**. By sending RAs with a lifetime of 0, a router still informs connected hosts of its presence, but tells connected hosts not to use it to reach hosts off the subnet.

If, for some reason, you wanted to hide the presence of a router entirely in terms of router advertisements, you can disable router advertisements on that router by issuing the **ipv6 nd suppress-ra** command.

Figure 20-4 shows how ND enables communication between two IPv6 hosts.

Figure 20-4   *Router Advertisements Make Hosts Aware of a Router's Presence and Provide Information Necessary for Host Configuration*

Src = Router Link-Local Address
Dst = All-Nodes Multicast Address
Data = Options, Prefix, Lifetime, Autoconfig flag

At startup, IPv6 hosts can send Router Solicitation (RS) messages to the all-routers multicast address. Hosts do this to learn the addresses of routers on a given link, as well as their various parameters, without waiting for a periodic RA message. If a host has no configured IPv6 address, it sends an RS using the unspecified address as the source. If it has a configured address, it sources the RS from the configured address.

Duplicate Address Detection

IPv6 DAD is a function of neighbor solicitation. When a host performs address autoconfiguration, it does not assume that the address is unique, even though it should be because the seed 48-bit MAC address used in the EUI-64 process should itself be globally unique.

To verify that an autoconfigured address is unique, the host sends an NS message to its own autoconfigured address's corresponding solicited-node multicast address. This message is sourced from the unspecified address, ::. In the Target Address field in the NS is the address that the host seeks to verify as unique. If an NA from another host results, the sending host knows that the address is not unique. IPv6 hosts use this process to verify the uniqueness of both statically configured and autoconfigured addresses.

For example, if a host has autoconfigured an interface for the address 2001:128:1F:633:207:85FF: FE80:71B8, then it sends an NS to the corresponding solicited-node address, FF02::1:FE80:71B8/ 104. If no other host answers, the node knows that it is okay to use the autoconfigured address.

The method described here is the most efficient way for a router to perform DAD, because the same solicited-node address matches all autoconfigured addresses on the router. (See the earlier section "IPv6 Address Autoconfiguration" for a discussion of solicited-node addresses.)

Neighbor Unreachability Detection

IPv6 neighbors can track each other, mainly for the purpose of ensuring that Layer 3 to Layer 2 address mapping remains current, using information determined by various means. Reachability is defined not just as the presence of an advertisement from a router or a neighbor, but further requires confirmed, two-way reachability. However, that does not necessarily mean that a neighbor has to ask another node for its presence and receive a direct reply as a result. The two ways a node confirms reachability are as follows:

- A host sends a probe to the desired host's solicited-node multicast address and receives an RA or an NA in response.

- A host, in communicating with the desired host, receives a clue from a higher-layer protocol that two-way communication is functioning. One such clue is a TCP ACK.

Note that clues from higher-layer protocols work only for connection-oriented protocols. UDP, for example, does not acknowledge frames and, therefore, cannot be used as a verification of neighbor reachability. In the event that a host wants to confirm another's reachability under conditions where no traffic or only connectionless traffic is passing between these hosts, the originating host must send a probe to the desired neighbor's solicited-node multicast address.

ICMPv6

Like ICMP for IPv4, ICMPv6 provides messaging support for IPv6. As you learned in the previous section, ICMPv6 provides all the underlying services for neighbor discovery, but it also provides many functions in error reporting and echo requests.

ICMPv6 is standardized in RFC 2463, which broadly classifies ICMPv6 messages into two groups: *error reporting* messages and *informational* messages. To conserve bandwidth, RFC 2463 mandates configurable rate limiting of ICMPv6 error messages. The RFC suggests that ICMPv6 may limit its message rate by means of timers or based on bandwidth. No matter which methods are used, each implementation must support configurable settings for these limits. To that end, Cisco IOS Software implements ICMP rate limiting by setting the minimum interval between error messages and allows credit to build using a token bucket.

To limit ICMPv6 error messages, use the **ipv6 icmp error-interval** command, in global configuration mode. The default interval is 100 ms, and the default token-bucket size is 10 tokens. With this configuration, a new token (up to a total of 10) is added to the bucket every 100 ms. Beginning when the token bucket is full, a maximum of 10 ICMPv6 error messages can be sent in rapid succession. Once the token bucket empties, the router cannot send any additional ICMPv6 error messages until at least one token is added to the bucket.

Unicast Reverse Path Forwarding

In IPv6, unicast RPF helps protect a router from DoS attacks from spoofed IPv6 host addresses. When you configure IPv6 unicast RPF by issuing the **ipv6 verify unicast reverse-path** command on an interface, the router performs a recursive lookup in the IPv6 routing table to verify that the packet came in on the correct interface. If this check passes, the packet in question is allowed through; if not, the router drops it.

Cisco IOS Software gives you the option of defining a sort of trust boundary. This way, a router can verify only selected source IPv6 addresses in the unicast RPF check. To do this, configure an access list on the router and call it with the **ipv6 verify unicast reverse-path** command.

In Example 20-4, the router will perform the RPF check on all IPv6 packets that enter the router's Fast Ethernet 0/0 interface. The router will then drop packets that meet both of these conditions:

1. The RPF check fails.

2. The source address is within the 2007::/64 range.

If either of these conditions is not met, the packet will be routed. If both conditions are met, the router drops the packet.

Example 20-4 *Unicast Reverse-Path Forwarding Configuration*

```
HiramMaxim(config)# ipv6 access-list urpf
HiramMaxim(config-ipv6-acl)# deny ipv6 2007::/64 any
HiramMaxim(config-ipv6-acl)# permit ipv6 any any
HiramMaxim(config-ipv6-acl)# interface fa0/0
HiramMaxim(config-if)# ipv6 verify unicast reverse-path urpf
HiramMaxim(config-if)# end
HiramMaxim# ipv6 interface fa0/0
FastEthernet0/0 is up, line protocol is up
  IPv6 is enabled, link-local address is FE80::207:85FF:FE80:7208
  No Virtual link-local address(es):
  Global unicast address(es):
    2002:192:168:1::1, subnet is 2002:192:168:1::/64
    2002:192:168:2::1, subnet is 2002:192:168:2::/64 [ANY]
  Joined group address(es):
    FF02::1
    FF02::2
    FF02::A
    FF02::D
    FF02::16
    FF02::1:FF00:1
    FF02::1:FF80:7208
  MTU is 1500 bytes
  ICMP error messages limited to one every 100 milliseconds
  ICMP redirects are enabled
```

Example 20-4 *Unicast Reverse-Path Forwarding Configuration (Continued)*

```
  ICMP unreachables are sent
  Input features: RPF
  Unicast RPF access-list urpf
    Process Switching:
      0 verification drops
      0 suppressed verification drops
    CEF Switching:
      0 verification drops
      0 suppressed verification drops
  ND DAD is enabled, number of DAD attempts: 1
  ND reachable time is 30000 milliseconds
  ND advertised reachable time is 0 milliseconds
  ND advertised retransmit interval is 0 milliseconds
  ND router advertisements are sent every 200 seconds
  ND router advertisements live for 1800 seconds
  ND advertised default router preference is Medium
  Hosts use stateless autoconfig for addresses.
```

For more information about how RPF checks work, see Chapter 16, "Introduction to IP Multicasting."

DNS

DNS for IPv6 is quite similar to DNS for IPv4; it provides resolution of domain names to IPv6 addresses. One key difference is the name used for DNS records for IPv6 addresses. In IPv4, these are known as A records; in IPv6, RFC 1886 cleverly terms them AAAA records, because IPv6 addresses are four times longer (in bits) than IPv4 addresses. RFC 1886 and RFC 2874 are both IPv6 DNS extensions. RFC 2874 calls IPv6 address records A6 records. Today, RFC 1886 is most commonly used; however, RFC 2874 expects to eventually obsolete RFC 1886.

IPv6 DNS extensions also provide the inverse lookup function of PTR records, which maps IPv6 addresses to host names.

CDP

Cisco Discovery Protocol provides extensive information about the configuration and functionality of Cisco devices. Because of its extensibility, it should be no surprise to you that CDP also provides information about Cisco IPv6 host configuration. To see IPv6 information transmitted in CDP frames, you must use the **detail** keyword for the **show cdp neighbor** command, as shown in Example 20-5.

Example 20-5 *IPv6 Information Available from CDP Output*

```
Rivers# show cdp neighbors detail
- - - - - - - - - - - - - - - - - - - - - -
Device ID: Mantle
Entry address(es):
  IP address: 10.7.7.6
  IPv6 address: FE80::207:85FF:FE80:7208  (link-local)
  IPv6 address: 2001::207:85FF:FE80:7208  (global unicast)
Platform: Cisco 1760,  Capabilities: Router Switch
Interface: Serial0/0,  Port ID (outgoing port): Serial0/0
Holdtime : 159 sec
(output omitted for brevity)
```

DHCP

One alternative to static IPv6 addressing, namely stateless autoconfiguration, was covered earlier. Another alternative also exists: *stateful autoconfiguration*. This is where DHCPv6 comes in. DHCPv6 is specified in RFC 3315.

Two conditions can cause a host to use DHCPv6:

- The host is explicitly configured to use DHCPv6 based on an implementation-specific setting.

- An IPv6 router advertises in its RA messages that it wants hosts to use DHCPv6 for addressing. Routers do this by setting the M flag (Managed Address Configuration) in RAs.

To use stateful autoconfiguration, a host sends a DHCP request to one of two well-known IPv6 multicast addresses on UDP port 547:

- FF02::1:2, all DHCP relay agents and servers

- FF05::1:3, all DHCP servers

The DHCP server then provides the necessary configuration information in reply to the host on UDP port 546. This information can include the same types of information used in an IPv4 network, but additionally it can provide information for multiple subnets, depending on how the DHCP server is configured.

To configure a Cisco router as a DHCPv6 server, you first configure a DHCP pool, just as in IPv4 DHCP. Then, you must specifically enable the DHCPv6 service using the **ipv6 dhcp server** *pool-name* interface command.

Access Lists and Traffic Filtering

Cisco IOS has the same traffic filtering and related concepts for IPv6 as for IPv4. Access lists serve the same purposes in IPv6 as in IPv4, including traffic filtering and access control for interface logins. You should be aware of a few key differences between access-list behavior for the two network layer protocols, however:

- Because Neighbor Discovery is such a key protocol in IPv6, access lists implicitly permit ND traffic. This is necessary to avoid breaking ND's ARP-like functionality. You can override this implicit-permit behavior using **deny** statements in IPv6 access lists.

- When IPv6 access lists are used for traffic filtering, the command syntax differs from that for IPv4. To configure an interface to filter traffic using an access list, use the **ipv6 traffic-filter** *access-list-name* {**in** | **out**} command.

- IPv6 access lists are always named; they cannot be numbered (unless you use a number as a name).

- IPv6 access lists are configured in named access-list configuration mode, which is like IPv4 named access-list configuration mode. However, you can also enter IPv4-like commands that specify an entire access-list entry on one line. The router will convert it to the correct configuration commands for named access-list configuration mode.

With these exceptions, access-list applications, behavior, and configuration are generally similar for IPv6 and IPv4.

Example 20-6 shows an access list that permits all Telnet traffic to a particular subnet and also matches on a DSCP setting of CS1. In addition, this entry logs ACL hits (and denies, for the second entry) for tracking purposes. The **show access-list** command is also shown to illustrate how similar IPv6 ACL behavior is to IPv4 ACLs.

Example 20-6 *IPv6 Access Lists*

```
cano(config)# ipv6 access-list restrict-telnet
cano(config-ipv6-acl)# permit tcp any 2001:1:2:3::/64 eq telnet dscp cs1 log
cano(config-ipv6-acl)# deny tcp any any log-input
cano(config-ipv6-acl)# line vty 0 4
! Next, the access list is applied inbound on VTY lines 0-4.
cano(config-line)# access-class restrict-telnet in
cano(config-line)# end
cano# show access-lists
IPv6 access list restrict-telnet
    permit tcp any 2001:1:2:3::/64 eq telnet dscp cs1 log (1 match) sequence 10
    deny ipv6 any any log-input (2 matches) sequence 20
cano#
```

IPv6 Static Routes

Now that we have laid the foundation for IPv6 addressing and basic services, the next section of this chapter focuses on routing. This section begins with static routes and then covers the two IPv6 routing protocols on the CCIE Routing and Switching qualifying exam blueprint, OSPFv3 and IPv6 EIGRP.

Static routing in IPv6 works almost exactly as it does in IPv4, but with several twists:

- An IPv6 static route to an interface has a metric of 1, not 0 as in IPv4.

- An IPv6 static route to a next-hop IP address also has a metric of 1, like IPv4.

- Floating static routes work the same way in IPv4 and IPv6.

- An IPv6 static route to a broadcast interface type, such as Ethernet, must also specify a next-hop IPv6 address, for reasons covered next.

As mentioned in the preceding list, IPv6 static routes that point to a broadcast interface must also specify a next-hop IP address. This is because, as you will recall from earlier in this chapter, IPv6 does not use ARP, and, therefore, there is no concept of proxy ARP for IPv6. A next-hop router will not proxy for a destination that is off the subnet. Therefore, static routes must specify the next-hop IP address in situations where you specify a broadcast interface as a next hop.

One valuable tip for real-life configuration work, especially where time is of the essence (as it is in the CCIE lab exam): Before you begin configuring routing processes or static routes, enable IPv6 routing debugging using the **debug ipv6 routing** command. This has the benefit of showing you all changes to the IPv6 routing table, including any that you may not intend!

Example 20-7 shows the configuration of a sample IPv6 static route and how it looks in the routing table.

Example 20-7   *IPv6 Static Route Configuration and* **show** *Commands*

```
Martin(config)# ipv6 route 2001:129::/64 2001::207:85FF:FE80:7208
Martin(config)# end
Martin#
Apr  2 19:22:30.191: %SYS-5-CONFIG_I: Configured from console by console
Martin# show ipv6 route
IPv6 Routing Table - 9 entries
Codes: C - Connected, L - Local, S - Static, R - RIP, B - BGP
       U - Per-user Static route
       I1 - ISIS L1, I2 - ISIS L2, IA - ISIS interarea, IS - ISIS summary
       O - OSPF intra, OI - OSPF inter, OE1 - OSPF ext 1, OE2 - OSPF ext 2
       ON1 - OSPF NSSA ext 1, ON2 - OSPF NSSA ext 2
       D - EIGRP, EX - EIGRP external
```

Example 20-7 *IPv6 Static Route Configuration and* **show** *Commands (Continued)*

```
C   2001::/64 [0/0]
      via ::, Serial0/0
L   2001::207:85FF:FE80:71B8/128 [0/0]
      via ::, Serial0/0
C   2001:128::/64 [0/0]
      via ::, Loopback0
L   2001:128::1/128 [0/0]
      via ::, Loopback0
C   2001:128:1F:633::/64 [0/0]
      via ::, FastEthernet0/0
L   2001:128:1F:633:207:85FF:FE80:71B8/128 [0/0]
      via ::, FastEthernet0/0
S   2001:129::/64 [1/0]
      via 2001::207:85FF:FE80:7208
L   FE80::/10 [0/0]
      via ::, Null0
L   FF00::/8 [0/0]
      via ::, Null0
Martin# ping 2001:129::1
Type escape sequence to abort.
Sending 5, 100-byte ICMP Echos to 2001:129::1, timeout is 2 seconds:
!!!!!
Success rate is 100 percent (5/5), round-trip min/avg/max = 28/30/32 ms
Martin#
```

Note in the output in Example 20-7 that the router automatically generates a /128 route in the IPv6 routing table, classified as Local, for each of its own interfaces.

A floating static route is configured in the same way as shown in Example 20-7, but floating static routes also include the administrative distance after the next hop. The full syntax of the **ipv6 route** command is included in the Cisco IOS command table at the end of this chapter. Additionally, you will find more detail on IPv6 static routing in the multicast coverage at the end of this chapter.

IPv6 Unicast Routing Protocols

The next two major sections of this chapter explore the details of the two IPv6 unicast routing protocols covered in the CCIE Routing and Switching qualification exam blueprint: OSPFv3 and EIGRP for IPv6. These routing protocols have a lot in common in terms of their Cisco IOS configuration. It is worth mention here that RIPng, which was removed from the CCIE Routing and Switching qualification exam blueprint at version 3, also shares many of these common configuration concepts.

Although OSPFv3 and IPv6 EIGRP operate quite differently, here are a few key aspects of configuring them that are helpful to understand as you study how these protocols work:

- In each of these IPv6 unicast routing protocols, enabling the protocol for a particular network in Cisco IOS is performed by issuing the appropriate **ipv6** interface configuration command. The command format, detailed in the "Foundation Summary" section at the end of the chapter, is **ipv6 {eigrp | ospf | rip}** followed by the necessary keywords and arguments.

- In router configuration mode, where the bulk of configuration is done for IPv4 routing protocols, IPv6 routing protocols require less configuration. The global configuration is also more intuitive because most of the configuration that is interface- or network-specific is done in interface configuration mode.

The next two major sections build heavily on the corresponding IPv4 protocol concepts, so it is important to study the EIGRP and OSPFv2 routing protocols in Chapters 8, "EIGRP," and 9, "OSPF," respectively, before working through the following sections of this chapter.

OSPFv3

The good news about OSPFv3 is that OSPFv2 was a mature routing protocol when development began on OSPFv3. The bad news about OSPFv3 is that it is more complex in some ways than OSPFv2. But mostly the two protocols are simply *different* because of the differences in the underlying Layer 3 protocol. Fortunately, RFC 2740, which defines OSPFv3, goes into quite a bit of detail in describing these differences. (And this RFC is well worth a read to gain a better understanding of OSPFv3 than this chapter can provide.)

Differences Between OSPFv2 and OSPFv3

OSPFv2 and OSPFv3 share many key concepts, including most of their basic operations and the concepts of neighbor relationships, areas, interface types, virtual links, metric calculations, and many others. However, you should understand the significant differences as well.

Key differences between OSPFv2 and OSPFv3 include these:

- **Configured using interface commands**—Cisco IOS enables OSPFv3 using interface subcommands, instead of using the OSPFv2 method (using the **network** command in router configuration mode). To enable OSPFv3 process ID (PID) 1 and area 2 on a given interface, the basic command is simply **ipv6 ospf 1 area 2**. Issuing this command also creates the **ipv6 router ospf 1** command in global configuration mode.

- **Advertising multiple networks on an interface**—If multiple IPv6 addresses are configured on an interface, OSPFv3 advertises all of the corresponding networks.

- **OSPFv3 RID must be set**—OSPFv3 can automatically set its 32-bit RID based on the configured IPv4 addresses, using the same rules for OSPFv2. However, if no IPv4 addresses are configured, OSPFv3 cannot automatically choose its router ID. You must manually configure the RID before OSPFv3 will start. By comparison, an OSPFv2 router ID is created automatically if any IP interfaces are configured on a router.

- **Flooding scope**—The scope for flooding LSAs is one of three specific types in OSPFv3:

  — **Link-local scope**—Used by the new LSA type, Link LSA.

  — **Area scope**—For LSAs flooded throughout a single OSPFv3 area. Used by Router, Network, Inter-Area Prefix, Inter-Area Router, and Intra-Area Prefix LSA types.

  — **AS scope**—LSAs of this type are flooded throughout the routing domain; this is used for AS External LSAs.

- **Multiple instances per link**—OSPFv3 supports multiple instances on a link. For example, suppose you have four routers on an Ethernet segment: routers A, B, 1, and 2. You want routers A and B to form adjacencies (become neighbors), and routers 1 and 2 to become neighbors, but you do not want routers A and B to form neighborships with routers 1 and 2. OSPFv3 supports this type of adjacency scoping. The range of instance numbers is 0–255, and the command format on the interface is, for example, **ipv6 ospf 1 area 0 instance 33**. The instance must match on all routers that are to become adjacent on a link.

- **Terminology**—OSPFv3 uses the term *link* for what OSPFv2 calls a *network*.

- **Sources packets from link-local addresses**—With the exception of virtual links, OSPFv3 uses link-local addresses for all communications between neighbors and sources packets from link-local addresses. On virtual links, OSPFv3 sources packets from a globally scoped IPv6 address.

- **Authentication**—OSPFv2 natively supports three authentication types: null, simple password, and MD5. OSPFv3, however, does not itself provide authentication, because IPv6 covers this requirement with its internal support for AH and ESP protocols, as described in more detail later in this chapter.

- **Networks in LSAs**—Whereas OSPFv2 expresses networks in LSAs as [address, mask], OSPFv3 expresses networks in LSAs as [prefix, prefix length]. The default router is expressed with a prefix length of 0.

Virtual Links, Address Summarization, and Other OSPFv3 Features

Many OSPFv3 features are conceptually identical to OSPFv2 and differ only slightly in their configuration. Some of these features include the following:

- Virtual links (which point to router IDs)

- Address summarization by area

- Address summarization in the routing process

- Stub area configuration

- NSSA configuration

- Advertising, or not advertising, a summary using the **area range** [**advertise** I **not-advertise**] command

- OSPF network types and interface configuration

- Router priority configuration for multiaccess networks, to influence DR and BDR elections

- Most OSPF **show** commands

OSPFv3 LSA Types

Most LSA functionality in OSPFv3 is the same as that in OSPFv2, with a few changes in the LSA names. In addition, OSPFv3 has two additional LSA types. Table 20-5 briefly describes each of the LSA types in OSPFv3. Compare this table to Table 9-4 for a better perspective on how OSPFv2 and OSPFv3 LSA types are similar to and different from each other. Note that OSPFv3 LSA types are basically the same as OSPFv2 LSAs, except for their slightly different names and the additions of type 8 and 9 LSAs to OSPFv3.

Table 20-5 *OSPFv3 LSA types*

LSA Type	Common Name	Description	Flooding Scope
1	Router LSA	Describes a router's link states and costs of its links to one area.	Area
2	Network LSA	Generated by a DR to describe the aggregated link state and costs for all routers attached to an area.	Area
3	Inter-Area Prefix LSA for ABRs	Originated by ABRs to describe interarea networks to routers in other areas.	Area
4	Inter-Area Router LSA for ASBRs	Originated by ASBRs to advertise the ASBR location.	Area
5	Autonomous System External LSA	Originated by an ASBR to describe networks learned from other protocols (redistributed routes).	Autonomous System
8	Link LSA	Advertises link-local address and prefix(es) of a router to all other routers on the link, as well as option information. Sent only if more than one router is present on a link.	Link
9	Intra-Area Prefix LSA	• Performs one of two functions: — Associates a list of IPv6 prefixes with a transit network by pointing to a Network LSA. — Associates a list of IPv6 prefixes with a router by pointing to a Router LSA.	Area

OSPFv3 in NBMA Networks

OSPFv3 operates in NBMA networks almost exactly like OSPFv2. In particular, each interface has an OSPF network type, with that network type dictating whether OSPFv3 needs to use a DR/BDR and whether at least one router needs to have an OSPF **neighbor** command configured. For example, when configuring Frame Relay with the IPv6 address on a physical interface or multipoint subinterface, the OSPF network type defaults to "nonbroadcast," which requires the use of a **neighbor** command:

```
Jackson(config-if)# ipv6 ospf neighbor 3003::1
```

OSPFv3 neighbor relationships over NBMA networks take a relatively long time to form (a minute or two), even on high-speed media, as they do in OSPFv2. This delay can lead to confusion and may cause you to spend time troubleshooting a nonproblem.

Invariably, at some point in your studies (or lab exams), you will configure OSPFv2 or v3 over an NBMA network and forget to include a **neighbor** statement. As a result, neighbors will not form and you will have to troubleshoot the problem. A useful crutch you can use to help you remember that NBMA OSPF peers require **neighbor** statements is the saying, "*n*onbroadcast *n*eeds *n*eighbors."

For completeness, you should be aware that it is possible to get OSPF neighbors to form over an NBMA network without **neighbor** statements, if you change the interfaces' network types from their defaults. This is done using the **ipv6 ospf network** interface command, as it is in IPv4. The same rules apply for IPv6, as explained in the Chapter 9 section "Designated Routers on WANs and OSPF Network Types."

Configuring OSPFv3 over Frame Relay

In IPv4 Frame Relay networks, you are likely to be familiar with mapping IP addresses to DLCI numbers. The configuration of **frame-relay map** statements is much the same in IPv6, but there is a twist: It requires two map statements instead of just one. One map statement points to the link-local address, and the other points to the unicast address of the next-hop interface. Only the link-local mapping statement requires the **broadcast** keyword (which actually permits multicast, as there is no such thing as broadcast in IPv6). In Example 20-8, the far-end interface's IPv6 unicast address is 2001::207:85FF:FE80:7208 and its link-local address is FE80::207:85FF:FE80:7208. The DLCI number is 708.

Example 20-8 *Frame Relay Mapping for IPv6*

```
frame-relay map ipv6 FE80::207:85FF:FE80:7208 708 broadcast
frame-relay map ipv6 2001::207:85FF:FE80:7208 708
```

If you configure only the link-local mapping, OSPFv3 will be happy; the neighbors will come up, the routers will become fully adjacent, and their routing tables will fully populate. However, when you try to send IPv6 traffic to a network across the Frame Relay cloud, it will fail because of Frame Relay encapsulation failures.

Of course, if you are able to use Inverse ARP, this issue does not impact your configuration. Inverse ARP works for IPv6 as it does for IPv4 and supports all configured IPv6 addresses on an interface.

Enabling and Configuring OSPFv3

Enabling OSPFv3 on a Cisco router is straightforward if you have a good grasp of OSPFv2. Once basic IPv6 addressing and reachability are configured and working, the OSPFv3 configuration process includes these steps:

Step 1 Identify the desired links connected to each OSPFv3 router.

Step 2 Determine the OSPF area design and the area to which each router link (interface) should belong.

Step 3 Identify any special OSPF routing requirements, such as stub areas, address summarization, LSA filtering, and virtual links.

Step 4 Configure OSPF on the interfaces.

Step 5 Configure routing process commands, including a router ID on IPv6-only routers.

Step 6 Verify OSPF configuration, routing tables, and reachability.

Figure 20-5 shows the network layout for this basic OSPFv3 routing example. Configuration details follow in Example 20-9 and Example 20-10.

Figure 20-5 *Topology for Basic OSPFv3 Routing Configuration Examples 20-9 Through 20-12*

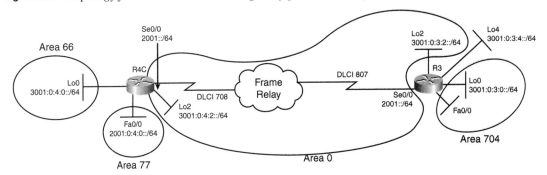

Example 20-9 *Configuring OSPFv3 on Router R3*

```
R3# show run
Building configuration...
! Lines omitted for brevity
!
! IPv6 unicast routing must be enabled to configure IPv6 features:
ipv6 unicast-routing
ipv6 cef
!
interface Loopback0
```

Example 20-9 *Configuring OSPFv3 on Router R3 (Continued)*

```
 no ip address
! IPv6 addresses are assigned to each OSPFv3 interface:
 ipv6 address 3001:0:3::/64 eui-64
! Next OSPFv3 is enabled on the interface and the interface is assigned to an area:
 ipv6 ospf 1 area 704
! IPv6 OSPFv3 draws its router ID from the IPv4 loopback address on
! interface Loopback 1:
interface Loopback1
 ip address 10.3.3.6 255.255.255.0
!
interface Loopback2
 no ip address
 ipv6 address 3001:0:3:2::/64 eui-64
! Like IPv4, setting the network type of a loopback address to point-to-point
! makes the route to this loopback appear in R4C's routing table as a /64
! network rather than as a /128 network (a host route):
 ipv6 ospf network point-to-point
 ipv6 ospf 1 area 0
! Note that interface Loopback 4 will be added later. Its use will be covered
! in another example later in this chapter.
!
interface FastEthernet0/0
 no ip address
 speed auto
! Assign an IPv6 address and perform OSPFv3 configuration on
! the interface:
 ipv6 address 2001:0:3::/64 eui-64
 ipv6 ospf 1 area 704
!
interface Serial0/0
 bandwidth 128
 no ip address
 encapsulation frame-relay
! On the serial interface, first configure the IPv6 address:
 ipv6 address 2001::/64 eui-64
! Next must specify a neighbor, because the interface is
! NBMA (frame relay in this case).
! Like OSPFv2, OSPFv3 in Cisco IOS requires a neighbor statement at
! only one end of the link:
 ipv6 ospf neighbor FE80::207:85FF:FE80:71B8
 ipv6 ospf 1 area 0
 clock rate 128000
 no fair-queue
 cdp enable
! Because this is a frame-relay interface, map the link-local address of
! the next hop. This allows OSPFv3 neighbors to form:
 frame-relay map ipv6 FE80::207:85FF:FE80:71B8 807 broadcast
```

continues

Example 20-9 *Configuring OSPFv3 on Router R3 (Continued)*

```
! Next, add a frame-relay map statement to the unicast address of
! the next hop on the serial link so that unicast IPv6 packets will
! reach their destination:
 frame-relay map ipv6 2001::207:85FF:FE80:71B8 807
! The ipv6 router ospf 1 global commands are created when OSPFv3 is
! enabled on the first interface:
ipv6 router ospf 1
 log-adjacency-changes
!
! Lines omitted for brevity
R3#
```

Example 20-10 *Configuring OSPFv3 on Router R4C*

```
R4C# show run
Building configuration...
 ! Lines omitted for brevity
!
ipv6 unicast-routing
ipv6 cef
!
!
interface Loopback0
 no ip address
 ipv6 address 3001:0:4::/64 eui-64
 ipv6 ospf 1 area 66
!
interface Loopback2
 no ip address
 ipv6 address 3001:0:4:2::/64 eui-64
! Like IPv4, setting the network type of a loopback address to point-to-point
! makes the route to this loopback appear in R3's routing table as a /64
! network rather than as a /128 network (a host route):
 ipv6 ospf network point-to-point
 ipv6 ospf 1 area 0
!
interface FastEthernet0/0
 no ip address
 speed 100
 full-duplex
 ipv6 address 2001:0:4::/64 eui-64
 ipv6 ospf 1 area 77
!
interface Serial0/0
 bandwidth 128
 no ip address
 encapsulation frame-relay
```

Example 20-10 *Configuring OSPFv3 on Router R4C (Continued)*

```
! Because the other neighbor has the neighbor statement, this side doesn't need one.
 ipv6 address 2001::/64 eui-64
 ipv6 ospf 1 area 0
 clock rate 128000
 no fair-queue
 cdp enable
! Here again, two frame-relay map statements are required:
 frame-relay map ipv6 FE80::207:85FF:FE80:7208 708 broadcast
 frame-relay map ipv6 2001::207:85FF:FE80:7208 708
 !
ipv6 router ospf 1
! Here, we must specify the OSPFv3 router ID, because
! this router has no IPv4 interfaces:
 router-id 99.99.99.99
 log-adjacency-changes
 !
! Lines omitted for brevity
R4C#
```

Note that this example configures several OSPF areas, so both intra-area and inter-area routes appear in the OSPFv3 routing tables. Routes with different network sizes and metrics will also be present. Example 20-11 confirms the OSPFv3 routing configuration by using **show** commands and ping tests.

Example 20-11 *Verifying OSPFv3 Configuration and Reachability*

```
! The show ipv6 interface brief command displays both
! the unicast and link-local addresses,
! which is useful during ping and traceroute testing:
R3# show ipv6 interface brief
FastEthernet0/0          [up/up]
    FE80::207:85FF:FE80:7208
    2001:0:3:0:207:85FF:FE80:7208
Serial0/0                [up/up]
    FE80::207:85FF:FE80:7208
    2001::207:85FF:FE80:7208
Loopback0                [up/up]
    FE80::207:85FF:FE80:7208
    3001:0:3:0:207:85FF:FE80:7208
Loopback1                [up/up]
Loopback2                [up/up]
    FE80::207:85FF:FE80:7208
    3001:0:3:2:207:85FF:FE80:7208
Loopback4                [up/up]
    FE80::207:85FF:FE80:7208
    3001:0:3:4:207:85FF:FE80:7208
```

continues

Example 20-11 *Verifying OSPFv3 Configuration and Reachability (Continued)*

```
R3#
! The show ipv6 protocols command gives the best summary of
! OSPFv3 configuration by interface and OSPF area:
R3# show ipv6 protocols
IPv6 Routing Protocol is "connected"
IPv6 Routing Protocol is "static"
IPv6 Routing Protocol is "ospf 1"
  Interfaces (Area 0):
    Loopback2
    Serial0/0
  Interfaces (Area 704):
    Loopback0
    FastEthernet0/0
R3#
! Next we'll look at the OSPFv3 interfaces in more
! detail to view the corresponding settings:
R3# show ipv6 ospf interface
Loopback2 is up, line protocol is up
  Link Local Address FE80::207:85FF:FE80:7208, Interface ID 10
  Area 0, Process ID 1, Instance ID 0, Router ID 10.3.3.6
  Network Type POINT_TO_POINT, Cost: 1
  Transmit Delay is 1 sec, State POINT_TO_POINT,
  Timer intervals configured, Hello 10, Dead 40, Wait 40, Retransmit 5
  Index 1/1/4, flood queue length 0
  Next 0x0(0)/0x0(0)/0x0(0)
  Last flood scan length is 0, maximum is 0
  Last flood scan time is 0 msec, maximum is 0 msec
  Neighbor Count is 0, Adjacent neighbor count is 0
  Suppress hello for 0 neighbor(s)
Serial0/0 is up, line protocol is up
  Link Local Address FE80::207:85FF:FE80:7208, Interface ID 3
  Area 0, Process ID 1, Instance ID 0, Router ID 10.3.3.6
  Network Type NON_BROADCAST, Cost: 781
  Transmit Delay is 1 sec, State DR, Priority 1
  Designated Router (ID) 10.3.3.6, local address FE80::207:85FF:FE80:7208
  Backup Designated router (ID) 99.99.99.99, local address
    FE80::207:85FF:FE80:71B8
  Timer intervals configured, Hello 30, Dead 120, Wait 120, Retransmit 5
    Hello due in 00:00:05
  Index 1/3/3, flood queue length 0
  Next 0x0(0)/0x0(0)/0x0(0)
  Last flood scan length is 1, maximum is 6
  Last flood scan time is 0 msec, maximum is 0 msec
  Neighbor Count is 1, Adjacent neighbor count is 1
    Adjacent with neighbor 99.99.99.99  (Backup Designated Router)
  Suppress hello for 0 neighbor(s)
Loopback0 is up, line protocol is up
```

Example 20-11   *Verifying OSPFv3 Configuration and Reachability (Continued)*

```
   Link Local Address FE80::207:85FF:FE80:7208, Interface ID 8
   Area 704, Process ID 1, Instance ID 0, Router ID 10.3.3.6
   Network Type LOOPBACK, Cost: 1
   Loopback interface is treated as a stub Host
 FastEthernet0/0 is up, line protocol is up
   Link Local Address FE80::207:85FF:FE80:7208, Interface ID 2
   Area 704, Process ID 1, Instance ID 0, Router ID 10.3.3.6
   Network Type BROADCAST, Cost: 1
   Transmit Delay is 1 sec, State DR, Priority 1
   Designated Router (ID) 10.3.3.6, local address FE80::207:85FF:FE80:7208
   No backup designated router on this network
   Timer intervals configured, Hello 10, Dead 40, Wait 40, Retransmit 5
     Hello due in 00:00:06
   Index 1/1/1, flood queue length 0
   Next 0x0(0)/0x0(0)/0x0(0)
   Last flood scan length is 0, maximum is 0
   Last flood scan time is 0 msec, maximum is 0 msec
   Neighbor Count is 0, Adjacent neighbor count is 0
   Suppress hello for 0 neighbor(s)
 R3#
 ! Now let's take a look at the IPv6 routing table's OSPF routes.
 ! Note the presence of two inter-area routes and one intra-area route.
 ! The intra-area route points to Loopback 0 on R4C, which is a /128 (host)
 ! route because LO0 has the default network type for a loopback interface.
 ! The others are /64 routes because of their network types.
 R3# show ipv6 route ospf
 IPv6 Routing Table - 15 entries
 Codes: C - Connected, L - Local, S - Static, R - RIP, B - BGP
        U - Per-user Static route
        I1 - ISIS L1, I2 - ISIS L2, IA - ISIS interarea, IS - ISIS summary
        O - OSPF intra, OI - OSPF inter, OE1 - OSPF ext 1, OE2 - OSPF ext 2
        ON1 - OSPF NSSA ext 1, ON2 - OSPF NSSA ext 2
        D - EIGRP, EX - EIGRP external
 OI  2001:0:4::/64 [110/782]
      via FE80::207:85FF:FE80:71B8, Serial0/0
 OI  3001:0:4::/64 [110/782]
      via FE80::207:85FF:FE80:71B8, Serial0/0
 O   3001:0:4:2:207:85FF:FE80:71B8/128 [110/781]
      via FE80::207:85FF:FE80:71B8, Serial0/0
 R3#
 ! A ping test proves reachability to an address on an inter-area route:
 R3# ping 3001:0:4:2:207:85FF:FE80:71B8
 Type escape sequence to abort.
 Sending 5, 100-byte ICMP Echos to 3001:0:4:2:207:85FF:FE80:71B8,
     timeout is 2 seconds:
 !!!!!
 Success rate is 100 percent (5/5), round-trip min/avg/max = 28/29/32 ms
 R3#
```

Next, Example 20-12 shows redistributing a new loopback interface into OSPFv3 on R3, filtered through a route map, to see the effect on R4C's routing table. Note the similarity in command syntax and output to OSPFv2.

Example 20-12 *Redistributing a Connected Interface into OSPFv3*

```
! First create the Loopback 4 interface on R3:
R3# conf t
R3(config)# interface Loopback4
R3(config-if)# ipv6 address 3001:0:3:4::/64 eui-64
! Next, create a route map to select only this new
! loopback interface for redistribution:
R3(config-if)# route-map Con2OSPFv3
R3(config-route-map)# route-map Con2OSPFv3 permit 10
R3(config-route-map)# match interface loopback 4
R3(config-route-map)# exit
R3(config)# ipv6 router ospf 1
R3(config-rtr)# redistribute connected route-map Con2OSPFv3
R3(config-rtr)# end
R3# show ipv6 protocols
IPv6 Routing Protocol is "connected"
IPv6 Routing Protocol is "static"
IPv6 Routing Protocol is "ospf 1"
  Interfaces (Area 0):
    Loopback2
    Serial0/0
  Interfaces (Area 704):
    Loopback0
    FastEthernet0/0
  Redistribution:
    Redistributing protocol connected route-map Con2OSPFv3
R3#
! On R4 the new redistributed route on R3 appears as an OE2 route, because
! type E2 is the default for redistributed routes, and the default
! metric is 20, as in OSPFv2.
R4C# show ipv6 route ospf
IPv6 Routing Table - 14 entries
Codes: C - Connected, L - Local, S - Static, R - RIP, B - BGP
       U - Per-user Static route
       I1 - ISIS L1, I2 - ISIS L2, IA - ISIS interarea, IS - ISIS summary
```

Example 20-12 *Redistributing a Connected Interface into OSPFv3 (Continued)*

```
        O - OSPF intra, OI - OSPF inter, OE1 - OSPF ext 1, OE2 - OSPF ext 2
        ON1 - OSPF NSSA ext 1, ON2 - OSPF NSSA ext 2
        D - EIGRP, EX - EIGRP external
OI  2001:0:3::/64 [110/782]
       via FE80::207:85FF:FE80:7208, Serial0/0
OI  3001:0:3:0:207:85FF:FE80:7208/128 [110/781]
       via FE80::207:85FF:FE80:7208, Serial0/0
O   3001:0:3:2::/64 [110/782]
       via FE80::207:85FF:FE80:7208, Serial0/0
OE2 3001:0:3:4::/64 [110/20]
       via FE80::207:85FF:FE80:7208, Serial0/0
R4C#
! Finally, verify reachability to the redistributed loopback interface:
R4C# ping 3001:0:3:4:207:85FF:FE80:7208
Type escape sequence to abort.
Sending 5, 100-byte ICMP Echos to 30
001:0:3:4:207:85FF:FE80:7208,
 timeout is 2 seconds:
!!!!!
Success rate is 100 percent (5/5), round-trip min/avg/max = 28/29/33 ms
R4C#
```

Authentication and Encryption

Key Topic

One area in which OSPFv3 is simpler than OSPFv2, at the protocol operation level, is that it uses IPv6's native authentication support rather than implementing its own authentication mechanisms. OSPFv3 uses Authentication Header (AH), beginning with Cisco IOS Release 12.3(4)T, and Encapsulating Security Payload (ESP) protocols for authentication, beginning with Cisco IOS Release 12.4(9)T. Both of these features require a Crypto feature set in the router.

To enable IPv6 OSPF authentication using AH, issue the command **ipv6 ospf authentication**. To enable encryption using ESP, issue the command **ipv6 ospf encryption**. These are interface configuration commands. Note that ESP provides both encryption and authentication. Also note that because AH and ESP are part of the IPsec protocol, you must also configure IPsec security policies to use them. The configuration details of IPsec are outside the scope of this book, but you can find related information on Cisco.com at http://www.cisco.com/en/US/products/sw/iosswrel/ps5187/products_configuration_guide_chapter09186a0080573b9c.html.

Here are three key things to know about OSPFv3 authentication and encryption:

- OSPFv3 can use AH for authentication.

- OSPFv3 can use ESP for authentication and encryption.

- OSPFv3 authentication and encryption can be applied per area or per link (interface); per-link configuration is more secure because it creates more layers of security.

EIGRP for IPv6

Like OSPFv3 compared to OSPFv2, EIGRP for IPv6 has a great deal in common with EIGRP for IPv4. In fact, EIGRP for IPv6 is very similar to EIGRP for IPv4. Of course, some differences exist, so this section covers the key differences before moving on to configuration.

Differences Between EIGRP for IPv4 and for IPv6

IPv6 EIGRP requires a routing process to be defined and enabled (**no shutdown**) and a router ID (in 32-bit IPv4 address format) to be manually assigned using the **router-id** command, both of which must be done in IPv6 router configuration mode before the IPv6 EIGRP routing process can start. These are two of the differences between EIGRP for IPv4 and IPv6. Some others include the following:

- **Configured on the interface**—As with OSPFv3 (and RIPng), EIGRP advertises networks based on interface commands rather than routing process **network** commands. For example, the command to enable IPv6 EIGRP AS 100 on an interface is **ipv6 eigrp 100**.

- **Must** no shut **the routing process**—When EIGRP for IPv6 is first configured on an interface, this action creates the IPv6 EIGRP routing process on the router. However, the routing process is initially placed in the shutdown state, and requires a **no shutdown** command in router configuration mode to become active.

- **Router ID**—EIGRP for IPv6 requires a 32-bit router ID (a dotted-decimal IPv4 address) to be configured before it starts. A router does not complain about the lack of an EIGRP RID, however, so remember to configure one statically when doing a **no shutdown** in the routing process.

- **Passive interfaces**—IPv6 EIGRP, passive interfaces are configured in the routing process only. That is, no related configuration commands are required on the interface.

- **Route filtering**—IPv6 EIGRP performs route filtering using only the **distribute-list prefix-list** command. IPv6 EIGRP does not support route filtering through route maps that call distribute lists.

- **Automatic summarization**—IPv6 EIGRP has no equivalent to the IPv4 (**no**) **auto-summary** command, because there is no concept of classful routing in IPv6.

- **Cisco IOS support**—EIGRP for IPv6 is supported in Cisco IOS beginning with Release 12.4(6)T.

Unchanged Features

All of the following EIGRP features work the same way in IPv6 as they do in IPv4. The only exceptions are the commands themselves, with **ipv6** instead of **ip** in interface commands:

- Metric weights

- Authentication

- Link bandwidth percentage

- Split horizon

- Next-hop setting, configured via the interface-level **ipv6 next-hop-self eigrp** *as* command

- Hello interval and holdtime configuration

- Address summarization (syntax differs slightly to accommodate IPv6 address format)

- Stub networks (syntax and options differ slightly)

- Variance

- Most other features

IPv6 EIGRP uses authentication keys configured exactly as they are for IPv4 EIGRP.

Route Filtering

IPv6 EIGRP uses prefix lists for route filtering. To filter routes from EIGRP updates, configure an IPv6 prefix list that permits or denies the desired prefixes. Then apply it to the EIGRP routing process using the **distribute-list prefix-list** *name* command.

Configuring EIGRP for IPv6

The basic steps required to configure IPv6 EIGRP are quite similar to those for IPv4 EIGRP, with several additions:

Step 1   Enable IPv6 unicast routing.

Step 2   Configure EIGRP on at least one router interface.

Step 3   In the EIGRP routing process, assign a router ID.

Step 4   Issue the **no shutdown** command in the EIGRP routing process to activate the protocol.

Step 5   Use the relevant **show** commands to check your configuration.

Next, let's look at a configuration example that includes IPv6 EIGRP routing between two routers connected across a Frame Relay cloud. Figure 20-6 shows the topology for this example; Example 20-13 covers the configuration details. Features exercised in this example include passive interfaces and redistribution. Example 20-13 is commented extensively to help you understand each feature being implemented. After the initial example, Example 20-13 adds route summarization to show its effect on the routing tables.

Figure 20-6 *Topology for Basic OSPFv3 Routing Configuration Example 20-13*

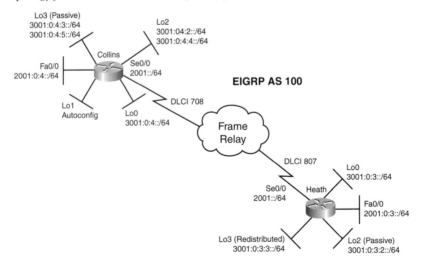

Example 20-13 *IPv6 EIGRP Routing Example Between Collins and Heath*

```
! After basic IPv6 configuration and EIGRP configuration on the
! appropriate interfaces, here's the base configuration:
Collins# show run
!
ipv6 unicast-routing
!
interface Loopback0
 no ip address
 ipv6 address 3001:0:4::/64 eui-64
 ipv6 eigrp 100
!
interface Loopback1
 no ip address
 ipv6 address autoconfig
 ipv6 eigrp 100
!
interface Loopback2
 no ip address
 ipv6 address 3001:0:4:2::/64 eui-64
 ipv6 address 3001:0:4:4::/64 eui-64
 ipv6 eigrp 100
!
interface Loopback3
 no ip address
 ipv6 address 3001:0:4:3::/64 eui-64
 ipv6 address 3001:0:4:5::/64 eui-64
 ipv6 eigrp 100
!
interface FastEthernet0/0
 no ip address
 speed 100
 full-duplex
 ipv6 address 2001:0:4::/64 eui-64
 ipv6 eigrp 100
!
interface Serial0/0
 bandwidth 768
 no ip address
 encapsulation frame-relay
 ipv6 address 2001::/64 eui-64
 ipv6 eigrp 100
 clock rate 128000
 no fair-queue
 cdp enable
 frame-relay map ipv6 FE80::207:85FF:FE80:7208 708 broadcast
 frame-relay map ipv6 2001::207:85FF:FE80:7208 708
! Note that Inverse ARP also would work here, since it is enabled by default.
```

continues

Example 20-13 *IPv6 EIGRP Routing Example Between Collins and Heath (Continued)*

```
!
! Now, in IPv6 EIGRP configuration mode, set the router ID, configure a
! passive interface, and issue a no shutdown on the routing process to begin
! EIGRP routing on Collins:
ipv6 router eigrp 100
 router-id 192.10.10.101
 no shutdown
 passive-interface Loopback3
!
! Once this is done, observe the results by viewing the IPv6 protocols running
! on Collins. Note the default metrics, which are the same as for IPv4 EIGRP, and
! how the Loopback 3 passive-interface configuration is indicated:
Collins# show ipv6 protocols
IPv6 Routing Protocol is "connected"
IPv6 Routing Protocol is "static"
IPv6 Routing Protocol is "eigrp 100"
  EIGRP metric weight K1=1, K2=0, K3=1, K4=0, K5=0
  EIGRP maximum hopcount 100
  EIGRP maximum metric variance 1
  Interfaces:
    FastEthernet0/0
    Serial0/0
    Loopback0
    Loopback1
    Loopback2
    Loopback3 (passive)
  Redistribution:
    None
  Maximum path: 16
  Distance: internal 90 external 170
Collins#
! Now switch to Heath and review the basic EIGRP interface commands.
Heath# show run
! (output omitted for brevity)
ipv6 unicast-routing
!
interface Loopback0
 no ip address
 ipv6 address 3001:0:3::/64 eui-64
 ipv6 eigrp 100
!
! Note that EIGRP is not configured on Loopback 2 or Loopback 3:
interface Loopback2
 no ip address
 ipv6 address 3001:0:3:2::/64 eui-64
!
interface Loopback3
```

Example 20-13 *IPv6 EIGRP Routing Example Between Collins and Heath (Continued)*

```
 no ip address
 ipv6 address 3001:0:3:3::/64 eui-64
!
interface FastEthernet0/0
 no ip address
 speed auto
 ipv6 address 2001:0:3::/64 eui-64
 ipv6 eigrp 100
!
interface Serial0/0
 bandwidth 128
 no ip address
 encapsulation frame-relay
 ipv6 address 2001::/64 eui-64
 ipv6 eigrp 100
 clock rate 128000
 no fair-queue
 cdp enable
 frame-relay map ipv6 2001::207:85FF:FE80:71B8 807
 frame-relay map ipv6 FE80::207:85FF:FE80:71B8 807 broadcast
!
! Next, configure the IPv6 EIGRP routing process and add a route map to
! select which connected interface to redistribute into EIGRP on Heath:
Heath(config)# ipv6 router eigrp 100
Heath(config-rtr)# router-id 192.10.10.1
Heath(config-rtr)# no shutdown
Heath(config-rtr)# passive-interface Loopback2
Heath(config-rtr)# redistribute connected metric 100000 100 255 10 1500
     route-map Con2EIGRP100
Heath(config-rtr)# exit
Heath(config)# route-map Con2EIGRP100 permit 10
Heath(config-route-map)# match interface Loopback3
Heath(config-route-map)# end
Heath#
! The appropriate show command provides a good high-level view of Heath's EIGRP
! settings:
Heath# show ipv6 protocols
IPv6 Routing Protocol is "connected"
IPv6 Routing Protocol is "static"
IPv6 Routing Protocol is "eigrp 100"
  EIGRP metric weight K1=1, K2=0, K3=1, K4=0, K5=0
  EIGRP maximum hopcount 100
  EIGRP maximum metric variance 1
  Interfaces:
    FastEthernet0/0
    Serial0/0
    Loopback0
```

continues

Example 20-13 *IPv6 EIGRP Routing Example Between Collins and Heath (Continued)*

```
     Loopback2 (passive)
  Redistribution:
     Redistributing protocol connected with metric 0 route-map Con2EIGRP100
  Maximum path: 16
  Distance: internal 90 external 170
Heath#
! On Collins, show commands display EIGRP neighbors and interfaces now that both
! neighbors are configured and up:
Collins# show ipv6 eigrp neighbor
IPv6-EIGRP neighbors for process 100
H   Address               Interface     Hold Uptime   SRTT   RTO  Q  Seq
                                        (sec)         (ms)       Cnt Num
0   Link-local address:   Se0/0         163 00:01:16   76    456  0  12
    FE80::207:85FF:FE80:7208
Collins# show ipv6 eigrp interface
IPv6-EIGRP interfaces for process 100

                     Xmit Queue  Mean  Pacing Time  Multicast    Pending
Interface    Peers   Un/Reliable SRTT  Un/Reliable  Flow Timer   Routes
Fa0/0        0       0/0         0     0/10         0            0
Se0/0        1       0/0         76    1/31         50           0
Lo0          0       0/0         0     0/10         0            0
Lo1          0       0/0         0     0/10         0            0
Lo2          0       0/0         0     0/10         0            0
! The routing table on Collins shows that we're learning four routes from Heath.
! Two are internal routes  and one is Heath's redistributed loopback (EX).
! Note the different administrative distances and metrics:
Collins# show ipv6 route eigrp
IPv6 Routing Table - 19 entries
Codes: C - Connected, L - Local, S - Static, R - RIP, B - BGP
       U - Per-user Static route
       I1 - ISIS L1, I2 - ISIS L2, IA - ISIS interarea, IS - ISIS summary
       O - OSPF intra, OI - OSPF inter, OE1 - OSPF ext 1, OE2 - OSPF ext 2
       ON1 - OSPF NSSA ext 1, ON2 - OSPF NSSA ext 2
       D - EIGRP, EX - EIGRP external
D   2001:0:3::/64 [90/3847680]
      via FE80::207:85FF:FE80:7208, Serial0/0
D   3001:0:3::/64 [90/3973120]
      via FE80::207:85FF:FE80:7208, Serial0/0
D   3001:0:3:2::/64 [90/3973120]
      via FE80::207:85FF:FE80:7208, Serial0/0
EX  3001:0:3:3::/64 [170/3870720]
      via FE80::207:85FF:FE80:7208, Serial0/0
Collins#
! On Heath, the routing table is more extensive:
Heath# show ipv6 route eigrp
IPv6 Routing Table - 18 entries
```

Example 20-13 *IPv6 EIGRP Routing Example Between Collins and Heath (Continued)*

```
Codes: C - Connected, L - Local, S - Static, R - RIP, B - BGP
       U - Per-user Static route
       I1 - ISIS L1, I2 - ISIS L2, IA - ISIS interarea, IS - ISIS summary
       O - OSPF intra, OI - OSPF inter, OE1 - OSPF ext 1, OE2 - OSPF ext 2
       ON1 - OSPF NSSA ext 1, ON2 - OSPF NSSA ext 2
       D - EIGRP, EX - EIGRP external
D   2001:0:4::/64 [90/20514560]
     via FE80::207:85FF:FE80:71B8, Serial0/0
D   3001:0:4::/64 [90/20640000]
     via FE80::207:85FF:FE80:71B8, Serial0/0
D   3001:0:4:2::/64 [90/20640000]
     via FE80::207:85FF:FE80:71B8, Serial0/0
D   3001:0:4:3::/64 [90/20640000]
     via FE80::207:85FF:FE80:71B8, Serial0/0
D   3001:0:4:4::/64 [90/20640000]
     via FE80::207:85FF:FE80:71B8, Serial0/0
D   3001:0:4:5::/64 [90/20640000]
     via FE80::207:85FF:FE80:71B8, Serial0/0
Heath#
! Verify reachability to the networks using ping. Only one ping test is shown
! for brevity, but hosts on all prefixes in the routing table are reachable.
Heath# ping 3001:0:4:5:207:85FF:FE80:71B8
Type escape sequence to abort.
Sending 5, 100-byte ICMP Echos to 3001:0:4:5:207:85FF:FE80:71B8,
    timeout is 2 seconds:
!!!!!
Success rate is 100 percent (5/5), round-trip min/avg/max = 28/29/32 ms
Heath#
! Now summarizing the two loopback addresses into one summary route on
! Collins's Serial 0/0 interface:
Collins# conf term
Enter configuration commands, one per line.  End with CNTL/Z.
Collins(config)# int s0/0
Collins(config-if)# ipv summary-address eigrp 100 3001:0:4:4::/63
Collins(config-if)# end
Collins# show ipv6 protocols
IPv6 Routing Protocol is "connected"
IPv6 Routing Protocol is "static"
IPv6 Routing Protocol is "eigrp 100"
  EIGRP metric weight K1=1, K2=0, K3=1, K4=0, K5=0
  EIGRP maximum hopcount 100
  EIGRP maximum metric variance 1
  Interfaces:
    FastEthernet0/0
    Serial0/0
    Loopback0
    Loopback1
```

continues

Example 20-13 *IPv6 EIGRP Routing Example Between Collins and Heath (Continued)*

```
   Loopback2
   Loopback3 (passive)
 Redistribution:
   None
 Address Summarization:
   3001:0:4:4::/63 for Serial0/0
     Summarizing with metric 128256
 Maximum path: 16
 Distance: internal 90 external 170
Collins#
! Heath's routing table reflects the difference, with one summary route instead
! of two separate routing table entries:
Heath# show ipv6 route eigrp
IPv6 Routing Table - 17 entries
Codes: C - Connected, L - Local, S - Static, R - RIP, B - BGP
       U - Per-user Static route
       I1 - ISIS L1, I2 - ISIS L2, IA - ISIS interarea, IS - ISIS summary
       O - OSPF intra, OI - OSPF inter, OE1 - OSPF ext 1, OE2 - OSPF ext 2
       ON1 - OSPF NSSA ext 1, ON2 - OSPF NSSA ext 2
       D - EIGRP, EX - EIGRP external
D   2001:0:4::/64 [90/20514560]
     via FE80::207:85FF:FE80:71B8, Serial0/0
D   3001:0:4::/64 [90/20640000]
     via FE80::207:85FF:FE80:71B8, Serial0/0
D   3001:0:4:2::/64 [90/20640000]
     via FE80::207:85FF:FE80:71B8, Serial0/0
D   3001:0:4:3::/64 [90/20640000]
     via FE80::207:85FF:FE80:71B8, Serial0/0
D   3001:0:4:4::/63 [90/20640000]
     via FE80::207:85FF:FE80:71B8, Serial0/0
Heath#
! Hosts on both summarized prefixes are still reachable:
Heath# ping 3001:0:4:4:207:85FF:FE80:71B8
Type escape sequence to abort.
Sending 5, 100-byte ICMP Echos to 3001:0:4:4:207:85FF:FE80:71B8,
   timeout is 2 seconds:
!!!!!
Success rate is 100 percent (5/5), round-trip min/avg/max = 28/30/32 ms
Heath# ping 3001:0:4:5:207:85FF:FE80:71B8
Type escape sequence to abort.
Sending 5, 100-byte ICMP Echos to 3001:0:4:5:207:85FF:FE80:71B8,
   timeout is 2 seconds:
!!!!!
Success rate is 100 percent (5/5), round-trip min/avg/max = 28/29/32 ms
Heath#
```

To summarize this section, you can see that IPv6 EIGRP is very similar to EIGRP for IPv4. You should find configuring it to be relatively easy once you have a good command of both IPv4 EIGRP and the basics of IPv6 addressing. Focus on the key differences between the two implementations and study the configuration examples in your pre-exam review.

Quality of Service

IPv6 QoS, like the routing protocols discussed in the two previous sections, has a great deal in common with IPv4 QoS. This is a result of Cisco's three-step, hierarchical strategy for QoS implementation. The same major QoS methods are available for IPv6 as for IPv4, and configuring them using the Modular QoS CLI (MQC) will also be familiar. Be sure that you are familiar and comfortable with QoS configuration for IPv4 before tackling this section of the chapter.

With respect to the Cisco IOS version, many of the IPv6 QoS features in this section have been implemented for some time, some as early as version 12.0. However, the IOS version on which this section is based is 12.4 Mainline.

Before getting into details, please note that these features are not available in IPv6 QoS implementation on Cisco routers:

Key
Topic

- Network Based Application Recognition (NBAR)

- Compressed Real-Time Protocol (cRTP)

- Committed access rate (CAR)

- Priority queuing (PQ)

- Custom queuing (CQ)

As you can see from this list, three of the five items, CAR, PQ, and CQ, are legacy QoS features. Supporting these features in a new implementation does not make sense, because the MQC handles the same functions. In IPv4, these technologies remain supported to avoid forcing users to migrate to the equivalent MQC-configured feature set. But because IPv6 is newer in Cisco IOS than CAR, PQ, and CQ, there is no reason to implement two methods of configuring these features; thus, the MQC feature implementations are the ones deployed in Cisco IOS for IPv6.

QoS Implementation Strategy

QoS for IPv6 in Cisco IOS includes packet classification and marking, queuing, traffic shaping, weighted random early detection (WRED), and policing. Each of these features is supported for both process switching and CEF switching in IPv6 in Cisco IOS.

Classification, Marking, and Queuing

Just as in IPv4, you must identify the network traffic you want to treat with QoS before configuring it. Once you have done that, the first step is to determine how a router can identify the traffic of interest; this is the classification phase, which is done through Cisco IOS class maps. If your network is running the same protocols on IPv4 and IPv6, it makes sense to classify traffic based on IP precedence and DSCP. If not, you can treat them independently using **match protocol ip and match protocol ipv6** instead. Cisco IOS has an additional match criteria for traffic specified in an IPv6 access list, **match access-group name**.

After you have configured class maps to match the desired traffic, you can mark the traffic in a policy map. The familiar **set dscp** and **set precedence** commands support both IPv4 and IPv6 in Cisco IOS.

Cisco IOS supports class-based and flow-based queuing for IPv6 traffic. Once you have configured classification and marking, which is covered in detail in Chapter 12, "Classification and Marking," you can queue the traffic using the same queuing tools available for IPv4 and described in Chapters 13 ("Congestion Management and Avoidance") and 14 ("Shaping and Policing"). Please refer to those chapters for more details.

Some IPv6 QoS feature configuration differs from IPv4, either because of IPv6's basic implementation differences from IPv4 or for other reasons, specifically the following:

- Because IPv6 access lists cannot be numbered, but rather must be named, Cisco IOS does not support the **match access-group** *xxx* command. Instead it supports the **match access-group** *name* command.

- The **match ip rtp** command identifies only IPv4 RTP transport packets. There is no equivalent for matching RTP packets in IPv6.

- The **match cos** and **set cos** commands for 802.1Q interfaces support only CEF-switched packets. They do not support process-switched or router-originated packets.

- The **match cos** and **set cos** commands do not support ISL interfaces, even for CEF-switched packets.

Congestion Avoidance

Like queuing, IPv6 WRED is identical to WRED for IPv4 both conceptually and in terms of the implementation commands. Cisco WRED supports both class- and flow-based (using DSCP or precedence) operation.

Traffic Shaping and Policing

Shaping and policing use many of the same configuration concepts and commands in IPv6 and IPv4 environments. One difference, however, is that IPv6 traffic shaping uses flow-based queuing by default, but you can use class-based WFQ to manage congestion if you choose. Cisco IOS also supports CB Policing, Generic Traffic Shaping (GTS), and FRTS for IPv6.

In Cisco IOS, you can use the **set-dscp-transmit** and **set-precedence-transmit** options for traffic policing for both IPv4 and IPv6 traffic to remark and transmit traffic as arguments for these actions:

- Conform action

- Exceed action

- Violate action

Tunneling Techniques

When IPv6 development and initial deployment began in the 1990s, most of the world's networks were already built on an IPv4 infrastructure. As a result, several groups recognized that there was going to be a need for ways to transport IPv6 over IPv4 networks, and, as some people anticipated, vice versa.

One of the key reasons for tunneling is that today's Internet is IPv4-based, yet at least two major academic and research networks use IPv6 natively, and it is desirable to provide mechanisms for hosts on those networks to reach each other over the IPv4 Internet. Tunneling is one of the ways to support that communication.

As you may gather, tunneling meets a number of needs in a mixed IPv4 and IPv6 world; as a result, several kinds of tunneling methods have emerged. This section looks at several of them and examines one in detail.

Tunneling Overview

Tunneling, in a general sense, is encapsulating traffic. More specifically, the term usually refers to the process of encapsulating traffic at a given layer of the OSI seven-layer model *within another protocol running at the same layer*. Therefore, encapsulating IPv6 packets within IPv4 packets and encapsulating IPv4 packets within IPv6 packets are both considered tunneling.

For the purposes of this book, which is to meet the CCIE Routing and Switching blueprint requirements, in this section we are mostly interested in methods of carrying IPv6 over IPv4 networks, not the other way around. This chapter also does not explore methods of tunneling IPv6 inside IPv6. However, you should be aware that both of these types of tunneling exist, in addition to the ones covered here. With that in mind, consider some of the more common tunneling methods, starting with a summary in Table 20-6.

Table 20-6 *Summary of Tunneling Methods*

Tunnel Mode	Topology and Address Space	Applications
Automatic 6to4	Point-to-multipoint; 2002::/16 addresses	Connecting isolated IPv6 island networks.
Manually configured	Point-to-point; any address space; requires dual-stack support at both ends	Carries only IPv6 packets across IPv4 networks.
IPv6 over IPv4 GRE	Point-to-point; unicast addresses; requires dual-stack support at both ends	Carries IPv6, CLNS, and other traffic.
ISATAP	Point-to-multipoint; any multicast addresses	Intended for connecting IPv6 hosts within a single site.
Automatic IPv4-compatible	Point-to-multipoint; ::/96 address space; requires dual-stack support at both ends	Deprecated. Cisco recommends using ISATAP tunnels instead. Coverage in this book is limited.

In case you are not familiar with implementing tunnels based on IPv4, take a moment to cover the basic steps involved:

Step 1   Ensure end-to-end IPv4 reachability between the tunnel endpoints.

Step 2   Create the tunnel interface using the **interface tunnel** *n* command.

Step 3   Select a tunnel source interface and configure it using the **tunnel source interface** {*interface-type-number* | *ip-address*} command.

Step 4   For nonautomatic tunnel types, configure the tunnel destination using the **tunnel destination** {*ip-address* | *ipv6-address* | *hostname*} command. To use the **hostname** argument, DNS or local hostname-to-IP-address mapping is required.

Step 5   Configure the tunnel IPv6 address (or prefix, depending on tunnel type).

Step 6   Configure the tunnel mode using the **tunnel mode** *mode* command.

Table 20-7 shows the Cisco IOS tunnel modes and the destinations for the tunnel types covered in this section.

Table 20-7 *Cisco IOS Tunnel Modes and Destinations*

Tunnel Type	Tunnel Mode	Destination
Manual	**ipv6ip**	An IPv4 address
GRE over IPv4	**gre ip**	An IPv4 address
Automatic 6to4	**ipv6ip 6to4**	Automatically determined
ISATAP	**ipv6ip isatap**	Automatically determined
Automatic IPv4-compatible	**ipv6ip auto-tunnel**	Automatically determined

Let's take a closer look at the methods of carrying IPv6 traffic over an IPv4 network.

Manually Configured Tunnels

This tunnel type is point-to-point in nature. Cisco IOS requires statically configuring the destination addresses of these tunnels. Configuring a manual IPv6 over IPv4 tunnel is almost identical to configuring an IPv4 GRE tunnel; the only difference is setting the tunnel mode. Example 20-14 and Figure 20-7 show a manually configured tunnel. IPv4 reachability has already been configured and verified, but is not shown.

Figure 20-7 *Manually Configured Tunnel*

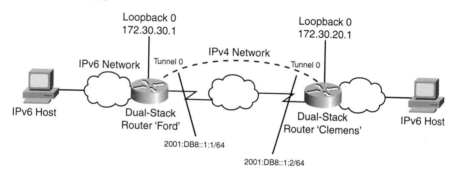

Example 20-14 *Manual Tunnel Configuration*

```
! In this example, Clemens and Ford are running IPv4 and OSPFv2 on their
! loopback 0 interfaces and the link that connects the two routers. This provides
! the IPv4 connectivity required for these tunnels to work.
!Configuration on the Ford router:
Ford# show run interface tunnel0
interface Tunnel0
 no ip address
 ipv6 address 2001:DB8::1:1/64
```

continues

Example 20-14 *Manual Tunnel Configuration (Continued)*

```
 tunnel source Loopback0
 ! In the tunnel destination, 172.30.20.1 is Clemens's Loopback0 interface:
 tunnel destination 172.30.20.1
 tunnel mode ipv6ip
Ford#
! Configuration on the Clemens router:
Clemens# show run interface tunnel0
interface Tunnel0
 no ip address
 ipv6 address 2001:DB8::1:2/64
 tunnel source Loopback0
 ! In the tunnel destination, 172.30.30.1 is Ford's Loopback0 interface:
 tunnel destination 172.30.30.1
 tunnel mode ipv6ip
 ! Demonstrating reachability across the tunnel:
Clemens# ping 2001:DB8::1:1
Type escape sequence to abort.
Sending 5, 100-byte ICMP Echos to 2001:DB8::1:1, timeout is 2 seconds:
!!!!!
Success rate is 100 percent (5/5), round-trip min/avg/max = 36/36/40 ms
Clemens#
```

Automatic IPv4-Compatible Tunnels

This type of tunnel uses IPv4-compatible IPv6 addresses for the tunnel interfaces. These addresses are taken from the ::/96 address space. That is, the first 96 bits of the tunnel interface addresses are all 0s, and the remaining 32 bits are derived from an IPv4 address. These addresses are written as 0:0:0:0:0:0:A.B.C.D, or ::A.B.C.D, where A.B.C.D represents the IPv4 address.

The tunnel destination for an IPv4-compatible tunnel is automatically determined from the low-order 32 bits of the tunnel interface address. To implement this tunnel type, use the command **tunnel mode ipv6ip auto-tunnel** in tunnel interface configuration mode.

IPv4-compatible IPv6 addressing is not widely deployed and does not conform to current global usage of the IPv6 address space. Furthermore, this tunneling method does not scale well. Therefore, Cisco recommends using ISATAP tunnels instead of this method, and for these reasons, this book does not explore this tunnel type further.

IPv6 over IPv4 GRE Tunnels

GRE tunnels provide two options that the other tunnel types do not—namely, encapsulating traffic other than IPv6 and support for IPsec. Like the manually configured variety, GRE tunnels are designed for point-to-point operation. With IPv6 as the passenger protocol, typically these tunnels are deployed between edge routers to provide connectivity between two IPv6 "islands" across an IPv4 cloud.

Configuring GRE tunnels for transporting IPv6 packets over an IPv4 network is straightforward. The only difference between GRE and the manual tunneling example shown in Example 20-14 is the syntax of the **tunnel mode** command, which for GRE is **tunnel mode gre ipv6**.

Automatic 6to4 Tunnels

Unlike the previous two tunnel types we have discussed, automatic 6to4 tunnels are inherently point-to-multipoint in nature. These tunnels treat the underlying IPv4 network as an NBMA cloud.

In automatic 6to4 tunnels, the tunnel operates on a per-packet basis to encapsulate traffic to the correct destination—thus its point-to-multipoint nature. These tunnels determine the appropriate destination address by combining the IPv6 prefix with the globally unique destination 6to4 border router's IPv4 address, beginning with the 2002::/16 prefix, in this format:

> 2002:*border-router-IPv4-address*::/48

This prefix-generation method leaves another 16 bits in the 64-bit prefix for numbering networks within a given site.

Cisco IOS supports configuring only one automatic 6to4 tunnel on a given router. Configuring these tunnels is similar to configuring the other tunnels previously discussed, except that the tunnel mode is configured using the **tunnel mode ipv6ip 6to4** command. Also, the tunnel destination is not explicitly configured for 6to4 tunnels because of the automatic nature of the per-packet destination prefix determination method that 6to4 uses.

In addition to the basic tunnel configuration, the extra step of providing for routing the desired packets over the tunnel is also required. This is usually done using a static route. For example, to route packets destined for prefix 2002::/16 over the tunnel0 6to4 tunnel interface, configure this static route:

> ipv6 route 2002::/16 tunnel 0

Example 20-15 and Figure 20-8 show a sample of a 6to4 tunnel and the routers' other relevant interfaces to tie together the concepts of 6to4 tunneling. In the example, note that the Fast Ethernet interfaces and the tunnel interface get the bold portion of the prefix 2002:**0a01:6401**:: from the Ethernet 0 interface's IPv4 address, 10.1.100.1. For this type of tunnel to work, the tunnel source interface must be the connection to the outside world, in this case the Ethernet 2/0 interface. Furthermore, each Fast Ethernet interface where hosts connect is (and must be) a different IPv6 subnet with the 2002:0a01:6401 prefix.

Figure 20-8 *Automatic 6to4 Tunnel Topology*

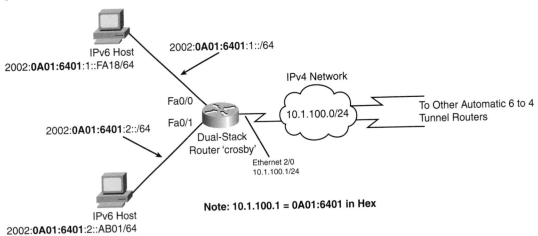

Note: 10.1.100.1 = 0A01:6401 in Hex

Example 20-15 *Automatic 6to4 Tunnel Configuration*

```
crosby# show running-config
! output omitted for brevity
interface FastEthernet0/0
 description IPv6 local host network interface 1 of 2
 ipv6 address 2002:0a01:6401:1::1/64
!
interface FastEthernet0/1
 description IPv6 local host network interface 2 of 2
 ipv6 address 2002:0a01:6401:2::1/64
!
interface Ethernet2/0
 description Ethernet link to the outside world
 ip address 10.1.100.1 255.255.255.0
!
interface Tunnel0
 no ip address
 ipv6 address 2002:0a01:6401::1/64
 tunnel source Ethernet 2/0
 tunnel mode ipv6ip 6to4
!
ipv6 route 2002::/16 tunnel 0
```

ISATAP Tunnels

ISATAP, short for Intra-Site Automatic Tunnel Addressing Protocol, is defined in RFC 4214. Like 6to4, ISATAP tunnels treat the underlying IPv4 network as an NBMA cloud. Therefore, like 6to4, ISATAP tunnels support point-to-multipoint operation natively and determine destination on a per-packet basis. However, the method they use for determining the addressing for hosts and the tunnel interface differs from 6to4 tunnels. Otherwise, ISATAP and automatic 6to4 tunneling is very similar.

ISATAP develops its addressing scheme using this format:

[*64-bit link-local or global unicast prefix*]:0000:5EFE:[*IPv4 address of the ISATAP link*]

The ISATAP interface identifier is the middle part of the address, 0000:5EFE.

For example, let's say that the IPv6 prefix in use is 2001:0DB8:0ABC:0DEF::/64 and the IPv4 tunnel destination address is 172.20.20.1. The IPv4 address, converted to hex, is AC14:1401. Therefore the ISATAP address is

2001:0DB8:0ABC:0DEF:0000:5EFE:AC14:1401

Configuring an ISATAP tunnel on a router differs slightly from configuring the previous tunnel types in that it uses a different tunnel mode (**ipv6ip isatap**) and in that it must be configured to derive the IPv6 address using the EUI-64 method. EUI-64 addressing in a tunnel interface differs from EUI-64 on a nontunnel interface in that it derives the last 32 bits of the interface ID from the tunnel source interface's IPv4 address. This method is necessary for ISATAP tunnels to provide a mechanism for other tunnel routers to independently know how to reach this router.

One other key difference in ISATAP tunnels is important to know. By default, tunnel interfaces disable router advertisements (RA). However, RAs must be enabled on ISATAP tunnels to support client autoconfiguration. Enable RAs on an ISATAP tunnel using the **no ipv6 nd suppress-ra** command.

NAT-PT

Although it is not technically a tunneling protocol, one of the methods of interconnecting IPv6 and IPv4 networks is a mechanism known as Network Address Translation-Protocol Translation (NAT-PT), defined in RFCs 2765 and 2766. NAT-PT works by performing a sort of gateway function at the IPv4/IPv6 boundary. At that boundary, NAT-PT translates between IPv4 and IPv6. This method permits IPv4 hosts to communicate with IPv6 hosts and vice versa without the need for those hosts to run dual protocol stacks.

Much like NAT and PAT (NAT overloading) for IPv4, NAT-PT supports static and dynamic translations, as well as port translation.

IPv6 Multicast

At the beginning of this chapter, multicast is introduced as one of the three address types in IPv6. This section goes into IPv6 multicast in more detail, starting with the equivalent to IGMP for IPv4: Multicast Listener Discovery.

Multicast Listener Discovery

Multicast receivers must inform their local subnet multicast router that they want to receive multicast traffic. Hosts perform this signaling using a protocol known as Multicast Listener Discovery, or MLD, which is based on IGMP and performs the same tasks as IGMP does in IPv4 networks. MLD also uses ICMPv6 messages in its operation.

In IPv6 networks, routers act as MLD queriers to determine which hosts want to receive traffic for a particular multicast group. Hosts are receivers, including routers, that want to receive that multicast traffic. MLD hosts send report messages to MLD queriers to inform them of their desire to receive that multicast traffic.

MLDv1 is based on IGMPv2; MLDv2 is based on IGMPv3. Like IGMP, MLDv2 is backward-compatible to MLDv1 hosts and allows for MLDv1-only, MLDv2-only, and networks with mixed MLDv1 and MLDv2 hosts.

In Cisco switches, MLD snooping provides the same functionality as IGMP snooping for IPv4. That is, it provides information to the switch about which connected hosts are members of a particular multicast group so that the switch can make decisions about whether, and on which interfaces, to allow traffic for that group to flow through the switch.

Configure a router interface to statically join a specific multicast group (in this case FF02::FE), regardless of whether any other group members are present on this interface, as follows:

```
DiMaggio(config-if)# ipv6 mld join-group ff02::fe
```

Explicit Tracking

Explicit tracking allows a multicast router to track the behavior of hosts within the IPv6 network. This feature also supports the fast-leave mechanism in MLDv2, which is based on the same feature in IGMPv3. Explicit tracking is disabled by default; you can enable it on an interface by using the command **ipv6 mld explicit-tracking** *access-list-name*.

PIM

In most respects, PIM for IPv6 operates exactly like PIM for IPv4. However, some differences are worth discussing here. Before reading this section, become familiar with PIM by studying Chapter 17, "IP Multicast Routing."

IPv6 PIM supports two modes of operation: sparse mode (SM) and source-specific multicast (SSM). PIM for IPv6 does not support dense mode. As is true in IPv4 PIM sparse mode, IPv6 PIM requires a Rendezvous Point (RP) to be statically defined at the RP router. However, other PIM-SM routers can learn about the RP using embedded RP support. This feature works by embedding information about RPs in MLD report messages and PIM messages. Routers then watch for the RP for each multicast group and use that RP for all PIM-SM activities. You can statically override embedded PIM information by specifying RPs on a per-group basis.

PIM DR Election

On broadcast interfaces, the PIM designated router (DR) is responsible for sending PIM Register, Join, and Prune messages toward the RP. In IPv6 PIM, DR election works exactly as in IPv4. That is, by default, the PIM router with the highest unicast IPv6 address becomes the DR. You can also statically configure the PIM DR by assigning priority values. (The highest priority wins the election.) If the DR fails, the PIM router with the highest remaining priority becomes the DR. The IPv6 address is again the tie-breaker.

Source-Specific Multicast

Source-specific PIM is derived from PIM sparse mode. It is more efficient than sparse mode. In sparse mode, a PIM Join message from a host results in sending traffic from all multicast sources toward that receiver. SSM instead uses the (S,G) model from the start to deliver multicast traffic to a particular group member from only one source, which the joining host specifies, rather than from all multicast senders for that group. SSM requires MLDv2 to operate, because MLDv1 messages do not contain the required information to support SSM. However, SSM mapping supports MLDv1 hosts by either DNS or static hostname-to-IPv6 address mappings. This allows routers to look up the source of a multicast stream when they receive an MLDv1 Join message. This feature permits extending SSM to MLDv1 hosts, in keeping with SSM's concept of maximizing multicasting efficiency.

SSM mapping must be enabled globally on a router by using the **ipv6 mld ssm-map enable** command. SSM mapping uses DNS by default. Disable DNS lookup for SSM mapping by using the **no ipv6 mld ssm-map query dns** command. Specify static mappings by using the **ipv6 mld ssm-map static** *access-list-name source-address* command.

PIM BSR

As in IPv4 PIM, every sparse-mode multicast group must be associated with the IPv6 address of an RP. PIM BSR performs this association automatically and adapts to changes in RP mappings to provide resiliency in the event of RP failures. For more on BSR, refer to Chapter 17.

Additional PIM Concepts and Options

All the IPv6 concepts of shared trees, shortest-path trees (SPT), switching between shared trees and SPTs, bidirectional PIM, and the RP behavior of tracking multicast groups and senders are identical to IPv4 PIM. The command structure for configuring PIM is also nearly identical to IPv4. In IPv6, the **ipv6** keyword precedes specific interface commands, instead of **ip**. Also, some additional command-line arguments exist for the IPv6 commands.

IPv6 Multicast Static Routes

Just as in IPv4, multicast routing fundamentally builds its routing table based on the unicast routing table. Before any multicast traffic can be routed, that traffic must pass the router's RPF check. That is, it must have arrived on the interface that the router's unicast routing table indicates is the correct path back toward the traffic source.

For tunnels, in particular, the RPF check can cause problems. If multicast traffic arrives over a tunnel instead of the physical interface over which the unicast routing table indicates that traffic should have arrived, then the router will discard that traffic. To prevent this behavior, you can configure static multicast routes to instruct the router as to which interface the traffic should arrive on. This will allow the RPF check to pass. In IPv6, unicast and multicast static routes use the same command, **ipv6 route**, but with different options.

For example, if you expect all multicast traffic on a router to arrive over the tunnel0 interface, configure the static multicast route as follows:

```
StewPerry (config)# ipv6 route ::/0 tunnel 0 multicast
```

Configuring Multicast Routing for IPv6

The first step in configuring multicast on a Cisco IOS router or switch is to enable multicast routing:

```
Jeter(config)# ipv6 multicast-routing
```

Once multicast routing is enabled, you can configure PIM on the desired interfaces, adjust MLD configuration, and enable any other necessary features such as BSR, MLD, and so forth. Cisco IOS IPv6 multicast configuration is so similar to IPv4 that its coverage ends here; refer to Chapter 17 for more details.

Foundation Summary

This section lists additional details and facts to round out the coverage of the topics in this chapter. Unlike most of the Cisco Press *Exam Certification Guides*, this "Foundation Summary" does not repeat information presented in the "Foundation Topics" section of the chapter. Please take the time to read and study the details in the "Foundation Topics" section of the chapter, as well as review items noted with a Key Topic icon.

Table 20-8 lists the protocols mentioned in or pertinent to this chapter and their respective standards documents.

Table 20-8 *Protocols and Standards for Chapter 20*

Name	Standardized In
IPv6 Addressing Architecture	RFC 2373
Internet Protocol, Version 6 Specification	RFC 2460
IPv6 Global Unicast Address Format	RFC 3587
Neighbor Discovery for IPv6	RFC 2461
IPv6 Stateless Address Autoconfiguration	RFC 2462
Source Address Selection for Multicast Listener Discovery (MLD) Protocol	RFC 3590
Multicast Listener Discovery Version 2 (MLDv2) for IPv6	RFC 3810
IPv6 Scoped Address Architecture	RFC 4007
ICMPv6 for the IPv6 Specification	RFC 2463
Stateless IP/ICMP Translation Algorithm (SIIT)	RFC 2765
Network Address Translation-Protocol Translation (NAT-PT)	RFC 2766
Generic Packet Tunneling in IPv6 Specification	RFC 2473
Transition Mechanisms for IPv6 Hosts and Routers	RFC 2893
Connection of IPv6 Domains via IPv4 Clouds	RFC 3056
Intra-Site Automatic Tunnel Addressing Protocol (ISATAP)	RFC 4214
DNS Extensions to Support IPv6	RFC 1886
DNS Extensions to Support IPv6 Address Aggregation and Renumbering	RFC 2874

Table 20-8   *Protocols and Standards for Chapter 20 (Continued)*

Name	Standardized In
DHCPv6	RFC 3315
IPv6 Prefix Options for DHCPv6	RFC 3633
OSPF for IPv3	RFC 2740
IAB/IESG Recommendations on IPv6 Address Allocation to Sites	RFC 3177

Table 20-9 lists some of the key IOS commands related to the topics in this chapter. Router-specific commands were taken from the IOS 12.4 Mainline command reference.

Table 20-9   *Command Reference for Chapter 20*

Command	Description
[no] ipv6 unicast-routing	Globally enables or disables IPv6 routing functionality.
show ipv6 interface {*type number*}	Displays configuration of all IPv6 interfaces or a selected interface, if specified in {*type number*}, including global unicast and link-local address, MTU, and other parameters.
show ipv6 interface brief	Displays a summary of IPv6 interfaces.
ipv6 address {*ipv6-address/prefix-length* | *prefix-name sub-bits/prefix-length* | autoconfig} {anycast | eui-64 | link-local}	Configures a global unicast (EUI-64 or non-EUI-64), link-local, or anycast address on an IPv6 interface.
[no] ipv6 route {*destination-prefix*} {*next-hop-ipv6-address* | *outgoing-interface*} {*next-hop-ipv6-address* | *administrative-distance* | **multicast** | *tag* | **unicast**}	Creates a static route to a prefix specifying an IPv6 address or interface, or both, as the next hop. Optionally configures administrative distance and route tag and qualifies this static route to be used for only multicast or for only unicast routing.
ipv6 multicast-routing	Enables IPv6 multicast globally.
ipv6 mld	Interface command for configuring Multicast Listener Discovery options.
ipv6 pim	Enables PIM on an IPv6 interface.
ipv6 ospf *process-ID* **area** *area-ID*	Activates OSPFv3 on an interface and sets the interface's OSPF area.

Table 20-9 *Command Reference for Chapter 20 (Continued)*

Command	Description
ipv6 eigrp *as-number*	Activates EIGRP on an interface.
ipv6 ospf neighbor *ipv6-address* [**priority** *number*] [**poll-interval** *seconds*] [**cost** *number*]	Specifies an OSPFv3 neighbor on an interface.
ipv6 router eigrp *as-number*	Enters global configuration mode for an EIGRP AS.
ipv6 router ospf *process-id*	Enters global configuration mode for an OSPF process.

Memory Builders

The CCIE Routing and Switching written exam, like all Cisco CCIE written exams, covers a fairly broad set of topics. This section provides some basic tools to help you exercise your memory about some of the broader topics covered in this chapter.

Fill in Key Tables from Memory

Appendix E, "Key Tables for CCIE Study," on the CD in the back of this book contains empty sets of some of the key summary tables in each chapter. Print Appendix E, refer to this chapter's tables in it, and fill in the tables from memory. Refer to Appendix F, "Solutions for Key Tables for CCIE Study," on the CD to check your answers.

Definitions

Next, take a few moments to write down the definitions for the following terms:

anycast, unicast, multicast, MLD, stateless autoconfiguration, link-local, stateful autoconfiguration, EUI-64, ND, RA, NA, NS, solicited-node multicast, AAAA, SSM, SM, BSR, 6to4, ISATAP, NAT-PT, GRE

Refer to the glossary to check your answers.

Further Reading

A good place to start for a further exploration of IPv6 in general is the main Cisco IPv6 technology support web page, located at http://www.cisco.com/go/ipv6.

Another great IPv6 reference library, including an RFC list, is located at http://www.ipv6.org.

The following link covers OSPFv3 implementation in detail, including encryption: http://www.cisco.com/univercd/cc/td/doc/product/software/ios123/123cgcr/ipv6_c/sa_ospf3.htm.

Part X: Appendixes

Answers to the "Do I Know This Already?" Quizzes

Chapter 1

1. C and E

2. A

3. C

   If a Cisco switch port has only **speed** or **duplex** configured, the interface still uses auto-negotiation Fast Link Pulses (FLP) to negotiate the setting that was not configured. There is no explicit command to disable auto-negotiation.

4. B and C

   Cisco switches disable auto-negotiation after the speed and duplex have been configured. The other switch attempts auto-negotiation and fails. However, the unconfigured switch can detect the speed even without auto-negotiation. By default, 10-Mbps and 100-Mbps ports use half duplex when they are unable to auto-negotiate a duplex setting.

5. C and D

   The half-duplex switch leaves its loopback circuitry enabled, erroneously detecting a collision when it is both sending and receiving a frame.

6. B and C

7. B

8. A, B, and D

Chapter 2

1. A

   The **switchport access vlan 28** command, entered in interface configuration mode, also creates the VLAN. The **vlan 28 name fred** command is valid in VLAN database mode but not in configuration mode.

2. A and B

   Of the three incorrect answers, one refers to VTP pruning, and another refers to VTP's ability to make VLAN configuration more consistent through the advertisement of VLAN configuration. Private VLANs do have a positive effect on the reduction of broadcasts, but that is not a primary motivation for using private VLANs.

3. C

   VTP works only for normal-range VLANs. Reserved VLAN numbers 1 and 1002–1005 cannot be pruned.

4. B

   Because the VTP client switch has a higher revision number than the existing switches, all client and server switches in the switched domain rewrite their VLAN databases and synchronize their revision numbers with the new client switch. VTP clients and servers can both overwrite VLAN configuration in a switched network. For this reason, be cautious about VTP settings whenever placing a new switch into your campus network.

5. B

   The new switch sends VTP updates with revision number 301, and the two original VTP servers sends updates with revision number 201. Because the new switch's revision number is higher, the older ten switches updates their configuration.

6. A

   VLAN 1 is the native VLAN by default. The switch ports to which the PCs connect also sit in VLAN 1 by default. 802.1Q does not add any header when passing frames in the native VLAN.

7.   A and B

The commands mentioned in the question have statically configured one switch to use 802.1Q trunking with no DTP auto-negotiation. Due to the **nonegotiate** option, the other switch must be statically configured to trunk, using **dot1q**, which requires the two commands that are listed as correct answers. The **nonegotiate** option is not required on the second switch, because both switches statically agree to the same trunking settings.

8.   A, B, and C

The subinterface number does not identify the VLAN, so either fa 0/1.1 or fa 0/1.2 could be used with the native VLAN. Also, native VLAN IP addresses can be configured under the physical interface as well.

9.   A, C, and D

802.1Q inserts a 4-byte tag, but it does not encapsulate the original frame. VTP Version 2, in and of itself, is restricted to normal-range VLANs. Finally, DTP chooses ISL over 802.1Q if both are enabled.

Chapter 3

1.   B

The root switch includes the Maxage timer in its advertised Hellos, with non-root switches using the timer value advertised by the switch. Maxage must expire before a non-root switch believes that connectivity to the root has been lost, thereby triggering reconvergence and the possible election of a new Root Port.

2.   C

The root switch includes the Forward Delay timer in its advertised Hellos. When receiving a Hello with TCN set, the non-root switch uses an aggressive time-out value for CAM entries based on the advertised Forward Delay timer.

3.   A and C

MST uses RSTP; RSTP waits three times the Hello time, as advertised in the Hello BPDU, before deciding to act. The timer settings on non-root switches, as usual, do not impact the process.

4. B and C

Multiple STP instances are certainly supported. The answer relating to multiple PVST+ domains is partially true. However, the mechanics involved use multicasts for each STP instance, instead of encapsulating in the native VLAN's Hellos, making that answer technically incorrect.

5. C

When STP converges, MAC address table entries need to be timed out quickly, because their associated interfaces may no longer be valid. The Topology Change Notification (TCN) BPDU from the non-root switch causes the root to react, marking a TCN bit in future Hellos, thereby making all switches time out their CAMs based on the Forward Delay timer.

6. D

All the links on one switch will become the Designated Port on their respective segments, making four ports forward. Only one of the ports on the other switch will be a Root Port, making the total five.

7. A

The links must all be in the same operational trunking state (trunking or not). If trunking, they must be using the same type of trunking. However, the settings related to trunk negotiation do not have to match.

8. C, D, and F

IEEE 802.1d (STP) uses states of forwarding, blocking, listening, learning, and disabled. IEEE 802.1w RSTP uses states of forwarding, learning, and discarding.

9. D and E

When grading yourself, if you did not pick the answer IEEE 802.1w, give yourself credit if you knew RSTP technically does not use Maxage, but instead waits three times the Hello interval instead of using Maxage.

10. B

UniDirectional Link Detection (UDLD) uses Layer 2 messaging to determine when it can no longer hear from the neighbor. These messages allow a switch to recognize a unidirectional link and react by error-disabling at least one end of the link. Loop Guard does not use messages, but rather it changes how a switch reacts to the loss of incoming Hellos. When they are no longer received, the port is placed into an STP loop-inconsistent state.

Chapter 4

1. D

2. C

Summary 10.1.1.0/21 would include addresses 10.1.0.0–10.1.7.255. Summary 10.1.0.0/22 would include 10.1.0.0–10.1.3.255, only including three of the four subnets listed in the question.

3. D

10.22.12.0/22 includes addresses 10.22.12.0–10.22.15.255, which covers exactly the same range of addresses as subnets 10.22.12.0/23 and 10.22.14.0/23 listed in the problem statement. Similarly, summary 10.22.16.0/22 covers exactly the set of IP addresses inside the other two subnets in the problem statement. As for the wrong answers, 10.22.12.0/21 is not actually a valid summary; 10.22.8.0/21 and 10.22.16.0/21 are valid. Summary 10.22.8.0/21 includes address 10.22.8.0–10.22.15.255, which includes address ranges not covered by subnets in the problem statement. Similarly, summary 10.22.16.0/21 includes IP addresses outside the listed subnets.

4. A and D

10.22.21.128/26 implies a range of 10.22.21.128–10.22.21.191; 10.22.20.0/23 implies a range of 10.22.20.0–10.22.21.255.

5. A

By definition, CIDR allows Internet routes to group large blocks of IP addresses, based largely on the assignment of IP network numbers to particular ISPs or to ISPs in particular worldwide geographic locations.

6. C and D

Port Address Translation (PAT) and dynamic NAT with overloading both refer to the same feature, in which each TCP or UDP flow is mapped to a small number of IP addresses by using different port numbers. The other terms do not refer to features that reduce the number of IP addresses used by NAT.

7. B

The four terms in the answers have two pair of contrasting words. The word "inside" implies a host inside the enterprise that is using NAT, whereas "outside" refers to a host outside the enterprise. The word "local" refers to an IP address used for packets as they flow through the enterprise (where local private addressing can be used), and "global" refers to an IP address used in packets as they flow over the Internet (which requires globally unique IP addresses). The question refers to a packet's destination address, with the packet going to a host inside the enterprise—hence the term "inside" is correct. The packet is on the Internet, per the question, so the term "global" also applies.

8.   A and B

Typically, a NAT overload configuration using a single public IP address would use the style that refers to the interface in the command. However, a NAT pool with a single IP address in the pool works the same and is valid.

Chapter 5

1.   C and D

LAN-attached hosts use Address Resolution Protocol (ARP) when they need to find the MAC address of another host, when the host thinks that the other host is on the same subnet. For R1 to have been performing a proxy ARP reply for PC2's ARP request, the request must have been for a host on a different subnet—most likely, an ARP looking for the web server's MAC address. For PC2 to make such an ARP request, PC2 must have believed that the web server was on the same subnet; if PC2's mask was 255.255.0.0, PC2 would have indeed thought that the web server was in the same subnet.

2.   A and E

When the router receives the DHCP request, it changes the destination IP address of the packet to the value set with the **ip helper-address** command. Because the PC does not yet have an IP address, the DHCP request (as sent by PC3) has an IP address of 0.0.0.0. The router then changes the source IP address so that the DHCP response packet can be routed back to the original subnet and then broadcast back onto that subnet. To make that happen, the router changes the source IP address of the DHCP request to be the subnet broadcast address for that subnet, namely 10.4.7.255.

3.   B and D

RARP and BOOTP require a static reservation of an IP address for each specific MAC address. Because BOOTP encapsulates its messages inside an IP packet, the packets can be routed to a BOOTP server; RARP does not use an IP header, so its messages cannot be routed. Also, RARP supports only the assignment of the IP address, whereas BOOTP allows the assignment of other settings, such as the mask and default gateway.

4. D

With default settings on R2, preemption would not be allowed. Therefore, even in cases for which R2 would have a better (higher) HSRP priority, R2 would not take over from R1 until R2 believed that R1 had failed.

5. D

Object tracking is a relatively recent Cisco IOS feature that replaces the individual tracking features that were previously built into HSRP, GLBP, and VRRP.

6. D

7. B and D

Routers using NTP server mode do not rely on outside devices for clock synchronization, so they do not need to know another NTP server's IP address. Routers in NTP broadcast client mode expect to receive NTP updates via LAN broadcasts, so they do not need to know an IP address of an NTP server to which to send NTP queries.

8. A, C, and D

SNMPv1 does not provide any means of securely passing SNMP passwords, which are known as *community strings* or simply *communities*. SNMP provides this support via MD5 hashes as well as many other security enhancements. One of those is support for encryption, which is often done with DES.

9. C

SNMP Inform messages came into SNMP with version 2. Version 3 is focused only on security features.

10. A

11. A

In a WCCP cluster, the lead content engine is elected based on which content engine has the lowest IP address.

Chapter 6

1. C

2. C, D, and E

The CEF FIB is populated based on the contents of the IP routing table. The two incorrect answers refer to events that do not change the contents of the IP routing table; rather, they change adjacency information. The three correct answers cause a change to the IP routing table, which, in turn, changes the CEF FIB.

3. D

Routers send InARP messages in response to learning that a new PVC is up. Routers learn that a PVC is up when they receive LMI messages stating that a previously inactive DLCI is now active. Although an InARP from another router may be received around the same time, it is the LMI notification of the now-active DLCI that drives the process.

4. A, C, and D

InARP is enabled by default on all three types of interfaces stated in the question. As a result, with the full mesh, all three routers will have the necessary mapping between the IP address and DLCI, and pinging will work between each pair of routers.

5. A, C, and E

InARP is enabled on all three types of interfaces by default. However, InARPs flow only across a PVC, and are not forwarded—so R2 and R3 have no way to inform each other of the correct mapping information. Additionally, R3's point-to-point subinterface usage actually changes R3's logic, whereby R3 does not rely on the received InARP information. Rather, R3 uses logic like "when forwarding to any address in 10.1.1.0/24, send it over the one PVC on that subinterface." R2, with a multipoint subinterface, does not use such logic and simply lacks the correct mapping information. As a result, when R2 pings R3, R2 does not know what DLCI to use and cannot send the Echo. R3, however, does know what DLCI to use, so when R3 pings R2, R3 actually sends the packet to R1, which then forwards it to R2. And R2 can't return the Echo Reply, so the ping fails.

6. C

The **ip classless** global configuration command tells the router to use classless IP forwarding/ routing. This means that if a packet's destination address does not match any specific subnet in the routing table, and a default route exists, the router will use the default route.

7. E

Of the incorrect answers, only the **ip address** command is a valid command; that command sets the IP address associated with the interface.

8. E

9. C

    The **set interface default** command tells policy routing to use the listed interface as if it were a default route, using it only if the IP routing table is not matched.

10. A and C

    The **default** option tells policy routing to first try to match the routing table and then to use the directions in the route map if no route exists in the routing table.

Chapter 7

1. A and C

    RIPv2 added VLSM support to RIPv1 by including the subnet mask with each route. RIP does not send Hellos. It defines infinity as 16 hops and uses either clear-text passwordsor MD5 for authentication.

2. A

    RIP sends full updates every 30 seconds, with those updates including all routes from the routing table, except for any routes omitted due to split horizon rules. The router actually adds 1 to the metrics shown in its routing table to the routes included in a routing update.

3. B and C

    R1's metric 16 route advertisement was a poisoned route. R1 would suspend split horizon rules for that route upon receipt of the metric 16 route, sending back a poison reverse route, metric 16. R1 would have sent back the metric 16 route whether split horizon was enabled or disabled on s0/0. Also, if the last received metric was 3, and then 16, the failed route would not have been caused by a counting-to-infinity problem.

4. A and B

    The Invalid timer is set per route, counting up from 0, and reset to 0 each time the same route is received in an update coming in the same interface as before. The timer is kept by a router and is not advertised. The **debug** commands show information about advertised and received updates, but because the Invalid timer is not transmitted in the network, these **debug** commands do not display the timer.

5. F

The **clear ip route** command is not complete and would be rejected by Cisco IOS. To delete all routes, the **clear ip route** * command would be used.

6. A, B, and E

The **network** command tells RIP to do three things on each interface in that classful network: Advertise the connected subnet, send updates, and process received updates. RIP does not have a Hello message. The **passive-interface** command does make RIP stop sending updates on an interface, but the command is a **router rip** subcommand, not an interface subcommand.

7. D

Cisco IOS disables split horizon by default on physical interfaces configured for Frame Relay, but it is enabled by default on Frame Relay multipoint interfaces. The default RIP authentication mode is simple text. RIP sends triggered updates when a route changes, and this feature cannot be disabled.

Chapter 8

1. C and D

EIGRP uses IP protocol 88, with no transport header following the IP header. It supports MD5 authentication, but not clear text. It first sends Update messages to 224.0.0.10 then sends them as unicasts if RTP requires retransmission.

2. A, C, and D

R2's K values differ from those of the other routers, so it will not become a neighbor. The Hello timer and Hold timer differences do not prevent EIGRP neighbor relationships from forming. Also, the different masks do not prevent neighborship, if each router believes that its neighbors are in the same primary subnet.

3. C

4. D

EIGRP Updates can be either full or partial. Although it is true that Reply messages include routing information, they often trigger the receiving router to use partial update messages to inform neighbors about the change in a route.

5. B

The **show ip eigrp topology** command lists successor and feasible successor routes, omitting routes that are neither. Because two of the routes are successors, only one of the three is a feasible successor.

6. B

R11's route through 10.1.11.2 is considered invalid, because the neighbor at that IP address failed. The topology table holds one feasible successor route to the subnet, so it can be used immediately, without requiring active Querying of the route.

7. B

An EIGRP router must wait on all Reply messages to be received before acting on the new information. The Active timer dictates how long the router should wait for all the Reply messages to come back.

8. C

The **network** command wildcard mask matches any interface with an address that starts with 10.1, with 0, 1, 2, or 3 in the third octet, and anything in the fourth octet. So, it will not advertise 10.1.4.0/24 or 10.1.5.0/24, because those interfaces are not matched with a **network** command. Because it is passive, no Hellos are sent out fa0/0, meaning no neighbor relationships are formed, and no routes are exchanged either in or out fa0/0.

9. A and D

The **passive-interface** command, by definition with EIGRP, tells EIGRP to not send EIGRP Hellos out the interface. A receive-only EIGRP stub router receives only routing updates, but to do so, it must form neighbor relationships with any routers, so it does send Hellos. Of course, if no **network** command matches an interface, EIGRP is not enabled for the interface at all.

Chapter 9

1. B and C

OSPF uses IP protocol 89, and does not use TCP. LSUs can be acknowledged by simply repeating the LSU or by using the LSAck packet.

2. **A and C**

   Multipoint interfaces default to use network type nonbroadcast, so the **ip ospf network non-broadcast** command would not show up in the configuration. This type defaults to 30-second Hello and 120-second Dead timers. The **neighbor** commands are required, but only one of the neighbors on either end of a PVC needs to configure the **neighbor** command. Network type nonbroadcast does require a DR. So for all routers to be able to communicate with the DR, router R-core needs to be the DR.

3. **C**

   The **ip ospf network non-broadcast** command, which is also the default on multipoint interfaces, requires a DR, as well as requiring **neighbor** commands.

4. **D**

   Unlike EIGRP, OSPF's Hello intervals on LANs must match, so R2 will not form any neighbor relationships. R1, R3, and R4 will not expect Hellos from R2, because it will not be a neighbor. R2 will not become a DR, because a router must form a neighbor relationship before performing DR election. R3 ties on highest priority among R1, R3, and R4, and it beats R1 with a higher RID, so it becomes DR, not BDR. R4's dead interval will default to four times hello, or 40 seconds.

5. **A**

   They must be in the same area, and must have the exact same stubby area type. The LSRefresh setting is not checked during the Hello process. Finally, the Hello and dead intervals must match before two routers will become neighbors.

6. **C and D**

   Routers in NSSAs inject type 7 LSAs; R1, being in the backbone area, cannot be in an NSSA, so it will inject a type 5 LSA for 200.1.1.0/24. R3 will indeed learn a route to 200.1.1.0/24, as area 0 is not a stub area. R2, an ABR, will forward the type 5 LSA created by R1 into area 1. Finally, every DR creates a type 2 LSA for the subnet and floods it throughout the area.

7. **A, B, and D**

   Routers in NSSA areas can inject type 7 LSAs into the NSSA area when redistributing into OSPF from external sources. However, because the area is totally NSSA, R2 will not forward type 5 or type 3 LSAs into totally NSSA area 1. Instead, R2 will inject a default route via a type 3 LSA into area 1. Finally, every DR creates a type 2 LSA for the subnet and floods it throughout the area.

8. B

The command configures area 55 as a totally stubby area, which means that no external type 5 (E1 or E2) LSA can be sent into the area by the ABR. Also, the ABR does not create type 3 summary LSAs for the subnets in other areas. The ABR does create and inject a default route into the area due to the **no-summary** option.

9. C

OSPF E1 routes include internal OSPF costs in the metric calculation; for E2 routes, the internal OSPF cost is not considered. R3's cost to reach 10.1.1.0/24 includes R3's cost to reach the ABR plus the cost stated in the type 3 LSA. When route summarization occurs, the summary uses the least cost of all the constituents subnets; however, this design does not use any route summarization.

10. A and E

The **network** command's mask works like an ACL wildcard, so the **network 10.0.0.0 0.0.0.255** command matches addresses beginning 10.0.0—so it does not match the LAN interface on R2. OSPF routers can use different process IDs and still become neighbors. OSPF costs can be asymmetric, meaning that routers can become neighbors without having the same OSPF costs. The cost value is not part of the DR election decision. Finally, with a reference bandwidth of 1000, R1 calculates the cost as 1000/100 = 10.

11. C and F

The **ip ospf dead-interval minimal** command sets the dead interval to 1 second and the Hello interval to (1/multiplier) seconds. The Hello interval defaults to 10 seconds on some network types, notably point-to-point and broadcast networks, and defaults to 30 seconds on other network types. The **ip ospf hello-multiplier** command is not a valid command.

12. A

The **ip ospf authentication** interface subcommand takes precedence over the **area 0 authentication message-digest** command, causing R1 to attempt OSPF type 1 (simple text) authentication, with the key being configured with the **ip ospf authentication-key** command.

Chapter 10

1. A, D, and E

   A **route-map** clause acts on items that match the parameters on the **match** command. For routes that do not match a clause's **match** command, the route map moves on to the logic in the next **route-map** clause. Route 10.1.1.0/24 was matched, and because the **route-map** clause had a **permit** action, the route was redistributed. 10.1.2.0/24 was not matched by the first **route-map** clause, so it would fall through to be considered in the next **route-map** clause. However, the question did not supply the rest of the information, so you cannot tell whether 10.1.2.0/24 was redistributed.

2. C and D

   10.128.0.0/9 defines the matching parameters on the prefix (subnet number), which matches subnets beginning with 10, and with 128–255 in the second octet. The **ge 20** implies that the routes must have a prefix length between 20 and 32, inclusive. Only 10.200.200.192 and 10.128.0.0 match both criteria.

3. A

   EIGRP requires that a metric be defined for any route redistributed into EIGRP, and no metrics have been defined. So, the **redistribute ospf 2** command does not cause any routes to be redistributed. OSPF defaults to use metric 20, with redistributed routes as type E2.

4. A and B

   The **redistribute eigrp 1 subnets** command looks for EIGRP routes and connected routes that match any EIGRP **network** commands.

5. C

   Because EIGRP treats external routes as AD 170 by default, R1 will not have any suboptimal routes as described in the question. For example, if subnet 1 was in the OSPF domain, and R2 injected it into EIGRP, the route would have administrative distance 170. R1, upon learning the EIGRP route to subnet 1, would prefer the OSPF (default administrative distance 110) route over the administrative distance 170 route.

6. A

   Table 10-7 summarizes the defaults for metric types and metric values when performing redistribution. OSPF defaults to external type 2, EIGRP defaults to external (but that is the only option), and RIP has no concept of route type—or has a single route type, depending on your perspective. OSPF defaults to external type 2 regardless of whether the route is redistributed via an ASBR inside a normal area or via an ADBR inside an NSSA area.

7. D

The three incorrect answers are classic descriptions of what route summarization does do. However, summary routes remove some details of the topology from the routing table, which in itself increases the possibility of suboptimal routes. It does nothing to help the generalized problem of suboptimal routing caused by redistribution.

8. A and C

Without the **always** keyword, OSPF requires that a route to 0.0.0.0/0 exists, but that route can be a dynamic or static route. EIGRP does not support the command.

Chapter 11

1. D

BGP neighbors must reach the established state, a steady state in which Update messages can be sent and received as needed.

2. C

Although eBGP neighbors often share a common link, there is no requirement that neighbors must be connected to the same subnet.

3. A and D

BGP sets TTL to 1 only for messages sent over eBGP connections, so the **ebgp-multihop** option is required only in that case. (The **ibgp-multihop** command does not exist.) The BGP router ID can be set to any syntactically valid number, in the format of an IP address, using the **bgp router-id** *id* command; it does not have to match another router's **neighbor** command.

4. D

When **no auto-summary** is configured, the **network** command must be an exact match of the prefix/prefix length. If omitted, the prefix length is assumed based on the default classful network mask—in this case, **network 20.0.0.0** would imply a mask of 255.0.0.0.

5. A and B

The **redistribute** command, when redistributing from an IGP, takes routes actually in the routing table as added by that IGP, or connected routes on interfaces matched by that IGP's **network** commands.

6.   C

The BGP **auto-summary** command affects only routes locally injected into a router's BGP table through redistribution or the **network** command. The **network** command, with **autosummary** enabled, needs to match only one subnet of the classful network, which it does in this case. The **aggregate-address** command creates the 9.0.0.0/8 aggregate, but without the **summary-only** keyword, it also advertises the component subnet 9.1.0.0/16.

7.   A and C

BGP routes must be considered to be **valid** and **best** before being advertised. With iBGP, the route also must not have been learned from another iBGP peer. Finally, the NEXT_HOP must be reachable, but the local router determines reachability by looking in its IP routing table for a matching route—not by pinging the NEXT_HOP IP address.

8.   A, D, and E

The **redistribute** command injects routes with an assigned ORIGIN value of incomplete, whereas routes injected with the **network** command are considered as IGP routes. The **aggregate-address** command, without the **as-set** option, always sets the ORIGIN code of the aggregate to IGP.

9.   D

For an iBGP-learned route, BGP synchronization requires that the NLRI (prefix/prefix length) be in the IP routing table, as learned via an IGP, before considering that BGP route as a candidate to be BGP's best route to that prefix. The other answers simply do not meet the definition of BGP synchronization.

10.   A and B

Confederations use eBGP rules for confederation eBGP peers regarding multihop and the advertisement of iBGP routes to eBGP (confederation) peers. Inside a confederation AS, a full mesh must be maintained.

11.   A, C, and E

NLRI 1.0.0.0/8 was learned via eBGP, so R1 advertises it to all iBGP peers—the route reflector logic has no impact on that logic. NLRI 3.0.0.0/8 shows normal route reflector operation for a route sent to the reflector by a client—it is reflected to all clients and nonclients. The NLRI 5.0.0.0/8 answer lists normal route reflector operation for routes received from a nonclient—it is reflected only to clients.

12. C

One of the challenges with migration to a confederation configuration is that the ASN is no longer configured on the **router bgp** command, but rather on the **bgp confederation identifier** command. Also, the **bgp confederation peers** command lists the confederation ASNs of routers in other confederation sub-autonomous systems, but it is required only on routers that have neighbor connections to routers in other confederation ASNs. As a result, R3 does not need the command.

Chapter 12

1. C

2. A and D

DSCP is the high-order 6 bits of the DS field, formerly known and the ToS byte. IPP occupies the high-order 3 bits of that same byte.

3. A, B, and E

CS3's first 3 bits purposefully match IPP 3. Also, with a value of binary 011000, CS3's decimal equivalent is 24.

4. B and D

AF31's binary value is 011010, so the first 3 bits, which comprise the same bits as the IPP field, are 011. Also, binary 011010 converts to decimal 26.

a. A

The **class-map** command defaults to use the **match-all** parameter, which means both **match** commands' conditions must be true to match the class.

5. A and B

ch cos 3 4 command uses OR logic between its two parameters, matching CoS 3 or 4. The **class-map c2** command uses match-any logic, so either **match** command can be true to match **class-map c2**. Finally, with match-all logic, **class-map c3** fails to match, because the frame has a CoS of 3, and the **match cos 2** command fails to match. The IPP and DSCP fields do not impact the actions taken by the listed configuration.

6. D

Each class map has an optional parameter of **match-all** (default) or **match-any**. With the default of **match-all**, both **match** commands in the class map must match, and a packet can't have both DSCP EF and AF31. After creating a set of class maps, and referring to them with **class** commands inside **policy-map barney**, you used the **service-policy input barney** command under **interface fa 0/0**. However, the **show policy-map interface fa 0/0** command shows that no packets match class fred.

7. B and E

Because the policy works for outgoing packets, the policy map cannot classify based on the DE bit, although the DE bit can be set. CoS and CLP do not exist in Frame Relay, so those fields cannot be set.

8. A

CB Marking requires that CEF be enabled globally, regardless of whether NBAR is being used. NBAR is in use in this case because the **match protocol** command tells Cisco IOS to use NBAR to match the parameters on that command. NBAR and the **match protocol** command can be used as an input or output function.

9. A and B

The **qos pre-classify** command can be issued in tunnel interface, crypto map, and virtual-template interface configuration modes.

Chapter 13

1. C

2. A and B

Multiple classes can be configured as LLQs with the **priority** command. Also, only one style of **bandwidth** command is allowed in a single policy map, making the last two answers incorrect.

3. B

To find the answer, take the configured interface bandwidth (100 kbps) and subtract 25 percent of the bandwidth (based on the default **max-reserved-bandwidth** of 75 percent). That leaves 75 kbps. Subtract 20 percent of the interface bandwidth (20 percent of 100 kbps) for the LLQ, which leaves 55 kbps. The *bandwidth remaining percent* feature then allocates percentages of the remaining bandwidth, which is 55 kbps in this case. 20 percent of 55 kbps is 11 kbps.

4. B

WRED increases the discard rate from 0 to 1/MPD as the average moves from the minimum threshold to the maximum threshold.

5. A and B

WRED defaults to using IPP, so **random-detect** enables it for IPP, as does the explicit version of the command (**random-detect precedence-based**).

6. A

The **priority-queue out** command enables the PQ (expedite queue) feature on a 3550 interface. The **wrr-queue bandwidth** command does not allow a 0 to be configured for any queue; 1 is the lowest allowed value. The queue for a frame is chosen based on CoS, not DSCP, and any CoS value(s) can be placed into the queue.

7. C

MDRR uses the term *quantum value* to indicate the number of bytes removed from each queue on each pass through the queues.

8. D

Chapter 14

1. C

CB Shaping adds Bc tokens to the bucket at the beginning of each shaping time interval (Tc). The presence of a non-0 Be means that the bucket is larger, as it is Bc + Be large, but it does not mean that more tokens are added at each Tc. (CB Policing adds tokens based on packet arrival.)

2. C

The formula is Tc = Bc/CIR. Shaping uses a unit of "bits" for Bc, so the units work out easily. In this case, Tc = 3200/128,000, or 1/40 of a second—25 ms.

3. A

shape peak actually shapes at a higher rate than the configured rate. CB Shaping defaults Be to be equal to Bc, so to make it 0; you must set it directly. Also, the shaping rate is configured in bps, not kbps.

4. A

The command could also have been used at point 2 in the configuration snippet—if the command was configured inside **class-default** inside **policy-map shape-question**. The answers beginning with **shape queue** are not valid commands.

5. E

The **show policy-map** command lists only the formatted configuration, with no calculated or statistical values. Tc = Bc/CIR = 5120/256,000 = 1/50th of a second, or 20 ms.

6. A

FRTS assigns settings based on the following order of precedence: the **class** command under the **frame-relay interface-dlci** command, the **frame-relay class** command under the subinterface, or the **frame-relay class** command under the interface.

7. D

The **frame-relay traffic-rate** command does not allow setting the Tc (the time interval), and FRTS normally defaults that value to 125 ms. To impact the Tc, the Bc must be set; to make Tc 62.5 ms, the rate and Bc must be chosen such that Bc/rate = 62.5 ms, or 1/16 second.

8. B and D

Shapers delay packets, and policers either discard packets or re-mark them.

9. C

CB Policing defaults its Be setting to 0 when it is configured as a two-color policer. That occurs when the **police** command does not have a **violate** action configured or an explicit Be value set. Also, the policing rate uses a unit of bps; both commands beginning **police 128** police at 128 bps, not 128 kbps. The **police 128k** command is syntactically incorrect.

10. A and C

CAR is always a single-rate, two-color policer, meaning that it supports only the conform and exceed actions. It does not use MQC commands. However, it does allow for policing supersets and subsets of interface traffic and can police packets going in either direction on an interface.

Chapter 15

1. B

The ANSI T1.617 Annex D LMI and the ITU Q.933 Annex A LMI are equivalent, using DLCI 0 for LMI flows and supporting a maximum of 976 PVCs/DLCIs. The Cisco LMI uses DLCI 1023 and supports 992 PVCs/DLCIs. Both ANSI and ITU LMI types can be autosensed, but so can the Cisco LMI type; the question asks for answers that apply only to ANSI and ITU LMI types.

2. C

The FECN signifies congestion from R1 to R2, so R2 would not slow down its adaptive shaping; R2 would slow down on receipt of a BECN. The receiver on the end of the PVC does not react to congestion; rather, the intermediate Frame Relay switches could react. To signal the congestion back to R1, R2 could be configured to "reflect" the FECN back to R1 by sending its next frame to R1 with BECN set; R1 could then adaptively shape to a lower rate. Finally, Cisco IOS policers cannot set FECN, but they can set DE.

3. B

The **encapsulation frame-relay** command defaults to **ietf** encapsulation; the **encapsulation frame-relay ietf** interface subcommand would achieve the same result. The **encapsulation cisco** command is syntactically incorrect, but the **encapsulation frame-relay cisco** interface subcommand would enable Frame Relay, with Cisco encapsulation, on the interface. However, the command is only a physical interface subcommand, not a subinterface subcommand. Encapsulation types can differ for each VC. Those without the encapsulation type listed on the **frame-relay interface-dlci** *dlci encapsulation-type* command use the encapsulation configured on the **encapsulation** interface subcommand; those with the encapsulation type on the **frame-relay interface-dlci** command use the specified type.

4. B

Frame Relay access links work when LMI is disabled on the router. Of the four answers with commands, the only valid command is **no keepalive**, which does indeed disable Frame Relay LMI.

5. B and D

Of the three options, only packet-by-packet uses a per-packet compression dictionary; only FRF.9 is standardized by a public standards body (Frame Relay Forum); and all three use the LZS algorithm. Any of the three types can be configured with the **frame-relay payloadcompress** command or the **frame-relay map** command.

6. A and E

The LMI messages do not contain any information about the router's subinterfaces, so the DLCI must be associated with each subinterface, with the **frame-relay interface-dlci** command being one method. The encapsulation type and the use of **frame-relay interfacedlci** and **frame-relay map** commands are unrelated. The FR network does not care about the headers past the LAPF header and, therefore, does not know about nor care to characterize the encapsulation type. Because the FR network does not care about the encapsulation type, different types can be mixed over the same access link.

7. A

A router can correlate a DLCI to a subinterface using two methods: a **frame-relay interface-dlci** command or a **frame-relay map** command. On the six subinterfaces with neither command configured, R1 will not know how to associate any DLCIs with the subinterfaces, so it cannot send traffic out those subinterfaces. The four subinterfaces with **frame-relay interface-dlci** commands do not need a **frame-relay map** command, because the router will receive InARP messages, see the DLCI listed, correlate that DLCI to the subinterface with the **frame-relay interface-dlci** command, and remember the associated next-hop address.

Chapter 16

1. B, C, D

Multicast packets are sent once from a source to many destinations, which eliminates traffic redundancy; hence, multicast uses less bandwidth than unicast. Multicast applications use UDP at the transport layer, which provides connectionless service.

2. C

A multicast address can be permanently assigned by IANA or can be temporarily assigned and relinquished. The multicast address range is 224.0.0.0 to 239.255.255.255. A multicast address is unstructured and does not use any subnet mask; therefore, it cannot be entered as an IP address on an interface of a router.

3. A and D

IANA reserves all the addresses in the range 224.0.0.0 to 224.0.0.255. Multicast routers do not forward packets with a destination address from this range. The addresses 224.0.1.39 and 224.0.1.40 are also reserved but routers can forward packets with these destination addresses.

4. D

An Ethernet multicast MAC address of 48 bits is calculated from a Layer 3 multicast address by using 0x0100.5e as the multicast vendor code (OUI) for the first 24 bits, always binary 0 for the 25th bit, and copying the last 23 bits of the Layer 3 multicast address.

5. D

Only hosts originate IGMP Membership messages, and only routers originate IGMP Query messages. Switches only forward these messages.

6. D

In IGMPv2, when a router receives a Leave message, it responds by sending a Group-Specific Query using the multicast address that was used in the Leave message as the destination address.

7. E

Chapter 17

1. C

When a multicast router receives a multicast packet, it first performs the Reverse Path Forwarding (RPF) check to determine whether the packet entered through the same interface it would use to go toward the source; if it did not, the router drops the packet.

2. D

When multiple PIM routers are connected to a LAN subnet, they send Assert messages to determine which router will be the forwarder of the multicast traffic on the LAN. Both PIM-DM and PIM-SM routing protocols use Assert messages.

3. D

When a PIM-DM router receives a Graft message after it has sent a Prune message, it will send a Graft message to the upstream router. It does not send a Prune message to the downstream router, and it does not have to re-establish adjacency with the upstream router.

4. C and E

A PIM-DM router sends Prune and Graft messages based on the demand for multicast group traffic. If nobody wants the group traffic, the PIM-DM router sends a Prune message to its upstream router. If somebody requests group traffic and the router is not receiving the traffic from its upstream router, it sends a Graft message to its upstream router.

5. A and C

The RP sends a Register-Stop message only when it does not need to receive the traffic, or when it does need to receive the traffic but the first-hop DR is now sending the multicast to the RP via the shortest-path tree to the RP.

6. C

R1 is not switching over from SPT to RPT. R1's upstream router on the shared tree will show the R flag only for its (S,G) entry.

7. B

The PIM Auto-RP messages will not reach all the PIM-SM routers if the **ip pim sparse-mode** command is configured on the interfaces of all the routers. Congestion is not a problem because all the routers show all the PIM neighbors, which means they are receiving multicast PIM Hello messages. The static RP configuration with an **override** option would show at least some RP mapping on the leaf routers. For an interface to be considered for use by PIM-SM, the **ip pim sparse-mode** command must be configured under the subinterface.

8. C and D

PIM-SM routers can maintain the forwarding state on a link only by periodically (default every 60 seconds) sending PIM Join messages. PIM-SM routers choose to send the periodic Joins for two reasons. First, Joins are sent to the RP if a host on a connected network is sending IGMP Report messages, claiming to want traffic sent to that multicast group. Second, Joins are sent to the RP if a router is receiving PIM Joins from a downstream router.

Chapter 18

1. D

AAA authentication for enable mode (privileged exec mode) only uses the default set of authentication modes listed in the **aaa authentication enable default group radius local** command. The **enable authentication wilma** and **aaa authentication enable wilma group**

fred local commands are not valid commands; the **enable** command can use only a default set of AAA authentication methods. Also, with the **aaa new-model** and **aaa authentication enable** commands as listed, the **enable secret** password is not used.

2. A

The **aaa authentication login fred line group radius none** command defines a set of methods beginning with **line**, which means using the **password** command listed in line configuration mode. The **login authentication fred** command refers to group fred. As a result, the router begins by just asking for a password and using the password listed in the **password cisco** command.

3. C

Because there is no **login authentication** subcommand under **line vty 0 4**, Telnet attempts to use the default methods defined in the **aaa authentication login default** command. The methods are tried in order: the servers in the default group of RADIUS servers and then the local set of usernames and passwords. Because barney/betty is the only defined username/password, if neither RADIUS server replied, barney/betty would be the required username/password.

4. A, B, and E

Several reference documents regarding security best practices are available at http://www.cisco.com/go/safe. The core SAFE document lists Dynamic ARP Inspection (DAI) as one best practice; it watches ARP messages to prevent many ARP-based attacks. Shutting down unused ports and enabling port security are also recommended. SAFE further recommends not using VLAN 1 for any traffic and disabling DTP completely; automatic mode would allow another switch, or a device masquerading as a switch, to use DTP to dynamically create a trunk.

5. D

Port security requires that each enabled port be statically configured as an access port or a trunk port. By default, port security allows only a single MAC address. Sticky-learned MACs are added to the running configuration only; dynamic-learned (nonsticky) MACs are used only until the next reload of the switch.

6. B

With 802.1X, the user device is the supplicant, the switch is the authenticator, and a RADIUS server is the authentication server. EAPoL is used between the supplicant and the authenticator. Until a port is authenticated, the switch forwards only 802.1X traffic (typically EAPoL), plus CDP and STP.

7. B and E

The **storm-control** command has numeric arguments that begin with the rising threshold for dropping packets of a particular type (in this case, broadcast), and end with the falling threshold. Therefore, a rising threshold of 0 pps and a falling threshold of 100 pps (or any falling threshold value) causes the port to drop all inbound broadcast traffic. Finally, the **storm-control action** command is per-interface.

8. D

Mask 0.0.1.255 matches 10.44.38.0 through 10.44.39.255. Mask 0.0.7.255 matches 10.44.32.0 through 10.44.39.255; in fact, if used as suggested, a **show run** command would have listed it as **access-list 1 permit 10.44.32.0 0.0.7.255**. Mask 0.0.15.255 would imply a range of 10.44.32.0 through 10.44.47.255; the resulting command output of **show run** would list **access-list 1 permit 10.44.32.0 0.0.15.255**. Finally, mask 0.0.5.255 uses discontiguous 0s and 1s, which is valid; however, it would not match IP address 10.44.40.18.

9. A and B

Routers will forward packets sent to subnet (directed) broadcast addresses, except for the router connected to the subnet; its action is predicated on the setting of the **ip directedbroadcast** command. An RPF check would also filter the packets, because a router's route to reach 9.1.1.0/24 would point into the enterprise, not toward the Internet, which is from where the packet arrived. Finally, a packet filter for all IP addresses in the subnet would filter both legitimate traffic and the attack.

10. B

TCP intercept can either watch the connections, monitoring them, or inject itself into the process. It injects itself by responding to TCP connection requests and then forming another TCP connection to the server—but only if the client-side connection completes. It is enabled globally, but it uses an ACL to define the scope of connections it processes. It is not specifically associated with an interface.

Chapter 19

1. A

LDP advertises a label to all neighbors for each prefix added as an IGP route to its routing table.

2.   D

LSRs forward unlabeled packets by examining the FIB and labeled packets based on the LFIB. To match the correct LFIB entry, an LSR compares the packet's outer label with the incoming label values of the LFIB entries.

3.   B

If no transport address is listed, LDP uses the neighboring router's IP address in the neighbor's LDP ID to form a TCP connection. The LDP ID does not have to be the IP address of the LAN interface. The LDP neighbors begin by sending Hellos, to 224.0.0.2, using UDP port 646. The ensuing TCP connection—one connection between each pair of neighbors—also uses port 646. (TDP uses port 711.)

4.   A and D

MPLS TTL propagation means that all IP packets' IP TTL field is copied into the MPLS TTL field at the ingress E-LSR. That process causes the IP addresses of the LSRs to be listed in the output of the **traceroute** command, regardless of from where it is used.

5.   B

MP-BGP defines the ability to define flexible extensions to the NLRI field of a BGP Update. MPLS defines a specific format called a Route Distinguisher (RD).

6.   B

The MPLS Route Target, specifically the import Route Target on the PE receiving a BGP Update, dictates into which VRF the receiving PE puts the routes.

7.   B

LSRs always process incoming unlabeled packets using a FIB (only). For MPLS VPNs, the FIB lists at least two headers: an outer label and an inner VPN label. Any intermediate P routers ignore the inner VPN label, instead forwarding based on the outer label.

8.   B and C

Penultimate hop popping (PHP) causes the second-to-last LSR to pop the outer label. As a result, the egress PE router label switches the packet using the (formerly) inner label, as opposed to the (formerly) outer label.

9. A and C

MPLS VPNs determine each FEC based on a prefix in the per-VRF routing table.

Chapter 20

1. B

Any IPv6 address pattern beginning with the bits 001/3 is an aggregatable global address.

2. A

Anycast addresses are indistinguishable from unicast addresses; they are derived from the unicast address pool. This permits multiple hosts to provide the shared services in a way that is transparent to hosts accessing those services.

3. B, C, and D

Modified EUI-64 format has two elements: the addition of 0xFFFE in the center of the host's MAC address and the flipping of the U/L bit in the MAC address. In routers with no Ethernet interfaces, Cisco IOS determines the interface ID from a pool of MAC addresses associated with the router.

4. D

IPv6 neighbor discovery, and a number of other functions in IPv6, uses ICMPv6.

5. C

IGMP's functions in IPv4 are handled in IPv6 by Multicast Listener Discovery (MLD).

6. D

OSPFv3 itself provides no authentication mechanism. Instead, it relies on IPv6's built-in authentication capability.

7. A and B

OSPFv3 introduces new LSA types of Link LSA and Intra-Area Prefix LSA. Inter-Area Prefix LSA is a distractor; this LSA type does not exist in OSPFv2.

8. **B**

In addition to the interface mode configuration, OSPFv3 also requires a router ID to begin operating on a router.

9. **A and B**

IPv6 EIGRP uses the same component metrics as EIGRP for IPv4. The defaults—bandwidth and delay—are also the same.

10. **C**

IPv6 EIGRP supports only classless operation, in the sense that there is no concept of classful addressing in IPv6, and, more importantly, IPv6 EIGRP packets that advertise routes always include prefix-length information.

11. **A and D**

Of the tunnel types listed, only manually configured and GRE tunnels are restricted to point-to-point operation. Automatic 6to4 tunnels and ISATAP tunnels both support point-to-multipoint operation.

12. **A**

Automatically configured tunnels are deprecated. Cisco recommends using ISATAP tunnels in similar applications instead.

13. **A**

SSM is a variation on PIM sparse mode.

Decimal to Binary Conversion Table

This appendix provides a handy reference for converting between decimal and binary formats for the decimal numbers 0 through 255. Feel free to refer to this table when practicing the subnetting problems in Appendix D, "IP Addressing Practice," which is on the CD.

Although this appendix is useful as a reference tool, note that if you plan to convert values between decimal and binary when doing subnetting-related exam questions, instead of using the shortcut processes that mostly avoid binary math, you will likely want to practice converting between the two formats before the exam. For practice, just pick any decimal value between 0 and 255, convert it to 8-bit binary, and then use this table to find out if you got the right answer. Also, pick any 8-bit binary number, convert it to decimal, and again use this table to check your work.

Decimal Value	Binary Value	Decimal Value	Binary Value	Decimal Value	Binary Value	Decimal Value	Binary Value
0	00000000	32	00100000	64	01000000	96	01100000
1	00000001	33	00100001	65	01000001	97	01100001
2	00000010	34	00100010	66	01000010	98	01100010
3	00000011	35	00100011	67	01000011	99	01100011
4	00000100	36	00100100	68	01000100	100	01100100
5	00000101	37	00100101	69	01000101	101	01100101
6	00000110	38	00100110	70	01000110	102	01100110
7	00000111	39	00100111	71	01000111	103	01100111
8	00001000	40	00101000	72	01001000	104	01101000
9	00001001	41	00101001	73	01001001	105	01101001
10	00001010	42	00101010	74	01001010	106	01101010
11	00001011	43	00101011	75	01001011	107	01101011
12	00001100	44	00101100	76	01001100	108	01101100
13	00001101	45	00101101	77	01001101	109	01101101
14	00001110	46	00101110	78	01001110	110	01101110
15	00001111	47	00101111	79	01001111	111	01101111
16	00010000	48	00110000	80	01010000	112	01110000
17	00010001	49	00110001	81	01010001	113	01110001
18	00010010	50	00110010	82	01010010	114	01110010
19	00010011	51	00110011	83	01010011	115	01110011
20	00010100	52	00110100	84	01010100	116	01110100
21	00010101	53	00110101	85	01010101	117	01110101
22	00010110	54	00110110	86	01010110	118	01110110
23	00010111	55	00110111	87	01010111	119	01110111
24	00011000	56	00111000	88	01011000	120	01111000
25	00011001	57	00111001	89	01011001	121	01111001
26	00011010	58	00111010	90	01011010	122	01111010
27	00011011	59	00111011	91	01011011	123	01111011
28	00011100	60	00111100	92	01011100	124	01111100
29	00011101	61	00111101	93	01011101	125	01111101
30	00011110	62	00111110	94	01011110	126	01111110
31	00011111	63	00111111	95	01011111	127	01111111

Decimal Value	Binary Value	Decimal Value	Binary Value	Decimal Value	Binary Value	Decimal Value	Binary Value
128	10000000	160	10100000	192	11000000	224	11100000
129	10000001	161	10100001	193	11000001	225	11100001
130	10000010	162	10100010	194	11000010	226	11100010
131	10000011	163	10100011	195	11000011	227	11100011
132	10000100	164	10100100	196	11000100	228	11100100
133	10000101	165	10100101	197	11000101	229	11100101
134	10000110	166	10100110	198	11000110	230	11100110
135	10000111	167	10100111	199	11000111	231	11100111
136	10001000	168	10101000	200	11001000	232	11101000
137	10001001	169	10101001	201	11001001	233	11101001
138	10001010	170	10101010	202	11001010	234	11101010
139	10001011	171	10101011	203	11001011	235	11101011
140	10001100	172	10101100	204	11001100	236	11101100
141	10001101	173	10101101	205	11001101	237	11101101
142	10001110	174	10101110	206	11001110	238	11101110
143	10001111	175	10101111	207	11001111	239	11101111
144	10010000	176	10110000	208	11010000	240	11110000
145	10010001	177	10110001	209	11010001	241	11110001
146	10010010	178	10110010	210	11010010	242	11110010
147	10010011	179	10110011	211	11010011	243	11110011
148	10010100	180	10110100	212	11010100	244	11110100
149	10010101	181	10110101	213	11010101	245	11110101
150	10010110	182	10110110	214	11010110	246	11110110
151	10010111	183	10110111	215	11010111	247	11110111
152	10011000	184	10111000	216	11011000	248	11111000
153	10011001	185	10111001	217	11011001	249	11111001
154	10011010	186	10111010	218	11011010	250	11111010
155	10011011	187	10111011	219	11011011	251	11111011
156	10011100	188	10111100	220	11011100	252	11111100
157	10011101	189	10111101	221	11011101	253	11111101
158	10011110	190	10111110	222	11011110	254	11111110
159	10011111	191	10111111	223	11011111	255	11111111

CCIE Routing and Switching Exam Updates: Version 1.0

Over time, reader feedback allows Cisco Press to gauge which topics give our readers the most problems when taking the exams. Additionally, Cisco might make changes to the CCIE Routing and Switching exam blueprint. To assist readers with those topics, the authors created new materials clarifying and expanding upon those troublesome exam topics. As mentioned in the introduction, the additional content about the exam is contained in a PDF document on this book's companion website, at http://www.ciscopress.com/title/1587201968.

This appendix presents all the latest updated information available at the time of this book's printing. To make sure you have the latest version of this document, visit the companion website to see if any more recent versions have been posted since this book went to press.

This appendix attempts to fill the void that occurs with any print book. In particular, this appendix does the following:

- Mentions technical items that might not have been mentioned elsewhere in the book

- Covers new topics when Cisco adds topics to the CCIE Routing and Switching written exam blueprint

- Provides a way to get up-to-the-minute current information about content for the exam

Always Get the Latest at the Companion Website

You are reading the version of this appendix that was available when your book was printed. However, given that the main purpose of this appendix is to be a living, changing document, it is important that you look for the latest version online at the book's companion website. To do so:

Step 1   Browse to http://www.ciscopress.com/title/1587201968.

Step 2   Select the Appendix option under the More Information box.

Step 3   Download the latest "Appendix C" document.

> **NOTE** Note that the downloaded document has a version number. Comparing the version of this print Appendix C (Version 1.0) with the latest online version of this appendix, you should do the following:
>
> ■ **Same version**—Ignore the PDF that you downloaded from the companion website.
>
> ■ **Website has a later version**—Ignore this Appendix C in your book and read only the latest version that you downloaded from the companion website.

Technical Content

The current version of this appendix does not contain any additional technical coverage.

224.0.0.2   The IP address to which Label Distribution Protocol (LDP) sends LDP Hellos. Also used in IP multicast to send packets to all multicast routers.

224.0.0.5   The All OSPF Routers multicast IP address, listened for by all OSPF routers.

224.0.0.6   The All OSPF DR Routers multicast IP address, listened for by DR and BDR routers.

2Way (OSPF)   A neighbor state that signifies the other router has reached neighbor status, having passed the parameter check.

6to4   An IPv6/IPv4 tunneling method that allows isolated IPv6 domains to be connected over an IPv4 network.

802.11a   A wireless LAN physical layer that operates at up to 54-Mbps data rates using OFDM in the 5-GHz band.

802.11b   A wireless LAN physical layer that operates at up to 11-Mbps data rates using DSSS in the 2.4-GHz band.

802.11g   A wireless LAN physical layer that is backward compatible with 802.11b and operates at up to 54-Mbps data rates using OFDM in the 2.4-GHz band.

802.11n   A prestandard (at the time of publication) wireless LAN physical layer that offers data rates in the hundreds of megabits per second.

802.1Q   The IEEE standardized protocol for VLAN trunking.

802.1Q-in-Q   A mechanism in which VLAN information can extend over another set of 802.1Q trunks by tunneling the original 802.1Q traffic with another 802.1Q tag. It allows a service provider to support transparent VLAN services with multiple customers, even if the customers use overlapping VLAN numbers.

AAA   *See* Authentication, authorization, and accounting.

AAAA   In IPv6 DNS, the IPv6 equivalent of an IPv4 DNS A record.

ABR   *See* Area Border Router.

Access Control Entry   An individual line in an ACL.

Access Control Server   A term referring generically to a server that performs many AAA functions. It also refers to the software product Cisco Secure Access Control Server.

access link   In Frame Relay, a link between a router and a Frame Relay switch.

access rate   The speed at which the access link is clocked. This choice affects the price of the connection and many aspects of traffic shaping and policing, compression, quality of service, and other configuration options.

ACE   *See* Access Control Entry.

Ack (EIGRP)   An EIGRP message that is used to acknowledge reliable EIGRP messages, namely Update, Query, and Reply messages. Acks do not require an Ack.

ACS   *See* Access Control Server.

active (EIGRP)   A state for a route in an EIGRP topology table that indicates that the router is actively sending Query messages for this route, attempting to validate and learn the current best route to that subnet.

active mode FTP   Defines a particular behavior for FTP regarding the establishment of data TCP connections. In active mode, the FTP client uses the FTP PORT command, over the FTP control connection, to tell the FTP server the port on which the client should be listening for a new data connection. The server uses well-known port 20, and initiates a TCP connection to the FTP client's earlier-declared port.

active scanning   Each 802.11 station periodically sends a probe request frame on each RF channel and monitors probe response frames that all access points within range send back. Stations use the signal strength of the probe response frames to determine which access point or ad hoc network to associate with.

actual queue depth   The actual number of packets in a queue at a particular time.

ad hoc mode   A wireless LAN that only includes wireless users and no access points. 802.11 data frames in an ad hoc network travel directly between wireless users.

adaptive shaping   A Frame Relay traffic shaping feature during which the shaping rate is reduced when the shaper notices congestion through the receipt of BECN or ForeSight messages.

Address Resolution Protocol   Defined in RFC 826, a protocol used on LANs so that an IP host can discover the MAC address of another device that is using a particular IP address.

adjacency (EIGRP)   Often used synonymously with neighbor, but with emphasis on the fact that all required parameters match, allowing routing updates to be exchanged between the routers.

adjacency table   A table used by CEF that holds information about adjacent IP hosts to which packets can be forwarded.

adjacent (OSPF)   Any OSPF neighbor for which the database flooding process has completed.

adjacent-layer interaction   On a single computer, one layer provides a service to a higher layer. The software or hardware that implements the higher layer requests that the next lower layer perform the needed function.

administrative scoping   Controls the distribution of multicast traffic for the private multicast address range 239.0.0.0 to 239.255.255.255 by configuring a filter and applying it on the interfaces.

administrative weight   A Cisco-proprietary BGP feature. The administrative weight can be assigned to each NLRI and path locally on a router, impacting the local router's choice of the best BGP routes. The value cannot be communicated to another router.

administratively scoped addresses   The range 239.0.0.0 through 239.255.255.255 that IANA has assigned for use in private multicast domains.

Advanced Encryption Standard   A superior encryption mechanism that is part of the 802.11i standard and has much stronger security than TKIP.

advertised window   *See* receiver's advertised window.

AES   *See* Advanced Encryption Standard.

AF   *See* Assured Forwarding.

aggregatable global unicast address   An IPv6 address format used for publicly registered IPv6 addresses.

aggregate route   Another term for summary route.

AGGREGATOR   An optional transitive BGP path attribute that, for a summary route, lists the BGP RID and ASN of the router that created the summary.

AIS   Alarm Indication Signal. With T1s, the practice of sending all binary 1s on the line in reaction to problems, to provide signal transitions and allow recovery of synchronization and framing.

All OSPF DR Routers   The multicast IP address 224.0.0.6, listened for by DR and BDR routers.

All OSPF Routers   The multicast IP address 224.0.0.5, listened for by all OSPF routers.

Alternate Mark Inversion   A serial-line encoding standard that sends alternating positive and negative 3-volt signals for binary 1, and no signal (0 V) for binary 0.

alternate mode   One of the two modes of MDRR, in which the priority queue is serviced between each servicing of the non-priority queues.

Alternate state   An 802.1w RSTP port state in which the port is not the Root Port but is available to become the root port if the current root port goes down.

AMI   *See* Alternate Mark Inversion.

anycast   An IPv6 address type that is used by a number of hosts in a network that are providing the same service. Hosts accessing the service are routed to the nearest host in an anycast environment based on routing protocol metrics.

AR   *See* access rate.

area (OSPF)   A contiguous group of data links that share the same OSPF area number.

Area Border Router   An OSPF router that connects to the backbone area and to one or more non-backbone area.

ARP   *See* Address Resolution Protocol.

AS number   A number between 1 and 64,511 (public) and 64,512 and 65,535 (private) assigned to an AS for the purpose of identifying a specific BGP domain.

AS_CONFED_SEQ   A type of AS_PATH segment consisting of an ordered list of confederation sub-ASNs through which a route has been advertised.

AS_CONFED_SET   A type of AS_PATH segment consisting of an unordered list of confederation sub-ASNs consolidated from component subnets of a summary BGP route created inside a confederation.

AS_PATH   A BGP path attribute that lists ASNs through which the route has been advertised. The AS_PATH includes four types of segments: AS_SEQ, AS_SET, AS_CONFED_SEQ, and AS_CONFED_SET. Often, this term is used synonymously with AS_SEQ.

AS_PATH access list   A Cisco IOS configuration tool, using the **ip as-path access-list** command, that defines a list of statements that match the AS_PATH BGP path attribute using regular expressions.

AS_PATH length   A calculation of the length of the AS_PATH PA, which includes 1 for each number in the AS_SEQ, 1 for an entire AS_SET segment, and possibly other considerations.

AS_PATH prepending   This term has two BGP-related definitions. First, it is the normal process in which a router, before sending an Update to an eBGP peer, adds its local ASN to the beginning of the AS_PATH path attribute. Second, it is the routing policy of purposefully adding one or more ASNs to the beginning of a route's AS_PATH path attribute, typically to lengthen the AS_PATH and make the route less desirable in the BGP decision process.

AS_SEQUENCE   A type of AS_PATH segment consisting of an ordered list of ASNs through which the route has been advertised.

AS_SET   A type of AS_PATH segment consisting of an unordered list of ASNs consolidated from component subnets of a summary BGP route.

ASBR   Autonomous System Boundary Router. An OSPF router that redistributes routes from some other source into OSPF.

ASN   *See* AS number.

Assert message   Sent by a PIM-DM or PIM-SM router when it receives a multicast packet for a group on a LAN interface that is in the outgoing interface list for the group; includes the administrative distance of the unicast routing protocol used to learn the network of the source with its metric value.

association ID   When a wireless station connects to an access point, the access point assigns an association ID (AID) to the station. Various protocols, such as power-save mode, make use of the association ID.

Assured Forwarding   A set of DiffServ PHBs that defines 12 DSCP values, with four queuing classes and three drop probabilities within each queuing class.

ATOMIC_AGGREGATE   A well-known discretionary BGP path attribute that flags a route as being a summary route.

authentication   With routing protocols, the process by which the router receiving a routing update determines if the routing update came from a trusted router.

authentication, authorization, and accounting   Three core security functions.

authentication method   A term referring generically to ways in which a router or switch can determine whether a particular device or user should be allowed access.

authentication server   In 802.1X, the computer that stores usernames/passwords and verifies that the correct values were submitted before authenticating the user.

authenticator   The 802.1X function implemented by a switch, in which the switch translates between EAPoL and RADIUS messages in both directions, and enables/disables ports based on the success/failure of authentication.

auto-negotiation   Ethernet process by which devices attached to the same cable negotiate their speed and the duplex settings over the cable.

autonomous system   In BGP, a set of routers inside a single administrative authority, grouped together for the purpose of controlling routing policies for the routes advertised by that group to the Internet.

Auto-RP   Auto-Rendezvous Point. Cisco-proprietary protocol that can be used to designate an RP and send RP-Announce messages that advertise its IP address and groups. Also, it can be used to designate a mapping agent that interprets what IP address RP is advertising and for what groups. A mapping agent sends this information in the RP-Discovery messages so that all PIM-SM routers can learn the IP address of the RP and groups it is supporting automatically.

average queue depth   Calculated measurement based on the actual queue depth and the previous average. Designed to allow WRED to adjust slowly to rapid changes of the actual queue depth.

B8ZS   *See* Bipolar 8 Zero Substitution.

backbone area (OSPF)   Area 0; the area to which all other OSPF areas much connect in order for OSPF to work.

BackboneFast   Cisco-proprietary STP feature in which switches use messaging to confirm the loss of Hello BPDUs in a switch's Root Port, to avoid having to wait for maxage to expire, resulting in faster convergence.

backup designated router   In OSPF, a router that is prepared to take over the designated router.

backup state   An 802.1w RSTP port state in which the port is an alternative Designated Port on some LAN segment.

Backward Explicit Congestion Notification   A bit inside the Frame Relay header that, when set, implies that congestion occurred in the direction opposite (or backward) as compared with the direction of the frame.

Bc   *See* Committed Burst.

Bc bucket   Jargon used to refer to the first of two buckets in the dual token bucket model; its size is Bc.

BDR   *See* backup designated router.

Be   *See* Excess Burst.

Be bucket   Jargon used to refer to the second of two buckets in the dual token bucket model; its size is Be.

beacon   An 802.11 frame that access points or stations in ad hoc networks send periodically so that wireless stations can discover the presence of a wireless LAN and coordinate use of certain protocols, such as power-save mode.

BECN   *See* Backward Explicit Congestion Notification.

BGP   *See* Border Gateway Protocol.

BGP decision process   A set of rules by which BGP examines the details of multiple BGP routes for the same NLRI and chooses the single best BGP route to install in the local BGP table.

BGP table   A table inside a router that holds the path attributes and NLRI known by the BGP implementation on that router.

BGP Update   A BGP message that includes withdrawn routes, path attributes, and NLRI.

Bipolar 8 Zero Substitution   A serial-line encoding standard that substitutes Bipolar Violations in a string of eight binary 0s to provide enough signal transitions to maintain synchronization.

Bipolar Violation   For some encoding schemes, consecutive signals must use opposite polarity in an effort to reduce DC current. A BPV occurs when consecutive signals are of the same polarity.

blocking state   An 802.1d STP port state in which the port does not send or receive frames, except for listening for received Hello BPDUs.

boot field   The low-order 4 bits of the configuration register. These bits direct a router to load either ROMMON software (boot field 0x0), RXBOOT software (boot field 0x1), or a full-function IOS image.

Boot Protocol   A standard (RFC 951) protocol by which a LAN-attached host can dynamically broadcast a request for a server to assign it an IP address, along with other configuration settings, including a subnet mask and default gateway IP address.

BOOTP   *See* Boot Protocol.

bootstrap router   In multicast (IPv4 and IPv6), the process that associates multicast groups with rendezvous points (RPs) in PIM BSR mode.

Border Gateway Protocol   An exterior routing protocol designed to exchange prefix information between different autonomous systems. The information includes a rich set of characteristics called path attributes, which in turn allows for great flexibility regarding routing choices.

BPDU Guard   Cisco-proprietary STP feature in which a switch port monitors for STP BPDUs of any kind, err-disabling the port upon receipt of any BPDU.

BPV   *See* Bipolar Violation.

broadcast address   Ethernet MAC address that represents all devices on the LAN.

broadcast domain   A set of all devices that receive broadcast frames originating from any device within the set. Devices in the same VLAN are in the same broadcast domain.

broadcast subnet   When subnetting a class A, B, or C address, the subnet for which all subnet bits are binary 1.

BSR   *See* bootstrap router.

CB Marking   *See* Class-Based Marking.

CBAC   *See* Context-Based Access Control.

CBWFQ   *See* class-based weighted fair queuing.

CDP Control Protocol   The portion of PPP focused on supporting the CDP protocol.

CDPCP   *See* CDP Control Protocol.

CE   *See* customer edge.

CEF   *See* Cisco Express Forwarding.

Cell Loss Priority   A bit in the ATM cell header that, when set to 1, means that if a device needs to discard frames, it should discard the frames with DE 1 first.

CGMP   *See* Cisco Group Management Protocol.

Challenge Handshake Authentication Protocol   An Internet standard authentication protocol that uses secure hashes and a three-way handshake to perform authentication over a PPP link.

CHAP   *See* Challenge Handshake Authentication Protocol.

CIDR   *See* classless interdomain routing.

CIR   *See* committed information rate.

Cisco Express Forwarding   An optimized Layer 3 forwarding path through a router or switch. CEF optimizes routing table lookup by creating a special, easily searched tree structure based on the contents of the IP routing table. The forwarding information is called the Forwarding Information Base (FIB), and by caching adjacency information is called the adjacency table.

Cisco Group Management Protocol   A Cisco-proprietary feature. After a Cisco multicast router receives IGMP Join or Leave messages from hosts, it communicates to the connected Cisco switches, telling them which hosts (based on their unicast MAC addresses) have joined or left each multicast group. Switches examine their CAM tables and determine on which ports these hosts are connected and either forward multicast traffic or stop forwarding on those ports only.

Class-Based Marking   An MQC-based feature of IOS that is used to classify and mark packets for QoS purposes.

class-based weighted fair queuing   A Cisco IOS queuing tool that uses MQC configuration commands and reserves a minimum bandwidth for each queue.

class map   A term referring to the MQC **class-map** command and its related subcommands, which are used for classifying packets.

Class of Service   A 3-bit field in an ISL header used for marking frames. Also, used generically to refer to either the ISL CoS field or the 802.1Q User Priority field.

Class Selector   A DiffServ PHB that defines eight values that provide backward compatibility with IP Precedence.

classful IP addressing   A type of logic for how a router uses a default route. A convention for discussing and thinking about IP addresses by which class A, B, and C default network prefixes (of 8, 16, and 24 bits, respectively) are considered.

classful routing   A type of logic for how a router uses a default route. When a default route exists, and the class A, B, or C network for the destination IP address does not exist in the routing table, the default route is used. If any part of that classful network exists in the routing table, but the packet does not match any existing subnet of that classful network, the packet does not match the default route and thus is discarded.

classless IP addressing   A convention for IP addresses in which class A, B, and C default network prefixes (of 8, 16, and 24 bits, respectively) are ignored.

classless interdomain routing   Defined in RFCs 1517–1520, a scheme to help reduce Internet routing table sizes by administratively allocating large blocks of consecutive classful IP network numbers to ISPs for use in different global geographies. CIDR results in large blocks of networks that can be summarized, or aggregated, into single routes.

classless routing   A type of logic for how a router uses a default route. When a default route exists, and no more specific match is made between the destination of the packet and the routing table, the default route is used.

Clear To Send   On a serial cable, the pin lead set by the DCE to tell the DTE that the DTE is allowed send data.

client tracking   Records client authentication and roaming events, which are sent to the CiscoWorks Wireless LAN Solution Engine (WLSE) to monitor client associations to specific access points.

CLP   *See* Cell Loss Priority.

CLUSTER_LIST   An optional nontransitive BGP path attribute that lists the route reflector cluster IDs through which a route has been advertised, as part of a loop-prevention process similar to the AS_PATH attribute.

collision domain   A set of all devices for which any frame sent by one of the devices would collide with any frames transmitted at the same time by any of the other devices in the set.

Committed Burst   With shaping, the number of bits allowed to be sent every Tc. Also defines the size of the token bucket when Be = 0.

committed information rate   In shaping and policing, commonly used to refer to the shaping or policing rate. For WAN services, a common reference to the bit rate defined in the WAN service business contract for each VC.

Common Spanning Tree   A single instance of STP that is applied to multiple VLANs, typically when using the 802.1Q trunking standard.

COMMUNITY   An optional transitive BGP path attribute used to store 32-bit decimal values. Used for flexible grouping of routes by assigning the group the same COMMUNITY value. Other routers can apply routing policies based on the COMMUNITY value. Used in a large number of BGP applications.

community VLAN   With private VLANs, a secondary VLAN in which the ports can send and receive frames with each other, but not with ports in other secondary VLANS.

component route   A term used in this book to refer to a route that is included in a larger summary route.

confederation   A BGP feature that overcomes the requirement of a full mesh of iBGP peers inside a single AS by separating the AS into multiple sub-autonomous systems.

confederation ASN   The ASN assigned to a confederation sub-AS.

confederation eBGP peer   A BGP peer connection between two routers inside the same ASN, but in different confederation sub-autonomous systems.

confederation identifier   In an IOS confederation configuration, the actual ASN as seen by eBGP peers.

configuration register   A 16-bit number set with a router **config-register** command. It is used to set several low-level features related mainly to accessing the router and what the router does when powered on.

conform   A category used by a policer to classify packets relative to the traffic contract. The bit rate implied by all conforming packets is within the traffic contract.

Congestion Avoidance   A method for how a TCP sender grows its calculated CWND variable, thereby growing the allowed window for the connection. Congestion Avoidance grows CWND linearly.

congestion window   A mechanism used by TCP senders to limit the dynamic window for a TCP connection, to reduce the sending rate when packet loss occurs. The sender considers both the advertised window size and CWND, using the smaller of the two.

Context-Based Access Control   Part of the Cisco IOS Firewall feature set, CBAC inspects traffic using information in the higher-layer protocols being carried to decide whether to open the firewall to specific inbound traffic. CBAC supports both UDP and TCP and multiple higher-layer protocols and can be applied inbound or outbound on an interface.

control plane   In IP routing, a term referring to the building of IP routing tables by IP routing protocols.

CoS   *See* Class of Service.

counting to infinity   A type of routing protocol convergence event in which the metric for a route increases slightly over time because of the advertisement of an invalid route.

CQ   *See* custom queuing

cross-over cable   Copper cable with RJ-45 connectors in which a twisted pair at pins 1,2 on the first end of the cable is connected to pins 3,6 on the other end, with a second pair connected to pins 3,6 on the first end and pins 1,2 on the other end.

CS   *See* Class Selector.

CSMA/CD   Carrier sense multiple access with collision detection. A media-access mechanism where devices ready to transmit data first check the channel for a carrier. If no carrier is sensed for a specific period of time, a device can transmit. If two devices transmit simultaneously, a collision occurs and is detected by all colliding devices. This collision subsequently causes each device to delay retransmissions of the collided frame for some random length of time.

CST   *See* Common Spanning Tree.

CTS   *See* Clear To Send.

custom queuing   A Cisco IOS queuing tool most notable for its reservation of a minimum bandwidth for each queue.

customer edge   An MPLS VPN term referring to a router at a customer site that does not implement MPLS.

CWND   *See* congestion window.

D4 framing   Another name for Superframe.

DAI   *See* Dynamic ARP Inspection.

Data Carrier Detect   On a serial cable, the pin lead set by the DCE to imply a working link.

data communications equipment   DCE devices are one of two devices on either end of a communications circuit, specifically the device with more control over the communications. Frame Relay switches are DCE devices. DCEs are also known as data circuit-terminating equipment (DTE).

Database Description   A type of OSPF packet used to exchange and acknowledge LSA headers. Sometimes called DBD.

Data-link connection identifier   A Frame Relay address used in Frame Relay headers to identify the VC

data plane   In IP routing, a term referring to the process of forwarding packets through a router.

data Set Ready   On a serial cable, the pin lead set by the DCE to imply that the DCE is ready to signal using pin leads

data terminal equipment   From one perspective, DTE devices are one of two devices on either end of a communications circuit, specifically the device with less control over the communications. In Frame Relay, routers connected to a Frame Relay access link are DTE devices.

Data Terminal Ready   On a serial cable, the pin lead set by the DTE to imply that the DTE is ready to signal using pin leads.

DCD   *See* Data Carrier Detect.

DCE   *See* data communications equipment.

DD   *See* Database Description.

DE   *See* Discard Eligible.

Dead Time/Interval   With OSPF, the timer used to determine when a neighboring router has failed, based on a router not receiving any OSPF messages, including Hellos, in this timer period.

default route   A route that is used for forwarding packets when the packet does not match any more specific routes in the IP routing table.

dense-mode protocol   A multicast routing protocol whose default action is to flood multicast packets throughout a network.

designated port   With Spanning Tree Protocol, the single port on each LAN segment from which the best Hello BPDU is forwarded.

designated router   With PIM on a multiaccess network, the PIM router with the highest IP address on the subnet. With OSPF, the OSPF router that wins an election amongst all current neighbors. The DR is responsible for flooding on the subnet, and for creating and flooding the type 2 LSA for the subnet.

DHCP   *See* Dynamic Host Configuration Protocol.

DHCP snooping   A switch feature in which the switch examines DHCP messages and, for untrusted ports, filters all messages typically sent by servers and inappropriate messages sent by clients. It also builds a DHCP snooping binding table that is used by DAI and IP Source Guard.

DHCP snooping binding database   The list of entries learned by the switch DHCP snooping feature. The entries include the MAC address used as the device's DHCP client address, the assigned IP address, the VLAN, and the switch port on which the DHCP assignment messages flowed.

Differentiated Services   A set of QoS RFCs that redefines the IP header's ToS byte, and suggests specific settings of the DSCP field and the implied QoS actions based on those settings.

Differentiated Services Code Point   The first 6 bits of the DS field, used for QoS marking.

differentiated tail drop   A term relating to Cisco LAN switch tail-drop logic, in which multiple tail-drop thresholds may be assigned based on CoS or DSCP, resulting in some frames being discarded more aggressively than others.

DiffServ   *See* Differentiated Services.

Diffusing Update Algorithm   A term referring to EIGRP's internal processing logic.

Digital Signal Level 0   Inside telcos' original TDM hierarchy, the smallest unit of transmission at 64 kbps.

Digital Signal Level 1   Inside telcos' original TDM hierarchy, a unit that combines multiple DS0s into a single channel—24 DS0s (plus overhead) for a T1, and 30 (plus overhead) for an E1.

Digital Signal Level 3   Inside telcos' original TDM hierarchy, a unit that combines multiple DS1s into a single channel—28 DS1s (plus overhead) for a T3, and 16 E1 DS1s (plus overhead) for an E3.

Dijkstra   Alternate name for the SPF algorithm, named for its inventor, Edsger W. Dijkstra.

direct sequence spread spectrum   A type of spread spectrum that spreads RF signals over the frequency spectrum by representing each data bit by a longer code. 802.11b specifies the use of DSSS.

disabled state   An 802.1d STP port state in which the port has been administratively disabled.

Discard Eligible   A bit in the Frame Relay header that, when set to 1, means that if a device needs to discard frames, it should discard the frames with DE 1 first.

discarding state   An 802.1w RSTP port state in which the port is not forwarding or receiving; covers 802.1d port states disabled, blocking, and listening.

distance vector   The underlying algorithms associated with RIP.

Distance Vector Multicast Routing Protocol   Operates in dense mode and depends on its own unicast routing protocol that is similar to RIP to perform its multicast functions.

distributed coordination function   The mandatory contention-based 802.11 access protocol that is also referred to as CSMA/CA.

distribution list   A Cisco IOS configuration tool for routing protocols by which routing updates may be filtered.

DLCI   *See* data-link connection identifier.

DMVPN   *See* Dynamic Multipoint VPN.

downstream router   The router that will receive the group traffic when a multicast router forwards group traffic to another router.

DR   *See* designated router.

DR election (OSPF)   The process by which neighboring OSPF routers examine their Hello messages and elect the DR. The decision is based on priority (highest), or RID (highest) if priority is a tie.

DROther   The term to describe a router that is neither the DR nor the BDR on a subnet that elects a DR and BDR.

DS field   The second byte of the IP header, formerly known as the ToS byte and redefined by DiffServ.

DS0   *See* Digital Signal Level 0.

DS1   *See* Digital Signal Level 1.

DS3   *See* Digital Signal Level 3.

DSCP   *See* Differentiated Services Code Point.

DSCP-to-CoS map   A mapping between each DSCP value and a corresponding CoS value, often used in Cisco LAN switches when performing classification for egress queuing.

DSCP-to-threshold map   A mapping between each DSCP value and a WRED threshold, often used in Cisco LAN switches when performing WRED.

DSR   *See* Data Set Ready.

DSSS   *See* direct sequence spread spectrum.

DTE   *See* data terminal equipment.

DTIM interval   The number of beacons that governs how often multicast frames are sent over a wireless LAN.

DTP   *See* Dynamic Trunking Protocol.

DTR   *See* Data Terminal Ready.

DUAL   *See* Diffusing Update Algorithm.

Dual FIFO   A Cisco IOS interface software queue queuing strategy implemented automatically when using either form of Frame Relay fragmentation. The system then interleaves packets from the high-priority queue between fragments of the medium-priority queue.

dual stack   An IPv6 migration strategy in which a host or router supports both IPv4 and IPv6 natively.

dual token bucket   A conceptual model used by CB Policing when using an excess burst.

dual-rate, three-color policer   Policing in which two rates are metered, and packets are placed into one of three categories (conform, exceed, or violate).

DVMRP   *See* Distance Vector Multicast Routing Protocol.

Dynamic ARP Inspection   A switch feature with which the switch watches ARP messages, determines if those messages may or may not be part of some attack, and filters those that look suspicious.

Dynamic Host Configuration Protocol   A standard (RFC 2131) protocol by which a host can dynamically broadcast a request for a server to assign to it an IP address, along with other configuration settings, including a subnet mask and default gateway IP address. DHCP provides a great deal of flexibility and functionality compared with RARP and BOOTP.

Dynamic Multipoint VPN   A method of providing dynamically configured spoke-to-spoke VPN connectivity in a hub-and-spoke network that significantly reduces configuration required on the spoke routers compared to traditional IPsec VPN environments.

Dynamic Trunking Protocol   A Cisco-proprietary protocol used to dynamically negotiate whether the devices on an Ethernet segment want to form a trunk and, if so, which type (ISL or 802.1Q).

E1   A name used for DS1 lines inside the European TDM hierarchy.

E1 route (OSPF)   An OSPF external route for which internal OSPF cost is added to the cost of the route as it was redistributed into OSPF.

E2 route (OSPF)   An OSPF external route for which internal OSPF cost is not added to the cost of the route as it was redistributed into OSPF.

E3   A name used for DS3 lines inside the European TDM hierarchy.

EAP   *See* Extensible Authentication Protocol.

EAP over LAN   The encapsulation of EAP messages directly inside LAN frames. This encapsulation is used between the supplicant and the authenticator.

EAPoL   *See* EAP over LAN.

eBGP *See* External BGP.

eBGP multihop A BGP feature that defines the IP TTL field value in packets sent between two eBGP peers. This feature is required when using IP addresses other than the interface IP address on the link between peers.

edge LSR An MPLS LSR that can forward and receive both labeled and unlabeled packets.

EF *See* Expedited Forwarding.

EGP *See* Exterior Gateway Protocol.

egress PE An E-LSR in an MPLS VPN network whose role in a particular discussion is to receive labeled packets from other LSRs and then forward the packets as unlabeled packets to CE routers.

ELMI *See* Enhanced Local Management Interface.

E-LSR *See* edge LSR.

enable password The password required by the **enable** command. Also, this term may specifically refer to the password defined by the **enable password** command.

enable secret The MD5-encoded password defined by the **enable secret** command.

encapsulation The process of taking a PDU from some other source and placing a header in front of the original PDU, and possibly a trailer behind it.

encoding The process of changing the electrical characteristics on a transmission medium, based on defined rules, to represent data.

enhanced editing The Cisco IOS feature by which special short key sequences can be used to move the cursor inside the current command line to more easily change a command.

Enhanced Local Management Interface A Cisco-proprietary LMI protocol, implemented in Cisco WAN switches and routers, through which the switch can inform the router about parameters for each VC, including CIR, Bc, and Be.

ESF *See* Extended Superframe.

established A BGP neighbor state in which the BGP neighbors have stabilized and can exchange routing information using BGP Update messages.

EUI-64   A specification for the 64-bit interface ID in an IPv6 address, composed of the first half of a MAC address, hex FFFE, and the last half of the MAC.

exceed   A category used by a policer to classify packets relative to the traffic contract. With two-color policers, these packets are considered to be above the contract; for three-color, these packets are above the Bc setting, but within the Be setting.

Excess Burst   With shaping and policing, the number of additional bits that may be sent after a period of relative inactivity.

expedite queue   A term used with Cisco LAN switches, referring to a queue treated with strict-priority scheduling.

Expedited Forwarding   A DiffServ PHB, based on DSCP EF (decimal 46), that provides low-latency queuing behavior as well as policing protection to prevent EF traffic from starving queues for other types of traffic.

Extensible Authentication Protocol   Defined in RFC 3748, the protocol used by IEEE 802.1X for exchanging authentication information.

Exterior Gateway Protocol   An exterior routing protocol that predates BGP. It is no longer used today.

exponential weighting constant   Used by WRED to calculate the rate at which the average queue depth changes as compared with the current queue depth. The larger the number, the slower the change in the average queue depth.

Extended Superframe   An enhanced version of T1 framing, as compared with the earlier Superframe (D4) standard.

External BGP   A term referring to how a router views a BGP peer relationship, in which the peer is in another AS.

external route   From the perspective of one routing protocol, a route that was learned by using route redistribution.

Fast Secure Roaming   Enables a wireless client to securely roam between access points in the same subnet or between subnets with access point handoff times within 50 ms.

fast switching   An optimized Layer 3 forwarding path through a router. Fast switching optimizes routing table lookup by creating a special, easily searched table of known flows between hosts.

FD   *See* feasible distance.

feasibility condition   With EIGRP, for a particular route, the case in which the RD is lower than the FD.

Feasible distance   With EIGRP, the metric value for the lowest-metric route to a particular subnet.

feasible successor   With EIGRP, a route that is not a successor route, but that meets the feasibility condition; can be used when the successor route fails, without causing loops.

FEC   *See* Forwarding Equivalence Class.

FECN   *See* Forward Explicit Congestion Notification.

FHSS   *See* frequency hopping spread spectrum.

FIB   *See* Forwarding Information Base.

finish time   A term used with WFQ for the number assigned to a packet as it is enqueued into a WFQ queue. WFQ schedules the currently lowest FT packet next.

flash updates   *See* triggered updates.

Flush timer   With RIP, a per-route timer, which is reset and grows with the Invalid timer. When the Flush timer mark is reached (default 240 seconds), the router removes the route from the routing table, and now accepts any other routes about the failed subnet.

ForeSight   A Cisco-proprietary messaging protocol implemented in WAN switches that can be used to signal network status, including congestion, independent of end-user frames and cells.

Forward Delay timer   An STP timer that dictates how long a port should stay in the listening state and the learning state.

Forward Explicit Congestion Notification   A bit in the LAPF Frame Relay header that, when set to 1, implies that the frame has experienced congestion.

Forwarding Equivalence Class   A set of packets in an MPLS network for which the MPLS network will apply the exact same forwarding behavior.

Forwarding Information Base   A neighbor state that signifies the other router has reached neighbor status, having passed the parameter check.

forwarding state   An 802.1d STP port state in which the port sends and receives frames.

fraggle attack   An attack similar to a smurf attack, but using packets for the UDP Echo application instead of ICMP.

fragmentation   In wireless LANs, a mechanism that counters issues related to RF interference by dividing a larger 802.11 data frame into smaller frames that are sent independently to the destination. See *also* LFI.

Frame Relay Forum   A vendor consortium that formerly worked to further Frame Relay common vendor standards.

framing   From a Layer 1 perspective, the process of using special strings of electrical signals over a transmission medium to inform the receiver as to which bits are overhead bits, and which fit into individual subchannels.

frequency hopping spread spectrum   A type of spread spectrum that spreads RF signals over the frequency spectrum by transmitting the signal at different frequencies according to a hopping pattern. One of the original 802.11 physical layers used FHSS to offer data rates of 1 and 2 Mbps.

FRF   *See* Frame Relay Forum.

FRF.5   An FRF standard for Frame Relay-to-ATM Service Interworking in which both DTEs use Frame Relay, with ATM in between.

FRF.8   An FRF standard for Frame Relay-to-ATM Service Interworking in which one DTE uses Frame Relay and one uses ATM.

FRF.9   An FRF standard for payload compression.

FRF.11-c   An FRF standard for LFI for VoFR (FRF.11) VCs, in which all voice frames are interleaved in front of data frames' fragments.

FRF.12   An FRF standard for LFI for data (FRF.3) VCs.

FT   *See* finish time.

full drop   A WRED process by which WRED discards all newly arriving packets intended for a queue, based on whether the queue's maximum threshold has been exceeded.

full duplex   Ethernet feature in which a NIC or Ethernet port can both transmit and receive at the same instant in time. It can be used only when there is no possibility of collisions. Loopback circuitry on NIC cards is disabled to use full duplex.

full SPF calculation   An SPF calculation as a result of changes inside the same area as a router, for which the SPF run must examine the full LSDB.

full update   A routing protocol feature by which the routing update includes the entire set of routes, even if some or all of the routes are unchanged.

fully adjacent (OSPF)   Any OSPF neighbor for which the database flooding process has completed.

Garbage timer   *See* Flush timer.

Gateway Load Balancing Protocol   A Cisco-proprietary feature by which multiple routers can provide interface IP address redundancy, as well as cause a set of clients to load-balance their traffic across multiple routers inside the GLBP group.

gateway of last resort   The notation in a Cisco IOS IP routing table that identifies the route used by that router as the default route.

generic routing encapsulation   A tunneling protocol that can be used to encapsulate many different protocol types, including IPv4, IPv6, IPsec, and others, to transport them across a network.

Get   In the context of SNMP, the Get command is sent by an SNMP manager, to an agent, requesting the value of a single MIB variable identified in the request. The Get request identifies the exact variable whose value the manager wants to retrieve. Introduced in SNMPv1.

GetBulk   In the context of SNMP, the GetBulk command is sent by an SNMP manager, to an agent, requesting the values of multiple variables. The GetBulk command allows retrieval of complex structures, like a routing table, with a single command, as well as easier MIB walking.

GetNext   In the context of SNMP, the GetNext command is sent by an SNMP manager, to an agent, requesting the value of a single MIB variable. The GetNext request identifies a variable for which the manager wants the variable name and value of the next MIB leaf variable in sequence.

GLBP   *See* Gateway Load Balancing Protocol.

global routing prefix   The first 48 bits of an IPv6 global address, used for efficient route aggregation.

GLOP addressing   The range 233.0.0.0 through 233.255.255.255 that IANA has reserved (RFC 2770) on an experimental basis. It can be used by anyone who owns a registered autonomous system number to create 256 global multicast addresses.

going active   EIGRP jargon meaning that EIGRP has placed a route into active status.

Goodbye (EIGRP)   An EIGRP message that is used by a router to notify its neighbors when the router is gracefully shutting down.

graceful restart (OSPF)   As defined in RFC 3623, graceful restart allows for uninterrupted forwarding in the event that an OSPF router's OSPF routing process must restart. The router does this by first notifying the neighbor routers that the restart is about to occur; the neighbors must be RFC 3623–compliant, and the restart must occur within the defined grace period.

Graft Ack message   Message sent by a PIM-DM router to a downstream router when it receives a Graft message from the downstream router; sent using the unicast address of the downstream router.

Graft message   Message sent by a PIM-DM router to its upstream router asking to quickly restart forwarding the group traffic; sent using the unicast address of the upstream router.

granted window   *See* receiver's advertised window.

GRE   *See* generic routing encapsulation.

half duplex   Ethernet feature in which a NIC or Ethernet port can only transmit or receive at the same instant in time, but not both. Half duplex is required when a possibility of collisions exists.

hardware queue   A small FIFO queue associated with each router's physical interface, for the purpose of making packets available to the interface hardware, removing the need for a CPU interrupt to start sending the next packet out the interface.

HDB3   *See* High Density Binary 3.

Hello (EIGRP)   An EIGRP message that identifies neighbors, exchanges parameters, and is sent periodically as a keepalive function. Hellos do not require an Ack.

Hello (OSPF)   A type of OSPF packet used to discover neighbors, check for parameter agreement, and monitor the health of another router.

hello interval   With some routing protocols, the time period between successive Hello messages.

Hello timer   An STP timer that dictates the interval at which the Root switch generates and sends Hello BPDUs.

High Density Binary 3   A serial-line encoding standard like B8ZS, but with each set of four consecutive 0s being changed to include a Bipolar Violation to maintain synchronization.

Hold timer   With EIGRP, the timer used to determine when a neighboring router has failed, based on a router not receiving any EIGRP messages, including Hellos, in this timer period.

Hot Standby Router Protocol   A Cisco-proprietary feature by which multiple routers can provide interface IP address redundancy so that hosts using the shared, virtual IP address as their default gateway can still reach the rest of a network even if one or more routers fail.

Holddown timer   With RIP, a per-route timer (default 180 seconds) that begins when a route's metric changes to a larger value.

HSRP   *See* Hot Standby Router Protocol.

I/G bit   The most significant bit in the most significant byte of an Ethernet MAC address, its value implies that the address is a unicast MAC address (binary 0) or not (binary 1).

iBGP   *See* Internal BGP.

IEEE 802.1X   An IEEE standard that, when used with EAP, provides user authentication before their connected switch port allows the device to fully use the LAN.

IGMP   *See* Internet Group Management Protocol.

IGMP snooping   A method for optimizing the flow of multicast IP packets passing through a LAN switch. The switch using IGMP snooping examines IGMP messages to determine which ports need to receive traffic for each multicast group.

IGMPv1 Host Membership Query   A message sent by the multicast router, by default every 60 seconds, on each of its LAN interfaces to determine whether any host wants to receive multicast traffic for any group.

IGMPv1 Host Membership Report   A message that each host sends, either in response to a router Query message or on its own, to all multicast groups for which it would like to receive multicast traffic.

IGMPv2 Group-Specific Query   A message sent by a router, after receiving a Leave message from a host, to determine whether there are still any active members of the group. The router uses the group address as the destination address.

IGMPv2 Host Membership Query   A message sent by a multicast router, by default every 125 seconds, on each of its LAN interfaces to determine whether any host wants to receive multicast traffic for any group.

IGMPv2 Host Membership Report   A message sent by each host, either in response to a router Query or on its own, to all multicast groups for which it would like to receive multicast traffic.

IGMPv2 Leave   A message sent by a host when it wants to leave a group, addressed to the All Multicast Routers address 224.0.0.2.

IGMPv3 Host Membership Query   A message sent by a multicast router, by default every 125 seconds, on each of its LAN interfaces to determine whether any host wants to receive multicast traffic for any group.

IGMPv3 Host Membership Report   A message sent by each host, either in response to a router query or on its own, to all multicast groups for which it would like to receive multicast traffic. The destination address on the Report is 224.0.0.22, and a host can specify the source address(es) from which it would like to receive the group traffic.

InARP   *See* Inverse ARP.

Inform   In the context of SNMP, the Inform command is sent by an SNMP manager to communicate a set of variables, and their values, to another SNMP manager. The main purpose is to allow multiple managers to exchange MIB information, and work together, without requiring each manager to individually use Get commands to gather the data.

infrastructure mode   A wireless LAN that includes the use of access points. Infrastructure mode connects wireless users to a wired network and allows wireless users to roam throughout a facility between different access points. All 802.11 data frames in an infrastructure wireless LAN travel through the access point.

ingress PE   An E-LSR in an MPLS VPN network whose role in a particular discussion is to receive unlabeled packets over customer links and then forward the packets as labeled packets into the MPLS network.

inner label   An MPLS term referring to the MPLS label just before the IP header. Also called the VPN label when implementing MPLS VPNs.

input event   Any occurrence that could change a router's EIGRP topology table, including a received Update or Query, a failed interface, or the loss of a neighbor.

Inside Global address   A NAT term describing an IP address representing a host that resides inside the enterprise network, with the address being used in packets outside the enterprise network.

Inside Local address   A NAT term describing an IP address representing a host that resides inside the enterprise network, with the address being used in packets inside the enterprise network.

inspection rule   A set of parameters for CBAC to perform in its traffic inspection process.

interface ID   64 bits at the end of an IPv6 global address, used to uniquely identify each host in a subnet.

Inter-Switch Link   Cisco-proprietary VLAN trunking protocol.

internal BGP   Refers to how a router views a BGP peer relationship, in which the peer is in the same AS.

internal DSCP   A term used with Cisco LAN switches, referring to a DSCP value used when making QoS decisions about a frame. This value may not be the actual DSCP value in the IP header encapsulated inside the frame.

internal router (OSPF)   A router that is not an ABR or ASBR in that all of its interfaces connect to only a single OSPF area.

Internet Group Management Protocol   A communication protocol between hosts and a multicast router by which routers learn of which multicast groups' packets need to be forwarded onto a LAN.

Invalid timer   With RIP, a per-route timer that increases until the router receives a routing update that confirms the route is still valid, upon which the timer is reset to 0. If the updates cease, the Invalid timer will grow, until reaching the timer setting (default 180 seconds), after which the route is considered invalid.

Inverse ARP   Defined in RFC 1293, this protocol allows a Frame Relay–attached device to react to a received LMI "PVC up" message by announcing its Layer 3 addresses to the device on the other end of the PVC.

IPCP   *See* IP Control Protocol.

IP Control Protocol   The portion of PPP focused on negotiating IP features—for example, TCP or RTP header compression.

IP forwarding   The process of forwarding packets through a router. Also call IP routing.

IP PBX   A component that interfaces with a phone using IP and provides connections to the Public Switched Telephone Network (PSTN).

IP Precedence   A 3-bit field in the first 3 bits of the ToS byte in the IP header, used for QoS marking.

IP prefix list   *See* prefix list.

IP routing   The process of forwarding packets through a router. Also called IP forwarding.

IP Source Guard   A switch feature that examines incoming frames, comparing the source IP and MAC addresses to the DHCP snooping binding database, filtering frames whose addresses are not listed in the database for the incoming interface.

IPv4   Version 4 of the IP protocol, which is the generally deployed version worldwide (at publication), and uses 32-bit IP addresses.

IPv6   Version 6 of the IP protocol, which uses 128-bit IP addresses.

ISATAP   An IPv6/IPv4 tunneling method that is designed for transporting IPv6 packets within a site where a native IPv6 infrastructures is not available.

ISL   *See* Inter-Switch Link.

isolated VLAN   With private VLANs, a secondary VLAN in which the ports can send and receive frames only with promiscuous ports in the primary VLAN.

Join/Prune message   Sent by a PIM router to its upstream router to either request that the upstream router forward the group traffic or stop forwarding the group traffic that is currently being forwarded. If a PIM router wants to start receiving the group traffic, it lists the group address under the Join field. If it wants the upstream router to stop forwarding the group traffic, it lists the group address under the Prune field.

joining a group   The process of installing a multicast application; also referred to as launching an application.

K value   EIGRP (and IGRP) allows for the use of bandwidth, load, delay, MTU, and link reliability; the K values refer to an integer constant that includes these five possible metric components. Only bandwidth and delay are used by default, to minimize recomputation of metrics for small changes in minor metric components.

label binding   In MPLS, the mapping of an IP prefix and a label, which is then advertised to neighbors using LDP.

Label Distribution Protocol   The RFC-standard MPLS protocol used to advertise the binding (mapping) information about each particular IP prefix and associated label. *See also* TDP.

Label Forwarding Information Base   An MPLS data structure used for forwarding labeled packets. The LFIB lists the incoming label, which is compared to the incoming packet's label, along with forwarding instructions for the packet.

Label Switch Router   An MPLS term referring to any device that can forward packets that have MPLS labels.

label switched path   The combination of MPLS labels and links over which a packet will be forwarded over an MPLS network, from the point of ingress to the MPLS network to the point of egress.

LACP   *See* Link Aggregation Control Protocol.

LAPF   *See* Link Access Procedure for Frame-Mode Bearer Services.

Layer 2 payload compression   The process of taking the payload inside a Layer 2 frame, including the headers of Layer 3 and above, compressing the data, and then uncompressing the data on the receiving router.

Layer 2 protocol tunneling   Another name for 802.1Q-in-Q. *See* 802.1Q-in-Q.

Layer *x* PDU   The PDU used by a particular layer of a networking model, with *x* defining the layer.

LCP   *See* Link Control Protocol.

LDP   *See* Label Distribution Protocol.

Lead Content Engine   The content engine in a WCCP cluster, which determines how traffic will be distributed within the cluster.

learning state   An 802.1d STP transitory port state in which the port does not send or receive frames, but does learn the source MAC addresses from incoming frames.

LFI *See* Link Fragmentation and Interleaving.

LFIB *See* Label Forwarding Information Base.

limiting query scope (EIGRP) An effort to reduce the query scope with EIGRP, using route summarization or EIGRP stub routers.

line coding *See* encoding.

Link Access Procedure for Frame-Mode Bearer Services An ITU standard Frame Relay header, including the DLCI, DE, FECN, and BECN bits in the LAPF header, and a frame check in the LAPF trailer.

Link Aggregation Control Protocol Defined in IEEE 802.1AD, defines a messaging protocol used to negotiate the dynamic creation of PortChannels (EtherChannels) and to choose which ports can be placed into an EtherChannel.

Link Control Protocol The portion of PPP focused on features that are unrelated to any specific Layer 3 protocol.

Link Fragmentation and Interleaving The process of breaking a frame into pieces, sending some of the fragments, and then sending all or part of a different packet, all of which is done to reduce the delay of the second packet.

link-local An address type in IPv6 networks that is used only on the local link and never beyond that scope.

Link-State Acknowledgment A type of OSPF packet used to acknowledge LSU packets.

link-state advertisement The OSPF data structure that describes topology information.

link-state database The data structure used by OSPF to hold LSAs.

link-state routing protocol Any routing protocol that uses the concept of using the SPF algorithm with an LSDB to compute routes.

Link-State Update A type of OSPF packet, used to communicate LSAs to another router.

listening state An 802.1d STP transitory port state in which the port does not send or receive frames, and does not learn MAC addresses, but does wait for STP convergence and for CAM flushing by the switches in the network.

LLQ *See* low-latency queuing.

LMI   *See* Local Management Interface.

local computation   An EIGRP router's reaction to an input event, leading to the use of a feasible successor or going active on a route.

local label   In MPLS, a term used to define a label that an LSR allocates and then advertises to neighboring routers. The label is considered "local" on the router that allocates and advertises the label.

LOCAL_AS   A reserved value for the BGP COMMUNITY path attribute that implies that the route should not be advertised outside the local confederation sub-AS.

Local Management Interface   The Frame Relay protocol used between a DCE and DTE to manage the connection. Signaling messages for SVCs, PVC Status messages, and keepalives are all LMI messages.

LOCAL_PREF   A BGP path attribute that is communicated throughout a single AS to signify which route of multiple possible routes is the best route to be taken when leaving that AS. A larger value is considered to be better.

LOF   *See* Loss of Frame.

Loop Guard   Protects against problems caused by unidirectional links between two switches. Watches for loss of received Hello BPDUs, in which case it transitions to a loop-inconsistent state instead of transitioning to a forwarding state.

loopback circuitry   A feature of Ethernet NICs. When the NIC transmits an electrical signal, it "loops" the transmitted electrical current back onto the receive pair. By doing so, if another NIC transmits a frame at the same time, the NIC can detect the overlapping received electrical signals, and sense that a collision has occurred.

LOS   Loss of Signal. A T1 alarm state that occurs when the receiver has not received any pulses of either polarity for a defined time period.

Loss of Frame   A T1 alarm state that occurs when the receiver can no longer consistently identify the frame.

low-latency queuing   A Cisco IOS queuing tool that uses MQC configuration commands, reserves a minimum bandwidth for some queues, provides high-priority scheduling for some queues, and polices those queues to prevent starvation of lower-priority queues during interface congestion.

LSA   *See* link-state advertisement.

LSA flooding   The process of successive neighboring routers exchanging LSAs such that all routers have an identical LSDB for each area to which they are attached.

LSA type (OSPF)   A definition that determines the data structure and information implied by a particular LSA.

LSAck   *See* Link-State Acknowledgment.

LSDB   *See* link-state database.

LSP   *See* label switched path.

LSP segment   A single label and link that is part of a complete LDP. *See also* label switched path.

LSR   *See* Label Switch Router.

LSRefresh   Link-State Refresh. A timer that determines how often the originating router should reflood an LSA, even if no changes have occurred to the LSA.

LSU   *See* Link-State Update.

LxPDU   *See* Layer *x* PDU.

LZS   The Lempel Ziv STAC compression algorithm is used in Frame Relay networks to define dynamic dictionary entries that list a binary string from the compressed data and an associated smaller string that represents it during transmission—thereby reducing the number of bits used to send data.

Management Information Base   The definitions for a particular set of data variables, with those definitions following the SMI specifications. *See also* SMI.

man-in-the-middle attack   A characterization of a network attack in which packets flow to the attacker, and then out to the true recipient. As a result, the user continues to send data, increasing the chance that the attacker learns more and better information.

map class   An FRTS configuration construct, configured with the **map-class frame-relay** global configuration command.

mark probability denominator   Used by WRED to calculate the maximum percentage of packets discarded when the average queue depth falls between the minimum and maximum thresholds.

marking down   Jargon referring to a policer action through which, instead of discarding an out-of-contract packet, the policer marks a different IPP or DSCP value, allowing the packet to continue on its way, but making the packet more likely to be discarded later.

MaxAge   An OSPF timer that determines how long an LSA can remain in the LSDB without having heard a reflooded copy of the LSA.

Maxage timer   An STP timer that dictates how long a switch should wait when it ceases to hear Hellos.

maximum reserved bandwidth   A Cisco IOS interface setting, as a percentage between 1 and 99, that defines how much of the interface's bandwidth setting may be allocated by a queuing tool. The default value is 75 percent.

Maximum Response Time   After a host receives an IGMP Query, the amount of time (default, 10 seconds) the host has to send the IGMP Report.

Maximum Segment Size   A TCP variable that defines the largest number of bytes allowed in a TCP segment's Data field. The calculation does not include the TCP header. With a typical IP MTU of 1500 bytes, the resulting default MSS would be 1460. TCP hosts must support an MSS of at least 536 bytes

maximum threshold   WRED compares this setting to the average queue depth to decide whether packets should be discarded. All packets are discarded if the average queue depth rises above this maximum threshold.

maximum transmission unit   An IP variable that defines the largest size allowed in an IP packet, including the IP header. IP hosts must support an MTU of at least 576 bytes.

MD5   *See* Message Digest 5.

MD5 hash   A term referring to the process of applying the Message Digest 5 (MD5) algorithm to a string, resulting in another value. The original string cannot be easily computed even when the hash is known, making this process a strong method for storing passwords.

MDRR   *See* Modified Deficit Round-Robin.

Measured Round-Trip Time   A TCP variable used as the basis for a TCP sender's timer defining how long it should wait for a missing acknowledgement before resending the data.

Message Digest 5   A method of applying a mathematical formula, with input including a private key, the message contents, and sometimes a shared text string, with the resulting digest being included with the message. The sender and the receiver perform the same math to allow authentication and to prove that no intermediate device changed the message contents.

metric   With routing protocols, the measurement of favorability that determines which entry will be installed in a routing table if more than one router is advertising that exact network and mask.

MIB   *See* Management Information Base.

MIB walk   In SNMP, the process of a manager using successive GetNext and GetBulk commands to discover the exact MIB structure supported by an SNMP agent. The process involves the manager asking for each successive MIB leaf variable.

MIB-I   The original standardized set of generic SNMP MIB variables, defined in RFC 1158.

MIB-II   The most recent standardized set of generic SNMP MIB variables, defined in RFC 1213 and updated in RFCs 2011 through 2013.

mincir   *See* minimum CIR.

minimum CIR   Jargon referring to the minimum value to which adaptive shaping will lower the shaping rate.

minimum threshold   WRED compares this setting to the average queue depth to decide whether packets should be discarded. No packets are discarded if the average queue depth falls below this minimum threshold.

MLD   *See* Multicast Listener Discovery.

MLP   *See* Multilink PPP.

MLP LFI   The PPP function for fragmenting packets, plus interleaving delay-sensitive later-arriving packets between the fragments of the first packet.

MLS   *See* Multilayer Switching.

Modified Deficit Round-Robin   A Cisco 12000 series router feature that combines the key features of LLQ and CQ to provide similar congestion-management features.

modified tail drop   A WFQ term referring to its drop logic, which is similar to tail-drop behavior.

Modular QoS CLI   The common set of IOS configuration commands that is used with each QoS feature whose name begins with "Class-Based."

MOSPF   *See* Multicast Open Shortest Path First.

MPD   *See* mark probability denominator.

MPLS Experimental (EXP)   A 3-bit field in an MPLS header used for marking frames.

MPLS TTL propagation   The MPLS feature by which an ingress E-LSR copies the IP packet's IP TTL field into the MPLS header's TTL field.

MPLS unicast IP routing   The simplest MPLS application, involving the advertisement of an IGP to learn IP routes, and LDP or TDP to advertise labels.

MPLS VPNs   An MPLS application that allows the MPLS network to connect to multiple different IP networks, with overlapping IP addresses, and provide IP connectivity to those multiple networks.

MQC   *See* Modular QoS CLI.

MRT   *See* Maximum Response Time.

MRTT   *See* Measured Round-Trip Time.

MSS   *See* Maximum Segment Size.

MST   *See* Multiple Spanning Trees.

MTU   *See* maximum transmission unit.

MULTI_EXIT_DISC (MED)   A BGP path attribute that allows routers in one AS to set a value and advertise it into a neighboring AS, impacting the decision process in that neighboring AS. A smaller value is considered better. Also called the BGP metric.

multi-action policing   In MQC and CB Policing, a configuration style by which, for one category of packets (conform, exceed, or violate), more than one marking action is defined for a single category. For example, marking DSCP and DE.

multicast   A type of IPv4 and IPv6 traffic designed primarily to provide one-to-many connectivity but unlike broadcast, has the capability to control the scope of traffic distribution.

multicast IP address range   IP multicast address range from 224.0.0.0 through 239.255.255.255.

multicast IP address structure   The first 4 bits of the first octet must be 1110. The last 28 bits are unstructured.

Multicast Listener Discovery   The IPv6 protocol used for the discovery of which hosts are listening for which multicast IP addresses for IPv6.

multicast MAC address   A 48-bit address that is calculated from a Layer 3 multicast address by using 0x0100.5E as the multicast vendor code (OUI) for the first 24 bits, always binary 0 for the 25th bit, and copying the last 23 bits of the Layer 3 multicast address.

Multicast Open Shortest Path First   A multicast routing protocol that operates in dense mode and depends on the OSPF unicast routing protocol to perform its multicast functions.

multicast scoping   The practice of defining boundaries that determine how far multicast traffic will travel in your network.

multicast state information   The information maintained by a router for each multicast entry in its multicast routing table, such as incoming interface, outgoing interface list, Uptime timer, Expire timer, etc.

multicasting   Sending a message from a single source or multiple sources to selected multiple destinations across a Layer 3 network in one data stream.

Multilayer Switching   A process whereby a switch, when making a forwarding decision, uses not only Layer 2 logic but other OSI layer equivalents as well.

Multilink PPP   A PPP feature used to load balance multiple parallel links at Layer 2 by fragmenting frames, sending one frame over each of the links in the bundle, and reassembling them at the receiving end of the link.

multipath   An issue whereby parts of the RF signal take different paths from the source to the destination, which causes direct and reflected signals to reach the receiver at different times, and corresponding bit errors.

Multiple Spanning Trees   Defined in IEEE 802.1s, a specification for multiple STP instances when using 802.1Q trunks

NA   *See* Neighbor Advertisement.

NAT   *See* Network Address Translation.

NAT-PT   *See* Network Address Translation-Protocol Translation.

native VLAN The one VLAN on an 802.1Q trunk for which the endpoints do not add the 4-byte 802.1Q tag when transmitting frames in that VLAN.

NBAR *See* Network Based Application Recognition.

NCP *See* Network Control Protocol.

ND *See* Neighbor Discovery Protocol.

neighbor (EIGRP) With EIGRP, a router sharing the same primary subnet, with which Hellos are exchanged, parameters match, and with which routes can be exchanged.

neighbor (OSPF) Any other router, sharing a common data link, with which a router exchanges Hellos, and for which the parameters in the Hello pass the parameter-check process.

Neighbor Advertisement In IPv6, the Neighbor Discovery message used by an IPv6 node to send information about itself to its neighbors.

Neighbor Discovery Protocol The protocol used in IPv6 for many functions, including address autoconfiguration, duplicate address detection, router, neighbor, and prefix discovery, neighbor address resolution, and parameter discovery.

Neighbor Solicitation In IPv6, the Neighbor Discovery message used by an IPv6 node to request information about a neighbor or neighbors.

neighbor state A state variable kept by a router for each known neighbor or potential neighbor.

Neighbor Type In BGP, either external BGP (eBGP), confederation eBGP, or internal BGP (iBGP). The term refers to a peer connection, and whether the peers are in different ASs (eBGP), different confederation sub-ASs (confederation eBGP), or in the same AS (iBGP).

nested policy maps An MQC configuration style by which one policy map calls a second policy map. For example, a shaping policy map can call an LLQ policy map to implement LLQ for packets shaped by CB Shaping.

Network Address Translation Defined in RFC 1631, a method of translating IP addresses in headers with the goal of allowing multiple hosts to share single public IP addresses, thereby reducing IPv4 public address depletion.

Network Address Translation-Protocol Translation As defined in RFCs 2765 and 2766, a method of translating between IPv4 and IPv6 that removes the need for hosts to run dual protocol stacks. NAT-PT is an alternative to tunneling IPv6 over an IPv4 network, or vice versa.

network allocation vector   A time value that each wireless station must set based on the duration value found in every 802.11 frame. The time value counts down and must be equal to zero before a station is allowed to access the wireless medium. The result is a collision-avoidance mechanism.

Network Based Application Recognition   A Cisco IOS feature that performs deep packet inspection to classify packets based on application layer information.

Network Control Protocol   The portions of PPP focused on features that are related to specific Layer 3 protocols.

network layer reachability information   A BGP term referring to an IP prefix and prefix length.

Network Time Protocol   An Internet standard (RFC 1305) that defines the messages and modes used for IP hosts to synchronize their time-of-day clocks.

network type (OSPF)   A characteristic of OSPF interfaces that determines whether a DR election is attempted, whether or not neighbors must be statically configured, and the default Hello and Dead timer settings.

Next Hop field   With a routing update, or routing table entry, the portion of a route that defines the next router to which a packet should be sent to reach the destination subnet. With routing protocols, the Next Hop field may define a router other than the router sending the routing update.

NEXT_HOP   A BGP path attribute that lists the next-hop IP address used to reach an NLRI.

NLPID   Network Layer Protocol ID is a field in the RFC 2427 header that is used as a Protocol Type field in order to identify the type of Layer 3 packet encapsulated inside a Frame Relay frame.

NLRI   *See* network layer reachability information.

no drop   A WRED process by which WRED does not discard packets during times in which a queue's minimum threshold has not been passed.

NO_ADVERT   A reserved value for the BGP COMMUNITY path attribute that implies that the route should not be advertised to any other peer.

NO_EXPORT   A reserved value for the BGP COMMUNITY path attribute that implies that the route should not be advertised outside the local AS.

NO_EXPORT_SUBCONFED   The RFC 1997 name for the reserved COMMUNITY path attribute known to Cisco IOS as LOCAL_AS. (*See* LOCAL_AS.)

not-so-stubby area   A type of OSPF stub area that, unlike stub areas, can inject external routes into the NSSA area.

NS   *See* Neighbor Solicitation.

NSSA   *See* not-so-stubby area.

NTP   *See* Network Time Protocol.

NTP broadcast client   An NTP client that assumes that a server will send NTP broadcasts, removing the requirement for the client to have the NTP server's IP address preconfigured.

NTP client mode   An NTP mode in which an NTP host adjusts its clock in relation to an NTP server's clock.

NTP server mode   An NTP mode in which an NTP host does not adjust its clock, but in which it sends NTP messages to clients so that the clients can update their clocks based on the server's clock.

NTP symmetric active mode   An NTP mode in which two or more NTP servers mutually synchronize their clocks.

OAM   *See* Operation, Administration, and Maintenance.

OFDM   *See* orthogonal frequency division multiplexing.

offset list   A Cisco IOS configuration tool for RIP and EIGRP for which the list matches routes in routing updates, and adds a defined value to the sent or received metric for the routes. The value added to the metric is the *offset*.

one-time password   Defined in RFC 2289, a mechanism by which a shared key and a secret key together feed into a hash algorithm, creating a password that is transmitted over a network. Because the shared key is not reused, the hash value is only valid for that individual authentication attempt.

OOF   *See* Out of Frame.

Operation, Administration, and Maintenance   A term referring to the processes and bits in the data stream used to manage the Telco TDM hierarchy.

optional nontransitive   A characterization of a BGP path attribute in which BGP implementations are not required to support the attribute (optional), and for which if a router receives a route with such an attribute, the router should remove the attribute before advertising the route (nontransitive).

optional transitive   A characterization of a BGP path attribute in which BGP implementations are not required to support the attribute (optional), and for which if a router receives a route with such an attribute, the router should forward the attribute unchanged (transitive).

ORIGIN   A BGP path attribute that implies how the route was originally injected into some router's BGP table.

ORIGINATOR_ID   Used by RRs to denote the RID of the iBGP neighbor that injected the NLRI into the AS.

orthogonal frequency division multiplexing   A technology that sends a high-speed data stream over multiple subcarriers simultaneously. It is highly immune to multipath interference. 802.11a and 802.11g specify the use of OFDM.

OTP   *See* one-time password.

Out of Frame   A T1 alarm state that occurs when the receiver can no longer consistently identify the frame. *See* LOF.

outer label   An MPLS term referring to the first of several labels when an MPLS-forwarded packet has multiple labels (a label stack).

Outside Global address   A NAT term describing an IP address representing a host that resides outside the enterprise network, with the address being used in packets outside the enterprise network.

Outside Local address   A NAT term describing an IP address representing a host that resides outside the enterprise network, with the address being used in packets inside the enterprise network.

overlapping VPN   An MPLS term describing designs in which one or more MPLS customer sites can be reached from multiple other VPNs.

overloading   Another term for Port Address Translation. *See PAT.*

P router   *See* provider router.

PAgP   *See* Port Aggregation Protocol.

PAP   *See* Password Authentication Protocol.

partial SPF calculation   An SPF calculation for which a router does not need to run SPF for any LSAs inside its area, but instead runs a very simple algorithm for changes to LSAs outside its own area.

partial update   A routing protocol feature by which the routing update includes only routes that have changed, rather than include the entire set of routes.

passive (EIGRP)   A state for a route in an EIGRP topology table that indicates that the router believes that the route is stable, and it is not currently looking for any new routes to that subnet.

passive mode FTP   Defines a particular behavior for FTP regarding the establishment of TCP data connections. In passive mode, an FTP server uses the FTP PORT command, over the FTP control connection, to tell the FTP client the port on which the server will be listening for a new data connection. The client allocates an unused port, and initiates a connection to the FTP server's earlier-declared port.

passive scanning   Each 802.11 station passively monitors each RF channel for a specific amount of time and listens for beacons. Stations use the signal strengths of found beacons to determine the access point or ad hoc network with which to attempt association.

Password Authentication Protocol   An Internet standard authentication protocol that uses clear-text passwords and a two-way handshake to perform authentication over a PPP link.

PAT   *See* Port Address Translation.

path attribute   A term generally describing characteristics about BGP paths that are advertised in BGP Updates.

payload compression   *See* Layer 2 payload compression.

PCM   *See* pulse code modulation.

PDU   *See* protocol data unit.

PE   *See* provider edge.

peak information rate   In two-rate policing, the second and higher rate defined to the policer.

peer group   In BGP, a configuration construct in which multiple neighbors' parameters can be configured as a group, thereby reducing the length of the configuration. Additionally, BGP performs routing policy logic against only one set of Updates for the entire peer group, improving convergence time.

penultimate hop popping   An MPLS VPN term referring to the more efficient choice of popping the outer label at the second-to-last (penultimate) LSR, which then prevents the egress PE from having to perform two LFIB lookups to forward the packet.

Per-Hop Behavior   With DiffServ, a DSCP marking and a related set of QoS actions applied to packets that have that marking.

permanent multicast group   The multicast addresses assigned by IANA.

permanent virtual circuit   A predefined VC. A PVC can be equated to a leased line in concept.

Per-VLAN Spanning Tree Plus   A Cisco-proprietary STP implementation, created many years before IEEE 802.1s and 802.1w, that speeds convergence and allows for one STP instance for each VLAN.

PHB   *See* Per-Hop Behavior.

PHP   *See* penultimate hop popping.

PIM Hello message   Sent by a PIM router, by default every 30 seconds, on every interface on which PIM is configured to discover neighbors, establish adjacency, and maintain adjacency.

PIM-DM   *See* Protocol Independent Multicast dense-mode routing protocol.

PIM-SM   *See* Protocol Independent Multicast sparse-mode routing protocol.

PIM-SM (S,G) RP-bit Prune   When a PIM-SM router switches from RPT to SPT, it sends a PIM-SM Prune message for the source and the group with the RP bit set to its upstream router on the shared tree. RFC 2362 uses the notation PIM-SM (S, G) RP-bit Prune for this message.

PIR   *See* peak information rate.

point coordination function   An optional contention-free 802.11 access protocol that requires the access point to poll wireless stations before they are able to send frames. Not commonly implemented.

Point-to-Point Protocol   An Internet standard serial data-link protocol, used on synchronous and asynchronous links, that provides data-link framing, link negotiation, Layer 3 interface features, and other functions.

poison reverse   With RIP, the advertisement of a poisoned route out an interface, when that route was formerly not advertised out that interface due to split horizon rules.

policing rate   The rate at which a policer limits the bits exiting or entering the policer.

policy map   A term referring to the MQC **policy-map** command and its related subcommands, which are used to apply QoS actions to classes of packets.

policy routing   Cisco IOS router feature by which a route map determines how to forward a packet, typically based on information in the packet other than the destination IP address.

Port Address Translation   A NAT term describing the process of multiplexing TCP and UDP flows, based on port numbers, to a small number of public IP addresses. Also called *NAT overloading*.

Port Aggregation Protocol   A Cisco-proprietary messaging protocol used to negotiate the dynamic creation of PortChannels (EtherChannels) and to choose which ports can be placed into an EtherChannel.

port security   A switch feature that limits the number of allowed MAC addresses on a port, with optional limits based on the actual values of the MAC addresses.

PortFast   Cisco-proprietary STP feature in which a switch port, known to not have a bridge or switch attached to it, transitions from disabled to forwarding state without using any intermediate states.

power-save mode   A mechanism for conserving battery power in wireless stations. The access point buffers data frames destined to sleeping stations, which wake periodically to learn from information in the beacon frame whether or not data frames are waiting for transmission. The radio card receives applicable data frames and then goes back to sleep.

PPP   *See* Point-to-Point Protocol.

PQ   *See* priority queue and priority queuing.

prefix   A numeric value between 0 and 32 (inclusive) that defines the number of beginning bits in an IP address for which all IP addresses in the same group have the same value. Alternative: The number of binary 1s beginning a subnet mask, written as a decimal value between 0 and 32, used as a more convenient form of representing the subnet mask.

prefix list   A Cisco IOS configuration tool that can be used to match routing updates based on a base network address, a prefix, and a range of possible masks used inside the values defined by the base network address and prefix.

priority (OSPF)   An administrative setting, included in Hellos, that is the first criteria for electing a DR. The highest priority wins, with values from 1–255, with priority 0 meaning a router cannot become DR or BDR.

priority queue   Jargon referring to any queue that receives priority service, often used for queues in an LLQ configuration that have the **priority** command configured.

priority queuing   A Cisco IOS queuing tool most notable for its scheduler, which always services the high-priority queue over all other queues.

private addresses   RFC 1918-defined IPv4 network numbers that are not assigned as public IP address ranges, and are not routable on the Internet. Intended for use inside enterprise networks.

private AS   A BGP ASN whose value is between 64,512 and 65,535. These values are not assigned for use on the Internet, and can be used for private purposes, typically either within confederations or by ISPs to hide the ASN used by some customers.

private VLAN   A Cisco switch feature that allows separation of ports as if they were in separate VLANs, while allowing the use of a single IP subnet for all ports.

process switching   A Layer 3 forwarding path through a router that does not optimize the forwarding path through the router.

promiscuous port   With private VLANs, a port that can send and receive frames with all other ports in the private VLAN.

protocol data unit   A generic term that refers to the data structure used by a layer in a layered network architecture when sending data.

Protocol Independent Multicast dense-mode routing protocol   PIM-DM is a method of routing multicast packets that depends on a flood-and-prune approach. PIM Dense Mode gets its name from the assumption that there are many receivers of a particular multicast group, close together (from a network perspective). Does not depend on any particular unicast routing protocol to perform its multicast functions.

Protocol Independent Multicast sparse-mode routing protocol   PIM-SM is a method of routing multicast packets that requires some intelligence in the network about the locations of receivers so that multicast traffic is not flooded into areas with no receivers. PIM Sparse Mode gets its name from the assumption that relatively few receivers of a particular multicast group, widely scattered (from a network perspective), want to receive that multicast traffic. Does not depend on any unicast routing protocol to perform its multicast functions.

provider edge   An MPLS VPN term referring to any LSR that connects to customers to support the forwarding of unlabeled packets, as well as connecting to the MPLS network to support labeled packets, thereby making the LSR be on the edge between the provider and the customer.

provider router   An MPLS VPN term referring to an LSR that has no direct customer connections, meaning that the P router does not need any visibility into the VPN customer's IP address space.

proxy ARP   A router feature used when a router sees an ARP request searching for an IP host's MAC, when the router believes the IP host could not be on that LAN because the host is in another subnet. If the router has a route to reach the subnet where the ARP-determined host resides, the router replies to the ARP request with the router's MAC address.

Prune Override   On a multiaccess network, when a PIM-DM or PIM-SM router receives a Prune message, it starts a 3-second timer. If it receives a Join message on the multiaccess network from another router before the timer expires, it considers the message as an override to the previously received Prune message and continues forwarding the group traffic on the LAN interface; otherwise, it stops forwarding the traffic on the LAN interface.

pruning   *See* VTP pruning.

public wireless LAN   A wireless LAN that offers connections to the Internet from public places, such as airports, hotels, and coffee shops.

pulse code modulation   An early standard from AT&T for encoding analog voice as a digital signal for transmission over a TDM network. PCM requires 64 kbps, and is the basis for the DS0 speed.

PVC   *See* permanent virtual circuit.

PVST+   *See* Per-VLAN Spanning Tree Plus.

quartet   A set of four hex digits listed in an IPv6 address. Each quartet is separated by a colon.

querier election   When multiple routers are connected to a subnet, only one should be sending IGMP queries. It is called a querier. IGMPv1 does not have any rules for electing a querier. In IGMPv2 and IGMPv3, a router with the lowest interface IP address on the subnet is elected as a querier.

Query (EIGRP)   An EIGRP message that is used to ask neighboring routers to verify their route to a particular subnet. Query messages require an Ack.

query scope (EIGRP)   The characterization of how far EIGRP Query messages flow away from the router that first notices a failed route and goes active for a particular subnet.

queue starvation   A possible side effect of a scheduler that performs strict-priority scheduling of a queue, which can result in lower-priority queues getting little or no service.

QV   *See* quantum value.

RA   *See* Router Advertisement.

QoS pre-classification   A process used in routers that are encrypting traffic to permit egress QoS actions to be taken on traffic that is being encrypted on that router. QoS pre-classification keeps a copy of each packet to be encrypted in memory long enough to take the appropriate egress QoS actions on that traffic as it leaves that router, because the encrypted traffic cannot be inspected for QoS actions.

quantum value   The number of bytes in a queue that are removed per cycle in MDRR. Similar to byte count in the custom queuing (CQ) scheduler.

radio management aggregation   Reduces the bandwidth necessary for radio management information, such as access point status messages, that is sent across the network by eliminating redundant management information.

RADIUS   A protocol, defined in RFC 2865, that defines how to perform authentication between an authenticator (for example, a router) and an authentication server that holds a list of usernames and passwords.

Rapid Per-VLAN Spanning Tree Plus   The combination of PVST+ and Rapid Spanning Tree. It provides subsecond convergence time and is compatible with PVST+ and MSTP.

Rapid Spanning Tree Protocol   Defined in IEEE 802.1w, a specification to enhance the 802.1d standard to improve the speed of STP convergence.

RARP   *See* Reverse ARP.

RD   *See* Reported distance or Route Distinguisher.

Ready To Send   On a serial cable, the pin lead set by the DTE to tell the DCE that the DTE wants to send data.

receiver's advertised window   In TCP, a TCP host sets the TCP header's Window field to the number of bytes it allows the other host to send before requiring an acknowledgement. In effect, the receiving host, by stating a particular window size, grants the sending host the right to send that number of bytes in a single window.

Red Alarm   A T1 alarm state that occurs when a device has detected a local LOF/LOS/AIS condition. The device in Red alarm state then sends a Yellow alarm signal.

regular expression   A list of interspersed alphanumeric literals and metacharacters that are used to apply complex matching logic to alphanumeric strings. Often used for matching AS_PATHs in Cisco routers.

Reliable Transport Protocol   A protocol used for reliable multicast and unicast transmissions. Used by EIGRP.

remaining bandwidth   A CBWFQ and LLQ term referring to the bandwidth on an interface that is neither reserved nor allocated via a **priority** command.

remote label   In MPLS, a term used to define a label that an LSR learned from a neighboring LSR.

rendezvous point   In the PIM-SM design, the central distribution point to which the multicast traffic is first delivered from the source designated router.

Reply (EIGRP)   An EIGRP message that is used by neighbors to reply to a query. Reply messages require an Ack.

reported distance   With EIGRP, the metric (distance) of a route as reported by a neighboring router.

request-to-send/clear-to-send   A mechanism that counters collisions caused by hidden nodes. If enabled, the station or access point must first send an RTS frame and receive a CTS frame before sending each data frame.

Report Suppression mechanism   When a Query is received from a router, each host randomly picks a time between 0 and the Maximum Response Time period to send a Report. When the host with the smallest time period first sends the Report, the rest of the hosts suppress their reports.

Response   In the context of SNMP, the Response command is sent by an SNMP agent, back to a manager, in response to any of the three types of Get requests, or in response to a Set request. It is also used by a manager in response to a received Inform command from another SNMP manager. The Response holds the value(s) of the requested variables.

Retransmission Timeout   With EIGRP, a timer started when a reliable (to be acknowledged) message is transmitted. For any neighbor(s) failing to respond in its RTO, the RTP protocol causes retransmission. RTO is calculated based on SRTT.

Reverse ARP   A standard (RFC 903) protocol by which a LAN-attached host can dynamically broadcast a request for a server to assign it an IP address. *See also* ARP.

RF channel   The specific frequency subband on which the radio card or access point is operating. The RF channel is set in the access point or ad hoc stations.

RGMP   *See* Router-Port Group Management Protocol.

RID   *See* router ID.

ROMMON   An alternative software loaded into a Cisco router, used for low-level debugging and for password recovery.

Root Guard   Cisco-proprietary STP feature in which a switch port monitors for incoming superior Hellos, and reacts to a superior Hello to prevent any switch connected to that port from becoming root.

root port   The single port on each nonroot switch upon which the best Hello BPDU is received.

Route Distinguisher   A 64-bit extension to the BGP NLRI field, used by MPLS for the purpose of making MPLS VPN customer routes unique in spite of the possibility of overlapping IPv4 address spaces in different customer networks.

route map   A configuration tool in Cisco IOS that allows basic programming logic to be applied to a set of items. Often used for decisions about what routes to redistribute, and for setting particular characteristics of those routes—for instance, metric values.

route poisoning   The process of sending an infinite-metric route in routing updates when that route fails.

route redistribution   The process of taking routes known through one routing protocol and advertising those routes with another routing protocol.

route reflector   A BGP feature by which a router learns iBGP routes, and then forwards them to other iBGP peers, reducing the required number of iBGP peers while also avoiding routing loops.

route reflector client   A BGP router that, unknown to it, is aided by a route reflector server to cause all iBGP routers in an AS to learn all eBGP-learned prefixes.

route reflector non-client   A BGP router in an AS that uses route reflectors, but that is not aided by any RR server.

route reflector server   A BGP router that forwards iBGP-learned routes to other iBGP routers.

Route Tag field   A field within a route entry in a routing update, used to associate a generic number with the route. It is used when passing routes between routing protocols, allowing an intermediate routing protocol to pass information about a route that is not natively defined to that intermediate routing protocol. Frequently used for identifying certain routes for filtering by a downstream routing process.

Route Target   In MPLS VPNs, a 64-bit Extended Community path attribute attached to a BGP route for the purpose of controlling into which VRFs the route is added.

routed interface   An interface on a Cisco IOS–based switch that is treated as if it were an interface on a router.

Router Advertisement   In IPv6, a Router Advertisement message used by an IPv6 router to send information about itself to nodes and other routers connected to that router.

router ID   The 32-bit number used to represent an OSPF router.

Router-Port Group Management Protocol   A Cisco-proprietary Layer 2 protocol that enables a router to communicate to a switch which multicast group traffic the router does and does not want to receive from the switch.

routing black hole   A problem that occurs when an AS does not run BGP on all routers, with synchronization disabled. The routers running BGP may believe they have working routes to reach a prefix, and forward packets to internal routers that do not run BGP and do not have a route to reach the prefix.

RP   *See* rendezvous point.

RPF check   Designed to solve the problems of multicast duplication and multicast routing loops. For every multicast packet received, a multicast router examines its source IP address, consults its unicast routing table, determines which interface it would use to go in the reverse direction toward the source IP address, compares it with the interface on which the packet was received, and, if they match, accepts the packet and forwards it; otherwise, the router drops the packet.

RPVST+   *See* Rapid Per-VLAN Spanning Tree Plus.

RSTP   *See* Rapid Spanning Tree Protocol.

RT   *See* Route Target.

RTO   *See* Retransmission Timeout.

RTP   *See* Reliable Transport Protocol.

RTP header compression   The process of taking the IP, UDP, and RTP headers of a voice or video packet, compressing them, and then uncompressing them on the receiving router.

RTS   *See* Ready To Send.

RTS/CTS   *See* request-to-send/clear-to-send.

RXBOOT   An alternative software loaded into a Cisco router, used for basic IP connectivity—most useful when Flash memory is broken and you need IP connectivity to copy a new IOS image into Flash memory.

SAFE Blueprint   An architecture and set of documents that defines Cisco's best recommendations for how to secure a network.

same-layer interaction   The two computers use a protocol with which to communicate with the same layer on another computer. The protocol defined by each layer uses a header that is transmitted between the computers to communicate what each computer wants to do.

scheduler   A queuing tool's logic by which it selects the next packet to dequeue from its many queues.

sequence number (OSPF)   In OSPF, a number assigned to each LSA, ranging from 0x80000001 and wrapping back around to 0x7FFFFFFF, which is used to determine which LSA is most recent.

sequence number   A term used with WFQ for the number assigned to a packet as it is enqueued into a WFQ. WFQ schedules the currently lowest SN packet next.

Service Interworking   The process, defined by FRF.5 and FRF.8, for combining ATM and FR technologies for an individual VC.

service policy   A term referring to the MQC **service-policy** command, which is used to enable a policy map on an interface.

service set identifier   Defines a particular wireless LAN. The SSID configured in the radio card must match the SSID in the access point before the station can connect with the access point.

Set   In the context of SNMP, the Set command is sent by an SNMP manager, to an agent, requesting that the agent set a single identified variable to the stated value. The main purpose is to allow remote configuration and remote operation, such as shutting down an interface by using an SNMP Set of an interface state MIB variable.

SF   *See* Superframe.

shaped mode   The operating mode of shaped round-robin that provides a low-latency queue with policing.

shaped round-robin   A packet-scheduling algorithm used in Cisco switches that provides similar behavior to CBWFQ in shared mode and polices in shaped mode.

shaping rate   The rate at which a shaper limits the bits exiting the shaper.

shared distribution tree   In PIM-SM, the path of the group traffic that flows from the RP to the routers that need the traffic. It is also called the root-path tree (RPT), because it is rooted at the RP.

shared mode   The operating mode of shaped round-robin that provides behavior like CBWFQ with bandwidth allocated between different traffic classes by a relative amount rather than absolute percentage of the available bandwidth.

shortest-path tree switchover   In the PIM-SM design, the process by which a PIM-SM router can build the SPT between itself and the source of a multicast group and take advantage of the most efficient path available from the source to the router as long as it has one directly connected group member. Once it builds an SPT, it sends a PIM-SM (S, G) RP-bit Prune toward the upstream router on the shared tree.

single-rate, three-color policer   Policing in which a single rate is metered, and packets are placed into one of three categories (conform, exceed, or violate).

single-rate, two-color policer   Policing in which a single rate is metered, and packets are placed into one of two categories (conform or exceed).

signal-to-noise ratio   The difference between the measured signal power and the noise power that a particular receiver sees at a given time. Higher SNRs generally indicate better performance.

Slow Start   A method for how a TCP sender grows its calculated CWND variable, thereby growing the allowed window for the connection. Slow Start grows CWND at an exponential rate.

Slow Start Threshold   A calculated TCP variable, used along with the TCP CWND variable, to dictate a TCP sender's behavior when it recognizes packet loss. As CWND grows after packet loss, the TCP sender increases CWND based on Slow Start rules, until CWND grows to be as high as the SSThresh setting, at which point TCP Congestion Avoidance logic is used. Essentially, SSThresh is the threshold at which Slow Start logic ends.

SLSM   *See* static length subnet masking.

SMI   *See* Structure of Management Information.

Smoothed Round-Trip Time   With EIGRP, a purposefully slowly changing measurement of round-trip time between neighbors, from which the EIGRP RTO is calculated.

smurf attack   A style of attack in which an ICMP Echo is sent with a directed broadcast (subnet broadcast) destination IP address, and a source address of the host that is being attacked. The attack can result in the Echo reaching a large number of hosts, all of which reply by sending an Echo Reply to the host being attacked.

SN   *See* sequence number.

SNMP agent   A process on a computing device that accepts SNMP requests, responds with SNMP-structured MIB data, and initiates unsolicited Trap messages back to an SNMP management station.

SNMP manager   A process on a computing device that issues requests for SNMP MIB variables from SNMP agents, receives and processes the MIB data, and accepts unsolicited Trap messages from SNMP agents.

SNR   *See* signal-to-noise ratio.

socket   A 3-tuple consisting of an IP address, port number, and transport layer protocol. TCP connections exist between a pair of sockets.

soft reconfiguration   A BGP process by which a router reapplies routing policy configuration (route maps, filters, and the like) based on stored copies of sent and received BGP Updates.

software queue   A queue created by Cisco IOS as a result of the configuration of a queuing tool.

solicited node multicast   In IPv6, an address used in the Neighbor Discovery (ND) process. The format for these addresses is FF02::1:FF00:0000/104, and each IPv6 host must join the corresponding group for each of its unicast and anycast addresses.

source DR   A designated router that is directly connected with a source of the multicast group.

source registration   In the PIM-SM design, the process by which a source DR, after it starts to receive the group traffic, encapsulates the multicast packets in the unicast packets and sends them to the RP.

source-based distribution tree   Method by which a dense-mode routing protocol distributes multicast traffic from a source to all the segments of a network. Also called shortest-path tree (SPT), because it uses the shortest routing path from the source to the segments of the network.

source-specific addresses   The range 232.0.0.0 through 232.255.255.255 that is allocated by IANA for SSM destination addresses and is reserved for use by source-specific applications and protocols.

source-specific multicast   IGMPv3 is designed to support source filtering. IGMPv3 allows a host to indicate interest in receiving multicast packets only from specific source addresses, or from all but specific source addresses, sent to a particular multicast destination address.

sparse-mode protocol   A multicast routing protocol that forwards the multicast traffic only when requested by a downstream router.

Spanning Tree Protocol   Defined in IEEE 802.1d, a protocol used on LAN bridges and switches to dynamically define a logical network topology that allows all devices to be reached, but prevents the formation of loops.

SPF algorithm   The algorithm used by OSPF and IS-IS to compute routes based on the LSDB.

SPF calculation   The process of running the SPF algorithm against the LSDB, with the result being the determination of the current best route(s) to each subnet.

split horizon   Instead of advertising all routes out a particular interface, the routing protocol omits the routes whose outgoing interface field matches the interface out which the update would be sent.

spread spectrum   A technology that enables frequency reuse. Two variants exist: frequency hopping (FHSS) and direct sequence (DSSS). Both techniques spread the signal power over a relatively wide portion of the frequency spectrum over time, to reduce interference between systems.

SRR *See* shaped round-robin.

SRTT *See* Smoothed Round-Trip Time.

SSID *See* service set identifier.

SSM *See* source-specific multicast.

SSThresh *See* Slow Start Threshold.

stateful autoconfiguration A method of obtaining an IPv6 address that uses DHCPv6. *See also* stateless autoconfiguration.

stateless autoconfiguration A method used by an IPv6 host to determine its own IP address, without DHCPv6, by using NDP and the modified EUI-64 address format. *See also* stateful autoconfiguration.

static length subnet masking A strategy for subnetting a classful network for which all masks/prefixes are the same value for all subnets of that one classful network.

sticky learning In switch port security, the process whereby the switch dynamically learns the MAC address(es) of the device(s) connected to a switch port, and then adds those addresses to the running configuration as allowed MAC addresses for port security.

storm control A Cisco switch feature that permits limiting traffic arriving at switch ports by percentage or absolute bandwidth. Separate thresholds are available per port for unicast, multicast, and broadcast traffic.

STP *See* Spanning Tree Protocol.

straight-through cable Copper cable with RJ-45 connectors in which the wire at pin 1 on one end is connected to pin 1 on the other end; the wire at pin 2 is connected to pin 2 on the other end; and so on.

strict priority A queuing scheduler's logic by which, if a particular queue has packets in it, those packets always get serviced next.

Structure of Management Information The SNMP specifications, standardized in RFCs, defining the rules by which SNMP MIB variables should be defined.

stub area An OSPF area into which external (type 5) LSAs are not introduced by its ABRs; instead, the ABRs originate and inject default routes into the area.

stub network (OSPF)   A network/subnet to which only one OSPF router is connected.

stub router (EIGRP)   A router that should not be used to forward packets between other routers. Other routers will not send Query messages to a stub router.

stub router (OSPF)   A router that should either permanently or temporarily not be used as a transit router. Can wait a certain time after OSPF process start, or after BGP notifies OSPF that BGP has converged, before ceasing to be a stub router.

stuck-in-active   The condition in which a route has been in an EIGRP active state for longer than the router's Active timer.

sub-AS   The term referring to a group of iBGP routers in a confederation, with the group members being assigned a hidden ASN for the purposes of loop avoidance.

subnet   A subset of a classful IP network, as defined by a subnet mask, which used to address IP hosts on the same Layer 2 network in much the same way as a classful network is used.

subnet broadcast address   A single address in each subnet for which packets sent to this address will be broadcast to all hosts in the subnet. It is the highest numeric value in the range of IP addresses implied by a subnet number and prefix/mask.

subnet ID   16 bits between the interface ID and global routing prefix in an IPv6 global address, used for subnet assignment inside an enterprise.

subnet mask   A dotted-decimal number used to help define the structure of an IP address. The binary 0s in the mask identify the host portion of an address, and the binary 1s identify either the combined network and subnet part (when thinking classfully) or the network prefix (when thinking classlessly).

subnet number   A dotted-decimal number that represents a subnet. It is the lowest numeric value in the range of IP addresses implied by a subnet number and prefix/mask.

subnet zero   When subnetting a class A, B, or C address, the subnet for which all subnet bits are binary 0.

successor route   With EIGRP, the route to each destination for which the metric is the lowest of all known routes to that network.

summary route   A route that is created to represent one or more smaller component routes, typically in an effort to reduce the size of routing and topology tables.

Superframe   An early T1 framing standard.

superior BPDU   Jargon used by STP mostly when discussing the root election process; refers to a Hello with a lower bridge ID. Sometimes refers to a Hello with the same bridge ID as another, but with better values for the tiebreakers in the election process.

supplicant   The 802.1X driver that supplies a username/password prompt to the user and sends/receives the EAPoL messages.

SVC   *See* switched virtual circuit.

switched interface   An interface on a Cisco IOS–based switch that is treated as if it were an interface on a switch.

switched virtual circuit   A VC that is set up dynamically when needed. An SVC can be equated to a dial-on-demand connection in concept.

synchronization   In BGP, a feature in which BGP routes cannot be considered to be a best route to reach an NLRI unless that same prefix exists in the router's IP routing table as learned via some IGP.

T1   A name used for DS1 lines inside the North American TDM hierarchy.

T3   A name used for DS3 lines inside the North American TDM hierarchy.

TACACS+   A Cisco-proprietary protocol that defines how to perform authentication between an authenticator (for example, a router) and an authentication server that holds a list of usernames and passwords.

Tag Distribution Protocol   The original MPLS protocol used to advertise the binding (mapping) information about each particular IP prefix and associated label. It is slightly different from LDP, but functionally equivalent. *See also* LDP.

tail drop   An event in which a new packet arrives, needing to be placed into a queue, and the queue is full—so the packet is discarded.

Tc   *See* Time Interval.

TDP   *See* Tag Distribution Protocol.

Time Interval (Tc)   Variable name for the time interval used by shapers and by CAR.

TCP code bits   Single-bit fields in the TCP header. For example, the TCP SYN and ACK code bits are used during connection establishment.

TCP flags   The same thing as TCP code bits. *See* TCP code bits.

TCP header compression   The process of taking the IP and TCP headers of a packet, compressing them, and then uncompressing them on the receiving router.

TCP intercept   A Cisco router feature in which the router works to prevent SYN attacks either by monitoring TCP connections flowing through the router, or by actively terminating TCP connection until the TCP connection is established and then knitting the client-side connection with a server-side TCP connection.

TCP SYN flood   An attack by which the attacker initiates many TCP connections to a server, but does not complete the TCP connections, by simply not sending the third segment normally used to establish the connection. The server may consume resources and reject new connection attempts as a result.

TDM   *See* time-division multiplexing.

TDM hierarchy   The structure inside telcos' original digital circuit build-out in the mid-1900s, based upon using TDM to combine and disperse smaller DS levels into larger levels, and vice versa.

Temporal Key Integrity Protocol   An enhanced version of WEP that is part of the 802.11i standard and has an automatic key-update mechanism that makes it much more secure than WEP. TKIP is not as strong as AES in terms of data protection.

terminal history   The feature in a Cisco IOS device by which a terminal session's previously typed commands are remembered, allowing the user to recall the old commands to the command line through a simple key sequence (for example, the up-arrow key).

time-division multiplexing   The process of combining multiple synchronized input signals over a single medium by giving each signal its own time slot, and then breaking out those signals.

Time to Live   A field in the IP header that is decremented at each pass through a Layer 3 forwarding device.

TKIP   *See* Temporal Key Integrity Protocol.

token bucket   A conceptual model used by shapers and policers to represent their internal logic.

ToS byte   *See* Type of Service byte.

totally NSSA area   A type of OSPF NSSA area for which neither external (type 5) LSAs are introduced, nor type 3 summary LSAs; instead, the ABRs originate and inject default routes into the area. External routes can be injected into a totally NSSA area.

totally stubby area   A type of OSPF stub area for which neither external (type 5) LSAs are introduced, nor type 3 summary LSAs; instead, the ABRs originate and inject default routes into the area. External routes cannot be injected into a totally stubby area.

traffic contract   In shaping and policing, the definition of parameters that together imply the allowed rate and bursts.

transient multicast group   Multicast addresses that are not assigned by IANA.

transit network (OSPF)   A network/subnet over which two or more OSPF routers have become neighbors, thereby being able to forward packets from one router to another across that network.

transit router (OSPF)   A router that is allowed to receive a packet from an OSPF router and then forward the packet to another OSPF router.

transmit power   The signal strength of the RF signal at the output of the radio card or access point transmitter, before being fed into the antenna. Measured in milliwatts, watts, or dBm.

Trap   In the context of SNMP, the Trap command is sent by an SNMP agent, to a manager, when the agent wants to send unsolicited information to the manager. Trap is not followed by a Response message from the receiving SNMP manager.

Triggered Extensions to RIP for On-Demand Circuits   Defined in RFC 2091, the extensions define how RIP may send a full update once, and then send updates only when routes change, when an update is requested, or when a RIP interface changes state from down to up.

triggered updates   A routing protocol feature for which the routing protocol sends routing updates immediately upon hearing about a changed route, even though it may normally only send updates on a regular update interval.

trunking   Also called VLAN trunking, a method (using either the Cisco ISL protocol or the IEEE 802.1Q protocol) to support carrying traffic between switches for multiple VLANs that have members on more than one switch.

TTL   *See* Time to Live.

TTL scoping   Controls the distribution of multicast traffic by checking the TTL values configured on the interfaces. It forwards the multicast packet only on those interfaces whose configured TTL value is less than or equal to the TTL value of the multicast packet.

Type of Service byte   A 1-byte field in the IP header, originally defined by RFC 791 for QoS marking purposes.

U/L bit   The second most significant bit in the most significant byte of an Ethernet MAC address, a value of binary 0 implies that the address is a Universally Administered Address (UAA) (also known as Burned-In Address [BIA]), and a value of binary 1 implies that the MAC address is a locally configured address.

UDLD   *See* UniDirectional Link Detection.

unicast MAC address   Ethernet MAC address that represents a single NIC or interface.

UniDirectional Link Detection   A protection against problems caused by unidirectional links between two switches. Uses messaging between switches to detect the loop, err-disabling the port when the link is unidirectional.

Update (EIGRP)   An EIGRP message that informs neighbors about routing information. Update messages require an Ack.

Update timer   With RIP, the regular interval at which updates are sent. Each interface uses an independent timer, defaulting to 30 seconds.

UplinkFast   Cisco-proprietary STP feature in which an access layer switch is configured to be unlikely to become Root or to become a transit switch. Also, convergence upon the loss of the switch's Root Port takes place in a few seconds.

upstream router   From one multicast router's perspective, the upstream router is another router that has just forwarded a multicast packet to that router.

User Priority   A 3-bit field in an 802.1Q header used for marking frames.

variance   An integer setting for EIGRP and IGRP. Any FS route whose metric is less than this variance multiplier times the successor's metric is added to the routing table, within the restrictions of the **maximum-paths** command.

variable-length subnet masking   A strategy for subnetting a classful network for which masks/prefixes are different for some subnets of that one classful network.

VC *See* virtual circuit.

violate A category used by a policer to classify packets relative to the traffic contract. These packets are considered to be above the traffic contract in all cases.

virtual circuit A logical concept that represents the path over which frames travel between DTEs. VCs are particularly useful when comparing Frame Relay to leased physical circuits.

virtual IP address The IP address used by hosts as the default gateway in a VRRP configuration. This address is shared by two or more VRRP routers, much as HSRP works.

virtual LAN A group of devices on one or more LANs that are configured (using management software) so that they can communicate as if they were attached to the same wire, when, in fact, they are located on a number of different LAN segments. Because VLANs are based on logical instead of physical connections, they are extremely flexible.

virtual link With OSPF, the encapsulation of OSPF messages inside IP, to a router with which no common subnet is shared, for the purpose of either mending partitioned areas or providing a connection from some remote area to the backbone area.

Virtual Router Redundancy Protocol A standard (RFC 3768) feature by which multiple routers can provide interface IP address redundancy so that hosts using the shared, virtual IP address as their default gateway can still reach the rest of a network even if one or more routers fail.

Virtual Routing and Forwarding table In MPLS VPNs, an entity in a single router that provides a means to separate routes in different VPNs. The VRF includes per-VRF instances of routing protocols, a routing table, and an associated CEF FIB.

VLAN *See* virtual LAN.

VLAN Trunking Protocol A Cisco-proprietary protocol, used by LAN switches to communicate VLAN configuration.

VLSM *See* variable-length subnet masking.

VoFR *See* Voice over Frame Relay.

Voice over Frame Relay Defined in FRF.11, an FR VC that uses a slightly varied header, as compared with FRF.3 data VCs, to accommodate voice payloads directly encapsulated inside the Frame Relay LAPF header.

VPN label   The innermost MPLS header in an packet traversing an MPLS VPN, with the label value identifying the forwarding details for the egress PE's VRF associated with that VPN.

VRF table   *See* Virtual Routing and Forwarding table.

VRRP   *See* Virtual Router Redundancy Protocol.

VRRP Master router   The router in a VRRP group that is currently actively forwarding IP packets. Conceptually the same as an HSRP Active router.

VTP   *See* VLAN Trunking Protocol.

VTP pruning   VTP process that prevents the flow of broadcasts and unknown unicast Ethernet frames in a VLAN from being sent to switches that have no ports in that VLAN.

WCCP   *See* Web Cache Communication Protocol.

WCCP cluster   A logical group of content engines running WCCP between them. The lead content engine determines the traffic distribution within the cluster, for optimum performance and scalability.

Web Cache Communication Protocol   The protocol used by content engines to manage traffic flow between routers configured for WCCP and between content engines. WCCP takes advantage of the fact that many web pages (and other content) are regularly accessed by users in a given network. Therefore, routers can redirect content requests to a cache engine or a cluster of cache engines to improve response time and reduce WAN usage for cached content before new requests are made across the WAN.

weight   A local Cisco-proprietary BGP setting that is not advertised to any peers. A larger value is considered to be better.

weighted fair queuing   A Cisco IOS queuing tool most notable for its automatic classification of packets into separate per-flow queues.

weighted random early detection   WRED is a method of congestion avoidance that works by dropping packets before the output queue becomes completely full. WRED can base its dropping behavior on IP Precedence or DSCP values to drop low-priority packets before high-priority packets.

weighted round-robin   A queuing scheduler concept, much like CQ's scheduler, in which queues are given some service in sequence. This term is often used with queuing in Cisco LAN switches.

weighted tail drop   A method that creates three thresholds per egress queue in the Cisco 3560 switch. Traffic is divided into the three queues based on CoS value, and given different likelihoods (weight) for tail drop when congestion occurs based on which egress queue is involved.

well-known discretionary   A characterization of a BGP path attribute in which all BGP implementations must support and understand the attribute (well known), but BGP Updates can either include the attribute or not depending on whether a related feature has been configured (discretionary).

well-known mandatory   A characterization of a BGP path attribute in which all BGP implementations must support and understand the attribute (well known), and all BGP Updates must include the attribute (mandatory).

WEP   *See* Wired Equivalent Privacy.

WFQ   *See* weighted fair queuing.

Wi-Fi Protected Access   A security standard that includes both TKIP and AES and was ratified by the Wi-Fi Alliance.

window   Typically used by protocols that perform flow control (like TCP), a TCP window is the number of bytes that a sender can send before it must pause and wait for an acknowledgement of some of the yet-unacknowledged data.

Wired Equivalent Privacy   The initial 802.11 common key encryption mechanism; vulnerable to hackers.

wireless LAN controller   Controls access to the Internet in public wireless LANs.

Wireless LAN Threat Defense Solution   An intrusion detection system that safeguards the wireless LAN from malicious and unauthorized access.

WLSE   *See* Cisco Wireless LAN Solution Engine.

WPA   Wi-Fi Protected Access. A security standard that includes both TKIP and AES and was ratified by the Wi-Fi Alliance.

WRED   *See* weighted random early detection.

WRR   *See* weighted round-robin.

WTD   *See* weighted tail drop.

Yellow Alarm   A T1 alarm state that occurs when a device receives a Yellow Alarm signal. This typically means that the device on the other end of the line is in a Red Alarm state.

Index

Symbols & Numerics

A

C

J-K

W-X-Y-Z

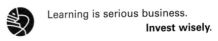

SEARCH THOUSANDS OF BOOKS FROM LEADING PUBLISHERS

Safari® Bookshelf is a searchable electronic reference library for IT professionals that features more than 2,000 titles from technical publishers, including Cisco Press.

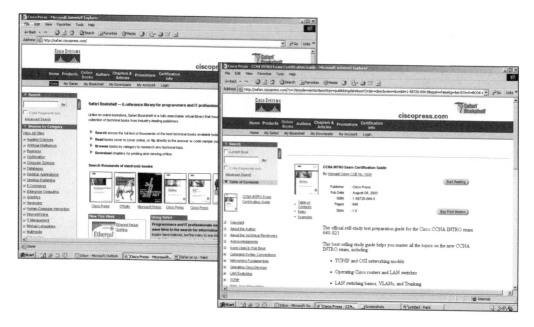

With Safari Bookshelf you can

- **Search** the full text of thousands of technical books, including more than 70 Cisco Press titles from authors such as Wendell Odom, Jeff Doyle, Bill Parkhurst, Sam Halabi, and Karl Solie.

- **Read** the books on My Bookshelf from cover to cover, or just flip to the information you need.

- **Browse** books by category to research any technical topic.

- **Download** chapters for printing and viewing offline.

With a customized library, you'll have access to your books when and where you need them—and all you need is a user name and password.

TRY SAFARI BOOKSHELF FREE FOR 14 DAYS!

You can sign up to get a 10-slot Bookshelf free for the first 14 days.
Visit **http://safari.ciscopress.com** to register.

THIS BOOK IS SAFARI ENABLED

INCLUDES FREE 45-DAY ACCESS TO THE ONLINE EDITION

The Safari® Enabled icon on the cover of your favorite technology book means the book is available through Safari Bookshelf. When you buy this book, you get free access to the online edition for 45 days.

Safari Bookshelf is an electronic reference library that lets you easily search thousands of technical books, find code samples, download chapters, and access technical information whenever and wherever you need it.

TO GAIN 45-DAY SAFARI ENABLED ACCESS TO THIS BOOK:

- Go to **http://www.ciscopress.com/safarienabled**
- Complete the brief registration form
- Enter the coupon code found in the front of this book before the "Contents at a Glance" page

If you have difficulty registering on Safari Bookshelf or accessing the online edition, please e-mail customer-service@safaribooksonline.com.